1-4-96   3   19.15

#2854183l

PENGUIN BOOKS

JUBA TO JIVE

Clarence Major is the author of seven novels and nine books of poetry. His three most recent novels —*My Amputations* (Western States Book Award, 1986), *Such Was the Season* (Literary Guild Selection, 1987/*The New York Times Book Review* "Summer Reading" Citation, 1988), and *Painted Turtle: Woman with Guitar* (*New York Times Book Review* "Notable Book of the Year" Citation, 1988)—received wide critical attention. His story collection *Fun & Games* (1990) was nominated for a *Los Angeles Times* Book Critics Award. His work has generally been the subject of many scholarly articles, dissertations, and two special issues of *African-American Review* (1979, 1993), and it has been translated into French, German, Italian, and other languages. Author of the much-quoted *Dictionary of Afro-American Slang* (1970), Major has edited two highly successful anthologies, *The New Black Poetry* (1969) and *Calling the Wind: Twentieth-Century African-American Short Stories* (Quality Paperback Book Club selection, 1993). He is the recipient of many awards, among them a National Council on the Arts Award (1970), a Fulbright (1981–1983), and two Pushcart prizes (1976, 1990). He reviews for *The Washington Post Book World* and has contributed to *The New York Times Book Review*, *The Los Angeles Times Book World*, *New York Post*, *The Baltimore Sun* magazine, *The Providence Sunday Journal*, *San Jose Mercury News*, *Denver Post*, *Essence*, *Ploughshares*, *The Kenyon Review*, *The American Review*, *The Review of Contemporary Fiction*, *The American Poetry Review*, *Michigan Quarterly Review*, *Massachusetts Review*, and more than a hundred other periodicals and anthologies in this country, Europe, South America, and Africa. In 1991 he served as fiction judge for the National Book Awards and has served twice on National Endowment for the Arts panels. He has traveled extensively and lived in various parts of the United States and for extended periods in France and Italy. A graduate (Ph.D.) of the Union Institute and a professor for more than twenty years, Major has lectured in dozens of U.S. universities as well as in England, France, Liberia, West Germany, Ghana, and Italy. Clarence Major is currently professor of African-American literature and creative writing at the University of California at Davis.

BOOKS BY CLARENCE MAJOR

My Amputations

Painted Turtle: Woman with Guitar

Such Was the Season

Reflex and Bone Structure

All-Night Visitors

NO

Fun & Games

Emergency Exit

Surfaces and Masks

Some Observations of a Stranger at Zuni in the Latter Part of the Century

Swallow the Lake

Inside Diameter: The France Poems

The Syncopated Cakewalk

The Cotton Club

Private Line

Symptoms & Madness

Dictionary of Afro-American Slang

The Dark and Feeling

The New Black Poetry

Parking Lots

Calling the Wind: Twentieth-Century African-American Short Stories

JUBA TO JIVE

A DICTIONARY OF AFRICAN-AMERICAN SLANG

EDITED AND WITH AN INTRODUCTION BY

CLARENCE MAJOR

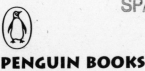

PENGUIN BOOKS

PENGUIN BOOKS
Published by the Penguin Group
Penguin Books USA Inc., 375 Hudson Street,
New York, New York 10014, U.S.A.
Penguin Books Ltd, 27 Wrights Lane,
London W8 5TZ, England
Penguin Books Australia Ltd, Ringwood,
Victoria, Australia
Penguin Books Canada Ltd, 10 Alcorn Avenue,
Toronto, Ontario, Canada M4V 3B2
Penguin Books (N.Z.) Ltd, 182–190 Wairau Road,
Auckland 10, New Zealand

Penguin Books Ltd, Registered Offices:
Harmondsworth, Middlesex, England

First published under the title *Dictionary of Afro-American Slang* by
International Publishers Co., Inc. 1970
Juba to Jive first published in simultaneous hardcover and paperback
editions by Viking Penguin and Penguin Books, divisions of Penguin
Books USA Inc. 1994

10 9 8 7 6 5 4 3 2 1

LIBRARY OF CONGRESS CATALOGING IN PUBLICATION DATA
Major, Clarence.
    Juba to jive: the dictionary of African-American slang/ Clarence
Major.
        p.   cm.
    Includes bibliographical references
    ISBN 0 14 05.1306 x
    1. Afro-Americans—Language (New words, slang, etc.)—
Dictionaries.   2. English language—United States—Slang—
Dictionaries.   3. Black English—Dictionaries.   4. Americanisms—
Dictionaries.   I. Title.
PE3727.N4M34   1994
427'973'08996—dc20   93–11748

Printed in the United States of America
Set in Postscript New Aster
Designed by Kathryn Parise

ACKNOWLEDGMENTS

I am indebted to many people, especially the early researchers, Albert Barrere, Charles G. Leland, John Bartlett, Frances Grose, Charles C. Jones, James A. Harrison, and John S. Farmer.

I also owe much to the pioneering work of Lorenzo D. Turner, Zora Neale Hurston, Geneva Smitherman, Edith Folb, Harry Middleton Hyatt, Ambrose Gonzales, Alan Lomax, Stephen Longstreet, Roger D. Abrahams, Cab Calloway, Dan Burley, Marcus H. Boulware, David Claerbaut, Frederick G. Cassidy, J. L. Dillard, Stuart Berg Flexner, Christina and Richard Milner, Robert Farris Thompson, Harold Wentworth, Robert S. Gold, and Joseph E. Holloway.

Fiction and autobiography were also important and dependable sources of research and verification. Works by the following authors have been especially useful: Louis Armstrong, Claude Brown, Billie Holiday, H. Rap Brown, Charles W. Chestnutt, Clarence L. Cooper, Ricardo Cortez Cruz, Ralph Ellison, Rudolph Fisher, Donald Goines, Chester Himes, Langston Hughes, Claude McKay, Mezz Mezzrow, Robert Dean Pharr, Iceberg Slim, Charles Wright, and Al Young.

Over the years since the publication of the first version of this book, *Dictionary of Afro-American Slang*, in 1970, I have saved words and phrases popular among black speakers I've come across with the intention of one day updating the book. I gathered nearly two thousand of them before 1990, when I decided to seriously work on a new edition.

At that time I had been employed in the Department of English at the University of California at Davis for one year—after teaching at the University of Colorado at Boulder for twelve. The Committee on Research at UC-Davis supported my plans to update the book by supplying me with a modest amount of money to pay for research assistants.

ACKNOWLEDGMENTS

A lot of people helped to make this dictionary a reality. I extend a very special thanks to Linda Raymond, who worked the longest with me as research assistant; and thanks also to Tiffany Anne Gardner, who also briefly served as a research assistant; to Susan Kancir, for typing the bibliography; thanks to Raleigh Elliott and the other librarians in Inter-Library Loan at UCD for being so patient and efficient; and to the earlier people—Sheila Silverstone, Corinna Fales, Nan Braymer, Jean Streiff, Max Gundy—who helped in one way or another with the first version. Thanks also to my friend and agent Susan Bergholz for her valuable advice and encouragement. And, finally, thanks to my editor, Dawn Seferian, and the other editors at Viking Penguin, for the expert work they performed on the manuscript.

CONTENTS

Terms

NOTE. American regionalism is an important factor in slang usage, especially before the large African-American migration north started after the Civil War. The loose distinctions I make between north and south, and sometimes between eastern and western parts of the country, in the matter of usage, are to be seen as only approximations. Because of black migration from the Old South to the northern ghettos throughout the latter part of the nineteenth and through the first half of the twentieth century, there can be no consistently and truly clear distinction drawn between, say, the slang of Harlem and that of black Savannah, Georgia, or Charleston, South Carolina.

But relative categories can be made. A user should keep in mind that the "use" category is meant only to suggest the group of speakers among whom the term is most frequently heard. "Southern northern use" (SNU)—the broadest category—roughly covers all classes and all age groups from teens up. Obviously categories will necessarily overlap. "Drug culture use" (DCU), for example, often borders on "Street culture use" (SCU) or "Pimp and prostitute use" (PPU). But, generally, categories are reliable.

Anglo-American slang. Terms clearly originating among white slang users, especially pejorative or derogatory terms such as "nigger," "Nigger War," "nigger jail," and "nigger fever," have been selected only in clear instances where such terms were adopted and altered by black speakers.

Drug culture. Terms from the drug culture are only those that originated among or were used excessively by black slang users in the drug culture.

Southern slang. I am well aware that there is a school of social linguists—J. A. Harrison, author of the famous essay "Negro Speech" (1881), for example—who believe, despite absolute proof to the contrary, that not only black slang but all of black speech is derived from Anglo-Saxon speech, or, more specifically, from Elizabethan English. This theory is based on the fact that Elizabethan forms and terms can be found in early white southern speech. I have, as a result, been extremely careful to avoid words and phrases too generally southern to be identified as black. When I have been able to detect black words and phrases clearly adapted to white southern use, I have been careful to point this out and to indicate other aspects of the differences and variations between white southern and black southern use.

Jazz and blues slang. Terms from the world of black music are used only when they clearly originated among or were used excessively by black musicians.

Prison slang. Terms from the world of penal life—which is closely connected with street, underworld, and hustling cultures—are used only when they clearly originated among or were used excessively by black prisoners.

Youth culture slang. Words and phrases from rap and hip-hop cultures—which are closely related to those of street and gang cultures—have been selected only when they seemed clearly to have started among black speakers or when they were adapted and altered by black speakers.

Etymologies

Despite the sometimes elusive nature of word origin I have given etymological information as often as possible. Most slang terms are closely linked to words in standard usage. Following the tradition of most other slang dictionaries, I have not given the etymologies for such words and phrases.

Cross reference

Words and phrases of similar nature and related meaning are indicated by cross referencing. The better-known terms or those with more significant historical roots carry the more extensive definitions.

Rare

When a term was never in wide use or was restricted to a certain geographical area I have characterized it as "Rare."

Abbreviations

PARTS OF SPEECH

Parts-of-speech abbreviations appear in single-word entries and in some few instances where a phrase can be clearly defined in terms of its parts of speech. No attempt has been made to define the parts of speech of most phrases because to do so would have been unnecessarily cumbersome—especially since slang, by its very nature, disrupts traditional usage. The following abbreviations for the parts of speech are used when appropriate.

adj.	adjective
adv.	adverb
exclam.	exclamation
imper.	imperative
interj.	interjection
n.	noun
prep.	preposition
pro.	pronoun
superl.	superlative
v.	verb
vi.	verb intransitive
vt.	verb transitive

GEOGRAPHICAL LOCATIONS

The following is a key to the most frequently used abbreviations of geographical locations where terms were most popular or to which they were native or restricted.

DCU	Drug culture use
JBWU	Jazz and Blues world use
JMFU	Jazz musician and fan use
MWU	Midwest use
NCU	Northern city use
NECU	Northeastern city use
NRU	Northern rural use

NU	Northern use
PPU	Pimp and prostitute use
PU	Prison use
SCU	Southern city use
SGU	Street culture (gang) use
SNCU	Southern and northern city use
SNU	Southern and northern use
SRU	Southern rural use
SU	Southern use
WCU	West coast use
YCU	Youth culture use

Sometimes combinations of any of the above may appear at the end of an entry.

When the location is even more restricted—as in the case of a single state, a couple of states close together, a particular region in a state, or a section of a well-known city (such as Harlem in New York)—the specific information is supplied at the end of each such entry.

Citations

The following works and those listed in the Bibliography have been my primary printed sources. I have cited only works I consider reliable in their grasp of African-American culture and only those parts of such works that suit the purposes of this dictionary. There were many occasions when I rejected potential entries. When previous slang dictionaries, glossaries, novels, stories, folktales, scholarly books, or essays, for example, contained words or phrases cited as having originated among African-American slang users or presented such as having been common in black speech in one period or another, I looked for verification. When I was unable to locate more than three sources to support the potential entry, and when I was not myself familiar with the word or phrase, or when it had not been verified by my field research and at least one print source, I rejected the entry.

FR (*field research*) stands for information gathered from direct verbal sources or for information given to me by African-Americans in all age and "culture" groups.

Abbreviations of cited printed sources follow:

RDA, DDJ; PB; TB
Abrahams, Roger D. *Deep Down in the Jungle*. Hatboro, Pa.: Folklore Associates, 1964.
———. *Positively Black*. Englewood Cliffs, N.J.: Prentice-Hall, 1970.
———. *Talking Black*. Rowley, Mass.: Newbury House Publishers, Inc., 1976.

ECLA, CS; NN
Adams, E. C. L. *Congaree Sketches*. Chapel Hill: University of North Carolina Press, 1927.
———. *Nigger to Nigger*. New York: Charles Scribner's Sons, 1928.

ALA, AL
Alexander, Adele Logan. *Ambiguous Lives: Free Women of Color in Rural Georgia 1787–1879*. Fayetteville: The University of Arkansas Press, 1991.

ILA, CS
Allen, Irving Lewis. *The City in Slang: New York Life and Popular Speech*. New York: Oxford University Press, 1993.

MA, PTO, BL
Andrews, Malachi, and Paul T. Owens. *Black Language*. Los Angeles: Seymour-Smith, 1973.

LA, SM
Armstrong, Louis. *Satchmo: My Life in New Orleans*. Englewood Cliffs, N.J.: Prentice-Hall, 1954.

HLB, LSS
Ballowe, Hewitt L. *The Lawd Sayin' The Same: Negro Folk Tales of the Creole Country*. Baton Rouge: Louisiana State University Press, 1947.

FB, STOS
Bancroft, Frederic. *Slave Trading in the Old South*. New York: Ungar Publishing Co., 1931, 1959.

AB, DSJC
Barrere, Albert, and Charles G. Leland. *A Dictionary of Slang, Jargon and Cant, etc.*, Vol. I: A–K; Vol. II: L–Z. London: George Bell and Sons, 1897.

JB, DA
Bartlett, John. *The Dictionary of Americanisms*. New York: Crescent Books, 1989. [reprint of the 1848 Bartlett & Welford edition]

BB, AW
Berry, Brewton. *Almost White*. New York: Macmillan Co., 1963.

WKB, JMC, PS
Bentley, William K., and James M. Corbett. *Prison Slang: Words and Expressions Depicting Life Behind Bars*. Jefferson, N. C.: McFarland and Co., 1992 ["Black Slang," pp. 48–51].

JMB, DG; WB
Brewer, John Mason. *Dog Ghost and Other Texas Negro Folk Tales*. Austin: University of Texas, 1958.
———. *The Word on the Brazos: Negro Preacher Tales from the Brazos Bottoms of Texas*. Austin: University of Texas Press, 1953.

CB, MPL
Brown, Claude. *Manchild in the Promised Land*. New York: Macmillan Co., 1965.

HRB, DND
Brown, H. Rap. *Die Nigger Die!* New York: Dial Press, 1969.

DB, OHHJ
Burley, Dan. *Dan Burley's Original Handbook of Harlem Jive*. New York: Dan Burley, 1944.

MHB, JS
Boulware, Marcus H. *Jive and Slang*. Hampton, Va.: Boulware, 1947. [an unpaginated copy examined at the Schomburg Library indicated in entries as np: no page number[s]]

CC, HDH; OMMM; NCCHD
Calloway, Cab. *Hi De Ho*. New York: Mills, n. d.
Calloway, Cab, and Bryant Rollins. *Of Minnie the Moocher and Me*. New York: Thomas Y. Crowell, Co., 1976. [contains the full text of *The New Cab Calloway's Hepsters Dictionary/Language of Jive*, 1944 edition]

XC
Cartier, Xam. *Muse-Echo Blues*. New York: Harmony Books, 1991.

FGC, DARE; JT
Cassidy, Frederick G. *Dictionary of American Regional English*, Vol. 1. Boston: Harvard University Press, 1985; vol. 2. Boston: Harvard University Press, 1991.
————. *Jamaica Talk: Three Hundred Years of the English Language in Jamaica*. London: Macmillan Education, 1961.

CWC, CW; WY
Chestnutt, Charles W. *The Conjure Woman*. Boston: Houghton Mifflin, Co., 1899.
————. *The Wife of His Youth*. Boston: Houghton Mifflin Co., 1899.

DC, BJ
Claerbaut, David. *Black Jargon in White America*. Grand Rapids, Mich.: William B. Eerdmans, 1972.

MC, NTH
Cliff, Michelle. *No Telephone to Heaven*. New York: E. P. Dutton, 1987.

CLC, TF; TS
Cooper, Clarence L. *The Farm*. New York: Crown, 1967.
————. *The Scene*. Greenwich, Conn.: Fawcett Publishing Co., 1961. [reprinted from the 1960 Crown Press edition]

HC, WSJ
Cooper, Helen. "Once Again, Ads Woo Teens with Slang." *The Wall Street Journal* (March 29, 1993): B1, B2.

RCC, SOC
Cruz, Ricardo Cortez. *Straight Outta Compton*. Boulder, Colo.: Fiction Collective Two, 1992.

CS, VOL. 3, NO. 2; VOL 3, NO. 3; VOL 4, NO. 1
Current Slang. Vol. 3, no. 2 (November 1968) ["The Slang of Watts," by Kathleen M. Grange, Ph.D.].
Also:
Volume 3, no. 3 (1969).
Volume 4, no. 1 (1969).

RHdeC, NB
deCoy, Robert H. *The Nigger Bible*. Los Angeles: Holloway House Publishing Co., 1967.

JLD, BN; LBE

Dillard, J. L. *Black Names*. The Hague: Mouton, 1976.
————. *Lexicon of Black English*. New York: Seabury Press, 1977.

RMD, ANF

Dorson, Richard M. *American Negro Folktales*. Greenwich, Conn.: Fawcett Premier Book, 1967. [reprint of the 1956, 1958 Indiana University Press edition]

RE, IM

Ellison, Ralph. *Invisible Man*. New York: Signet, 1960. [reprinted from the 1952 Random House edition]

JSF, AON

Farmer, John S. *Americanisms—Old and New. A Dictionary of Words, Phrases and Colloquialism Peculiar to the United States, British America, the West Indies, etc.* London: Thomas Poulter and Sons, 1889.

LF, EJ

Feather, Leonard. *Encyclopedia of Jazz*. New York: Horizon, 1955.

RF, WJ

Fisher, Rudolph. *The Walls of Jericho*. New York: Alfred A. Knopf, 1928.

SBF, IHAT

Flexner, Stuart Berg. *I Hear America Talking: An Illustrated Treasury of American Words and Phrases*. New York: Van Nostrand Reinhold, Co., 1976.

EF, BVV; RDSL

Folb, Edith. *Black Vernacular Vocabulary*. Los Angeles: The UCLA Center for Afro-American Studies, 1972.
————. *Runnin' Down Some Lines: The Language of Black Teenagers*. Cambridge: Harvard University Press, 1980.

HLF, RJPD

Foster, Herbert L. *Ribbin', Jivin', and Playin' the Dozens: The Unrecognized Dilemma of Inner City Schools*. Cambridge, Mass.: Ballinger Publishing Co., 1974.

DG, BG; BGL; CP; CR; DC; DL; D; ER; ICH; KE; KLH; SP; W

Goines, Donald. *Black Gangster*. Los Angeles: Holloway House Publishing Co., 1977.

——. *Black Girl Lost*. Los Angeles: Holloway House Publishing Co., 1973.

——. *Crime Partners*. Los Angeles: Holloway House Publishing Co., 1978.

——. *Cry Revenge*. Los Angeles: Holloway House Publishing Co., 1974.

——. *Daddy Cool*. Los Angeles: Holloway House Publishing Co., 1974.

——. *Death List*. Los Angeles: Holloway House Publishing Co., 1974.

——. *Dopefiend*. Los Angeles: Holloway House Publishing Co., 1971.

——. *Eldorado Red*. Los Angeles: Holloway House Publishing Co., 1974.

——. *Inner City Hoodlum*. Los Angeles: Holloway House Publishing Co., 1975.

——. *Kenyatta's Escape*. Los Angeles: Holloway House Publishing Co., 1974.

——. *Kenyatta's Last Hit*. Los Angeles: Holloway House Publishing Co., 1975.

——. *Street Players*. Los Angeles: Holloway House Publishing Co., 1973.

——. *Whoreson*. Los Angeles: Holloway House Publishing Co., 1972.

RSG, JL; JT
Gold, Robert S. *A Jazz Lexicon*. New York: Alfred A. Knopf, 1964.
——. *Jazz Talk*. New York: Bobbs-Merril Co., 1975.

HEG, DAUL
Goldin, Hyman E., Frank O'Leary, and Morris Lipsius. *Dictionary of American Underworld Lingo*. New York: Twayne Publishers, 1950.

AEG, BB
Gonzales, Ambrose E. *The Black Border: Gullah Stories of the Carolina Coast*. Columbia, S.C.: State, 1922.

KG, JV
Grimes, Kitty. *Jazz Voices*. London: Quartet Voices, 1983.

FG, DVT
Grose, Frances. *1811 Dictionary of the Vulgar Tongue*. Chicago: Follett Publishing Co., 1971. [reprint of the 1788 F. Leach/Mat. Drew edition, London]

SH, GL

Hall, Susan. *Gentleman of Leisure: A Year in the Life of a Pimp*. New York: New American Library, 1972.

JAH, MLN; PBE

Harrison, James A., "Negro English." *Modern Language Notes* 7 (February 1881).

————. "Negro English." *Perspectives on Black English*. Edited by J. Dillard. The Hague: Mouton, 1975. [reprinted from Anglia, 1884]

JH, PBL

Haskins, Jim, and Hugh F. Butts. *The Psychology of Black Language*. New York: Barnes and Noble Books, 1973.

RH, SK, NN

Hauge, Ron, and Sean Kelly. *Nick Names*. New York: Collier Books, 1987.

CH, CFS; IHHLHG; P

Himes, Chester. *Cast the First Stone*. New York: Coward-McCann, 1952.

————. *If He Hollers Let Him Go*. New York: Thunder's Mouth Press, 1986. [reprint of the 1945 Doubleday edition]

————. *Pinktoes*. New York: Dell Publishing Co. and G. P. Putnam's Sons, 1966. [reprint of the 1965 G. P. Putnam's Sons/Stein and Day edition]

BH, LSB

Holiday, Billie. *Lady Sings the Blues*. New York: Doubleday, 1956.

JEH, AAC; AHAE

Holloway, Joseph E., ed. *Africanisms in American Culture*. Bloomington and Indianapolis: Indiana University Press, 1990.

Holloway, Joseph E., and Winifred K. Vass. *The African Heritage of American English*. Bloomington and Indianapolis: Indiana University Press, 1993.

LH, LKFC; BNF

Hughes, Langston. *Laughing to Keep from Crying*. New York: Henry Holt, 1952.

Hughes, Langston, and Arna Bontemps. *The Book of Negro Folklore*. New York: Dodd, Mead, 1958.

ZNH, DTR; JGV; MM; TEWG; SS; AM

Hurston, Zora Neale. *Dust Track on a Road*. New York: Harper-Collins Publishers, 1991. [reprint of the 1942 J. B. Lippincott edition]

————. *Jonah's Gourd Vine*. New York: HarperCollins Publishers, 1990. [reprint of the 1934 J. B. Lippincott edition]

————. *Mules and Men*. Philadelphia: J. B. Lippincott, 1935.

————. *Their Eyes Were Watching God*. New York: HarperCollins Publishers, 1990. [reprint of the 1937 J. B. Lippincott edition]

————. *Seraph on the Suwanee*. New York: HarperCollins Publishers, 1991. [reprint of the 1948 Scribner's Sons edition]

————. "Story in Harlem Slang." *American Mercury*, 55 (July 1942): 84–96.

HMH, HCWR
Hyatt, Harry Middleton. *Hoodoo—Conjuration—Witchcraft—Rootwork: Beliefs According to Many Negroes and White Persons, These Being Orally Recorded among Blacks and Whites*. Vol. 1 and 2. New York: Memoirs of The Alma Egan Hyatt Foundation, 1970.

HJ, ILSG
Jacobs, Harriet. *Incidents in the Life of a Slave Girl*. Boston: n. p., 1861.

KCJ, JS
James, Kelvin Christopher. *Jumping Ship and Other Stories*. New York: Villard Books, 1992.

BJ, BLH, SD
Jones, Bessie, and Bess Lomax Hawes. *Step It Down: Games, Plays, Songs and Stories from the Afro-American Heritage*. Athens: University of Georgia Press, 1972.

CCJ, NMGC
Jones, Charles C. *Negro Myths from the Georgia Coast*. Boston and New York: Houghton Mifflin Co., 1888.

REK, BC; G
Kennedy, Emmet R. *Black Cameos*. New York: Boni, 1924.

————. *Gritny*, 1927.

SK, PC
Kennedy, Stetson. *Palmetto Country*. New York: Duell, Sloan and Pearce, 1942.

RRL, DAZ
Lingeman, Richard R. *Drugs from A to Z: A Dictionary*. New York: McGraw-Hill, 1969.

EXPLANATORY NOTES

AL, LWBB; MJR; RS

Lomax, Alan. *The Land Where the Blues Began.* New York: Pantheon Books, 1993.

———. *Mister Jelly Roll.* New York: Duell, Sloan and Pearce, 1950.

———. *The Rainbow Sign: A Southern Documentary.* New York: Duell, Sloan and Pearce, 1959.

SL, RJON

Longstreet, Stephen. *The Real Jazz Old and New.* Baton Rouge: Louisiana State University Press, 1956.

CM, CW

Major, Clarence, ed. *Calling the Wind: Twentieth Century African-American Short Stories.* New York: Harper Perennial, 1993.

MM, NYT

Marriott, Michel. "Cheap High Lures Youths to Malt Liquor '40's." *The New York Times.* Vol. CXLII, No. 49, 303 (April 16, 1993).

HM, GL

Max, H. *Gay(s) Language: A Dic(k) tionary of Gay Slang.* Austin, Tex.: Banned Books, 1988.

CMc, HH

McKay, Claude. *Home to Harlem.* New York: Pocket Books, 1956. [reprint of the 1928 Harper and Brothers edition]

TMC, DA; WE

McMillan, Terry. *Disappearing Acts.* New York: Viking Penguin, 1989.

———. *Waiting to Exhale.* New York: Viking Penguin, 1992.

MM, RB

Mezzrow, Milton, with Bernard Wolfe. *Really the Blues.* New York: Random House, 1946.

CRM, BP

Milner, Christina, and Richard Milner. *Black Players.* Boston: Little, Brown and Co., 1971.

WM, DBD

Mosley, Walter. *Devil in a Blue Dress.* New York: Pocket Books, 1991. [reprint of the 1990 W. W. Norton and Co. edition]

JM, WPC

Mowry, Jess. *Way Past Cool.* New York: Farrar, Straus and Giroux, 1992.

PM, UCLAS
Munro, Pamela. *U.C.L.A. Slang: A Dictionary of Slang Words and Expressions Used at U.C.L.A.* Los Angeles: UCLA Occasional Papers in Linguistics 8/Department of Linguistics, UCLA, 1989.

FN, JS
Newton, Francis. *The Jazz Scene.* London: McGibbon and Kee, 1959.

EP, DU
Partridge, Eric. *A Dictionary of the Underworld, British and American, Being the Vocabularies of Crooks, Criminals, Racketeers, Beggars and Tramps, Convicts, the Commercial Underworld, the Drug Traffic, the White Slave Traffic, Spivs.* New York: Bonanza Books, 1961. [reprint of the 1949 Macmillan Co. edition]

RDP, SRO
Pharr, Robert Dean. *S. R. O.* New York: Doubleday, 1971.

RP, C
Price, Richard. *Clockers.* Boston: Houghton Mifflin Co., 1992.

NNP, FBSN
Puckett, Niles Newbell. *Folk Beliefs of the Southern Negro.* Chapel Hill: University of North Carolina Press, 1926.

DR, BASL
Rose, Dan. *Black American Street Life: South Philadelphia, 1969–1971.* Philadelphia: University of Pennsylvania Press, 1926.

TR, AGD
Rosengarten, Theodore. *All God's Dangers: The Life of Nate Shaw.* New York: Alfred A. Knopf, 1974.

EBR, MUS
Ruther, Edward Byron. *The Mulatto in the United States.* New York: Negro Universities Press/Greenwood Publishing Corp., 1969. [reprint of the Richard G. Badger 1918 edition]

LS, GYY
Saxon, Lyle., comp. *Gumbo: Ya-Ya: A Collection of Folktales.* Boston: Houghton Mifflin Co., 1945.

SGS, BG
Stoney, Samuel Gaillard, and Gertrude Matthew Shelby. *Black Genesis.* New York: Macmillan Co., 1930.

IS, PSML; TB

Slim, Iceberg. *Pimp: The Story of My Life*. Los Angeles: Holloway House Publishing Co., 1969.

———. *Trick Baby: The Biography of a Con Man*. Los Angeles: Holloway House Publishing Co., 1969.

GS, TT

Smiterman, Geneva. *Talkin' and Testifyin': The Language of Black America*. Boston: Houghton Mifflin Co., 1977.

LAS, RL

Stanley, Laurence A., ed. *Rap: The Lyrics*. New York and London: Penguin Books, 1992.

TT, NFR

Talley, Thomas. *Negro Folk Rhymes*. New York: Macmillan Co., 1922.

MT, DAF

Tallman, Marjorie. *Dictionary of American Folklore*. New York: Philosophical Library, 1959.

RFT, FS

Thompson, Robert Farris. *Flash of the Spirit: African and Afro-American Art and Philosophy*. New York: Random House, 1983.

LDT, AGD

Turner, Lorenzo D. *Africanisms in the Gullah Dialect*. Ann Arbor: University of Michigan Press, 1973. [reprint of the 1949 University of Chicago Press edition]

AW, CP

Walker, Alice. *The Color Purple*. New York: Harcourt Brace Jovanovich, 1982.

WF, DAS

Wentworth, Harold, and Stuart Berg Flexner. *Dictionary of American Slang*. New York: Thomas Y. Crowell Co., 1967.

RW, AAGYRS

Westmacott, Richard. *African-American Gardens and Yards in the Rural South*. Knoxville: University of Tennessee Press, 1992.

TW, CH; CK

Williams, Terry. *Crackhouse*. Reading, Mass.: Addison-Wesley Publishing Co., 1992.

———. *The Cocaine Kids: The Inside Story of a Teenage Drug Ring*. Reading, Mass.: Addison-Wesley Publishing Co., 1989.

DW, TL
Wepman, Dennis, Ronald Newman, and Murry B. Binderman. *The Life: The Lore and Folk Poetry of the Black Hustler*. Philadelphia: University of Pennsylvania Press, 1976.

CW, TM; TW
Wright, Charles. *The Messenger*. New York: Farrar, Straus and Giroux, 1963.
————. *The Wig*. New York: Farrar, Straus and Giroux, 1966.

CVV, NH
Vechten, Carl Van. *Nigger Heaven*. New York: Alfred A. Knopf, 1926.

AY, S
Young, Al. *Snakes*. New York: Holt, Rinehart and Winston, 1970.

INTRODUCTION

Slang has never had a consistently good reputation. Often it is characterized as much by arrogance, bigotry, sexism, and self-contempt as by humor, compassion, and wisdom. But it also happens to be the most alive aspect of our language. My goal, then—at least in part—is to help bring to the language we call slang a better name, a better reputation; and also to suggest, by the example of this dictionary, how intrinsic it is to the quest of human culture to express and to renew itself.

Also, there is the sense that slang is tolerated because, for the most part (in the minds of some critics), it belongs to the young, the youth culture, and there is the sense, or hope, that they will eventually grow out of it, advance to standard speech, which, the official guardians of the culture seem to hope, will signal their acceptance of the status quo. J. L. Dillard makes the point [in *Lexicon of Black English*, 1977] that the word *slang* itself has caused many people to take lightly or negatively a complex and rich language.

> The general public has long associated slang with a transitory stage in the language development of teenagers, soon to be dropped by all except those few who never enter the adult, mainstream world. "Slang" was, for the average American, an exotic language phenomenon primarily for children—outside the domain of working language and not really to be considered seriously. (p. 17)

Kids aside, maybe the case is more pervasive and serious than that. Slang has always been considered, by official watchers of culture, to be a threat to not only "proper" language but to "proper" society as well. Irving Lewis Allen, in his *City in Slang: New York Life and Popular Speech* (1993), takes a broader view:

Around 1850 the word slang, while in English a century earlier, became the accepted term for "illegitimate" and other unconventional speech. Disapproving comment on low speech forms, fueled by class anxieties in the changing city, probably helped establish the word slang in the United States. By 1900 the term had all its present meanings, including that of a vocabulary regarded as below standard and that threatened proper, genteel usages. . . . Street speech . . . expressed the troublesome spirit of the social underside of the industrial city: unconventional, experimental without license, insubordinate, scornful of—or merely careless of—authority. These locutions spread rapidly and began to be noticed, recorded, and deemed something of a social problem. (pp. 22–23)

The way black jazz and blues musicians have been talking, say, since the latter part of the nineteenth century, might be seen as an outstanding example of this rebellion Allen speaks of. In fact, Robert S. Gold, in his introduction to *A Jazz Lexicon* (1964), supports Allen's claim, saying that there is an "essential rebelliousness at the heart of both the music and the speech" (xviii). And I would go so far as to say that *all* alive art is rebellious, and *all* alive speech, slang or otherwise, is rebellious, rebellious in the healthy sense that they challenge the stale and the conventional.

African-American slang cuts through logic and arrives at a quick, efficient, interpretative solution to situations and things otherwise difficult to articulate. It serves as a device for articulating every conceivable thing imaginable—the nature of sex, the taste of food, social relationships, life itself, and death. Just as the word "Watergate" explains a vast and complex incident, a word like "bondage," to refer to being "in debt," or a phrase like "jump the broom," to explain that somebody will get married, makes the point quickly with a strong, clear, symbolic gesture, and a sense of vibrant, alive humor.

Black slang is a living, breathing form of expression that changes so quickly no researcher can keep up with it. A word or phrase can come into existence to mean one thing among a limited number of speakers in a particular neighborhood and a block away it might mean something else or be unknown entirely—at least for a while.

One group of speakers—such as a gang, a social club, or even a whole neighborhood—may feel the need for secrecy from another gang, social club, or neighborhood only just around the corner. At this point, when it is most private, this mode of speech thrives and is at its most effective. It is the classic example of a secret tongue. At the same time, both groups will feel the need to maintain a rapidly changing vocabulary unknown to the larger, mainstream culture—known generally or loosely as white America. The need for secrecy is part of the reason for the rapid change.

Since the days of slavery, this secrecy has served as a form of cultural self-defense against exploitation and oppression, constructed out of a combination of language, gesture, body style, and facial expression. In its embryonic stages during slavery, the secrecy was a powerful medium for making sense out of a cruel and strange world. African-American slang is a kind of "home talk" in the sense that it was not originally meant for listeners beyond the nest.

As always the case with informal private talk, it becomes, formally speaking, *informal* language—slang—when it reaches the larger speaking population. In other words, slang is, in a sense, a corruption of the more private forms of informal speech, such as cant, argot, or jargon. This evolution from private to public is natural for the words and phrases strong enough to survive for any considerable length of time.

But once such a transition is made, original meanings are very often lost. For example, "up tight" in the fifties, among the original group of black speakers who created the term, had a specific sexual reference. Once the phrase fell into general use, it took on a psychological meaning, referring to some sort of mental disturbance.

This evolution from private to public is not only essential to the vitality at the crux of slang, but inevitable. By this I mean, African-American slang is not only a living language for black speakers but for the whole country, as evidenced by its popularity decade after decade since the beginning of American history. The most recent example of this popularity is rap and hip-hop during the 1980s and the 1990s.

One important aspect of this "aliveness" is its onomatopoeic tendency. How words *sound* has always interested black speakers. Zap, yacky-de-yack, bop, bebop, ticktock, O-bop-she-bam, hoochy-choochy, honkytonk—all have been popular at one time or another. Perhaps even more than any other type of slang words, onomatopoeic words deliver the pleasure of immediacy—the "sock!" (as in "sock it to me").

In a similar way, the rhyming jargon of black slang gives the same sort of satisfaction—especially for the pleasures of syncopated sound—as do rhyming terms such as Muhammad Ali's "rope-a-dope." Related in form is the language of rap and hip-hop. Rappers and would-be rappers carry on a tradition—just as the break dancing of the eighties followed the flash dancing of the forties—that started with pre–twentieth century forms of playful, informal African-American speech.

Some rap and hip-hop words and phrases will enter the canon, just as in the past hip and jive words such as "dude" and "cool" ended up in general use and in dictionaries.

While a certain vocabulary or idiom might please and serve one decade or generation, it will not necessarily work for the next. Changes in black slang word forms take place continually. It happens when speakers drop syllables, usually from the end or sometimes from the beginning of a word, such as "Bama" for Alabama, "cap" for "backcap," "bam" for "bambita," "bro" for "brother," or "head" for "crackhead."

Other changes occur through shifts in the function of African-American slang words. A noun, for example, might be used as a verb: "He *boozed* himself to death" or "I *jived* my way to Brooklyn." Black speech is fluid in this way because it remains open to the influences of verbal forces from every conceivable direction.

And it is important to remember that it is anonymous speakers who create and sustain the initial contents and shape of this language. Black social groups across the country are the homes of such anonymous speakers. Their talk draws on many levels of language, and popular culture in general, for its storehouse of words and phrases.

Let me return to an earlier point in order to complete the thought. The private talk of an African-American gang or social club becomes slang when it reaches the larger African-American community or communities. It continues to be slang from that point on as it moves out into the general American speaking public. But African-American slang is *not* colloquialism; it is not dialect, not argot, not jargon or cant. Black slang is composed of or involves the use of redundancies, jive rhyme, nonsense, fad expressions, nicknames, corruptions, onomatopoeia, mispronunciations, and clipped forms.

In this way, the collective verbal force of black speakers throughout the many black communities in America carries on the tradition of renewing the American language—while resisting and using it. Yet African-American informal speech and slang are quite distinct in many essential ways from common American speech and slang. There is a basic grammatical difference between black speech and American English. Today, in the 1990s, nouns, for example, tend to be repeated within a single sentence along with pronouns as they were a hundred and fifty years ago. At the same time, the overall shape of African-American slang is also influenced—through exchange and conflict—by American English words and phrases that are adjusted to the African forms.

Again, for example, "This guy, he come at me out of nowhere." Or, "The mayor, he done the best he could with an impossible situation." Past, present, and future tenses are often not present in the expected order. No matter the subject, it gets the same verb form. Plurals are employed where in English structure they are not required. Sentences are commonly structured without the *to be* verb forms.

To say it yet another way, what I am calling African-American slang *includes* black dialect, but slang and idiom are not the same thing as dialect. Black speakers generally sound like other speakers of their regions. We know this as dialect. But African-American slang, late as the 1920s, 1930s, and 1940s, was still largely regionalized. If, in the thirties, a southern black speaker of slang came into contact with a northern black speaker of slang, neither one usually had any idea what the other was talking about.

Today, in the nineties, just about every segment of the country is in touch with every other, due to television and radio, air travel and telephones, faxes and computers, so a homogenized form of African-American slang has been emerging since the 1950s while dialects seem less altered by extra-regional influences.

This makes for a fertile language environment and for even more accelerated change in African-American slang. It evolved over the decades best when the social and political atmospheres were most fluid and creative. A social environment that is accommodating is necessary for the evolution of any form of slang. African-American communities have been generally receptive to slang, although it has had to evolve in a moral war zone between the secular position of street culture and the sacred position of the sisters and deacons of the black church.

American society generally is receptive to slang. Slang never evolves in isolation. Black slang in particular uses the receptive American atmosphere to its own advantage while creating and maintaining a private language with its own center of gravity, integrity, and shape.

Many of the words and phrases are borrowed from very specific cultural pockets in the country—from the drug scene, prison life, street life, entertainment, and especially the areas of blues and jazz.

These categories are important areas upon which black slang draws. They are every bit as essential to the vitality of black slang as is the presence of the mainstream American cultural scene.

This also means that, even when there is relatively little direct outside contact or communication between African-Americans and other American social and racial subgroups, cross-fertilization—by way of television or whatever—is essential for the continuation of a private black alternative language—one that is, to some extent, destined to return to the white public area from which it has borrowed.

So it is useless to ask, Why an alternative language? Why not *one* American tongue for every ethnic or social group? Most African-Americans, like most Americans of any ethnic group, are skilled in what is called the common American culture—and the American language is the instrument of that culture. Each group's individual cultural identity is essentially established through the bond of its own distinctive expression. As is the case for other subcultures, African-Americans are *also* skilled in their own racial culture. Informal speech is part of that culture, and they have many effective uses for informal speech. In daily life there are situations so sensitive or painful that slang often seems the only way to deal with them.

One of the primary functions of this language is its quest to create a coherent cultural construct of positive self-images. Though many of the words and phrases may sound harsh and even obscene to outsiders, the language is essential to the cultural enrichment of African-Americans.

Black speakers, in self-mockery, can call each other "nigger" and, in a sense, make null and void racial slurs of white bigots. As James Baldwin often said, "I told you *first*." But the effectiveness of such a strategy, and its long-term psychological benefits, remains open to question. Yet it is a social phenomenon that has significant historical consensus simply by virtue of its long practice.

American English, perhaps more than any other language, has borrowed from other tongues, period. Black slang is a form of black speech and black speech is a form of American English, but in the early stages, say, in the sixteenth century, black speech was still close to its African roots. Such African words and phrases as "okra," "coca-cola," "turnip," "jazz," "gorilla," "banana," and "juke" (as in "juke-box"), for example, became common symbols in American English.

More important, African-American speech and slang have contributed to the ultimate formation of formal American English. And not only through the process of African nonslang words entering the language, but also as slang words and phrases, such as "ace boon coon," "Afro," "attitude," "bad," "not," and so on, enter the mainstream formal language. Stuart Berg Flexner, in *I Hear America Talking* (1976), says:

> When we heard America talking, we heard Blacks talking. . . . The "we" is Black and White. . . . The Blacks have influenced the American language in two major ways (1) by using many of their native (Black African) words and speech, and (2) by causing, doing, being, influencing things that have had all America talking, often using terms created or popularized by the Black presence and experience. (p. 31)

There are roughly four areas of African-American slang: (1) the early southern rural slang that started during slavery, (2) the slang of the sinner-man/black musician of the period between 1900 and 1960, (3) street culture slang out of which rap and hip-hop evolved, and (4) working class slang. All areas are fully represented in this dictionary, from the beginnings of black people in this country to the present.

The point, of course—and it's a pity to have to stress it—is that not all black speech is "street speech." But a surprisingly large number of Americans believe this to be so. "There are now thousands, perhaps millions, of black Americans who . . . have limited contact with vernacular black speech," says John Baugh in *Black Street Speech* (1983). "Dialect boundaries therefore don't automatically conform to racial groups. Then collectively, black Americans speak a wide range of dialects, including impeccable standard English" (p. 127).

Not only has there been, historically speaking, geographically determined diversity to African-American slang, but the Africans who made up the language out of Portuguese Pidgin, Bantu, and Swahili, primarily, created what was known early on as Plantation Creole. The persistence of Africanisms in the formation of black slang and African-American culture generally can be seen as a grand testimony to the strength of the human spirit and to the cultural strength of that polyglot group of Africans dumped, starting in 1619, on this continent to work the land.

But make no mistake, this is not another African language. And I am not pushing an Afrocentric program by spelling out the origins of this language. Black slang is an *American* language with distant roots in the ancient coastal tribes of central west Africa, as well as, indirectly, in Anglo-Irish culture and elsewhere.

But perhaps more important than any of the above is this: African-American speech and slang form is, in a sense, one of the primary cutting edges against which American speech—formal and informal—generally keeps itself alive.

A Note on This Book

The earlier version of this book, *Dictionary of Afro-American Slang*, appeared in 1970, at a time when research in this area was still extremely scarce. Today there is much scholarly work on African-American speech, but to my knowledge there is no substantial reference dictionary of African-American words, phrases, and expressions. This volume contains at least three times the number of entries as were in the first volume.

In looking through hundreds of dictionaries, I've discovered that most of them have brief or no introductions. In my original introduction, I felt that I needed to spend some time justifying the book, so I talked about the function of African-American slang and a little bit about its history. Here I have tried to do as much and more, while keeping in mind that a dictionary needs little or no introduction.

But since a reader will need to know how to use a book, let me explain the format of the entries. The date following the entry generally refers to the period during which the word, phrase, or expression was most popular.

Information on part of speech indicates the way a word or phrase or expression was most often used in a sentence.

The definitions themselves, I hope, are clear and to the point.

Then there is an example of usage, in instances where an example seemed necessary. The final section of a typical entry gives the area or areas of the country where the word or phrase or expression was first most popular.

But I've made no attempt to nail down precisely the time of origin of words, phrases, or expressions, except by implication. It would be extremely difficult, for example, to indicate precisely when "back door," as a symbol, entered African-American culture, or when "bamboo," meaning clothes, spread from plantation to plantation in the vocabulary of slaves. But I've relied on a vast body of research, which has been thoroughly explored.

And, as might be expected, the research is often contradictory. Given this situation, I believe I settled for the most likely periods of popularity. In most instances, the word or phrase started at the earliest period of the time indicated.

Finally, I have compiled African-American words and phrases that, in some cases, are more than two hundred years old, as well as the most recent ones—many rap and hip hop terms—I could locate. The entries represent African-American speakers in every section of the country, from as early as the 1620s through to the 1990s. In gathering these words, phrases, and expressions, I have relied heavily on hundreds of sources spoken and printed (see bibliography at the end of the dictionary) and from my own cultural experience.

JUBA
TO
JIVE

A adj. (1950s–1960s) that which is emphatically correct. Example: "You fucking A, man." Midwest and southern use.

ABC n. (1950s–1990s) abbreviation for "ace boon coon." (EF, RDSL, p. 227.) SNU.

Abear v. (1940s–1950s) tolerate; endure. (FGC, DARE, p. 3.) Example: "I never could abear such loud talk." SNU, MWU.

Abie n. (1930s–1940s) Harlem tailor, usually Jewish, but in any case white (probably pejorative). (DB, OHHJ, p. 12; FGC, DARE, p. 4.) Harlem use.

Abortion n. (1970s) an utter fiasco. (FR.) Example: "The project was a total abortion." Rare. New York City use.

Abraham Lincoln; Abe n. (1950s–1960s) a five-dollar bill. (FR.) Example: "Can you lay an Abe Lincoln on me till payday?"

Absofuckinglute(ly) adj., adv. (1960s–1970s) without doubt; emphatic. Here, as in many other instances, the swear word serves as an intrinsic all-purpose intensifier. (RCC, SOC, p. 17.) Example: "It's the absofuckinglute truth." NCU.

Acapulco [gold] n. (1960s) a high-quality grade of marijuana. (CS, vol. 3, no. 2, p.8; EF, RDSL, p. 227.) SNU.

Ace n. (1940s–1990s) early in the forties ace was used to refer to a dollar bill. By the early fifties it meant one's best friend; one's lover. Picked up from card-playing use, the ace being the card the player often relies on to change the odds. Short for "ace boon coon." Form of address for a friend. (WKB, JMC, PS, p. 48.) Examples: "I spent my last ace"; or, "Hey! Ace! How're you doing?" SNU.

Ace boon coon n. (1930s–1950s) a black expression of friendship. The expression takes the white racial slur "coon" and combines it with "ace" (from card playing) to make an ironically positive reference. (CB, MPL, p. 77.) Example: "You are my ace boon coon." NECU, MWU.

Ace boom boom n. (1980s–1990s) a variant of "Ace boon coon"; one's best friend. (EF, RDSL, p. 227.) SNU.

Ace-coon n. (1960s–1970s) This phrase is used ironically and refers to an important man. Often it used to refer to a "token" black person employed in what is essentially otherwise an all-white place of business. (FR.) Example: "He's the ace-coon here." SNU. See "Big Shot."

Ace-deuce n. (1940s) three. Limited use, mainly the south and midwest. (DB, OHHJ, p. 133.) Example: "We been married ace-deuce years." Southern and midwest use. See "acey-deucey."

Ace in the hole n. (1970s) hidden plan of action. The expression does not refer to an actual object. The meaning of "ace" by the 1970s had changed dramatically. In the midwest, especially, it took on this far more restricted meaning. (FR.) Example: "Don't worry, I got an ace in the hole." SNU, MWU.

Ace-lover n. (1940s) number one; most important member of the opposite sex. A woman's expression used to refer to her husband or pimp. Limited use, mainly the south and midwest. (FR.) Example: "I might fool around on the side when somebody looks good to me, but Johnny is my one and only ace-lover." Southern and midwest use.

Ace out v. (1970s–1980s) to best; to surpass someone in competition. This was primarily an east coast phrase. The use of "ace" in this context still had clear connections with its earlier meanings. (FR.) Examples: "Did you see Jackson ace out in last night's game?"; or, "She aced out everybody in the foot race." NECU.

Ace up one's sleeve n. (1970s) This expression has a much clearer connection with the language of card games and gambling. It refers to a hidden plan of action. (FR.) Example: "The dude had an ace up his sleeve. That's how he won." SNU.

Acey-deucey adj. (1970s) Complex; unstable; composed of opposites. (FR.) Example: "I can't stay here and keep this place for you, Grover, because it's a very acey-deucey situation." See "ace-deuce." SU, MWU.

Aching for a side of beef (1990s) said of a woman when she desires a man. (RP, C) NECU.

Acid rock n. (1960s–1970s) white music, especially hard rock. (CS, vol. 3, no. 2, p. 8.) Northern and southern college student and city use. WCU, SNU.

Acknowledge n. (1920s) misuse of the word "knowledge." (FR.) Example: "He's got the acknowledge to get us out of here." SU.

Action n. (1960s–1990s) the vitality or force of a situation, plan, or proposition; excitement; gambling; sexual intercourse; music. The word "action" has changed little over the recent four decades. Also, in drug culture, "action" refers to plenty of drugs available on the scene. (CS, vol. 3, no. 2, p. 8; RSG, JL, pp. 4–5.) Examples: "Tonight, let's go where the action is"; or, "Let's get some action going here." Or, "I want some action." SNCU.

Actor n. (1980s) a faker. Unlike "movie star," this term has a negative connotation because in the eighties greater importance was placed on so-called "truth" as opposed to "fiction." Popular among black speakers but probably not of black origin. (FR.) Example: "The guy is just an actor—he's not for real." SNCU.

Action on a solid half traction (1940s) to be ready for anything. (DB, OHHJ, p. 133.) Harlem use.

Advantage v. (1920s) take advantage of; to cheat. The word in this context is misused. (FR.) Example: "I don't want you to try to advantage him."

Afeared (1650s–1890s) scared; from Old English. (JSF, AON, p. 7.); picked up from white southern use.

A-forty n. (1990s) a forty-ounce bottle of Old English 800 Malt Liquor. (MM, NYT, p. 1.) Bronx use.

Afrika Bambaataa [and The Soul Sonic Force] an early rap artist [and group]; came to prominence with the hit "Planet Rock" (1982).

African; Africky n. (1620s–1920s) anger; bad temper. It makes sense that, from the seventeenth century to the latter part of the nineteenth century and even up to the 1960s, this word would have a negative connotation, especially since Africa was offered as a negative symbol, associated with the uncontrollable forces of nature, wildness, the uncivilized. The 1920s were simply the period of Africa's highest overtly conscious negative rating in American speech. This period gave rise to the Tarzan-inspired British and American views of Africa, and they were picked up by blacks from popular American culture. (AEG, BB, p. 36.) Example: "Don't go getting your African up." SU.

African dominoes n. (1920s–1930s) a form of dice playing originating among black gamblers in New Orleans. (FR.) Example: "Let's throw some African dominoes." SU.

African golf ball n. (1980s–1990s) a watermelon. (EF, RDSL, p. 227.) SNU.

African grape n. (1970s–1990s) a watermelon. (EF, RDSL, p. 227.) Example: "Leroy wouldn't be caught dead eating an African grape out on the lawn so people driving by can see him." SNU.

Afro n. (1960s–1970s) a "natural" hair style that became popular among African-Americans in the early 1960s. The hair is allowed to grow long and is left woolly. Example: "That's a bad afro, girl!" SNU.

Afroed adj. (1970s) wearing a "natural," Afro hairstyle. (FR.) Example: "Both the men and the women were Afroed." SNCU.

Afromobile n. (1880s–1890s) a three-wheel passenger carriage used at Palm Beach for tourists. The vehicle was pedaled by black men. Picked up from white use. (FGC, DARE, p. 17.) Palm Beach, Florida, use.

After hours n. (1930s–1940s) a term used by jazzmen to refer to those times away from public places when they can play without restrictions or inhibitions; very private social gatherings in the wee hours of the morning. (RSG, JT, p. 2.) JBWU.

After-hours club n. (1930s–1990s) a social club where musicians and party-goers meet, often a private home; in the eighties and nineties a crackhouse, usually a converted private home. (RSG, JT, p. 2; TW, CH, p. 146.) JBW, SCU.

AG n. (1980s) the Attorney General. (FR.) Example: "Who you think you are, the AG?" East coast use mainly.

Agent n. (1960s–1970s) any policeman or policewoman. (CS, vol 3, no. 2, p. 8.) NCU.

Agg n. (1850s–1880s) variant of "egg." (CCJ, NMGC, p. 167.) Georgia use.

Agogo n. (1650s–1990s) *ngongo* (Bantu); a-go-go; a bell; bell sound. (HV, AHAE, p. 155.) SNU.

A grip n. (1990s) expensive; difficult. (FR.) Example: "I'd get my own apartment if it wasn't such a grip." WCU, SNCU.

Ah-ah n. (1920s) a stupid person; one who is unaware. (CMc, HH, p. 30.) Example: "The man's just a white man's ah-ah." May have roots in the West Indies. Harlem use.

A-head n. (1980s) a heavy user of amphetamines. (RRL, DAZ, p. 4.) Example: "The dude's a major A-head." Mainly east coast and drug culture use.

Ain't v. (1620s–1990s) do not; does not; am not. "Ain't" is a dialectal contraction of "not" in its various forms: am, is, has, have. (AEG, BB, p. 287.) Example: "I ain't coming." Or, "This ain't right. You got to do it again." SNU

Ain't coming (1940s–1950s) statement of refusal. (FR.) Example: "There's too much work here for one person. You gotta get somebody else to help me, or else I ain't coming." Coming, in this context, does not refer to actual physical motion but to mental activity. SNU.

Ain't holding no air (1980s–1990s) without substance; without basis; without importance or authority. (EF, RDSL, p. 227.) WCU.

[Your money] Ain't long enough (1980s–1990s) to have a limited amount of money. (EF, RDSL, p. 227.) SNU.

Ain't it [the truth] (1940s–1960s) exclamation for "Isn't it true?" Or, "There's something making you mad, ain't it?" (FR.) Example: in response to a statement that seems valid, the listener would say, "Ain't it the truth!" SNU.

Ain't nothing to it (1960s–1970s) said in response to "How are you doing?" Implies that life is all right or at least not a total disaster. This expression was also used to explain how simple a process or procedure might be. (FR.) Example: "Ain't nothing to it but to do it." SNU.

Ain't shit (1950s–1990s) without value; the worst possible condition, person, or thing. (EF, RDSL, p. 228.) SNU.

Air bags n. (1940s) the human lungs. So used because, at least in X rays and drawings, the lungs resemble bags. (DB, OHHJ, p. 133.) Example: "That joker knocked all the wind out of Max's air bags." Harlem use.

Airish adj. (1840s–1940s) to put on airs; cold, windy, cool, chilly. (FGC, DARE, pp. 28–29.) Example: "It's rather airish today, don't you think?" SNU.

Air out v. (1920s–1990s) to go for a walk; to leave, especially abruptly. (ZNH, AM, p. 85, 94.) Example: "Come on, sugar, let's air out on the boulevard." SNU.

Airy; airily adj., adv. (1960s) to put on airs; conceited. This term is less distinctly "black" than, say, "dicty." See "Dicty." (FR.) Example: "She sure is an airy bitch, isn't she." SNU.

AK n. (1990s) an AK-47 assault rifle. (FR.) NCU.

Akimbo; akimboing adj. or adv.; v. (1880s–1940s) to saunter, especially with hands in pockets or on hips. (JMB, DG, p. 55.) SU.

Alabama n. (1900s–1990s) nickname for a person from that state. The practice of using such nicknames was of course not exclusively black, but blacks in the midwest certainly practiced it rigorously. (ZNH, AM, p. 91.) NU. See "Bama."

Alarm clock n. (1940s) a college professor. The expression refers to early class hours and/or to one who wakes up a student who has fallen asleep in class. (MHB, JS, np.) Southern Negro college use.

Al Capone ride n. (1980s–1990s) any old car, especially one in need of repair or junking. (EF, RDSL, p. 228.) Los Angeles use.

Ali shuffle n. (1960s) Boxer Muhammad Ali described his in-the-ring footwork—a kind of dance—as the "Ali shuffle." SNU.

All-both pron. (1620s–1940s) both; of African and Gullah origin. (ECLA, CS, p. 8) SU. See "All-two."

All hid (1940s–1950s) children's hide-and-seek game. Phrase used as a question. (FGC, DARE, p. 41.) Example: "All hid? Ready or not, here I come." SNU.

Alley n. (1640s–1870s) the row between planted vegetables. (LDT, AGD, p. 283.) SU.

Alley[way] n. (1980s) corridor in a hospital. The negative association stems from the presence of hundreds of homeless, destitute people often left waiting for hours in the corridors of public hospitals. (FR.) NECU.

Alley rat n. (1980s) a demoralized, corrupt, thieving person. Phrase is both a drug culture term and a black street culture reference. NCU.

Alley tidde n. (1890s–1930s) an earthy style of playing the violin. (FR.) Example: "When Buck gets that alley tidde sound of his going, you can't help but put your hoe down and dance." JBW.

Alligator n. (1920s–1930s) a usually though not necessarily pejorative term probably coined by Louis Armstrong to describe white musicians who stole ("followed") the ideas of black players. It's a term used by black jazzmen, particularly in New Orleans, referring to white jazzmen and white jazz fans, jive black people, or jitterbugs (CC, OMMM, NCCHD, p. 252; DB, OHHJ, p. 133; RSG, JT, p. 3.). See "Gate" and "Gator." SNU.

Alligator-bait n. (1940s) a Negro in or from Florida. The expression refers to the brutal idea that white men in the Florida area used blacks as "alligator-bait." (DB, OHHJ, p. 133.) Harlem use.

All in the Kool Aid [and don't even know the flavor] (1990s) nosy, prying, inquisitive. (FR.) YCU, SCU.

All-originals n. (1980s) a social gathering of black people. (FR.) Example: "We're having an all-originals tonight at the club." SNU.

All-originals scene n. (1980s) an all-black affair. (FR.) SNU.

All reet adv., adj. (1930s–1940s) This is a variant pronunciation of "all right," spoken playfully. (FR.) SNU.

All she wrote n. (1930s–1940s) the end; the finish. (FR.) Example: "I can't tell you any more about it. That's all she wrote. The pencil broke." SU, MWU.

All that adj. (1970s–1990s) short for "all that much." (FR.) Example: "You been bragging on your boyfriend for days, girl—I know he can't be all that." SNCU.

All-two adj. (1700s–1940s) Gullah word meaning both or each; "a pleonastic negro corruption." (JJSF, AON, p. 13; AEG, BB, p. 287.) Example: "Here, take all-two wid you, you gon em." South Carolina and Georgia use. See "All-both."

Aloose adj. (1880s–1890s) variant of "loose." Example: "She's one of them aloose womens." (FR.) SU.

Amen bench n. (1890s–1940s) bench in the "Amen corner." See "Amen corner."

Amen corner n. (1890s–1940s) the front seats to the left or right of the pulpit in a "Negro" church. (FGC, DARE, p. 56.) SNU.

American Business College n. (1940s) liquor store, from "A.B.C.," or Alcoholic Beverage Commission. (MHB, JS, np.) Example: "Sonny? Naw. Only college he know anything about is the American Business College." Rare. Southern Negro college student use.

Ambulance chaser n. (1930s–1950s) a crooked lawyer who patrols the streets in search of accidents and their victims as clients. Sometimes these lawyers create situations to encourage accidents. (FR.) NCU.

A'monlar n. (1960s) a greeting. (CS, vol. 3, no. 2, p. 8.) Watts, Los Angeles, use.

Angel dust n. (1970s–1980s) a homemade drug in powder form sniffed through a straw or tube; the drug phencyclidine (PCP), which has been used to tranquilize livestock in preparation for surgery. (FGC, DARE, p. 63.) Example: "Wanna get off on some angel dust?" DCU.

Angel dust hero n. (1980s–1990s) a person who is hooked on cocaine. (KCJ, JS, p. 152.) DCU

Angel liquor n. (1940s) variant of "angelica," a type of sweet, fortified wine. Example: "Pour me a nice glass of angel liquor." California use.

Angel's turnip n. (1890s–1920s) apocynum androsoemifolium; a conjure potion; dogbane. (NNP, FBSN, p. 245.) Example: "She fixed him good with angel's turnip." SU.

Angle(d) up adj. (1900s–1920s) to confuse or be confused. (ECLA, NN, p. 263.) Example: "He's all angled up." Used in South Carolina and other southern areas.

Anigh prep. (1630s–1890s) close or near. (CCJ, NMGC, p. 64.) Example: "We had to get all our stuff out cause the fire was getting too anigh and next minute everything woulda been gone." SU.

Ankle v. (1940s) to walk. (MHB, JS, np.) Example: "You have to ankle over there. I can't lend you my car because it's in the shop." Southern use.

Ann; Miss Ann n. (1940s–1960s) coded term for any white female. "His mama washes clothes on Wednesday for Miss Ann." SNU.

Anxious adj. (1940s) This word was deliberately misused to refer to a fine state of affairs; anything good. (DB, OHHJ, p. 133.) Example: "They were jamming late and it was an anxious night." Harlem use.

[Get] Any n. (1930s–1940s) refers to sexual activity, especially sexual intercourse. (FR.) Example (one male to another): "Did you get any last night?" SNU.

Anywhere n. (1950s–1970s) This word is used in friendly conversation among drug addicts referring to drugs. (RRF, DAZ, p. 10; JH, PBL, p. 83.) Example: "Are you anywhere?"; in other words, "Do you possess any drugs we can share?" DCU, SCU.

Ape; ape-shit adv. (1950s) to be extremely excited, angry, or "crazy." Example: "He went ape-shit over her." SNU.

Apollo play n. (1940s) the planet earth. (DB, OHHJ, p. 133.) Example: "The cat is so out there he's not even part of the Apollo play." Harlem use.

Apron n. (1920s–1950s) negative expression for a woman; a wife; a bartender (DB, OHHJ, p. 133). Example: "Bob's apron won't let him out tonight. We have to play a three-way game of cards, fellas"; or, "The apron wouldn't serve me another drink, and it was only five minutes before closing time." Harlem, SNU.

Apple n. (1930s–1960s) New York City. "Apple" was commonly used among black speakers in the thirties and forties to refer to New York City. The term "Big Apple" was later widely used among many ethnic groups, especially those concentrated in New York City. Also, to a lesser degree, the term is used to refer to the "earth" or "this planet." (DB, OHHJ, p. 133; CC, OMMM, NCCHD, p. 252; HLF, RJPD, p. 169.) NSU. See "Big Apple."

Apple n. (1960s–1970s) money. (JH, PBL, p. 83.) New York City, UCU.

Apple n. (1980s–1990s) the vagina. (EF, RDSL, p. 228.) Watts and South-central Los Angeles use.

Apple [in the white folk's yard] n. (1900s–1920s) an expression used by one black person to refer to another who is looked upon with unusual favor by white folk. (ECLA, NN, p. 263.) Example: "That old boy is a real apple in his white folks' yard." Used in South Carolina and other southern areas.

Applejack n. (1930s–1950s) liquor, especially bootleg liquor, so called because apples were used as the primary ingredient from which the alcohol was made. (FR.) Example: "Let's get happy on some applejack." SU.

Applejack n. (1950s–1960s) all-purpose tag name for dances; the latest dance step. (FR.) SNU.

Apple hat n. (1980s–1990s) a large floppy cap like those associated with the 1930s. (EF, RDSL, p. 228.) Watts and South-central Los Angeles use.

Apples n. (1980s–1990s) a woman's breasts. (EF, RDSL, p. 228) Watts and South-central Los Angeles use.

Application n. (1950s–1960s) the first conversation a pimp has with a potential prostitute. During this conversation he determines whether or not she is suitable. (CRM, BP, p. 295.) Example: "No ho work for me less she pass my application, know what I'm saying." San Francisco Bay Area and Los Angeles use.

Are [one's] boots laced (1930s–1940s) inquiry as to whether or not things are in their proper order, or, more vaguely, an inquiry as to whether or not one understands whatever is in question. (FR.) Example: "I got the potato salad made for the party. Are your boots laced?" Rare. SU.

Arey; aruh n. (1700s–1940s) of Gullah origin, meaning "each" or "either." (AEG, BB, p. 288.) Example: "If arey one of them chilluns turn ginst her she won't ever gets it." South Carolina and Georgia use.

Argufy v. (1700s–1940s) of Gullah origin; to argue. (AEG, BB, p. 287; FGC, DARE, p. 85; JSF, AON, p. 21.) Example: "He likes confusion. He always be argufying with everybody." SU.

Arm n. (1950s–1960s) penis. (CRM, BP, p. 296.) Example: "Man, I gave that ho so much arm I thought it was gonna go all the way up and come out through her mouth." San Francisco Bay Area use.

Armstrong n. (1940s–1950s) a very high note or series of them, especially on a trumpet. The term refers to Louis Armstrong's manner of playing the trumpet. (CC, OMMM, NCCHD, p. 252; DB, OHHJ, p. 133.) Example: "He can hit them armstrongs all night long." Jazz culture and black nightlife use.

Arnchy adj., n. (1920s) pretentious, putting on airs. Anyone who puts on excessive airs. (CCV, NH, p. 285.) SNU. See "Dicty," "Stuck-up," "Airy."

Around the way girl n. (1990s) a neighborhood girl; ghetto girl; girl who follows the so-called "inner city" fads, such as wearing big hooped gold earrings, and is comfortable with "ghetto" slang. (FR.) WCU, SNCU.

[Take] Around the world (1950s–1960s) licking of a person's whole body during lovemaking. (DW, TL, p. 183.) SNU.

Arter adv., prep., conj., adj. (1850s–1880s) variant of "after." (CCJ, NMGC, p. 167.) Georgia use.

Ass n. (1930s–1990s) an all-purpose intensifier with almost no meaning outside the chosen context in which it is used. One's self or a dumb person. (JH, PBL, p. 83) Examples: "It was a bad-ass short"; or, "If you don't pay me by Friday your ass is mine." SNU. See "Ass off."

Ass off (1940s–1960s) an all-purpose intensifier. (FR.) Example: "She can really cook her ass off!" SNU.

Ass on [one's] shoulder (1930s–1950s) to act superior. (ZNH, AM, p. 89) Example: "My boss at work really got her ass on her shoulder this morning, so my whole day was a drag." SNU. See "airy," "arnchy," and "dicty."

Ass peddler n. (1950s) one who sells him or herself sexually. (FR.) Example: "That bitch? She's an avenue ass peddler." SNU, SCU, PPU.

Assbackwards adv. (1930s) backward; confused. The implication here is the same as putting the cart before the horse. (FR.) Example: "Bobby always gets everything assbackwards every time his mother sends him to the store without a note." SNU.

Assed adj. (1960s–1970s) an all-purpose intensifier used to give emphasis: bad-assed, high-assed, tight-assed, etc. (FR.) Example: "He's a bad-assed dude." SNU.

Assed-out adj. (1980s–1990s) to be dead or killed. An all-purpose intensifier in the sixties and seventies. SNU, SCU.

Associates n. (1990s) casual friends or acquaintances. (FR.) Example: "I got lots of associates on the job and in school." SNU.

Astorperious adj. (1930s–1940s) haughty. (ZNH, AM, p. 94.) Rare. Harlem use. See "Dicty."

Attic n. (1940s) the human head. (DB, OHHJ, p. 133.) Example: "You better listen to the man. He's got a lot up in the attic." Harlem use.

Attitude n. (1970s–1980s) a negative disposition; antisocial; unjustified anger. (HLF, RJPD, p. 169; PM, UCLAS, p.16.) Example: "That guy has an attitude. I'd keep my distance." SNU.

Attitude n. (1990s) a haughty disposition. The meaning shifts from "antisocial" in the seventies and eighties to "stuck-up" or "dicty," but with a nasty disposition, in the nineties.

A Tribe Called Quest (1980s–1990s) a popular rap group.

Audi 5000 v. (1990s) to leave. (HC, WSJ, p. B1.) Example: "Catch you later, gotta Audi 5000 for the crib." Northern and southern city youth culture use.

August ham n. (1920s) watermelon. (CVV, NH, p. 285.) Example: "After church Mama and her sister, Aunt Cora, and all them relatives, get together and cook friend chicken, biscuits, greens and hamhocks, and for dessert they serve big old sweet August hams." SNU.

Aunt n. (1700s–1940s) an old "Negro" woman. Picked up from white use. (JSF, AON, p. 26.) SU.

Aunt Hagar n. (1900s–1940s) the African-American people. (ZNH, AM, p. 94.) SNU.

Aunt Hagar's Children n. (1900s–1940s) black people; the black race; African-Americans. According to Genesis 21:9, Hagar was Ishmael's mother and the wife of Abraham. (ZNH, AM, p. 94.) SNU.

Aunt Jane n. (1960s–1970s) a female Uncle Tom. A female member of a black church. This is a variant not only of the male "Uncle Tom" but also an attempt to define the elderly black woman whose whole world is sacred, as opposed to secular. Such a person, for example, believes that the blues, movies, comic books, and many other aspects of the world beyond the church are sinful. Any black woman accused of racial disloyalty. (DC, BJ, p. 57.) Example: "Her name ain't Carrie, honey, it's Aunt Jane: she think she white, acting all high and mighty." SNU. See "Aunt Jemima," "Aunt Sally," and "Uncle Tom."

Aunt Jemima n. (1940s–1980s) female Uncle Tom. Aunt Jemima is truly a secular icon of the happy darkie in southern white mythology. The image, like most other American images of black people, has little or nothing to do with black people themselves. On the other hand, they reflect the state of mind of white Americans. Black people use the term ironically. SNU. See "Aunt Tomasina."

Auntjemimablack adj. (1960s) very black psychologically. This expression was created by Black Nationalist poets in the sixties. It never gained wide use. (FR.) Midwest and east coast use.

Aunt Sally n. (1960s) a female Uncle Tom. (CS, vol. 3, no. 2, p. 8.) SNU. See "Aunt Jane."

Aunt Thomasina n. (1960s) female Uncle Tom, a variant of Aunt Jemima. (FR.) Rare. NECU. See "Aunt Jemima."

Avenue-tank n. (1940s) the double-decker style public transportation bus on the New York City Fifth Avenue route. (DB, OHHJ, p. 133.) Harlem use.

Awful adv. (1800s–1990s) excessive or very large or extensive. (FR.) Example: "That's awful nice of you." SNU.

Ax v. (1500s–1990s) a variant pronunciation of "ask." (CCJ, NMGC, p. 167.)

Ax; axe n. (1930s–1960s) any musical instrument, but usually a saxophone, probably a variant of "sax." From the fifties through the sixties, a knife, especially a switchblade used in street fights. (DC, BJ, p. 57; RSG, JL, p. 8.) SNU.

Axle grease n. (1940s) any stiff pomade for the hair made in a base of lye. Probably originally a euphemism. (FR.) Example: "The boys put that axle grease on their hair and, man, you shoulda seen them crying holy Jesus to get it off." SNU.

B

B n. (1940s–1950s) code language for benzedrine. Example: "He's a B-head." DCU.

Baby; babe n. (1900s–1990s) term of address for one's lover or spouse, but also a word used in general, irrespective of the sexual identity or the personal or social relationship. "Baby" was especially popular socially during the sixties. Any "girl." Example (Adam Clayton Powell): "Keep the faith, baby!" (CS, vol. 3, no. 2, p. 8.) SNU.

Baby jazz drummer Warren Dodds (1898–1959). Brother of Johnny Dodds. Worked with Jelly Roll Morton, Sidney Bechet, et al.

Baby Benz n. (1980s–1990s) Mercedes-Benz model 190E. (TW, CK, p. 135.) Example: "I got me a bad Baby Benz." SNU.

Baby-child n. (1920s–1980s) any infant, male or female. (REK, G., p. 14.) Example: "She a good baby-child." SU.

Baby-kisser n. (1940s–1950s) a politician. (DB, OHHJ, p. 133.) Example: "I'm sick of these baby-kissers coming around here trying to get my vote." Harlem, SNU.

Babylon n. (1960s) a negative expression for the United States, with intended biblical implications. (DC, BJ, p. 57.) Example: Black Nationalist speaking: "Babylon, with its racism, luxury, and vice, will be destroyed. The day of judgment will come." NCU.

Back; backing n. (1940s–1950s) the musical accompaniment given a jazzman doing a solo. (FR.) Examples: "The bass was a great back." And, "The fellows gave me great backing." JBWU.

[From way] Back adj. (1930s–1950s) well established; traditional; having been a long while in existence or of amazing time-tested skill. (FR.) Example: "The dude knows what he's talking about. He's from way back." SNU.

Back alley n. (1930s–1950s) any popular street in a rundown, disreputable area. (FR.) Example: "We partied in the back alley. It was a gas." SNCU.

Backbeat n. (1920s–1940s) in jazz, rhythmic accent of a secondary nature; also, in the forties, one's heart movement. (DB, OHHJ, p. 133; RSG, JT, p. 8.) Harlem, JBWU.

Backbeat of the trey thirty n. (1940s) the third day of the month. (DB, OHHJ, p. 133.) Harlem use.

Backcap; cap n. (1930s–1950s) a sharp reply, associated with The Dozens, a highly ritualized game designed to test emotional strength. (DB, OHHJ, p. 133.) SNCU. See "Dirty Dozens" and "Cap [on]."

Back door n. (1890s–1990s) the back door seems to be a permanent fixture, metaphorically speaking, in black culture, especially in the blues. The idea of the sun, for example, shining in one's back door "someday" is well known. The "backdoor" man, as a secret lover, is also well known. The back door as an entrance/exit for blacks working in white homes during and after slavery perhaps gave the idea of the back door a great presence in the psyches of African-Americans. In black culture, it rarely refers to the anus, as it does in popular American culture. (FR.) SNU.

Backdoor artist n. (1950s–1960s) a devious drug addict who cheats or robs other drug addicts. (CS, vol. 3, no. 2, p. 9.) Watts, Los Angeles, use.

Back-gate parole n. (1920s–1940s) death in prison; to leave prison as a corpse; death in prison. The word "parlor" is short for "funeral parlor." This expression refers to both capital punishment and murder or death by "natural" causes. To die in prison is seen as a great misfortune. (DB, OHHJ, p. 133; HEG, DAUL, p. 21.) Example: "Joe left this morning by way of a back-gate parole." Harlem, SCU, PU.

Back off interj. (1940s–1990s) a command to stop intimidating or teasing someone. (WM, DBD, p. 132.) Example: "I'm warning you, now. Back off!" NSU.

Back talk v. (1800s–1940s) rebuff; to repel. (JSF, AON, p. 30.) SU.

Back-to-back adj. (1980s–1990s) side-to-side; together, as in friendship. (EF, RDSL, p. 228.) Example: "Raymond and me, we back-to-back through thick and thin." SNU.

Bacon n. (1940s) the good life; symbol of prosperity. (WM, DBD, p. 27.) Example: "If we play our cards right, we'll be in the bacon next year." SNCU.

Bactize v. (1850s–1890s) variant form of "baptize." (CCJ, NMGC, p. 167.) Example: "We bactized George last Sunday." Georgia use.

Bad adv. (1700s–1940s) much. (FR.) Example: "I hate him as bad as you do." SU.

Bad adj. (1700s–1990s) positive to the extreme; *a ka nyi ko-jugu* (Mandingo/Bambara); *a nyinata jaw-ke* (Mandingo/Bambia); *gud boad* (Sierra Leone); a simple reversal of the white standard, the very best; good. (HV, AHAE, p. 137; HLF, RJPD, p. 170; CS, vol. 3, no. 2,

p. 9; SH, GL, p. 212; PM, UCLAS, pp. 16–17.) SNU. See "Bad boy," "Bad mouth," "Bad-ass."

Bad-ass adj. (1900s–1990s) a positive, all-purpose intensifier. (ARD, DDJ, p. 79; PM, UCLAS, p. 17; FGC, DARE, p. 126.) Examples: "That's a bad-ass short." Or, "He's a bad-ass dude." Or, "Get your bad-ass self over here and give me a kiss." SNCU.

Bad-ass(ed) nigger n. (1900s–1990s) positive, courageous person; troublemaker; mean person. (EF, RDSL, p. 228.) SNU.

Bad boy n. (1980s–1990s) used to refer to almost anything good or impressive. (FR.) Example: In reference to his new car parked in the driveway, a young black man might say, "Just look at that bad boy! Isn't it a motherfucker?" SNCU.

Bad-doing adj. (1960s) excellent; the best. This is a variant of "bad-ass," usually with the slight exception that its reference is often an event rather than an object. (FR.) SNU.

Bad eye n. (1680s–1990s) a threatening glance; a threat; threatening; *nyejugu* (Mandingo). The expression is not unrelated to "bad mouth" and possibly even "reckless eyeballing." But "bad" is used in this context in its usual mainstream negative way, not in the usual black positive way as in the case of terms like "bad nigger" or "bad rags." (HV, AHAE, p. 137.) Example: "You don't want to be 'round when Old Bill give the bad eye, 'cause he can curse you sho as hell." SU.

Bad hair n. (1800s–1950s) kinky hair. (ZNH, AM, p. 94.) SNU.

Bad Henry baseball player and home-run champion Hank Aaron (born 1934).

Bad in the head (1980s–1990s) to be emotionally or psychologically dislocated. (EF, RDSL, p. 228.) South-central Los Angeles use.

Bad man n. (1700s–1890s) the (Christian) Devil. (JAH, MLN, p. 277.) SU.

Bad mouth n. (1680s–1920s) a spell; a curse; *da jugu* (Mandingo). (HV, AHAE, p. 137.) Example: "The conjure woman put the bad mouth on him and he died two days later." The meaning of "bad mouth" changed gradually by the thirties. See next entry for the same expression.

Bad mouth n. (1930s–1990s) malicious gossip. The way "bad mouth" came to be used in the 1930s has not changed over the seven decades of its twentieth-century use. Also, a hip, fast-talking style. (RDA, TB, pp. 77–78; JH, PBL, p. 83; LDT, AGD, p. 233; GS, TT, p. 45.) Example: "The dude is always putting the bad mouth on somebody. If he ain't careful, he's going to get iced." SNU.

Bad-mouth v. (1960s–1970s) to best someone on a verbal level. (RDA, TB, pp. 17, 77–78.) SNU.

Bad news n. (1960s) any negative experience or situation. (CS, vol. 3, no. 2, p. 9.) Example: "The minute Roy threw that chair at the window I knew it was bad news from there on."

Bad news n. (1970s–1980s) an unpleasant place or thing. "Bad" is used in its usual mainstream negative way in this context. Picked up from white use—"the good news is . . . the bad news is . . ." SNCU.

Bad news n. (1980s–1990s) any person thought to be a problem; a problem person. (EF, RDSL, p. 228.) SNU.

Bad nigger n. (1700s–1990s) an unruly slave; a rebellious black person—usually male—who refuses to be subservient. Picked up from white overseer or "driver" use and general plantation use during slavery and lingered in the vocabulary—especially in the south —for decades into the twentieth century. In the twentieth century, "Bad nigger" is a black person who refuses to be meek or who rejects the social terms of poverty and oppression the culture designs for him; (1960s) a black person who is respected by other blacks. In the 1990s singer-dancer Michael Jackson made a video for a song called "Bad," which further popularized the African-American reversal of the meaning of the word "bad." (CB, MPL, p. 281.) SNU.

Bad place n. (1880s–1960s) Hell, in the biblical sense. Before the turn of the century, this phrase was commonly used by adults in conversation with small children. The "bad place" was where they would go for all eternity if they did not behave. After the turn of the century, and after the great migration north in the thirties and forties, the reference to hell was less frequent but lingered on into the 1960s. Now it's rare. (JAH, MLN, p. 277.) SNU.

Bad rags n. (1960s) very stylish or good-looking clothes. (DC, BJ, p. 57.) Example: "Miles Davis wears some bad rags, Jim." SNU.

Bad scene n. (1960s) an unpleasant or unwanted experience or situation. (DC, BJ, p. 57.) Example: "I got out of there fast. It was a bad scene—with Bobby throwing up and the rest of them fighting like dogs." NCU.

Bad talk n. (1960s) positive revolutionary or radical ideas. This was a Black Nationalist phrase. (FR.) Example: "We got to cut the bad talk and get to some action." SNU.

Bad trip n. (1960s–1970s) any bad experience with drugs; a bad experience; a troublesome person. (CS, vol. 3, no. 2, p. 9.) Examples: "Man, I had a bad trip on that acid you gave me." Or, "Going to school this semester is a bad trip." Or, "Man, you is a bad trip, you know that." NCU.

Bag n. (1930s–1990s) "Bag," in the thirties, was more literal than it later became. Its referent was an actual thing, a bag, usually containing bootleg liquor; and later, in the fifties and sixties, its referent was a bag of drugs. In Watts, Los Angeles, in the sixties, "bag" sometimes meant any "problem." After the sixties the word took on a more complex meaning, referring to a person's disposition or mood or behavior; to one's life-style, vocation, hobby, interests; a social coterie or clique. Earlier example: "Bring your own brown bag." Later example: "What's your bag?" (CS, vol. 3, no. 2, p. 9; CLC, TS, p. 254; RRL, DAZ, p. 13; WF, DAS, p. 14; CRM, BP, p. 296.) DCU, SCU.

Baggie bags n. (1980s–1990s) small plastic sandwich bags a dealer uses to package drugs. (TW, CK, p. 135.) SNU, DCU.

Bagman n. (1950s–1960s) a dealer or pusher; the one in possession of drugs. (CLC, TS, p. 254; RRL, DAZ, p. 13.) Example: "Did the bagman make his stop yet?" DCU. See "Clocker."

Bagpipe n. (1940s) a vacuum cleaner. (DB, OHHJ, p. 133.) Example: "Get the bagpipe and do the floor." Harlem use.

Bague n. (1850s–1890s) variant form of "beg." (CCJ, NMGC, p. 167.) Georgia use.

Bahama mama n. (1980s–1990s) any fat black woman. (EF, RDSL, p. 228.) South-central Los Angeles use.

Bait n. (1980s–1990s) a girl or woman with bad body odor. (EF, RDSL, p. 228.) South-central Los Angeles, SU.

Bald-headed adj. (1880s–1960s) deliberately deceptive; a secondary meaning is silly or foolish. This expression has been around in black popular speech for a long time. (FR.) Example: "You're telling a bald-headed lie!" SNU.

Bale of straw n. (1960s) white female, usually blonde. The reference is to hair color. (FR.) Example: "The dude be screaming kill whitey and all the while he's sleeping with a bale of straw." SNU.

Ball; balling n., v. (1930s–1970s) sexual intercourse; a loud, uninhibited drinking party; to have fun. Also, to have social or sexual fun or both. Also used as a verb, roughly between the thirties and the fifties, meaning to attend a party. Drugs and/or alcohol are usually involved. (RDA, DDJ, p. 263; HLF, RJPD, p. 170.) Examples: "We're gonna have a ball tonight." Or, "We're balling tonight." NCU. See "Party."

Ballad n. (1950s–1990s) any slow tempo accompanying a song. (KG, JV, p. 181.) JBWU.

Ball and chain n. (1950s–1970s) a wife; a sweetheart; a restricting situation. Picked up from prison work farm use. (JH, PBL, p. 83.) Example: "Is your ball and chain going to let you out tonight?" SNU.

Ball face n. (1800s–1890s) a black pejorative term for a white person. (JSF, AON, p. 34.) NU.

Balling v. (1930s–1940s) having fun, especially at a party. (ZNH, AM, p. 94.) SNU.

Balloon v. (1960s) the act of packaging drugs—especially heroin—in quantities to be sold. (CS, vol. 3, no. 2, p. 9.) Watts, Los Angeles, use.

Balloon room n. (1940s–1950s) a place where marijuana is smoked. (FR; WF, DAS, p. 17; DB, OHHJ, p. 133.) Example: "Let's go fly high in the balloon room." NCU.

Ballroom without a parachute n. (1940s) marijuana den where no marijuana is available. (DB, OHHJ, p. 133.) Example: "You talked me into coming over here to get high and this is a ballroom without a parachute." Harlem, NCU, SCU.

Balls n. (1700s–1980s) the human testicles. Unlike its popular mainstream use—to refer to courage, vitality, or stamina—this word in black culture is used literally. (FR.) SNU.

Ball the jack n., v. (1930s–1940s) a Negro dance involving vigorous hand clapping and chanting or singing. The emphasis is more on group participation in fun than on the fun of couples or individual fun. In that sense, it's related to the American barn dance. Secondary meaning: to go; to work swiftly. (BJ, BLH, SD, pp. 44–45.) SU.

Ball [one] up; balled up v. (1960s–1970s) confuse; mixed up; messed up. (FR.) Example: "Lay off, man. You're balling me up." Or, "On the talk show she was all balled up." SNU.

Balm of Gilead n. (1870s–1890s) In black culture, "Balm of Gilead" does not refer to the fragrance of a garden plant. Negroes, before the turn of the century, used this expression to refer to a salve made from the bud of the gilead tree, but it was also loosely used to refer to money. (FR.) SU.

Balloons n. (1960s–1970s). Derogatory expression for a woman's breasts. (FR.) Example: "Hey! Look at the balloons on that chick!" SCU.

Bam v. (1970s–1990s) to strike a person. (FR.) Example: "He went bam, bam, bam, right in the mouth. You should've seen it, man." SCU.

Bam; bambita n. (1970s–1980s) amphetamines. (RRL, DAZ, p. 13.) Example: "Wanna get up on some bams?" DCU, SCU.

Bama n. (1930s–1960s) short for "Alabama"; a country person with "uncool" ways, from Alabama or any place in the southeast. (ZNH, AM, p. 94.) Example: "He's a Bama, right from the South." MWU.

Bambache n. (1890s–1920s) a wild-drinking good time, especially at a social gathering; an all-night drunken party. (LS, GYY, p. 203.) SU.

Bambi v. (1650s–1950s) to lie down in the grass, especially to hide in the grass; *mubambi* (Bantu). (HV, AHAE, p. 137.) SNU.

Bamboo n. (1830s–1860s) any clothing made from cotton, wool, or other fabric. Very likely a backhanded reference to bamboo material out of which garments were made in some parts of Africa. (FR.) SU.

Banda n. (1990s) an infant or small child who is a member of a poor family in a large city ghetto. (FR.) NCU.

Banana n. (1560s–1940s) originally a West African word with possible Arabic roots, meaning "toe" or "finger." Also, fruit (Wolof). As black slang, "banana" came to mean a light-complexioned and attractive Afro-American female, a mulatto, quadroon, or octoroon.

The reference is to the yellow color of the fruit as representative of the skin color of the girl or woman. (HV, AHAE, p. 137; SBF, IHAT, p. 32; DB, OHHJ, p. 133.) SNU.

Band; ban n. (1920s–1930s) a girl or woman. Probably a variant of "bantam." If so, it is likely also a variant of "chick." (FR.) SNU.

Band man n. (1930s–1940s) a jazzman who functions better with a group than as a soloist. (FR.) Example: "He's strictly a band man." JBWU; SNU.

Bang n. (1950s–1960s) an excited reaction to an injection of narcotics or a sniff of cocaine; also sex or any excitement. (RRL, DAZ, p. 14; IS, PSML, p. 313.) Example: "I really got a bang outta that coke last night." DCU, YCU.

Banjo; banjar n. (1630s–1930s) a stringed musical instrument (banjar) captured Africans brought from West Africa to the so-called New World, used frequently in social and religious gatherings. "[The] Banjar, brought from Africa . . . [is the] origin of the guitar" (Thomas Jefferson, 1781). Probably derived from the word *mbanza* (Angola Kimbubdee), which refers to an instrument much like the banjo. In the 1940s the word "banjo" was also sometimes used to refer to the penis; a "Negro" expletive. (HV, AHAE, p. 138, 155; JSF, AON, p. 36; SBF, IHAT, p. 32; JH, PBL, p. 83.) SU.

Bank n. (1930s–1940s) a euphemism for "toilet." (DB, OHHJ, p. 133.) Example: "Excuse me while I make a little trip to the bank to make a deposit." NCU.

Bank n. (1990s) money. (FR.) Example: "You can put your bank on that horse 'cause she can run even in mud and a snowstorm." Rare. NECU.

Banta issue n. (1940s) "banta" is a variant of "bantam" ("chick") and refers to any attractive young woman in the military. This was an expression of black soldiers during World War II. (DB, OHHJ, p. 133.) Example: "Let's go pick up some banta issue." SNU. See "Band" and "Bantam."

Bantam n. (1930s–1940s) a girl or young woman. Variant of "chick." (DB, OHHJ, p. 133.) SNU. See "Band" or "Banta issue," or "Banter play built on a coke frame."

Banter play built on a coke frame n. (1930s–1940s) an attractive girl or young woman. "Banter" is a variant of "bantam" (which is a variant of "chick"); and "coke frame" refers to the shape of a Coca-Cola bottle as representative of the shape of an attractive female body. (DB, OHHJ, p. 133.) Example: "Man! You see that banter play built on a coke frame? Sure would like to know her name." Harlem, NCU.

Banty adj. (1860s–1930s) saucy. (JSF, AON, p. 37.) SU.

Barbecue; bar-B-Q n. (1940s–1950s) an attractive female; probably an attractive female as an object for oral sex. This reference was especially popular during the forties and lingered on into the fifties. The emphasis is on the sense of taste and oral sex. Blues singers in the forties picked it up and spread the use in songs about lovemaking. (CC, OMMM, NCCHD, p. 253; DB, OHHJ, p. 133.) SNU.

Barbecue Bob blues guitar player Robert Hicks (1902–1963).

Bardacious adj. (1920s) anything wonderful, delightful. (CVV, NH, p. 285.) Sometimes pronounced "bo-dacious." Example: "I like going to the Happy Hour Club 'cause they play all that bardacious music and everybody real friendly." Harlem, NCU.

Barge; barged n., v. (1940s) in the forties, southern black speakers used this word in a highly restricted way, taking one sense of it—that is, to move clumsily forward, to force entry, to bump into things, to barge in without being invited—and confining it to the narrow meaning of "to jump." (MHB, JS, np.; CS, vol. 3, no. 2, p. 9.) Example: "He barged over the fence." Usage was never widespread. Also, later (1960s) in Watts, Los Angeles, and possibly other northern cities, "barge" meant a Cadillac or any unusually large automobile. SNU.

Bark n. (1940s) human skin, especially dark skin. The color of most tree bark became an ideal metaphor for the various colors of black people. (DB, OHHJ, p. 133.) Example: "She's got beautiful bark and all she ever uses on it is Vaseline." Harlem, SNU.

Barkers n. (1940s) shoes that hurt. Derived from the reference to feet as "dogs," the idea of shoes being "barkers" refers to shoes that are too tight and are, therefore, hurting—as represented by barking—the feet. (DB, OHHJ, p. 133.) Example: "Hold on, let me take off my barkers. They're killing me." Harlem, SNU.

Barley n. (1960s) beer. (DC, BJ, p. 57.) MWU.

Barn door n. (1900s–1990s) the fly of a pair of trousers. Example: "Your barn door is open." SNU.

Barrel punishment n. (1830s–1860s) to place a person over a barrel and viciously beat him or her, sometimes to death. Many slaves were punished in this manner, often for "misconduct" such as stealing food or refusing to work when ill. (FR.) SU.

Barrelhouse n., v. (1890s–1930s) a cheap saloon; unpretentious, rough music played in such a place; hot music; a syncopated "free and easy," seductive style of piano playing. (RSG, JT, pp. 10–11; DB, OHHJ, p. 133; CC, OMMM, NCCHD, p. 253.) Examples: "Let's barrelhouse tonight"; Or, "Let's go to a barrelhouse." Or, "I want to hear some barrelhouse tonight." SNU.

Barruh n. (1850s–1890s) variant form of "barrow." (CCJ, NMGC, p. 167.) Georgia use.

Bary n. (1930s–1940s) short for "baritone saxophone" or the sound the instrument makes. (FR.) Example: "That bary backup is a gas!"

Base adj., n. (1960s–1990s) a term used to ridicule, harass, disparage, or insult someone. Also, cocaine from which hydrochloride has been removed. (TW, CK, p. 135; EF, RDSL, p. 228.) Examples: "I did some base last night that knocked me out." And, "That dude is really base; I wouldn't give him the time of day." DCU. See "Dissing" and "Freebase."

Base crazies n. (1980s) sometimes called "picking," according to Terry Williams, this phrase refers to "a kind of hallucination that leads a person to search for the smallest particle of cocaine or crack." (TW, CK, p. 135.) DCU.

Base galleries See "Basing gallery."

Basehead n. (1980s–1990s) a person who smokes freebase crack cocaine. (FR.) Example: "All his friends are baseheads. I wonder about him." DCU, SCU. See "Pipehead."

Basehouse n. (1970s–1990s) house where drug users buy and freebase crack cocaine. (FR.) Example: "The cops busted that basehouse on the corner last night." DCU, SCU.

Baser n. (1880s–1950s) In African-American cultural terms of call and response, this is the responding line sung by a gospel group. (FR.) SU.

Basing v. (1980s–1990s) to smoke freebase cocaine. Example: "They all be basing in there together." (TW, CK, p. 135.) DCU.

Basing gallery n. (1970s–1980s) a house where drug users gather to smoke cocaine. This term was dropped in the mid-eighties in favor of the more effective "basehouse." (FR.) DCU.

Basket n. (1920s–1930s) short for "bread basket," which refers to the stomach. In the sixties and after, "basket" was also used by black (and white) gay men to refer to the groin. In black culture, the earlier use was far more common. (DB, OHHJ, p. 133.) See "Bread basket." NCU.

Basket name n. (1890s–1920s) of Gullah origin; the child's nickname given at birth usually by the nurse who tends the infant. It is meant to ward off evil spirits. It is a name used while the child is still in the basket, or cradle. Used on the coasts of South Carolina and Georgia.

Basting v. (1950s–1960s) to vilify or ridicule someone behind their back or to their face. (HLF, RJPD, p. 170.) NCU. See "Cap" and "Dozens."

Bastille n. (1960s) any jail or prison. (CS, vol. 3, no. 2, p. 9.) Watts, Los Angeles, use.

Bat n. (1940s–1960s) an ugly woman; a derogatory term used to refer to an elderly, usually unattractive woman interested in young men. The association probably has more to do with the animal than a baseball bat. Also, a job; an ugly girl. (HLF, PJRD, p. 170; DB, OHHJ, p. 133; JH, PBL, p. 83.) Example: "Man, I saw you dancing with some old bat last night." SNU. See "Battle."

Bato n. (1980s–1990s) pejorative term for a Chicano or Latino male or female. (EF, RDSL, p. 228.) South-central Los Angeles use.

Battle n. (1940s–1950s) in jazz, musical competition between instrumentalists; also an unattractive woman, especially an elderly woman. That these two uses existed simultaneously is perhaps not surprising since "battle" of instruments, while known and used among jazz fans, was essentially restricted to the world of musicians and their fans. "Battle" is short for "battle ax." There is also some evidence that "battle" was, in the south and here and there in the midwest, used to refer to unattractive young women and girls as well. (RSG, JT, pp. 11–12; DB, OHHJ, p. 133.) JMFU, SU, MWU.

Battle-hammed adj. (1930s–1940s) to be ill-shaped, especially from the hips down. (ZNH, AM, p. 94.) Rare. Harlem, SNU.

Battling stick n. (1800s–1860s) slave term; a long, slender stick used to beat slaves. Same stick also used to stir clothes boiling in a boiler pot. (SK, PC, p. 67.) SU.

Bayoo n. (1870s–1890s) "Negro American for a man of whom Quashie thinks very little." From white use; used with self-irony. (JSF, AON, p. 44.) SU.

Bazuca; bazooka n. (1980s–1990s) an especially potent and thickly rolled cigarette laced with cocaine. (TW, CK, p. 135.) Example: "The dude can smoke two bazucas, drink a pint of whiskey, do some hash, and go on the stand and blow half the night." DCU.

Bazuco n. (1980s–1990s) the oily substance in freebase cocaine. (TW, CH, p. 149.) Example: "That shit you sold me, man, had too much bazuco in it." DCU.

BB head n. (1940s–1950s) a boy with a "knotty" head. (FR.) SU.

BB head n. (1980s–1990s) pejorative term for a female with very kinky short hair. (EF, RDSL, p. 228.) SNU.

B-boy n. (1980s–1990s) any young black male break dancer. (FR.) SNU.

BC n. (1960s–1980s) contraceptives or birth control pills. (RRL, DAZ, p. 21.) Example: "Are you on BC?" SNU.

B-DAC n. (1980s–1990s) Bureau of Drug Abuse Control. (FR.) DCU.

Beat adj. (1960s–1990s) ugly. (PM, UCLAS, p. 19.) SNU.

Beat with an ugly stick (1960s–1990s) ugly; ugliness. (PM, UCLAS, p. 18.) Example: "You see that bitch, man, she look like somebody beat her with an ugly stick." SNU.

Be; been (1750s–1990s) to exist. "Be" is used to indicate both future and habitual events; "been" is used to throw emphatic emphasis on the event. (FR.) Examples: "I be going to school and this gang attack me." Or, "Tomorrow I be on my way." Also: "Man, I been through all that stuff." SNU. See "be done" and "be down with it."

Beagle n. (1700s–1940s) of Gullah origin; a foxhound. (AEG, BB, p. 289.) South Carolina and Georgia use.

Beam v., n. (1940s) to look; also, the sun. Dan Burley's "bean," meaning "sun," is probably a printer's error. The reference is to the beam of a car's headlights. (DB, OHHJ, p. 133.) Example: "They be beaming me when I walk by." Harlem, NCU.

Beamer(s) n. (1980s–1990s) a person who smokes crack cocaine freebase. (TW, CH, p. 146.) Example: "The place is full of beamers." DCU.

Beaming v. (1980s–1990s) getting high on drugs, especially cocaine. (TW, CK. p. 135.) Example: "Do you have to always be beaming?" DCU. See "Beam[ing] up."

Beam(ing) up v. (1980s–1990s) getting high on crack cocaine. (TW, CH, p. 146.) Example: "They were beaming up when I got back from school." DCU. See "beaming."

[The] Bean jazz saxophone player Coleman Hawkins (born 1904). Worked with Dizzy Gillespie, Charlie Parker, and others.

Bean n. (1940s–1950s) the human head. (FR.) Example: "He's always got his bean slicked down with axle grease." NCU.

Bean n. (1980s–1990s) pejorative term; a Chicano or Latino. (EF, RDSL, p. 229.) South-central Los Angeles use.

Bean choker n. (1980s–1990s) pejorative term; a Chicano or Latino. (EF, RDSL, p. 229.) South-central Los Angeles use.

Bear n. (1930s–1950s) unpleasant life-style; an ugly woman. (DC, BJ, p. 57; JH, PBL, p. 83.) Examples: "Man, going to work and coming home to this neighborhood is a bear." And, "It was a blind date, but I didn't know she was going to be a bear." SNU.

Bear adj. (1960s–1990s) short for "booger bear"; any difficult situation or thing. (CS, vol. 3, no. 2, p. 10.)

Bear down v. (1940s–1950s) to play with great emotional impact. Example: "Charlie Parker really bears down." JMFU.

Beard n. (1940s–1950s) a female's pubic hair; (1950s) an intellectual or far-out person. (FR.) Examples: "The stripper shaved her beard." And, "I can't stand the dude—he's such a beard." NCU.

Beast n. (1960s–1980s) a white person. This term was popular among Black Nationalists in the sixties, lapsed in the seventies, and gained popularity again among the young in the eighties. (CS, vol. 3, no. 2, p. 10.) SNCU.

Beastie Boys n. (1980s–1990s) a rap group (*Paul's Boutique*).

Beat n., v. (1900s–1990s) accent or stress in musical forms like jazz and rhythm and blues; highly developed rhythm that has nothing to do with 2/4 or 4/4 or 6/8 time and is unlimited as to number of beats in a bar; also, ugly, tired, worn; also, "beat" in Watts, Los Angeles, in the sixties meant to rob, cheat, or deceive someone. (CS, vol. 3, no. 2, p. 10; RSG, JL, pp. 14–15; CC, OMMM, NCCHD, p. 253; DB, OHHJ, p. 134.) SNU.

Beat artist n. (1980s–1990s) a person who sells counterfeit drugs. "Beat" is short for "deadbeat." (TW, CK, p. 135.) Example: "Don't do business with Little Willie. He's a beat artist." DCU.

Beat [one's] chops v. (1940s) to talk—especially excessively. (CC, OMMM, NCCHD, p. 253; MHB, JS, np.) Example: "My wife and her friend get together and all they do is beat their chops." SU.

Beat down n. (1980s–1990s) a fist fight or a scuffle. (WKB, JMC, PS, p. 48.) SNU.

Beat [one's] dummy [meat] v. (1940s) male act of masturbating. (FR.) Example: "The boy spends too much time beating the dummy." Rare. See "Beat off" and "Jack off."

Beater n. (1940s) short for deadbeater; person who refuses to pay his or her debts. (FR.) Example: "The cat's a beater with a mouth full of gimmie [give me]." SNU.

Beat for adj. (1940s–1960s) to be short on money; broke. (DW, TL, p. 60.) Example: "I'm beat for some bread." NCU.

Beat for the yolk (1940s) short of cash. (DB, OHHJ, p. 134.) Example: "Can you lay a dime on me? I'm beat for the yolk." Harlem, NCU.

Beat [one's] gums v. (1930s–1940s) to talk excessively. (ZNH, AM, p. 94.) Example: "You invite Jack up here all he gone do is beat his gums all night." SNU.

Beat it v. (1940s–1980s) to depart; go away. The reference is to the slap of shoe bottoms against pavement. "Beat It" was also the title of a popular song by Michael Jackson. (FR.) Example: "If we're gonna get there in time we've got to beat it." SNU.

Beat off v. (1960s–1970s) to masturbate. This is a male expression. "Beat off" replaced "jack off," common during the thirties through the fifties. (FR.) See "Jack off."

Beat out some licks v. (1930s–1960s) to drum on drums. (WF, DAS, p. 26.) Example: "Let's go down in the basement and beat out some licks." JMFU.

Beat [one's] skin v. (1940s) clap hands, applaud. (DB, OHHJ, p. 134.) Example: "You should have heard the audience beating skin when we finished." Harlem use.

Beat the rocks v. (1930s–1940s) to walk on the sidewalk. "Beat" refers to the slap of leather against pavement. This expression was especially relevant to walking the streets looking for employment during the Depression and after. (FR.) Example: "I beat the rocks all day and found nothing."

Beat to the socks n. (1930s–1940s) weariness. This expression throws emphasis on the feet and legs as instruments of motion. (RSG, JT, p. 13.) Example: "I beat the rocks all day looking for work, and now I'm beat to the socks." Harlem, NCU.

Beat [one's] time (1940s–1950s) to cheat or be cheated in romance. (FR.) Example: "He was trying to beat my time with my baby." SNU.

Beat-up adj. (1940s–1950s) dilapidated, disheveled. (FR.) Example: "He tried to sell me his old beat-up Ford." SNU.

Beaver n. (1940s) the vagina. The association has to do with the supposed similarity between a beaver's coat and the female pubic hair. (RF.) SNU.

Beber n. (1850s–1890s) variant form of "beaver." (CCJ, NMGC, p. 167.) Georgia use.

Bebop n. (1940s–1950s) radical jazz form replaced by "Bop." It employs West African rhythms and the intricacies of European and American harmony. An onomatopoeic word applied to the music of Charlie Parker, Kenny Clarke, Dizzy Gillespie, Bud Powell, and Thelonious Monk. (RSG, JT, pp. 13–14.) JMFU; SNU. See "Bop."

Bebop singer Joe Carroll (born 1919). Vocalist with Dizzy Gillespie's band.

Bebop glasses n. (1940s) fashionable, thick-framed dark eyeglasses or "shades" made popular by jazzmen such as Dizzy Gillespie. JMFU; SNU.

Bebopper n. (1980s–1990s) a person who tries to be "hi" but is actually inexperienced. (EF, RDSL, p. 229.) SNU.

Bebop Santa n. (1960s) Santa Claus; hero of a song done as a take-off on "The Night Before Christmas." (FR.) SNU.

Be done (1830s–1990s) future perfect, serves as "will have." (FR.) Example: "By tomorrow I be done with all my exams. Summer here I come!" SNU. See "Be's."

Bedbug n. (1920s–1930s) a black Pullman porter. This term may have been picked up from derogatory white use and used ironically as so many such terms were. The dark-skinned porters on trains turned back the beds for white passengers. Also, an unpleasant person. (ZNH, AM, p. 92.) SNU.

Bedhouse n. (1920s–1930s) a whorehouse. (FR.) Example: "I'm not going to spend the rest of my life working in a bedhouse."

Bedout adj. (1850s–1890s) variant form of "without." (CCJ, NMGC, p. 166.) Georgia use.

Be down with it (1990s) to be supportive; to be in agreement. (FR.) Example: "It's cool; he be down with it." See "Down." SNCU.

Bee n. (1950s–1960s) an addict's habit; an idea. (CLC, TS, p. 254.) Example: "The dude's bee is so heavy it stings him every day." DCU.

Bee-luther-hatchee; B. Luther Hatchett n. (1920s–1940s) a far-away, damnable place; the next station after the stop for the biblical hell; an absurd place or an ironic situation located in a particular place; a mythical place, like "Ginny Gall." (ZNH, MM, p. 190; ZNH, AM, p. 94; SK, PC, pp. 153–154.) Example: "He always be over in Bee-luther-hatchee or somewhere." Florida and southern coastal use. See "Diddy-wah-Diddy," "Ginny Gall," "Guinea Gall," "West Hell," and "Zar."

Beef n. (1930s–1940s; 1960s–1970s) an "old" word dating back to general criminal use in the thirties. For young blacks in the sixties and later it meant roughly the same as it had earlier: a complaint or argument; a disagreement in progress. (IS, PSML, p. 313; CC, OMMM, NCCHD, p. 252; MHB, JS, np.; CS, vol. 3, no. 2, p. 10.)

Example: "Them two dudes get together they always got a beef going on." NCU.

Beef n. (1980s–1990s) penis. (EF, RDSL, p. 229) South-central Los Angeles use, SNU.

Before Abe n. (1940s) any time prior to January 1, 1863, the official day of Emancipation of slaves in the United States. (FR.) Harlem use. See "Before Abe Jive."

Before Abe Jive n. (1940s) hard, thankless work; slave labor. (DB, OHHJ, p. 134.) Harlem use.

Before day creep n. (1920s–1940s) a secret journey in the night or early morning to see a lover. (Lightnin' Hopkins, "Lightnin's Love," *The Lost Texas Tapes, Volume 1*, Collectables, 1990.) SU. See "Creep."

Behani ghani (1980s–1990s) hello; what's up?; how are you?; from Swahili *"Abari gani."* (EF, RDSL, p. 229.) South-central Los Angeles use.

Behavish(ness) adj., n. (1980s–1990s) unruly; bad behavior. (FR.) Example: "He's a behavish motherfucker." SNU. See "Attitude."

Behind n. (1940s–1970s) buttocks; afterward; that which follows. (CRM, BP, p. 296; OR, BASL, p. 174.) Examples: Mother to child: "You better get your behind in this house." Or, "I can take her quitting me, taking my money, but lying to my mother is too much. How am I suppose to act behind that?" SNU.

Behind the scales n. (1980s–1990s) place of the drug seller. The person who sells drugs often does it from behind a desk where he or she weighs the goods in plastic bags on a scale. (TW, CH, p. 146.) DCU.

Beige n. (1930s–1940s) a light-skinned Negro. (FR.) Rare. MWU. See "Yellow."

Beiging v. (1980s–1990s) a process that deliberately alters the color of cocaine to light brown, making it appear purer than it is. (TW, CK, p. 135.) DCU.

Bell n. (1950s–1960s; 1980s–1990s) reputation attached to one's name or position. (IS, PSML, p. 313.) Example: "You can hear Mister Jones's bell coming a mile away." NCU.

Bells n. (1940s–1950s) any pleasant sound. Coined by Lester Young: "Bells to my ears"; short for wedding bells; an expression of approval. (FR.) Examples: Jazz fan: "The cats were ringing some bells last night, man." A bridegroom to his best friend: "I guess I finally hear bells." JMFU.

Belly fiddle n. (1900s–1940s) guitar. (FR.) Example: "Leadbelly get a hold of his belly fiddle—look out!" JBWU, SU.

Belly habit n. (1980s–1990s) gnawing withdrawal stomach pains from the use of physically addictive drugs. (RRL, DAZ, p. 21.) Example: "She sick with a belly habit." DCU.

Beluthahatchie n. (1920s–1940s) see "Bee-luther-hatchee."

Bend n. (1940s–1950s) in jazz, a scooping pitched sound made by working the lips on, say, a saxophone, so that one turns the base pitch down or up or muddles it—on purpose. (RSG, JT, p. 14.) JMFU.

Bend [one's] ear v. (1980s–1990s) to tell someone something; to whisper some message to a person. (FR.) Example (a woman to her female friend): "I had to bend his ear, he was so embarrassing." SNU.

Bender(s) n. (1940s) the human arm; elbows; legs; knees. (DB, OHHJ, p. 134.) Example: "I had my benders full of goods when the coppers busted in." Harlem use.

Benjamin n. (1940s–1950s) an overcoat. The jazz expression was "benny," short for "Benjamin." But this particular use was derived from an earlier 1920s referent: a man's straw hat. (CLC, TS, p. 254; RSG, JL, pp. 17–18.) Example: "You see Miles in his bad Benjamin last night?" NCU, JMFU.

Bennies n. (1960s) nickname for Benzedrine, a popular street drug during the sixties. (CS, vol. 3, no. 2, p. 10.) DCU.

Benny n. See "Benjamin."

Bent out of shape (1960s–1970s) angry, out of control, or socially uncool. (FR.) Example: "I got home late and my wife was bent out of shape." NCU.

Be out (1990s) an expression of support; encouragement. (FR.) Example: "I heard you were going to a Halloween party dressed as a big duck. Well, go on and be out!"

Berries (1920s) an expression of approval. (CVV, NH, p. 285.) Rare. Harlem use.

Berries n. (1980s) a woman's nipples, especially if dark brown or dark red in color. (FR.) NCU.

[The] Berries n. (1980s–1990s) wine. (EF, RDSL, p. 229.) South-central Los Angeles use.

Be's v. (1750s–1990s) that which is; to share the human condition; exists; is. (FR.) Example: "Things just be's that way." SNU.

Bet (1990s) short for "you bet." (FR.) YCU.

Bi n. (1960s) one who practices sex with both genders. (CS, vol. 3, no. 2, p. 10.) Example: "In my world, I expect everybody I meet to be bi." Watts, Los Angeles; SNCU.

Bichy n. (1680s–1850s) kola nut; slave and slave trader term. (HV, AHAE, pp. 152–153.) Slave trade, SU.

Bible n. (1920s–1940s) the truth. This term was better known in big cities such as Chicago, Philadelphia, and New York. Possibly related to swearing on the Bible. (CC, OMMM, NCCHD, p. 253; DB, OHHJ, p. 134.) Example: "I'm talking Bible to you, man, when I say I saw the cats take your piano out of here." SNU.

Biddie; biddy n. (1940s) an attractive little girl or small old woman. "Little biddie" was often the common expression. (DB, OHHJ, p. 123; FGC, DARE, p. 229.) Example: "Daddy's little biddie baby." Or, "My baby's a little biddie mama, but she can raise enough hell to bring down heaven." SNU.

Bidness n. (1850s–1990s) variant form of "business." (CCJ, NMGC, p. 167.) Georgia use.

Bid whist n. (1930s–1940s) during this type of whist the players take turns bidding to name the trump card. (FGC, DARE, p. 229.) SNU.

Big eye adj. (1650s–1990s) greedy; covetous; *anya uku* (Igbo). (HV, AHAE, p. 138.) SU.

Big adj. (1920s–1940s) to be pregnant. (FR.) Example: "Girl, you mean to tell me you're big again?" SU.

Big A n. (1990s) refers to the disease Acquired Immunodeficiency Syndrome (AIDS). (TW, CH, p. 146.) Example (one pimp to another):

"Half of these bitches on the block got the Big A. Better keep your women clean, man." SNU.

Big Apple n. (1930s–1990s) any big northern city, but especially New York; term originated among widely traveled jazzmen. New York is the apple and Harlem the "stem." Also, "Big Apple" was a loose-hipped "Negro" dance. (*Life*, August 9, 1937, p. 22; CC, HDH, p. 16; CC, OMMM, NCCHD, p 252.) SNU. See "Apple" and "Big Red with the Long Green Stem."

Big band n. (1920s–1950s) any group of musicians composed of from fourteen to twenty persons, such as Cab Calloway's, Duke Ellington's, or Count Basie's big bands. (RSG, JT, p. 15.) JMFU.

Big Bill blues singer William Lee Conley Broonzy (1893–1958).

Big Boy n. (1800s–1940s) a foolish young or reckless man. (ZNH, AM, p. 94.) SU.

Big bit; bit n. (1930s–1950s) an extremely long, unjust prison term. (WKB, JMC, PS, p. 18.) Example: "I can take a year or two but a big bit would kill me." PU, SCU.

Big britches fit little Willie (1920s–1930s) This expression means a time of reckoning is at hand. (ZNH, MM) Example: "There been two lynchings in this county already this year. These is times when big britches fit little Willie." Florida and southern coastal use.

Big Daddy n. (1940s–1950s) often any black man over the age of thirty who has power and influence in his community. (DC, BJ, p. 57.) SNU.

Big Daddy Kane (1980s–1990s) Antonio Hardy, a rap artist.

Big do; big doing n. (1900s–1920s) any unusually exciting or frenzied event; a pompous person; a show-off; a bully. (ECLA, NN, p. 263.) Examples: "You going to the big doing tonight?"; and, "That boy a big do on the plantation—watch what you say 'round him." South Carolina; SU.

Big Foot Country n. (1940s–1960s) the deep South; southeastern United States—Georgia, Alabama, Mississippi, et al. (IS, TB, p. 311.) Chicago; MWU.

Biggity adj. (1860s–1920s) putting on airs; "a negro term." (JSF, AON, p. 53.) SU.

Big gut n. (1930s–1940s) the stomach. (ZNH, AM, p. 85.) SNU.

Big house n. (1930s–1950s) refers to any prison. Example: "Big shot Gerald got a big bit in the big house." NECU.

Big John n. (1970s–1990s) any policeman. (EF, RDSL, p. 229.) Watts and South-central Los Angeles use.

Big Juice n. (1960s–1970s) any white underworld leader, especially one with paid police protection. (JH, PBL, p. 83.) New York; SCU.

Big Mama n. (1920s–1960s) one's grandmother, "big" implying "older" rather than "larger"; but if the grandmother was in fact larger then all the better; an aged flapper. (SBF, IHAT, p. 309.) SNU.

Big Mama blues singer Willie Mae Thornton (1926–1984).

Big man (1940s–1990s) the behind-the-scenes drug wholesaler who supplies neighborhood pushers. An especially vivid representation of this trickster figure can be found in a much-underrated novel, *The Scene* (1960), by Clarence L. Cooper, Jr. (FR.) DCU, SCU.

Big Neck George Walker Nicholas. Tenor saxophone player, born August 22, 1922. Worked with Dizzy Gillespie, et al.

Big Red with the Long Green Stem n. (1920s–1940s) Seventh Avenue in New York City. Phrase coined by jazz musicians. ("Big Red is an elliptical form of the Big Red Apple; green is money, long green is much money; and stem, a slang for a main street" [ILA, CS, p. 74.]) Example: "Saturday night I fall out sharp on Big Red with the Long Green Stem in my hundred-dollar threads and my fifty-dollar black-and-white kicks." Harlem use. See "Big Apple."

Big shot n. (1930s–1940s) any self-important person. This term was borrowed from the white criminal world. Originally, in the 1920s, it meant the leader of a gang, a leading shooter; but very often it was used ironically. When black speakers picked it up in the thirties, the irony remained and the term began to apply to any person who took himself or herself too seriously. (FR.) See "Big Timer."

Big Spender n. (1940s–1950s) any person, usually male, who flaunts his money. Used ironically and in a mocking way. (FR.) See "Big Timer" and "Big Shot."

Big time n. (1960s) a "stiff" or long prison sentence. (CS, vol. 3, no. 2, p. 10.) Watts, Los Angeles; SCU, PU.

Big Timer n. (1940s–1950s) one who flaunts himself or his money or both; often a phrase used mockingly for a square or naïve person. See "Big Spender" and "Big Shot."

Big Top n. (1940s–1990s) the Illinois state prison system. (IS, TB, p. 311.) Chicago; MWU.

Big Windy (Wind) n. (1940s–1990s) the phrase refers to the mighty winds that sweep in on Chicago from Lake Michigan. (DB, OHHJ, p. 134.) Chicago; NCU. See "Hawk."

Bigger Thomas n. (1960s) "bad nigger"; a person whose dominant emotion is fear; one who reacts out of fear with violence; character in Richard Wright's novel *Native Son*; a so-called bad nigger. The reference became popular briefly among black students on the east coast. (FR.) Example: "The dude pulled a Bigger Thomas, smashing all the furniture, and got away with it." See "Bad nigger."

Bill n. (1940s–1950s) one-dollar bill or a hundred-dollar bill. More often it referred to a hundred dollars. (IS, PSNL, p. 313.) Example: "Can you lay a bill on me till payday?" SNU. See "C note."

Billiken adj. (1930s–1950s) a rare word, but apparently at least among some Negro college students in the south it meant "cheap" (etym. unknown). (MHB, JS, np.) SU, MWU.

Billy Seldom n. (1800s–1860s) African-American slave name for wheat bread. (JLD, BN, p. 8.) Southern plantation use.

Bimeby adv. (1700s–1920s) before long; soon. A corruption of by and by. This term originated in pidgin and Creole and remained current throughout the centuries of slavery. Example: "Going to the Promised Land bimeby." (AEG, BB, p. 290.) SU.

Binge; binging v. (1990s) to prolong crack cocaine use. To binge on food was a well-known idea in the decades of the seventies and eighties, especially among diet-conscious Americans. Participants in the drug and black street cultures picked up the term and applied it to excessive use of crack cocaine. (TW, CH, p. 146.) Example: "Tess be binging so much she gonna one of these days kill herself." DCU.

Binner v. (1850s–1890s) variant form of "was" or "were." (CCJ, NMGC, p. 167.) Georgia use.

Bip bam, thank you, ma'am (1950s–1960s) descriptive phrase expressing gratitude to a woman after lovemaking, from a popular song. (FR.) SNU.

Bird jazz artist Charlie Parker (1920–1955), also known as Yardbird. Early in his career he worked with Jay McShann, Dizzy Gillespie, and Earl Hines, and recorded for Decca and Savoy. Parker is considered the most influential jazz innovator, generally regarded as one of the greatest, perhaps the greatest, instrumentalist in American music. (FR.) See "Yardbird."

Bird n. (1970s–1990s) a girl or young woman. (EF, RDSL, p. 229.) South-central Los Angeles use.

Birdie n. (1900s–1950s) like the sound of a bird; from the forties on, in jazz, a grace note. (RSG, JT, p. 16.) JMFU, SU.

Birdland n. (1950s) a famous nightclub in New York City, named for Charlie Parker; a life-style with after-hours connotations. (FR.) SNU.

Birdwood n. (1940s) marijuana. The reference is to the smell of burning marijuana. (DB, OHHJ, p. 134) DCU. See "Weed" and "Grass."

Biscuit(s) n. (1930s–1940s; 1980s) symbol of sustenance; also the human skull; a bed pillow. This image of the skull probably stems from the round shape in silhouette. In terms of image, the pillow may only be an extension of the head. In any case, in black culture, biscuit is primarily a general sustenance symbol. Biscuit, in other cultural pockets of America, was variously known as a woman's hairdo, a flitter tree, etc. From about the mid-fifties to the end of the seventies "biscuit" dropped out of use, but the word was reintroduced into the language in the eighties to mean "buttocks." (DB, OHHJ, p. 134.) Example: "Get off your biscuits and go to work." MWU.

Bit n. (1950s–1960s) a prison sentence; personality trait; one's attitude. (IS, PSNL, p. 313.) Examples: "I got a long bit to do, and God knows I don't deserve it." And, "He came in here with his bit and I put him out." NECU.

Bitch n. (1800s–1990s) in other cultural pockets, "bitch" has previously been known to refer variously to a dog or a hand-carried makeshift lamp, a difficult task, a prostitute, or a woman in general, but black speakers have used this word to refer either specifically to mean-spirited women in the sporting life or more commonly (in a nonmalicious way) to refer to any woman; or to flaunting male homosexuals. It is also used to refer to any difficult or formidable situation or person. (CRM, BP, p. 296; PM, UCLAS, p. 21.) SNU.

Bitching adj. (1960s) anything good or wonderful. (CS, vol. 3, no. 2, p. 10.) Example: "That's a bitching Cadillac you got there, Max." Rare. Watts, Los Angeles, use.

Bite n. (1940s–1950s) the price of a thing, especially something expensive, such as a car. (IS, PSML, p. 313.) Example: "What's the bite on that new Caddy of yours?" NCU.

Bite; bit v. (1940s–1950s) to be cheated or misused in some way. (1980s–1990s) In music, and behavior, to imitate another's style. (TW, CK, p. 135.) Examples: "He got bit real bad in that transaction." And, "The cat always biting Charlie Parker." NCU.

Biting; bitin' v. (1990s) to copy someone. This is a hip-hop expression probably with origins in the idea of "taking a bite out of someone." (FR.) SNCU.

Bitter mouth n. (1930s–1940s) related to "bad mouth" and the idea of a bitter tongue; "bitter mouth" refers to cynical or mean talk, but this phrase was rare and confined mainly to the south. (FR.) SU. See "Bad mouth."

Bittle(s) n. (1700s–1940s) food; variant form of "victuals." (CCJ, NMGC, p. 167; AEG, BB, p. 290.) South Carolina and Georgia use. See "Grub" and "Pecks."

Biz Markie (1980s–1990s) Marcel Hall, a rap artist ("Goin' Off").

BJ (Blowjob) (1990s) fellatio; oral sex. (TW, CH, p. 146.) Example: "She gives a great BJ." SNU. See "Derby."

Black n. (1940s) night; the use of the word "black" as slang was rare. In the midwest and some degree in the south it replaced the word "night." (FR.) Example: "Wait till black and ask her to the dance." SU, MWU.

Black-and-tan n. (1860s–1870s) from the tanning and beating of slaves; during the Civil War, the South was called—by Northerners —black-and-tan. (AB, DSJC, p. 117.) NU.

Black and tan n. (1920s–1940s) "dark and light-colored folks" (CC, OMMM, NCCHD, p. 253). NCU.

Black-and-tan resort n. (1900s–1920s) any black nightclub in Harlem, called by Walter Winchell "sepia sin spots." (ILA, CS, p. 74.). Picked up from white use. Harlem, NECU. See "Black joints."

Black-assed pea n. (1940s–1980s) black-eyed peas; soul food. (FGC, DARE, p. 253.) SNU.

Black Babe Ruth baseball player Josh Gibson (1911–1947) of the Negro League.

Black beauties n. (1960s) biphetamine capsules. (RRL, DAZ, p. 24.) DCU.

Black Beauty Joe Louis (Barrow). See "Brown Bomber."

Black bird n. (1960s–1970s) any dark-skinned person. The term was picked up from white negative use and used in a positive way. (RSG, DARE, p. 255.) Example (one young lover to another): "You are my sweet black bird." South Carolina and Georgia use.

Blackbirder n. (1620s–1860s) a ship transporting black people from Africa to America to be sold into slavery; the captain of a ship transporting shackled black people from Africa to America. (SBF, IHAT, p. 35.) SNU.

Black Boogaloo n. (1960s) a dance of the sixties, but the term had other connotations referring to a certain cultural rhythm and/or the feeling of blackness. (FR.) NU.

Black Bottom n. (1920s–1960s) the area where the "nitty-gritty" black population of any town or city resides; a popular dance among black people. This dance, originating in the late twenties, was so "nasty" it had to be kept from outsiders. The chosen area was usually on the other side of the tracks or in the low area of town, as opposed to a hillside. Blues songs refer to the term, and it turns up in early African-American fiction. Same as "Buttermilk Bottom." (FGC, DARE, p. 256.) SU. See "Buttermilk Bottom."

Black Codes n. (1860s–1870s) laws first made by Bienville, French colonial governor of Louisiana, regarding the relation of master and slave, and which were retained by the Crown of Spain in 1769 to restrict rights of Negroes; these laws were enforced vigorously after the Civil War in a desperate effort to keep newly freed black people from gaining essential civil rights. Attempting to combat these laws, Congress passed the 1867 Reconstruction Act, in itself a compromise with the South. (SBF, IHAT, p. 298; JSF, AON, p. 57.) SNU.

[The] Black Eagle of Harlem Col. Hubert F. Julian, mercenary fighter.

Black fay (o'fay) n. (1960s) a term used to accuse a black person of acting like a white person. To some lesser degree the term was also used to refer to a black person who acted in a meek or servile or subservient manner in the presence of whites. The phrase is not similar to Norman Mailer's "white Negro." (FR.) Example: "I can't stand the dude. He's such a black fay." (FGC, DARE, p. 260.) MWU. See "Uncle Tom."

Blackfellow n. (1620s–1860s) a black man; picked up from white use. (JSF, AON, p. 57.) SU.

Black gunion n. (1950s–1970s) a very strong, gummy grade of marijuana. (IS, PSML, p. 313.) NCU.

Black is back (1990s) a rallying phrase, much like "Power to the people!" or "Black Power!" The implication was that racial consciousness, as felt in the sixties, had returned in the nineties. (FR.) SNU.

Black joint n. (1900s–1920s) any black nightclub catering to "slumming" white patrons in Harlem. Picked up from white use. (ILA, CS, p. 74, 152.) New York use. See "Black-and-tan resort."

Black justice n. (1980s–1990s) self-determination; a term used by young college-educated blacks. Implication: there is little or no justice for blacks in the courts or in society in general. (FR.) SNU.

Black moat n. (1980s–1990s) a dark form of marijuana. (EF, RDSL, p. 229.) DCU, WCU.

Black nigger n. (1620s–1950s) term of abusive address by one "colored" man to another. (JSF, AON, pp. 58–59.) SNU.

Black-out; blackout n. (1940s) derisive phrase referring to a very dark-complexioned person. (MHB, JS, np.) Example: "The broad was such a blackout I couldn't even see her in the dark when I took her to the picture show." SU.

Black Patti Sissieretta Jones, a popular vaudeville performer.

Black pimp n. (1930s–1940s) a telephone operating free of charge on a party line. Party lines were common, especially in rural areas of America, during the early part of the twentieth century. It was possible to cheat the local telephone company by rigging up one's own telephone line and hooking it to an open line used by several other families. (MHB, JS, np.) SU.

Blackplate n. (1960s) backbones and dumplings, baked grits, scrambled pork brains, chitlins and cornbread, cracklin' biscuits, fried catfish, fried tripe, etc. (FR.) See "Soul food."

Black power handshake n. (1960s) a greeting expressed by bringing the hands together so that the thumbs cross. (DC, BJ, p. 58.) NCU.

Black Sheep (1990s) a rap group.

Black stuff n. (1950s–1960s) a code term for opium. The term refers to the brownish yellow color and possibly even to the bitter taste. It is not likely that any racial pun was intended. It was possible for junkies to discuss the drug without uninformed nearby listeners knowing the nature of their discussion. (RRL, DAZ, p. 25.) Example: "Let's go check out some black stuff." NCU.

Blacksploitation; blaxploitation [films] (1970s–1980s) highly commercial Hollywood films (*Shaft* [1971], *Super Fly* [1972], *Black Caesar* [1973], *Blacula* [1973], *Black Samson* [1974], *The Black Godfather* [1974]) that sensationalize stories about black characters. (FR.) SNU.

Black three-hundred-and-sixty degrees (1960s; 1980s) to describe a black person, profoundly black in a psychological sense. The concept was popular in the sixties, fell out of favor during the seventies, and reemerged in the eighties. (FR.) Example: "The dude is Black three-hundred-and-sixty degrees." NCU.

Blade n. (1930s–1940s) a switchblade knife. Example: "Back off, motherfucker, or I'll cut you with my blade."

Blame adj. (1680s–1930s) sure; unmistakable. (JAH, PBE, p. 172.) Example: "She was a blame idiot for going off and leaving them children like that." SU.

Blan adj. (1850s–1890s) "in the habit of, accustomed to" (CCJ, NMGC, p. 167.) Georgia use.

Blanco n. (1980s–1990s) a white person. This reference was picked up by blacks from the sometimes close association of African-American and Hispanic (or Latino) peoples in large urban areas such as New York and Los Angeles. (FR.) NCU.

Blank n. (1980s–1990s) any nonnarcotic powder sold as a drug. (RRL, DAZ, p. 25.) Example: "The dude charged me fifty dollars and gave me a blank [bag of tooth powder]." NECU.

Blanket party n. (1940s–1990s) a violent game played in prisons or dorms or halfway houses where a newcomer is covered by a blanket and kicked and pounded with fists. Picked up from military use. (EF, RDSL, p. 229.) SNU, PU, DCU.

Blanks; blants v. (1850s–1890s) form of "belongs to." (CCJ, NMGC, p. 167.) Example: "I blanks to you, baby." SU.

Blanked up v. (1980s–1990s) to be tricked or even murdered. (FR.) Example: "They blanked up on Bobby and left him in the alley." SNCU.

Blanshed; blanched v. (1980s–1990s) to be ruined socially. It's a variant of "blanched," which means to whiten, to make pale or colorless. The original meaning has been deliberately altered to make an ironic—and perhaps even hidden racial—statement about the conflict between appearance and reality. (FR.) SNU.

Blarey-eyed adj. (1970s) having froglike eyes; walleyed. The term was used to insult. (FGC, DARE, p. 277.) Example: "Boy, get your blarey-eyed self outta my face." New York City and New Jersey use.

Blast v. (1940s–1990s) to smoke marijuana; from the eighties through the nineties, to deeply inhale smoke from a freebase pipe (TW, CH, p. 146); insult; disparage; also, to play a musical instrument without restraint; to smoke marijuana, especially in a group— a "blast party." (RRL, DAZ, p. 25.) Example: "Rhonda blasted him for coming on to her like that." SNCU, DCU.

Blast n. (1990s) any song, especially of rap or rock music. (FR.) Example: "Let's get high and listen to some blasts." SNU.

Blast party n. (1940s–1960s) a gathering of marijuana smokers. (RRL, DAZ, p. 25.) SNCU, DCU.

Blaze on v. (1980s–1990s) to suddenly and without warning strike someone; an unexpected blow. (EF, RDSL, p. 229; FGC, DARE, p. 422.) Example: "He and his gang came around the corner and blazed on me 'fore I had a chance to blink." NCU. See "Fire."

Bleed n. (1980s–1990s) a black person. This is another code reference, a variant of "blood," which means African-American or black person. (EF, RDSL, p. 229.) Example: "Hey, Bleed, how you doing?" SNU. See "Blood."

Blewy; blooey n. (1940s) this term was, even in the forties, rather obscure in jazz circles but common enough in New Orleans and New York to qualify as slang. It means an out-of-place note. (FR.) Example: "The cat kept blowing them blewies all night, I had to leave." Limited northern and southern use.

Bliggey; bliggey-de-bliggey interj. (1960s) an alternative to using a swear word. (CS, vol. 3, no. 2, p. 10.) Example: "Well, I'll be a bliggey-de-bliggey." Watts, Los Angeles, use.

Blind adj. (1960s–1990s) originally uncircumcised (largely black homosexual use); after the eighties, unaware; unable to understand what's obvious. (FR.) Example: "The folks are blind to the injustice that's being handed to them."

Blinders n. (1930s–1940s) a loosely used term, it referred to the human eyes or eyelids. The referent was horse blinders. (FR.) Example: "I swear, that boy always got blinders on. If a snake had been in front of him it would've bit him." Southern use primarily.

Blindfolded lady with the scales (1940s–1950s) The image or symbol here is what counts. It refers to the idea of justice or the legal system in the United States or to any American court building and its transactions. (DB, OHHJ, p. 134.) Example: "The blindfolded lady with the scales had me by the balls. I got a big bit." NECU, MWU.

Blip n. (1930s–1950s) loosely used term meaning any astonishing or disappointing fact; anything inscrutable or at least strange, possibly even good. In earlier times, among white speakers, it meant a nickel. Black speakers may have picked it up as early as the twenties, but the meaning did not shift firmly for them till the thirties. Also, among southern Negro college students in the forties, "blip" apparently was used to refer to "a nickle." (MHB, JS, np; DB, OHHJ, p. 134; CC, OMMM/ NCCHD, p. 253.) Example: "Ain't this a blip? Look what the hairdresser done to my hair." SNU.

Blizzard n. (1990s) the cloudy white substance seen in a cocaine-smoker's pipe. (TW, CH, p. 147.) Example: "Don't let the blizzard bother you." NECU, DCU.

Blockbuster n. (1960s; 1980s–1990s) barbiturates, usually Nembutal. In the fifties and sixties Nembutal was known as Yellow Jackets, because of the yellow color of its capsule. (RRL, DAZ, p. 25.) Example: "I got stoned on a blockbuster." NECU, DCU, YCU. See "Yellow Jacket."

Blockbusting v. (1980s) one gang attacking another on its own turf. (KCJ, JS, p. 139.) Example: "The Lynxs, man, they always be blockbusting on everybody else's turf." NSU, SCU.

Blood n. (1950s–1990s) often a term of address by one black person to another. The implication of kinship by blood, here, stands for racial or ethnic or cultural kinship. More frequent among black male speakers than among females. "Blood" also, but rarely, means wine. (FR; CS, vol. 3, no. 2, p. 10; JH, PBL, p. 83.) Example: "Hey, Blood! How you doing?" SNU. See "Youngblood."

Blood brother; bloodbrother n. see "Blood."

Bloods n. (1960s–1980s) fellow black males; used as a euphemism for "brothers." (FR.) SNU.

Bloods (1980s–1990s) Los Angeles–based street gang. (FR.) Los Angeles use.

Bloodynoun n. (1870s–1950s) is an onomatopoeic expression ("blood an' 'ounds") referring to a large bullfrog with a deep croak. Of Gullah origin. (FGC, DARE, p. 291). Charleston, South Carolina, use.

Blow v., n. (1920s–1950s) originally carried a jazz connotation but came to mean any performance: a writer, for example, "blows" a typewriter; to speak well; to smoke marijuana; to leave; to lose something. To have one's mind "blown" is to be astonished. (CB, MPL, p. 220; CS, vol. 3, no. 2, p. 10; RSG, JL, pp. 24–25.) Example: "She had to blow her job after her boss got under her skin one too many times." SNCU.

Blow n. (1950s–1980s) originally a shot of heroin into the skin that was ineffective because it missed the vein. In the sixties, "blow" came to mean marijuana. From the seventies into the eighties, "blow" still seemed to refer marijuana—to what was done with the smoke. (CLC, TS, p. 254; MM, RB, p. 330.) DCU.

Blow n. (1980s–1990s) cocaine. (TW, CK, p. 135; DG, D, p. 27; DR, BASL, p. 127.) Examples: "Don't hit me a blow again like that; my arm is already black and blue." And, "Want to smoke some blow?" SNU, DCU. See "Girl" and "Coke."

Blow a gut (1950s–1960s) to explode with laughter. Example: "I laughed so hard I thought I would blow a gut." (FR.) NCU.

Blow ass v. (1980s–1990s) to run. (EF, RDSL, p. 229.) SNCU, SCU.

Blow away v. (1950s–1960s) to impress or to be astonished. (FR.) Example: "Her singing blew me away!" JMFU, SNU.

Blow [one's] ass off (1940s–1950s) to make great and very moving music in a public place such as a nightclub. (RSG, JT, pp. 19–20.) Example: "Diz and Bird blow their asses off." JMFU.

Blow black v. (1960s) to talk or write along the lines of Black Consciousness. This phrase was used primarily by Black Nationalist poets and musicians of the period. "Blow" was borrowed from jazz talk and applied to writing and everyday life. (FR.) Example: "Ellison is blowing black!" SNCU. See "Blow change."

Blow change v. (1960s) Like "Blow black," this phrase was limited to use by Black Nationalist poets and their readers. It meant to think, talk, along the lines of revolutionary principles. (FR.) Example: "Don Lee is blowing change!" SNCU.

Blow Charlie v. (1960s–1970s) to sniff cocaine. Cocaine is a white powdery substance. "Charlie" was the old expression for white folk. The idea of "blowing" refers to what happens to the smoke. Hence, to "Blow Charlie" was to snort a white substance. (FR.) Example: "Let's go blow Charlie." DCU, YCU.

Blow [one] down v. (1930s–1950s) to win in a musical competition; a battle between saxes. Often such battles took place late at night just before joints were about to close. Bean (Coleman Hawkins) blew down a lot of other saxophone players. (RSG, JT, p. 20.) See "Battle."

Blow [one] out v. (1930s–1950s) in jazz, to win in a musical competition between two instrumentalists. (BH, LSB, p. 55.) JMFU.

Blow [one's] wig v. (1930s–1940s) to experience excitement or enthusiasm. (CC, OMMM, NCCHD, p. 253.) NCU.

Blower n. (1940s–1950s) a handkerchief; a soloist. In the forties the use of "blower" in this sense was pretty much confined to the south and the midwest. "Blower" meaning a soloist did not enjoy widespread use among black jazz and blues musicians—although enough to qualify entry here. (RSG, JT, pp. 21–22.) JMFU, SNU.

Blow fire v. (1980s–1990s) to show great skill in performing a task. (EF, RDSL, p. 229.) SNCU.

Blowing v. (1940s–1960s) playing a saxophone or another type of reed instrument; but in the fifties and sixties, "blowing" came to refer to the playing of any musical instrument. (FR.) Example: "The cat's blowing his heart out." See "Blow."

Blowing room n. (1950s) time allowed jazzmen to improvise during recording sessions or in a concert. (RSG, JT, pp. 21–22.) Example: "Hey, man, I got to have some blowing room before we take it home [reach closure]." East coast and west coast use primarily; JMFU.

Blowing session n. (1950s) a jazz session where improvisation is the theme. Example: "Max, Diz, and Bird were on time for the blowing session."

Blowjob n. (1920s–1990s) oral-genital sex; fellatio, specifically. Like many other slang expressions, this one defies logic but works nonetheless. "Blowing," strictly speaking, is not a motion present in this sort of sexual activity. But the word "blow"—as loosely used in music circles—may have been borrowed from this sexual context. (WF, DAS, p. 46; EP, DU, p. 51.) Example: "She gives a great blowjob." Commonly used throughout the country and in other English-speaking countries. SNU. See "Head" and "Derby."

Blow, Gabriel, blow (1860s–1940s) This expression stems from a well-known African-American folktale with many versions. One of the best-known concerns an incident involving a Methodist preacher, his congregation, and a small black boy. During a sermon concerning the angel Gabriel, the preacher called out, "Blow, Gabriel, blow," and a boy, playing in the church attic, just happened at that moment to toot his toy horn. The preacher and his congregation, terrified, believing Gabriel in Heaven had responded, all shot out of the church pronto. (RMD, ANF, p. 231; JMB, WB, pp. 98–100.) SU.

Blow gage (gauge) v. (1950s–1960s) to smoke marijuana. The idea of "blowing" refers, as in the case of "Blow Charlie," to what the smoker does with the smoke. (FR.) Example: "Let's go blow some gage." East coast use; DCU, NCU. See "Blow snow."

Blow heavy v. (1980s–1990s) borrowed from jazz use; to perform in an impressive manner; to say meaningful things. (EF, RDSL, p. 230.) Example: "Rev. Donald blow heavy when he gets up in the pulpit and starts talking to the congregation." JMFU, SCU, SNCU, SNU.

Blow [one's] mind n. (1950s–1970s) originally, to get high on a hallucinogenic drug. Later the expression was used loosely to refer to the intensified mental state caused by any kind of experience, such as seeing a good movie or painting or the sunrise, etc.; to lose self-control or composure; to do something irrational, impolite; to be overwhelmed or deeply moved. Originally a black expression, once it moved into wider use, black speakers abandoned it immediately. (FR.) Examples: "LSD will blow your mind." And, *"On the Waterfront* blew my mind." SNU.

Blow [one's] mind roulette n. (1960s) a game wherein a variety of pills are thrown on a table or in the middle of a floor in a dark room and the players grope for and swallow the pills they find. They then wait for their own reactions to see what they've chanced upon. (RRL, DAZ, p. 25.) NECU, WCU.

Blowoff v. (1950s) "to get rid of a mark after he's been fleeced" (IS, TB, p. 311). Chicago, MWU.

Blow [one's] cool v. (1950s–1960s) (CW, TW, p. 72.) See "Blow [one's] top."

Blow out n. (1980s–1990s) a fancy hairdo. (EF, RDSL, p. 230.) SNCU.

Blow out the afterglow v. (1930s–1940s) to turn off electric lights. Memory of candlelight and kerosene light, in the south, was still vivid among many African-Americans as late as the thirties and forties. The idea of "blowing out" a light made as much sense as horsepower in a car or calling a refrigerator an icebox. (MHB, JS, np.) Example: "Blow out the afterglow and let's go to sleep." SU, MWU.

Blow [one's] pipes v. (1970s–1990s) to suddenly hit the accelerator and make a car screech or bark a loud tailpipe complaint. (EF, RDSL, p. 230.) South-central Los Angeles use.

Blow snow v. (1960s) to inhale cocaine through the nose. (RRL, DAZ, p. 25.) Northern city drug culture and street use.

Blow some tunes v. (1980s–1990s) to perform cunnilingus. (EF, RDSL, p. 230.) SNCU.

Blow [one's] soul v. (1950s–1960s) in jazz, to perform with tremendous skill and emotion; to do creative work with great passion and honesty. Picked up from the vocabulary of jazz and blues, the idea of "blowing" soul—cultural blackness—spread to other areas of black professional and artistic life. (RSG, JT, p. 20.) Example: "Jacob Lawrence is blowing soul in his Frederick Douglass series." JMFU, SNCU, WCU.

Blow [one's] top v. (1930s–1950s) to become unstable or violent. To blow one's "top" (head) was to go "crazy," or to become mentally unstable. Black speakers came to use the word as a noun ("blowtop"). To be completely overcome with enthusiasm or delight or pure emotion; insanity—same as flip, "flip one's lid," etc. Later, in the sixties, white speakers used this term as a substitute for "crack up" or to refer to a nervous breakdown, loss of sanity. ("Crack up" among black speakers never meant loss of sanity but uncontrollable laughter.) (CC, OMMM, NCCHD, p. 253; ZNH, AM, p. 94.) Example: "Look at Smitty over there in the corner smoochin' that broad by the jukebox. If his wife comes in here now she's going to blow her top." JMFU, NECU, WCU. See "Crack up."

Blow the gig v. (1950s–1960s) to lose a job for any reason (initially, usually because of failure to appear on time). This was originally an expression used in the music business, then show business. In the late fifties and early sixties the phrase spread into general use. (DB, OHHJ, p. 134; RSG, JT, p. 20; RSG, JL, pp. 24–25.) Example: "Marvin didn't even show up for the first reading. He blew the gig from the gitgo." East coast and west coast use primarily.

Blow the roof off (1930s–1940s) an expression used to describe an especially lively jam session where the playing is intense and loud. (RSG, JT, p. 20; RSG, JL, p. 25.) Example: "You going to hear Jug tonight? He's gonna blow the roof off." JMFU. See "Blow up a breeze (storm)."

Blowtop n. See "Blow [one's] top."

Blow up a breeze (storm) v. (1930s–1940s) to play a musical instrument with great spirit and skill, especially in a group setting. (RSG, JT, p. 21.) See "Blow the roof off."

Blue n., v., adj. (1890s–1990s) closely related, in the African-American historical memory, with blackness. The word use may have its origins in the concept of blue-black skin, or black skin that seems to reflect blue light or has a blue cast to it. Although it is pure speculation, the concept of the blues may have its origin in this idea. In Louisiana and Virginia, black speakers referred to African-Americans of Anglo, Indian, and African blood as "Blues." The reference was to the prominence of blue veins in the light skin. (For white speakers in America, as early as the 1800s, "blue" meant "drunk," perhaps because, when intoxicated, one's skin, especially the tip of the nose, might appear blue. White speakers also used the word to refer to the sky.) But "blue," in the latter part of the twentieth century, was also used to refer to feeling low or to the quality of the blues; music sung or played in a blues manner. (SL, RJON, p. 17; RSG, JT, p. 23; FGC, DARE, p. 296; WF, DAS, p. 48.) Examples: "That nigger so black he blue." Or, "She's such a high tone. You know how uppity the blues are." SNU, JMFU. See "Blues," "Blue funk," "Blue boy's" and "Blueblack."

Blue trumpet player Richard Allen Mitchell (born March 13, 1930). Worked with Earl Bostic, Sarah Vaughan, Horace Silver, and others.

Blue and white n. (1960s–1990s) a Los Angeles police bar. (EF, RDSL, p. 230.) South-central Los Angeles use.

Blue balls n. (1920s–1950s) a testicular condition caused by unrelieved sexual tension; also a venereal disease. (ZNH, MM, p. 341.) SNU.

Blue boy n. (1950s) an African-American male; a "Nigger male." (RHdeC, NB, p. 29.) SNU. See "Blue."

Blue Broadway n. (1940s) the concept of Heaven as it is associated with the sky; also, the Milky Way. (DB, OHHJ, p. 134.) Example: "When I lay my burden down I'll be climbing the Blue Broadway." Harlem; New York City.

Bluebird n. (1900s–1930s) a policeman. The association was made between the color of the officer's uniform and the color of the bird. (FR.) Example: "There's a bluebird on every corner of Harlem these days." NECU.

Blueblack adj., n. (1890s–1990s) a skin color that is so black it has or seems to have a blue overtone to it. (FR.) SU. See "Blue."

Bluecat n. (1960s) a policeman. (DW, TL, p. 60.) Rare. NCU.

Blue-eyed soul brother n. (1960s) any white male who empathizes with black people or the Black Struggle. (DC, BJ, p. 58; EF, RDSL, p. 230.) NU.

Blue-eyed soul sister n. (1960s) any white female who empathizes with black people or the Black Struggle. (DC, BJ, p. 58.) NU. See Grace Halsell's *Soul Sister* and *Black/White Sex*, 1972.

Blue funk n. (1950s–1960s) mental depression; extreme loss of will. (FR.) Example: "I wake up in the morning and I'm in a blue funk." NECU, MWU.

Blue heavens n. (1960s) Amytal barbiturate in a blue capsule. (CS, vol. 3, no. 2, p. 10.) Watts, Los Angeles; DCU.

Blue john; Blue-john n. (1890s–1930s) skimmed milk. The milk appears to have a blue overtone to it. Zora Neale Hurston refers to "blue john" several times in her writings. (FGC, DARE, p. 306.) Example: "Biscuits made with blue-john are lighter than those you make with buttermilk." Florida, North Carolina, and Georgia use.

Blue note n. (1890s–1990s) in jazz, an off or flat note; notes flattened third and seventh degrees; a moderately flattened third or seventh note of the scale that cannot be demonstrated in written music. This term probably has origins in the way early blues was played on the (bottleneck) guitar. (JEH, AAC, p. 187; RSG, JL, p. 27.) JMFU.

Blues n. (1890s–1990s) Out of "Negro" work songs, hollers, and spirituals, this special type of music became popular through the vocal style of W. C. Handy around 1912. As the blues moved into the cities, many other forms of jazz, such as boogie-woogie and bebop, grew out of it. Among black speakers and others, "blues" has come to mean a state of sadness or depression. Also, "blues," in Watts, Los Angeles, and other black communities, sometimes was used by those in the drug culture to refer to blue capsules of Amytal barbiturate. Also—and apparently on a limited basis—"blues" (from "blue chips") meant "money" in some northeastern cities. (CS, vol. 3, no. 2, p. 11; DW, TL, p. 60.) Examples: "He sings some mean blues." Or, "I got the blues this morning." SNU.

Blue Vein Circle n. (1890s–1920s) an unofficial guild of mulattoes in such places as Virginia, North Carolina, and Washington, D. C. (CVV, NH, p. 285.) Example: "Those Blue Vein Circle people feel like they better than anybody darker." SNU.

Bluff cuffs with the solid senders n. (1940s) trousers with large ballooning cuffs. This expression refers to a particular fashion of the forties. (DB, OHHJ, p. 134.) Example: "Hey, baby bro', you look like

49

you about to take off and go into orbit wearing them bluff cuffs with the solid senders." Harlem; NCU.

Blunt n. (1980s–1990s) a blunted capsule containing secobarbital compound. (EF, RDSL, p. 230.) DCU.

Blunt n. (1990s) a cigar filled with marijuana and cocaine. (TW, CH, p. 147.) Example: "He blew himself away last night with a blunt." Los Angeles, DCU. See "Coke blunt."

Blunted up adv. (1990s) high on marijuana and coke. (Queen Latifah, *Essence*, 1992, p. 116.) Hip hop and drug culture use.

BMW (1990s) stands for "break my windows." BMW (Bavarian Motor Works) cars are a type often burglarized, hence the expression. (FR.) Rare. Los Angeles use.

Board v. (1930s–1940s) to eat; the expression was somehow derived from the concept of a lodger who is supplied with regular meals. (FR.) Example: "I'm hungry. You ready to board?" MWU, SU.

Boat n. (1960s) a Cadillac or any large car. (DC, BJ, p. 58.) NCU. See "Short."

Bodacious; bowdacious adj. (1680s–1990s) extreme; exceedingly excessive; grand; *botesha* (Bantu). (HV, AHAE, p. 138.) Example: "Man, that dude be bodacious; he just wants right in and takes what he wants and dare anybody to say anything." SNU.

Bodacious tatas n. (1980s–1990s) large breasts. (PM, UCLAS, p. 22.) SNCU, YCU.

Body bag n. (1990s) condom. This cynically comic social expression is the product of the Age of AIDS. (FR.) Example: "You don't go on a date these days without a body bag." NECU, MWU.

Bof conj. (1850s–1990s) variant form of "both." (CCJ, NMGC, p. 167.) SU.

Bogard (Bogart) v., n. (1950s–1960s) to act in a forceful manner; black people growing up during the fifties identified easily with tough guys like Humphrey Bogart. By the mid-seventies Bogart had lost some of his popularity (and so had insensitive, violent behavior) so the meaning of the expression changed, to signify a bully. (JH, PBL, p. 83; DC, BJ, p. 58; FGC, DARE, p. 319.) Examples: "Don't bogard me, man, if you know what's good for you." Or, "He's too much of a bogart for my taste." MWU, NECU.

Bogish; Boguish adj. (1930s–1940s) bogus. This expression was a variant of "bogus," both out of ignorance and on purpose. It may have started out as a mispronunciation but was picked up and made fashionable for awhile. But it remained of limited use. (ZNH, MM, p. 56; FGC, DARE, p. 322, JLD, LBE, p. 153.) Example: "You can't sell me that bogish meat. Look at the color!" See "Bogus (bogish) beef." NECU, MWU.

Bogue adj. (1890s–1960s) phony; fake; deceitful; also, sick from lack of a narcotic. The effect is a burning sensation in the pit of the stomach, sweating and weakness, desire for something sweet such as candy. (CLC, TS, p. 254; FGC, DARE, p. 322.) Example: "He's too bogue to walk to the hospital." NCU.

Bogus adj. (1930s–1990s) false; fraud; *boko, boko-boko* (Hausa). (HV, AHAE, p. 138, PM, UCLAS, pp. 22–23.) SNCU.

Bogus (bogish) beef n. (1930s–1990s) groundless complaint or chatter. (FR; JH, PBL, p. 83.) Example: "She's always got some bogish beef!" NECU, MWU.

Boiling down n., v. (1880s–1890s) a tongue lashing or scolding; to tell off or to correct. This expression is a variant of "blessing out," "telling off," and "boiling out." (JAH, MLN, p. 123.) SU.

Boiling water n. (1940s) the wake following a boat. During World War II, this expression started among African-American soldiers who described the churning water following a boat as "boiling." (FGC, DARE, p. 325.) Example: "We landed at Normandy with moonlight on the boiling water so pretty." Limited, but some use beyond military.

Bold adj. (1980s–1990s) aggressive; powerful. (FR.) Example: "I was bold, man, when I went for the interview. They respected me." SNCU.

Bolito n. (1920s) a gambling game popular in Harlem during the 1920s. (CVV, NH, p. 285.) Harlem use.

Bomb n. (1950s–1960s) a drug of high potency, especially a fat reefer. (CLC, TS, p. 254.) Examples: "I smoked a bomb last night— blew me away." And "She always rolls bombs that look like blimps for her parties." MWU, DCU. See "Bombed out" and "Bomber."

Bombed out adj. (1950s–1960s) overcome or dominated by an excess of narcotics. (RRL, DAZ, p. 26.) Example: "I was bombed out for twelve hours after last night's bender." NECU; MWU. See "Bomb(s)" and "Bomber."

Bomber n. (1950s–1960s) a very thick reefer (marijuana). (FR; CS, vol. 3, no. 2, p. 11.) See "Bomb(s)" and "Bombed out."

Bombershay n. (1890s) a dance of the Gay Nineties. Example: "We did the Bombershay till the police raided the place." (RSG, JT, p. 23.) JMFU, SU.

Bombs n. (1940s) word used to explain the effect of Kenny Clarke's drum accent after bebop became simply bop. Lester Young also told Louis Bellson to stop dropping bombs behind him. (RSG, JT, pp. 23–24; RSG, JL, p. 28.) Example: "Klook be knocking back some heavy bombs." Los Angeles, JMFU.

Bondage n. (1940s) debt. (DB, OHHJ, p. 134.) Example: "Child, I got so much bondage I don't know what to do." Harlem, NECU.

Bone n. (1900s–1930s; 1960s–1990s) short for "trombone"; from the forties to the nineties, "bone" was used to refer to the male sex organ; it was also, to a lesser degree, used during the forties to refer to persons of mixed Anglo-Irish–African ancestry. "Bone," as a reference to the penis, unlike the racial reference, continued. "Bone" also, in the sixties in northeastern cities, was used to refer to a dollar bill. (DW, TL, p. 60; *Down Beat* [March 30, 1961], p. 17.) JMFU, SNU. See "Boner" and "Boneing."

Boner n. (1960s–1990s) erect penis. (FR.) Example: "That's some boner!" NECU, MWU.

Boning v. (1960s–1990s) sexual intercourse. In Spike Lee's movie about a black college campus, *School Daze*, there was a special room for "boning" in one fraternity house. (FR.) Example: "He does more boning than anybody I know." NECU, MWU.

Bone out v. (1990s) to leave quickly. (FR.) SNCU, YCU.

Bones n. (1930s–1950s) dice. (DC, BJ, p. 58.) Example: "I knowed my chance of getting outta there alive was cut in half the minute I saw snake eyes on them bones." SU, MWU. See "Galloping dominoes."

Boneset n. (1890s–1940s) a plant used for medicinal purposes; natural medicine for arthritis. (RW, AAGYRS, p. 84.) SU.

Bonfire n. (1940s) a cigarette or its stub. (DB, OHHJ, p. 134.) Example: "Can you spare a bonfire?" Harlem; MWU.

Boo n. (1930s–1950s) a bad scare; corruption of "jabooby" (marijuana), so called because it sometimes induced anxiety or fear in the user—what is meant by a "bad experience." Also, to a limited extent, "boo" was used to refer to marijuana. (DC, BJ, p. 58.) Example: "I got a bad boo last night." NECU, MWU.

Booboo n. (1950s–1990s) blunder; error; *mbubu* (Bantu). (HV, AHAE, p. 138.) SNU.

Boo-boo n. (1960s–1980s) any mistake, such as accidentally dropping something. Although this term was used during the sixties, it was not till the middle of the seventies that it became widely used. Its use declined in the mid-eighties. (FR.) Example: "Oh, I made a boo-boo when I tried to carry all those plates myself; now they're smashed." SNU.

Boobus n. (1980s–1990s) pejorative term for flat or small breasts. (EF, RDSL, p. 230.) South-central Los Angeles use.

Boodle n. (1950s) a fake—padded—roll of money flashed to impress a sucker. (IS, TB, p. 311.) Example: "I showed him my boodle and the sucker grinned and took out his wallet." Chicago, MWU.

Boody n. (1650s–1990s) sex; "ass"; sometimes a pejorative term; buttocks; usually a male term; *buedi* (Bantu). (HV, AHAE, p. 138.) Example: "Hey, little mama, when you gone give me some of that boody?" SNU.

Boody; Booty n. (1920s–1950s) rear end; sex; body; refers to female sexuality; sex; the buttocks. Although this usage continued beyond the fifties in a limited manner, its other, earlier, formal sense, meaning "plunder" or "loot," was never challenged or lost ground. (CVV, NH, p. 285.) SNU. See "Hootchie-pap."

Boody call n. (1990s) a telephone call, especially late at night. (FR.) Example: "I swear my boyfriend ain't got no sense, he thinks nothing of making a boody call at three in the morning when I'm dead asleep." YCU, SCU.

Boodylicious adj. (1990s) stunning; mildly unpleasant; outstanding; wonderful. (FR.) YCU, SCU.

Boogaloo n. (1960s) a dance of the sixties. (FGC, DARE, p. 333.) See "Black Boogaloo," "Hully Gully," and "Jerk."

Booger n. (1940s–1990s) anything difficult; a burden; tough situation. (In the late eighties and early nineties, "booger" also had another meaning, limited mainly to Oakland and the Bay Area in California. It was used as a playful variant of "burger," as in hamburger. (FGC, DARE, p. 333; JM WPC.) Examples: "Give me a Booger King special." And, "School this year was a booger." YCU, SCU. See "Booger Bear" and "Booger Boo."

Booger Bear n. (1800s–1960s) a hobgoblin; an unattractive girl or woman. While black speakers also used the word "booger" to variously refer to nasal mucus, a ghost ("hant"), or a burden or bad scare, "booger," in this context, remained current for many years. (FGC, DARE, p. 334.) Example: "Don't set me up with no Booger Bear." SNU, NECU, MWU.

Boogerboo n. (1940s–1960s) a deceptive person or a difficult task or situation. (FR.) SNU. See "Booger Bear."

Boogie v. (1700s–1990s) to move quickly. (PM, UCLAS, p. 23.) SNU.

Boogie n. (1940s–1990s) sexual intercourse. (EF, RDSL, p. 230.) NSU.

Boogie Down Productions a rap group ("Criminal Minded").

Boogie-Woogie v., n. (1650s–1990s) early meaning: to beat a drum (Mande); *buga* (Hausa); *mbuki-mvuki* (Bantu); a fast-stepping blues in which the bass figure comes in double time, traditionally associated with Kansas City jazz; also, the type of dancing done to that music. Musician Dan Burley describes "boogie-woogie" as "barrelhouse" and "a manner of life." Also, it's been described as harmony with an accented base; in some parts of the south, a case of syphilis. Some people believe blues musician Cow-Cow Davenport coined the phrase and that it refers to the Devil, the "boogie," and all the troubles associated with him. (HV, AHAE, p. 138; ZNH, AM, p. 94; JH, PBL, p. 83; RSG, JL, pp. 29–30; CC, OMMM, NCCHD, p. 253; DB, OHHJ, p. 134.) SNU.

Boogler n. (1960s) anybody who frequents parties and get-togethers. (CS, vol. 3, no., 2, p. 11.) Example: "He's the worst boogler in Watts." Watts, Los Angeles, use.

Boohoo v. (1880s–1990s) to weep. This onomatopoeic term remained popular for so long because of its effective representation of its referent. Very often it is used in a mocking or playful manner. (FR.) Example: "She boohoos at the drop of a hat." SNU.

Boojy; Boojie adj. (1950s–1960s) short for "bourgeois." A derogatory term, it's used to refer to middle-class blacks, especially those who do not live in the ghetto. (CRM, BP, p. 297.) Example: "These folks are so boojy they make me sick." NECU, MWU.

Book n., v. (1920s–1990s) repertoire of a musical group; to leave. "Book it," in the seventies, when large numbers of young blacks started going to college, was used to refer to studying. "Book" also —at least on the west coast in the hustling life—referred to "a supply of tricks' names, addresses, and telephone numbers written in a book." "The book" refers to the oral tradition in pimping, its "rules and principles." To "book" somebody was, in the sixties, to look at him or her. But "book" also generally has been used to refer to any magazine since the twenties, and remains current (1990s). "Magazine" itself was not a commonly used word in southern and midwestern black communities. (CRM, BP, p. 297; CS, vol. 3, no. 2, p. 11; RSG, JL, p. 30.) Examples: "All my bitches are high-class call girls. We work strictly from the book." And, "Catch ya later! I gotta go home and book it." SNU. See "Bookity-book."

Book it v. (1980s–1990s) to move fast; to run; to leave suddenly. (RCC, SOC, p. 19.) SNCU, SCU, DCU.

Boo-koos; Boo-kooing n., v. (1920s–1960s) a large amount of anything; also, the kind of loud talking called bullying or woofing; probably from the French word *beaucoup*. (ZNH, MM, p. 30; IS, PSML, p. 313; ZNH, MM, p. 30.) Examples: "The joint was full of boo-kooing way into the night"; and, "I got boo koos of love for you, baby." Southern coastal Florida and Georgia use, SNU.

Book learning n. (1890s–1930s) formal education. (JMB, WB, p. 48.) Example: "That girl got lots of book learning. She's going to be a big success up there in Chicago." SNU.

Bookie n. (1950s–1990s) a person who takes bets. (FR.) Example: "She can't go a day without seeing her bookie." SNU.

Bookity-book v. (1880s–1990s) an echoic sound, and, as such, an onomatopoeic term meaning to run or move quickly; to move swiftly.

(FR.) Example: "You should have seen that dude bookity-booking it out of here." SNCU, SCU, DCU. See "Book it."

Boolhipper n. (1980s–1990s) a black leather coat. (FR.) Example: "He come in here strutting in his bad boolhipper." SNU.

Boom! (1980s–1990s) expression of approval; eureka! (FR.) Example: in response to the statement, "Sure is hot today!" a respondent would say, "Boom!" SNU.

Boom boom n. (1940s) a pistol or shotgun; a western movie. (MHB, JS, np.; DB, OHHJ, p. 134.) Examples: "He got his boom boom on the guy." And, "Let's go catch a boom boom." SNU.

Boom box; boombox n. (1980s–1990s) a radio with powerful speakers; a high-powered, portable radio–tape deck player, known as a "ghetto blaster" in the eighties. (TW, CH, p. 147.) SNU. See "Ghetto blaster" and "Ghetto box."

Boom! Pow! Bam! (1990s) an exclamation used in ordinary conversation by the members of rap culture. (See Lawrence A. Stanley's *Rap: The Lyrics*, 1992.) Example: "Yo! I got this call from this chick. Boom! I was over. Then she came on with this jive about Ray. Pow! Bam! My dream shot down." SNCU.

Boo-reefer n. (1950s) marijuana cigarette. (DC, BJ, p. 58.) MWU. See "Joint" and "Boo."

Boost v. (1950s–1990s) to shoplift; to improve one's condition; "a brace of shills for a flat joint." (IS, TB, p. 311; CS, vol. 3, no. 2, p. 11; CLC, TS, p. 254; IS, PSNL, p. 313.) Example: "Boosting is her profession. Then she sells the stuff on the boulevard." NCU, MWU, NECU. See "Booster."

Booster n. (1930s–1990s) an expert thief, especially in department stores. (FR.) See "Boost."

Boost up v. (1990s) turn up. (FR.) Example: "Boost up the stereo." NCU.

Boot n. (1920s–1950s) a black person; "colored" person; a "Negro"; to explain or tell or listen; to give; one black person to another, especially male. The reference to race comes from the black color of boots. (CC, OMMM, NCCHD, p. 253; RDP, SRO, p. 3; IS, PSML, p. 313; DB, OHHJ, p. 134; IS, TB, p. 311.) Example: "You ain't got no loot, but you my favorite boot." SNU.

Boot v. (1940s–1950s) In a more restricted sense, "boot" was also used in the thirties to refer to the making of exciting music. Both uses were concurrent during the period of their greatest popularity. (RSG, JL, pp. 30–31.) SU, MWU. See "Booting" and "Booted (one)."

Booted [on] v., adj. (1900s–1940s) to be informed; hip. (FR.) Example: "I got booted while I was down there talking with them yesterday." NECU.

Booted [one] v. (1940s) to introduce or be introduced. (DB, OHHJ, p. 134.) Example: "Dig! She booted me to her best friend." NECU.

Bootie drought n. (1980s–1990s) a period of no sexual activity. (PM, UCLAS, p. 23.) Los Angeles, YCU.

Booting n., v. (1920s–1930s) lovemaking. Southern use, especially in the Mississippi Delta area. Also, in drug culture, "booting" was used (1960s) to refer to the high that comes from injecting, say, heroin. (RRL, DAZ, p. 27; Kokomo Arnold, "Busy Booting," 1936.) Example: "We were booting all night." DCU, NCU.

Boot-snitch n. (1900s–1940s) information; especially damaging information given, commonly, by a gossip; one who gossips; also, a dictionary or lexicon. (DB, OHHJ, p. 134.) Example: "You going to listen to that boot-snitch rather than to me?" Harlem; NCU. See "Booted (on)."

Bootie Mitchell Wood, Jr., trombone player, born December 27, 1919; worked with Lionel Hampton, Erskine Hawkins, Count Basie, Duke Ellington, et al.

Booty n. (1950s–1990s) the female body or female rear end; the vagina. (EF, RDSL, p. 230.) SNU.

Booty busting v. (1990s) having anal sex. (FR.) YCU, SCU.

Bop v. (1800s–1860s) to hit, especially on the top of the head. Female slaves were often "bopped" (with a battling stick) on the head rather than beat or horsewhipped on the backsides. (SK, PC, p. 67.) SU. See "Battling stick."

Bop n. (1940s–1970s) an innovative form of jazz started in the forties by Charlie Parker (the Prince of Bop), Bud Powell, Richie Powell, Max Roach, Dizzy Gillespie, Kenny Clarke, Thelonious Monk, and others. In "bop," innovation was the key: melody and harmony were open-ended; anything could happen in bop. The word "bop" replaced "bebop." It generally also referred to a style of scat singing or unconventional playing of an instrument. It also meant to strike someone, a lively walk, or to dance. (RSG, JL, pp. 32–33.) JMFU. See "Bebop" and "Booper, bopster."

Bopper, bopster n. (1940s–1950s) person who is devoted to bop music. (RSG, JL, p. 33.) SNU. See "Bebop."

Border reds n. (1980s–1990s) barbiturate compound in a capsule with red borders. (EF, RDSL, p. 230.) DCU.

Borrowing v. (1980s–1990s) stealing. (TW, CK, p. 135.) DCU.

Boss adj. (1960s) the very best of anything; excellent; very fine. (FR; CS, vol. 3, no. 2, p. 11; IS, PSML, p. 313.) Example: "Man! That's a boss short you're driving." SNU.

Boss player n. (1960s) any black person (but especially male) who succeeds in white America; an expert pimp. (CRM, BP, p. 297.) WCU. See "Player."

Boston n. (1900–1930s) "way up north," an accented bass piano style such as that practiced by Eubie Blake. (See Andre Hodein, *Jazz: It's Evolution and Essence*, 1956, p. 213; RSG, JL, pp. 34–35; RSG, JT, p. 28.) Example: "He plays great Boston piano." JMFU.

BOT; B.O.T. n. (1950s–1990s) balance of (imprisonment) time. (RRL, DAZ, pp. 27–28.) PU, SCU.

Both two pron. (1620s–1990s) both. A double negative used for emphasis and possible humor. (FGC, DARE, p. 346.) Example: "Both two came in here talking that talk and I got rid of them." SU.

Botherate; Botheration v., n. (1700s–1960s) so-called "negroism"; annoyance; to menace. (FGC, DARE, p. 346.) Example: "I can't stand no more botheration." SU, MWU.

Botherment n. See "Botheration."

Bottle it v. (1920s) a command to shut up; stop talking. (CVV, NH, p. 285.) Example: "All right, all right, that's enough, just bottle it." Harlem and other northern city use.

Bottle(s) n. (1980s–1990s) vial. Clockers and junkies call the vials cocaine comes in "bottles." (RP, C, p. 6.) DCU.

Bottle up and go v. (1930s–1940s) to leave, especially in an unhappy or unpleasant manner resulting from a disagreement. This expression was intrinsic to the Depression years but was never widely used. The reference to "bottle" as a euphemism for or variant on "pack" may refer to liquor. (HMB, JS, np.) Example: "You people don't know how to act. I'm going to bottle up and go." SU, MWU.

Bottom n. (1870s–1930s) the black (Negro? colored?) section of town; a rundown, disreputable area in a black community; low land. Also known (especially by whites) as "Coon Bottom." (FGC, DARE, pp. 348–349.) SU. See "Buttermilk Bottom."

Bottom v. (1980s–1990s) basketball term, usually shouted, meaning to shoot a three-pointer. (FR.) Basketball players and fans' use.

Bottom woman n. (1950s–1960s) in a pimp's stable of prostitutes, the "bottom woman" is the favorite and the one he can most depend on. (IS, PSML, p. 313; SH, GL, p. 212.) Example: "I got bitches out there bringing in long bread, but I don't trust none of them like I do my bottom woman." PPU.

Boulevard cowboy n. (1940s) the type of reckless taxicab driver that is common in New York City and on the South Side of Chicago. (DB, OHHJ, p. 134.) Example: "You can't even get across the street without fear of some boulevard cowboy running over you." East coast and midwestern city use. See "Boulevard westerner."

Boulevard westerner n. (1940s) a reckless taxicab driver. (DB, OHHJ, p. 134.) NCU. See also "Boulevard Cowboy."

Bounce n. (1930s–1940s) a lightweight, fast-tempo style of music. This sound was closely associated with bebop in the forties, which later, in the fifties, became known as bop. An example of this would be Bud Powell's composition "Bouncing with Bud," on the album by the same title (Delmark DL 406) recorded in Copenhagen, April 26, 1962. (See Barry Vlanov, *A History of Jazz in America*, 1952, p. 350.) JMFU.

Bouncy in [one's] deuce of benders (1900s–1940s) Uncle Tom mannerisms. (DB, OHHJ, p. 134.) Example: "He is bouncy in his deuce of benders when he's around white folks." Rare. SNU.

Bound and sot (set) (1880s–1890s) said of a dead person's spirit when it has been bound by a spell to its place of burial. Example: "Ain't no black cat oil going to get him out of that grave: he's bound and sot." Southern use.

Bow-wow n. (1930s–1970s) In "redneck" or "cracker" jargon this expression referred to a lame cow or inferior beef. During the same period black speakers used it to refer to a gun (DB, OHHJ, p. 134); the expression of course is derived from the sound a gun makes. By the late sixties the term was revived to mean an ugly woman. (FGC, DARE, p. 353.) SNU.

Box n. (1920s–1940s) "Box" meant a piano during the twenties and into the early thirties. Later, from the late thirties and into the forties, the word was used to refer to any string instrument; in the fifties, a phonograph or stereo or television set. It was also, at the same time, used by some male speakers to refer to the vagina. Other referents were house, apartment, room, radio. (DB, OHHJ, p. 134; RSG, LJ, p. 34; DC, BJ, p. 59; CS, vol. 3, no. 2, p. 11.) SNU.

Box-ankled adj. (1900s–1950s) a derogatory expression referring more to a manner of walking than to ill-shaped ankles; describes ankles that rub together or strike each other when the person walks. Example: "He's knock-kneed, humpbacked, cross-eyed, box-ankled, and he stutters something crazy. I feel sorry for him." SU.

Boxed adj. (1930s–1940s) overcome by narcotics or liquor. "Boxed" may refer to "coffin," implying a certain deadness easily associated with an induced state of drunkenness; or it may refer to the idea of being knocked out as from being hit in boxing. Example: "I was boxed out of my mind." NCU.

Box fire n. (1940s) cigar or cigarette. (DB, OHHJ, p. 134) Example: "I love to light up a box fire after dinner." Harlem use.

Boy n. (1920s–1940s) heroin, so called because of the sexual sensation it gives. The word "boy" may have originated among female speakers or among male homosexuals. (CLC, TS, 254; IS, PSML, p. 313.) Examples: Female speaker: "The doctor told me boy will kill me, but he didn't say when." DC.

Boys n. (1930s–1940s) hustlers or street-corner men; gang members. (DB, OHHJ, p. 134.) NCU.

Bozo n. (1650s–1990s) a stupid person; a big and dumb person; *bozo* (Bantu). (HV, AHAE, p. 138.) SNU.

Brace of broads n. (1890s–1940s) the human shoulders. (DB, OHHJ, p. 134.) Example: "I worked the fields for thirty years using my brace of broads to carry every load." SNU.

Brace of hookers n. (1890s–1940s) the human arms. (DB, OHHJ, p. 134.) Example: "In those days we didn't have forklifts, just these brace of hookers." Harlem, SNU.

Brace of horned corns n. (1890s–1940s) aching feet. (DB, OHHJ, p. 134.) Example: "My brace of horned corns are killing me." Harlem; SNU.

Brad n. (1950s–1960s) a piece of metal placed on the bottom of a shoe to prevent wear; tap. (FR.) Example: "The Nicholas Brothers got some great-sounding brads." SNU.

Bradys n. (1990s) white kids or young whites in the middle class, especially living in the suburbs; from the "Brady Bunch" television show. (HC, WSJ, p. B1.) YCU, SNCU.

Brand X n. (1980s–1990s) marijuana. (EF, RDSL, p. 230.) DCU.

Brass ankles n. (1880s–1930s) persons of both black and white ancestry, so called because they seemed "brass" in color. (BB, AW, pp. 36–37.) South Carolina use.

Brass wigs (1940s) army officers on southern "Negro" college campuses during World War II. (MHB, JS, np.) "Negro" college students use.

Bread n. (1930s–1960s) money. Black speakers used this word to refer literally to money as an essential means for basic survival in a capitalist society. (JH, PBL, p. 83; RSG, JL, p. 37.) Example: "How much bread will they pay me if I take that gig?" SNU. See "Long bread."

Break n., v. (1900s–1940s) among jazzmen, to stop while playing without missing the beat. As a form of innovation, "breaks" were in a category with licks and riffs. (FN, JS, p. 290.) JMFU.

Breakdown, break-down n. (1920–1940s) a very popular and exciting dance started by black people in the south, picked up by whites; done to fast, loud, and jazzy music; also, to explain something, "break it down." (Listen to Duke Ellington's "Birmingham Break-down," 1927.) SU.

Break [one's] balls v. (1930s–1950s) to overexert oneself at a task. "Balls," of course, refers to testicles. (FR.) Example: "I was breaking my balls on that job." SNU.

Break [one's] brim v. (1950s–1960s) to turn a felt hat at a catty or rakish angle. (DW, TL, p. 60.) Example: "Joey, break your brim a little to the left. That's it, that's cool!" NECU.

Breaking adj. (1980s–1990s) to be obsessive about something or to go to extremes. (TW, CK, p. 135.) DCU.

Breaking Luck n. (1930s–1950s) the first trick of the evening for a prostitute. (CRM, BP, p. 297; IS, PSML, p. 313.) Example (prostitute): "I walked the block for only five minutes before I had my breaking luck." PPU.

Break it down v. (1930s–1950s) to get excited; to swing; to get hot while playing music; a cry of excitement, often shouted from the audience at a jazz band. (FR.) Example: "Break it down! Break it down! Swing! Get hot!" Harlem; NCU.

Break (broke) it up v. (1930s–1940s) to earn great applause. As Cab Calloway explains this term, "to stop the show" with an overwhelming performance. Dan Burley: "to score heavily" (DB, OHHJ, p. 134; CC, OMMM, NCCHD, p. 253.) Example: "We really broke it up last night at the Cotton Club." SNCU.

Break [one] off some v. (1990s) to give; especially drugs. (FR.) YCU, SCU.

Break (broke) out with v. (1940s–1950s) to suddenly come forth with something such as an idea, a thing, or a performance. This expression did not have its origins in musical circles. (FR.) Example: "He broke out with this new sound nobody had heard before." NECU.

Break out with v. (1980s–1990s) to do, say, present, wear. (PM, UCLAS, p. 24.) YCU.

Break [it] up v. (1940s–1950s) to earn applause (CC, OMMM, NCCHD, p. 253); also, to explode with convulsive laughter. Example: "The jive dude really broke me up with his jokes." Large city use coast to coast. See "Crack up."

Break wide (1980s–1990s) a command to desist, to leave the scene. (WKB, JMC, PS, p. 48.) Arizona State Prison; PU, SCU.

Break yourself (1990s) a mugger's command that a victim turn over his money. (*Sacramento Bee*, July 25, 1993, p. A2.) SCU.

Breath-and-britches n. (1920s–1930s) a worthless man, "trashy nigger," (ZNH, TEWG.) Example: (wife to husband regarding daughter) "If I can help it she ain't going to end up marrying no breath-and-britches." SU.

Bree n. (1930s) a girl. (CC, OMMM, NCCHD, p. 253.) Rare. Harlem use.

Breeder n. (1700s–1860s) a black slave woman who was used primarily for giving birth to new slaves. "The stronger and most intelligent Negroes were selected as breeders. . . . The white slave-owners and overseers also mated with the breeders, and their mulatto offspring were valued as house servants" (SK, PC, p. 74). SU.

[Up a] Breeze adj., n. (1930s–1990s) the utmost, as in "blowing music" or "planting trees" or "walking" up a breeze. Also, in the sixties, "to leave." From the eighties to the nineties, a very hip or cool person. (WKB, JMC, PS, p. 48; HLF, RJPD, p. 170; listen to Chuck Berry's *Blowing Up a Breeze*, Columbia C-541.) Examples: "He worked that breath harp up a breeze." Or, "Pete is a real breeze." SU.

Bref n. (1850s–1990s) variant form of "breath." (CCJ, NMGC, p. 167.) SU.

Brer; buh n. (1650s–1990s) male form of address; older brother; *kckc* (Mandingo). (HV, AHAE, p. 138.) SNU.

Br'er Rabbit n. (1880s–1950s) a tricky or deceptive person; from one of the many stories about a rabbit. The rabbit had always been a central figure in the folktales of many African cultures. As slaves in "the land of the free," black folk continued to make up stories about trickster rabbits who were able to survive the threat or attack of far larger animals. It was a type of tale that said something meaningful to the black heart. One of the most popular examples of this type of story was written by Joel Chandler Harris, a white writer of the Plantation Tradition. (RMD, ANF, pp. 66–123; NNP; FBSN, pp. 75, 149, 157, 472, 496, 504; Mrs. E. M. Bacus, *Tales of the Rabbit from Georgia Negroes*, 1899; W. H. Barker, *West African Folk-Tales*, 1917.) SNU.

Bresh n., v. (1850s–1890s) variant form of "brush." (CCJ, NMGC, p. 167.) SU.

Brew house n. (1980s–1990s) beer or liquor store. (EF, RDSL, p. 231.) WCU.

Brick composer and guitar player Jacob Roger Fleagle (born August 22, 1906). He worked with Fletcher Henderson, Chick Webb, and Jimmie Lunceford.

Brick n. (1960s–1990s) about two pounds of marijuana, sometimes in loaf form. (EF, RDSL, p. 231; CS, vol. 3, no. 2, p. 11.) DCU, SCU.

Brick n. (1990s) basketball shot lacking finesse. (FR.) Example: "He shot a brick." SNU.

Bricking v. (1960s) A rare term, it referrs literally to throwing bricks—especially at the police or National Guard—during an act of civil disobediance. (DC, BJ, p. 59.) Example: "Man, me and Timmy was down on Ellis Avenue bricking them pigs left and right." MWU.

Bricklayer n. (1960s–1990s) a mud dauber wasp. In the nineties, a basketball player who lacks finesse. (FR.) Example: "I won't play with a bricklayer." SNU. See "Brick."

Brick-presser n. (1920s–1930s) any person who spends time on the sidewalk; a hobo; a tramp; a street person. (CVV, NH, p. 285.) Harlem; NCU.

Bright n. (1920s–1930s) day; daylight. (CC, OMMM, NCCHD, p. 253.) Example: "Catch you two brights from now." SNU.

Bright adj. (1940s–1950s) the color of a light-complexioned Negro; describes daylight. (FR.) Examples: "She's real bright like her mama." Or, "It's real bright today." SU. See "Brightening," "Yellow," and "Yellow (girl, boy)."

Brightening n. (1940s) early morning. (FR.) Example: "I always get up at the first brightening." SU.

Bright-skin n. (1700s–1950s) light-colored skin; high yellow. (GS, TT, p. 251.) SNU.

Bring [one] down v. (1930s–1940s) The earliest use of this expression was positive, as in "bring my love down," to make someone feel good, but by the late thirties it meant to depress or sadden; in the fifties and sixties, to help sober a person; or to come down from drugs. Also, at the same time, the expression was used to refer to a joy-killing person, a person who was a "drag." (RRL, DAZ, p. 28; CC, OMMM, NCCHD, p. 253; PM, UCLAS, p. 25.) Examples: "Monk can really bring me down." Or "We brought him down with coffee." See "Drag."

Bring [one] out v. (1940s–1950s) to introduce an uninformed person to the in-group life-style; or to "hip" a "square" to what's happening on the "scene." Same as "turn (him or her) on." (FR.) NCU. See "Turn on."

Bring your own brown bag (1960s) used to encourage invited party guests to bring contributions of liquor. (FR.) SNU.

Brim n. (1950s) a hat, especially one made of felt with a silk band. (DC, BJ, p. 59.) MWU.

Bro n. (1960s–1970s) short for "brother," a term of male address. (CS, vol. 3, no. 2, p. 11.) Example: "Yo! Bro! How ya doing?" SNU.

Broad n. (1930s–1950s) a girl, woman; originally, in the early thirties, it meant specifically a plump, shapely female; the shoulders. (MHB, JS, np.; CLC, TF, p. 153; CS, vol. 3, no. 2, p. 11) Examples: "Will there be any broads there tonight?" And "He can carry anything on his broads." SNU. See "Chick."

Broadus n. (1870s–1920s) surplus; the overflow; a small quantity; a few drops. This word was common among slaves and ex-slaves working the markets in the south. It probably has origins in African pidgin and Carribean Creole. The reference to a small quantity probably also implies high quality or generosity. (FR.) Example: "She filled my sack so full the broadus spilled out on the ground."

Broke adj. (1930s–1960s) to be without cash. (WF, DAS, p. 64; CS, vol. 3, no. 2, p. 11.) Example: "Man, I'm flat broke." SNU.

Broke arm n. (1920s–1930s) leftovers from a big party or Saturday night fish fry. (LA, SM, p. 29.) Example: "The next morning Jennie took all the broke arms over to Nancy's and her kids went to town eating." SU.

Broke up v. (1850s–1890s) to leave. (CCJ. NMGC, p. 167.) Example: "We broke up at midnight and all went home." Georgia use.

Bronco n. (1650s–1990s) one who works with cattle; *bronco* (Ibiblio). (HV, AHAE, p. 153.)

Bronco Jim nickname of an American Negro cowboy from Texas who was a skilled horsebreaker.

Bronco Sam nickname of an American Negro cowboy and bronco buster.

Broom v. (1940s) to walk or run, especially quickly. (DB, OHHJ, p. 135.) Harlem; NCU. See "Broom to the slammer that fronts the drape crib."

Broom n. (1940s) cigar. (DB, OHHJ, p. 135.) Harlem; NCU. See "Broom to the slammer that fronts the drape crib."

Broom to the slammer that fronts the drape crib v. (1940s) one of those "cute" (or hip?) expressions so popular since the forties. It simply means to walk to the clothes closet. "Broom" is to walk; "slammer" loosely used can be a door or closed space, such as a prison cell, but in this case clearly refers to the closet; to "front" is to present; "drape" means clothes; and "crib" means home. See "Broom," "Slammer," "Front," "Drape," and "Crib." (DB, OHHJ, p. 135.) Harlem use.

Brooks n. (1950s) a Brooks Brothers shirt, but also any expensive shirt, especially one made of silk. Sometimes used to refer to suits, also made by Brooks Brothers. (DC, BJ, p. 59.) MWU.

Brother n. (1940s–1990s) form of address. (FR.) SNU. See "Blood brother" and "Blood[s]."

Brother in black(ness) n. (1800s–1990s) term of address for one black male to another. (ZNH, AM, p. 94; MHB, JS, np; JH, PBL, p. 83.) Harlem; SNU.

Brotherman n. (1960s–1990s) form of address; another black man; blood brother. (FR.) Example: "Hey! Brotherman, what's happening?" SNU. See "Brother," "Blood brother," and "Blood(s)."

Brown Abe n. (1930s) a penny. This expression was popular during the Depression years. (DB, OHHJ, p. 135.) Example: "Say, brother, can you spare a few brown Abes for a cup of coffee?" NCU.

Brown Abes and Buffalo heads n. (1930s–1940s) pennies and nickels. (DB, OHHJ, p. 135.) SNCU.

Brown Bomber prizefighter Joe Louis (1914–1981), heavyweight champion from 1937 to 1949. Commonly used throughout the country.

Brown Embalmer Joe Louis. See "Brown Bomber."

Brown eye n. (1970s–1990s) anal intercourse. (EF, RDSL, p. 231; HM, GL, p. 5.) SNU.

Brownies n. (1930s–1960s) cookies containing marijuana. (DB, OHHJ, p. 135; CS, vol. 3, no. 2, p. 11.) Example: "Sue actually served her special brownies to all them high-class folk, and they never knew the difference." NCU.

Brownie arcade n. (1940s) an amusement shooting gallery characterized by one-cent slot machines. (DB, OHHJ, p. 135.) Example: "The boys hang out at the brownie arcade all day playing." Harlem; NCU.

Brown powder n. (1950s–1960s) heroin. (DG, CR, p. 47.) DCU.

Brownskinned service n. (1930s–1940s) "Negro" or black hospitality. This is similar to so-called "southern hospitality," in that it is social in nature. (FR.) Example: "Home folk give you some great brownskinned service." SU, MWU.

Brown stuff n. (1950s–1960s) heroin. (DG, CR, p. 47.) DCU. See "Brown powder."

Brown Sugar n. (1900s–1930s) an African-American woman, especially a beautiful one. (FR.) SU.

Bruise v. (1860s–1940s) variant of "browse"; to move about in a seemingly aimless manner. (JAH, MLN, p. 263.) SNU.

Brujera n. (1700s–1890s) hoodoo; a religion whose deity is Olorum, King of Heaven; a religion practiced by Florida Negro slaves; a form of hoodoo or voodoo introduced in Palmetto County, Florida, by slaves transported from Cuba. Later, elements of Christianity were mixed with the "brujera" worship. (SK, PC, pp. 175–179.) Palmetto County, Florida, use.

Brush n. (1940s) mustache. (DB, OHHJ, p. 135.) Harlem use.

Brush [one's] teeth v. (1980s–1990s) to perform cunnilingus. (EF, RDSL, p. 231.) Watts and South-central Los Angeles use.

Brush; brushing; brush off v. (1850s–1950s) to beat with a stick or switch; mustache; short for "brush off." The earliest use of this word by slaves was picked up from slaveholders who referred to a whipping of a slave as a "brushing." In the nineteenth century it came to mean a mustache—which had some presence among black speakers. But brush as in "brush off" was far more common among black speakers. (FR.) SU.

Brushes n. (1920s–1950s) wire brushes; in jazz, thin drumsticks that, when used on the drum's surface, create a delicate, muted effect. (RSG, JL, pp. 41–42; WF, DAS, p. 65.) JMFU.

Brush mouth n. (1860s–1940s) a sip of whiskey. (LDT, AGD, p. 232.) SU.

Bubba n. (1800s–1920s) form of address for a brother; a male sibling. (FR; AEG, BB, p. 291.) SU.

Bubber jazz trumpter James Miley (1903–1932).

Bubble n. (1960s) an allergic skin reaction in the form of a small oval swelling caused by careless injection of heroin. (CS, vol. 3, no. 2, p. 11.) DCU, NCU.

Bubble dancing v. (1940s) washing dishes. (MHB, JS, np.) Example: (mother to daughter) "You'd better get in that kitchen and do some bubble dancing." SU, MWU.

Bucca White blues singer Booker T. Washington White (1906–1977); worked with Napoleon Hairiston, "Miss Minnie," and Washboard Sam.

Buck; nigger buck n. (1700s–1930s) a young, strong black male. "Nigger buck"—the male equivalent of the female wench—was a vulgar and derogatory slaveholder expression picked up by slaves and carried over and used ironically in black speech. A cynical, snide, white belief in black male virility is implicitly expressed in the use of the word. Black use of it moved from the ironic stance to total rejection by the turn of the century. (FGC, DARE, pp. 405–406.) Southern plantation use; SU.

Buck jazz trumpter Wilbur Clayton (born 1911); played with Count Basie.

Buck-and-gag v. (1800s–1860s) a method for punishing slaves; the slave was bound and gagged and beaten severely; then left to "roast" in the hot sun all day. (SK, PC, p. 68.) SU.

Buck-and-wing n. (1840s–1940s) a tap dance step originating among "Negros." (Edna Feber, *Show Boat*, p. 25.) Sometimes known, among whites, as "buckdancing." SU.

Buckaroo n. (1650s–1990s) a poor white man or woman; *buckra* (Ibibio). (HV, AHAE, p. 153.) SNU.

Buckhead n. (1860s–1940s) any person of both white and black ancestry. (BB, AW, p. 27.) South Carolina use.

Bucket n. (1930s–1990s) a car, so called because of the sense of being in a container; a thing used to carry something. This quality was not present in the horse-and-wagon or horse-and-buggy many African-Americans in the south still knew during the thirties and forties. (FR.) Example: "Hop in my bucket and let's go for a spin." Southern and midwestern use. See "Buggy," "Hog," and "Struggle buggy."

Buck [ass] naked adj. (1830s–1950s) naked; fully naked. (FGC, DARE, p. 42.) Example: "I saw the boy buck ass naked run outta the house that time his daddy was beating him with the strap." Southern rural use. See "Buck paddle."

Buck-off v. (1990s) to kill someone. (Queen Latifah, *Essence*, September 1992, p. 87.) SNCU.

Buck paddle v., n. (1850s–1900s) to place someone across a log and beat them across the buttocks; a paddle used for punishment. (HJ, ILSG, np; FGC, DARE, p. 421.) Example (white slaveholder): "I buck paddle my niggers good to keep them in line." Southern plantation and rural use.

Buckra n. (1700s–1940s) white man; used in the same way as "massa" for "master" but with a very different meaning. John Bartlett: "In the language of the Calabar Coast, *buckra* means devil; not, however, in the sense we apply to it, but that of a demon." (JB, DA, p. 51; SBF, IHAT, p. 32; ECLA, NN, p. 263; CCJ, NMGC, p. 167; AEG, BB, p. 291; JB, DA, p. 51; CVV, NH, p. 285; JSF, AON, pp. 96–97; JH, PBL, p. 83.) SU.

Buckra-nigger n. (1700s–1860s) derogatory expression for a slaveholder's favorite slave. (AEG, BB, p. 291.) SU.

Buck the saw v. (1960s) to overcome difficult odds. (DW, TL, p. 60.) Example: "You'll have to buck the saw to get these people in this neighborhood to vote for you again." NCU.

Buckwheat n. (1890s–1960s) the idea of buckwheat as a plantation and rural southern staple meant that it had served as a metaphor for many things—truth, hard facts, etc.—in African-American life in the south. Often it was used as a nickname for boys. Because of its light brown color, black people sometimes called light-skinned friends and relatives "buckwheats." (EF, RDSL, p. 231; CS, vol. 3, no. 2, p. 12.) SU.

Buddha; buda n. (1980s–1990s) crack cocaine mixed with marijuana. (TW, CK, p. 135.) DCU.

Buddha-head n. (1970s–1990s) Japanese or Chinese person; anyone of Asian descent. (EF, RDSL, p. 231.) Los Angeles use.

Budhead n. (1950s) anyone who loves to drink beer. (DC, BJ, p. 59.) MWU.

[Do like] Buddy Brown, lay back down (1930s–1950s) expression reflecting sadness, the blues, despair; also, an expression of contentment. (Hear Sleepy John Estes, "Buddy Brown Blues," 1935, *I Ain't Gonna Be Worried No More*, 1929–1941, Yazoo, 1992; Lightnin' Hopkins, "I Went to Louisiana," *Lightnin' Hopkins Strikes Again*, 1990).) SU.

Buddy Ghee n. (1930s–1940s) term of address by a male for a male friend. (CC, OMMM, NCCHD, p. 253.) Rare. Harlem use.

Buffalo soldier(s) n. (1870s–1890s) two African-American cavalry and two infantry regiments west of the Rockies that served after the Civil War on and around reservations for thirty years. "Buffalo soldier" became the Native-American nickname for black soldiers. Native Americans saw a similarity between the black man's short, curly hair and the buffalo's tightly knit curls, hence the name. (SBF, IHAT, p. 66.) Blacks picked up the use of the name from Native Americans. SNU.

Buffer n. (1890s–1990s) male or female who performs oral sex in exchange for cocaine. (TW, CH, p. 147.) NCU.

Bug v. (1650s–1990s) to fight; wiggle; twitch; to annoy or irritate, in the way that a bug on the neck might; *baga-baga* (Mandingo); *bog-bog* (Sierra Leone); *jito-bag* (Mandingo); *baga* (Mandingo); *bug-aboo* (Liberia). (HV, AHAE, p. 139; LS, GYY, p. 455; CS, vol. 3, no. 2, p. 12; JH, PBL, 83; LA, SM, p. 164; SL, RJON, p. 147.) Example: "Get on away from here. Don't bug me." SNU. See "Bug [in ear]."

Bug [in ear] n. (1940s–1980s) an idea. (FR.) Example: "He put a bug in my ear that turned into a million dollars." SNU. See "Bug."

Bugaloo n. (FGC, DARE, p. 435.) See "Boogaloo."

Bugged on adj. (1940s–1950s) extremely enthusiastic about something. "Bug," in this context, took on a positive connotation, but with the sense that obsession is implied. And to the extent that obsession might be considered less than positive—an itch, an irritation, an unrelenting burden—"bug" retains some of its earlier negative quality. (FR.) NCU.

Bug(ged) out v. (1960s) to go away; in the nineties, to get angry. (CS, vol. 3, no. 2, p. 12.) Example: "Now you've really bugged me out!" NCU.

Buggy n. (1920s; 1990s) in the twenties and thirties a "buggy" was an automobile. Why "buggy"—to mean car—should become current again in the nineties remains a mystery, but it has. (WF, DAS, p. 69; FGC, DARE, p. 437.) See "Struggle buggy" and "Bucket."

Bugle n. (1940s) the human nose, so called because of the sound made when blown hard. (DB, OHHJ, p. 135; FGC, DARE, p. 439.) Example: "He blows his bugle at the dinner table. It's so disgusting." Harlem use.

Building n. (1950s) any place of residence, not only an apartment building but a family home of any type. (DC, BJ, p. 59.) MWU. See "Crib" and "Pad."

Bull n. (1940s–1950s) lesbian, short for "bull dyke" or "bulldagger." See both.

Bulldagger; bulldag n. (1940s–1950s) variant of "bull dyke"; lesbian (or even a tomboy); or an especially aggressive female homosexual; (1960s) negative term for a female homosexual. This term and "bull dyke" generally declined in use during the early sixties. (CS, vol. 3, no. 2, p. 12; JH, PBL, p. 83.) SNU.

Bulldogger n. (1980s–1990s) a man who forces his will on others; a tough or mean man; a bully. (WKB, JMC, PS, p. 49.) Example: "Nestor a bad bulldogger, man, he make a little sapsucker like you wear lipstick and put on a dress for him." PU.

Bull dyke; bulldyker n. (1920s–1950s) lesbian. (CVV, NH, p. 285.) Example: "Yeah, man, a bull dyke took my wife from me. Talk about rotten luck." See "She-he" and "Bulldagger."

Bull-jive v. (1970s–1990s) to put someone on; to kid. (RDA, TB, p. 55) Example: "Carl, don't bull-jive me, man, I can see straight through you, little daddy." SNU.

Bull Moose bandleader and singer Benjamin Clarence Jackson (born 1919). He retired and ran a bar in Philadelphia in the late fifties.

Bull of the woods n. (1940s) derogatory term for the president or dean of a college. The metaphor is not without humor. (MHB, JS, np.) Example: "The bull of the woods says school costs will increase next year." Hampton Institute; southern Negro college student use.

Bull scare n. (1940s–1950s) the aggressive manner and "wolfing" of a bluff. (IS, PSML, p. 313.) NCU.

Bullskating v. (1940s) to brag. (ZNH, AM, p. 94; MHB, JS, np.) Example: "He always be bullskating around his friends." SNU.

Bull's wool n. (1900s–1940s) stolen clothes. One of the earliest (1900s) white uses of this expression referred to cheap or homemade clothing. Black speakers no doubt used it this way too, but later, among black speakers, the expression came to specifically mean stolen clothes. (DB, OHHJ, p. 135; FGC, DARE, p. 454.) SU, MWU.

Bum-beefed v. (1960s) to be framed by the police as in the case when drugs are planted in one's pocket by the arresting officer. (CS, vol. 3, no. 2, p. 12.) DCU.

Bummy adj. (1990s) dirty and raggedy; disheveled. (RP, C.) Example: "Lots of bummy people hanging around Times Square." New York City; NECU.

Bump n. (1950s–1960s) a dance in which partners bump hips. (FR.) SNU.

Bump n., v. (1980s–1990s) robbery; to rob. (FR.) SCU.

Bump [bumpty-bump-the-bump] n. (1900s–1960s) phrase voiced while doing a dance where people bump hips. (FR.) SNCU.

Bump [and grab] v. (1990s) to deliberately drive into someone's moving car for the purpose of stalling and robbing them. (FR.) SNCU. See "Smash and grab."

Bumper n. (1930s–1940s) a nickel. (SK, PC, p. 135.) Example: "Don't see how daddy gone take you to the fair, sugar, he ain't got a bumper to his name." Florida; SU.

Bumping adj. (1990s) to be having a "rocking" good time; same as "jumping" in "the joint is jumping." (FR.) YCU, SCU.

Bumps n. (1900s–1970s) rash, especially on the face. (FGC, DARE, p. 457.) SNU.

Bumptious adj. (1880s–1920s) easy to anger; hot-tempered. (FGC, DARE, p. 458.) SU.

Bum rush; bumrush n. (1980s–1990s) a sudden police raid; mob action; to stampede, especially to get into a theater or a sports event. (TW, CK, p. 135.) New York City; DCU, YCU, SCU.

Bum trip n. (1960s) a negative psycho-physical reaction to ingesting drugs. (CS, vol. 3, no. 2, p. 12.) DCU.

Bunch-of-fives n. (1940s) the fists, especially as used in a fistfight. (DB, OHHJ, p. 135.) Example: You want this bunch-of-fives against your nose?" NCU.

Bunnyhug n. (1900s–1920s) jazz dance originating on the Barbary Coast. (FR.) SNU.

Bunk composer and instrumentalist William Geary Johnson (1879–1949).

Buns n. (1960s) the buttocks. (HLF, RJPD, p. 170.) Example: "If you'd get off your buns and get a job you wouldn't be so depressed." NCU. See "Cakes" and "Rusty-dusty."

Bunt n. (1970–1990) a short drive of the golf ball. (HLF, RJPD, p. 170; GS, TT, p. 58.) Black golf players' use.

Buppies n. (1980s–1990s) the African-American middle class in the United States. (XC, MEB, p. 4.) SNU.

Bups n. (1980s–1990s) short for "buppies." See "Buppies."

Burn v. (1920s; 1950s–1960s) the earliest use referred to someone who cheated at cards; to cheat in a drug transaction; to burn someone is to abuse them in any way but especially to borrow or steal money. Also "burn" means to cook, especially well. (FR; CS, vol. 3, no. 2, p. 12; CLC, TS, p. 254; RRL, DAZ, p. 32.) Examples: "That dude burned me for my last dollar." And, "Can't nobody outdo Sue when she gets in the kitchen to burn." SNCU, DC. See "Burnt."

Burn artist n. (1960s) a pusher who habitually cheats drug users. (CS, vol. 3, no. 2, p. 12; RRL, DAZ, p. 32.) DC.

Burn(ed) out v. (1950s) to suffer a loss or defeat of some type, or to inflict such a loss. Also, to be arrested as a result of a police stool pigeon. (DC, BJ, p. 59; RRL, DAZ, p. 32.) Example: "The Ravens burned me out while I was in the joint." MWU.

Burn some rubber v. (1970s–1990s) See "Burn some wheels."

Burn some wheels v. (1970s–1990s) to drive a car in a fast and reckless manner, especially stopping and starting fast. (FR.) YCU, SCU.

Burnt v. (1960s) to have been cheated or robbed. (CS, vol. 3, no. 2, p. 13.) DCU.

Burnt-out vein n. (1960s) a collapsed vein due to overuse from shooting drugs. (CS, vol. 3, no. 2, p. 13.) DCU.

Burrito n. (1970s–1990s) pejorative term for a Chicano or Latino person. (EF, RDSL, p. 231.) Watts and South-central Los Angeles use.

Bush n. (1960s) a "natural" hairstyle. (HLF, RJPD, p. 170.) SNU. See "Afro."

Bush n. (1970s–1990s) female pubic hair. (EF, RDSL, p. 231.) SNU.

Bushbitch n. (1980s–1990s) an ugly girl or young woman. (Eddie Murphy, *Eddie Murphy Raw*, 1987.) SNCU.

Bush devil n. (1700s–1860s) a "worldly representation" of "supernatural forces, personifying the will of God and mysteries of life" (JEH, AAC, p. 78). SU.

Business n. (1940s) penis. (WM, DBD, p. 132.) Example: "That joker crazy; he'd put his business in anything with a hole in it." SNU.

Busk; busking v. (1960s–1990s) to play music by heart; performing music without the benefit of a score. (KG, JV, p. 181.) Example: "That dude been busking since back in the forties and never missed a lick." JMFU.

Bust; busted v. (1900s–1990s) to arrest; to be arrested and/or convicted; penniless; to fail. (IS, PSML, p. 313; WF, DAS, pp. 79–80; CS, vol. 3, no. 2, p. 12; JEH, PEB, p. 175.) SNCU, SCU. See "Burn."

Bust a sweat (1980s–1990s) refers to sexual excitement—not an orgasm, but the excitement leading up to it. (JM, WPC) Example: "Every time I touch that chick I bust a sweat." SNCU, SCU.

Bust [one's] conk v. (1930s–1940s) to work very hard, especially mentally. (CC, OMMM, NCCHD, p. 253.) Example: "I busted my conk on that test this morning in physics." NCU. See "Conk buster."

Buster n. (1990s) an informer; a "snitch." (FR.) YCU, SCU.

Bust [one's] nuts v. (1940s–1950s) ejaculation; orgasm. (DW, TL, p. 60.) Example: "He busted his nuts the minute he got started." NCU.

Bust some booty v. (1980s–1990s) male term; to take an aggressive or very active role in sexual intercourse. (EF, RDSL, p. 231.) SNU.

Buster blues clarinetist William C. Bailey (born 1902); played with W. C. Handy's orchestra.

Busters n. (1980s–1990s) the police. Rap culture use.

Busting suds v. (1960s–1970s) to wash dishes. (JH, PBL, p. 83.) NCU.

Butch n. (1940s–1950s) lesbian; female homosexual. See "Bull dyke" and "Bulldagger."

Butter n. (1980s–1990s) the posterior. (EF, RDSL, p. 231.) SNU.

[Big] Butter-and-egg man n. (1900s–1920s) Walter Winchell held that the expression was coined by Harry Richman, others say Texas Guinan (of the Waldorf-Astoria Hotel restaurant), but no one disagrees with the fact that Louis Armstrong made it famous with his 1924 song "The Butter-and-Egg Man"; and a year later George S. Kaufman's play of the same title opened on Broadway. A "butter-and-egg man" is a sugar daddy or a back-door man; sometimes also used as a sarcastic phrase for vulgar, showy men who thought themselves bigshots. (ILA, CS, p. 77.) SNU.

Butter baby n. (1980s–1990s) a woman with a big rear end and large breasts. (EF, RDSL, p. 231.) SNU.

Butterhead n. (1940s) a "Negro" who is considered an "embarrassment" to his race. (FR.) SNU.

Butterfly n. (1940s) a good-looking young woman. (DB, OHHJ, p. 135.) SNU.

Buttermilk bottom n. (1920s–1940s) a black neighborhood in Atlanta (and in other southern black communities) located at the base of a hill on the East Side. (FR.) SU. See "Black Bottom."

Button n. (1960s) a capsule containing heroin or opium. (CS, vol. 3, no. 2, p. 13.) DCU.

Button [one's] lips v. (1930s–1940s) to refrain from speaking. NCU.

Butt out interj. (1960s; 1990s) a command to go away, or to mind one's business, especially addressed to a would-be interrupter of a conversation. (CS, vol. 3, no. 2, p. 13.) NCU.

Butt-sprung adj. (1930s–1940s) describes an ill-fitting garment, especially as viewed from the rear. (ZNH, AM, p. 94.) Example: "Child, you shoulda seen Marsha come in in her butt-sprung outfit last night looking like she thought she was into something." SNU.

Buttwhipping n. (1950s) a spanking. Usually used in addressing a misbehaving child. (DC, BJ, p. 59.) SU, MWU.

[To] Buy a woof [wolf] ticket v. (1980s–1990s) to call someone's bluff; to intimidate. (EF, RDSL, p. 231.) Example: "Listen, man, if you want to buy a woof ticket just come right on and put up your dogs." Watts and South-central Los Angeles use.

By golly! (1800s–1990s) a common oath. (JSF, AON, p. 111.) SU.

Buzz n. (1930s–1950s) the first effects of smoking marijuana or using some other kind of dope; from the forties to the fifties, a telephone call. (CS, vol. 3, no. 2, p. 13.) NSU.

Buzzard lope n. (1660s–1860s) a dance done by slaves and ex-slaves on plantations in which the dancer makes buzzardlike flying movements. (HV, AHAE, p. 156.) SU.

Buzz mute n. (1930s) in jazz, an unusual instrument that creates a sound like a cross between a trumpet and a razor. (RSG, JL, p. 46.) JMFU.

BYO n. (1960s) initials for "*Bring your own brown bag.*" (CS, vol. 3, no. 2, p. 13.) SNU. See "Bring your own brown bag."

C n. (1970s–1990s) code for cocaine. (WF, DAS, p. 83; IS, PSML, p. 314.) DCU.

C and H n. (1960s–1990s) cocaine and heroin; a play on the brand name of the product C and H cane sugar. (EF, RDSL, p. 231; RRL, DAZ, p. 34.) DCU.

C and M n. (1960s–1990s) cocaine and morphine. (RRL, DAZ, p. 34.) DCU.

Cab singer and bandleader Cabell Calloway (born 1907); famous scat singer of songs such as "Minnie the Moocher." See also "Cabbage."

Cabbage Cab Calloway's nickname.

Cabbage n. (1940s–1950s) money. (DC, BJ, p. 60.) Example: "Sitting here with no cabbage, waiting till my baby come home." NCU. See "Scratch."

Cack; kack v. (1900s–1940s) to brag or flaunt one's good fortune. (ZNH, AM, p. 89.) SNU. See "Cack-broad."

Cack-broad n. (1900s–1940s) variant of "cackle," referring to a Sugar Hill type of society lady who brags or flaunts her wealth. (ZNH, AM, p. 89.) SNU.

Caddy n. (1940s–1950s) a Cadillac automobile. (FR.) SNU.

Café au lait n. (1920s–1930s) a light-skinned Harlem woman, especially in the Cotton Club's chorus line. (Donald Bogle, *Brown Sugar*, 1980, p. 35.) Harlem use.

Cage of anger n. (1980s–1990s) prison. (KCJ, JS, p. 133.) PU.

Caint v. (1800s–1990s) a form of "cannot" (can't). SNU.

Cake n. (1960s) money. (JH, PBL, p. 83.) NCU.

Cakes n. (1960s) the buttocks. (HLF, RJPD, p. 170.) Example: "Get off your cakes and make some money like other men do." NCU.

Cakewalk n. (1870s–1920s) a syncopated dance originating among African slaves on plantations in the deep south; actually, a mockery and caricature of white folk waltzing or minueting. It was later used to refer generally to a social gathering at which the guests might entertain themselves by offering a cake as a prize to the guest who can dance most elegantly and impressively around the cake. (HV, AHAE, p. 156; RSG, JL, p. 47.) SNU. See "Take the cake."

Cakewalk wedding n. (1990s) a dance designed to dramatize the Billie and Willie Farrell song (about Miss Dora Dean) of the same title. (Ann Charters, *Nobody: The Story of Bert Williams*, p. 35.) SNCU.

Caledonia n. (1920s–1950s) pejorative term for a black woman who refuses to adjust to a morally acceptable traditional role. (FR.) SNU.

California bankroll n. (1980s–1990s) a roll of singles covered by a large bill—such as a hundred-dollar bill—and used to impress friends or "suckers." (EF, RDSL, p. 231.) Watts and South-central Los Angeles use.

Call n. (1960s) the first response to injected drugs. (CS, vol. 3, no. 2, p. 13.) Example: "Hey! I just got a call." DCU.

Call [one's] name v. (1890s–1920s) to mention or to know a person's name. (FR.) Examples: "I think I loved him before I could call his name." And, "What they call your name?" SU.

Call [one] out v. (1980s–1990s) to challenge someone to a fistfight or a gun battle. (EF, RDSL, p. 231.) SCU.

Call [one] out of [one's] name v. (1900s–1940s) most popular in the thirties, this expression refers to the business of insult through name-calling. (FR.) Example: "If you call me out of my name again I'm going to knock your head off." Southern use.

Call [oneself] v. (1900s–1940s) to intend to do something. (FR.) Example: "I call myself taking care of things at home, but I miss my wife." SU.

Call(ing) hogs v. (1930s–1940s) to snore. (MM, RB, p. 331; FGC, DARE, pp. 517–518.) Example: "That man of mine calls hogs all night so bad I can't sleep half the time." SU.

Call off all bets (1930s–1940s) to die. (DB, OHHJ, p. 135.) Example: "You hear about Joseph McGhee calling off all bets last week?" SNU.

Calling the wind (1700s–1880s) slaves working in cotton or corn fields often called the wind to help in a particular task; wind was also depended on to carry one's voice across the distance of a field. (FR.) SU. See "Come wind."

Camel walk n. (1900–1940s) a dance step in which the emphasis is in imitating the shoulder and back movements of a camel in motion. Most popular during the twenties, at the time of Snake Hips, the Buzzard Lope, and the Fishbone. (CVV, NH, p. 242.) SNU.

Camp ground n. nineteenth-century expression for free land; a symbol of Heaven. After slavery, many blacks formed and met in small bands, usually in remote forest areas, and survived in such small units. The settled areas were called camp grounds. See "Canaan" and "Jubilee."

Camp meeting n. (1900s–1940s) an open-air revival meeting.

Campy adj. (1950s) cozy to the point of absurdity. (FR.) Example: "They sho are a couple of campy dudes." SNU.

Can n. (1890s–1930s) the buttocks or hips, but the obvious connection with toilet or toilet seat as "the can" is inescapable. (ZNH, MM) Example: "Get off your can and clean up this house." SNU.

Can n. (1960s) an ounce of marijuana. Also, a person's rear-end. (IS, PSML, p. 314; CS, vol. 3, no. 2, p. 14.) Examples: "I'll never buy a can from Jake again." And "Get off your can and go to the store for me." DCU.

Canaan n. (1800s–1930s) a place-name found frequently in the spirituals; a nineteenth-century expression for free land; a symbol of Heaven. (FR.) See "Camp ground" and "Jubilee."

Canary n. (1920s–1940s) any female jazz vocalist, especially one who sings with a band. (CC, OMMM, NCCHD, p. 253; DB, OHHJ, p. 135.) Example: "We got two canaries coming out tonight and four cats on saxes." JBWU.

Candlelight n. (1760s–1940s) of Gullah origin; dusk; twilight. (TT, NFR, p. 74; FGC, DARE, p. 867.) Example: "Will you be home by candlelight, John?" South Carolina and Georgia; SU.

Candle-sperm n. (1920s) a voodoo term. According to R. Emmet Kennedy, author of *Black Cameos* (1924), this expression referred to wax from a spermaceti candle. (REK, G, p. 119.) Example: "Somebody was burning a candle over her to keep bad luck in her way. She was sure of it, because she found red pepper and buzzard feathers and candle-sperm tracks on her front door steps." SU.

Candy n. (1870s–1940s) sex; heard often in the blues as a sexual reference. (FR.) SNU.

Candy n. (1960s–1990s) heroin. (EF, RDSL, p. 231.) DCU.

Candy n. (1980s–1990s) any attractive person; an attractive woman. (EF, RDSL, p. 231.) SNCU.

Candy butt n. (1980s–1990s) pejorative term for any young man or woman who is not "hip" or "cool" on the "scene." (EF, RDSL, p. 231.) SNCU.

Candy man n. (1870s–1970s) a woman's lover or man; a pimp who sells *himself* sexually; a sexually assertive man. (JH, PBL, p. 83.) SNU.

Candy man n. (1950s–1990s) drug pusher. (JH, PBL, p. 83.) Example: "Catch ya later. I got an appointment with the candy man." SNU.

Can I get a witness? (1960s) a plea for affirmation. (FR.) Example: "Hey, can I get a witness that I didn't have some bow-wow on my arm Saturday night?" SNCU.

Canned heat n. (1960s) crude alcohol produced for heating purposes but drunk by down-and-out alcoholics. (DW, TL, p. 60.) Example: "Them cats in the alley keep warm on that canned heat." NCU.

Cannibal n. (1960s–1980s) derogatory expression referring to one who indulges in oral-genital sex. SNCU.

Cannon n. (1920s–1950s) a pickpocket. This word probably is related to "cannonball," which is the vault in a safe. Urban blacks picked up the usage from white underworld lingo. (HEG, DAUL, p. 40; IS, TB, p. 311; IS, PSML, p. 314.) Example: "Johnny's the best cannon on Sixty-third and Cottage." MWU.

Cannonball saxophonist and trumpeter Julian Edward Adderley (born 1928).

Canoe; canoeing v. (1920s–1950s; 1980s–1990s) to have sex; to make love; to be intimate; to cuddle. The interior shape of the canoe suggests the curves of an embrace. Louis Armstrong uses the word in his autobiography, *Satchmo*, 1954. Also, in the eighties and nineties: a cigarette or reefer burning abnormally lengthwise rather than evenly around. (TW, CK, p. 135.) Example: "Sugar, let's canoe." SU, MWU.

Cans n. (1970s–1990s) recording studio earphones. (KG, JV, 181.) JMFU.

Can to can't n. (1700s–1860s) slave term for "sunup to sundown." (HLB, LSS, p. 50.) Example: "We worked from can to can't." SU. See "Can't-see."

Can't-see n. (1840s–1930s) the period of darkness before sunrise and after sunset. (JMB, DG, p. 104.) Example: "Times were hard for us. I was working from can't-see in the morning to can't-see at night." SU.

Canyon n. (1980s–1990s) the vagina; a large vagina. (EF, RDSL, p. 231.) SNCU.

[Dive in the] Canyon v. (1980s–1990s) to perform cunnilingus. (EF, RDSL, p. 231.) SNCU.

[Grin in the] Canyon v. (1980s–1990s) to perform cunnilingus. (EF, RDSL, p. 231.) SNCU.

[Yodel in the] Canyon v. (1980s–1990s) to perform cunnilingus. (EF, RDSL, p. 231.) SNCU.

Cap v. (1990s) to kill or murder someone. (FR.) Example: "Don't send Woody, 'cause they'll cap him before he can get his hand out of his pocket." NECU, SCU.

Cap n. (1980s–1990s) glycerin container for drugs. (IS, PSML, p. 314; RRL, DAZ, p. 37; CLC, TS, p. 254.) Example: "Caps all over the ground in the projects." NCU.

Cap on; capped on; capped v. (1940s–1950s) to verbally put down someone; to censure; to insult. (CC, OMMM, NCCHD, p. 253; AY, S, p. 16; MM, RB, p. 331; DC, BJ, p. 60.) Example: "That boy so bad he'd cap on his mama." See "Dirty Dozens."

Cape n. (1980s–1990s) condom. (FR.) Example: "If you want to fly with me you got to wear yourself a cape." SNCU.

Capon n. (1930s–1940s) a pejorative term for an effeminate male, with obvious derogatory reference to the fact that a capon is a castrated rooster. (DB, OHHJ, p. 135.) SNU.

Capping n. (1940s–1950s) ritual of verbal insult; besting someone. (AY, S, p. 16; RDA, TB, p. 48.) SNU. See "Cap" and "Dirty Dozens."

Caravan n. (1980s–1990s) to go on a joy ride in more than one car —stolen or otherwise. (EF, RDSL, p. 232.) Watts and South-central Los Angeles; SCU.

Carfare n. (1940s–1990s) busfare. (FR.) Example: "I ain't even got carfare to go look for work." SNCU.

Carga n. (1960s) drug users' word for heroin. (CS, vol. 3, no. 2, p. 14.) Watts, Los Angeles; WCU.

Carmelite n. (1963) a person of Indian, Black, and Anglo-Saxon racial ancestry. According to the Federal Writer's Project Guide for Ohio, 1940, this word originated among blacks in Carmel, Ohio. (BB, AW, p. 19.) Regional Ohio use.

Carouse v. (1940s–1950s) to be loud and intoxicated. (FR.) Example: "Man, when you gone stop your drinking and carousing?" SU, MWU.

Carry n. (1780s–1940s) a wagon for hauling produce; "Negro" word. (JSF, AON, p. 125.) SU.

Carry v. (1780s–1940s) to lead. Heard in "Negro song." (JSF, AON, p. 125.) Example: "Y'all come on and carry me back to the farm, hear." SU.

Carry power v. (1930s) to carry power is to possess it. Zora Neale Hurston used the phrase frequently in her books. (FR.) Example: "That old woman carry power. She can put a spell on anybody she wants to." SU

Carrying v. (1960s–1980s) short for "Are you carrying drugs?" This word usually referred to users and not to someone who was a drug runner or a clocker possessing narcotics. (RRL, DAZ, p. 38.) Example: "Don't get caught out here carrying 'cause these cops don't play."

Carrying on v. (1930s–1950s) misbehaving; having an illicit affair. (FR.) Examples: "If he ain't carrying on over here he's carrying on over there." Or, "That man's always carrying on something terrible." SU, MWU.

Carve v. (1920s–1940s) to outplay another musician in a musical competition. (AL, MJR, p. 145.) Example: "Pres carved me up [like a turkey] last night." JMFU.

Carving Contest n. See "Cutting Contest."

Cascos n. (1780s–1920s) the offspring of a quadroon and a white parent. (EBR, MUS, p. 13.) SU. See also "Metif."

Case n. (1960s–1990s) a person's personal affairs or life. (EF, RDSL, p. 232.) Example: "I'm gone stay on your case, boy, till you admit you were wrong." SNCU.

Case v. (1970s) to look at someone. (FR.) Example: "The dude was out there casing everybody in sight." NCU. See "Pen."

Casey Brown (KC Brown) n. (1890s–1940s) a mythic and brave outlaw willing to risk his life to fight racial oppression. (ZNH, MM, p. 306.) SU.

Cashmere n. (1940s–1950s) any sweater of any material. (RDA, DDJ, p. 264.) Example: "I fell into the ballroom dap wearing my bad cashmere and my stingy-brim and all the chicks was casing me." NCU.

Casper n. (1950s) a pejorative term for a light-skinned black person. The word refers to the cartoon character Casper the Friendly Ghost, who is snow-white. (EF, RDSL, p. 232.) Example: "Them casper women think they too good for a black man." MWU.

Castle n. (1930s–1940s) one's home or house. (DB, OHHJ, p. 135.) Example: "I gotta hit the castle and dig on some pecks." NCU.

Cat n. (1900s–1950s) a prostitute or infrequently the female sex organs; from the twenties to the forties, a jazzman, a musician in a swing band; from the forties to the fifties, generally, any one male. (IS, PSML, p. 314; DB, OHHJ, p. 135; EF, RDSL, p. 232; DR, BASL, p. 127; CC, OMMM, NCCHD, p. 253.) Example: "Hey, cat! How ya doing?" SNCU. See "Cathouse" and "Dude."

Cat trumpet player William Anderson (born September 12, 1916). Worked with Duke Ellington, 1944–1947.

Catch n. (1960s) a woman. (CS, vol. 3, no. 2, p. 14.) Example: "I got me a nice catch last night to add to my stable." PPU, SCU.

Catch; catching v. (1890s–1900s) "to lure a victim into the first stage of a con game"; to "score" with a member of the opposite sex; to reach or come into the possession of something; to discover something or someone; from the twenties to the fifties, to listen to or observe someone. (EF, RDSL, p. 232; IS, TB, p. 311.) Examples: "I gotta catch me a woman"; or "I caught him on the way out the door," meaning "I stopped him" or "I spoke with him"; or "Hey, did you catch the show last night?" PPU, SCU.

Catch action n. (1960s) young women—often runaways—on the streets who may be potential prostitutes. (CS, vol. 3, no. 2, p. 14.) PPU, SCU.

Catching v. (1980s–1990s) to win over a young woman for the purpose of prostitution. (CRM, BP, p. 247.) Example: "His Mack talk so strong he be catching a new woman every night." PPU, SCU. See "Catch."

Catching sense n. (1600s–1860s) During slavery certain "invisible [African] institutions" remained in place, in the communal life of the slaves. "Catching sense" was the term for membership into the plantation's religious community ("plantation membership and praise house" [JEH, AAC, p. 79]).

Catch up bass n. (1900s) expression for the left-hand effect created by a jazz bassist. (FR.) JMFU.

Catercawner (catter corner) adv., adj. (1900s–1940s) diagonally across from; variant of "catercorner." Example: "Mr. Thomas's barn is cattercawner from mine." SU.

Catfaces n. (1930s–1950s) unpressed wrinkles in one's clothing. (FR.) Example: "We'll leave for market as soon as I iron these catfaces out of my dress." SU.

Catfish trouble n. (1860s–1890s) from a nineteenth-century Louisiana folktale; a person's dog might have, instead of fleas, crabs; and by the same "logic" it was not improbable that a trouble-ridden person might one day get lucky and catch in his mousetrap a catfish rather than a mouse. The expression spoke to the absurdity in life. (MT, DAF, p. 57.) SU.

Catfish row n. (1860s–1890s) a poor community of African-Americans; a series of shacks clustered together where black families live. (See Gershwin and Heyward, *Porgy and Bess*, 1933; FGC, DARE, p. 566.)

Cathouse n. (1900s–1930s) a whorehouse; barrelhouse; a style of music heard in brothels in New Orleans, Atlanta, and other cities of the south. (FR.) SU. See "Cat" and "Catting."

Catnip n. (1970s–1990s) weak, diluted, or false marijuana. (EF, RDSL, p. 232.) DCU.

Cat on the peek port (1940s) the lookout man. (DB, OHHJ, p. 135.) Example: "We had two cats on the peek port and still got caught." Harlem use.

Cat-o'-nine-tails n. (1650s–1860s) a leather whip used during slavery to beat slaves; picked up from white use. (FR.) SU.

Cat sense n. (1930s–1940s) common sense. It was a common Chicago South Side expression but had roots in the south. (FR.) Example: "The boy ain't got enough cat sense to come in from the rain." SNU.

Catterwalling v. (1930s–1950s) to make a loud noise or to wail like a cat. (FR.) Example: "You should have seen her catterwalling out of here this morning." SU, MWU.

Catting v. (1900s–1930s) when a man is out searching for available women, especially prostitutes. (FR.) Example: "Every payday Milton takes his paycheck and go catting." SU. See "Tomcat."

Cattle train n. (1940s–1950s) a Cadillac, a very popular car among black people during the forties and fifties. The expression is a commentary on the large size of the Cadillac compared to most other cars. (DB, OHHJ, p. 135.) Example: "Mack pick up all the cats in his cattle train and they go out to the dogs every Saturday afternoon." SNCU.

Catty-cat; kitty-cat n. (1970s–1990s) vagina. (EF, RDSL, p. 232.) SNU.

[The] Cat Woman actress and singer Eartha Kitt (born 1928).

Caution sign n. (1980s–1990s) anyone dressed in loud or gaudy colors. (EF, RDSL, p. 232.) Watts and South-central Los Angeles use.

Cave n. (1930s) a room; pad; where one lives. (FR.) Example: "Let's hit my cave and dig some jams." Rare. SNCU.

Cease v. (1890s–1920s) a contraction of "decease"; stop. (FGC, DARE, p. 576.) Example: "Flora Belle, she gone cease if she don't stop working so hard." SCU.

Cent n. (1960s–1970s) dollar. (CS, vol. 3, no. 2, p. 14.) Example: "Hey, Buddy, can you lay two cents on me till next week?" SNCU.

Century n. (1900s–1930s) a hundred-dollar bill or a hundred dollars in bills. Picked up from white use. (FR.) Example: "I saved up to a century to buy you this birthday present." SU, MWU.

Cha-cha n. (1940s–1990s) sex; sexual intercourse. (EF, RDSL, p. 232.) SNU.

Chain-lightning n. (1890s–1930s) a strong, homemade liquor that quickly affects the senses. (SGS, BG, p. 154.) Example: "We was sitting out back with a jug of chain-lightning and feeling pretty good." SNU. See "White-lightning."

Chalk n. (1980s) usually a person of Anglo-Irish descent; a white person. (EF, RDSL, p. 232.) Example: "I felt a draft when the chalks came in." NCU.

Chalking v. (1980s–1990s) to lighten the color of cocaine with a chemical so that potential buyers will think it's pure. (TW, CK, p. 136.) DCU.

Chamber lye n. (1890–1940) human urine sprinkled around a garden to keep deer away; chamberpot urine. (RW, AAGYRS, p. 84.) SU.

Chamber of commerce n. (1940s) a toilet. (DB, OHHJ, p. 135.) Example (mother to child): "Go to the chamber of commerce before you go to bed." Harlem use.

Champ n. (1950s–1960s) a junkie who will not cheat or inform the police on other junkies. (CLC, TS, p. 254.) Example: "Fletcher is a champ. You can trust him with the bag." NCU.

Change n. (1920s–1950s) any amount of money, paper, or coins. In jazz, since about 1925, the word has also meant an interlude during which a key change is made. (RSG, JL, p. 50.) JMFU, SNU.

Changes n. (1950s–1970s) originally from jazz world use; to "go through" or to "put through" changes; and, contemporary use in jazz world, chord sequence of a piece of music; on a personal basis, to have problems or to undergo a change of life-style; Richard Perry, *Changes*, 1974: "Put Someone through changes: To make a person uncomfortable by doing or saying something that contradicts his understanding of reality"; emotional or psychological problems. (RSG, JL, p. 51; KG, JV, p. 181.) Example: "I been through so many changes this year I don't even want to see next year." NCU.

[Go through] Changes v. See "Changes."

[Put through] Changes v. See "Changes."

[Run the] Changes v. (1940s–1950s) in jazz, to perform harmonic progressions as straight work, without genuine inspiration. (RSG, JL, p. 51.) JMFU.

Channel v. (1940s–1950s) to cause two things to happen because of a particular initial move; a bridge, connecting separate entities. (LF, EJ, p. 346.) Example: "If you channel your money my way, I can make you rich and me rich, too." SNU.

Charcoal n. (1870s–1900s) a musical passage between two separate musical themes; also, affectionate expression used by one black person to another. (FGC, DARE, p. 593; CVV, NH, p. 285.) Example: "Hey, charcoal!" Picked up from derogatory white use and converted. SU.

Charge n. (1930s) a thrill, especially from drugs. (FR.) Example: "Girl gives me a charge like sex." SNCU.

Charging v. (1960s–1990s) to verbally put someone down. (RDA, TB, p. 50.) SCU; YCU. See "Signify," "Dirty Dozens," and "Cracking."

Charles n. (1800s–1960s) any white man; variant of "Charley" or "Charlie." SNU. See "Charlie" and "Chuck."

Charles Coke n. See "Charlie" (cocaine).

Charlie n. (1850s–1960s) any white man; corruption of "Mister Charlie"; originally and primarily a southern term referring to the overseer or boss during slavery and the following period up through Reconstruction. Also, but rarely, "charlie" meant "a dollar." (RRF, DAZ, p. 39; FGC, DARE, p. 594; FR.) SNU. See "Mister Charlie," "Charlie Goons," "Charlie Nebs," "Sylvester."

Charlie n. (1960s) cocaine, because of its white color. (RRL, DAZ, p. 39.) Charlie as a reference for cocaine did not gain wide acceptance. (FR.) NCU.

Charlie Goon(s) n. (1960s) policemen. Derived from "Mister Charlie" or "Charlie." This term was in common use among blacks and counterculture people during the sixties. (FR.) Example: "We kept up a peaceful protest till the Charlie Goons picked us up and carried us to the paddy wagons." NCU.

Charlie Nebs n. (1960s) policemen. See "Charlie Goons."

Charm n. (1830s–1920s) variant of "chime"; heard in some of the spirituals. (FR.) SU.

Chart n. (1950s–1960s) in jazz, a written arrangement. (RSG, JL, p. 53; KG, JV, p. 181.) Example: "He write out his own charts." SNU.

Chase [chorus] n. (1940s–1960s) jazz term; players in turn take a series of choruses each and go through a range of bars. (FN, JS, p. 22.) JMFU.

Chaser n. (1990s) a frequent crack cocaine freebase user. (TW, CH, p. 147.) Example: "That sucker's the worse chaser in the hood." DCU.

Chasing the bag v. (1960s) actively seeking heroin. (RRF, DAZ, p. 39.) DCU.

Cheat; cheating v. (1900s–1920s) in jazz, stretching harmonic or rhythmic variations to cover limited musical skill. (MM, RB, p. 173.) Example: "He be out there blowing like a champ, but, you know, if you listen real close, he be cheating all the time." SNU.

Cheaters n. (1930s) dark eyeglasses; later, in the forties, supplanted by "shades." (FR.) Example: "He wear some mean cheaters. You can't see his eyes." SNU. See "Shades."

Check v. (1960s–1990s) notice; look; focus; listen; to keep in line; pay attention. (FR.) NSU.

Check [this, it] out v. (1960s–1990s) an invitation to observe or to try something; to closely observe; pay attention. (Originally, "check" was used as a command to desist.) (PM, UCLAS, p. 28.) Example: "It's a great show. Check it out." SNU. See "Check the war."

Check the war v. (1940s) command to stop arguing or fighting. (MHB, JS, np.) Example: "Hey! You two been it at long enough. Check the war!" SU.

Check [one's] nerves (1940s) command to keep cool. (MHB, JS, np.) SU.

Check [one's] self (1960s–1990s) a warning to stay in or to get back in line with what is expected. (FR.) SNU.

Cheeb; cheeba; sheeba n. (1980s–1990s) marijuana. (WKB, JMC, PS, p. 48.) NSU.

Cheeks n. (1960s) the buttocks. (HLF, RJPD, p. 170.) SNU.

Cheese n. (1970s) a light-skinned, yellow complexioned, or creamy complexioned person; mulatto. (FGC, DARE, p. 602.) Example: "He don't want him no cheese 'cause too many mens be eyeballing her." SU.

Cheese-eater n. (1950s–1960s) an informer, a snitch, a double-crosser. The reference to "rat" or "ratting" is implicit. (FGC, DARE, p. 603.) Example: "That cat is the worse cheese-eater on the block." SNU.

Cheezy adj. (1960s) anything cheap; stingy; ugly. (CS, vol. 3, no. 2, p. 15.) SNU.

Chemicals n. (1970s) code for street drugs. (RRL, DAZ, p. 39.) Example: "Got any chemicals?" NCU.

Cherokee Bill a Negro cowboy, born in 1876 at Fort Concho, Texas; a black cowboy, woman-charmer, and infamous murderer who met his end on the gallows at age twenty.

Cherokee Mariah Lilly (1800s–1850s) nickname for Susan Hunt, "free woman of color" (ALA, AL, pp. 28–29.) Georgia use.

Cherry n. (1930s–1950s) virginity; a female virgin; a person who is inexperienced. (HEG, DAUL, pp. 42–43; DW, TL, p. 60.) Examples: "I'd give my right arm to be the one to get her cherry"; or "He's such a cherry he don't even know how to hold his liquor." SNU.

Chesapikers n. (1780s–1800s) Georgia settlers from Maryland and Virginia. (ALA, AL, p. 20.) Georgia use.

Chew; chewed v. (1950s) to abuse or defeat verbally or physically. From "chew out," no doubt. (DW, TL, p. 60.) Example: "Eric chewed Dan up, man. You should've dug it." MWU.

Chewers n. (1940s) teeth or false teeth. (DB, OHHJ, p. 135.) Example: "Her kids got chewers big just like hers." MWU.

Chewtobaccy n. (1900s–1940s) a piece of chewing tobacco. (FR.) Example: "He spits his old nasty chewtobaccy everywhicha-where." SU.

Chib; chiv n. (1940s) an especially long and sharp switchblade knife. (FR.) Example: "Keep out of the way of his chib or he might cut you." SU.

Chica n. (1700s–1860s) *tshika* (Bantu), a dance done by African captive slaves on southern plantations in which the woman partner shakes her hips rhythmically while the male dances suggestively around her. (HV, AHAE, p. 157.) SU.

Chicago bankroll n. (1970s–1990s) a roll of singles topped by a big bill. (EF, RDSL, p. 232.) Chicago, Los Angeles; PPU, SCU, DCU. See "California bankroll."

Chicago green n. (1980s–1990s) a "medium to dark green" type of marijuana associated with the Chicago scene. (EF, RDSL, p. 232.) DCU.

Chick n. (1920s–1960s) any young woman, especially an attractive one. Usually not derogatory. "Chick" (meaning "woman" or "female") has been a word used most frequently among black speakers. (CC, OMMM, NCCHD, p. 253; MHB, JS, np.; FGC, DARE, p. 611; JH, PBL, p. 83.) SNU.

Chickama v. (1650s–1990s) to sit down; have a seat; sit in this place; word black children use in a game song; *shikama, shikamaku* (Bantu). (HV, AHAE, p. 139.) SU.

Chickenbone special n. (1950s) metaphor for anything that is inferior, but originally it referred to a bag of greasy fried chicken southern Negroes took on train trips probably because food from the diner was unavailable to them. The phrase is believed to have originated in Philadelphia among black students at Temple University. (FGC, DARE, p. 613.) NECU.

Chicken butt n. (1960s) a playful response: "What's up?" meaning "forget it." (MA, PTO, BL, p. 73.) WCU.

Chicken feed n. (1940s–1950s) an insufficient amount of money. The expression originated in the south but quickly became popular on the streets of such cities as Philadelphia and New York. (MHB, JS, np.) Example: "He's a chicken feed chump! Can't even show a woman a good time." SNU.

Chicken-head n. (1900s–1990s) an aggressively unpleasant woman. (EF, RDSL, p. 232.) SNU.

Chicken-preacher n. (1890s–1940s) short for "chicken-eating preacher." (FR.) Example: "Mama always have that chicken-preacher here every Sunday eating up all our food." SU. See "Fry-meat preacher."

Chicken scratch n. (1940s–1950s) a small amount of money. (FR.) SNU. See "Scratch."

Chicken scratch n. (1950s) nappy hair. (CM, CW, Gayl Jones, "White Rat," p. 375.) Kentucky use; SU.

Chicken scratching v. (1940s–1950s) an ineffective beginning. (FR.) Example: "You call this cleaning up the backyard? This ain't nothing but chicken scratching." SNU.

Chickenshit v. (1940s–1950s) very little and insufficient action or anything unacceptable or disagreeable. This expression probably didn't have its origins in any black community but became a common street expression in the south and the midwest during the forties and lasted into the fifties. (RDA, DDJ, p. 264; WF, DAS, p. 99.) SU, MWU.

Chico drummer Foreststorn Hamilton (born 1921). Worked with Count Basie and others.

Chico n. (1960s–1990s) pejorative term for Chicano or Latino male or female. (EF, RDSL, p. 232.) See "Bato."

Chigger; chigo; chego; chiego n. (1650s–1990s) originally from the West African Wolof word *jiga*, which means "insect"; "chigger," as used by African-Americans and other Americans, is a corruption of the Caribbean *chigo*, for flea or mite, sometimes called "chinch," or "bedbug"; variant of West African word for jigger mite; *jiga* (Wolof). (HV, AHAE, p. 139; SBF, IHAT, p. 32.) SU. See "Jigger."

Child n. (1620s–1950s) an informal term of address; form of address by an older person to a younger person or by one woman to another. (FR.) Example: "Child, if you don't get yourself in this house I'm going to skin you alive." Originally primarily used in the south. SNU.

[This] Child n. (1650s–1950s) a term of self-address. (JSF, AON, p. 137.) Example: "This child is gonna live till she dies! Yes, Lord!" SU.

Chili v. (1940s–1950s) to ignore. This may be a corruption of "chill," meaning to kill. (FR.) SNCU.

Chili Bean n. (EF, RDSL, p. 232.) See "Bato."

Chili pimp n. (1940s–1950s) one who plies his trade with only one prostitute. (IS, PSML, p. 314.) Example: "Roy? He ain't nothing but a chili pimp. Ain't got a pot to piss in." NCU.

Chill; chilling n., v. (1940s) murder; murdering. (HEG, DAU, p. 43.) Example: "The cops put a chill on Bobby right in the doorway of his own house, man." NCU.

Chill; chilling v. (1980s–1990s) relaxing; cooling it. (WKB, JMC, PS, p. 48; TW, CK, p. 136.) Example: "I'm just here chilling and sipping something cool. How ya doing?" SNCU. See "Cool."

Chill out; chill interj., v. (1980s–1990s) a command to desist from an action or to be calm; v. to relax. (WKB, JMC, PS, p. 48.) Example: "Chill out, motherfucker!" East and west coast use.

Chillun n. (1850s–1890s) variant form of "children." (CCJ, NMGC, p. 167.) SU.

Chilly most adj. (1990s) extremely calm or relaxed. (WKB, JMC, PS, p. 48.) Rare. Arizona state prison use.

Chime n. (1940s) In the nineteenth century "chime," as slang, meant false praise. Black use of it as slang started roughly in the 1940s and it referred to an hour or the time according to the clock. (CC, OMMM, NCCHD, p. 253; DB, OHHJ, p. 135; WF, DAS, p. 100; EP, DU, p. 120.) Example: "I'll be back in one chime." Rare. Harlem use.

Chimer n. (1940s) any sort of timepiece but especially an alarm clock; the human heart (ticker). "Chime" as slang for the ticking of the human heart is certainly much more inventive and imaginative than the clock reference, but this latter use was actually quite rare. (FR.) Example: "I gotta weak chimer. Gotta take it easy." SU, MWU. See "Ticker," "Tick-tock," and "Tick."

Chimney n. (1920s–1940s) a hat; the human head. (DB, OHHJ, p. 135.) Example: "Randy, that boy wears some mean chimneys." SNU.

Chimney chops n. (1620s–1800s) In England, "Chimney chops" was "an abusive appellation for a negro." Picked up from white use. Also, "chimney" was an underworld term meaning the top pocket on one's shirt (FG, DVT, np; EP, DU, 1949, p. 120; AB, DSJC, p. 232.) Rare. SU.

Chinch n. (1860s–1950s) a small red bug commonly called a bedbug. You can hear the word in some early blues recordings. (CLC, TS, p. 254; SL, RJON, p. 148.) Example: "I got chinches in my bed big as cows. Lord have mercy on me." SU, MWU. See "Chinchpad" and "Chigger."

Chinch-bug n. (1650s–1950s) any sort of small bug or insect; bedbug; worm or caterpiller; *tshishi* (Bantu). (HV, AHAE, p. 139.) SU.

Chinchpad n. (1890s–1950s) a rundown rooming house or hotel. (DB, OHHJ, p. 135.) Example: "His father died in one of them chinchpads downtown by the railroad track." SNU. See "Chinch" and "Chigger."

Chinchy adj. (1650s–1950s) stingy; mean; irritable; *tshinji* (Bantu). (HV, AHAE, p. 139.) Example: "He's so chinchy he wouldn't even give him poor old mama a decent burial." SNU.

Chine n. (1950s–1960s) short for "machine," meaning automobile. (FR.) Example: "Come on, hop in my chine, and let's go for a spin." MWU.

Chining v. (1950s–1960s) from "machine-ing," meaning to drive a car. (FR.) Example: "Me and Buddy went chining and picked up a couple of fine chicks last night." MWU.

Chingazo n. (1970s–1990s) sexual intercourse; *chingar*: fuck; sexual activity. Picked up from the Spanish-speaking community. (EF, RDSL, p. 232.) South-central Los Angeles use.

Chip n., v. (1940s) a sip, as in a sip of liquor; also to sip (liquor). (WM, ARD, p. 121.) SNU.

Chippie singer Bertha Hill (1905–1950). She worked with Louis Armstrong and King Oliver.

Chippie see "Chippy."

Chippy; chippying n., v. (1930s–1940s) according to Dan Burley, a "chippie" was a "glamour girl, play girl, slender, young girl of the racy, bony type," in Harlem before the fifties. The general slang-speaking population used the word to refer to a promiscuous woman or a delinquent girl. Also, on the drug culture scene, this use: one who dabbles or only occasionally uses hard drugs. By the eighties, black street-culture speakers in large cities used the word to refer to a young woman who infrequently used strong drugs. (DB OHHJ, 135; WF DAS, 101; RRL, DAZ, p. 55; IS, PSML, p. 314.) SNU. See "Dabbling."

Chirp n., v. (1930s–1940s) generally, jazz musicians used this term to refer to female vocalists, but it was rare after about 1935. (CC,

OMMM, NCCHD, p. 254; RSG, JL, 56.) Example: "Lil [Armstrong] never chirps." SNU. See "Canary."

Chitlins n. (1840s–1950s) chitterlings; hog bowels or intestines. Actually, the word "chitterling" has origins in Old English. It's a traditional soul food made from pork innards, considered waste by the slaveholder and therefore given to slaves, who ritualized it and turned it into a delicacy. (FG, DVT, np; AB, DSJC, p. 234.) SNU. See "Gutbucket," "Soul Food," and "High on the Hog."

Chitlins 101 n. (1960s–1970s) Used primarily by blacks themselves, this was a derogatory phrase applied to any black studies course in U.S. schools. College students; SNCU, YCU.

Chits n. (1940s–1950s) short for "chitterlings." No relation to Anglo-Indian word "chit." (AB, DSJC, p. 234.) SNU.

Chocker n. (1940s) necktie. (DB OHHJ, 135.) Example: "You can spot him 'cause he'll be wearing a bright yellow jive chocker." NECU.

Chocolate rock n. (1990s) the dark pipe substance that mixes with crack cocaine free base. (TW, CH, p. 147.) DCU.

Chocolate thunder n. (1980s–1990s) any black basketball player. Obvious color association. May or may not be originally associated with "chocolate soldier" (children's candy). (FR.) Example: "Chocolate thunder struck that white boy from every direction." SNU.

Choice adj. (1940s–1950s) in jazz circles but not exclusively so—anything good or excellent. (RSG, JL, p. 56.) Example: "Miles Davis played made some choice sounds tonight." JMFU.

Choked-down adj. (1980s–1990s) to be beautifully or handsomely dressed. (EF, RDSL, p. 232.) SNCU.

Choked up [tight] adj. (1960s) the appearance of being formally—and therefore uncomfortably—dressed, as in a suit and tie. (DW, TL, p. 60.) NCU.

Cholly n. (1940s) a dollar bill. May be associated with "Charlie" (for white man), who was associated with power (money). (DB, OHHJ, p. 135.) Example: "Hey, Skeets, lay a cholly on me." Harlem; NCU.

Choose v. (1950s–1960s) when a woman makes a voluntary selection of a pimp. (SH, GL, p. 212.) PPU.

Choose off v. (1980s–1990s) an expression used to taunt one to fight. (EF, RDSL, p. 232.) Watts, South-central Los Angeles; SCU.

Chop v., n. (1950s–1960s) to "cap"; a retort. (RDA, TB, p. 35.) NCU.

Chop-axe; chopping axe n., v. (1890s–1930s) cutting wood; any axe used for cutting wood. (FR.) Examples: "Get the chop-axe and cut the wood, boy"; or "Go on out in the backyard, like I told you, and chop-axe me some wood." SU.

Chopping high v. (1950s) living well. The expression is similar to "Living high on the hog." (FR.) Example: "I see you chopping high these days. Last time I saw you you were on unemployment." NCU.

Chop[s] n. (1920s–1930s; 1980s) one's musical technique; lips or the mouth; a musician's lips; Louis Armstrong's nickname. (KG, JV, p. 181; RSG JL, p. 56.) Example: "The man's got powerful chops and he can really let them fly." SNU.

Chops n. (1960s) teeth. (DC, BJ, p. 60.) Example: "You see the chops on that man over there?" Rare. MWU.

Chopstick n. (1960s–1990s) any Asian male or female. (EF, RDSL, p. 232.) South-central Los Angeles use; YCU.

Chorus n. (1930s–1980s) in jazz, a solo on the tune; the unit of music played. (KG, JV, p. 181; RSG, JL, p. 57.) JMFU.

Chow down; chowing down v. (1940s–1960s) to eat vigorously; picked up from military use: "To eat a meal." (WF, DAS, p. 103.) Example: "Boy, you should have seen them kids chowing down." SNCU.

Christian's path; Christian path n. (1650s–1930s) slave term for a good, upstanding life-style. Term can be heard in early spirituals. SU, SNU.

Christmas tree(s) n. (1960s–1990s) colorful capsules—blue, red, white, green—containing barbiturates. (EF, RDSL, p. 232; CS, vol. 3, no. 2, p. 15.) DCU.

Chronic n. (1990s) marijuana. (FR.) DCU, YCU.

Chrome n. (1970s–1990s) a gun. (FR.) SCU.

Chu Berry a tenor saxman (1910–1941) who worked with Fletcher Henderson, among other outstanding artists.

Chubby Checker singer Ernest Evans (born 1941).

Chubbyfat adj. (1940s–1950s) to describe extreme obesity. (FR.) MWU.

Chuck n. (1960s–1970s) any white man. (CS, vol. 3, no. 3, p. 5; JH, PBL, p. 83.) SNU. See "Charlie."

Chuck D (1980s–1990s) lead rapper in the group Public Enemy; called rap "black America's CNN." (*USA Weekend*, February 5–7, 1993, p. 18.)

Chuck it v. (1960s) to give up something. (FR; MHB, JS, np.) Example: "Billy gotta chuck his hoss habit or it going to kill him." SCU, YCU.

Chucklehead(ed) n., adj. (1920s–1930s) fathead; fatheaded. (CM, CW, Zora Neale Hurston, "The Guilded Six-Bits," p. 71.) SU.

Chump n. (1950s–1960s) a square; a victim; a dupe. Term derived from earlier use; "an underworld novice." May also be associated with the much earlier (1650s) "Chum: a chamber-fellow . . . in prison." (FG, DVT, np; CLC, TS, p. 254; CRM, BP, p. 297; HEG, DAU, p. 44; SH, GL, p. 212.) Example: "He's a chump for being in the way. He deserves what he got." NCU. See "Sucker" and "Chump change."

Chump change n. (1950s–1960s) any small amount of money. (IS, PSML, p. 314; CRM, BP, p. 297.) DCU, YCU. See "Chump."

Chump job n. (1960s) any low-paying job; "square" work. (CRM, BP, p. 297.) DCU, YCU.

Chump squeeze v. (1950s–1960s) "a momentary five-fingered punch on the arm or shoulder that meant whatever you wanted it to" (AY, S, p. 48). Detroit; NCU.

Chumpy adj. (1960s) unusual or strange behavior. (CS, vol. 3, no. 2, p. 15.) Example: "He come in here acting all chumpy—liked to scared me to death." Watts, Los Angeles, use.

Chunk v. (1880s–1930s) to throw. In some parts of the south the term was generally used by white speakers to refer to a block or beam of wood. (FGC, DARE, p. 663.) Example: "Mama, Juneboy chunked a rock and hit me in the head." SU.

Church-called adj. (1920s–1950s) feeling compelled to become a preacher. (FR.) SNU.

Churchfolk(s) n. (1920s–1950s) any person or persons who attend church on a regular basis. (FR.) Example: "They good churchfolks." SNU.

Cigar-box fiddle n. (1940s) a musical instrument made from an ordinary cigar box, string, and strips of wood. (AL, LWBB, pp. 427–428.) SU.

Cigarette pimp n. (1950s–1960s) any pimp who stoops to solicit for his woman ("ho"). (CRM, BP, p. 33.) PPU, SCU. See "Player."

[The] Cincinnati Cobra boxer Ezzard Charles, heavyweight champion (1949–1951).

Circus; circus love n. (1900s–1950s) an erotic or obscene dance performed by naked women in a whorehouse; an orgy in a whorehouse. In the fifties, an orgy, especially one involving various types of sexual activity. (AL, MJR, pp. 47, 118; IS, PSML, p. 314.) SNCU.

Circus house n. (1900s–1930s) a whorehouse of the type native to New Orleans, where some forms of blues and jazz originated. (AL, MJR, p. 47, 118.) SU, JBWU.

Citizen n. (1890s–1930s) probably short for "white citizen"; any square or prosaic white person. May have been picked up from white use of the word meaning an uncouth person. (FGC, DARE, 673.) Example: "My boss, he's a real citizen, man. I try to keep out of his way." SU.

C-jame n. (1960s) cocaine. (CS, vol. 3, no. 2, p. 15.) Watts, Los Angeles, use. DCU.

Clam n. (1940s–1950s) in jazz, a misplaced note. (RSG, JL, p. 59.) Example: "The band isn't in good shape tonight. Too many clams." JMFU. See "Clambake."

Clambake n. (1930s–1950s) an "ad lib [jam] session . . . not in the groove"; a "swing" or jam session; (1950s) a jazz or rhythm-and-blues musical affair that doesn't come off well. (RSG, JL, p. 58; CC, OMMM, NCCHD, p. 253; DB, OHHJ, p. 136.) SNU. See "Clam."

Clapper(s) n. (1700s–1950s) a settlement of people of "Negro"-Indian-white ancestry living in Schoharie County, New York. (BB, AW, pp. 21–23.) Upstate New York use.

Clapper(s) n. (1920s–1940s) a "Negro" church. (AB, DSJC, p. 240; FGC, DARE, p. 678.) SU.

Clap-trap n. (1960s–1970s) derogatory word for the human mouth. This and other rhyming slang terms were especially popular among black speakers. (AB, DSJC, p. 240.) SNU.

Class n. (1960s) a quality of an attractive, well-dressed, and cool person. (CS, vol. 3, no. 2, p. 15.) Example: "The cat's got class. See how he treats his women?" SNCU, SCU.

Classis Chassis (Classy Chassis) n. (1950s–1960s) an attractive young woman's body. This and other rhyming slang terms were especially popular among black speakers. Especially popular among musicians and in clubs. (WF, DAS, 107.) JBWU, SNCU.

Claw(s) n. (1940s) fingers. Among white slang speakers, "claw" generally referred to a pickpocket, or to policemen (WF, DAS, p. 107; DB, OHHJ, p. 136; HEG, DAU, p. 45.) NCU.

Clay-eater n. (1620s–1940s) one who eats chunks of earth—red dirt—which is rich in iron and potassium; a pejorative term used by blacks (and whites) in the south; a white native of the lowlands of Georgia and South Carolina. (JSF, AON, p. 152.) SU.

Clean adj. (1930s–1990s) not using drugs; well-dressed, dressed up; a clean performance—technically precise, such as in music. Since about 1925 "clean" meant, to general slang users, having no money. In the thirties it came to mean being free of drug addiction or innocent of possessing illegal goods; and in the fifties and sixties, free from suspicion, generally. Also, well-groomed. (RRL, DAZ, p. 42; CRM, BP, p. 298; RSG, LJ, p. 59; WF, DAS, p. 108.) Examples: "The dude was clean as a whistle"; or "Bird and Pres are clean players"; or, regarding drug use, "He's been clean now for a whole year." SNCU.

Cleaners (1930s–1950s) See "Take [one] to the Cleaners." SNCU.

Cleaner than the board of health (1960s–1970s) to be flashy in appearance; dressed in expensive garments. (JH, PBL, p. 84.) SNCU.

Clean out of sight (1950s) unusually impressive. (FR.) SNCU. See "Out of sight."

Clean up v. (1960s) to confess, especially to failure or deceit. (CS, vol. 3, no. 2, p. 16; CRM, BP, p. 298.) Watts, Los Angeles; WCU.

Clear adv. (1650s–1990s) completely. (JAH, PBE, p. 171.) Example: "He got his bags and got clear away before she got back from the polling place." SU.

[A] Clear field n. (1960s–1970s) opportunity, especially an opportunity for "hitting on" a member of the opposite sex for, say, a date. (CS, vol. 3, no. 2, p. 8.) YCU.

Cleo-May n. (1920s–1930s) a conjuring potion used by women to compel men to fall in love with them. (ZNH, MM, p. 337.) Florida use.

Click n., v. (1960s–1990s) variant of "clique"; a private club or neighborhood gang. From the eighties to the nineties, to have something go right or to have someone come through for you at the right moment. (HLF, RJPD, p. 170; TW, CK, p. 136.) Examples: "When Simon comes over, everything will click." SNU, SNCU.

Clink n. (1930s–1940s) a "Negro," usually male; black man. Black slang speakers used the term to refer to themselves. May be related to the fact that black men were so frequently imprisoned ("clink": jail or prison) during the thirties and forties. (HEG, DAU, p. 45; DB, OHHJ, p. 136; WF, DAS, p. 109.) SNCU, PU. See "Boot."

Clinker n. (1930s–1950s) in jazz, an error in playing; at one time also referred to the leg that bound one convict to another in a chain gang. (RSG, JL, pp. 59–60; HEG, DAU, p. 45.) JMFU, SU.

Clip n. (1990s) a particular quantity of cocaine bottles gathered to be sold. (RF.) DCU.

Clip; clipped v. (1940s) to steal something, especially to pick someone's pocket. (HEG, DAU, p. 45; DB, OHHJ, p. 136.) Example: "He can clip you before you know it. Got them smooth slender hands." NCU.

Clip; clipped v. (1990s) to shoot someone without mortally wounding them. (FR.) YCU, SCU.

Clip side of big moist (1940s) on the other side of the Atlantic Ocean, where World War II was going on. (DB, OHHJ, p. 136.) Harlem use.

Clock n. (1940s–1990s) the human heart; in the nineties, to observe and understand; comprehend. (DB, OHHJ, p. 136.) Harlem; SNU. See "Clocker."

Clock n. (1990s) to "score," "hit," or accomplish something. (FR.) Example: "He can clock better than anybody out there." SCU, DCU, YCU.

Clock a grip v. (1990s) to suddenly make a lot of money, especially selling drugs or in some other illegal way. (FR.) YCU, DCU, SCU.

Clocker n. (1980s–1990s) a drug runner who works for a drug dealer. "They were there around the clock" (Richard Price, "Fresh Air," *National Public Radio*, September 22, 1992.) DCU. See "Clock," "Clocking; clocking out," and "Clockwork."

Clocking; clocking out v. (1980s–1990s) to say inappropriate, malicious things; also, to be mentally disturbed; to do "crazy" things (TW, CK, p. 136). Examples: "Is he clocking?"; and "Is she clocking out?" DCU.

Clockwork n. (1940s–1990s) the human brain; one's mind; in the nineties, dependability in delivering drugs. (MHB, JS, np.) See "Clock," "Clocker(s)," and "Clocking; clocking out."

Clodhopper; clodhoppers n. (1930s–1940s) a country rustic; feet; shoes. Unlike white slang speakers in the south, black speakers frequently referred to the feet themselves as "clodhoppers." (AB, DSJC, p. 243; FGC, DARE, p. 690.) Example: "Get your muddy clodhoppers off my clean rug, boy." SNCU.

Close as ninety-nine is to a hundred (1930s–1940s) very close. (ZNH, AM, p. 88.) SNU.

Closet baser n. (1990s) secret crack cocaine user. (TW, CH, p. 147.) Example: "You'd never know she was strung out, but she's a closet baser." DCU.

Cloud n. (1990s) crack cocaine high or sometimes the smoke from the pipe. (TW, CH, p. 147.) DCU.

Cloud [followed by a number] n. (1950s–1960s) expresses contentment, the kind of ease associated with the floating lightweightedness of clouds. Examples: "Cloud 7" or "Cloud 9." (WF, DAS, pp. 110–111.) SNU.

Clow n. (1990s) a dice game. (FR.) SNCU.

Clown n. (1940s–1950s) a foolish person; a "typical" down-home nigger; a white man's nigger; any "Negro" or black person who grins and shuffles, so to speak, for white folks. (FR.) Example: "That clown is a disgrace to his race." SNU. See "Nigger."

Clubbing v. (1980s–1990s) going from club to club; bar hopping. A hip-hop culture term for a night out on the town. (FR.) SNCU.

Cluck adj., n. (1940s) black or very dark; a very black "Negro." Rarely used among black speakers; picked up from derogatory white speech. (WF, DAS, p. 111.) SU.

Clucker n. (1990s) a person who uses crack cocaine. (FR.) DCU.

Clueless adj. (1980s) unaware; does not understand. (FR.) Example: "He's clueless." NECU, MWU.

Cluff v. (1800s–1880s) to cut into two parts; past tense of "cleave." (JAH, MLN, p. 252; FGC, DARE, p. 697.) SU.

Clyde n. (1940s) an uninformed person; a square. (FR.) Rare. MWU.

C note n. (1950s–1960s) a hundred-dollar bill. (CRM, BP, p. 296.) Example: "Hey, Cornbread, lay a C note on me till tomorrow." San Francisco and Bay Area; WCU.

Coal n. (1940s) a black person. (ZNH, AM, p. 89.) See "Charcoal."

Coal-scuttle blond n. (1930s–1950s) originally a bonnet (Quaker); a black woman who wears a blonde wig. (FGC, DARE, p. 700; ZNH, AM, p. 94; AB, DSJC, p. 246.) Example: "George, some old coal-scuttle blond came in the barbershop other day looking for you." Harlem; NECU, MWU. See "Rag."

Coast v. (1960s; 1980s–1990s) In the sixties "coast" sometimes meant to relax or to take it easy or to nod while on drugs. In the eighties and later, it referred to the feeling of being high or stoned, utter relaxation as a result of using drugs. (RRL, DAZ, p. 43; IS, PSML, p. 314; CS, vol 3., no. 2, p. 16.) SNCU, DCU.

Cock n. (1620s–1990s) vagina; female genitalia. "Cock" is generally used to refer to the male genitalia by northern whites and many southern whites. Black country slang users and black speakers on the streets of northern cities use it to refer to the female genitalia—also known among blacks as "pussy" and "tail." The male genitalia, among blacks—in street talk—is called "dick." (EF, BVV, p. 42; EF, RDSL, p. 232; RDA, DDJ, p. 267; CRM, BP, p. 298; RDA, DDJ, p. 264.) Example: "Baby you got a cock. This here is a cock-opener."— Charles Mingus, *Beneath the Underdog: His World as Composed by Mingus*, 1971, p. 167. SNU.

Cock block; CB n. (1980s–1990s) any interference with a male's attempt to have sex with a particular female. (EF, RDSL, p. 232.)

Example: "Her mother is nice to me, but she's a real cock block every time I think something is about to happen." SNCU.

Cockhound n. (1960s) any man who is more interested in sex than in making money or gaining power. (CRM, BP, p. 298.) SNU.

Cock-of-the-walk n. (1960s–1990s) an aggressive and flashy male style of walking; a strutting, flashy male. (EF, RDSL, p. 233; RCC, SOC, p. 14.) SNU.

Cock-opener n. (1920s–1940s) penis. (FR.) See "Cock."

Cock pluck v. (1970s–1990s) to stimulate a female with a dildo or with one's hand. (EF, RDSL, p. 233.) SNU.

Cocksman n. (1960s) Among most white and black slang users this word was understood to refer to men who were popular with women or who were on a female sexual conquest. Black speakers used it in the same way; a male whore. (FR.) SNCU.

Cocksucker n. (1950s–1970s) abusive, all-purpose, male-to-male term, with no special reference to sexual activity. Black use of this term was always more general than it was among white speakers. (WF, DAS, 113.) Example: "Tell the cocksucker if he come back up here his ass is mine." SNU.

Cocktail v. (1950s–1960s) to stick the last bit of marijuana ("roach") into the cleaned-out end of a regular cigarette because it is too short to hold by hand. Also, the roach may be wrapped into the torn-off flap of a book of matches to achieve the same end. (IS, PSML, p. 314; RRL, DAZ, p. 46; JH, PBL, p. 84.) DCU.

Coffee-bag n. (1920s) a coat pocket. This rarely used term originated among tramps and hobos—black and white—who sometimes slept on burlap bags of coffee in box cars on long-distance freight trains. Probably they carried away in their coat pocket as much coffee as possible. (WF, DAS, 113; EP, DU, 136; DB, OHHJ, p. 136.) SNU.

Cogs n. (1930s–1940s) sunglasses. (CC, OMMM, NCCHD, p. 254.) Harlem; NCU.

Cohoot n. (1850s–1890s) agreement. (CCJ, NMGC, p. 167.) Georgia use.

Coins n. (1900s–1950s) in black street talk, any amount of money, in coins or paper. (WF, DAS, p. 114.) Example: "I got some coins. Let's go down to the Royal and check out the scene." SNU.

Coffee-coolers n. (1950s) human lips. (DC, BJ, p. 60.) (FR.) Example: "That dude got some giant coffee-coolers on his face." Rare. MWU.

Coke n. (1900s–1990s) cocaine. Popular reference for cocaine among black and white speakers through the decades; "Coke" is also used to refer to Coca-Cola, a soft drink. (CLC, TS, p. 245; CRM, BP, p. 298; SH, GL, p. 212.) DCU, SCU, YCU, SNU.

Coke bar; coke joint n. (1980s–1990s) a tavern or nightclub where patrons openly engage in the use of crack cocaine. (TW, CH, p. 147; CRM, BP, p. 298.) DCU.

Coke blunt n. (1990s) see "Blunt."

Coke-frame n. (1940s) shapely female body; compared to the contours of a Coca-Cola bottle. (DB, OHHJ, p. 136.) SNU.

Coke-head n. (1950s–1990s) cocaine addict. (WF, DAS, p. 114; RRL, DAZ, p. 47.) Example: "He's such a coke-head he'll fall asleep with a lit cigarette and burn the house down." SNU.

Coke party n. (1960s–1990s) a gathering of cocaine users in an apartment or house. (CRM, BP, p. 298.) DCU.

Coke stare n. (1980s–1990s) a fixed gaze; evil look. (EF, RDSL, p. 233.) DCU.

Cold adj. (1960s–1990s) unfeeling or cruel behavior; in the nineties, the absolute truth; well done; excellent. (FR; CRM, BP, p. 298; ZNH, AM, p. 94.) Examples: "That's some cold shit, man, her coming in here like that at four in the morning"; and "He put it out there cold, man, so everybody could dig on the hard truth." SNU. See "Cold shot."

Cold-blooded adj. (1950s–1960s) heartless. (DW, TL, p. 179; CRM, BP, p. 298; TMc, DA, p. 1.) Example: "This here nigger is so cold-blooded he wouldn't give you the time of day." SNU.

Cold case n. (1980s–1990s) any negative or unpleasant situation or attitude. (EF, RDSL, p. 233.) South-central Los Angeles; NCU.

Cold facts n. (1990s) the truth. (FR.) Example: "They lack the cold facts." See "Cold."

Cold hand; cold in hand adj. (1940s) to be without money. Harlem use.

Cold lamping v. (1990s) shedding light on murky, unclear matters; spreading truth. (FR.) Example: "You want to know how it is? Listen to me. I'm cold lamping." SNU, YCU.

Cold meat party n. (1940s) a funeral. (FR.) Example: "Man, it was the happiest cold meat party I ever been to. Everybody was eating and drinking and laughing like nobody died." Rare, NCU.

[A] Cold one n. (1950s) beer. (FR.) Example: "Give me a cold one, bartender." MWU.

Cold shot (1950s–1970s) a mean action or deed; insult; incident or experience. (FR.) See "Cold."

Cold turkey adv. (1940s–1990s) to kick a physically addictive drug habit without tapering off. (WF; CLC, TS, p. 254; DAS, p. 115; RRL, DAZ, p. 47; RCC, SOC, p. 57.) Example: "They sent the sucker down to Lexington this time, but the first time he had to go cold turkey." DCU, SCU, SNCU.

Collar v. (1930s–1940s) to give or receive something; to obtain; to understand or explain. (CC, OMMM, NCCHD, p. 254; ZNH, AM, p. 85.) Example: "Excuse me, I think I'll go collar myself some dinner." SNU.

Collar a broom v. (1930s–1940s) to leave quickly, as if flying away on a broom like a witch. (DB, OHHJ, p. 136.) Example: "I'm gonna collar a broom. You people are too jive." Rare. SNU.

Collar(ing) a duster up the ladder (1930s–1940s) to climb steps. (DB, OHHJ, p. 136.) Example (tired man at the bottom of a long stairway talking with neighbor): "Joe, I'm gonna collar a duster up the ladder; catch you in the morning." Rare. SNU.

Collar(ing) a hot v. (1940s) to eat lunch or supper, especially very fast. (MHB, JS, np; ZNH, AM, p. 94.) Example: "I'm gonna collar a hot and get to work." Negro college student; SNU.

Collar(ing) a nod v. (1930s–1940s) to sleep. Zora Neale Hurston used the phrase in her stories. (WF, DAS, p. 115; ZNH, AM, p. 94.) Example: "Every time I see old Buster he be collaring a nod." SNU.

Collar(ing) the jive v. (1930s–1940s) to grasp what is happening in a situation. (MHB, JS, np.) Example: "You meatheads collar the jive I'm putting down?" Negro college student; SNU.

College n. (1900s–1970s) prison. In prison a certain kind of "education" is obtained. Picked up from underworld use, blacks—many of them in prison—used the term to refer to the fact that one could learn a lot about life and crime, too, in prison. In other words, it was a place where one got a "higher" degree of learning. (HEG, DAU, p. 47; WF, DAS, 115.) YCU, SNCU.

College-called adj. (1950s–1960s) feeling compelled to go to college. A takeoff on "church-called" or "Christ-called." (FR.) College students; YCU, SNCU.

Colly v. (1920s–1940s) to comprehend; to understand. Picked up from underworld lingo and used on the streets of Harlem and in other northern black communities, "colly" is probably a corruption of "collar" (see "Collar") or of the French word *compree*. The origin is much more likely "collar" in the sense that one thug grabs another by the collar and shakes some sense (understanding) into him. (EP, DU, p. 140.) NU.

Showing [one's] Color n. (1950s–1960s) ironic usage meaning acting like a "Negro" or an Uncle Tom. (FR.) Example: "He's showing his color." SNU.

Colored adj. (1620s–1950s) African-American; Afro-American; black American; Black American; "Negro"; Negro American. (JSF, AON, p. 159.) SNU.

Colored people's time (CP time) n. (1920s–1940s; 1960s) one to two hours later than the appointed time. (FR.) Example: "He'll never get a good job because he's always operating on CP time." SNU.

Color guard n. (EF, RDSL, p. 233.) See "Caution sign."

Color scale n. (1930s–1940s) the range of African-American skin colors from white to jet black. (ZNH, AM, p. 94.) Example: "We every color in the color scale." SNU.

Color-struck; colorstruck adj. (1920s–1930s) refers to a black person who prefers a light-skinned companion. In a way, the opposite of color blind—another American social abnormality. (FR.) Example: "He's so color-struck he dates only light-skinned women." SNU.

Colt n. (1930s–1940s) a young man. The friskiness of the colt is associated with the spunk and virility of the young man. (FR.) Example: "He be running round the neighborhood like a young colt trying to hit on every chick he see." SU.

Combo n. (1930s–1940s) abbreviation for "combination," a small musical group as opposed to a big band. Jazz musicians use the term to refer to any small group of musicians. (FR; RSG, JL, p. 61.) Example: "Bud had just a little combo back then. He was always at his best with a trio." JMFU.

Come; cum v. (1700s–1990s) to have an orgasm; to ejaculate. (FR.) SNU.

Come across v. (1880s–1920s) to realize; to occur to a person. (FGC, DARE, p. 733.) Example: "I was out there plowing and it come across my mind that I been taken for the biggest fool this side of Jackson." SU.

Come again v. (1940s) a request to repeat or restate what has been said. Sometimes the speaker would cup an ear and lean toward the person of whom the request is being made. (DB, OHHJ, p. 136.) SNU.

Comeback n. (1980s–1990s) nickname for a chemical used in the making of crack cocaine. (TW, CH, p. 147.) DCU.

Come down v. (1930s–1940s) to start sobering up from the body-and-mind effects of drugs, including liquor. (IS, PSML, p. 314; RRL, DAZ, p. 48.) Example: "I was so high it took me two days to come down." SNU. See "Come off" and "Comedown."

Comedown n. (1950s–1970s) any poor condition. (FR.) Example: "Baby, this sure is a comedown for me, no money in my pockets, all my stuff in the pawnshop. I was hoping you wouldn't see me like this." SNU. See "Come down."

Come down front (1950s–1960s) a request or command to tell the truth or to be forthright or confess. (DW, TL, p. 179.) Example: "I'm on the level with you, baby, why don't you come on down front with me." NECU, MWU.

Come down on v. (1950s) to insult or "loud talk" someone. (DC, BJ, p. 60.) Example: "The bitch came down on me so bad I wanted to waste her." NCU.

Come-freak n. (1950s–1970s) anybody—male or female—who is obsessed with sex. (CRM, BP, p. 298.) SNCU.

Come-loving adj. (1950s–1970s) to be obsessed with sex. (DG, W, p. 157.) SNCU. See "Come-freak."

Come off v. (1930s–1940s) to return to normal from the effects of a drug stimulant; to stop. (FR.) Example: "When I came off that drunk, I swore I'd never touch another drop of liquor." SNU.

Come on; come(ing) on: v. (1930s; 1960s; 1990s) in jazz circles in the thirties and later, a musician was said to "come on" in a certain way, which meant he played a certain way. At the same time, and especially in the sixties, "come on" meant the way a person approached something or somebody. Flirting, for example, was a form of "coming on." (MM, RB, p. 331.) JMFU, SNCU.

Coming on bad v. (1960s–1970s) showing verbal courage; upstaging or besting someone. (RDA, TB, p. 85.) SNCU.

Come(s) on like gangbusters v. (1940s) to do something in a very fast and stunning way. During the forties a popular radio program called "Gangbusters" always started with a bang. Hence the saying. (DB, OHHJ, p. 136; WF, DAS, p. 117.) SNU. See "Come[s] on like a test pilot."

Come(s) on like a test pilot v. (1940s) to do something in a quick and efficient manner. (CC, OMMM, NCCHD, p. 254.) Harlem show business use. See "Come[s] on like gangbusters."

Come on strong v. (1950s–1990s) exhibiting positive behavior; complimentary; in the eighties and nineties, negative behavior; uncomplimentary. (FR.) Examples: (positive) "He's the right man for this company because he comes on strong"; (negative) "He comes on far too strong to ever get a good girl interested in him." SNCU.

Come on with it (1980s–1990s) a taunting command used to dare someone. (WKB, JMC, PS, p. 48.) Example: "Come on with it, put up your dukes—come on with it, I dare you." SNCU.

Come out v. (1850s–1890s) to announce one's faith in God or Christ; to join the church; from the seventies to the nineties, to be introduced to the "happenings" in the hip world. (FGC, DARE, p. 737.) Examples: "Sister Mary stood up last Sunday in church and came out for Christ as her savior"; and, "The dude come out on the scene real strong." SNU.

Come up weak v. (1960s) to disappoint or to fall short of expectations. (DW, TL, p. 179.) Example: "I waited two hours for that joker the last time, and this time I just know he's gonna come up weak again." NECU, MWU.

Come wind n. (1700s–1880s) a cry that was customary among black people during slavery when a task was dependent on wind currents. The wind was also often depended upon to carry the voice across the distance of a field. (FR.) SU. See "Calling the wind."

Coming from v. (1960s–1990s) point of view or position. (FR.) Examples: "Where you coming from, man?"; or, "I want a divorce. That's where I'm coming from." SNU.

Coming on bad v. (1950s–1960s) aggressive and verbal "wolfing" at someone. (RDA, TB, pp. 77–78.) SNU.

Coming up v. (1930s–1950s) growing up or being raised. (DC, BJ, p. 61.) Example: "Back when I was coming up, people didn't do that sort of thing, not out in the open." SNU.

Comp; comps; comping v. (1940s) in jazz, a shortening of "accompany." (RSG, JL, pp. 63–64) Example: "I got this new boy comping and he's a gas." JMFU.

Compy v. (1940s) variation on the word "comprehend" or "compree." (FR.) Example: "I'm through with you. You compy?" Rare. NCU.

Con; conned; con game n., v. (1920s–1950s) any confidence game played on an unsuspecting person; short for convict; but after the forties it fell into more general use and, while still used in the previous ways, also meant to trick, persuade, or promote in someone's mind an idea he or she may not have previously entertained. Variations: On the con; con along. Example: "Terry runs a real smooth con game. Babes fall for his shit all the time." (WF, DAS, p. 117; RSG, JL, p. 64; HEG, DAU, p. 47.) PPU, SCU. See "Murphy."

Con-con n. (1990s) the oily substance remaining in a pipe after free base has been smoked. (TW, CH p. 147.) DCU.

Confession n. (1940s) a conference with a teacher; takeoff on the Catholic confession. (MHB, JS, np.) Rare. Southern "Negro" college student; SU.

Congo Square n. (1800s–1990s) variant of La Place du Congo in New Orleans, so named officially by the city government on October 15, 1817; also known as Place Congo and associated with African (American) Congo culture; location of an annual ancestral festival. (Robert Farris Thompson; JEH, AAC, pp. 148–149; George W. Cable, *The Dance in Place Congo*, 1886, pp. 1–2, 6; HV, AHAE, p. 157.) New Orleans use.

Conjunct v. (1850s–1890s) agree to; conclude. (CCJ, NMGC, p. 167.) Example: "Me and Mister Willis conjunct all right on the price for the work I did for him." Georgia use.

Conjuring lodge n. (1620s–1930s) sacred house; church; stemming from their belief in the power of the conjurer, black Americans during slavery held this as a place in which mediumistic rites and principles could be respected and practiced. It is not unlike the Zuni and Hopi kiva. (FR.) SU.

Conk n. (1930s–1950s) pomade for the hair; a hairstyle; the human head itself; brains or intelligence. In general white use during the same time period, this term referred mostly to the human head or the face or the nose, and to the act of hitting someone on the head. (WF, DAS, p. 119; DB, OHHJ, p. 136.) SNU. See "Wig."

Conk-buster; conk busting n., adj. (1930s–1950s) anything proving mentally difficult; also sometimes referred to what drugs or liquor did to the mind; from the forties into the fifties, cheap whiskey or wine. (WF, DAS, p. 119; ZNH, AM, p. 94.) Example: "That cat comes up with some conk-busting questions." SNU.

Conkpiece n. (1940s) the head or a hat. (DB, OHHJ, p. 136.) NCU. See "Conk."

Connect n. (1980s–1990s) short for "connection"; a drug dealer (RRL, DAZ, p. 49); one who sells drugs; a contact person for narcotics. (TW, CH, p. 147.) Example: "He meets his connect two or three times a week; that's how heavy his habit is these days." DCU. See "Connection."

Connection n. (1950s–1960s) a drug dealer. (CLC, TS, p. 254.) DCU. See "Connect."

Conniggeration n. (1940s–1950s) apparently invented by Robert H. DeCoy for his book *The Nigger Bible*. He says it means, in essence, the love of black people for each other—the process of demonstrating affection and interest in the interrelations between what he calls "Nigrites." (RHdeC, NB, pp. 29–30.) Extremely rare. NCU.

Contact habit n. (1950s–1960s) an addict's term for the high a non-using pusher gets from dealing with drug addicts. (RRL, DAZ, p. 49.) DCU.

Contact high n. (1950s–1960s) to get a "buzz" from the secondhand smoke of marijuana. (DC, BJ, p. 61.) Example: "You can walk by that chick's door and get a contact high, she smokes so much dope." NCU.

Contraband n. (1850s–1860s) a black person. (JSF, AON, p. 159, 165.) SU.

Cooch n. See "Coochie."

Coochie n. (1990s) female genitalia. (FR.) YCU.

Cook; cooking v. (1930s–1940s) in jazz, to play with great inspiration; to be in the spirit of a situation; also, a method of dissolving heroin with water in a spoon over a flame. (RSG, JL, p. 64.) Example: "Diz was really cooking last night." JMFU. See "Cook up."

Cook v. (1990s) to heat cocaine until it hardens into free base. (FR.) DCU.

Cooker n. (1950s) a hip or swinging person (rare); (1980s–1990s) one who cooks cocaine. (TW, CH, p. 147; RRL, DAZ, p. 50.) See "Cook up."

Cookie n. (1950s) variant of "oreo" (black on the outside, white on the inside); any black person perceived by his or her community to be guilty of racial disloyalty. "Guilt" can consist of anything from merely being middle class to being an out-and-out Uncle Tom or a head-scratching, grinning Sambo. "Cookie" has also been used (rarely) to refer to the female genitalia. Also (rarely) used as a word for cocaine. (DC, BJ, p. 61.) SNU. See "Oreo."

Cooking v. (1980s–1990s) heating cocaine to get it hard enough to form crack free base. (TW, CH, p. 147.) DCU.

Cook-pot n. (1920s–1930s) a pot for cooking, especially one used for cooking soul food such as neck bones, greens, hamhocks, black-eyed peas, and so on. (FR.) Example: "Mama put on the cook-pot and burn from way back." SU, MWU.

Cook up v.i. (1930s–1950s) to cook heroin; to get in the swing of things; to swing with the music; getting in the groove. (RRL, DAZ, p. 50; DW, TL, p. 179.) DCU.

Cook-stove n. (1700s–1930s) a stove for cooking food. (FR.) SU.

Cook-woman n. (1700s–1930s) a woman who cooks food. (FR.) SU.

Cook(ing) with gas v. (1940s) variant of "cook" or "cooking"; to be really informed and in the spirit. The use of the gas range was fairly new, rare, and popular in the forties. To cook with gas was to be in style. (FR.) SNU.

Cool adj., v. (1650s–1990s) "gone out" (Mandingo); fast (Mandingo); "far out"; "gone, man, gone." "Cool" appears to have been in use in England as early as the 1590s, and in the 1930s American tramps and criminals were using it to refer to the act of killing someone; to be under great self-control. At various times "cool" has meant roughly the same thing as "bad" or "boss" or "hip" or "together"; loosely used, but generally it means anything favorably regarded; a word of agreement, consent, or affirmation; also, a cool person is one who is detached, aloof. In the forties "cool" music was fashionable, just as it was fashionable for the listener—and everybody else!—to be cool. "Cool" was the opposite of hot. (JAH, PBE, p. 172; HV, AHAE, p. 139; RSG, JL, pp. 65–66; WF, DAS, p. 121; EP, DU, p. 147; JAH, MLN, p. 257.) SNU, ZMFU, SCU, YCU. See "Cool as a cucumber," "Cooling (it)," "Cool it," "Cool jazz," "Cool out," and "Cool papa."

Cool as a cucumber adj. (1950s) very stylish; calm; sporty; very cool. (FR.) SNU.

Coolie n. (1980s–1990s) a cigarette in which cocaine is mixed with the tobacco. (TW, CH, p. 147.) SNCU.

Cooling-board n. (1850s–1990s) a flat, wide board—usually pine— where a dead body is placed for viewing during a slave's or ex-slave's wake. (ECLA, NN, p. 264.) South Carolina; SU.

Cooling it v. (1950s–1960s) taking it easy; a jazz expression picked up and used in street culture. (RDA, DDJ, pp. 164–165; RSG, JL, p. 67.) JMFU, SNU.

Cool it (1950s–1960s) relax; take it easy; go slow. (FR.) Example: "Cool it, man. Don't get upset." SNU.

Cool jazz n. (1940s–1950s) a style of jazz associated with musical developments on the west coast; usually mellow and restrained; sometimes referred to as intellectual music. (RSG, JT, pp. 56–57.) See "Cool." JMFU, SNCU.

Cool out (1980s) a command to be calm or to use restraint. (FR.) Example: "We'll be there soon. Just cool out." SNCU. See "Chill out" and "Cool."

Cool papa n. (1940s) a nonchalant male. (FR.) Example: "All the women dig him 'cause he's such a cool papa." See "Cool."

Cool Papa James Bell, outfielder in the Negro Leagues.

Cooling [it] (1930s–1940s) in jazz context, not employed. Toward the end of the forties, "cooling it," took on the more general meaning, relaxing. (CC, HDH, p. 16; RSG, JL, p. 67.) JMFU; SNCU.

Coon n. (1650s–1940s) black use of "coon" was picked up from derogatory white use probably as early as the 1650s. Blacks used "coon" with the same sort of self-irony and affection with which they used words such as "nigger" and "sambo." (WF, DAS, p. 122.) SU.

Coon Bottom n. See "Bottom" and "Buttermilk Bottom."

Cooncan n. (1920s–1950s) Con Quien: a type of rummy card game played by "Negroes" in the south. (RDA, DDJ, p. 265; DW, TL, p. 179.) SU.

Coon dick n. (1920s–1930s) alcoholic drink made of "grapefruit juice, cornmeal mash, beef bones and a few mo' things" (ZNH, MM, p. 32). Eatonville, Florida; SU.

Coonering See "Junkanoo."

Coon-ey Island n. (1890s) Coney Island; a vaudeville skit; also a song sang by Black Patti and her Fifty Troubadours. (Ann Charters, *Nobody: The Story of Bert Williams*, 1970, p. 44.) SNU.

Cooning v. (1890s–1930s) "cooning" originated among white speakers, meaning stealing as opposed to robbing. (WF, DAS, p. 122.) Although "cooning" may to some degree refer to the fact that racoons were known to steal food, it probably also stems from the widespread southern mythic belief that all blacks were thieves, hence to steal something was to "coon." (WF, DAS, p. 122.) Rare. SU.

Coon jigger n. (1650s–1930s) a "Negro" child. Picked up from white use and used ironically. (FGC, DARE, p. 765.) SU.

Coonjine adj. (1900s–1940s) White speakers used "coonjine" to refer to the way black dock workers walked. Some black self-ironic use but rare among black speakers. (FGC, DARE, p. 765; HLB, LSS, p. 89.) SU.

Coon juice n. See "Coon dick."

Coonjun; coongiv v. (1900s–1940s) to be exploited; used with an apparent ironic twist. SU.

Coonshine n. (1870s–1900s) this term originated among white speakers, meaning a night party. Some black self-ironic use but rare among black speakers. (FGC, DARE, p. 766.) SU.

Coon shout; shouting n., v. (1680s–1900s) this term originated among white speakers, meaning to imitate black singing or shouting. (FGC, DARE, p. 766; MM, RB, p. 146.) SU.

Cooper n. (1890s) black roustabout working the hogsheads at the Louisville tobacco auctions at the end of the nineteenth century. There were many of them. Picked up from white use. (MT, DAF, p. 73.) Kentucky use; SU.

Cooter; coota n. (1650s–1990s) originally from the West African word *kuta*; or possibly from *nkuda* (Kongo), meaning a "box turtle," or a hard-backer turtle; terrapin. West African word *kuts*: a box turtle. (JH, PBL, p. 84; HV, AHAE, p. 139; SBF, IHAT, p. 32; ECLA, NN, p. 264; FGC, DARE, p. 769.) South Carolina, Georgia, Alabama; SU.

Cootie Crawl n. (1900s–1940s) a popular jazz dance. (FR.) SNU.

Coo-yon n. (1860s–1930s) one who is mentally unbalanced; crazy person. (FR.) Louisiana use.

Cop n., v. (1820s–1990s) to receive or obtain drugs. Originally, as early as the 1820s, "cop" meant "to arrest," but by the 1850s the meaning had shifted to the policeman himself. "Cop" was popular among black slang users from the beginning. The original use of "cop," that is, to obtain something, also remained popular among black speakers. (FGC, DARE, 771; CS, vol. 3, no. 2, p. 19; RRL, DAZ, p. 50; DB, OHHJ, p. 136; CLC, TS, p. 254; IS, PSML, p. 314; EP, DU,

p. 148.) Examples: "Go cop me a bag of grapes"; or, "Here's a nickel, go cop me a weed." SNU, DCU, YCU, SCU.

Cop v. (1950s–1960s) refers to how a pimp talks a woman into working for him. (SH, GL, p. 212.) Example: (one pimp to another) "See that broad there? I can cop her in five minutes." PPU.

Cop a broom v. (1940s) to leave in a hurry. (DB, OHHJ, p. 136.) Example: "That cat was so scared, he copped a broom faster than you could say jackrabbit." Harlem; NCU.

Copacetic adj. (1920s–1960s) all right; Harlem variant of *copissettic* (Italian); excellent, fine, very good. *Copesetique* (Creole-French). Carl Van Vechten defines "kopasetee" in *Nigger Heaven*, 1926, to mean "an approbatory epithet somewhat stronger than all right." (CVV, NH, p. 286.) Example: "When you're loving me, mama, everything is copacetic." Harlem; SNU.

Cop [a/her] cherry v. (1940s) to deflower or ravish a woman or girl of her virginity. (WF, DAS, p. 123.) SNU.

Cop a drill v. (1940s) to leave at a walking pace. (DB, OHHJ, p. 136.) Example: "I was cool, but I copped a drill the minute the cops arrived on the scene." See "Cop."

Cop a heel v. (1940s–1960s) to run away fast. (IS, TB, p. 311.) Chicago; MWU.

Cop and blow v. (1950s) for a pimp, to recruit as many new "whores" as leave; in the "short-money game," a pimp tries to make as much off a temporary "ho" as possible (IS, PSML, p. 314; CRM, BP, p. 298). SCU, PPU, NCU.

Cop a nod v. (1940s–1950s) to take a nap, to sleep. (MHB, JS, np.) NECU, MWU. See "Cop" and "Cop z's."

Cop a plea v. (1930s–1960s) to plead guilty to a lesser charge; to be verbally evasive; to plead for mercy; to apologize. (FR.) Example: "Her mother was back there copping a plea just as loud as she was." NECU, MWU. See "Cop."

Cop a squat v. (1940s) to sit down. (DC, BJ, p. 61.) MWU. See "Cop."

Copman n. (1980s–1990s) a drug runner. (TW, CK, p. 136.) New York City use.

Cop out v. (1950s–1960s) to make excuses for oneself; evasiveness; to rely on alibi. (DC, BJ, p. 61.) NECU.

Copper n. See "Cop."

Copper-nose(d) n., adj. (1890s–1940s) although not of black origin, common among black speakers of the period; a drunk, so called because, among heavy black drinkers, the tip of the nose turns a dark purple. (DB, OHHJ, p. 136; AB, DSJC, p. 259.) Example: "When Rudy comes in here all copper-nosed, I don't even serve him." NCU.

Copper pox n. (1920s–1930s) syphilis. Some southern rural blacks, mainly in Florida, believed that if one held two copper pennies under the tongue during intercourse, it was possible to infect one's partner with syphilis (copper pox). (FGC, DARE, p. 773.) Florida use.

Copping Z's v. See "Cop z's."

Copping zone(s) n. (1980s–1990s) area in a city where cocaine dealers meet users. (TW, CH, p. 147.) DCU.

Cop z's v. (1950s–1960s) to sleep; doze; nap. Picked up from cartoons where characters sleep with a row of z's—suggesting snoring —in a balloon above their heads. (DC, BJ, p. 61; CM, DAAS; RSG, JL, p. 70; CVV, NH, p. 286.) Example: "After the football game, I went home and copped some z's." NECU, MWU.

Corn; corny n., adj. (1900s–1950s) money; homemade corn whiskey (especially cheap whiskey); bad jazz or any bad music; anything out of fashion. (CC, OMMM, NCCD, p. 254; RSG, JL, p. 70; WF, DAS, p. 124; DB, OHHJ, p. 136.) Examples: "We was in the wagon hitting a jug of corn and everybody was singing and carrying on"; and, "I stopped going to Sady's 'cause all they got on the jukebox is this old corny jazz from ten years back." SNU.

[The] Corner n. (1940s–1950s) intersection where young black men gather on the sidewalk to socialize and to make "business" transactions. (FR.) Example: "Meet you on the corner half past ten, then you can tell me all about where you been." SNU.

Cornfield hollers n. (1700s–1890s) a loose phrase for Negro work songs. (FR.) SU.

Cornfield Negro [nigger] n. (1800s–1890s) any slave who works the fields. Picked up from white use. (FGC, DARE, pp. 783–784.) SU.

Cornpone n. (1800s–1940s) cornbread. (FR.) SU.

Corn-pone n. (1930s–1940s) person from the south or one with a southern way of talking; a rustic. (FR.) Example: "The corn-pones come up here and they shocked to see toilets inside the houses, and they step in an elevator, they think they going to heaven." Harlem; NECU.

Corn rolls; cornrolls n. (1800s–1990s) tightly braided hair; a hairstyle consisting of many narrow, closely woven, tight braids arranged close to the scalp. Traditional among black women and girls for many generations. (EF, RDSL, p. 233.) SNU.

Corn song n. (1830s–1860s) a slave work song usually sung during corn harvest or while shucking corn. (FGC, DARE, p. 788.) SU.

Corn-stalk fiddle n. (1800s–1890s) a homemade banjo. (JSF, AON, p. 171.) Example: "Can't nobody stop Poppa once he gets holt of his corn-stalk fiddle and a jug of shine." SU.

Corperation n. (1920s–1930s) large stomach on a man. (CM, CW, Zora Neale Hurston, "The Guilded Six-Bits," p. 71.) Example: "He looks just like a rich white man with his corperation sticking out like that." SU.

Corroded adj. (1980s–1990s) unpleasant; ugly. (EF, RDSL, p. 233.) Example: "Man, picking you up like this so early in the morning is some corroded shit." South-central Los Angeles; NCU.

Cotch (1930s) a card game. (ZNH, MM, p.) Florida; SU.

Cotton n. (1930s–1990s) the hair of a black woman's pudendum. (RDA, DDJ, p. 265; EF, RDSL, p. 233.) NCU.

[The] Cotton Curtain n. (1950s) the south; southeastern United States. (FR.) Example: "Man, I'll never go back behind the Cotton Curtain now that I'm out of there and free." NU.

Cottonmouth n. (1960s) a mouth dried out from excessive marijuana smoke. (CS, vol. 3, no. 2, p. 18.) Watts, Los Angeles; NCU.

Cotton Negro [nigger] n. (1800s–1960s) a slave who works in cotton fields in Georgia. Picked up from white use. (FB, STOS, p. 254.) SU.

Cotton pickers n. (1780s–1930s) hands. (FR.) Example: "Keep your cotton pickers to yourself." Probably originated during slavery in Georgia and/or Alabama. SU. See "Cotton picking."

Cotton picking [hands] adj. (1900s–1930s) an insult, referring to either the actual hands of a person or to that person's presence. (FR.) Examples: "That's my dress, Sadie, so keep your cotton-picking hands off it"; or, "When I say run I want you to get your cotton-picking ass in the wind. You hear me?" SNU.

Cotton black n. See "Cotton slave."

Cotton slave n. (1700s–1860s) a black person who works in the cotton fields on a slave plantation. (SBF, IHAT, p. 35.) SU. See "Cotton black."

Couldn't hardly v. (1780s–1990s) barely. (DG, DC, p. 49.) Example: "When I was up there I couldn't hardly see who all was there 'cause the light was so bad." SNU.

Counsellor n. (1920s) a Harlem or black ghetto lawyer. (CVV, NH, p. 285.) NCU.

Count Basie born William Basie, 1904, in Red Neck, New Jersey; world-famous band leader, composer, pianist; winner of many jazz polls and mentor of an impressive number of now-famous singers and instrumentalists.

Count it off (1940s–1990s) to make clear the expected tempo. (KG, JV, p. 181.) Example: "Go on, count it off and I'll pick it up." JBWU.

Country cracker n. (1750s–1950s) boastful, poor, uneducated, white storyteller; a rustic white person of the Deep South, especially Georgia or South Carolina. (JB, DA, p. 96; ECLA, NN, p. 264; GS, TT, p. 252; AB, DSJC, p. 264; CMc, HH, p. 49.) Example: "Don't pay that old country cracker no mind." SNU. See "Cracker" and "Redneck."

Couple of cents n. (1960s) two dollars. (DC, BJ, p. 61.) Example: "Hey, Jack, lay a couple of cents on me till payday." MWU.

Courting house n. (1860s–1940s) a place—usually an abandoned shack—where young couples went to make love. (SK, PC, p. 67.) Palmetto County, Florida, use.

Cowboy n. (1680s–1860s) an African slave who tended the cows on a plantation in the southern territories or states. Colonial period term. White men were known as "cattle*men*." The word "cowboy" was later used to refer to white cattlemen of the West. (HV, AHAE, pp. 153–154.) SU.

Cowboy n. (1960s–1990s) a "badass nigger." (EF, RDSL, p. 233.) Watts and South-central Los Angeles use. See "Bad ass[ed] nigger."

Cowboy(ed) v. (1960s–1990s) any wildly executed crime, such as the robbery of a bus or train or a bank. (CS, vol. 3, no. 2, p. 18.) Example: "Rodney and Champ cowboyed the whole supermarket payroll just as a Brinks truck was making their pickup." Watts, Los Angeles; NCU.

Cow Cow Charles Davenport, singer and piano player, born 1894 at Anniston, Alabama, and died in Cleveland, Ohio, December 2, 1955; as pianist and singer, he toured (1914–1930) the vaudeville circuit; author of the famous "Cow-Cow Boogie."

Cow express n. (1940s) shoes. (FR.) Example: "I had to go to work by cow express this morning 'cause my car wouldn't start." NCU.

Cowpeas n. (1850s–1990s) *Vigna sinensis*; black-eyed peas. (HV, AHAE, p. 150.) SU.

Cowpea soup n. (1850s–1960s) soul food vegetable often cooked with ham bones and onions. (FR.) SU.

Cozy born William Cole, drummer, in East Orange, New Jersey, October 17, 1909; first recordings were done with the famous Jelly Roll Morton in 1930; later worked with Louis Armstrong and Benny Goodman.

CPT n. (1900s–1960s) "colored people's time"; sooner or later. (FR.) Example: "I'll be there four o'clock CPT." SNCU. See "Colored people's time."

Crab n. (1940s) college freshman. (MHB, JS, np.) Southern Negro college student use.

Crab-apple switch n. (1930s–1940s) a long slender twig torn from a crab apple tree used for whipping children. (FGC, DARE, p. 823.) SU.

Crabs n. (1930s–1940s) genital lice. (HEG, DAU, p. 51; RDA, DDJ, p. 265.) SNU.

Crack v. (1890s–1940s) to joke; insult; to tease. (ZNH, DTR, p. 112; AB, DSJC, p. 264; SH, GL, p. 212.) SNU. See "Cracking."

Crack n. (1980s–1990s) a mixture of cocaine, baking soda, and lidocaine, and any variety of other substances. (TW, CH, pp. 147–148.) DCU.

Crack attack n. (1990s) the sudden craving for crack cocaine. (TW, CH, p. 148.) DCU.

Crack diet n. (1990s) small serving of sweets (candy, cookies, sweet rolls) with a soda or bottle of juice. (TW, CH, p. 148.) DCU.

Cracked-ice n. (1940s) diamonds. (FR; DB, OHHJ, p. 136.) SNU.

Cracker n. (1860s–1940s) usually a poor white man but sometimes any white person; any poor, uneducated white person, usually of Georgia or one of the Carolinas. One theory holds that it's a term from the nineteenth-century backcountry of Georgia, coined by black people—a reference to the whip-*cracking* slaveholder. Another theory is that it comes from the white soda cracker as opposed to, say, ginger cookies. (JSF, AON, p. 179; ECLA, NN, p. 264; EF, RDSL, p. 233; FGC, DARE, p. 826; JB, DA, p. 96; AB, DSJC, p. 264; CMc, HH, p. 49.) SNU.

Crack gallery n. (1980s–1990s) a house or an apartment where a user can buy crack free base. (TW, CK, p. 136.) SNU.

Crackhead; head n. (1980s–1990s) a heavy user of crack or free base cocaine. (TW, CH, p. 148.) SNU.

Crackhouse n. (1980s–1990s) a house where drug users gather to smoke cocaine. (TW, CK, p. 136; RCC, SOC, p. 56.) SNU.

Cracking v. (1890s–1990s) to verbally and playfully put someone down; to insult; to convey factual information though in a playful—if not mean-spirited—manner. (ZNH, AM, p. 95; RDA, TB, p. 50; RDA, TB, p. 45.) SNU. See "Capping," "Charging," and "Dirty Dozen."

[One may be] Cracking but [one is] facking (fact-ing) (1930s–1940s) a statement supporting the notion that one is conveying factual information though in a playful manner. (ZNH, AM, p. 95.) SNU. See "Cracking."

Cracking shorts v. (1930–1940) breaking into cars to steal them or their contents. (RRL, DAZ, p. 51.) DCU.

Crackling biscuits (bread) n. (1900s–1940s) oven-cooked bread containing dried pork skin, a soul food. (FR.) SU.

Crack of day n. (1800s–1940s) the first light; early morning. (AEG, BB, p. 294.) SU.

Crack [one's] sides (1930s–1950s) to laugh vigorously. (JMB, WB, p. 66.) Example: "We cracked our sides when Betty slapped that nigger." MWU. See "Crack up."

Crack up n. (1940s–1950s) originally meant to praise or celebrate someone; but for black slang users it meant convulsive with laughter; go crazy; become insane; because of wild laughter, remotely associated with "crack up," meaning to go crazy. (FR; AB, DSJC, p. 264; RSG, JL, p. 71.) Example: "Boy, I really crack up when I hear them two in there with their mess." SNU.

Crack-wise n. (1940s–1950s) an obvious square who uses a profusion of hip terms in an effort to be accepted on the "scene"; a would-be hipcat not yet fully accepted on the scene; a novice hipcat who is looked upon with suspicion. (IS, PSML, p. 314.) NCU, SCU.

Cram n., v. (1960s) to leap up and literally insert or push a basketball through the hoop. (DC, BJ, p. 61.) Sports fans; MWU.

Cramp [one's] style v. (1950s) to annoy or anger or offend in some way. (FR.) Example: "My little brother cramps my style when he wears my leather jacket without asking." SNCU.

Crank n. (1990s) another word for speed (amphetamines). (FR; TW, CH, p. 148.) DCU. See "Speed."

Crank it up v. (1990s) to intensify, especially in volume (while listening to music). (FR.) Example: "That's great music, but crank it up so I can get the full effect." SNCU.

Crap n. (1960s) nonsense. (FR.) Example: "I don't want to hear none of that crap." SNU.

Crash v. (1960s–1990s) come down from a drug high; to sleep; in the eighties and nineties, to hit someone, especially in the face. (TW, CK, p. 136.) SNU.

Crazy adj. (1940s–1990s) excellent or first-rate; in the nineties, a great quantity; a large amount. Anything or any person or place that is beautiful; the *n*th!; great or good. (RSG, JL, pp. 71–72.) Example: "He's making crazy dollars selling drugs." SNCU.

Crazy as a betsey bug adj. (1920s–1940s) irrational; insane; unconventional; variant of "Crazy as a bedbug." (AW, CP, p. 189.) SU.

Crazy rim (brim) n. (1960s) a handsome hat. (RDA, DDJ, p. 265.) NCU. See "Brim."

Creaker n. (1900s–1940s) an old person. (LH, BNF, p. 482; DB, OHHJ, p. 136.) SNU.

Creel n. (1890s–1940s) a racially mixed person of South Carolina. (FGC, DARE, p. 842.) South Carolina use.

Creep n., v. (1920s–1940s) a clandestine mission usually for the purpose of a romantic meeting between male and female; to creep is to carry on a clandestine affair, usually with a married person. (EF, RDSL, p. 233; FGC, DARE, p. 882; TMc, WE, p. 271.) SNU.

Creeper n. (1920s–1940s) a man involved in a clandestine affair; a man who sneaks to visit a married woman in her bed. (CVV, NH, p. 285; JH, PBL, p. 84.) SNU.

Creole state (1860s–1890s) Louisiana. (JSF, AON, pp. 413–414.) SNU.

Crew n. (1980s–1990s) a group of young women or men forming a loosely knit organization, sometimes known as a gang. (TW, CH, p. 148.) New York City use.

Crib n. (1940s–1990s) one's home or room, rare after coinage of "pad"; in the nineties, a basketball lay-up shot; easy shot; but also still used to refer to one's apartment or house. Prisoners call their cell the "crib." (WKB, JMC, PS, p. 48; FR; HLF, RJPD, p. 170.) SNCU, PU. See "Pad."

Cribbing v. (1960s–1990s) the act of going about one's daily life; living at home. (DC, BJ, p. 62.) Example: "Ain't nothing happening, man, just cribbing and waiting till payday." SNCU.

Crick n. (1930s–1940s) sometimes pronounced "crink," a form of creak. (FR; FGC, DARE, p. 849, p. 851.) Example: "I've got a crick in my neck." SNU. See "Crook."

Crimey n. (1980s–1990s) a buddy; a friend or "partner in crime." (TW, CK, p. 136.) New York City; NCU.

Cripple n. (1980s–1990s) an athlete who is ineffective. (EF, RDSL, p. 233.) SNU.

Cripple Clarence Lofton. Piano player and singer, born March 28, 1896, and died January 28, 1956.

Crips (1980s–1990s) street gang based in Los Angeles area. (FR.) Los Angeles use.

Croak v. (1950s) Mainstream slang users use this word to refer to someone dying. It means to die. In black street culture in the fifties it meant to kill someone. (IS, PSML, p. 314.) Example: "Johnny is a bad dude, he'll croak a motherfucker with one shot through the left eye." NCU; SCU.

Croak [on someone] v. (1980s–1990s) to slam dunk despite being well guarded. (FR.) Basketball players' and fan use.

Croatan n. (1880s–1930s) a native of North Carolina or South Carolina whose ancestry consists of black, Indian, and white. (FGC, DARE, p. 854 BB, AW, p. 25.) North Carolina, South Carolina; SU.

Crook n. (1930s–1940s) alternate of "crick." Example: "I've got a crook in my neck." SU. See "Crick."

Crooklyn n. (1990s) variant of "Brooklyn," a county in New York City. (FR.) Brooklyn use.

Cross v. (1940s–1990s) short for double-cross; to deceive or mislead or confuse. (IS, PSML, p. 314; FR; WF, DAS, p. 131.) NCU.

Crow Jane n. (1900s–1920s) a very black or especially dark-complexioned woman. (Hear Frankie Jaxon, "It's Heated," 1929, *Tampa Red/Bottleneck Guitar, 1928–1937*, Yazoo.) SU, SNU.

Cruise; cruising v. (1930s–1990s) strutting; walking with style; out for fun; looking for or making contact for sexual relations. (ZNH, AM, p. 94.) NCU.

Crumbcrusher; crumbcruncher n. (1930s–1950s) a baby or small child. (JH, PBL, p. 84; RF, DB, OHHJ, p. 136; IS, TB, p. 311; EF, RDSL, p. 233.) Example: "She got a house full of crumbcrushers." Harlem; SNU.

Crumb-hall n. (1930s–1940s) a dining room. (DB, OHHJ, p. 136.) Example: "You should see the GIs hit the crumb-hall at six." Harlem use.

Crumb-stash n. (1930s–1940s) a kitchen. (DB, OHHJ, p. 136.) Example: "Mama won't let nobody in the crumb-stash while she's cooking." Harlem use; SNU.

Crumbs n. (1950s) an insubstantial amount of money. (FR.) See "Bread" and "Two cents."

Crumbsnatcher n. (1930s–1950s) See "Crumbcrusher."

Cruncher n. (1930s–1940s) a small child who eats a lot (FR); the sidewalk. (DB, OHHJ, p. 136.) See "Crumbcrusher."

Crunt n. (1950s–1960s) dried semen or anything filthy or unclean. Variant of "crud." (RDA, DDJ, p. 265.) SNU.

Crush n. (1930s–1940s) a hat, especially a felt one. (MHB, JS, np.) SU. See "Brim."

Crutch n. (1960s–1990s) a tweezers-like device for holding a marijuana "roach" (smoked-down cigarette). (EF, RDSL, p. 233.) DCU.

Crutch n. (1940s) car. (FR.) Example: "The dude can't get along without his crutch." NCU.

Cry baby n. (1920s–1990s) complainer or one who cannot take criticism. (FR; WF, DAS, p. 133.) SNU.

Crying buddy n. (1960s) one's best friend; a "running" buddy. (HLF, RJPD, p. 170.) Example: "Me and Joe Joe, we crying buddies through thick and thin." NCU.

Crying shame n. (1930s–1950s) a disgrace; any misfortune; injustice. (FR.) Example: "Girl, it's a crying shame the way that man treats that woman." SNU.

Crystal n. (1960s) Methedrine, amphetamine sulphates, or desoxyn. (RRF, DAZ, p. 53.) DCU.

Cub n. (1930s–1950s) a small room. (WF, DAS, p. 133.) See "Cubby (hole)."

Cubby [hole] n. (1930s–1950s) a room or small apartment where one lives. (FR.) SU.

Cubes n. (1960s–1990s) morphine. (EF, RDSL, p. 233.) DCU.

Cubs n. (1890s–1920s) "fixed" playing cards. (FR.) SU.

Cuckle burks; cuckle burr n. (1790s–1940s) variant of "cockle-burr;" hair, especially nappy hair. (ECLA, NN, p. 264; FR.) SU.

Cudjo n. (1620s–1890s) one of the seven day names for an African male used during the slave period. (AB, DSTC, p. 480.) SNU.

Cue n. (1940s–1950s) a tip, money given to a waitress or waiter as a token of gratitude. (FR.) Also, variant of "clue," meaning to inform someone (WF, DAS, p. 111.) SNU.

Cuff n., v. (1930s–1990s) to punch or to fight; also, a job or employment; from thirties underworld use: to swindle. (EF, RDSL, p. 233; HEG, DAUL, p. 54.) SNCU.

Cuffee n. (1630s–1890s) *Kofi* (Akan); black man; male born on Friday; form of brotherly address. (HV, AHAE, p. 140.) SU.

Cuffey n. (1630s–1890s) variant of "Cuffee"; in common use among blacks and whites in the colonies before the Civil War. (ECLA, NN, p. 264; FGC, DARE, p. 876.) SU. See "Cuffee."

Cuffy n. (1700s–1890s) *Kofi* (Akan); form of address. There is evidence of some modern limited use of the word in such cities as Chicago. Territories and slave states use. (HV, AHAE, p. 140.) SU. See "Cuffee."

Cultural fruit n. (1970s–1990s) watermelon. (EF, RDSL, p. 233.) See "African grape."

Cupcake n. (1840s) a pretty girl. (MHB, JS, np.) Southern Negro college student use, SU.

Cups n., adj. (1840s–1950s) sleep; asleep; usually referring to drunken sleep. Meaning stretched from "in [one's] cups." (CC, OMMM/ NCCHD, p. 254; WF, DAS, p. 134.) Examples: "When she's in her cups, you can't wake her if the place was on fire"; and, "He's in his cups," meaning, sleeping off a drunk. SU.

Cush; cushie n. (1970s–1940s) from the Gullah word *kush* (Arabic: *kusha*; corruption: "couscous"); meaning fried cake made from sugar and cornmeal. (SBF, IHAT, p. 32.) SU.

[To the] Curb adj. (1990s) without money and desperate. (HC, WSJ, p. B1.) SNU. See "Kick [one] to the curb."

Cure v. (1960s) to age marijuana; also, the opposite of "cutting" (diluting). To cure drugs also refers to mixing two or more drugs to increase the total effect. (CS, vol. 3, no. 2, p. 19.) DCU.

Curiossome adj. (1840s–1900s) curious or strange. (FGC, DARE, p. 885.) Example: "That house by the road always been a curioussome sight for folks round here." SU.

Curl n. (1980s–1990s) derogatory term, short for Jheri Curl. (FR.) Example: "Betty still got the curl, girl, we should clown her." YCU, SCU.

Cut; cutting v., n. (1920s–1960s) in jazz, to outdo a competitor in playing a solo; in the thirties, the tapes done during a recording session; "cut": from the forties to the sixties, to disappear, so to speak, to leave the scene; from the fifties to the sixties, to dilute drugs; "cut"—short for "cut out"—to leave a place immediately; also in the sixties, any musical work or theatrical performance. Also "cutting" referred, in the sixties and later, to diluting drugs (ZNH, AM, p. 94; RSG, JL, p. 74; DB, OHHJ, p. 136; HLF, RJPD, p. 170; CS, vol. 3, no. 2, p. 19; CLC, TS, p. 254.) Example: "That cat got the reputation for cutting his stuff." SNU, JMFU.

[The] Cut n. (1990s) from "cut," as with a knife; a rough section of a city or town; the ghetto. (FR.) WCU.

Cut a hog v. (1900s–1930s) to make a mistake. (ZNH, TEWG, p. 149.) Example: "This is the last time you gone come in my house and cut a hog then turn around and like you ain't done nothing wrong." Florida use.

Cut a rug v. (1930s–1940s) to dance, especially to jitterbug; originally a jitterbug expression. (WF, DAS, p. 136.) SNCU.

Cut a side n. (1980s–1990s) sexual intercourse; probably picked up from musician's slang. (EF, RDSL, p. 234.) Los Angeles; YCU.

Cut a swath v. (1750s–1900s) accomplishing anything impressive. Stems from early field-hand use to characterize any great amount of work done with a scythe. Picked up from general white use in rural areas. (MT, DAF, p. 85.) SU.

Cute suit with the loop droop n. (1940s) a flashy, drapelike suit of clothes. (DB, OHHJ, p. 136.) Harlem use.

Cut [one's] eyes v. (1930s–1940s) to look with contempt at someone; to look askance. (FR.) Example: "You see that chick cut her eyes at me?" SNU.

Cut-down adj. (1850s–1880s) of Gullah origin; to feel dejected, blue, unhappy. Example: "I feel so cut-down here lately since my baby left." (AEG, BB, p. 295; CCJ, NMGC, p. 92.) Georgia, South Carolina; SU. See "Take down."

Cut [no] ice (1960s) the failure to convince, win, or impress someone. (FR.) NCU. See "Cutting ice."

Cut loose v.i. (1950s–1960s) to make a break with a situation or person. (IS, PSML, p. 314; FR; DW, TL, p. 60; CRM, BP, p. 299.) DCU, SNCU.

Cut out v. (1940s–1960s) to leave; to depart quickly. (MHB, JS, np.; DC, BJ, p. 62; FR; CC, OMMM, NCCHD, p. 254.) Example: "Both brothers cut out before we had a chance to ask their names." SU, MWU.

Cutouts n. (1960s–1970s) sandals. (FGC, DARE, p. 898.) North Carolina use.

Cut-rate adj. (1930s–1940s) cheap or poor in quality; insignificant; to belittle someone; "to play cheaply." (DB, OHHJ, p. 136; CH, IHHL, p. 84; CC, OMMM, NCCHD, p. 254.) Examples: "She's such a cut-rate person—you see them trashy shoes?"; and "Don't cut-rate me! I don't play that shit." Harlem use.

Cut [some] sides v. (1930s–1960s) to make a phonograph recording, usually at one's own expense. (DC, BJ, p. 62; RSG, JL, p. 278; FN, JS, p. 10.) Example: "Me and Benny and Cleveland and Juicehead cut some sides last year and sold them from door to door out of a shopping bag." JMFU, SNU.

Cut [one] some slack v. (1960s) to give or to be given an easier time of it—a break, so to speak. (DC, BJ, p. 62.) Examples: "Micky, if you don't cut me some slack, pretty soon I'm gone start thinking you ain't my friend no more"; and, "Hey, baby, don't do me like this, cut me some slack." MWU.

Cut the cheese v. (1950s) cutting the cheese usually refers to a children's game, but among black children the expression was used to refer to flatulence; to "pass gas." (FGC, DARE, p. 900.) SU.

Cut the fool v. (1860s–1940s) silly or stupid behavior. (ZNH, DTR, p. 229.) Southern use.

Cut-throat n. (1980s) rebellious male. (FR.) Example: "That sucker ain't nothing but a cut-throat who gone end up in prison." (FR.) SNU.

Cutting v. (1930s–1940s) to stab someone with a switchblade knife. (FR.) SNU.

Cutting contest n. (1930s–1940s) in jazz, a "battle" between musicians wherein the applause of the listeners serves as a grading system. (RSG, JL, p. 75.) JMFU, SNU.

Cutting ice v. (1960s–1970s) succeeding in an impressive way. (FR.) See "Cut (no) ice."

Cutting man n. (1950s–1960s) a man's best male friend. "Cutting" is derived from jazz world use referring to the competition between individual musicians giving their all to a performance. (RDA, DDJ, p. 265; RGS, JL, p. 75.) JMFU, SCU.

Cut the pigeon wings n. (1700s–1850s) to perform a dance done by plantation slaves. (HV, AHAE, pp. 157–158.) Example: "Every Saturday night after we get washed up and everything, we gather in the quarters and be cutting the pigeon wings and singing and carrying on."

Cut under (1890s–1930s) an insult. (LA, SM, p. 212.) SNU.

Cut up; cutting up v. (1860s–1960s) to make a lot of noise; to complain; dancing; fighting. (FGC, DARE, p. 901.) SNU.

Cutty n. (1970s–1990s) one's best friend. (EF, RDSL, p. 234.) SNU.

Cutware bottoms up adv. (1940s) the act of holding a drinking glass upside down to the mouth in order to drain it of its last drops. (DB, OHHJ, p. 136.) NCU.

Cuz n. (1960s; 1980s–1990s) form of address, short for "cousin," meaning friend; usually a male term; term of address used by Los Angeles Crips, a gang. (WKB, JMC, PS, p. 49; EF, RDSL, p. 2324.) SNU.

Cyclops n. (1960s) a television set—because of the one-eye appearance. (DC, BJ, p. 62.) Example: "I got a new cyclops, and all the kids want to do is sit in front of it." MWU.

Cypress Hill n. (1990s) gang rape. (FR.) Example: "Them suckers got that bitch so drunk they pulled a Cypress Hill on her." NCU.

Dabbling v. (1950s–1990s) to make moderate use of narcotics such as heroin. (RRL, DAZ, p. 55.) Example: "He wasn't really strung out at first; he was just dabbling." DCU. See "Chippying."

Dad n. (1930s–1940s) word of address by one male to another. (CW, TM, p. 107; EF, RDSL, p. 234.) Example: "What's happening, Dad?" SNU.

Dada Mama n. (1920s–1930s) a sustained drum roll, so called because of the double-roll effect. (RSG, JT, p. 65.) JMFU.

Daddy n. (1630s–1990s) paternal father; also a woman's term of address to her male lover, boyfriend, or husband. (CVV, NH, 285; FGC, DARE, p. 3.) SNU.

Daddy Week n. (1940s) "Daddy" was the nickname for Frank Schiffman, managing director of Harlem's Apollo Theater, and "week" refers to the usual span of time bands and acts were employed. (FR.) Example: "What's Daddy Week got lined up next?" Harlem use.

Daddy-O n. (1930s–1940s) term of address by one male to another, demonstrating affection, respect, and sympathy; made popular by radio disc jockey Daddy-O Daily (FR.) Example: "Hey, Daddy-O, give me some skin." SNCU.

Dagger n. (1960s–1990s) short for "bulldagger"; lesbian. (EF, RDSL, p. 234.) SNU.

Dagger-pointed goldies n. (1940s) yellow, sharp-toed style of shoes. (DB, OHHJ, p. 136.) Example: "Here comes Jimmy strutting down the block in his zoot suit tapping along in his bad dagger-pointed goldies." SNCU. See "Kicks."

Dairies n. (1970s–1990s) a woman's breasts. (EF, RDSL, p. 234.) South-central Los Angeles use.

Daisy-beaters n. (1940s) feet; shoes. (FR.) Example: "I picked up some bad daisy-beaters at Stacy Adams yesterday." Harlem use.

Damaged adj. (1960s) drunk. Example: "Clark was too damaged last night to drive home. Trish drove him home." SNU. See "Twisted."

Damblack adj. (1930s–1940s) very dark. (ZNH, AM, p. 94.) See "Dark black."

Damper n. (1950s) savings bank or safe-deposit box; also, to stop or inhibit something or someone. (IS, PSML, p. 314.) Examples: "Mack and Grady stuck up a damper"; and, "She comes in here, and every time she puts a damper on the place." SNU.

Dance in the sandbox (1960s) to jive, to scheme. Rare. (FR.) PPU.

Dance on [one's] lips [face] (1980s–1990s) to strike one in the face; to pounce on the face. (EF, RDSL, p. 234.) South-central Los Angeles; SCU.

Dang interj. (1950s) variant of "damn"—spoken in frustration. (FR.) SNU.

Dank n. (1990s) marijuana. (*USA Weekend*, August 13–15, 1993, p. 10.) YCU, WCU.

Dap adj. See "Dapper."

Dap n. (1990s) credit given where credit is due. (FR.) SNCU. See "Props."

Dap daddy n. (1950s–1990s) handsomely dressed male. (EF, RDSL, p. 234.) SNCU.

Dapped down adj. (1950s–1990s) dressed in a sharp, flashy manner. (EF, RDSL, p. 234.) SNCU.

Dapped to a tee (EF, RDSL, p. 234.) See "Dapped down."

Dapper v., adj. (1950s; 1980s–1990s) in the fifties a dapper person dressed in style. In the eighties and nineties, it still meant that but was also used to verbalize agreement during a friendly handslap. (FR; DC, BJ, p. 62; CS, vol. 3, no. 2, p. 19.) SNCU.

Dapt adj. See "Dapper."

Dashiki adj., n. (1950s–1960s) loose; corruption of the Yoruba word *danshiki*; a loose pullover shirt worn in the sixties by black men and women as a symbol of pride in their African cultural and racial heritage. (HV, AHAE, p. 140; SBF, IHAT, p. 32.) SNU.

Dark black n. (1930s–1940s) any very black person. (ZNH, AM, p. 94.) SNU.

Dark brown shit n. (1950s–1960s) inferior heroin. (DG, NDA, p. 119.) DCU.

Darktown n. (1900s–1930s) a black section of a city; a word often used in entertainment and in headlines in black newspapers. Probably picked up from white use. (FGC, DARE, p. 14.) Examples: "Darktown Strutters Ball" and "Darktown Frolics Company." SNU.

Date n. (1920s–1950s) recording appointment for musicians; also came to mean a gig; also, the arrangement a prostitute makes with a trick. (RSG, JL, pp. 78–79; CS, vol. 3, no. 2, p. 19.) JBWU; PPU.

Davy Crockett n. (1940s) draft board official. (DB, OHHJ, p. 136.) Example: "Guess I'll get on down to see Davy Crockett and sign up and get my butt shipped over the big dip." Harlem use.

Day gig n. (1940s–1960s) also known as a "slave"—a nonmusical job a musician is forced to take for need of money. (MM, RB, p. 370; LF, EJ, p. 346.) Example: "Half the cats in the band working a day gig." SNU, JMFU.

Day-day (1900s–1930s) farewell, good-bye, spoken with lightheartedness or in a childish manner. "Day-day" is similar to "night-night" or "bye-bye." SU.

Deadbeat n. (1900s–1990s) one who cheats or "cons" someone out of money or other valuables. (FGC, DARE, pp. 18–19, 22.) Example: "Stu is the kind of deadbeat who takes you to dinner, then you end up paying the bill—and worse than that, he keeps selling that worthless jewelry to unsuspecting women." SNU.

Dead-Eye Dick Nat Love, black gunfighter, cowboy. See "Deadwood Dick."

Dead-head n. (1930s–1950s) a drunk or stupid person. (FG, DARE, p. 23.) Example: "Marvin ain't nothing but a dead-head, and his mama's gonna kick him out of the house one of these days." SNU.

Deadly adj. (1960s) excellent. (FR.) Example: "That's a deadly suede jacket, Tommy. Where'd you get it?" SNU.

Deadman's fingers n. (1880s–1930s) the gills or lungs of a crab, considered poisonous. (FGC, DARE, p. 25.) NSU.

Dead president(s) n. (1940s) any paper certificate of money. (MHB, JS, np.) Example: "Hey, man, lay a couple of dead presidents on me till payday." SNU.

Dead thing n. (1960s) a Black Nationalist phrase used to refer to any white idea or manner or custom or artifact. (FR.) Example: "Western society is a dead thing." NCU.

Deadwood Dick believed to have been a Negro cowboy, Nat Love, a slave born in Tennessee (1854 or 1855?). He left home at fifteen to work with a cattle outfit. The men of Deadwood City (Dakota Territory), because he won a very popular shooting contest, bestowed upon him the name "Deadwood Dick." In the 1870s many adventure stories about Deadwood Dick began to appear and were read mostly by boys, but Nat Love in 1907 published a book about his real adventures.

Deal (1780s–1920s) See "Devil."

Deal n. (1960s–1970s) any woman. (JH, PBL, p. 84.) New York City; SCU.

Deal; dealing v. (1920s–1990s) selling illegal drugs. (CLC, TS, p. 254; RRL, DAZ, p. 57.) Example: "Hotshot knows how to deal without attracting attention to himself." NCU.

Dealer n. (1920s–1990s) one who trafficks in illegal drugs. See "Deal" and "Pusher."

Deal in coal v. (1900s–1940s) to take an interest in very dark-skinned women. (ZNH, AM, p. 95.) Example: "Sorry, man, I don't deal in no coal." SNU.

Deal in dirt v. (1970s–1990s) to gossip. (EF, RDSL, p. 234.) South-central Los Angeles; SNU.

Deal in zeroes v. (1960s) to draw a blank; to experience failure at something or with someone. (DW, TL, p. 180.) NCU, SCU.

Dealt [one] v. (1960s) to trick or be tricked. (DC, BJ, p. 62.) Example: "The sucker was dealt with quickly and we got our money back." MWU.

Death rain n. (1940s) a sudden and sustained downpour; heavy rain on a dark day. Example: "Baby got caught in a death rain and came home looking like a plucked chicken."

Deece n. (1940s) a dime. (DB, OHHJ, p. 136.) Harlem use.

Deeda n. (1960s–1970s) LSD-25. (RRL, DAZ, p. 58.) Harlem use.

Deemer n. (1950s) a dime. (IS, PSML, p. 311.) Rare. NCU.

[Going] Deep v., adj. (1960s–1970s) referring to a profound philosophical point; serious and surprisingly interesting. (RDA, TB, p. 3.) See "Heavy."

Deb n. (1950s) short for "debutante"; girl member of a gang. (PT, DMS, p. 315.) Example: "Mary Jo was our deb till she got pregnant. Now she won't speak to us." SNU.

Deck n. (1960s) quantity of narcotics. (FR.) Example: "Trudy gets her deck every Friday night down there in Boslow Park." DCU.

Decked out adj. (1940s–1960s) the particular way one is dressed. (FR.) Example: "The two brothers come in here on the weekends all decked out in their fine rags trying to pick up women." SNU.

Deep hole n. (1970s–1980s) problem situation. (FR.) Example: "This debt has me in a deep hole, man." SNU.

Deep six n. (1940s) a grave. (DB, OHHJ, p. 136.) Example: "Every living person got to one day get down into a deep six and be quiet." Harlem use; SNU.

Deep sugar n. (1940s) a very passionate kiss; a French kiss. (DB, OHHJ, p. 136.) Example: "Hey, little mama, how about some deep sugar?" SNU.

Deep yellow n. (1900s) light-skinned African-American. "She was a deep yellow woman." (TR, AGD, p. 8.) SU. See "Yellow."

Def adj. (1980s–1990s) short for "definitely"; first rate; anything good or wonderful; excellent; the highest praise. (TW, CK, p. 136; PM, UCLAS, p. 33.) Example: "This tape has a lot of def jams." SNU.

Defense plant on a square's dim (1940s) amateur night at Apollo Theater in Harlem. (DB, OHHJ, p. 136.) Harlem use.

Def jams n. (1990s) good music. See "Def."

De la Soul n. (1990s) rap group (*3 Feet High & Rising*).

Dem (1700s–1990s) deliberate corruption of "them"; refers to white people. (ECLA, NN, p. 265.) SNU.

Demo n. (1980s) a crack cocaine pipe. (FR.) DCU. See "Stem."

Demon n. (1940s) dime. (DB, OHHJ, p. 137.) Example: "Sucker ain't got even a demon in his pocket and he acting like he owns the world." Harlem use; MWU.

Den n. (1940s) one's home. (DB, OHHJ, p. 137.) Example: "I been laying low in the den, cooling it." Harlem; MWU.

Derby n. (1950s) the reference is to the human head engaged in oral copulation. (IS, PSML, p. 314.) Example: "She gives great derby." NCU.

Desk piano n. (1940s) typewriter. (DB, OHHJ, p. 137.) Example: "This dude Chester Himes plays some mean desk piano. You ever catch one of his stories?" Harlem use.

Deuce n. (1920s–1940s) two dollars or a two-dollar bill; a pair. (DB, OHHJ, p. 137.) Example: "Roger, how about laying a deuce on me till later tonight when my luck change?" SNCU.

Deuce 25 n. See "[The] Deuce and a Quarter."

[The] Deuce and a Quarter n. (1960s) the Buick Electra 225. (DC, BJ, p. 62; EF, RDSL, p. 234.) Example: "He be cruising up and down the boulevard in his bad Deuce and a Quarter." Rare. MWU.

Deuce of benders n. (1930s–1940s) knees. (DB, OHHJ, p. 137; MHB, JS, np.) Example: "You should have seen that long-legged cat's deuce of benders in the wind as he booted it out of here." Harlem use.

Deuce of haircuts n. (1930s–1940s) two weeks. (DB, OHHJ, p. 137.) Example: "I see my supplier every deuce of haircuts." Harlem use.

Deuce of nods on the backbeat n. (1940s) Example: "It was exactly deuce of nods on the backbeat that I last saw Mack." Harlem use.

Deuce of peekers n. (1930s–1940s) two eyes. (DB, OHHJ, p. 137.) Example: "I saw her with my own deuce of peekers. I swear!" Harlem use; MWU.

Deuce of ruffs [russ] n. (1930s–1940s) twenty cents. (DB, OHHJ, p. 137.) Example: "Can't talk about me. He ain't got deuce of ruffs in his pockets." Harlem use; MWU.

Deuce of ticks n. (1930s–1940s) two minutes. (DB, OHHJ, p. 137.) Example: "Just hold on. I'll be there in deuce of ticks." Harlem use; MWU.

Devil n. (1700s–1990s) a troublesome Christian deity associated with wrongdoing. (FR.) SU.

Devil n. (1950s–1970s) white man; sometimes used by some Black Nationalists to describe any white person, especially white males, and more especially white police. (CS, vol. 3, no. 2, p. 20; JH, PBL, p. 84.) SNU.

Devil and Tom Walker exclam. (1940s–1960s) an expression of annoyance; euphemism for or variant of such; picked up from white use; exclamation, as, "What in the dickens . . . ?" (FGC, DARE, p. 46.) New England; NRU.

[The] Devil is beating his wife (1900s–1940) in African-American folklore, when the sun appears while it's raining. It was believed that if you stick a pen into the ground and place your ear to it you can hear the blows. (FR.) SU.

Devilment n. (1700s–1940s) malicious mischief; evil. (FG, DARE, p. 48.) Example: "You kids come on in this house before you get into some devilment." SU.

Devil's dick n. (1980s–1990s) the pipe crack cocaine users smoke. (TW, CH, p. 148.) DCU.

Devil's snuff n. (1850s–1940s) natural powdery spores found in the forests in the south, used by conjurers. (HMH, HCWR, p. 179.) SU.

Devil's stool [footstool] n. (1900s–1940s) a larger-than-average mushroom. (FGC, DARE, p. 56.) SU.

Devil's songs n. See "Corn songs."

Devil's work n. See "Hoodoo."

Dewbaby n. (1960s) an especially dark-skinned (blue-black) male child. (DC, BJ, p. 62.) MWU.

Dew sore n. (1820s–1880s) lower leg sores thought to be caused by walking through wet grass. (FGC, DARE, p. 59.) Virginia; North Carolina; SU.

Dex n. (1960s) Dexedrine, an amphetamine sulfate that, when taken, stimulates the central nervous system. (RRL, DAZ, p. 61.) NCU.

Dexies n. (1960s) nickname for Dexedrine—amphetamine sulfate. (CS, vol. 3, no. 2, p. 20; RRL, DAZ, p. 61.) DCU.

Dey n. (1700s–1990s) variant of "they"; white people. See "Dem."

Diaper n. (1980s–1990s) a woman's expression for a sanitary napkin. (EF, RDSL, p. 234.) SNU.

Diaper the baby v. (1970s–1990s) a woman's expression meaning to put on a sanitary napkin. (EF, RDSL, p. 234.) South-central Los Angeles; SNU.

Diasticutis n. (1930s) the human posterior or buttocks. (ZNH, TEWG, p. 53.) Example: "Get off your rusdy diasticutis and help me shuck this corn." SU.

Dick n. (1820s?–1900s; 1930s–1940s; 1960s–1990s) the penis. Possibly a variant of "prick." Black slang users almost never used the word "cock" but have favored "dick" from an unknown early time (1820s?). In the thirties and forties, "dick" was a term of address among beboppers; later replaced by Jack or Jim (RSG, JL, p. 79). "Dick" remains current in hip-hop, drug, and street cultures. (TW, CH, p. 148; WF, DAS, p. 146; RDA, DDJ, p. 265.) See "Johnson."

Dick v. (1900s–1990s) sexual intercourse or sexual activity involving the penis. (FR.) Example: "That dude thinks he can dick everyone in sight." SNU.

Dickhound n. (1980s) a woman who has many sexual partners; a slut. (FR.) SNU.

Dicky check v. (1980s–1990s) police inspection of male genital area for possible hidden drugs. (RP, C, p. 12.) Example (narcotics agent speaking): "Open your pants, hotshot. Dicky check time." DCU.

Dicty; Dickty; Dictee adj., n. (1890s–1920s) snobbish or pretentious; high-class or snobbish-acting person or a way of acting haughty. (NH, DTR, p. 225; CVV, NH, p. 285; DB, OHHJ, p. 137; CC, OMMM, NCCHD, p. 254.) SNU.

Diddly n. (1920s–1960s) the Christian hell; distance; something of little or no value. (ZNH, AM, p. 94.) Example: "I don't give a diddly whether you come back or not." SNU.

Diddly damn n. (1920s–1950s) insignificant amount. (FR.) Example: "I don't give a good diddley damn whether you believe me or not." SNU. See "Diddly squat" and "Doodly-squat."

Diddly squat n. (1950s) insignificant amount. (FR.) Example: "I don't give a diddly squat if I never see you again." SNU. See "Diddly Damn" and "Doodly-squat."

Diddy-popper n. (1980s–1990s) pejorative term for any young black person who does not live in the ghetto; a young middle-class African-American. (EF, RDSL, p. 234.) South-central Los Angeles; YCU.

Diddy-wah-diddy n. (1920s–1960s) expression often used in an insult; a distant place without value; a faraway, damnable place. (ZNH, AM, p. 94; SK, PC, pp. 153–154.) See "Bee-luther-hatchee," "Diddly," "West Hell," and "Zar."

Dig v. (1650s–1990s) from the word *deg* or *dega*, (Wolof/African); to understand; to call attention to; a call for attention or an expression of understanding; to appreciate. (Probably no relation to the 1880s white American use: "a diligent student.") "Plant you now and dig you later": a common black expression. (JSF, AON, p. 200; HV, AHAE, p. 140; DB, OHHJ, p. 137; CRM, Bp, p. 299; CC, OMMM, NCCHD, p. 254; HLF, RJPD, p. 170; CS, vol. 3, no. 2, p. 20; DG, BG, p. 44; PM, UCLAS, p. 34.) Example: "Hey! Dig, man, that's a mean leather coat you sporting." SNU.

Dig the dip on the four and two (1940s) to take a bath every Saturday night. (DB, OHHJ, p. 137.) Example: "This old country-time dude digs the dip on the four and two—never heard of taking a bath every night." Harlem use.

Dig you later (1930s–1960s) an expression of farewell; it was shortened to "later." (FR.) Example: "I gotta go down to the drugstore. Dig you later." SNU.

Digital Underground (1990s) rap group. (*Sex Packets*.)

Digits n. (1990s) telephone numbers; a telephone number. (HC, WSJ, p. B1.) Example: "Hey, girl, why don't you lay your digits on me so I can sound on you later." YCU.

Dillinger front n. (1970s–1990s) a double-breasted suit. (EF, RDSL, p. 234.) South-central Los Angeles; SCU.

Dim n. (1920s–1940s) nighttime or evening. (CC, OMMM, NCCHD, p. 254.) Example: "Catch you in the dim." SNU.

Dilly dude n. (1960s) a person who doesn't fit in; an outsider; weird person. (CS, vol. 3, no. 3, p. 5.) Ohio use.

Dime n. (1960s) a ten-dollar bill; ten-year prison term. (DW, TL, p. 180; RRL, DAZ, p. 63; CRM, BP, p. 299; CS, vol. 3, no. 2, p. 20; KCJ,

JS, p. 138.) Example: "Steve got a dime for killing his father; they called it manslaughter." SNCU.

Dime bag; dime's worth n. (1960s–1970s) a quantity of marijuana or morphine narcotics that costs ten dollars. (FR.) DCU.

Dime note n. (1930s–1940s) ten dollars. (DB, OHHJ, p. 137; CC, OMMM, NCCHD, p. 254.) Example: "Here's a dime note—go get me a fifth of Dirty Bird." SNU.

Dims and brights (1920s–1940s) days and nights. (DB, OHHJ, p. 137.) Example: "That ho be out here walking these streets dims and brights." SNU.

Dinge n. (1650s–1920s) a black person; *den-ke* (Mandingo); *den, din* (Mandingo). (HV, AHAE, p. 140; CVV, NH, p. 285.) SNU.

Dingy adj. (1960s) stinginess; to be broke; penniless. (CS, vol. 3, no. 2, p. 20.) Watts, Los Angeles, use.

Dinky; rinky-dinky adj. (1950s–1960s) poor quality. (FR.) Example: "You wouldn't catch me in none of the dinky Sears clothes she wears." SNU.

Dinosaur n. (1980s–1990s) penis. (EF, RDSL, p. 234.) South-central Los Angeles; YCU.

[The Beale Street] Dip n. (1900s–1920s; 1960s) jazz dance in vogue. A "dip" became known generally in black communities by the sixties as any party or social gathering, especially of teenagers or young adults. (HLF, RJPD, p. 170.) SNU.

Dip n. (1940s) a hat. (DB, OHHJ, p. 137.) Harlem use. See "Brim."

Dip n. (1960s) "Dip" was obsolete as a term for a pickpocket as early as the late forties, but was found to be again in current use in Watts, Los Angeles, in the sixties. (CS, vol. 3, no. 2, p. 20; HEG, DAUL, p. 59.) SNU.

Dipping v. (1900s–1940s) picking pockets. (HEG, DAUL, p. 59.) Example: "That cat is so smooth at dipping, you wouldn't even know he'd touched you." SNU.

Dip the fly v. (1980s–1990s) to perform sexual intercourse. (EF, RDSL, p. 234.) South-central Los Angeles use.

Dirt n. (1920s–1950s) gossip; an objectionable person; earthy jazz usually played by small bands. (RSG, JL, pp. 81–82.) Example: (said ironically) "Man, you ought to be ashamed of yourself playing that dirt like you do." JMFU, SNU.

Dirt farm n. (1980s–1990s) anyplace where gossip originates. (EF, RDSL, p. 234.) Example: "This house ain't nothing but a dirt farm." South-central Los Angeles; SNU.

Dirt nap v. (1990s) to take a dirt nap is to die or be buried; to knock out or be knocked out by someone. (JM, WPC, p. 7.) Example: "If you don't stay away from my woman you gone be taking yourself a long dirt nap." SCU, WCU.

Dirty adj., v. (1920s–1950s) good; bad, mean, or terrible as good; also, possessing incriminating evidence. (RSG, JL, p. 82; IS, PSML, p. 314; RRL, DAZ, p. 63.) Examples: "He so dirty I swear I can't see why she put up with him"; and, "They got some dirty stuff on him." SNU.

Dirty Bird n. (1940s–1950s) nickname for Old Crow whiskey. (FR.) SNU.

Dirty dog n. (1940s–1950s) any man who mistreats a woman—definitely a woman's expression. (FR.) Example: "That man is a dirty dog. The way he treats her is a crying shame." SNU.

Dirty Dozens n. (1900s–1950s) a very elaborate verbal rhyming game traditionally played by black boys, in which the participants insult each other's relatives—in twelve censures—especially their mothers. The object of the game is to test emotional strength. The first person to give in to anger is the loser. Variously described as "bad talk," "capping," goading. "Dirty Dozens" is an indigenous verbal folk game. (ZNH, TEWG, p. 123; HRB, DND, p. 27, ZNH, TEWG, p. 123.) SNU. See "Cap" and "Signify."

Dirty hearts n. (1960s–1970s) the Hearts card game for three players; "frequent among black speakers" (FGC, DARE, p. 82). Michigan; MWU.

Disappearing act n. (1950s–1990s) when one's lover or spouse leaves without any formal notice; to leave a note and vanish for a short or extended period. (TMc, DA, title page.) Example: "He pulled his disappearing act again this month, girl." SNU.

Disband v. (1930s–1940s) to discard a playing card while playing a game of cards. (FGC, DARE, p. 83.) SNU.

Dis Con n. (1950s–1960s) a disorderly conduct charge; often the legal ruling under which prostitutes were arrested. (SH, GL, p. 212.) PPU.

Discounting v. (1890s–1920s) to express low regard for something or somebody, especially in a contemptuous manner. (ECLA, NN, p. 265.) Example: "I'm not discounting Jessie just 'cause he ain't here." SU.

Dishrag n. (1860s–1950s) a small cotton cloth used for drying plates and other dishes. (FR.) SU.

Disneyfied adj. (1990s) mythic; unreal. Example: "He lives a Disneyfied life." SNCU.

Disrecognize v. (1930s) to not recognize someone or something. (FR.) Example: "I walked right by her disrecognizing her." SU.

Disregardless v. (1850–1940) regardless. Although identified as chiefly Appalachian, this term was common among black speakers in the forties and fifties but not as common as "irregardless." (FGC, DARE, p. 87.) Example: "I want you back here by ten, disregardless of how much fun you might be having." SU. See "Irregardless."

Disremember v. (1630s–1900s) not to remember. (FGC, DARE, p. 87.) Example: "I'm getting so I just disremember even what I did yesterday." SU.

Dissing v. (1980s–1990s) short for disrespect; to insult, usually verbally, though a scornful look is also a form of dissing. (TW, CH, p. 148.) Example: "Man, they were dissing us, so we jumped them." SNCU.

[The] District n. (1900s–1920s) the section of New Orleans known as Storyville, famous as a place where early jazz went through its urban birth pains. (FR.) New Orleans use.

Ditch n. (1960s) the fleshy area on the body side of the elbow where heroin addicts often inject the drug into the large, visible vein there. (CS, vol. 3, no. 2, p. 20.) Watts, Los Angeles; DCU.

Dittybop n. (1960s) a young person who crudely and foolishly displays hip mannerisms that are out of key with his or her personality. (DW, TL, p. 61.) NCU.

Divine Miss Sarah Sarah Vaughan. See "Sassy."

[One with] Divine rights n. (1980s–1990s) the police. (EF, RDSL, p. 234.) South-central Los Angeles use.

Dixie (1800s–1880s) "an indigenous northern negro refrain common upward of eighty years ago" (JSF, AON, pp. 204–205). NCU, NRU.

Dixie [land] n. (1900s–1930s) name of the first or one of the first jazz bands to appear in New Orleans restaurants around 1917; a style of music characterized by the combined tonal effects of a sax, a trumpet, a clarinet; pre-Swing music. (RSG, JL, pp. 82–83.) SNU.

Diz; Dizzy John Birks Gillespie, born in Cheraw, South Carolina, October 21, 1917; trumpet player, composer, singer, jazz-band leader; a very famous jazz personality and musician who (in 1951) started his own recording company.

DMT n. (1960s) nickname for LSD-25; lysergic acid diethylamide tartrate 25. (CS, vol. 3, no. 2, p. 20; RRL, DAZ, pp. 128–129.) DCU.

Do n. (1940s–1950s; 1980s–1990s) short for a processed hairdo or for curled hair; a woman's hair, especially just after a trip to the hairdresser. (PM, UCLAS, p. 34.) Example: "Where'd you get a bad do, girl."

Do adv. (1850s–1930s) in southern speech sometimes used as "otherwise." (FR.) Example: "Be here by four do everything will be put away and you won't get to see any of it." SU.

Do n. (1970s) a fancy party. (FR.) Example: "Are you going to the big do tonight?" SNU.

Do a number v. (1960s–1990s) to manipulate unfavorably; to take advantage of someone. (FR.) Example: "He did a number on her, and she wound up broke." NCU.

Do-up(s) v., n. (1960s–1990s) the process of injecting a narcotic into the flesh, especially the arm. (CS, vol. 3, no. 2, p. 20.) Example: "We help each other with the do-ups." DCU.

Doberman n. (1960s) a dishonest, cowardly, or deceitful person. (DC, BJ, p. 63.) Example: "That dude's a doberman, Jim, he'll come up behind your back and stab you." MWU.

Do Cap n. (1980s–1990s) a plastic shower cap used by black men to protect their hair *do*. (WKB, JMC, PS, p. 49.) SNU.

Doc Cheatham Aldolphus Anthony Cheatham; trumpet player; born in Nashville, Tennessee, June 13, 1905; worked with Cab Calloway, Herbie Mann, and Billie Holiday.

Doc Paul Wesley Evans. Cornet player, born June 20, 1907. Worked with Bunk Johnson, Eddie Condon, and others.

Doctoring v. (1920s–1930s) practicing voodoo or hoodoo. (FR.) Example: "That old woman been down there in her cabin by the creek doctoring since back in the days of slavery." SU.

Doctor lady n. (1920s–1930s) a conjuring woman. (FR.) SU. See "Doctoring" and "Doctor woman."

Doctor woman n. (1920s–1930s) a conjuring woman. (FR.) See "Doctoring" and "Doctor lady."

Dodge City n. (1980s–1990s) the ghetto in Venice, California; so called because of a local reputation for violent crimes. (EF, RDSL, p. 234.) Los Angeles use.

Dog exclam. (1930s–1960s) said in frustration or disappointment; "dag" is a variant of "dog." (HLF, RJPD, p. 170.) Example: "Dog! I thought sure I'd hit the number this time!" SNU.

Dog n. (1940s–1950s) a woman's name for an abusive or offensive man; a young or older "whore" (FR; CRM, BP, p. 299; PM, ULCAS, p. 34; IS, PSML, p. 314; EF, RDSL, p. 235). SNU. See "Dirty" and "Dirty dog."

Dog n. (1960s) an especially brutal policeman. (CS, vol. 3, no. 2, p. 20.) Watts, Los Angeles, use.

Dog v., n. (1940s–1960s; 1980s) in the forties and fifties, to mistreat; in the sixties, an ugly female, an old whore, an unfair man, and, rarely, an exceptional person; in the eighties, to discredit. (CS, vol. 3, no. 2, p. 20.) Example: "Why that man got to dog her like that? It's cruel." SNU.

Dog v. (1960s) residue from opium or heroin of poor quality. (CS, vol. 3, no. 2, p. 20.) Watts, Los Angeles; DCU.

Dog finger n. (1920s–1930s) the middle finger or index finger of either hand; an unlucky finger; tabooed finger. (HMH, HCWR, p. 609; BJ, BLH, SD, p. 12.) Example; "He stuck his dog finger in the pie and that really made me mad." SU.

Dog food n. (1960s) a cash bribe for a policeman, district attorney, or judge. (CS, vol. 3, no. 2, p. 21.) Watts, Los Angeles; SCU.

Dog food n. (1980s–1990s) heroin. The term is used by black drug addicts and ex-addicts both in and out of prison. (WKB, JMC, PS, p. 49; EF, RDSL, p. 234.) DCU, PU. See "Boy," "Horse," and "Smack."

Doggish adj. (1930s–1960s) woman's term for a disgusting, sexually irresponsible man. (CS, vol. 3, no. 2, p. 21.) SNU.

Doggone exclam. (1700s–1950s) same as "dog my cats"; an exclamation of dissatisfaction, frustration, bewilderment, astonishment. (JAH, PBE, p. 172; FGC, DARE, p. 112; CMc, HH, p. 24.) SU.

Doghouse n. (1940s–1950s) bass violin or string bass. (RSG, JL, p. 84; CC, OMMM, NCCHD, p. 254.) Rare. JMFU.

Dog house n. (1980s–1990s) black prison inmates' term for solitary confinement; any jail cell. (WKB, JMC, PS, p. 49.) PU.

Dogies n. (1680s–1880s) cattle; little things; small; *kidogo, dodo* (Kimbundu). (HV, AHAE, p. 154.) SU.

Dogie; doojee; duji n. (1950s–1960s) heroin. (PT, DMS; RRL, DAZ, p. 65.) Spanish Harlem use; DCU.

Dog(ging) it; dogged; dogging; doggish v., n. (1940s–1990s) to "dog it" refers to sexual intercourse performed on the knees with the male behind the female; "dogged" and "dogging," to mistreat or mistreating someone; "doggish," brutishly lustful, lecherous. "Dogging" —in the nineties—refers to the sexual performance, for money, of teenage girls hooked on hard drugs. (MM, RB, p. 332; CB, MPL, p. 370; TW, CK, p. 136.) Examples: "He's a doggish man, eyeing everything that walks by"; and, "He dogged her so long her knees got weak." SNU.

Dog juice (1980s–1990s) cheap wine. (EF, RDSL, p. 234.) South-central Los Angeles; DCU, YCU, SCU.

Dog sick v. (1840s–1930s) to be sick in the stomach, especially after having eaten something disagreeable. (FR.) SNU. See "Sick as a dog."

Dog my cats (1890s–1940s) an expression of astonishment or surprise. Example: "Well, dog my cats! If one more thing go wrong today I'm just gone sit down and cry." (CMc, HH, p. 24.) SU. See "Doggone."

Dog tune n. (1940s) a jazz song of poor quality. (RSG, JL, p. 84.) Example: "You ain't never gone catch them playing no dog tune." JMFU.

[Suck a] Dog's dick v. (1950s–1960s) an expletive for the lowest thing a human being can do; the most degenerate act. (DG, W, p. 104.) SCU, PPU, DCU.

Dog's howl n. (1700s–1950s) a warning of coming disaster, especially if it occurs at night. (FR.) Example: "I heard that dog's howl last night and my heart jumped up in my mouth." SU.

Dogs n. (1900s–1940s) one's feet. (CVV, NH, p. 285.) Example: "My dogs are killing me after pounding the pavement all day." SNU.

Dogs n. (1990s) fists. (FR.) Example: "You think you can whip me, just put up your dogs and try." (FR.) YCU.

Do it v. (1920s–1930s) a phrase often cried out from a black audience to encourage performers. (RSG, JL, pp. 83–84.) SNCU.

Do-it fluid n. (1980s–1990s) liquor. (EF, RDSL, p. 235.) SNCU, SCU, YCU.

Doing a hundred (1940s–1950s) in very fine shape. (FR.) Example: "He got himself a good job now and he's doing a hundred." SNU.

Doing the dirt v. (1950s–1960s) See "Dirt."

Do-less adj. (1950s) lazy. (FR.)

Dollies n. (1960s) pills of Dolophine, used by heroin addicts to combat withdrawal. (CS, vol. 3, no. 2, p. 21; RRL, DAZ, p. 65.) Example (addict who's just been sentenced to do time): "I need me some dollies to come down so I can get ready to do this bit." DCU.

Dolo Charles Mitchell Coker. Piano player, born November 16, 1927; worked with Lou Donaldson, Dexter Gordon, et al.

Dolo n., adj. (1990s) a solo; on one's own. (FR.) Example: "Bud is something when he's into his dolo." JBWU.

Dolo n. (1950s–1960s) Dolophine; a synthetic opiate drug used to kick a hard-drug habit. (RRL, DAZ, p. 65.) DCU.

Dome n. (1960s) the human head. (DC, BJ, p. 63.) Example: "He be always going upside her dome when he gets that mess in him." MWU.

Dome n. (1940; 1980s–1990s) the human head. Popular in the forties, this work nearly vanished from the vocabulary of black slang users then resurfaced in the eighties. (FR.) SNU.

Domie; Domi; Dommy n. (1930s) one's home or apartment. (FR.) Rare. SU, MWU.

Dominickes n. (1860s–1930s) a person of black and white ancestry who is native to the Ponce de Leon, Florida, area. (FGC, DARE, p. 128.) Florida; SU.

Done v. (1620s–1990s) past action for "did"; an all-purpose intensifier referring to completing something. (FR.) Examples: "He had done gone and come back before daylight"; and, "She done all right in school." SNU.

[Been] Done v. (1920s–1990s) past complete marker; *doon* (Wolof). The African origin of "done" converging with the English "done" may help to explain the black American particular use of the word. (HV, AHAE, p. 140.) Example: "I don't know what you talking about, I been done finished the dishes." SNU.

Don't adv. (1700s–1940s) otherwise. (FR.) Example: "Take the basket if you want it don't you can leave it alone." SU.

Don't-care-ish(ified) adj. (1930s–1950s) without concern; indifference. Example: "He and his cousins all are just a bunch of don't-care-ish young men." SU.

Don't let your mouth buy what your ass can't pay for (1980s–1990s) advice to keep quiet, especially in a delicate situation. (EF, BVV, p. 44.) South-central Los Angeles; SNCU.

Don't let your mouth overload your ass (1980s–1990s) advice to keep quiet, especially in a delicate situation. (EF, BVV, p. 44.) South-central Los Angeles; SNCU.

Don't let your mouth write a check your ass can't cash (1980s–1990s) advice to keep quiet, especially in a delicate situation. (EF, BVV, p. 44.) South-central Los Angeles; SNCU.

Don't make bahn-nahn (1900s–1940s) a request not to be let down or disappointed. (FR.) Example (one lover to another): "Don't make a bahn-nahn and come home late again." Possibly limited to New Orleans.

Don't pay [one] no rabbit foot (1900–1940) literally, to ignore someone. (FR.) Example: "Sally Mae, don't pay him no rabbit foot, 'cause he's always in here in somebody's face." SU.

Don't play [one] cheap (1940s–1960s) a request or plea that one be taken seriously. (FR.) SNU.

Don't sweat it (1950s) a request or command to not worry; relax; take it easy. (FR.) SNU.

Doodeysquat adj., n. (1940s–1960s) without value. (AY, S, p. 16.) Example: "You can ask all night, but I don't give doodeysquat how long you beg; you won't make me change my mind." SNU.

Doodle; doodling v. (1900s–1930s) in jazz, to play with great informality; possible sexual implications (RSG, JL, p. 85). Example: "When the Dixieland Jazz Band starts doodling, everybody wants to just relax." JMFU.

Doodly-squat; doodley squat adj. (1930s–1960s) without value; worthless; nothing. (ZNH, JGV, p. 217; ZNH, MM, RB, p. 92.) SNU. See "Diddley-squat."

Dooflus n. (1930s–1980s) an ineffectual male. (FR.) Example: "He's such a dooflus, he ain't got even enough sense to come in from the rain." NU.

Doo-hickey n. (1800s–1950s) generalized name for any object (usually a mechanical device); sometimes one whose name has been momentarily forgotten. (FR.) SU.

Dookie n. (1930s–1950s) feces. (FR.) SNU.

Do [one's] thing v. (1680s–1960s) to follow one's "bliss" or quest after one's dreams; to do what one most wants to do; to be comfortable in giving expression to one's sincerest desires. The concept, as used by blacks, may have origins in Mandingo *ka a fen ke*. (DC, BJ, p. 63; HV, AHAE, p. 140; CS, vol. 3, no. 2, p. 21.) SNU.

Doorshaker n. (1950s–1960s) a private security guard. (CLC, TS, p. 254.) Example: "They got this big doorshaker in the Kitty Kat to make sure nobody starts acting up." SNU.

Door sign n. (1830s–1900s) a talisman; luck object; any object (such as a horseshoe) placed above a black family's doorway out of respect for the particular beliefs of the people within; a very old custom going back to and beyond the ancient Jews, who considered the doorway (as a symbol of the "doorway of life") sacred and best protected by magic. (MT, DAF, p. 97.) SNU.

Dope n. (1980s–1990s) Mainstream American slang users in the thirties used "dope" to refer to food or to information and only occasionally used it in connection with drugs. It was revived in the eighties as a term for illegal drugs and used frequently on the black street culture scene. (FR.) SNU.

Dope n., adj. (1870s–1990s) information; at times also used to refer to illegal drugs but mainly in mockery of "square" usage; by the 1980s it was being used as an adjective, meaning good or outstanding. (HEG, DAUL, p. 60; WF, DAS, p. 156.) Examples: "You get the dope on the situation and we'll take it from there." SNU.

Dope crew n. (1990s) a team of workers who gather and process and sell illegal narcotics. (FR.) Example: "Big Daddy got his dope crew out on the street round the clock." DCU.

Dope fiend n. (1950s–1960s) any user of "heavy" drugs, especially heroin or morphine. A term from "straight" culture, black drug addicts often use it in jest. (CS, vol. 3, no. 2, p. 21; RRL, DAZ, p. 65.) DCU, SNU.

Dope house n. (1990s) any apartment or house where illegal drugs are sold. (FR.) DCU, SNCU.

Doper n. (1960s–1970s) a dope fiend; any user of heavy drugs. DCU, SNCU. See "Dope fiend."

Do-rag n. (1940s–1960s) a cloth tied around the head to protect a processed hairdo; a stocking cap used to hold greased or straightened hair in place; scarf for covering and protecting processed hair. The do-rag keeps the "do" from "going back." (GS, TT, p. 66; DC, BJ, p. 63.) SNU. See "Head handkerchief."

Do-right(s) n. (1950s–1960s) inmates' nickname for cooperative and well-behaved patients at the drug rehabilitation facility at Lexington, Kentucky. (RRL, DAZ, p. 67.) PU, DCU.

Dosing v. (1900s–1950s) to receive or administer medical treatment. (HMH, HCWR, p. 205.) SU.

Do tell exclam. (1840s–1930s) exclamation of astonishment, usually in response to surprising news. (FR.) Example: "Do tell! You finally getting married, huh?" SU.

Dots n. (1920s–1960s) in jazz, first referred to musical notes on sheet music and later to the sheet music itself. (KG, JV, p. 181; RSG, JL, p. 85.) Example: "I don't read dots, but I can play anything I hear." JMFU.

Double v. (1920s–1940s) musician's word meaning to double the brass section (from circus use for "double in brass"); to double the string or fiddle section. (RSG, JL, pp. 85–86.) JMFU.

Double-headed n. (1860s–1930s) an intelligent person; a voodoo or hoodoo doctor. (HMH, WCWR, p. 150.) SU.

Double master blaster v., n. (1980s–1990s) for a male to ejaculate or reach orgasm while being fellated and smoking crack cocaine at the same time; an orgasm achieved under such conditions. (TW, CH, p. 148.) DCU.

Double-maw [-mother] n. (1920s–1960s) grandmother. (ZNH, SS, p. 247.) SU.

Double shuffle n. (1860s–1940s) a tap dance done in syncopation style. SNU.

Double team v. (1850s–1950s) to cause extra pressure or force upon something or someone. (ZNH, MM, p. 206; AEG, BB, p. 69.) SU.

Dough n. (1950s–1960s) money, though "bread" was much more commonly used. (CS, vol. 3, no. 2, p. 21.) See "Bread."

[The] Doughnut v., n. (1980s–1990s) driving a car fast and turning quickly so that it spins around in a circle. The doughnut is usually done in a stolen car. (JM, WPC.) WCU.

Do up v. (1940s–1950s) to cause something to happen; to effect change; tie a cord around the arm to distend a vein for the injection of heroin. (FR.) DCU, SNU.

Dout prep. (1880s–1950s) variant of "without." (FR.) SU.

Dower negro n. (1750s–1860s) a black person, usually a woman, given to a white bridegroom's family as part of a young white bride's dowery. (SBF, IHAT, p. 35.) SU.

Do what? interrog., exclam. (1900s–1990s) an expression of mock disbelief but more generally a request for clarity: "What did she say?" (FR.) (TR, AGD, p. 49.) SNU. See "Say what?"

Do which? See "Do What?"

Down adj., v. (1950s–1970s) word of approval, exciting, excellent, especially in a person's character; in the seventies, to be very hip, classy, cool, smart, handsome, intelligent, brave. "Down" was replaced by "together" in the sixties. Also to come "down" from a drug high; the control a pimp exerts over his prostitutes; to put one "down" means to attack one's self-esteem. (RDA, DDJ, p. 265; DW, TL, p. 61; FR; DC, BJ, p. 63; CRM, BP, p. 299; CS, vol. 3, no. 2, p. 21; IS, PSML, p. 314.) DCU, SNU, JMFU.

Downers n. (1960s) barbiturates or tranquilizers; frequently used to combat the frenzied effects of amphetamines. (RRL, DAZ, p. 66; CRM, BP, p. 199; CS, vol. 3, no. 2, p. 21.) DCU.

Down front adj. (1950s–1960s) to be nonsecretive; to disclose all. (DW, TL, p. 61.) SNCU. See "Come down front."

Down home; downhome n. (1930s–1950s) an honest, unpretentious life-style or personality; the simple life; "gutbucket"; country style; in jazz, an earthy way of playing; any single or all of the Southeastern states in the United States; the old country for black Americans. (RSG, JL, p. 88; JH, PBL, p. 84.) NU.

Down on adj. (1940s–1960s) to be disappointed with someone or something; also, with "to go," oral sex. (CS, vol. 3, no. 2, p. 21.) Examples: "I'm down on that cat, man, he fucked up with me last week when he didn't drop the shit where I told him"; and, "She went down on me on the first date." SNU.

Downtown; downtowning n., adj., v. (1920s–1990s) anywhere south of Harlem; to live or work there. (DW, TL, p. 61.) Example: "Hey, man, I hear you've moved up in life, you're downtown these days." Harlem use.

Down with [it] adj. (1930s–1940s; 1980s–1990s) to be in command of something; to understand a subject completely; to comprehend; to empathize. (DB, OHHJ, p. 15; MM, RB, p. 369; LH, BNF, p. 483.) Examples: "Give me some jams, and I can really get down with it"; and, "Miles, he be down with his shit, man." SNU.

Down with [one's] ax (1950s–1960s) in jazz, to be skilled in the professional use of an instrument; proficiency in working with one's materials. (RSG, JT, p. 75.) JMFU.

[The] Dozens n. (JH, PBL, p. 84.) See "Dirty Dozens."

Dozzing; Dossing v. (1930s–1990s) sleeping or napping, especially as a result of the effects of drugs. (FR.) Example: That cat always be dozzing and talking shit." DCU.

Draft n. (1930s–1940s) code word among blacks, used to indicate that a white person has just entered the room. (BH, LSB.) Example: "The minute we felt a draft, we changed the subject." SNU.

Drag v., n. (1900s–1920s) a musician who lags behind the beat "drags" it; a blues style; a tempo. (LH, BNF, p. 483.) JBWU.

Drag n. (1930s–1980s) a bore; a dull person, place, or incident. (HMH, HCWR, p. 808.) Example: "He a real drag. People kind of stop feeling good when he come around." SNU.

Drag n. (1940s–1990s) feminine attire when worn by a male. (DW, TL, p. 61.) SNU.

Drape(s) n. (1930s–1940s) a keenly draped zoot suit; to be draped was to be attired in the best of Harlem fashion. (CC, OMMM, NCCHD, p. 254; DC, BJ, p. 63.) Example: "That cat wears drapes big as his Ida Mae's bloomers." SNCU.

Drape shape n. See "Zoot suit."

Dreadlocks n. (1950s–1970s) braids; a hairstyle consisting of matted locks; originating in Jamaica, Caribbean. (FR.) SNU.

Dreambox n. (1940s) the human head. (DB, OHHJ, p. 137.) Example: "She got a dizzy dreambox on her shoulders." SNU.

Dreamers n. (1930s–1940s) sheets and blankets for the bed. (CC, OMMM, NCCHD, p. 254.) Rare. Harlem use.

Dress-and-breath n. (1920s–1930s) a lazy woman, especially a lazy housewife. (CM, Zora Neale Hurston, "The Guilded Six-Bits," p. 71.) SU.

Dr. Feelgood (1960s–1970s) a good feeling; name of a song by Aretha Franklin; to feel beautiful and fulfilled; to feel blessed. SNU. See "Happy."

Dribble; dribbling n. (1940s) to stutter. (DB, OHHJ, p. 137.) Example: "Adam always be dribbling. Make me want to choke it outta him." SNU.

Dribble-lip; dribbled-lipped n., adj. (1980s–1990s) a bottom lip that hangs excessively; to describe such a lip. (JM, WPC.) Example: "I can't kiss that dribble-lipped fool!" SCU, WCU.

Dried-barkers n. (1940s) furs. (DB, OHHJ, p. 137.) Harlem use.

Drift n. (1950s–1960s) one's style or meaning. (FR.) Example: "Do you get my drift?" SNU

Drill; drilling n., v. (1940s) walking; probably picked up from military use. (FR.) Example: "I was late for work and I had to drill all the way." NSU.

Drilling [for oil] v. (1940s) to have sexual intercourse. When the blues was still in the barrelhouses and the whorehouses in the 1900s and the 1920s, the music contained direct and blunt references to sexual activity, but when black musicians fell under the restrictions of recording studios, euphemisms and metaphors for sex began to multiply. This expression—one among hundreds of euphemisms for sex—can be heard in blues songs (Eddie "Cleanhead" Vinson, "Oil Man Blues," *Eddie "Cleanhead" Vinson and His Orchestra 1946–1947*, Bee Music Co., 1947). SNU.

Drink n. (1940s) any large body of water like an ocean or river. In the forties the term was used most frequently in reference to the Atlantic Ocean. (FR.) SNU.

Drink at the fuzzy cup v. (1980s–1990s) to perform cunnilingus. (EF, RDSL, p. 235.) South-central Los Angeles; SNCU.

Drink like a fish v. (1940s–1950s) to drink (usually alcohol) excessively. (FR.) Example: "He ain't good for nothing; all he do is drink like a fish." SNU.

Drinking muddy water v. (1930s–1950s) blues phrase; symbolic of having a difficult time or a hard life. (FR.) Example: "I ain't long for this world. I been sleeping in a hollow log and drinking muddy water." SNU.

Drive-by; drive-byed v. (1980s–1990s) to shoot at or to be shot at from a passing car. (JM, WPC, p. 7.) Example: "Billy got drive-byed last night. He's in the hospital." WCU.

Driver n. (1760s–1860s) a whip-carrying overseer on a slave plantation. (FGC, DARE, p. 200.) SU.

Driving pigs v. (1940s) snoring. (FR.) SU.

Dr. J basketball player Julius Erving.

Drop n. (1900s–1940s) a light rainfall. (FGC, DARE, p. 204.) SU.

Drop n. (1930s–1950s) a passenger in a taxi. (WF, DAS, p. 163.) Harlem use.

Drop; drap n. (1860s–1920s) an orphan, especially one whose parents are unknown. (CWC, CW, p. 155.) Example: "Nobody knowed she was pregnant, then she left her drap on Miss Howard's doorstep." SU.

Drop; dropped; dropping v. (1960s) to take drugs orally. (CS, vol. 3, no. 2, p. 23.) Example: "We dropped acid last night." DCU.

Drop a dime v. (1980s–1990s) to inform; confess; to set someone up for arrest; to call the police for the purpose of informing on someone. (TW, CK, p. 136; EF, RDSL, p. 236.) Examples: "Don't trust that dude, man, he'll drop a dime quick as you can bat your eyes"; and, "Man, you know, that sucker dropped a dime on me." DCU.

Drop [one's] drawers v. (1940s–1950s) a request or command to prepare for sexual activity, usually addressed by a male to a female; to take off panties. (DW, TL, p. 180.) SNU.

Drop a rack v. (1980s–1990s) to swallow a variety of narcotic pills at once. (EF, RDSL, p. 236.) DCU.

Dropper n. (1950s–1970s) an eyedropper used by a heroin addict as part of his "works." (CS, vol. 3, no. 2, p. 22.) See "Works." DCU.

Dropping dimes v. (1980s–1990s) to shoot three-pointers. (FR.) Basketball players' and fan use.

Dr. Thomas (1960s–1990s) a black man who identifies with white middle-class culture; a play on Uncle Tom; pejorative when referring to an educated black person, especially one with a Ph.D. (EF, RDSL, p. 235.) SNU.

Drugstore stuff n. (1960s) synthetic opiates obtained by an addict from a pharmacy; a substitute for heroin. (CS, vol. 3, no. 2, p. 22.) Example: "Man, I've been reduced to drugstore stuff." Watts, Los Angeles, use.

Drumstick(s) n. (1940s) the human leg or legs. (DB, OHHJ, p. 137.) Example: "Look at that joker running on them long drumsticks." SNU.

Drunk n. (1700s–1990s) drunkenness. (HMH, HCWR, p. 13.) SU.

Drunk as a Cooter adj. (1900s–1940s) to be falling down drunk. Example: "Him and Willie Boy get drunk as a cooter and can't nobody do nothing with them." Georgia and Alabama use. SNU. See "Cooter."

Drunk as a dog adj. (1850s–1960s) describing a person who vomits from too much alcohol. (FGC, DARE, p. 109.) SU.

Drunk as Cooter Brown adj. (1900s–1940s) to be extremely intoxicated. (FR.) Georgia and Alabama use. See "Cooter" and "Drunk as a Cooter."

Druthers n. (1790s–1990s) preference. (JMB, WB, p. 80.) SU.

Dry adj. (1900s–1960s) to have something dry is to have it plain; used especially in the case of food. (REK, G, p. 15.) Examples: "He just came right out and told me the dry truth, just like that"; and, "I couldn't eat that old dry peanut butter sandwich she made for me." SNU.

Dry bridge n. (1890s–1940s) an overpass or a bridge over a dry riverbed. (FGC, DARE, p. 214.) Example: "They finally put up a dry bridge over Cotter Creek." SU.

Dry drought n. (1880s–1960s) a period of excessive dry weather. (CCJ, NMGC, p. 7.) Example: "We ain't had nothing but dry drought all this year." SU.

Dry goods n. (1920s–1930s) clothing; zoot suit "drapes." Southern and northern use. (DB, OHHJ, p. 137; CC, OMMM, NCCHD, p. 254.) Example: "We take our dry goods down to Mister Handy's Cleaners on Forty-seventh and Cottage." SNU.

Dry long so adv. (1700s–1950s) plainly; without ornamentation or frills. (ZNH, TEWG, p. 71; AEG, BB, p. 298.) Example: "Every day was the same. We was going dry long so." SU. See "Dry so long."

Dry so adj., n. (1700s–1940s) plain; so so; okay but not great; dullness; fate. (AEG, BB, p. 298.) South Carolina and Georgia; SU. See "Dry long so" and "Dry so long."

Dry so long adv., adj. (1700s–1940s) variant of "dry long so"; dullness or fate. SU. See "Dry long so."

D.T. n. (1980s) city detective, especially a narcotics agent. (TW, CK, p. 136.) DCU.

Dubee n. (1980s–1990s) a marijuana cigarette. (EF, RDSL, p. 236.) DCU.

Ducat n. (1990s) money. (FR.) Example: "Last year I was into some big ducats when I had me a little hustle going." NCU.

Duckhead n. (1980s–1990s) a woman with short, nappy hair. (EF, RDSL, p. 234.) NCU. See "B.B. Head."

Ducks n. (1940s–1950s) tickets to any social event. (DB, OHHJ, p. 137.) Example: "Go down and stand in front of the stadium, somebody always down there selling ducks." NCU.

Ducking the card v. (1970s) to score below par. (GS, TT, p. 58.) Black golf players' use.

Dud n. (1960s–1990s) anything or anybody that is boring. (CS, vol. 3, no. 2, p. 22.) SNU.

Dud trumpet player Wilbur Odell Bascomb; (born 1916); Soloist for Erskine Hawkins's band.

Dude n. (1960s–1980s) black male term of address; any sharp, smart, respected man or boy. Derived from "duds"; a "dudsman" dealt in clothes (TMc, DA, p. 111; EP, DU, p. 213; CRM, BP, p. 299; CS, vol. 3, no. 2, p. 22; PM, UCLAS, p. 36.) Example: "Hey, Dude! How are you?" SNU. See "Duds."

Duds n. (1940s–1950s) one's finest clothes. (DB, OHHJ, p. 137.) Example: "He must have a boss job 'cause he's always decked out in some hip duds." NCU.

Due n. (1980s) residue trapped in a pipe after smoking base cocaine. (TW, CH, p. 148.) DCU. See "Con-con."

Dues n. (1940s–1960s) the ups and downs of life; one's responsibilities or commitments. (FR.) Example: "Man, I've paid my dues, I'm telling you, I shouldn't have to put up with no more shit." SNU.

Duffers n. (1990s) young women who perform fellatio as payment for crack cocaine. (FR.) DCU.

Duke Edward Kennedy Ellington, composer, pianist, band leader; born in Washington, D.C., April 29, 1899; in himself, a living institution of modern American culture; famous as the composer of such classics as "Sophisticated Lady," "Solitude," "In a Sentimental Mood," and "I Got It Bad and That Ain't Good."

Duke(s) n., v. (1930s–1940s) the fists or to fight with the fists. In mainstream American culture—if there is such a thing—"dukes," as early as the twenties, referred to the hands, the clenched fists, especially as they related to playing cards; black speakers used the word the same way (CC, OMMM, NCCHD, p. 254; DC, BJ, p. 62.); especially the fists, but—rarely—also refers to the knees (DB, OHHJ, p. 137). NCU.

Duking v. (1950s–1960s) fistfighting, especially on the street. (DC, BJ, p. 63.) MWU.

Dummy n. (1900s–1960s) stupid or dumb person (Redd Foxx frequently used the word). (FR.) Example: "If you can't help me, get outta my way, dummy." SNU.

Dump v. (1960s) to throw up from drug sickness. (CS, vol. 3, no. 2, p. 22.) Example: "The poor boy was so sick, he went in the toilet to dump." DCU.

Dump v. (1950s–1960s) to physically attack someone. (CRM, BP, p. 299.) Example: "Smitty dumped Joe in the first round." SCU, WCU.

Dumps n. (1940s–1980s) a state of sadness; to have the blues. (FR.) Examples: "I wish she wasn't always down in the dumps." See "Blues."

Dunk sauce n. (1920s–1940s) leftover cooking liquid. (FR.) Example: "The way you eat this stuff is you tear off yourself a piece of bread and just stick it here in this dunk sauce." SU.

Duppy n. (1750s–1960s) of Bantu origins; the spirit of a dead person; a ghost; featured often in African-American folktales; also used in the Caribbean. (HLB, LSS, p. 6; MC, NTH, p. 210.) SU.

Dust v. (1930s–1940s) to leave quickly, as if to raise a cloud of dust (EP, DU, p. 217; DB, OHHJ, p. 137; JH, PBL, 84.) SNU.

Dust n. (1930s–1990s) money (DC, BJ, p. 63; DR, BASL, p. 122.) Example: "You got any dust till payday?" MWU.

Dust v., adj. (1980s–1990s) to be defeated or rejected; finished. (PM, UCLAS, p. 18.) Los Angeles; SNCU.

Dust n. (1800s–1950s) dark-skinned black person. (FR.) SU.

Dust n. (1930s–1970s) a "dust" of something is a pinch or a small amount; "dust" is also snuff (FGC, DARE, p. 240.) SU.

Dust-bin n. (1940s) a grave. (DB, OHHJ, p. 137.) Example: "We all gotta go to the dust-bin one of these days, Lord knows." SNU.

Dusted adj., v. (1930s–1940s) to be killed, murdered, or buried, usually as an act of revenge. (DC, BJ, p. 62.) Example: "Them cats dusted James and just left him there in the alley." NCU.

Dusted adj., v. (1960s–1990s) to be defeated or hurt. (CS, vol. 3, no. 2, p. 22.) Watts, Los Angeles, use; YCU.

Duster n. (1920s–1940s) the buttocks. (FR.) Example: "If you'd get off your duster sometime you might feel better." SU. SNU. See "Rusty Dusty."

Dusty behind n. (1800s–1990s) rear end; variant of black ass. (RCC, SOC, p. 27.) See "Duster."

Dusty-butt n. (1900s–1940s) an ineffective, ugly prostitute; also a short person whose rear end, as the term implies metaphorically, drags along the ground. (ZNH, AM, p. 94.) Example: "Here come Dusty-butt, looking all evil and mean." SNU.

Dusty line n. (1980s–1990s) an old or obsolete expression or slang term. (JM, WPC, p.) Example: "One dusty line after another come outta his mouth." WCU, SCU.

Dutchess n. (1930s) form of address for any woman or girl. (CC, OMMM, NCCHD, p. 254.) Rare. SNU.

[To] Dirty dishes v. (1930s–1940s) to eat. (ZNH, AM, p. 85.) Example: "Come on, Mary, let's go down to the Soup Spoon and dirty some dishes." SNU.

Du-wah (1950s–1990s) a "soul" expression meaning nothing in particular, often used in rhythm and blues and black rock and roll songs of the fifties and later. (FR.) SNU.

Dyke n. (1950s–1960s) a lesbian; less common than "bulldagger," the most common black expression for a female homosexual. (CS, vol. 3, no. 2, p. 22.) SNU. See "Bulldagger" and "Bulldyke."

Dynamite n. (1960s–1990s) relatively undiluted drugs such as marijuana or heroin; the powerful effects of such drugs. (RRL, DAZ, p. 70; CLC, TS, p. 254.) DCU.

Dyno n. (1960s–1990s) any uncut, strong, and pure form of heroin. (RRL, DAZ, p. 70.) DCU.

Eagle n. (1940s–1950s) money. (GS, TT, p. 72) SNU.

Eagle fly (flies) on Friday; eagle-fly v. (1950s–1960s) to get paid on Friday. (FR; GS, TT, p. 72.) Example: "I can't wait till the eagle fly on Friday so I can make the scene and check the haps." SNU.

Eagle Rock v., n. (1920s–1940s) to dance; a dance, making the motions of an eagle in flight. (LS, GYY, p. 491.) Example: "Look at that sweet little mama Eagle Rock." SNU.

Ear man n. (1900s–1940s) musician who does not read sheet music, who plays "by ear." (Frederic Ramsey, Jr., and Charles Edward Smith, ed., *Jazzmen*, 1939, p. 190.) JMFU.

Ear music n. (1900s–1940s) improvisational music. (RSG, JL, p. 94.) Example: "The cat's a natural the way he just sits down and makes great ear music any time of the day or night." JMFU.

Early beam n. (1930s–1940s) morning; in the morning. Early morning is a mythical time in the blues. (DB, OHHJ, p. 137.) Example: "Catch you in the early beam." SNU. See "Early bright."

Early black n. (1940s) in the evening. (CC, OMMM, NCCHD, p. 255; DB, OHHJ, p. 137.) Example: "Catch you in the early black." SNU.

Early bright n. (1930s–1940s) the first daylight of the morning; dawn. Early morning is a mythical time in the blues. (CC, OMMM, NCCHD, p. 255; DB, OHHJ, p. 137.) Example: "Be here by early bright if you're going fishing with us." SNU.

Early candlelight n. (1900s–1940s) early evening; a way of measuring evening time before watches and clocks became common household objects. (FGC, DARE, p. 255.) SU.

Ears n. (1940s–1950s) to listen. (FR.) Example: "I got ears for what you're saying" (implies approval for what is being heard). SNU.

Earth pads n. (1940s) feet or shoes. (MHB, JS, np.) Example: "That cat's earth pads so big he can't find no shoes to fit him." Harlem use.

Ease v. (1930s–1990s) to be "cool," especially while leaving a scene. "Ease" can be heard often in the blues. (HLF, RJPD, p. 170.) Examples: "Raise the window, baby, let me ease on out of here. There's a man downstairs at your front door"; and, "I'm gone ease on out of this here place, catch you suckers later." SNU.

Easter rock n. (1920s–1940s) a very lively church ceremony held on Easter Sunday. The participants sing, shout, dance, and strut around the seats in the church, and later they gather outside and eat a big lunch of fried chicken, biscuits, sweet potatoes, greens, and fruit pies. (RF; FGC, DARE, p. 261.) Example: "You should see the sisters and the decons with their hand clapping and tambourine beating when Easter rock time come around." SU.

Eastman n. (1900s–1920s) a pimp; a man who is supported by a woman or women. (CVV, NH, p. 285.) Example: "Not many of these chicks out here think they can get along without an Eastman behind them who suppose to be looking out for them." Harlem use.

Easy adj., adv. (1930s–1950s) without effort; predisposed to; with a tendency toward. (AL, RS, p. 112.) Examples: "Me? I'm just hanging out easy waiting for my old lady to come home"; and, "Take it easy, Greasy." SNCU.

Easy-E n. (1980s) rapper and rap production company owner.

Easy ride n. (1980s–1990s) a loose woman. (EF, RDSL, p. 236.) South-central Los Angeles; SNU.

Easy rider n. (1900s–1950s) a ladies' man; a man sexually attractive to women; a sexually available woman. Originated among black speakers. (SL, RJON, p. 150; FGC, DARE, p. 262.) SNU.

Easy walker(s) n. (1920s–1940s) comfortable shoes. (LA, SM, p. 47.) SU.

Eat acorns v. (1930s–1940s) according to Zora Neale Hurston, "eat acorns" literally means "I give you one point." It is similar to the expressions "Eat dirt" and "Eat crow." "Eat acorns" was an expression used by rural black speakers; a baiting phrase; a command to take on one's responsibility to "put up or shut up." (ZNH, MM, pp. 222–223.) SRU. See "Eating dirt."

Eat cheese v. (1940s–1950s) originally a black expression; to ingratiate oneself with another. (FGC, DARE, p. 265.) SU.

Eat a fur burger v. (1980s–1990s) to perform cunnilingus. (EF, RDSL, p. 236.) South-central Los Angeles; SCU, YCU.

Eat dirt; eating dirt v. (1980s–1990s) to be humiliated. (FR.) Example: "Girl, you know Betty, she's gonna make that dog eat dirt if she catch George hitting on that young cherry." See "Eat acorns."

Eatings n. (1920s–1930s) food. (FR.) Example: "I ain't got no eatings in the house, man, but I can treat you at the restaurant around the corner." SNU.

Eat it up v. (1950s–1960s) to enjoy anything immensely. (FR.) Example: "I catch Mingus and every time I eat it up." SNU.

Eat out v. (1980s–1990s) to perform cunnilingus. (EF, RDSL, p. 236.) South-central Los Angeles; SCU, YCU.

Eat pie v. (1980s–1990s) to perform cunnilingus. (EF, RDSL, p. 236.) South-central Los Angeles; YCU, SCU.

Eat pussy v. (1950s–1960s) often used in a negative manner; to perform cunnilingus. (FR.) Example: "Go eat pussy! Get outta my face!" SNU. See "Eat dirt."

Ebonics n. (1980–1990) essentially a Creole language; black speech; Black English. (JEH, AAC, p. 22.) Scholarly use.

[Mister] Eddie n. (1920s) a white man; companion of Miss Ann or Miss Mary. (CVV, NH, p. 286.) Harlem use.

Edge n. (1960s) a knife, usually a switchblade, carried in the pocket as a concealed weapon. (DC, BJ, p. 63.) Rare. MWU.

Educated Pussy n. (1950s–1960s) a weak or ineffective man. (RDP, SRO, p. 4) Harlem; PPU, SCU.

Eel-ya-dah (1940s–1950s) black existential verbal jazz sounds originating in bebop. (RSG, JL, p. 95.) See "Oo-bla-dee." JMFU.

Eh, eh! exclam. (1700s–1940s) a Gullah expression of excitement or alarm. (AEG, BB, p. 299; RCC, SOC, p. 14.) South Carolina and Georgia use.

Ego tripping v. (1970s) to flaunt one's sense of self-importance. (GS, TT, pp. 159–160.) SNU.

Egyptian Paradise Seed n. (1920s–1930s) seed of Amonium Melegreta used in the conjuring quest for success. It is used to feed a saint symbolically. (ZHH, MM, p. 337.) SU.

Eight-ball n. (1950s) a "square" person; an unsophisticated person. (FR.) Example: "That sucker ain't nothing but a eight-ball, always hanging around trying to be cool." SNU.

[An] Eighth n. (1950s–1960s) short for an eighth of heroin; about sixty grains of morphine. (DW, TL, p. 180; RRL, DAZ, p. 70.) DCU.

Eight-rock n. (1930s–1950s) derogatory term for a very dark-skinned black person. (ZNH, AM, p. 94.) Example: "Her mama wouldn't let her marry Billy 'cause he such a eight-rock." SNU.

Eight-to-the-bar adv., adj. (1930s–1940s) describing dancing the Boogie-Woogie; a dance done to boogie-woogie music. (RSG, JL, p. 96.) Example: "You shoulda seen everybody cutting up eight-to-the-bar last night." Rare. SNCU.

Eighty-eight (88) n. (1940s) a piano. (DB, OHHJ, p. 137; RSG, JL, p. 95.) Example: "Man, you see how that cat handled that eighty-eight?" JMFU.

El D n. (1960s–1990s) short for Cadillac "El Dorado." (EF, RDSL, p. 234.) South-central Los Angeles; SNCU, YCU, SCU.

Eleanor Club n. (1940s) a mythic organization of black women working as domestics in the southeastern states. The name refers to Eleanor Roosevelt, a fighter for the rights of black women and men. (FGC, DARE, p. 284.) SU. See "Elizabeth Club."

Element n. (1870s–1890s) the sky or the atmosphere. (CCJ, NMGC, p. 168.) Example: "They couldn't put the fire out and the smoke got all up in the element." SU.

Elephant fair n. (1900s–1920s) a jumping game and song played by black children in the south. (BJ, BLH, SD, p. 61, p. 220.) SU.

Elephant year n. (1940s–1950s) any year filled with bad luck. (FGC, DARE, p. 287.) Example: "I shoulda knowed we'd loose the house, 'cause this here is elephant year." Virginia use.

Eleven-card n. (1920s–1930s) a card game—a type of coon-can—played in the south, usually for two players. (ZNH, MM, p. 37.) Example: "Both of us get together and play eleven-card every Friday night." SU.

Eleven-card players n. (1920s–1930s) coon-can players. (ZNH, MM, p. 222.) SRU. See "Eleven-card."

Eleventy-eleven; leventy-leven n. (1890s) eleven. (RSG, JL, p. 288.) Example: "If I done told you one time I done told you eleventy-eleven times to chop some wood before you come in the house." Southern use.

Elizabeth Club n. (1940s) a mythic organization of black women working as domestics in the southern states. SU. See "Eleanor Club."

Elsehow conj. (1900s–1940s) a Gullah form of "or else" or "how else." (AEG, BB, p. 224.) Example: "If you not here by six I don't see elsehow you gone get to go with us." SU.

Elseways adv. (1900s–1940s) a Gullah form of "otherwise." (FGC, DARE, p. 291.) Example: "Don't miss the train elseways you have to take the bus." SU.

Empress of the Blues Bessie Smith, blues singer; born April 15, 1894 in Cattanooga, Tennessee, and died in Clarksdale, Mississippi, on September 26, 1937.

Enamel n. (1940s) the human skin. (DB, OHHJ, p. 137.) Example: "She got some pretty enamel. I just love to look at her." Harlem use.

[The] End superl. (1950s) of the highest order. (FR.) Example: "The show, man, was the end!" NCU.

Ends n. (1950s–1960s) money needed to live on; a payment or reward. (CLC, TS, p. 254.) Example: "Sorry, I just ain't got the ends to pay the rent this month." SNU.

Endways adj., adv. (1900s–1940s) backwards. (FR.) Example: "You got the damned thing endways, no wonder it won't go in." SNU.

Entitle n. (1860s–1880s) variant of title; entitlement; a person's name; especially refers to the name a slave gave himself or herself. (Booker T. Washington, *Up from Slavery*, p. 24.) Example: "After slavery I took the entitle of Hawkins 'cause I never liked the master's name nohow." SU.

Enty interrog. exlam. (1840s–1920s) a Gullah exclamation. Probably a corruption of "Ain't it so" or "Ain't it the truth." (William Gilmore Simms, *Eutaw*, p. 210.) South Carolina and Georgia coastal use.

Equipped adj. (1960s) to be in proper shape; dressed well; to be "cool" or "hip." (DC, BJ, p. 63.) Example: "She always falls on the scene equipped." MWU.

Ervine n. (1960s) a policeman—stemming from the "E" on the license plates of Los Angeles police cars. (CS, vol. 3, no. 2, p. 23.) Watts, Los Angeles, use.

Essence of Bend-over n. (1920s–1930s) a conjuring potion used to conquer someone sexually. (ZNH, MM, p. 337.) SU.

Essence of St. Michael n. (1920s–1930s) a conjuring potion. (ZNH, MM, p. 336.) SU.

Essence of Van n. (1920s–1930s) a conjuring solution made with oil of lemon grass. (ZNH, MM, p. 336.) SU.

Essence of Van Van n. (1920s–1930s) a good-luck potion made from alcohol and lemon grass; used in conjuring work. (ZNH, MM, p. 336.) SU. See "Essence of Van."

[Great] Est; -est superl. (1860s–1960s) of Gullah origin; a suffix used as though it were a word itself, meaning the greatest, the best, the most ("more-est"); the nth degree. (AEG, BB, p. 314; CC, CW, p. 134; RSG, JT, p. 138.) SU.

Ethiopian n. (1940s) an African-American. (WF, DAS, p. 55; FGC, DARE, p. 310.) Picked up from white use. SNU.

Ethiopian opera n. (1840s) minstrel show. Picked up from white use. (FGC, DARE, p. 310.) SNU.

Ethiopian paradise n. (1900s–1930s; 1950s) alternate for "Nigger Heaven" or Harlem or any black community; before the fifties, the top floor of a theatre—reserved for black people. (FGC, DARE, p. 310.) SNU.

Eve and Adam (1900–1930) black speakers in the south would often reverse the names of the biblical first couple, so that the female preceded the male. (FR.) SU.

Evenwhich pron. (1900s–1930s) variant form of "whichever." (FR.) Example: "Take evenwhich one you like best." SU.

Everybody and they momma n. (1940s–1950s) every conceivable person; all. (FR.) Example: "Everybody and they momma was out of there before the law came." SNU.

Every last one n. (1920s–1940s) everyone. (FR.) Example: "Every last one of us was out of there before the whistle stopped blowing." SNU.

Every once in a while (1840s–1900s) at intervals. (FR.) Example: "Every once in a while you get to thinking something is wrong out here." SNU.

Every post man on his beat n. (1930s–1940s) kinky hair that stands in strands or patches. (ZNH, AM, p. 94.) SNU.

Every tub [on its own black bottom] n. (1920s–1940s) in jazz, improvisation independent of any prearrangement. (RE, IM, p. 472.) JMFU.

Every-which-way; everywhicherway prep. (1830s–1930s) of Virginia slave origin; whichever; going in many different directions at once; crazy; confusion. (FR; ECLA, NN, p. 265.) SU.

Evil; evilling adj., v. (1930s–1990s) usually a reference to a particular person or an "unnatural" effect, meaning bad or very terrible; disillusioned; disappointed; angry; mean. (DB, OHHJ, p. 137; FGC, DARE, p. 320; CC, OMMM, NCCHD, p. 255.) Example: "Sallie Mae can't do nothing with that boy—he's always out in the streets with that gang of his, and you know they ain't up to nothing but studying evilling night and day out there." SNU.

Evil eye n. (1700s–1900s) refers to the superstitious belief that the eye(s) of a person can generate evil enough to jinx or even kill, as, "If looks could kill." Probably stems from the notion that the eye reveals true human emotions; although especially believed by black American slaves, this superstition occurs in many cultures. (FR.) SNU.

Exoduster n. (1878–1980s) any ex-slave who migrated north after the Civil War. (FGC, DARE, p. 323.) Example: "We was all exodusters after Mister Lincoln changed the law." SU.

Expense n. (1940s) a newborn baby. (DB, OHHJ, p. 137.) Example: "I see you folks got another expense in the cradle." Harlem use.

Explosion n. (1940s) in jazz, a very loud burst of chords. (RSG, JL, p. 98.) Example: "If you sat up close you could hear better when the band really hit one them beautiful explosions." JMFU.

Extry adj. (1860s–1950s) a variant form of extra. (FGC, DARE, p. 325.) Example: "I need extry time to do this job." SU.

Eyeball; eyeballing v. (1900s–1960s) to look; to see; originally used by black speakers (FGC, DARE, p. 327; ZNH, MM, p. 160). Example: "Everybody was eyeballing me when I walked in the joint." SNU. See "Reckless Eyeballing."

Eyefuck v. (1970s–1980s) obvious ogling of the opposite sex. See "Reckless eyeballing."

Eyes n. (1940s–1950s) an expression of approval or desire. "No eyes" expresses aversion or disapproval; also short for "four-eyes"—referring to eyeglasses. (FR.) Example: "I got eyes for her."

Eyes bigger than [one's] stomach (1930s–1950s) greediness; often used by a parent regarding a child who has piled more food than he or she can eat onto their plate. SNU.

F

Face(s) n. (1930s–1940s) a stranger, especially an unknown white person. (DB, OHHJ, p. 138; ZNH, AM, p. 88.) Example: "I don't know any white people, man, they just faces to me." Harlem use.

Face bowl n. (1800s–1950s) shallow pan; bathroom sink. (FR.) SNU.

Fab adj. (1990s) short for "fabulous." (FR.) YCU.

Fade; fade away v., n. (1940s–1990s) to be quiet or to leave; depart; in the nineties, a type of haircut for males that gradually becomes shorter in back; a Negro who fades into a white way of life. (MHB, JS, np) SNU.

Faded adj. (1990s) to be drunk or intoxicated from drugs. (FR.) YCU, SCU, WCU.

Faded boogie n. (1950s) a black informer; a "white nigger." (FR.) SNU.

Fag n. (1900s–1950s) a cigarette. (WF, DAS, p. 176.) SNU.

Faggot; fag n. (1900s–1950s) derogatory expression for a male homosexual. (WF, DAS, p. 176; DC, BJ, p. 64; RDA, DDJ, p. 265; RCC, SOC, p. 42.) SNU.

Fagingy-fagade n. (1920s) a white person. Pig Latin. (CVV, NH, p. 285.) Harlem; SNU.

Faintified adj. (1930s) faint; dizzy; weak. (FGC, DARE, p. 335.) SU.

Fairy n. (1940s) a male homosexual. (FR.) SNU.

Fake v. (1900s–1950s) etymology unknown; to improvise the forgotten notes of a song; from the twenties to the forties, in music, to make the best of a lean situation; to sing or play without other musical backing. (RSG, JL, p. 99.) JMFU, SNU.

Fake book n. (1920s–1930s) a record book of chord progressions used by jazz musicians working at dances. (RSG, JL, p. 100.) JMFU.

Faker n. (1920s–1940s) a musician with no command of written music. (RSG, JL, p. 101.) JMFU.

Fake [the] funk v. (1990s) to pretend to be "in the know," or "hip"; to pretend to feel what one does not feel. (FR.) YCU.

Fake on [one] v. (1980s–1990s) on the west coast, to shun or avoid one; on the east coast, to deceive or humiliate. (EF, RDSL, p. 236.) SNCU.

Fake out v. (1960s–1990s) to mislead; to deceive or humiliate. (FR.) SNCU. See "Fake on [one]."

Fall v. (1950s–1960s) to be arrested. (CLC, TS, p. 140; DW, TL, p. 180) Example: "Bobby fell last week, and look at him, he's back on the street Monday morning." SCU.

Fall by [in; up] v. (1890s–1940s) act of arriving. (FR.) Example: "Ya'll fall by when you down our way, you hear." SNU.

Fallout; falling out n. (1740s–1860s) Some slaves sometimes met around a camp fire on plantations to hold religious ceremonies. When the sisters and brothers felt happy or at one with God, they would "fall out." Falling out consisted of convulsive shouting and flailing, rolling on the ground or floor from religious ecstasy. (SK, PC, p. 77.) SU.

Falling star n. (1700s–1940s) believed by many (black and white) to represent the spirit of someone who has made a pact with the devil. (MT, DAF, p. 108; FR.) SNU.

Fall off; drop off v. (1920s–1940s) in jazz, to lower the instrumental tone by playing or blowing, which reduces the volume. (RSG, JL, pp. 101–102.) Example: "I dug the hip way the brass section fell off just before Bird came in with his solo." JMFU.

Fall out v. (1930s–1960s) to be surprised or overcome; to be upset; to engage in an angry argument; to argue; to suddenly laugh with great vigor. (CC, OMMM, NCCHD, p. 255; DB, OHHJ, p. 138.) Example: "Girl, when I saw him come in looking like that I fell out." SNU.

False n. (1920s–1940s) a lie. (REK, G, p. 20; HMH, HCWR, p. 12.) Example: "She told her mother a false." SU.

False [fake] fingers adj. (1920s–1940s) in jazz, a way of "choking" the trumpet with the fingers to produce certain desired effects. (RSG, JT, p. 88.) JMFU.

Familious adj. (1880s–1920s) variant of "familiar." (CC, CW, p. 112.) SU.

Family n. (1950s–1960s) a pimp and the women who are in his "care." (SH, GL, p. 212.) PPU.

Fan v. (1890s–1940s) to flaunt one's self; to speak or hit. (FR; FGC, DARE, pp. 352–353.) SU.

Fancy girl n. (1680s–1860s) a slave girl or woman used by a slave-owner for sexual pleasure; such a girl invariably worked in the "big house." (Joel Williamson, *New People: Miscegenation and Mulattoes in the United States*, 1980, pp. 68–69.) SU.

Fancy stroll n. (1980s) the main drag where street life is at its most intense; any city. (FR.) SNU.

Fangs n. (1950s) a musician's lips and teeth and fingers; also, his skill. (RSG, JL, p. 102.) JMFU. See "Chops."

Fanner n. (1850s–1880s) a small and shallow basket. (CCJ, NMGC, p. 168.) Example: "Go pick some grapes and put them in this fanner." Georgia and the Carolinas use.

Far out adj. (1950s–1960s) extremely good; wonderfully satisfying; something that defies any convention or established mode. (RSG, JL, pp. 102–103.) SNCU.

Farina Allen Clayton Hoskins. Child actor in "Our Gang" shorts.

Farm n. (1930s–1950s) prison; short for work farm. (FR.) SU, MWU.

Fast Aleck n. (1930s) a fast-moving male or female. (ZNH, MM, p. 217.) SU.

Fast luck; fast luck oil n., v. (1920s–1930s) a good-luck potion used in hoodoo rituals; conjuring solution made with oil of citronella. New Orleans. (ZNH, MM, p. 336.) SU.

Fast Scrubbing Essence n. (1920s–1930s) a conjuring solution made of thirteen different oils and used for business success. (ZNH, MM, p. 336.) SU.

Fast track n. (1960s) (FR.) SNU. See "Track" and "Slow track."

Fat adj. (1930s–1950s) in jazz, a full tone; also wealthy. (RSG, JL, p. 103.) JMFU.

Fat around the heart adj. (1930s) to react with fear; scared. (ZNH, MM)

Fat cat n. (1900s–1980s) impressive, wealthy person. (FR.) SNU.

Fat city n., adj. (1940s–1960s) fine state of affairs; good luck; wealth. (FR.) NCU.

Fathead alto and tenor saxophone player David Newman (born February 24, 1933); worked with Ray Charles and others.

Fatha; Father jazz pianist Earl Hines (born December 28, 1905).

Father's Day n. (1960s) day a father must appear in domestic court regarding child support. (FR.) SNCU.

Father Divine George Baker, evangelist; born 1880, died 1965.

Fat lip n. (1940s–1960s) obnoxious talk. (FR.) Example: "Don't give me any fat lip." SNU.

[Bet a] Fat man v. (1950s–1960s) an oath. (RSG, JT, pp. 137–138.) Example: "I'll bet a fat man he doesn't make it back by tomorrow." SNU.

Fat Meat n. (1940s–1960s) the truth. (FR.) Example: "She don't believe fat meat is greasy, but if she comes around here messing with my man again she's going to find out what the real world is like." SNU.

Fatmouth; fat mouth v. (1650s–1990s) to talk excessively; the concept of "fat-mouth": *da-baa* [Mandingo]. (HV, AHAE, p. 140; FGC, DARE, p. 368.) SNU.

Father Neptune Harlem name for clarinet player Milton Mesirow (better known as Mezz Messrow) in the 1930s and 1940s. See "Mezz Messrow."

Fat nuts n. (1980s–1990s) a quality of a mean, forceful man; courage. (WKB, JMC, PS, p. 49.) Example: "That dude, Maddog, he got some fat nuts man, you see the way he made Lindo pick up that fork." Prison and northern and southern street culture use.

Fats Antoine Domino. Piano player, singer, and songwriter; born February 26, 1928.

Fats n. (1900s–1930s) jazzmen in general. (FR.) Rare. JMFU.

Faust n. (1930s–1940s) an ugly girl or woman; a blind date; an ugly person, male or female.

Favor v. (1880s–1940s) to resemble. (HMH, HCWR, p. 360.) Example: "She favors her mother." SU.

Fay n. (1920s–1950s) short for ofay: a white person. (MM, RB, p. 62.) SNU.

Feature v. (1930s–1940s) to comprehend; understand; an expression of enthusiastic approval; to resemble. (FG, DARE, p. 378.) Example: "She sure feature her mama." SNU.

Federal joint n. (1950s–1960s) a federal state prison. (CLC, TF, p. 155.) PU, SCU.

Fed up adj. (1920s–1950s) bored; disgusted. (FR.) SNU.

Feed vt. (1940s) in jazz, chords backing a soloist. (RSG, JL, p. 104.) JMFU.

Feel [one's] stuff v. (1930s–1940s) to operate out of one's deepest and truest feelings. (FR.) SNU.

Feel a draft v. (1940s–1950s) Lester Young's phrase; the sensing of racism in a white person; to sense the presence of hostility or racism. (RSG, JL, p. 105.) Example: two black men at a table with a white man, and the white man makes a statement one of the black men takes to be racist; this black man says to the other black man, "Is it just me? I feel a draft." NCU.

Feeler n. (1900s–1930s) the water "scout" for the minister at a baptism. He checks the river bottom for danger—rocks or pits or anything else to be avoided. (FR.) SU.

Feelers n. (1940s) fingers. (DB, OHHJ, p. 138.) Example: "Get your feelers off me—they're cold." Harlem use.

Feeling n. (1930s–1940s) emotional honesty. (FR.) See "Soul."

Feeling good v. (1920s–1940s) the first euphoric stage of intoxication. (FR.) SNU.

Feets n. (1880s–1930s) feet. (ECLA, CS, p. 6; ZNH, AM, p. 92.) SU.

Fell; fall v. (1940s–1960s) to be put in prison or to endure any terrible condition. (CLC, TS, p. 254.) SCU, DCU.

Fellow n. (1930s–1940s) any white man. The reverse of white use, which characterized Negroes as black "fellows." (JSF, AON, p. 57.) SU. See "Black fellow."

Fence n. (1930s–1990s) a very old term, dating back to the 1690s; person or place dealing in stolen goods. (EP, DU, 235.) SNCU.

Fend; fen v. (1920s–1930s) to defend. (AEG, BB, p. 301; HMH, HCWR, p. 147.) Example: "I can fend you today, sho, but what you gone do tomorrow when I'm gone." SU.

Fender benders n. (1970s–1980s) capsules of barbiturates. (EF, BVV, p. 44.) South-central Los Angeles; DCU.

Fessor n. (1900s–1930s) form of "professor"; any intelligent man. (FGC, DARE, p. 392.) SNU.

[Jungle] Fever n. (1950s–1990s) originally "the fever" referred to those members of the white race obsessively attracted to black men or women. After the appearance of the movie *Jungle Fever*, the term came to refer to any black man attracted to white women or vice versa. (FR.) YCU, SCU, SNU.

Few tickers n. (1940s) a few (clock) minutes (ticks). (DB, OHHJ, p. 138.) Example: "How tight. I'll be there in just a few tickers." Harlem use. See "Ticks."

Fews and twos n. (1940s) a small sum of money. (DB, OHHJ, p. 138; CC, OMMM, NCCHD, p. 255.) Example: "How you expect me to buy you a drink when here I am skating on fews and twos?" Harlem use.

Fey n. (1940s–1970s) a white person. (DR, BASL, p. 127.) SNCU.

Fey cat(s) n. (1940s–1970s) a white boy or man. (DR, BASL, p. 127.) SNCU.

Fiddle cases n. (1940s) shoes. (DB, OHHJ, p. 138.) Example: "He come in here with them big fiddle cases tracking up my new carpet, I could've killed that joker." (FR.) Harlem; South Side, Chicago use.

Fiddle song n. (1860s–1890s) a nonreligious rag song, known otherwise as a sinful song or devil song. (FGC, DARE, p. 402). SU. See "Corn songs."

Field nigger [Negro] n. (1630s–1960s) originally a black slave who worked crops, as opposed to one who worked in the home of the slaveholder. Malcolm X extended and popularized the concepts: a field nigger was more likely to become a revolutionary while the house nigger was more likely to be an Uncle Tom. (SBF, IHAT, p. 35; Malcolm X, "The Old Negro and the New Negro," speech, 1971, [in *The End . . .* 1989], pp. 86–87.) SNU. See "Field darky" and "Hoe nigger."

Fiend; fiendish; fiendish-back n., adj. (1960s) any thing or person of positive quality; outstanding. (CS, vol. 3, no. 2, p. 23.) Watts, Los Angeles, use.

Fifteenth Amendment Persuasion (1860s) a black person; picked up from white use during the Civil War. (JSF, AON, p. 159, 252.) SU.

Fifty-cents bag n. (1980s–1990s) a five-dollar bag of marijuana. (EF, RDSL, p. 237.) DCU.

Fifty-eleven; fifty-'leven n. (1890s–1950s) a profuse or uncountable quantity. (FR.) SNU.

Fight dirty v. (1980s) to fistfight without observance of any sort of honor code. (KCJ, JS, p. 122.) SNU.

File; filed; filing v. (1960s) may be a variant form of "vile"; contemptuous treatment; meanness; cruelty. (CS, vol. 3, no. 2, p. 23; WF, DAS, pp. 181–182.) Example: "He get around his boys he always filing, but you get him alone he just as nice as a puppy." Watts, Los Angeles, use.

Filled up v. (1800s–1950s) filled. Example: "Go see for yourself, the bucket is filled up like I told you." (FR.) SU.

Filling station n. (1980s–1990s) liquor store. (EF, RDSL, p. 237.) SNU.

Fillmill n. (1940s) a tavern. (DB, OHHJ, p. 138.) Example: "Nobody can get Buddy out of that fillmill once he gets his paycheck cashed." Rare. SNU.

Fill up the windows v. (1930s–1940s) in jazz, to follow a phrase by another musician with a refrain or filler phrase. Buck Clayton (in the film *Lady Day: The Many Faces of Billie Holiday*, 1990) said he always let Billie do her number, then he'd just come in at the end and "fill up the windows." (FR.) JMFU.

Filly n. (1940s) a young woman. (DB, OHHJ, p. 138.) Example: "He thinks if he puts on his gladrags every filly on the block will fall for him." SNU.

Fin n. (1930s–1940s) a five-dollar bill. (MHB, JS, np; CS, vol. 3, no. 2, p. 23.) Example: "Hey, jack, can you lay a fin on me till day after tomorrow?" SU.

Final v. (1940s) to leave the scene; also, in street culture, to dump or get rid of the person hired to work a con on somebody. (IS, TB, p. 311; CC, OMMM, NCCHD, p. 255; DB, OHHJ, p. 138.) Example: "Cab copped a final and didn't come back till three in the morning." Harlem use.

Finale n. (1940s) death; to die. (DB, OHHJ, p. 138.) Harlem use. See "Final thrill."

Final thrill n. (1940s) death. (DB, OHHJ, p. 138.) Example: "When I feel that final thrill I'll be ready, but until then I'm getting every thrill I can get."

Finally at last (1920s–1950s) finally; at the end. (FR.) SNU.

Find a stump to fit [one's] rump (1900s–1960s) spoken with irony; a friendly invitation to sit down, usually on a chair or a couch. (DW, TL, p. 181.) SNU.

Fine v. (1930s–1950s) often a woman's term for handsome; pretty; good-looking. (DB, OHHJ, p. 138.) Example: "He's so fine!" SNU.

Fine and mellow adj. (1930s–1950s) very satisfying. (FR.) See "Fine." SNU.

Fine as wine adj. (1930s–1950s) quite pleasing. (FR.) SNU.

Fine banana n. (1930s–1940s) any light-complexioned "colored" girl or woman. (DB, OHHJ, p. 138.) SNU.

Fine brown frame n. (1930s–1940s) the shapely body of any attractive African-American woman. (MHB, JS, np.) Example: "My baby got a fine brown frame, so fine she keeps me tame." SNU.

Fine dinner n. (1940s) any attractive female. (CC, OMMM, NCCHD, p. 255; DB, OHHJ, p. 138.) Harlem use. See "Fine brown frame" and "Fine fryer."

Fine fryer n. (1940s) an attractive young woman. (DB, OHHJ, p. 138.) SNU.

Fine props n. See "Props."

Fine thing n. (1940s) any attractive young woman. (MHB, JS, np.) SNU.

Fine weather n. (1940s) any attractive girl or young woman. (MHB, JS, np.) Southern Negro college student use. See "Freezing weather."

Finger-artist n. (1940s–1950s) a lesbian. (FR.) SNCU.

Fingerfuck(ing) v. (1960s–1970s) finger fondling of the female genitals. (FR.) SNU.

Finger popper; finger-popping n., v. (1950s–1960s) excited snapping of fingers in time to music; a very spirited listener is said to be finger-popping—probably originally used more by white jazzmen than black but became extremely popular among black musicians in the late fifties, early sixties. (RSG, JL, p. 106; WF, DAS, p. 183.) JMFU.

Finger root n. (1780s–1890s) root of an ash tree used in hoodoo ceremonies. (FR.) New Orleans use.

Fingers n. (1930s–1950s) a jazz pianist; sometimes also means pickpocket. (FR.) SNU.

Fire v. (1880s–1990s) to discharge from paid employment; to throw someone out of place by force; in the forties, a cigarette (DB, OHHJ, p. 138; DC, BJ, p. 64). See "Blaze on."

Fire-eater n. (1840s–1880s) any white southerner opposed to freeing the slaves. (JSF, AON, p. 240.) NU.

Firefight n. (1990s) gun battle, especially on the streets or in an alley. Term used in rap songs. (FR.) WCU.

Fire on v. (1970s–1990s) to hit another person suddenly and/or unexpectedly; asking questions in a rapid-fire manner. (DC, BJ, p. 64; EF, RDSL, p. 237.) Example: "If you go up there they will fire on you 'fore you can blink." SCU, YCU. See "Blaze on" and "Fire."

Fire [one] up v. (1960s) to light one's cigarette or reefer. (CS, vol. 3, no. 2, p. 24.) Example: "Hey, man, fire your girl up; her joint burned out." DCU.

First base n. (1930s–1970s) a woman's breasts. Example: "After he got to first base he knew he could go all the way." SNU.

First dark n. (1650s–1890s) twilight. (FR.) SU.

First fowl-crow n. (1700s–1880s) around one or two in the morning; the time when the rooster begins crowing just after midnight. (FR.) SU.

First Lady of Swing Ella Fitzgerald, singer; born April 25, 1918, in Newport News, Virginia; worked with Duke Ellington, Louis Armstrong, and many others.

First thirty n. (1940s) the month of January—a common phrase despite the fact that January has thirty-one days. (DB, OHHJ, p. 138.) Harlem use.

Firsts n. (1870s–1990s) traditionally, African-Americans first of their race to occupy a given position of prestige in any American career. (FR.) SNU.

Fish n. (1930s–1960s) a woman; sex. (JH, PBL, p. 84; EF, RDSL, p. 237.) Example: "Going down to Butler Street and get me some fish." SNU.

Fish-hooks n. (1940s) fingers. (DB, OHHJ, p. 138.) Example: "Keep your nasty fish-hooks outta my plate." SNU.

Fish horn n. (1940s) a saxophone. (DB, OHHJ, p. 138.) Example: "Nobody handles a fish horn like Bird." JMFU.

Fishing for food (1940s) gossiping. (MHB, JS, np.) Example: "Mary Alice is always fishing for food." SU.

Fist junction n. (1980s–1990s) the moment at which a fistfight starts. (EF, RDSL, p. 237.) Watts and South-central Los Angeles use.

Fit n. (1950s–1960s) short for "outfit"; any good-looking apparel, especially while being worn. (DC, BJ, p. 64.) SNU.

Five-and-dime adj. (1980s–1990s) sleezy or without class. (EF, RDSL, p. 237.) Example: "Girl, you seen Susie with that five-and-dime outfit on last night?" SNU.

[To give one] Five v., n. (1930s–1950s) to slap hands together as a form of greeting; the five fingers on a hand. (HLF, RJPD, p. 170.) SNU. See "Skin."

Five-by-five adj. (1950s) short and fat. (FR.) SNU.

Five calendars n. (1960s–1970s) five months. (JH, PBL, p. 84.) Example: "If I haven't lost this weight in five calendars I'm going to a fat farm." New York use.

Five-cent paper n. (1960s) a small amount—less than one ounce —of heroin sold in a folded piece of paper for five dollars. (RRL, DAZ, p. 76.) DCU.

Five-dollar bag n. (1960s) short for a five-dollar bag of heroin— about an eighth of a teaspoon. It is usually diluted with quinine or milk sugar. (RRL, DAZ, p. 76.) DCU.

Five-O n. (1980s–1990s) the police. (TW, CK, p. 136.) New York City use; WCU.

[The] Fives (1920s–1940s) a "bluesy" piano style; sad; funky. Also, "the fives" refers to the fingers of a single hand. (RSG, JL, p. 96; DB, OHHJ, p. 138.) JMFU.

Fives n. (1960s) Benzedrine or amphetamine tablets. (RRL, DAZ, p. 76.) DCU.

Fix n. (1940s–1960s) usually an injection of heroin; a bribe. (IS, PSML, p. 314; CLC, TS, p. 254; RRL, DAZ, p. 76.) Example: "If you wanna know what went down, Golden Boy died from the fix Joey gave him." DCU.

Fixing v. (1840s–1950s) preparing for an occasion; imminent; about to occur. (FR.) Example: "I was fixing to go to the market just before you came." SNU.

Fizzical culturist n. (1940s) a bartender. (DB, OHHJ, p. 138.) Harlem use.

Flag spot n. (1930s–1940s) bus stop. (FR.) Example: "Sadie be out at the flag stop at seven every morning; you can set your watch by her." SNU.

Flag stop (1940s) a bus stop. (DB, OHHJ, p. 138.) SNU. See "Flat spot."

Flagwaver; flagwaving n. (1930s) the high point in a jazz performance.

Flake(s) n. (1980s–1990s) small particles of cocaine, smaller than "rocks." (TW, CK, p. 136.) DCU.

Flake out v. (1980s–1990s) to pass out, as from a narcotic high. (EF, RDSL, p. 237.) DCU.

Flam n. (1930s–1960s) an onomatopoeic jazz term meaning a rapid exchange of beats. (RSG, JT, p. 94.) JMFU.

Flam n., v. (1960s–1970s) a con game; to deliberately misrepresent a situation. (FR.) SNU.

Flame cooking v. (1980s–1990s) smoking cocaine base by putting the pipe over a stove flame. (TW, CK, p. 136.) DCU.

Flapper(s) n. (1900s–1940s) popular term among black speakers; from the beginning, in the first decade of the century, a "flapper" was a young prostitute; later, any young woman who refused to follow the prescribed code of conduct; seen as "wild," refusing to wear a corset; a young woman who smoked cigarettes in public, who danced to jazz music, who believed in what was later, in the sixties, called free love. (SBF, IHAT, p. 309; MHB, JS, np.) SNU.

Flappers n. (1930s–1940s) arms. (FR.) SNU.

Flapping eagle n. (1930s) a flashy type of dance step done by flapping one's arms like the wings of an eagle. Malcolm X discusses it in his autobiography. (FR.) NCU.

Flaps n. (1940s) ears. (MHB, JS, np; DB, OHHJ, p. 138.) Example: "Look at the flaps on that joker's head." SNU.

Flapper steaks n. (1940s) pig ears. (MHB, JS, np.) See "Soul food."

Flare up n., v. (1940s–1950s) in jazz, the point, or to reach a point, of intensity by repetition of chords; an expression of or expressing anger. (RSG, JT, p. 94.) JMFU.

Flash n. (1950s–1960s) any cheap jewelry "flashed" at a "sucker" in order to lure him or her to a desired location for the purpose of further exploiting him or her. (IS, TB, p. 311; SH, GL, p. 212.) SCU, PPU.

[One's] Flash n. (1960s–1990s) a roll of money made conspicuous to impress. (EF, RDSL, p. 237.) PPU, DCU.

Flash-sport n. (1950s) an unusually stylish man. (FR.) Example: "Albert's really out there, man, a true flash-sport, scoring every day." SNCU, YCU.

Flat n., adj. (1930s–1960s) in the thirties, a nickle, five cents; in the forties and fifties, an apartment; in the sixties, without money. (DW, TL, p. 181; DB, OHHJ, p. 138; CS, vol. 3, no. 2, p. 24.) SNU.

Flatback v. (1940s–1990s) to engage in face-to-face sex. (CRM, p. 247; TW, p. 148.) PPU, WCU, SNU.

Flat-backer n. (1940s–1990s) heterosexual prostitute; the "lowest" class of prostitute, one who works in a sleezy whorehouse, or one who is "honest" enough to give the customer what he has paid for rather than stealing his money. (CRM, p. 247; TW, CH, p. 148; IS, PSML, p. 315.) Example: "She won't give no head, she a flat-backer from way back." PPU.

Flat-footed adj. (1820s–1920s) unequivocal; straightforward. (FR.) See "Flat out."

Flat out adj., adv. (1930s–1940s) unequivocal; straightforward. (FR.) Example: "I told her flat out I wont about to bring that heavy thing back up these steps—even if she paid me." See "Flat-footed."

Flavor n. (1980s–1990s) superior cocaine; good-tasting cocaine. (TW, CH, p. 148.) DCU.

Flavor Flav (1980s) rapper for Public Enemy.

Fleamale n. (1920s–1940s) play on "female"; any young woman who identifies with the flapper image; a flapper; a fickle young woman. (MHB, JS, np.) Example: "Look at all these fleamales running around campus in those sack dresses." Rare. Southern Negro college student use.

Flex n. (1990s) spunk; energy. (RP, C, p. 15.) Example: (drug dealer to a runner) "Anybody work for me got to have flex." SCU.

Flibbertigibberty adj. (1860s–1930s) agitated; fussy; scattered; restless. (FGC, DARE, p. 475.)

Flibbogibbet adj. See "Flibbertigibberty."

Flick; flicker n. (1940s–1950s) a motion picture; the theater itself. (DC, BJ, p. 64; MHB, JS, np.) SNU.

Flink v. (1880s) variant of "flinch"; to retreat in a cowardly manner; to act cowardly; shirk responsibility. (FGC, DARE, p. 478.) SU.

Flimflam v. (1950s) any type of con game worked on "suckers." (IS, TB, p. 311.) SCU.

Flip v. (1940s–1960s) originally to overwhelm; to inform on someone; to "rat" on an acquaintance; from the thirties to the fifties, either enthusiastic response or violent response; to lose one's head; to go crazy; in the sixties, flighty, breezy, lacking in seriousness. (FGC, DARE, p. 254; WF, DAS, p. 190; CLC, TS, p. 254.) SNU.

Flip n. (1980s–1990s) any passive male homosexual; gentle gay male. (WKB, JMC, PS, p. 49.) PU, SCU.

Flip [one's] lid [top] v. (1940s–1950s) popular among black slang users but not of black origin; to go crazy; to be insane. (FR.) SNU.

Flip out v. (1940s–1960s) to have a temporary psychotic reaction to a drug; to go crazy. (RRL, DAZ, p. 77.) SNU. See "Flip [one's] lid [top]."

Flippers n. (1930s–1940s) ears. (DB, OHHJ, p. 138.) Example: "Hey! Look at the flippers on that cat!" Harlem; SNU.

Flipping out v. (1960s–1980s) to have a violent reaction to something, especially drugs; temporary psychotic reaction to drugs. (JH, PBL, p. 84.) SNCU.

Flip side n. (1920s–1940s) the opposite side of a wax record of recorded music. (RSG, JL, pp. 109–110.) JMFU, SNCU.

Flooding n., v. (1920s–1930s) menstruation; menstruating. (ZNH, MM, p. 342.)

Floorburners n. (1950s–1960s) shoes; dancing shoes—in the sense that vigorous dancing causes the floor to "burn." (DC, BJ, p. 64.) MWU.

Floored v. (1950s–1960s) to be knocked down so that one hits the floor, literally. (DC, BJ, p. 64.) SNCU.

Flub v. (1990s) to cause problems; to "screw up." (XC, MEB, p. 9.) SNCU.

Fluff v. (1930s–1940s) especially in jazz, to play a false note; to goof; to get rid of someone or something; to snub. (RSG, JL, p. 110.) JMFU.

Fluff n. (1980s–1990s) a woman's vagina. (EF, RDSL, p. 237.) SNU.

Flummadiddle n. (1860s–1940s) anything silly or foolish. (FGC, DARE, p. 500.) Example: "That is just about the most fummadiddle thing I ever did heard tell of." SNU.

Flunky n. (1860s–1930s) subordinate, especially in a work situation; a doormat. (FGC, DARE, pp. 501–502.) SU.

Flusteration n. (1860s–1930s) confusion. (CC, CW, p. 19.) SU.

Fly; flew v. (1880s–1990s) originally a Gullah term; to be fast and ecstatic; brash; good or great. In the 1970s the term was especially popular because of the *Super Fly* movies. (AEG, BB, p. 301; DC, BJ, p. 64; CWC, CW, p. 147; PM, UCLAS, p. 39; SH, GL, p. 212.) SNU.

Flycar n. (1980s–1990s) any fancy car. (FR.) NCU. See "Fly."

Flychick n. (1930s–1940s) a pleasure-loving, party-going young female. (DB, OHHJ, p. 138.) Harlem; SNU. See "Fly."

Fly coy v. (1960s–1970s) to suddenly become coy. (JH, PBL, p. 84.) NCU.

Flyer with the roof slightly higher n. (1940s) a modified version of a ten-gallon Stetson hat. (DB, OHHJ, p. 138.) Harlem; NCU.

Flygirl n. (1980s–1990s) an attractive girl. SNU. See "Fly" and "Flychick."

Fly hot v. (1900s–1930s) to show quick anger. (FR.) Example: "She can fly hot in a minute if you so much as look at her sideways." See "Fly."

Focus v., n. (1940s) to look, especially with great interest; to gaze; to see; also sight or eyes. (MHB, JS, n.p.; CC, OMMM, NCCHD, p. 255.) Example: "Dig Bobby's focus on that new girl Sherry whenever she walks by—somebody could steal his shirt and he wouldn't even know it." SU, NCU.

Fold [one's] ears v. (1960s) to advise, especially at great length; also, simply to talk impressively to someone. (FR.) SNU.

Folding green n. (1970s) paper money. (FR.) SNU.

Folks n. (1980s–1990s) a single African-American or a group of African-Americans. (EF, RDSL, p. 237.) Examples: "Man, you are fine folks, you know that?" and, "I got to be around me some folks or I loose my rhythm." SNU.

Follow-me-girl [-boy] oil n. (1930s–1940s) a conjuring potion used to attract the opposite sex; sold commercially in New Orleans and other southern cities and towns. (FR.) SU.

Fonk; fonky n., adj. (1960s–1990s) variant (pronunciation) of "funk." (CRM, BP, p. 300; CS, vol. 3, no. 2, p. 24.) SCU, PPU. See "Funk."

Fonk; fonky adj., v. (1980s–1990s) positive; also negative; praise; good; also, to embarrass or snub; outdo someone; upstage; insult, depending on context. (EF, RDSL, p. 237.) Example: "Lala was always trying to fonk me out so I don't have nothing to do with her no more." YCU. See "Front."

Fonky-fresh adj. (1990s) the most sophisticated; the most attractive; the smartest; the best; the finest. (FR.) See "Fonk."

Food n. (1940s) gossip. (MHB, JS, np.) SU. See "Fishing for Food."

Foo-foo (fu-fu) n. (1620s–1880s) mush; West African origin (Ewe); mashed plantains; batter made from flour. Southern plantation; SU.

Fool n., adj. (1900s–1990s) a foolish person; in the fifties, foolish. (FR.) Example: "What kind of fool plan is that?" SNU.

Fool around v. (1950s) to tease. (FGC, DARE, p. 520.) SNU.

Foolishment n. (1940s) nonsense; silliness; foolishness. (FGC, DARE, p. 522.) SNU.

Fool with v. (1750s–1950s) to annoy. (JAH, PBE, p. 175.) Example: "Don't fool with me, boy, I'll knock you clear out to the road." SU.

Foop; fooping v. (1920s) to dance without restraint. (CMc, HH, p. 30.) Example: "All of 'em out there on the floor fooping and hooping and hollering something crazy." Harlem; YCU. See "Jig-jogging."

Football n. (1950s–1970s) dance step. (GS, TT, 256.) SNU.

Foot it; footing it v. (1950s–1960s) to walk, especially a considerable distance. (DC, BJ, p. 64.) SNCU.

Foot-loosing around v. (1940s) wasting of time. (MHB, JS, np.) SNU.

Footprints n. (1700s–1860s) as pertaining to the belief that one's footprint held magic. If the area of dirt holding the print was preserved, it could be used by a conjurer to manipulate the person who left the print. (MT, DAF, p. 118.) SU.

Foots n. (1880s–1930s) see "Feets."

Foots Walter Purl Thomas, tenor saxophone player and composer; born October 2, 1907; worked with Jelly Roll Morton, Cab Calloway, et al.

Foot-washing Baptist [Church] n. (1880s–1940s) a church where the practice of foot washing is a common ceremony. (JMB, WB, p. 34.) SU.

For days adj. (1950s–1970s) any extreme; extensive; a long period of time; that which is true. (EF, RDSL, p. 237; CS, vol. 3, no. 2, p. 24.) Example: "She kissed me for days" (indicating a long kiss). SNCU.

Fore; fo adv., prep. (1620s–1990s) form of "before." (ECLA, CS, p. 13; FGC, DARE, p. 531.) SU, SNU.

Foreign adj. (1900s–1940s) refers to what are considered unnatural sex acts. (FR.) SU.

Forget [one] v. (1950s–1960s) variant of "fuck [one]"; an expression of contempt. (HLF, RJPD, p. 170.) Example: "Man, forget you." SNU.

Forget it v. See "Forget [one]."

Forks n. (1940s) fingers. (DB, OHHJ, p. 138.) Harlem use.

For real adj. (1960s–1970s) real; serious; trustworthy; dependable; to be without a scheme or a "game." (CRM, BP, p. 300.) SNCU.

Forteyed adj. (1990s) drunk or intoxicated. (Queen Latifah, *Essence*, 1992, p. 116.) YCU.

Forty n. (1980s–1990s) forty-ounce beer. (FR.) YCU, SCU.

Forty-'leven [eleven] (1800s–1960s) many in number; numerous; "sounds like a negroism." (JSF, AON, p. 251.) SU, SNU. See "Fifty-eleven."

Fotch; fotched (1680s–1880s) southern black variant of "fetch" and "fetched." (JSF, AON, p. 251.) SU.

Foul v. (1960s) anything unpleasant; usage probably picked up from sports ("foul line"). (CS, vol. 3, no. 2, p. 25.) Example: "That sure was some foul shit Jason got Glenda mixed up in." SNCU.

Four and one n. (1940s–1950s) the fifth working day; payday; Friday. (DB, OHHJ, p. 138.) Harlem use.

Four-headed adj. (1930s) possessing great mental or magical abilities. New Orleans use mainly. (HMH, HCWR, 1785.) SU.

Four sister's on thumb street n. (1970s–1990s) one's hand used in masturbation. (EF, RDSL, p. 237.) SNU.

Four Thieves Vinegar n. (1920s–1930s) a conjuring solution made with vinegar and used to gain power over someone, to create domestic chaos, to break up a relationship, to steal another person's mate, or to drive someone insane. (ZNH, MM, p. 337.) SU.

Fowl-crow n. (1880s) early morning, just after midnight. (CCJ, NMGC, p. 161; SGS, BG, p. 170.) SU. See "First fowl-crow."

Fowl hawk n. (1880s–1900s) of Gullah origin; a chicken hawk. (AEG, BB, p. 303.) SU.

[Stone] Fox n. (1940s–1970s) a beautiful black girl; "fox" is often used alone, but when "stone" is added it implies "solid" or the presence of an irrefutable "fox." (DC, BJ, p. 64; CRM, BP, p. 300; CS, vol.

3, no. 2, p. 25; JH, PBL, p. 84.) Example: "You see April? She's a stone fox." SNU.

Fox trot n. (1900) a phrase that attempted to define a type of jazz dance and rhythm. (RSG, JL, pp. 111–112.) SNU. See "Camel walk."

Foxy adj. (1930s–1960s) from the thirties to the forties, to be clever or cunning; from the fifties to the sixties, female beauty, especially black; good-looking; beautiful; attractive. (DW, TL, p. 181; CC, OMMM, NCCHD, p. 255; CS, vol. 3, no. 2, p. 25.) SNU. See "[Stone] Fox."

Fraid adj. (1700s–1990s) variant of "afraid"; cowardly; scared. (REK, G, p. 67.) SU.

Frail; frailing n., v. (1700s–1940s) variant of "flail"; to whip or beat someone or an animal; in the forties, a thin girl. (FGC, DARE, pp. 555–556). SU.

Frail eel n. (1930s–1940s) pretty girl; any good-looking woman. (FR; FGC, p. 556; ZNH, AM, p. 94.) Harlem; SU.

Frame n. (1940s–1950s) the body; a suit of clothes. (CC, OMMM, NCCHD, p. 255.) SNU. See "Fine brown frame."

Frames n. (1950s) eyeglasses. (DC, BJ, p. 64.) Example: "Dizzy wear them thick bebop frames and you can't see his eyes." SNU.

Frantic adj. (1940s–1950s) "jump tune" music; anything exciting and satisfying. (RSG, JT, p. 98.) JMFU, SNU.

Freak n. (1920s–1950s) in jazz, a musician who possesses the skill to play high brass notes for an impressive length of time. (RSG, JL, p. 112; CS, vol. 3, no. 2, p. 25.) Example: "That freak can hold a high note longer than the Mississippi River." JMFU.

Freak n. (1950s–1990s) a person who obviously enjoys sex; homosexual. (IS, PSML, p. 315; DW, TL, p. 181; DC, BJ, p. 64; CRM, BP, p. 300; RDA, DDJ, p. 265; PM, UCLAS, p. 40.) Example: "That chick is a freak; she wants every pair of pants she see." SNU.

Freakish adj. (1940s–1950s) weird or homosexual; describing oral or anal sex. (FR.) Example: "You see them two guys holding hands? They must be freakish or something." SNU.

Freak-fuck n. (1980s–1990s) anal intercourse. (EF, RDSL, p. 238.) SNU.

Freak-off; freaking off v. (1960s–1970s) to express enjoyment; to make something beautiful. (CRM, BP, p. 300.) Examples: "Ward really freaks off when Hilda comes around"; and, "Sanders believes in freaking off his apartment with all kinds of expensive antique furniture and shit. You should see it." NCU.

Freak-off; freaking off v. (1980s–1990s) the practice of "unconventional sex." (EF, RDSL, p. 238.) Example: "Those dudes down in the Village like to freak off." SNU.

Freakology n. (1950s–1960s) the "study" of being unusual, of being homosexual, of being different. (FR.) Rare. SNCU.

Free adj. (1800s–1940s) to be honest; truthful; sincere. (FGC, DARE, p. 559.) Example: "I want you to be free with me." SU, SNU.

Free base n. (1980s–1990s) cooked cocaine. (TW, CK, p. 136.) DCU.

Freebasing v. (1980s–1990s) smoking cocaine that has been mixed with other drugs. Free base cocaine is cocaine minus the hydrochloride. (TW, CH, p. 148.) DCU. See "Free base."

Freebee n. (1900s–1960s) a thing or idea that does not cost money. (JH, PBL, p. 84; CC, OMMM, NCCHD, p. 255.) Example: "You can come back if you like, but no more freebees." SNU.

Freehanded adj. (1700s–1940s) of Gullah origin; unselfish; kind; generous. (AEG, BB, p. 302.) South Carolina and Georgia use. See "Free" and "Freehearted."

Freehearted adj. (1900s–1940s) generous; compassionate. (FR.) SU. See "Freehanded."

Free issue n. (1860s–1890s) any African-American of mixed racial heritage, especially the offspring of a white woman and a black man; any black person freed by manumission and the Civil War. (BB, AW, p. 34; ECLA, CS, p. 59.) SU.

Freemale n. (1870s–1920s) of Gullah origin; any black female. (AEG, BB, p. 302.) SU.

Freeman n. (1860s–1890s) short for legally free black man; any black person set free by the Emancipation Proclamation and by the Civil War. (FR.) SNU. See "Black issue" and "Free man of color."

Free man [woman] of color n. (1860s–1900s) a free Black person born during slavery; mulatto. (ECLA, CS, p. 56.) SU. See "Issue."

Free papers n. (1830s–1860s) a document carried by free blacks and freed slaves that states that the possessor is legally free. (SBF, IHAT, p. 35.)

Free school n. (1900s–1940s) a public school; the term is derived from the derogatory expression "free schools, pretty yellow teachers and dumb Negroes." (ZNH, AM, p. 94.) SU.

Freeway Freddy n. (1970s–1990s) a highway patrolman in southern California. (EF, RDSL, p. 238.) California use.

Free woman of color n. See "Free man of color."

Freewheeling v. (1930s–1940s) see "Cruise." (ZNH, AM, p. 94.) Harlem; SNU.

Freeze n., v. (1850s–1930s) the cold shoulder; to ignore someone. (FGC, DARE, p. 536.) Example: "That boy gave me the freeze when I spoke to him this morning." SNU.

Freeze v. (1950s–1960s) often an imperative command; to stop, especially to stop in one's tracks. (DC, BJ, p. 64.) MWU, NCU.

Freeze on v. (1980s–1990s) to ignore a person or situation. (FR.) Example: "Dawn's group freeze on Ruth when she walks by." SNU.

Freezed v. (1850s–1930s) variant of "froze." (FR.) Example: "When we found him he was freezed liked this." SNU.

[Miss] Freezing Weather n. (1930s–1940s) any unattractive girl or young woman. (MHB, np.) Example: "Betty is fine, but she hangs out with Miss Freezing Weather." Southern Negro college student use; SU.

Fresh adj. (1980s–1990s) complimentary, meaning to look good; original; very contemporary; fine appearance; positive; good. (TW, CK, p. 137.) Example: "It's real fresh the way you take care of the shop." YCU.

Fresh-cool adj. (1990s) the best; the finest; the newest. (FR.) YCU. See "Fonky-fresh."

Fresh cut n. (1980s–1990s) a close and neat haircut. (WKB, JMC, PS, p. 49.) PU.

Fresh hide n. (1980s–1990s) a new man or woman as a sexual mate. (EF, RDSL, p. 238.) South-central Los Angeles; YCU.

Fresh water trout n. (1940s) good-looking girls. (DB, OHHJ, p. 138.) Harlem; SNU.

Frick and frack n. (1980s–1990s) testicles. (EF, RDSL, p. 238.) Watts and South-central Los Angeles; SNCU.

Fried, dyed and to the side adj. (1970s–1980s) said of straightened and dyed hair, especially hair dyed blonde or red. (EF, BVV, p. 45.) Watts and South-central Los Angeles; SNCU.

Friend n. (1900s–1990s) female term for menstruation; also, male term for his own penis; female term for her own vagina. (AW, CP, p. 161.) SNU. See "Business," "Dick," and "Johnson."

Friend-boy n. (1900s–1940s) boyfriend. (FR.) SU.

Friend-girl n. (1900s–1940s) girlfriend. (FR.) SU.

Fri-high-day n. (1990s) any drinking day for a teen. (MM, NYT, p. 1.) Bronx, New York, use.

Frimpted adj. (1940s) unattractive. (FR.) Rare.

Fringe; fringing v. (1940s) to get by, by begging or sponging. (MHB, JS, np.) Southern Negro college student; SU.

Frisking the whiskers v. (1930s–1940s) the warm-up playing musicians do before swinging into a full jam session. (CC, OMMM, NCCHD, p. 255; DB, OHHJ, p. 138.) JMFU.

Frizzly adj. (1840s–1930s) unruly. (LS, GYY, p. 537.) Example: "He got frizzly hair." Louisiana; SU. See "Frizzly chicken."

Frizzly chicken n. (1840s–1930s) a barnyard chicken with unruly feathers. (LS, GYY, p. 537.) Louisiana; SU.

Fro n. (1960s–1970s) short for "Afro"; a bushy, sculptured hairstyle symbolic in the sixties and seventies as a sign of black pride. (DC, BJ, p. 64.) SNU. See "Natural."

Froe n. (1890s–1930s) a damaged knife. (ZnH, MM, p. 221.) SU.

Frog bread n. (1890s–1940s) wild mushroom; toadstool. (HMH, HCWR, p. 72.) SU. See "Toad frog bread."

Frog up adj. (1920s–1930s) to be misled or duped; confused or deceived; "negro use." (WF, DAS, p. 202.) Example: "Old man Bowsworth will frog up anybody just to get them to bring their cotton to him first." SU.

Frogstool n. See "Toadstool" and "Frog bread."

Frolic pad n. (1940s) a nightclub or dance hall. (DB, OHHJ, p. 138.) MWU.

From prep. (1700s–1990s) for; the results of; to avoid; after; because of; "from" is a word used frequently and in interesting ways by many black speakers. (DC, BJ, p. 64; EF, RDSL, p. 109; ERK, G. p. 58; FGC, DARE, pp. 586–587.) Example: "I can't help from crying every time I think about it." SNU.

From hunger adv. (1930s) inferior; for money; to appeal to popular tastes. (FR.) Example: "He just playing music from hunger." JMFU.

From the get-go adv. (1950s–1960s) from the beginning. (FR.) See "[From] Jump street."

From way back adj. (1940s–1950s) distance in time. (FR.) Example: "He's a friend from way back." SNU. See "Back."

Frone n. (1940s) any unattractive woman. (MHB, JS, np.) SU.

[Out] Front; front adj. (1940s–1950s) from the very beginning. (RSG, JL, pp. 114–115.) JMFU, SNCU.

Front n. (1930s–1960s) a suit of clothes, particularly an expensive one (WF, DAS, p. 202; DW, TL, p. 181; MHB, JS, np; DC, BJ, p. 64; CC, OMMM, NCCHD, p. 255; CRM, BP, p. 300; HLF, RJPD, p. 170); (1950s–1960s) false appearance (WKB, JMC, PS, p. 80). SNCU.

Front n. (1950s–1960s) the persona or facade one shows the public. (CW, TM, p. 12.) New York City; NECU.

Front v. (1960s–1970s) to insult, outdo, or snub; to belittle; upstage. (FR.) NCU. See "Fonk."

Front; fronting v. (1980s–1990s) to take narcotics on "consignment." (TW, CK, p. 137.) DCU.

Front door n. (1900s–1940s) vagina. See "Jelly roll."

Fronter n. (1970s–1980s) one who shows off. See "Front."

Fronting v. (1960s) to appear other than one is; to misrepresent oneself. (DC, BJ, p. 64.) NCU.

Fronting v. (1980s–1990s) selling drugs on consignment; disparaging; insulting. (TW, CK, p. 137.) Example: "I don't like those dudes, they're still fronting on us." DCU.

Front-off v. (1970s–1980s) to upstage. (EF, RDSL, p. 109.) SNCU. See "Front."

Front street n. (1980s–1990s) straightforwardness. (FR.) Example: "I expect you to deal on front street with me like I do with you." SNU.

Front yard n. (1940s) pubic hair. (FR.) SNU.

Fruit v. (1930s–1960s) to "jive" around; kidding; clowning. (CRM, BP, p. 300.) SNU.

Fruit n. (1970s–1990s) homosexual male. (EF, RDSL, p. 238.) SNCU.

Fruiting v. (1930s–1940s) being promiscuous. (DB, OHHJ, p. 138.) Harlem; SNCU.

Frump; frumpy n., adj. (1940s) any unattractive girl or woman; ugliness. (MHB, JS, np; CC, OMMM, NCCHD, p. 255) SNU.

Fry v. (1930s–1940s) to straighten the hair with a hot iron; to have one's hair processed professionally at a barbershop or to have it done at home by a friend or a relative. In the seventies, to execute in the electric chair (WF, DAS, p. 203; DW, TL, p. 181; CC, OMMM, NCCHD, p. 255.) SNU.

Fry-bacon n. (1700s–1940s) of Gullah origin; fried bacon; also, the sound a pond frog makes. (AEG, BB, p. 302.) South Carolina and Georgia use. See "Fry-frog."

Fry [one] for lambchops v. (1950s–1960s) to abuse; to be put to death by the state. (CLC, TF, p. 156.) PU, SCU.

Fry-frog n. (1700s–1940s) of Gullah origin; the pond frog whose croak sounds like "fry bacon, tea table." (AEG, BB, p. 302.) South Carolina and Georgia use. See "Fry-bacon."

Fry-meat preacher n. (1900s–1940s) a small-time preacher who preaches in return for a meal. (FGC, DARE, pp. 595–596.) SU.

Fryings n. (1900s–1940s) the juice or fat from cooking meat. (FR.) SNU.

Fucked up adj. (1940s–1970s) confused or experiencing great misfortune, or both. (FR.) SNU.

Fuck it interj. (1800s–1990s) expletive marking a rejection of something; to [the] hell with it. (FR.) SNU.

Fuck off interj. (1940s–1990s) expletive marking a rejection of someone; go to hell. (FR.) SNU.

Fuck up v. (1940s–1990s) to ruin or spoil. (FR.) SNU.

Fuck-up n. (1940s–1990s) ineffective person. (FR.) SNU.

Fugitive slave n. (1700s–1860s) a term used only ironically by black people; any black person who has managed to free himself or herself from slavery. (SBF, IHAT, p. 35.) SNU.

Fugley adj. (1980s–1990s) absolutely unattractive. Derived from "fucking ugly." (PM, UCLAS, p. 41.) Example: "I don't care how many generations it was handed down through, you won't catch me dead or alive in this fugley wedding dress." YCU, SNCU.

Fulafafa n. (1900s–1960s) a woodpecker. (JH, PBL, p. 84.) Rare. New York City; SNU.

Full adj. (1800s–1990s) filled; having overeaten. (FR.) SNU.

Full moon n. (1800s–1990s) time of a woman's menstruation. (FR.) Example: "It's the full moon time." SNU.

Full of shit (1940s–1990s) a profane interjection used to dismiss what someone has said; misinformation; malicious exaggeration. (FR.) Example: "Man, get outta my face—you full of shit." SNU.

Full up v., adj. (1800s–1950s) to fill; to be full. (HMH, HCWR, p. 678.) Example: "Rita, you go full up the jar." SU.

Fulling station n. (1930s–1950s) filling station; gas station. (JLD, LBE, p. 109.) SU.

Function n. (1900s–1940s) a dance party held in a small room. (ZNH, AM, p. 94.) Example: "Sure is some funky folks at this function." SNU.

Funeral clothes n. (1930s–1950s) see "Sunday-go-to-meeting clothes."

Funfetti n. (1980s–1990s) any of various types of candy eaten by drug users because of their "sweet tooth." (RCC, SOC, p. 16.) DCU, YCU.

Funk; funky n. (1640s–1990s) probably from *lu-funki* (Ki-Kongo and Bay Kongo) for "bad body odor"; down-to-earth; "for real"; in touch with the essence of being human; body odor; an offensive or unpleasant smell or thing; also, attractive or beautiful. (RFT, FS, p. 104; DW, TL, p. 181; CRM, BP, pp. 300–301; CS, vol. 3, no. 2, p. 25; DG, SP, p. 76.) SNU. See "Fonk."

Funk n. (1950s–1990s) the "soul" quality in black music; the melancholy mood of the blues; also known as South, hard bop, and down-home. (RSG, JL, p. 116; James Baldwin, *Tell Me How Long the Train's Been Gone*, 1968, p. 117.) JMFU. See "Fonk."

Funked-up adj. (1990s) something splendid or wonderful; "cool"; sophisticated. (*Essence*, November 1992, p. 26.) Example: "Geneva gets herself all funked-up and you wouldn't even know her if you saw her on the street." YCU. See "Funk" and "Fonk."

Funk on a dunk (1990s) to be insincere; to joke; from a phrase coined by basketball player Shaquille O'Neal, "don't fake the funk on a nasty dunk." (HC, WSJ, p. 38.) YCU.

Funky adj. (1950s–1970s) a nitty-gritty, truly felt blues mood in jazz and therefore in the people who produce this art form; sometimes called "a sense of tragedy" in Euro-American logic. (RDA, TB, p. 8.) JMFU, SNU. See "Funk" and "Fonk."

Funky Broadway n. (1950s) the main street where the underbelly in any city shows. (FR.) NCU.

Funky chicken n. (1960s–1970s) a dance done with chickenlike motions of the arms and feet; a dance made popular by teen dancers on the television show *Soul Train*; the arms are flapped like a chicken flaps its wings. (FR.) SNU.

Funky dude n. (1950s–1960s) a "sucker" or a fool; victim of a pimp's scheme. (DG, CR, p. 47.) PPU.

Funny adj. (1950s–1960s) strange; homosexual. (DC, BJ, p. 65) Example: "He's funny, he comes in here loping and his eyes popping out of his head"; and, "She always looking at women, she must be funny or something." SNU.

Funny bone n. (1880s–1950s) a mythic "bone" in the body that responds to humor. (JMB, DG, p. 38.) SU.

Funny-looking adj. (1950s–1960s) odd; strange; crazy. (FR.) SNU.

Fur; fa prep. (1620s–1990s) the Gullah form of "for." Originally African but later Gullah and general southern black use. (FGC, DARE, pp. 528–530.) SU.

Fur n. (1960s) a woman, possibly because of long hair and pubic hair. (HLF, RJPD, p. 170.) New York city use.

Fur n. (1950s–1960s) a woman's wig. (DC, BJ, p. 65.) See "Rat."

Fur good adv. (1800s–1950s) for always. (FGC, DARE, p. 529.) Example: "I want to be yo husband fur good." SU.

Fur soul (for soul) adj. (1800s–1950s) of Gullah origin; from the heart; truly; sincere. (AEG, BB, p. 303.) Example: "When I took my marriage vows it was fur soul." SU.

Fuss [at] v. (1700s–1990s) to nag someone; cry; cause confusion. (ECCLA, CS, p. 24; DC, BJ, p. 65.) Example: "All you do is fuss all the time." SU.

Fussful adj. (1880s–1930s) ill-tempered. (HMH, HCWR, p. 549.) SU.

Fuss up v. (1890s–1920s) to cause excitement or confusion. (ECLA, NN, p. 265.) Example: "They fuss up every time they gets together." South Carolina use.

Fuzz; furze n. (1900s–1940s) police; also, facial hair. (DC, BJ, p. 65.) Examples: "Quick, hide! Here comes the fuzz"; and, "When you gone shave that fuzz off your face?" NCU.

G

G n. (1940s–1950s) a thousand dollars. (IS, PSML, p. 315; WF, DAS, p. 206.) Example: "You can pick up an easy five G's if you do this job for me." SCU.

G v. (1990s) to have sexual intercourse. (FR.) YCU.

Gabriel n. (1700s–1890s; 1930s–1940s) mythical figure in Negro culture; the angel Gabriel, a biblical personality, featured large in the minds of African-American slaves because he would be the one who'd blow the horn alerting everybody to the arrival of Judgment Day. He is featured in the spirituals and in folk songs and in the blues. Also, in modern times and in jazz, "Gabriel" stands for any trumpet player, especially professional. (FR; AEG, BB, p. 303; CC, OMMM, NCCHD, p. 255.) SNU.

Gage v. (1650s–1920s) form of "engage." (CCJ, NMGC, p. 130; AEG, BB, p. 303.) SU.

Gage; gauge n. (1930s–1950s) marijuana; liquor. (RSG, JL, p. 118.) New York City; DCU. See "Gauge."

Gagement n. (1650s–1920s) form of "engagement." See "Gage."

Gaff n. (1930s–1950s) a crooked scheme, especially in gambling where a gambling device might be "fixed" to diminish the gamblers' chances of winning. (HEG, DAU, p. 76; WF, DAS, p. 206; DW, TL, p. 181; IS, TB, p. 312.) SCU, PPU, PU.

Gaffle n. (1990s) defeat or betrayal. (FR.) YCU.

Gallery n. (1900s–1950s) a large porch. (LA, SM, p. 160.) SU.

Galloping dominoes n. (1950s–1960s) dice. (DC, BJ, p. 65.) See "Bones."

Galloping piano n. (1920s–1930s) in jazz, a rhythm that sounds much like a horse's gallop. (RSG, JL, pp. 118–119.) JMFU.

Gal n. (1650s–1950s) a girl; not pejorative before the 1960s. (AEG, BB, p. 222.) SNU.

Gal officer(s) n. (1940s–1950s) pejorative for "harpies"; lesbians. (DB, OHHJ, p. 138.) Harlem use.

[The] Galveston Giant Jack Johnson, heavyweight prizefighter. See "Big Smoke."

Gam; gamming v. (1920s–1940s) from the old word "gamon," as in "gamon and patter"; usually—and as early as the sixteenth century—the term meant lively (but commonplace) talk, uncontrollable chatter, humbug, lies, or deceit; but black slang users, by the 1920s, were using the term to refer to bragging and showing off, or even flirting. (DB, OHHJ, p. 138; FG, DVT, np; CC, OMMM, NCCHD, p. 255.) SNU.

Gam cases n. (1940s) stockings. (DB, OHHJ, p. 138.) Harlem; SNU.

Game n. (1950s–1960s) a pimp's tactics or philosophy on the hustling life. (SH, GL, p. 212.) PPU.

Game-making v. (1890s–1920s) to kid or joke with or ridicule someone. (ECLA, NN, p. 265.) South Carolina use.

[The] Game n., v., adj. (1930s–1990s) hipcat's life-style; sporting life; a deceptive act; a manipulative attempt; a philosophy of trickery; also, the process of courting with jive talk. (Queen Latifah, *Essence*, September 1992, p. 120; DC, BJ, p. 65; CRM, BP, p. 301; DW, TL, p. 182; HLF, RJPD, p. 170.) Examples: "He can game his way into anything"; "He'll game after her, then she'll fall for him"; "She can make a lot of bread off suckers at the pussy game"; and, "I'm getting out of the game for good." SNCU.

[Run a] Game v. See "[The] Game."

[Pussy] Game n. See "[The] Game."

[To] Game v. See "[The] Game."

Games n. (1880s–1990s) a network of schemes worked on an "innocent" victim or a "sucker." (TW, CH, p. 148; EF, RDSL, p. 71.) DCU.

Gaming v. (1890s–1990s) playing a trick on an unsuspecting victim or "sucker." (TW, CH, p. 148; EF, RDSL, p. 70.) DCU. See "Games."

[Get one's] Game together v. (1960s) to present to the world a convincing persona, especially one appealing enough to fool potential "suckers." (CRM, BP, p. 301.) SNCU.

Gander v. (1940s) to walk. (IS, TB, p. 312; MHB, JS, np.) Example: "The professor takes a gander across campus every morning before anybody else is up." SNU.

Gang n. (1930s–1950s) group; pack; a large amount of anything. (FGC, DARE, p. 628.) See "Boo Koos."

Gang bang v. (1950s–1980s) to participate in gang fighting. (DC, BJ, p. 65.) MWU, YCU, SCU.

Gangbangers n. (1950s–1960s) violent gang members. (DC, BJ, p. 65.) Example: "The gangbangers messed him up bad." NCU.

Gangster n. (1950s–1960s) marijuana, especially a rolled joint; also, in the midwest, sometimes a cigarette. (CLC, TS, p. 255; DC, BJ, p. 65.) DCU.

Gangster doors n. (1980s–1990s) any four-door car. (EF, RDSL, p. 238.) South-central Los Angeles; YCU.

Gangster front n. (1980s–1990s) a double-breasted suit like those worn by gangsters in the Hollywood movies of the thirties. (EF, RDSL, p. 239.) South-central Los Angeles; YCU.

Gangster pills n. (1960s) barbiturates in the form of pills. (WKB, JMC, PS, p. 81.) DCU.

Gangster stick n. (1950s–1990s) marijuana cigarette. (EF, RDSL, p. 239.) South-central Los Angeles; DCU, YCU, SCU.

Gangster walls n. (1980s–1990s) white-walled tires on a fancy car. (EF, RDSL, p. 239.) South-central Los Angeles; YCU; SCU.

Gaper n. (1930s–1940s) a mirror. (DB, OHHJ, p. 138.) Example: "Every time I see you you in front of the gaper—you must think you pretty or something." Harlem use.

Gapper n. (1950s–1960s) narcotics. (DG, D, p. 21.) PPU, DCU.

Gappings n. (1930s–1940s) pay; salary; wages. (RSG, JL, p. 119.) JMFU.

Garage door n. (1940s–1960s) a man's trouser fly. (FGC, DARE, p. 633.) SNU.

Garbage n. (1950s–1960s) diluted or contaminated heroin. (RRL, DAZ, p. 81.) Example: "Bobby died from some old garbage Billy sold him on a humbug." DCU.

Garbage n. (1980s–1990s) insignificant or unimportant events; trivia. (FR.) Example: "Ella Mae always into everybody's business, gossiping, nosing around, whispering about people. Don't she know decent folk don't care nothing about all that old garbage she talking about?" YCU.

Gas n., v. (1930s–1950s) anything enormously surprising, exciting, and satisfying; by the mid-fifties word was stretched and lost much of its character, coming to mean anything very unusual or amusing. (CC, OMMM, NCCHD, p. 255; DC, BJ, p. 65; CS, vol. 3, no. 2, p. 25; DB, OHHJ, p. 138.) Example: "I love the way you dance—it's a gas!" SNU.

Gas buggy n. (1930s–1940s) automobile. (DB, OHHJ, p. 138.) SNU.

Gashead n. (1960s) derogatory term for a person with a processed or straightened hairstyle. (DC, BJ, p. 65; CS, vol. 3, no. 2, p. 25.)

Example: "Carl's such a gashead—his hair so slick a fly that tried to land on it went into a skid and crashed." NCU.

Gas meter n. (1940s) a quarter. (FR.) NCU.

Gasper(s) n. (1930s–1940s) a cigarette. (MHB, JS, np; DB, OHHJ, p. 139.) Example: "He thinks he's cool smoking his gaspers." SNU.

Gas pipe n. (1940s) a trombone. (DB, OHHJ, p. 139.) Harlem use.

Gasser n. (1930s–1940s) anything excellent. (FR; CC, OMMM, NCCHD, p. 255; DB, OHHJ, p. 139.) See "Gas."

Gassing up [one's] head v. (1980s–1990s) smoking crack cocaine. (RP, C, p. 5.) Example: "Two thirds of the jokers you see standing there on the corner be gassing up their heads every chance they get." New Jersey and New York; DCU.

Gat n. (1900s–1990s) a firearm, especially one that is easy to carry concealed in a pocket or a holster; may be derived from "Gatling Gun." (WF, DAS, p. 209; DW, TL, p. 182; RDA, DDJ, p. 265; EP, DU, p. 280.) SCU, PU.

Gate; gatemouth n. (1920s–1940s) short for "gatemouth"; gator-faced; jazz musician or any hip male person; Louis Armstrong says he was the first to use the term "gatemouth." (CC, HDH, p. 16; RSG, JT, pp. 104–105.) JBWU.

Gatemouth blues singer Clarence Brown (born 1924).

Gates n. (1940s–1950s) term of address by one male to another. (MHB, JS, np.) Example: "Hey! What's happening, gates?" SNU.

Gator n. (1880s–1940s) short for "alligator"; a negro corruption of alligator; term of address from one male friend to another; from the 1930s to the 1940s, a jazz fan. (JSF, AON, p. 260.) SU.

Gauge/gage; gaga; ghanja n. (1930s–1960s) an especially strong type of marijuana grown in Jamaica and elsewhere; a powerful marijuana cigarette. (WKB, JMC, PS, p. 81–82; WF, DAS, p. 207.) New York; DCU.

Gazer n. (1930s–1940s) a window. (DB, OHHJ, p. 139.) Harlem use; SNU.

Gee adj. (1700s–1930s) to the right as opposed to the left; opposite of "haw." (AEG, BB, p. 193.; BJ, BLH, SD, p. 208.) SU.

Gee n. (1930s–1940s) male friend or any male. (FR.) SNU.

Gee n. (1950s–1960s) a paper device a junkie uses to secure the needle to the eyedropper in preparation for an injection of heroin. (DW, TL, p. 182.) DCU. See "Geeze."

Geechee n. (1700s–1990s) Gullah; "ogeechee"; a language derived from a mix of Mandingo, Bantu, Fante, Wolof, Ewe, Twi, Yoruba, Ibo, and other West African languages; a language of the coast of Guinea; also, of Kissi County, Liberia. It has its own well-focused grammar and syntax. This term has also been used by whites in a derogatory way to refer to any "very black" southern "Negro" (HV, AHAE, p. 141; WF, DAS, p. 210–211; LDT, AGD, pp. 31–205). See "Gullah."

Geechee n. (1700s–1990s) any black (and sometimes nonblack) person from the coastal area of Georgia or North Carolina. (MM, RB, p. 333.) SU.

Geechee n., adj., v. (1900s–1980s) a derogatory term for a southern person whose speech is not easily understood; unable to speak clearly; to speak with a heavy accent. (FGC, DARE, p. 648.) SU.

Geek n. (1970s–1990s) a "weird" person; an intellectual. (EF, RDSL, p. 239.) SNU, YCU.

Geets; geetus n. (1940s) power or money or both. (FGC, DARE, p. 650.) SNU.

Geeze; geezing v. (1960s–1990s) the act of injecting heroin into a vein. (EF, RDSL, p. 239; CS, vol. 3, no. 2, p. 26.) Example: "Here, hold the needle, help me with this geeze." DCU.

George n. (1860s–1890s) any "Negro" Pullman porter; picked up from white use and derived from George Pullman, who invented the cars. (FR.) SNU.

George Walker v. (1900s–1940s) walking on stilts. (LS, GYY, p. 18.) SU.

Georgia buggy n. (1930s–1940s) a hand-pushed cart or wheelbarrow; "what niggers say" (FGC, DARE, p. 655). SNU.

Georgia cracker n. (1700s–1990s) a white person from Georgia; probably from "cracking," as in cracking jokes. (CMc, HH, p. 49; GS, TT, p. 252.) Example: "If you're going down South, you got to watch out for them Georgia crackers. They ain't nothing but trouble." SNU.

Georgiaed v. (1930s–1960s) a northern city con game played on innocent blacks, men and women, fresh up from the south. To be seduced into sexual activity by a woman. (CLC, TS, p. 255; IS, PSML, p. 315.) Example: "The minute Mae got up here from Alabama, she got Georgiaed by her first so-called trick. He didn't give her one red penny." NCU. See "Murphy."

Georgia ham n. (1940s–1970s) watermelon. (JH, PBL, p. 84.) SCU.

Georgia Skin n. (1920s–1930s) a card game, any number can play. (ZNH, MM, pp. 307–308; RDA, DDJ, p. 266.) NSU.

Georgy n. (1850s–1950s) variant pronunciation of "Georgia." (ZNH, AM, p. 90.) SU.

Get a clue v. (1960s) become aware. (FR.) Example: "I told him to get a clue." SNU.

Get a move on v. (1930s–1940s) a command to move fast. (FR.) SU.

Get around v. (1930s–1940s) to overcome a difficulty. (FR.) SU.

Get beautiful v. (1980s–1990s) to get high on narcotics. (EF, RDSL, p. 239.) DCU.

Get busy v. (1990s) sexual intercourse; intense physical activity. (FR.) Example: "All the ladies are after me. I can get busy any time I feel like." YCU.

Get down dirty v. (1970s–1990s) to tell someone off in a very loud and abusive manner. (EF, RDSL, p. 239.) SNU, YCU, SCU.

Get down [heavy] v. (1930s–1970s) to "feel" the music; to respond to the party mood or spirit of the dance; have a good time; lose all pretensions; to perform well; to be intensely involved, especially with music or the spirit of a party; also, to do anything to the fullest. (DW, TL, p. 183; CS, vol. 3, no. 2, p. 26; SH, GL, p. 212; GS, TT, p. 55.) Example: "You got to get down to get over, and when you get over, come to see me." SNU. See "Down."

Get [one's] drift v. (1970s–1980s) to understand; to comprehend. (FR.) SNU.

[From the] Get-go; git go n. (1950s–1960s) the beginning. (CRM, BP, p. 301.) Example: "The whole thing was wrong right from the get-go." SNU.

Get happy See "Get [the] spirit."

Get [one's] hat v. (1940s–1960s) go; leaving a house or location; sometimes an imperative, most often not; means to leave, especially quickly. (FGC, DARE, p. 663; CS, vol. 3, no. 2, p. 26.) Examples: "Sorry, Trudy, I got to get my hat; I can't stand any more of this"; "When I saw her husband coming, I got my hat"; and, "If he comes in here with any more tricks I'm gonna make him get his hat." SNCU.

Get high behind v. (1950s–1960s) to become intoxicated after smoking or using drugs or after drinking liquor; refers to the effects of being "behind" (under the influence of) a specific drug. (FR.) SNCU.

Get hot v. (1920s–1950s) in jazz, to play with great excitement; in gambling, to have a streak of luck. (MM, RB, p. 141.) JMFU.

[To] Get in [one's] eye(s) v. (1970s–1990s) to hit one in the eye or the face; to crowd a person's personal space; to shout in one's face. (FR.) YCU.

Get in there exclam., v. (1930s–1940s) shouted at musicians; a cry to give it "all you got"; a command to become active toward a positive end. (CC, HDH, p. 16.) SNU.

Get in the wind v. (1950s–1960s) to leave, especially quickly. (DW, TL, p. 182.) See "Split."

Get it exclam., v. (1920s–1950s) a cry of encouragement to musicians on a stage or to one engaged in doing something exciting. (RSG, JL, p. 122.) JMFU. See "Get in there."

Get it on v. (1960s) a command to start; start moving; start playing music; get started; to up the tempo. (DC, BJ, p. 65; CS, vol. 3, no. 2, p. 27.) Example: "Let's get it on." NCU. See "Get it" and "Get in there."

Get it together v. (1960s) get organized; get focused. (DC, BJ, p. 65.) NCU.

Get [one's] jollies v. (1950s–1970s) to have fun, experience pleasure. (FR.) SNU.

Get [one's] kicks v. See "Get [one's] jollies."

Get next to v. (1950s–1970s) to impress favorably; to anger; to become involved romantically. (DR, BAS1, p. 222.) Example: "I sure would like to get next to you, baby." NCU.

Get [one's] nose cold v. (1970s–1990s) to get high on cocaine or crack cocaine. (EF, RDSL, p. 239.) DCU.

Get [one's] nuts off v. (1940s–1950s) sexual release; implies ejaculation more than orgasm. (FR.) SNU.

Get [one's] mind right v. (1950s–1960s) think straight; clear thoughts; to agree with someone. (DG, KE, p. 73.) SNU, DCU, PPU, SCU.

Get off v. (1930s–1940s) jazz musical improvisation. (RSG, JL, p. 122.) Example: "When Bird gets up there he can really get off." JMFU.

Get off v. (1960s–1990s) to experience the release of injected drugs, especially after a taxing hassle to come by the stuff; as a sexual reference, ejaculation or orgasm; high from alcohol. (RRL, DAZ, p. 82; DC, BJ, p. 66.) SNCU.

Get off [one's] back v. (1970s) command to desist; "Stop bothering me." (FR.) SNU.

Get on [one's] case v. (1960s–1980s) to verbally attack; punish. (DC, BJ, p. 65; RDA, TB.) Example: "If he stays out all night, she'll really get on his case." SNCU.

Get-out n. (1940s–1950s) a person's clothing; an outfit. (FR.) Example: "You see Fox? He's got up in a bad get-out, man." YCU, SNU.

Get out of [one's] face imper. (1940s) an expression meant to warn the listener that the speaker's aura is being unacceptably invaded. (FR.) Example: "If you don't get out of my face with that garbage, you gonna be sorry." SNU.

Get out of town interj. (1980s) exclamation of friendly disbelief. (FR.) SNU.

Get over v. (1940s–1960s) to succeed at a task; sexual conquest; to overcome difficulty; to survive hardship; to get by. (CS, vol. 3, no. 2, p. 26; CD, BJ, p. 66; EF, RDSL, 77.) Example: "I can get over without working too hard." YCU, SNU.

Get previous v. (1950s–1960s) to act in a very forward manner. (FR.) Rare. South Side, Chicago, use.

Get real imper. (1980s–1990s) a command to be serious; to deal soberly with a situation. (FR.) Example: "Get real, Ricky." SNU.

Get [one's] rocks off v. (1960s) to enjoy immensely; to achieve orgasm. (FR.) SNU.

Get [one's] rug beat v. (1940s) to get a haircut. (MHB, JS, np.) Example: "Boy, you need to run down to Mister Sammy's and get your rug beat." SU.

Get [one's] self together v. (1960s–1970s) to get organized. (DR, BASL, p. 28.) SNCU.

Get sloppy v. (1980s–1990s) to get drunk. (PM, UCLAS, p. 43.) YCU.

Get some kick v. (1940s) to obtain money. (FR.) See "Kick."

Get some of this imper. (1990s) command or invitation to participate; to partake. (FR.) Example: "You can come and get some of this, if you think you can handle it." SNU.

Get someone told v. See "Get [one] told."

Get some trim v. (1950s–1990s) male term; obtain sexual intercourse. (PM, UCLAS, p. 43.) SNU. See "Trim."

Get [the] spirit; getting the spirit (1800s–1990s) to be possessed by strong emotions or supernatural force; to believe one is in touch with one's God or with supernatural forces. (GS, TT, p. 57.) SNU. See "Get happy."

Get stupid v. (1990s) act silly; to have a good time; to be slightly intoxicated. (FR.) SNU.

Get the fuck out of here exclam. (1980s–1990s) expression of friendly disbelief. (TMc, DA, p. 383.) Example: in response to being told he has just won thirty million in the lottery, a man might say, "Get the fuck out of here." SNU.

Get [one's] thing together v. (1950s–1970s) mainly to orient one's thinking and living to whatever the popular political and social notions happen to be. (FR.) SNU.

Get to v. (1950s–1960s) affect; listen to; watch; observe. (FR.) Example: "Sure he made me mad, but I'm not going to let it get to me." SNU.

Get [one] told v. (1930s–1950s) to level unpleasant criticism at someone. (FGC, DARE, p. 665.) SNU.

Get to this v. (1950s–1960s) exclamation; request to listen. (FR.) SNU.

Getting happy v. (1870s–1930s) showing spiritual possession; church shouting; feeling the spirit of a deity; getting the spirit; "religious hysteria." In the Deep South, long before the end of slavery, blacks normally got "happy" in church. It remained a tradition through the twentieth century. (JEH, AAC, p. 109.) SNU.

Getting [one's] v. (1990s) getting one's share of the good things in life. (FR.) Example: "For far too long everyone's been getting theirs; now I'm going to get mine!" SNU.

Getting on v. (1960s) getting drunk or high. (FR.) SNCU.

Getting on [one's] case v. (1960s–1970s) to tell someone off. (RDA, TB, p. 41.) SNCU.

Getting on some stiff time v. (1930s–1940s) to succeed, especially at any illicit, money-making activity. (ZNH, AM, p. 94.) SNU.

Getting over the hump v. (1950s–1960s) overcoming a difficulty—a specific difficulty, or generally speaking. (FR.) SNU.

Getting place n. (1890s–1930s) not necessarily a real place; used as a response to an unwanted question. (FR.) Example: "I could tell she was jealous when she asked me where I got my shoes, so I just said, 'The getting place.'" SNU.

Get up [off] v. (1930s–1950s) to get high; or to refrain from something; to release or relinquish something of value. (ZNH, AM, p. 95.) Examples: "He takes care of his friends. He got up off a hundred dollars when I was broke"; or "She got up off some of that good loving of hers." SNU.

Get with it v., imper. (1970s–1980s) to show enthusiasm or interest; to be physically and psychically in fashion or in the spirit of what is happening; usually a command. (FR.) SNU.

Get with the program imper. (1970s–1980s) command to go along with another's proposal. (FR.) SNCU.

GFC n. (1980s–1990s) Los Angeles gang: Godfather Crips. (EF, RDSL, p. 238.) Watts and South-central Los Angeles use.

Ghetto blaster n. (1980s) radio with powerful speakers. (FR.) SNU. See "Ghetto box."

Ghetto box n. (1980s–1990s) radio with powerful speakers. (FR.) See "Ghetto Blaster" and "Boom box."

Ghetto goddesses The Supremes; rhythm-and-blues group consisting of Diana Ross, Mary Wilson, Florence Ballard; Motown recording artists of the sixties.

Ghetto thing n. (1990s) anything culturally native to black communities. (FR.) Example: often told to those not familiar with black people or the community or the neighborhood, "You don't get it because it's a ghetto thing." NCU.

Ghostbusting v. (1980s–1990s) desperately searching—such as on the floor—for cocaine particles. (TW, CH, p. 148.) DCU.

Ghost move v. (1990s) to move quickly. (FR.) Example: "You see that motherfucker make his ghost move down the alley?" SCU.

Ghost note v. (1920s–1940s) a soft, almost unheard jazz note in a series of louder ones. (FR.) SNU.

Ghosts n. (1990s) white particles sometimes confused with crack cocaine. (FR.) DCU. See "Ghostbusting."

Gibby n. (1960s) a reckless, devil-may-care type of person, especially male. (CS, vol. 3, no. 2, p. 26.) Watts, Los Angeles, use.

Gig; gigging n., v. (1700s–1960s) trick; tease; to rock back and forth; a child's pacifier; rectum or vagina; also, a jazzman's job (later "gig" came to mean any kind of job). (DC, BJ, p. 66; KG, JV, p. 181; RDA, DDJ, p. 266; FG, DVT, n.p; RDA, DDJ, p. 266; FGC, DARE, p. 672.) SNU. See "Gig(ging) around."

Gig(ging) around v. (1900s–1960s) working at any number of jobs. (RSG, JL, pp. 123–124; CLC, TS, p. 255.) JMFU. See "Gig."

Gigi n. (1660s–1890s) of African origin; any object (toy, blanket) a child carries around like a fetish. (FR.) SU.

Gims n. (1940s) the eyes. (DB, OHHJ, p. 139.) Harlem use.

Gimming v. (1940s) gazing; sizing up someone; rudely gaping at someone. (DB, OHHJ, p. 139.) Harlem use.

Gin; ginning v. (1930s–1960s) to make the thrashing motion of a cotton gin's circular motion; to fight; a street fight or melee. (DC, BJ, p. 66; FGC, DARE, p. 676.) Example: "Allen and Garner ginned it out on the playground." SNU.

Gingerbread [cake] n. (1880s–1920s) the color of African-Americans of mixed Indian or Anglo and African ancestry; "ginger cake negro." (CWC, CW, p. 18.) SU.

Gingertown n. (1890s–1930s) a black community; section of a city populated by African-Americans. (FR.) SNU.

Gin mill n. (1880s–1940s) a run-down nightclub, especially where a jazz musician finds himself working, grudgingly. Musicians who have experienced drugs have contempt for the sloppiness of heavy drinkers or any drinking crowd. (FR.) JBWU, SNCU.

Ginny n. (1720s–1930s) a pejorative term used by Americans to refer to anybody with dark skin; probably with origins in the word "Guinea"; picked up from white use. (EP, DU, p. 287.) SNU.

Ginny n. (1980s) vagina. (FR.) SNU.

Ginny Gall n. (1900s–1940s) West Hell; a mythical, remote area in the biblical hell; an unpleasant, faraway place; also known as "Guinea Gall." (SK, PC, pp. 153–154; ZNH, AM, p. 95; TWT, NFR, p. 205.) Example: "I'd rather be an outcast in Ginny Gall than to give you another chance." SU. See "Guinea Gall."

Girl n. (1940s–1950s) cocaine, so called by males because of the sexlike feeling it gives; also, a male homosexual; from the thirties to the sixties, form of address for one woman to another; a woman. Example: "Girl, you should have seen them suckers run." (IS, PSML, p. 315; CLC, TS, p. 255; IS, TB, p. 312.) DCU.

Girlfriend n. (1980s) a somewhat aggressive term of female-to-female address; lesbian term of address (FR.) SNU.

Git; gits v. (1700s–1990s) of Gullah origin; form of "get." (AEG, BB, p. 51, 248.) Examples: "I told you once, I'm telling you twice—now git!"; and "When I gits there you better be ready to go." SNU.

Git-box; gitbox n. (1920s–1930s) a guitar. (ZNH, MM, p. 113.) SU.

Git-down; get down imper., n. (1960s–1970s) both an imperative and a descriptive phrase. As a command it means simply to experience what is happening, get "with it," get into the rhythm of the moment, feel the music (the beat); and as a descriptive phrase (as it was used on the hustling scene) it refers to the time for action, the time to steal money, or to turn tricks, to gamble, and so on. (CRM, BP, p. 301.) SNCU.

Git-go n. See "[From the] Get go."

Give a fuck v. (1950s–1990s) to care or be concerned. (FR.) Example: "Who gives a fuck about it?" SNU.

Give a shit v. (1970s–1990s) to care or be concerned, usually negated. (FR.) Example: "I don't give a shit." SNU.

Give [one] five imper., v. (1940s–1950s) a physical show of approval or greeting, enacted when two people slap their hands together. (FR.) SNU.

Give him his head v. (1970s) let a person do what he thinks best; also, to fight; metaphorically speaking, to knock one's head off and hand it to one. (FR.) SCU; YCU; SNCU.

Give it up imper. (1980s–1990s) a command for applause. (RCC, SOC, p. 20.) Example: "Give it up for our next guest." JMFU.

Give it up imper., v. (1990s) an aggressive request for a woman to surrender sexual favors. (FR.) YCU, SCU.

Give me five [on the sly] imper., v. (1950s–1990s) a request to slap hands together in agreement or approval. (EF, RDSL, p. 240.) SNCU.

Give me five [on the soul side] imper., v. (1950s–1990s) a request to slap hands together in agreement. (EF, RDSL, p. 240.) SNCU.

Give out v. (1930s–1940s) an outpouring of feeling or talk. (RSG, JL, p. 124.) Example: "Charlie really give out a lot, man, when he's on the stand." JMFU.

Give [one] some skin imper., v. (1940s–1950s) a request to slap hands in agreement. (CC, OMMM, NCCHD, p. 255; MHB, JS, np.) SNU. See "Five," "High five," and "Skin."

Give [one] some slack imper., v. (1960s–1990s) a command or request to desist pressure, criticism; to show restraint; a plea for more sympathy and understanding. (FR.) SNCU.

Give [one] some sugar imper., v. (1930s–1950s) a command or request for a kiss or to give someone a kiss. (FR.) SNU.

Give the drummer some imper., v. (1940s–1950s) a call for applause for the drummer in a small jazz group. (FR.) JMFU.

[Don't] Give [one] the jive v. (1950s–1960s) don't kid or deceive one; a request for one to be forthcoming and honest. (FR.) SNCU, YCU, SCU.

Glad pad[s] n. (1920s–1940s) dance hall or some other lively place. (DB, OHHJ, p. 139.) Harlem; SNCU.

Glide v. (1990s) to walk; move; arrive; leave. (EC, MEB, p. 11.) Example: "I'll glide in in this outfit and everybody will flip." SNU.

Glim; glimming v. (1890s–1940s) from southern folk speech, the act of seeing, especially in a glimpse. (CC, OMMM, NCCHD, p. 256.) Example: "When Heloise came through here, you should've seen Wirth glimming her—man, oh, man!" NU.

Glims; glimmers n. (1890s–1940s) the eyes. (CC, OMMM, NCCHD, p. 256; FGC, DARE, p. 688.) Example: "Victor's got big glims for Beatrice. Look at 'em!" NU.

Globetrotter n. (1960s) an addict who moves fast and frequently in search of high-quality drugs. (RRL, DAZ, p. 82.) DCU.

Glory n. (1700s–1930s) the "Negro" slaves' term for the Christian concept of Heaven. (FR.) SU.

Glory roll n. (1930s–1940s) a large roll of money carried in the pocket, especially to impress others with. (DB, OHHJ, p. 139.)

Glue-sniffing v. (1950s) inhaling the fumes of model airplane glue in order to get stoned. (FR.) SCU.

Gnat butter n. (1900s–1940s) decayed skin tissue; smegma under foreskin or clitoris. (FGC, DARE, p. 694.) Georgia use.

Go v. (1630s–1950s) pronounced "gwine"; to go. (AEG, BB, p. 305.) SU.

Go vi. (1920s–1940s) an enthusiastic expression of encouragement, especially to a jazz performer making music. (RSG, JL, p. 125.) Example: "The first time he caught Miles live, Little Johnny was so blown away, man, that dude jumped up, knocking over chairs, yelling, 'Go, man, go!' " JMFU.

Go along with v. (1950s–1970s) to agree with. (FR.) Example: "I'll go along with that."

Goat-hair n. (1940s–1950s) homemade whiskey or liquor; bootleg liquor. (RDA, DDJ, p. 266.) Philadelphia use; SCU, PPU.

[Hair] Go back v. (1900s–1950s) for the pressed or processed hair to return to its normal state. (FR; GS, TT, p. 65.) Example: "Babette won't go out the house when her hair go back." SNU. See "Nappy edges."

Gobble v. (1920s–1940s) to talk. (FR.) SU. See "Gobble-gobble."

Gobble-gobble n. (1920s–1940s) to talk. (MHB, JS, np.) Example: "When Miss Lou Lou come over to the house all she and Mama do is gobble. I can't stand it, so I get outta there." SNU.

God George Baker, born 1874, died 1965 on Hutchinson's Island, Georgia; known as Father Divine or Minister. His followers believed he was God.

[The] Godfather of Soul James Brown, singer; born around 1936. See "Soul Brother Number One."

God [has] gone to Jersey City (1930s–1940s) an oath, applied to an impossibility. (ZNH, AM, p. 89.) Example: "If I'm lying, God done gone to Jersey City." Harlem use.

God made dirt and dirt don't hurt (1970s–1990s) a children's saying used after they drop food on the ground or floor and brush it off and eat it. (FR.) Very young child use.

Go(es) down; went down v.i. (1950s) anything occurring. (DW, TL, p. 182) Examples: "If you pull that shit again you'll see what go down"; and, "I'm telling you exactly what went down." SCU, YCU, PPU.

Go-down n. (1940s) a basement apartment. (DB, OHHJ, p. 139.) Harlem use.

Go down [on] v. (1940s–1970s) to perform cunnilingus or fellatio; from the sixties to the seventies, that which happens; to occur. (FR.) SNU.

God's amount n. (1900s–1930s) of Gullah origin; a great number or quantity of anything; large amount or abundance. (HMH, HCWR, p. 1098.) SU.

God's plenty n. See "God's amount."

Gofer; go-for n. (1940s–1960s) one who approves of something; person excited about carrying out a task; someone who shows enthusiasm for anything. (JH, PBL, p. 84.) SNU.

Go for v. (1950s) to be considered for. (FR.) Example: "I'm going for the president's job. Wish me luck."

Go for soul v. (1930s–1940s) an all-out expression of deeply felt excitement. (FR.) JMFU.

Go home v. (1920s–1940s) an agreement among jazzmen to do the final chorus of a number, to "ride out" to the end. (RSG, JT, p. 110.) JMFU. See "Take it home."

Go in and out the window n. (1900s–1940s) a British children's game and song black children in the south played to African rhythms. (BJ, BLH, SD, pp. 76–77.) SU.

Going back v. (1900s–1970s) processed or straightened hair returning to its natural state. (FR.) SNU. See "Do" and "Do-rag."

Going down vi. (1950s–1960s) that which is happening; event; occurrence. (DG, W, p. 103.) Example: "I swear I don't understand what's going down." SCU, YCU.

Going down the river (1900s–1940s) going to the state prison in Mississippi. (AL, LWBB, p. 258.) SU, PU.

Going through changes v. (1960s–1970s) experiencing mood swings; changing one's outlook. (FR.) Example: "I don't like to go back home to visit my mother and father 'cause they still be going through changes they went through when I was a kid at home. I get sick of it." SNCU. See "Changes."

Goldberg n. (1930s–1960s) sometimes derogatory, sometimes not; any Jewish merchant running a business in any black neighborhood. (CRM, BP, p. 301; EF, RDSL, p. 240.) See "Abe."

Golded; golded-up v. (1800s–1940s) gilded, as in a gilded spittoon or gold-plated grandfather clock. (SK, PC, p. 154; ZNH, TEWG, p. 76.) SU.

Golden girl n. (1970s–1980s) high-quality cocaine. (EF, RDSL, p. 240.) South-central Los Angeles; DCU.

Golden leaf n. (1920s–1940s) very good marijuana. (FR.) NCU.

Gold fish n. (1940s) sliced peaches. (MHB, JS, np.) Example: "Seem like they serve them canned gold fish in the cafeteria every day in the week." SU.

Gold fish bowl n. (1950s–1960s) a married woman, especially one seduced by a man who is not her husband. (James Alan McPherson, "The Story of a Scar," CM, CW, p. 355.) Example: "Lots of men like to fish in gold fish bowls 'cause they know they don't have to give the woman nothing or marry her." SNU.

Golliwog n. (1890s) an emblem in the form of a grotesque wide-eyed black youth. The term originated among Anglo-Saxon speakers but was widely used among black people and first appeared in children's books by Bertha and Florence Upton. (FGC, DARE, p. 722.) SNU.

Go-long n. (1920s–1940s) unpleasant circumstances; a truck used by policemen to transport large numbers of arrested people to jail; a paddy wagon. (ZNH, TEWG, p. 159; ZNH, AM, p. 92.) SU. See "Dry so long."

Go-man-go v. (1940s) a cry of encouragement, especially to a performer of one kind or another. (RSG, JL, p. 125.) JMFU. See "Go."

Gon v. (1620s–1990s) a form of "going to." (FR.) SNU.

Gone v. (1890s–1950s) exhausted from hard work or illness; from the 1940s to the 1950s, anything unusually exciting and good, sometimes to the extent of being unreal; in a trance; crazy. (MM, RR, p. 370.) JMFU, SNCU.

Goner n. (1650s–1950s) one who is close to dying; one who is in serious trouble. (FR.) SNU.

Gonest vi. (1940s–1950s) the best. (RSG, JT, p. 111.) JMFU.

Go north interj. (1860s–1940s) advice to leave the South—the stronghold of slavery and black oppression. A common expression among the newly freed slaves, it held on from the 1860s till the 1940s when the great black migrations north began to taper off. (DC, BJ, p. 66.) Example: "Go north, man, go north!" SU.

Goo n. (1920s–1950s) sticky food or human blood. (DB, OHHJ, p. 139.) SNU.

Goo-goo watch n. (1930s–1940s) the early hours of the morning. (DB, OHHJ, p. 139.) SU.

Goober n. (1700s–1940s) peanut; from the Bantu word *nguba*; of African origin; a person who can work magic, cast a spell. (HV, AHAE, p. 141; FGC, DARE, p. 725; SBF, IHAT, p. 32.) SNU.

Goober dust (goofer dust; geube dust; gubi dust; gibi dust) n. (1700s–1940s) of African origin; graveyard dust; the bone dust of a black cat; dirt to which magical powers have been assigned. (DW, TL, p. 182; FGC, DARE, p. 725.) SU.

Goobers n. (1650s–1940s) peanuts; *nguba* (Bantu). (LDT, AGO, p. 194.) SU.

Goodest adj. (1890s–1940s) the best. (FR.)

Good fashion adv. (1700s–1950s) of Gullah origin; to do something completely and to the fullest satisfaction; completely and effectively done. (AEG, BB, p. 304.) SU.

Good hair n. (1800s–1950s) straight or almost straight hair (a concept that began to disappear in the early sixties with the renewal of black consciousness); silky straight hair. (GS, TT, p. 64; ZNH, AM, p. 95.) Example: "Semar won't hardly go with no girl who ain't got good hair." SNU.

Good shit n. (1980s) excellent-quality drugs. (KCJ, JC, p. 155.) DCU.

Go off on v. (1960s–1980s) to become angry enough to deliver an impassioned lecture to someone who is offensive. (FR.) SCU, DCU, PPU, PU.

Good people n. (1950s–1970s) someone who's considered honest or "for real"; a decent person; a friendly person. (CS, vol. 3, no. 2, p. 27.) Example: "She's good people, man, stick by her, 'cause if you don't I'm gonna be trying to get next to her." SNU.

Good stick n. (1980s–1990s) nausea and vomiting after use of heroin; considered not unpleasant. (FR.) DCU.

Goody bread n. (1700s–1940s) crackling bread; a bread with a sprinkling of pork rinds; "a favorite dish of the negroes." (JSF, AON, p. 175.) SU.

Goof n., v. (1940s–1950s) a mistake; to make a mistake; a stupid person. (FR.) SNU.

Goof doctor n. See "Goofer," "Hoodoo," "Hoochie-choochie (man or woman)." (FR.) SNU.

Goof ball(s) n. (1940s–1950s) a narcotic in the form of a pill. (FR.) DCU.

Goofer v. (1880s–1920s) conjure; to cast a spell or bewitch someone; n. (1920s–1930s) grave dust or dirt; peanut (Bantu origin). (CC, CW, p. 11; HMH, HCWR, p. 222; NNP, FBSN, p. 215; FGC, DARE, p. 729.) SU.

Goofer [dirt or dust] n. (1620s–1930s) dirt from a grave or from a graveyard used in conjure work; from the verb *kufwa* (Ki-Kongo), which means "to die." (RFT, FS, p. 105; CC, CW, p. 11, 15; NNP, FBSN, p. 215; HV, AHAE, p. 141.) SU.

Goofer-bag n. (1700s–1940s) a bag of charms or conjuring objects; *kufwa* (Bantu), which means providing for death or protection from bad luck or death. (HV, AHAE, p. 141.) SU.

Goo-gobs adj. (1930s–1950s) plenty; an excessive amount. (FR.) SNU.

Goola n. (1900s–1940s) piano. (DB, OHHJ, p. 139.) JMFU.

Goon squad n. (1960s) mediocre political leadership; cops. (FR.) SNCU.

Gopher n. (1920s–1930s) land tortoise; in the sixties, one who is excited about something, who works hard to accomplish something. (DC, BJ, p. 66.) Example: "I've been a gopher for that position too long to give up now." SU. See "Gofer."

Gorgeous adj. (1900s–1940s) pungent and rich in flavor; the taste of rabbit or possum meat. (FGC, DARE, p. 743.) Georgia use. SU.

Gorilla v. (1900s–1950s) to strong-arm someone; to use physical force. (IS, PSML, p. 315; EF, RDSL, p. 240; IS, PSML, p. 315.) Example: "If you gorilla that sonofabitch he'll stay outta your way." SCU, PU, PPU.

Gorilla pimp n. (1940s–1960s) a stupid, crude, tactless hustler; any stupid pimp who uses more muscle than brains. (IS, PSML, p. 315; CRM, BP, p. 302; EF, RDSL, p. 240.) Example: "Paul ain't nothing but a dumb gorilla pimp; no wonder his bitches don't respect him." PPU, SCU, PU. See "Mack man."

Gospel n. (1680s–1950s) the Negro slaves' term for the Truth; the absolute truth. (FR.) SU.

Gospel bird n. (1930s–1940s) barnyard chicken, so called because in the south fried chicken was a favorite on Sunday, the Christian holy day, especially if the preacher was coming to dinner. (ZNH, MM, p. 32; JLD, LBE, p. 58.) SU.

Gospel plow n. (1680s–1860s) the Negro slave's term for the Righteous Way of living. (FR.) SU.

Got [one's] boots on adj. (1940s) to be wise, hip; also, to use a condom. (CC, OMMM, NCCHD, p. 256.) Example: "You can't play Sapphira for no fool, she got her boots on." Harlem; YCU, SNCU.

Got down v. (1960s) to perform in a superior way. (FR.) Example: "Man, the way he plays! He really got down." JMFU. See "Down" and "Get down."

Got [one's] glasses on adj. (1930s–1940s) derogatory term meaning to appear intellectual; smart; alert; high-class. (CC, OMMM, NCCHD, p. 256.) Example: "When Selene got her glasses on you can't tell her nothing—she thinks she knows everything." SNU.

Got [one's] nose open adj. (1950s–1960s) to be in love. (HLF, RJPD, p. 171.) Example: "He's really got his nose open for her." SNCU. See "Nose open."

Got it going on adj. (1990s) refers to anything timely; that which is fashionable; looking good. (FR.) Example: "She's really got it going on with her fine self." YCU.

Go to town v. (1930s–1950s) in music, to perform vigorously; any musical activity accompanied by extreme excitement; in general, to passionately commit oneself to something. (RSG, JT, p. 110.) Examples: "That boy sure does go to town at the table when Grandma serve fried chicken and peach pie." JMFU, SNU.

Gots v. (1700s–1940s) variant of "got." (AEG, BB, p. 51, 248.) See "Git."

Go-up n. (1920s–1950s) an upstairs apartment. (DB, OHHJ, p. 139.) SCU, YCU.

Go up Salt River v. (1900s–1940s) to die. (DB, OHHJ, p. 139.) SU.

Go upside [one's] head v. (1950s–1960s) to strike. (FR.) YCU, SCU.

Go when the wagon comes v. (1930s–1940s) the outcome of any situation beyond one's control; everybody will be arrested when the police wagon (van) comes. (ZNH, AM, p. 95.) SNCU.

Go with v. (1960s) to date. (FR.) Example: "I know I love you, baby. Want to go with me?" SNU.

Grab n. (1930s–1990s) a term that dates back to the 1750s; an arrest by police. (EP, DU, p. 302.) Example: "The goons came in the hood and made a grab early Sunday morning when nobody expected them." New Jersey and New York; DCU, PPU, PU, SCU, NCU.

Grab a sitdown v. (1970s–1980s) take a seat; sit down. (FR.) SNU.

Grab a stump to rest [one's] rump v. (1940s–1960s) See "Find a stump to fit [one's] rump."

Grabbers n. (1940s–1950s) the hands; the fingers. (FGC, DARE, p. 752.) See "Meathooks."

Gracious to goodness adj. (1800s–1940s) a large amount; massive; mighty. (FR.) "This is a gracious to goodness lot of food, Mama, I can't eat all this—take some of it back." SU.

Grafty adj. (1950s–1970s) mean and stingy. (FGC, DARE, p. 754.)

G-rag n. (1960s) a tiny cloth for an opium pipe. (CS, vol. 3, no. 2, p. 25.) Watts, Los Angeles, use.

Grand n. (1780s–1950s) grandchild. (AEG, BB, p. 304.) SU.

Grand n. (1930s–1950s) a thousand dollars. (WF, DAS, p. 226; IS, PSML, p. 315.) See "G."

[Do a] Grand v., n. (1950s–1960s) to succeed; fine results. (CS, vol. 3, no. 2, p. 20.) Example: "She did a grand when she made my mother feel right at home." Watts, Los Angeles, use.

Grandbaby n. (1700s–1990s) grandchild. (FR.) Example: "This here my grandbaby, ain't she cute?" SU.

Granddaddy n. (1700s–1990s) grandfather. (FGC, DARE, p. 757.) SNU.

Grandma [grandmama; grandmomma; grandmammy] n. (1700s–1990s) grandmother. (FR; AEG, BB, p. 304.) SNU.

Grandma change (1930s–1940s) see "Money's mammy." (ZNH, AM, p. 92.) SNU.

Grandmaster Flash and the Furious Five (1990s) rap group specializing in the hip-hop style.

Grand theft n. (1960s) a large sum of stolen money. (CS, vol. 3, no. 2, p. 27.) SCU, PPU, PU.

Granny Grunt n. (1930s–1940s) a matriachal (and funny) mythic figure to whom members of the Harlem community could address questions regarding difficulties in the future. (ZNH, AM, p. 95.) Harlem use.

Grape(s) n. (1960s–1970s) money. (JH, PBL, p. 84.) Rare. New York City use.

Grape-cat n. (1940s) a male who drinks a great deal of wine. (DB, OHHJ, p. 139.) SCU.

Grape-chick n. (1940s) a female who drinks a great deal of wine. (DB, OHHJ, p. 139.) SCU.

Grapes n. (1930s–1960s) hemorrhoids (HEG, DAU, p. 86); wine (DC, BJ, p. 66). Example: "Netty and Alva sure like their grapes. They sit in the kitchen all afternoon sharing a bottle and gossiping." SNU.

Grape Society n. (1930s–1950s) any street gathering of cheap wine drinkers. (FR.) NCU.

Grapes of wrath n. (1940s) wine; phrase taken from the Scriptures and also a play on John Steinbeck's popular novel of the same title (MHB, JS, np.) Example: "They be back there in the back room gambling, cussing, and in their grapes of wrath."

Grapevine telegraph [telephone] system n. (1860s–1920s) the chain of verbal communication in a black community. A pre–Civil War expression, referred to in Margaret Mitchell's *Gone with the Wind*. (FGC, DARE, p. 768.) SU.

Grass n. (1930s–1970s) marijuana; also white folks' hair. (CS, vol. 3, no. 2, p. 27.) DCU. See "Silk."

Grasshead n. (1960s) a heavy smoker of marijuana. (CS, vol. 3, no. 2, p. 27.) Watts, Los Angeles; DCU.

Grassing v. (1930s–1940s) outdoor sexual horseplay; intercourse on the grass. (FGC, DARE, p. 769.) Florida use.

Graveyard dirt n. (1620s–1930s) dirt lifted from a grave's pit or site to be used in conjuring or hoodoo ceremonies. (FGC, DARE, p. 778.) SU. See "Goofer."

Gravy n. (1940s–1990s) money or the power it generates; overtime on the job at double pay; also, in the 1980s "gravy" came to mean heroin. (CC, OMMM, NCCHD, p. 256.) SNU.

Gravy on [one's] grits adj. (1930s–1940s) to be in good shape; successful. (SK, PC, p. 288.) Example: "He won't even hardly speak to us now that he got gravy on his grits and all." SU.

Gray [boy; dude; chick; broad] n. (1950s–1980s) a white person, male or female; in the eighties, includes light-skinned Spanish-speaking people in the Los Angeles area; also a light-skinned black person, but rare. (RHDeC, NB, p. 31; DC, BJ, p. 66; CRM, BP, p. 302; JH, PBL, 84; CB, MPL, p. 166; EF, RDSL, p. 54; DB, OHHJ, p. 139.) SNU.

Gray dog n. (1970s–1980s) the police. (EF, RDSL, p. 240.) Watts and South-central Los Angeles; SCU.

Graze v. (1950s) to eat. See "Grease."

Grease; grease [one's] chops n. (1920s–1970s) a black man; black person; v. to eat, especially greasy food [Gullah]. (FGC, DARE, p. 789; FR; HLF, RJPD, p. 170; DB, OHHJ, p. 139.) Example: "Billy Joe so fat 'cause all he think about is eating. That boy grease his chops more than any six little boys put together." SNU. See "Peck" and "Scarf."

Grease back v. (1940s–1950s) to eat with great ceremony and vigor or voraciously. (MHB, JS, np.) Example: "Steve is one you can count on to grease back when his grandma gets in the kitchen to burn." SNU. See "Grease."

Grease [one's] chops v. (1930s–1960s) to eat. See "Grease."

Grease [one's] mouth v. (1850s–1920s) a Gullah term meaning to eat greasy meat, especially pork. (AEG, BB, p. 304.) Example:

"Daddy roast a pig. I'm gon grease my mouth." South Carolina and Georgia use.

Greaser n. (1920s–1970s) one who engages in eating food, especially with relish. (FR.) SNU.

Greasy aces n. (1930s–1940s) a special paper treatment which allows the card cheat to detect the aces. (HEG, DAUL, p. 86.) Example: "Myron don't need no card up his sleeve, man, he got greasy aces to depend on." SNU.

Greasy fingers n. (1930s–1940s) a pickpocket. (FR.) SCU, PPU, PU.

Greasy junkie n. (1960s) a shiftless, lazy junkie. (RRL, DAZ, p. 86.) DCU.

Greasy spoon n. (1920s–1970s) a restaurant serving boiled, oily, and fried foods, specifically associated with black culture; soul-food restaurant. (FR.) SNU.

[The] Greatest heavyweight boxing champion Muhammad Ali; born Cassius Clay, January 17, 1942, in Louisville, Kentucky. See "Louisville Lip."

Great getting up morning n. (1700s–1940s) Christian Judgment Day. This phrase is common in the spirituals. (FR.) SNU.

Great white father n. (1930s–1940s) used ironically or in jest, this term usually refers to the president of the United States, but actually can be used for any extremely powerful authoritarian figure who happens to be white. (DB, OHHJ, p. 139.) SNU.

Greeks n. (1920s–1940s) persons of black, Indian, and Anglo ancestry. (BB, AW, p. 36.) South Carolina use.

[Long] Green n. (1950s–1960s) money; sometimes, a considerable sum of money. (CS, vol. 3, no. 2, p. 27.) Example: "You need that long green to make it in the Big Apple." SNU.

Green banana n. (1930s–1940s) a young light-skinned woman or girl. (DB, OHHJ, p. 139.) Harlem; SNU.

Green door n. (1960s–1970s) the execution chamber door in New York state prisons. (DW, TL, p. 182.) PU.

Greens n. (1800s–1960s) leafy part of root vegetables; collards, mustard. (FR.) SNU.

Green shit n. (1950s–1960s) money, especially a roll of bills. (DG, NDA, p. 48.) Example: "You ain't nowhere less you got a roll of green shit like this." PPU, DCU, SCU.

Grey n. see "Gray."

Greyhound v. (1940s–1950s) to run fast. (FR.) Example: "Look at that boy greyhound it; look just like a jackrabbit." SU.

Greyhounding v. (1960s) dating a white person. (DC, BJ, p. 67.) Example: "That dude's got a complex. He's always greyhounding." MWU.

Griffa n. (1960s) marijuana cigarette. (FR.) DCU.

Griffe n. (1780s–1920s) the offspring of a full-blooded African and a mulatto; the child of white and black parents; the offspring of two mulattoes. (FGC, DARE, p. 811; EBR, MUR, p. 12.) SU. See "Marabou."

Grill n. (1940s) the stomach. (MHB, JS, np.) Example: "That joker will eat anything that won't crawl back up out of his grill." Southern Negro college student; SU. See "Bread basket."

Grind [on]; grinding v. (1950s–1960s) the hip motion made during sexual intercourse; also close dancing, belly-rubbing dancing; a common reference in the blues. (HLF, RJPD, p. 170; RDA, DDJ, p. 266; CS, vol. 4, no. 2, p. 6.) SNU.

Grine salt v. (1850s–1880s) to fly around in a circle as a bird might do. (CCJ, NMGC, p. 169.) Georgia and the Carolinas use.

Grip v. (1960s) to brag, then back down after boasting. (DC, BJ, p. 67.) Example: "Don't grip now, man, you've got 'em all going."

Gris-gris n. (1700s–1940s) a charm to protect against evil—worn or carried on the body. (HV, AHAE, p. 141.)

Grit n., v. (1940s–1960s) food; or to eat. (HLF, RJPD, p. 170.) Example: "She ain't got grit the first in the house to feed all them children"; and, "I'm hungry, I wanna grit." SNU. See "Gritting."

Grits and grease n. (1930s–1960s) hominy grits seasoned with bacon grease. (DC, BJ, p. 67.) SNU.

Gritting v. (1990s) eating; eating hominy grits. (Listen to Black Sheep, "Flavor of the Month," William McLean and Andres Titus. (c)

1991 Peep Bo Music/RRL Music, Inc. ASCAP.) Example: "They be gritting way back down at McDonald's." SNU.

Grizzly Bear n. (1910–1920) a jazz dance. (RSG, JT, p. 114.) JMFU.

Groan box n. (1900s–1920s) Accordion; bass fiddle. (DB, OHHJ, p. 139.) Harlem; JMFU. See "Squeeze box."

Grog n. (1940s–1960s) from Old English, meaning liquor; beer. (FGC, DARE, p. 815; DC, BJ, p. 67.) MWU.

Groove n., v. (1940s–1950s) in jazz, one's style or manner of playing; any type of excellent music; generally, any good feeling or thought. (RSG, JL, p. 130.) Examples: "Bud's melodic groove is complex and intense"; and "Going to the fair, now that's something I can groove on." JMFU, SNU.

Groovy adj. (1930s–1950s) excellent; enjoyable; smart; stylish; alert. Rare among black speakers after the fifties but popular among white users of slang during the sixties and after. (FR, AY, S, p. 82; CC, OMMM, NCCHD, p. 256; CS, vol. 3, no. 2, p. 27; JH, PBL, p. 84.) NU.

Ground apple n. (1940s) a brick or rock or stone. (DB, OHHJ, p. 139.) Harlem; SNU.

Ground grabbers; grippers n. (1930s–1940s) shoes, especially new ones. (CC, OMMM, NCCHD, p. 256; DB, OHHJ, p. 139.) SNU.

Groundpads [bags] n. (1930s–1940s) feet or shoes or socks. (DB, OHHJ, p. 139.) Harlem; SNU.

Groundpad spade n. (1930s–1940s) a shoehorn. (DB, OHHJ, p. 139.) Harlem; SNU.

Ground rations n. (1930s–1940s) sexual intercourse. (ZNH, AM, p. 95.) Harlem; SNU.

Grounds n. (1960s) the residue from heroin. (CS, vol. 3, no. 2, p. 27.) DCU.

Growl v., n., adj. (1920s–1940s) in jazz, a crude tone produced on the trumpet, thought of as the nitty-gritty, gut-bucket, funky, down-in-the-dirt sound. (RSG, JL, p. 131; CC, OMMM, NCCHD, p. 256; DB, OHHJ, p. 139.) Rare. JMFU.

Grub; grubbing n., v. (1800s–1960s) food; originally a variant of "scrub"—for underbrush, stumps, and roots—but later used by cow-boys and the military and black speakers to mean food. (ECLA, NN, p. 266; FGC, DARE, p. 831; DC, BJ, p. 67; PM, UCLAS, p. 45.) SNU.

Gruesome twosome n. (1940s) a couple in a steady relationship. (FR.) SNU.

Grunt n. (1960s) a bowel movement; a foot soldier during the Vietnam war; a meal (WF, DAS, p. 688; DC, BJ, p. 67). Military; MWU.

GT Granville Hogan, drummer; born in Galveston, Texas, on January 16, 1929. He has worked with Bud Powell and Randy Weston.

Guided missile n. (1990s) the erect human penis. (TW, CH, p. 149.) New York City; DCU.

Guinea n. (1780s–1860s) a black sold into slavery from the coast of Guinea; any black slave on a southern plantation. During the early stages of slavery, slaves were called by the region from which they came. After a hundred years or so that practice vanished. (SBF, IHAT, p. 55.) Example: "Bring that Guinea in here, but make sure he washes his feet first." SU.

Guinea Gall n. (1850s–1940s) West Hell; a horrible place; far away. (TWT, NFR, p. 205.) SU. See "Ginny Gall."

Guinea Paradise n. (1920s–1930s) conjuring seeds. (ZNH, MM, p.) See "Egyptian Paradise Seed." SU.

Gullah n. (1680s–1990s) African-Americans of coastal Georgia and South Carolina; probably from the Ngola-Angola (Bantu) ethnic group; or from Gola, a tribe in Liberia. (HV, AHAE, p. 141; SBF, IHAT, p. 32.) SU.

Gullah n. (1680s–1990s) a type of plantation Creole spoken off coastal South Carolina and Georgia and the nearby islands. Probably a variant of the West African word *Gola*. (HV, AHAE, p. 141; SBF, IHAT, p. 32.) SU. See "Geechee."

Gullah Jack (1820s) a well-known conjure and root doctor and also an insurrection leader. (JEH, A, p. 37.) SU.

Gully-low adj. (1900s–1950s) in jazz, much the same meaning as "growl"; a gut-bucket, low-down sound; in general use it refers to a poverty-ridden, unsophisticated life-style. (RSG, JL, p. 132.) JBWU, SNU.

Gum beating n. (1930s–1990s) silly talk; excessive talk. (RCC, SOC, p. 17.) SNU.

Gum-beating v. (1940s–1950s) talking, especially excessively. (MHB, JS, np; ZNH, AM, p. 95.) Example: "I can't stand to go there 'cause they always gum-beating somebody to death." SNU.

Gumbo n. (1800s–1990s) soup; from *kingombo* (Bantu/Tshiluba); a thick soup of okra and shrimp and spiced with filè. (SBF, IHAT, p. 32; HV, AHAE, p. 151.) New Orleans; SU, SNU.

Gumbo file n. see "Gumbo."

Gumdrop(s) n. (1970s–1990s) narcotics in capsule form. (EF, RDSL, p. 241.) DCU.

Gumshoe n. (1950s) policeman. (CW, TM, p. 105.) SCU, PU.

Gun; gunning v. (1930s–1940s) to look, especially forcefully or openly and rudely. (DB, OHHJ, p. 139.) Example: "See how that joker's gunning Mary Jo?" SNCU.

Gungeon; Jamaican ganga; gunja n. (1930s–1960s) potent marijuana, either from Africa or Jamaica. (RRL, DAZ, p. 87.) Harlem; DCU. See "Gauge."

Gunny n. (1960s) marijuana; may be variant of "bag" (gunny sack) as in "carrying the bag [marijuana]." (CS, vol. 3, no. 2, p. 28.) Watts, Los Angeles; DCU.

Gunpowder n. (1900s–1930s) gin. (FR.) SNU.

Guns n. (1980s–1990s) breasts. (EF, RDSL, p. 241.) South-central Los Angeles; YCU, SCU.

Gusto n. (1960s) beer. (DC, BJ, p. 67.) MWU.

Gut n. (1890s–1920s) a natural ditch, channel, or narrow stream, dry or full; usually in the swamps. (ECLA, CS, p. 113.) SU.

Gutbucket; gut-bucket n., adj. (1890s–1950s) bucket used to carry beer; a dive for drinking; from about 1900 to 1950 or so, "gutbucket" meant a low-down, nitty-gritty blues style of jazz originally played in gin mills, barrelhouses, whorehouses, and honky-tonks. The word referred to the smaller bucket placed beneath the larger liquor barrels to catch the gin leakage in such places. (CC, OMMM, NCCHD, p. 256; RSG, JL, p. 132; RSG, JT, p. 116; ZNH, AM, p. 95.) SNU.

Gut food n. (1930s–1940s) fallen arches. (ZNH, AM, p. 95.) NSU.

Guts n., adj. (1930s–1950s) short for "gutbucket," that raw, cultural feeling that characterizes the blues; emotional and spiritual honesty coming from the very bottom of the self; down-to-earth playing or "blowing." (RSG, JL, p. 133.) JBWU, SNU. See "Soul."

Gutterings n. (1890s–1920s) the "droppings" from liquor barrels in the barrelhouses and honky-tonks of cities such as New Orleans, where jazz and blues formally started. (FGC, DARE, p. 855.) JMFU, PPU. See "Gutbucket."

Gutter music n. (1900s–1930s) a type of black music originating in New Orleans; low-down, nitty-gritty music. (RSG, JL, p. 133.) New Orleans; JMFU, SU.

Gutter talk n. (1900s–1950s) talk considered offensive in polite society; barrelhouse talk. (FR.) SNU. See "Gutbucket," "Guts," "Gutter music," and "Gutty."

Gutty adj. (1930s–1940s) of the gutter. (RSG, JL, p. 133.) SNU. See "Gutter music" and "Guts."

Gwyne; gwine v. (1700s–1990s) of British and Gullah origin; a form of "going." (CCJ, NMGC, p. 15; LDT, AGD, pp. 225–275; AEG, BB, p. 103.) SU.

Gwinter v. (1700s–1990s) going to. (FGC, DARE, p. 696.) SU.

H

H n. (1930s) heroin. (WF, DAS, p. 238; IS, PSML, p. 315.) DCU.

Habit n. (1930s–1960s) drug habit; usually refers to the heavy use of heroin. (RRL, DAZ, p. 88.) Example: "Marla got a habit so bad it keeps her from having a normal relationship with her husband." DCU.

Hack n. (1850s–1960s) known among black speakers in North Carolina as an evil spell; anger or annoyance; a white person; a prison guard; embarrassment. (MM, RB, p. 333; CH, CFS, p. 295; FR; RRL, DAZ, p. 8; CB, MPL, p. 239; DW, TL, pp. 182–183.) PU, SCU.

Hacked adj. (1940s–1950s) irritated; exhausted. (FR.) SNU.

Hag n. (1620s–1890s) of Gullah origin; an evil spirit; the skinless body of a ghost. (HMH, HCWR, p. 158; LDT, AGD, p. 275.) Georgia, Virginia, South Carolina use.

Hag-hollering n. (1760s–1940s) of Gullah origin; a vicious night cry; crowing; screaming; also, midnight. (FGC, DARE, p. 867.) South Carolina; SU.

Hagfish adj. (1760s–1940s) bad or rotten fish contaminated by a hag or evil spirit. (FGC, DARE, p. 867.) South Carolina use.

Hagride v., n. (1900s–1940s) to nag; torment verbally; harass while asleep; a nightmare about a witch. (HMH, HCWR, p. 135, 143.) Example: "His aunt hagrode him awake every time he fell asleep." South Carolina; SU.

Haim (haiming; hame; hime) n., v. (1950s–1960s) a job other than in music; any modest-paying job; also, to be employed at such a job. (CLC, TS, p. 255; DC, BJ, p. 67; LF, EJ, p. 346.) Example: "Man, I'm sick of haiming at Ludlow's for chicken feed." DCU. See "Hang" and "Slave."

Haint n. (1690s–1940s) may be defined as ghost, spirit, specter, phantom, apparition, a disembodied spirit; probably a corruption of haunt. (AEG, BB, p. 305.) SU.

Haircut v. (1900s–1940s) to be robbed or cheated; to be abused in some way by a woman (from the biblical story of Samson and Delilah); to feel a physical cut or scraping of the penis or vagina during sexual intercourse. (FR.) SNU.

Hairdick n. (1830s–1940s) an unbranded calf. (SK, PC, pp. 222–223.) Palmetto County, Florida, use.

Haiti n. (1850s–1950s) the black section of some northern cities or towns; in the 1950s, the black sections of Pittsburgh and Uniontown, Pennsylvania; picked up from white use. (FR.) Philadelphia use.

Half a man n. (1980s–1990s) derogatory expression for an effeminate homosexual. (WKB, JMC, PS, p. 49.) Example: "You get a dude come in here half a man he going to catch hell from everybody." PU, SCU.

Half-and-half n. (1930s–1960s) hermaphrodite; in the sixties, person of black and white parentage; after the brand-name dairy product Half & Half. (FR.) SNU.

Half-ass(ed) adj. (1900s–1990s) careless; ineffective; inadequate; to exert a halfhearted effort at a task; insufficiently done; poor in quality. (FGC, DARE, p. 876.) SNU. See "Piss-poor."

Half a stretch away n. (1930s–1940s) the distance of one half of a city block. (DB, OHHJ, p. 139.) NU.

Halfer(s); halvers n. (1870s–1930s) one who shares half of the profits, as from cotton or corn farming. After the Civil War, blacks entered agreements with white farmers to share farming profits but rarely got their share. (JMB, WB, p. 69; AL, RS, p. 92; FGC, DARE, p. 881.) Sharecroppers; SU.

Half-in-two adj., v. (1890s–1930s) in two parts or sections; break in half. (ZNH, MM, p. 93.) SU.

Half past a colored man n. (1940s) 12:30 AM; usually stated as a response to a request for the time. (FR.) SNU.

Half set n. (1950s–1960s) a less-than-acceptable offer—usually in illegal drug dealings. (DG, CR, p. 48.) DCU.

Half strainer n. (1750s–1940s) a person anxious to move up the social ladder; a particularly ambitious social climber. (FGC, DARE, p. 879.) SU.

Hall n. (1900s–1940s) short for "dance hall"; anyplace where jazz musicians gather to perform. (RSG, JT, pp. 118–119.) JMFU.

Ham n. (1700s–1940s) in Christianity, Noah considered Ham the ancient ancestor of black people; picked up from white use. (FR.) SNU.

Hambone n. (1890s–1940s) probably a reference to the human thigh and the hip; word used in children's jingles ("Hambone, Hambone, where you been?"); from the late nineteenth century through the thirties, an all-purpose metaphor for black cultural experience; variously known to refer to rhythm, the penis, hard times. (JLD, LBE, p. 33; BJ, BLH, SD, p. 34.) SNU.

Ham buggy n. (1940–1950) variant of "hamburger." (Hear Big Mama Thornton, "School Boy," *Ball 'n' Chain*, 1989, Arhoolie Productions.) SNU.

Ham fat n. (1900s–1930s) mediocre person or thing. (MM, RB, p. 58.) SNU.

Hamhocks n. (1950s–1990s) a woman's legs and ankles. (EF, RDSL, p. 241.) SNU.

Ham kick n. (1900s–1930s) a social game in a dance hall or social club designed to give men a peek at the underpants or thighs of young women; the woman who could kick a ham that was hung high up won the meat. (RSG, JL, p. 136; RSG, JT, p. 119.) Example: "I don't want my girl to go to the ham kick tonight, but I sure would like to go myself." JMFU, SNU.

Hammer n. (1950s–1960s) any attractive girl or woman. (DC, BJ, p. 64; JH, PBL, p. 84.) Example: "Mercedes is a real hammer; every dude on the block wants to get next to her." SNU.

Hammer n. (1970s) a golf club. (GS, TT, p. 58.) Black golf players' use.

Hammer-man n. (1960s–1970s) a man in authority; penis. (FR.) SNU.

Hammers n. (1960s–1980s) female thighs. (EF, RDSL, p. 241.) South-central Los Angeles; SCU, NCU.

Hams n. (1930s–1940s) human legs. (DB, OHHJ, p. 139.) Example: "Hey, big fine mama, you sure got some nice hams on you." SNU.

Ham scam n. (1920s–1930s) a hard or difficult time.

Ham-snatcher; ham-snatching n., v. (1960s–1990s) anyone who steals from stores during riots; looting. (FR.) Example: "Ham-snatchers come in all colors. During the L.A. riots, man, everybody —whites, Latinos, blacks—everybody was ham-snatching." NCU.

Hanch n. (1800s–1940s) haunch. (AEG, BB, p. 34.) SU.

Hand n. (1700s–1940s) a good-luck charm; amulet. (HMH, HCWR, p. 192.) SU.

Handcuffs n. (1930s–1940s) an engagement ring or wedding ring. (MHB, JS, np.) Example: "Magdaline let that nigger put handcuffs on her; now look at her—he keeps her barefoot and pregnant." SNU.

Handjive n. (1900s–1940s) body-slapping during dancing or playing. (BJ, BLH, SD, p. 22.) YCU, SCU, SNU.

Handkerchief head n. (1900s–1960s) an Uncle Tom; one who wears a handkerchief or a rag on his head to preserve his expensively processed hairdo. (DC, BJ, p. 67; CS, vol. 3, no. 2, p. 28; ZNH, AM, p. 95.) SNU.

Hand running adv. (1890s–1920s) continuously; in sequence; in succession. (FGC, DARE, p. 890.) SNU.

Handsome ransom n. (1930s) a large quantity of money. (FR.) PPU, SCU.

Hang v., n. (1960s–1990s) to endure; to stick with an unpleasant situation; a job—especially one taken on halfheartedly or grudgingly. (XC, MEB, p. 12; CS, vol. 3, no. 2, p. 28.) Examples: "I couldn't hang in that scene anymore. It was getting me down."; and, "Willard found this hang for me, and I don't know how to tell him I can't accept it." SCU, PPU, SNCU.

Hang crepe on [one's] door v. (1860s–1930s) door signs have always featured largely in magic or voodoo works; hanging crepe on one's door is an indication of death; to threaten; a symbolic way of telling one (such as a deceitful lover) that he or she can expect to die soon. (Son House, "Government Fleet Blues," *Travelin' Man, The Complete Library of Congress Sessions 1941–1942*, Interstate Music, Ltd., England.) SU.

Hang loose interj., v. (1960s–1980s) relax; take it easy. (DC, BJ, p. 68; CS, vol. 3, no. 2, p. 28.) SNU.

Hangout n. (1890s–1950s) a place for illicit sexual relations; meeting place for a gang; picked up from hobo and underground use. (WF, DAS, p. 242; JH, PBL, p. 84.) SNU.

Hang-up n. (1960s–1970s) a psychological block or problem. (JH, PBL, p. 84; CS, vol. 3, no. 2, p. 28.) Example: "Leonarda got this hang-up, man—she can't stop chewing gum and twitching when she talks." SNU.

Hang up v. (1960s–1970s) to get rid of something or someone. Probably originally a cowboy term referring to the symbolism of hanging up one's saddle, boots, fiddle, gear, or spurs; in the sixties it was used by young black speakers in a similar manner—as a request, declaration, or imperative to desist. (FGC, DARE, p. 895.) Example: "I wish Asher would hang up drugs. If he did that, I'd marry him for sure." SNU.

Hant n., v. (1700s–1940s) from "haunt"; a supernatural being; a ghostlike presence; to haunt. (ECLA, NN, p. 266; FGC, DARE, p. 921; AEG, BB, p. 305.) SU.

Happening n., v. (1880s–1960s) any spontaneous event; chance occurrence; origin probably not black. (FGC, DARE, p. 897; CS, vol. 3, no. 2, p. 28.) Examples: "Lola and Herman, they always happening by just when I take Jo-Jo out for his walk"; and, "It was really amazing how all my friends showed up at my place at the same time, when I wasn't expecting any company, and the whole afternoon turned into a real happening." SU.

Happenings n. (1940s–1950s) usually refers to any significant incident or situation of the moment. This has been an extremely popular word in black street and youth cultures. Examples: Often used in the form of question—"What's happenings?"; "What's the happenings?"; or "What's the haps?"—and especially as a form of address. (CW, TW, p. 30.) SNU. See "Haps."

Happy Albert Caldwell, tenor sax; born in Chicago, July 25, 1903; played with Bernie Young's Creole Jazz Band (c. 1922).

Happy adj. (1700s–1900s) feeling religious joy or the spirit through hand clapping and shouting. To get happy in church is to feel the spirit, to be deeply moved both mentally and physically; to know a sincere appreciation of life, of existence; to feel true, joy, bliss. (RDA, PB, p. ix; GS, TT, p. 72.) SNU.

Happy dust n. (1920s) cocaine. (CVV, NH, p. 285.) Harlem use.

Happy shop n. (1960s–1970s) a liquor store. (JH, PBL, p. 84.) SCU, SNCU.

Haps n. (1950s–1960s) short for "happening" or "happenings." (CW, TW, p. 30.) Example: "Hey, baby, ain't seen you in awhile—what's the haps?" SCU, SNU.

Hard adj. (1930s–1940s) in jive talk, like the word "bad"; for black people, "hard" has a positive connotation; terribly good. (CC, OMMM, NCCHD, p. 256; WF, DAS, p. 243; FGC, DARE, p. 899; DB, OHHJ, p. 139.) Example: "Claudia, that's a hard hairdo you got there." SCU, YCU, PPU, PU, JMFU.

Hard as lard (1940s–1960s) an expression of exceptional delight; anything that's smooth; excellent; very positive. (DW, TL, p. 183.) Example: "My luck's hard as lard! I hit the number!" PPU, SCU, SNU.

Hard bop; hard bop–funky n. (1950s–1960s) a blues-type bop, closer to an earlier form—hot jazz—than to straight bop. (RSG, JT, p. 121.) JMFU. See "Funky."

Hard bopper n. (1950s–1960s) one who "digs" hard bop. See "Hard bop."

Hard down adj. (1930s) true or pure. (AL, RS, p. 113.) Example: "Webster is a hard down, true as blue man."

Hardest adj. (1930s) difficulty. (FR.) SNU.

Hardhead n. (1930s–1980s) usually a rebellious or strong-willed male; also, blacks have thought of whites as hardheaded and vice versa. (WF, DAS, p. 243; CS, vol. 3, no. 2, p. 28.) Example: "Darcy a hardhead; I can't even get him to wash his hands before he comes to the table for supper." SNU.

Hardheaded adj. (1930s–1980s) obstinate or stubborn. (ZNH, AM, p. 85.) See "Hardhead."

Hard-hitting adj. (1930s–1940s) timely; in style; anything excellent. (DB, OHHJ, p. 139.) SNCU.

Hard John n. (1930s–1940s) an FBI agent. (DB, OHHJ, p. 139.) Harlem use.

Hardleg n. (1940s–1950s) any man; any aging prostitute; an ugly woman. (IS, PSML, p. 315; MHB, JS, np.) SCU.

Hardlegs n. (1960s) a male child. (DC, BJ, p. 68.) NCU.

Hard-oil n. (1940s) lard or oleomargarine. (DB, OHHJ, p. 139.) Harlem use.

Hard skull-fry n. (1940s–1950s) a heavily greased and shiny conked hairdo. (DB, OHHJ, p. 139.) SNCU.

Hard spiel n. (1930s–1940s) jive talk. "Spiel" clearly picked up from tramp and underworld lingo; in use by 1899. (CC, OMMM, NCCHD, p. 256; EP, DU, p. 666; DB, OHHJ, p. 139.) Harlem; NCU.

Hard swing n. (1950s–1960s) a very intense form of swing music. (RSG, JL, pp. 138–139.) Example: "Bring me some true boppers, not any of these hard swing players." JMFU.

Hard up adj. (1960s) in difficult circumstances. (FR.) Example: "They're so hard up, they don't have food." SNU.

Harky imper. (1800s–1880s) variant of "Hark!"; a call to attention. (CCJ, NMGC, p. 30.) SU.

Harlem oil n. (1920s–1940s) kerosene used in a mixture of sugar as a medicine for children; picked up from white use. (FGC, DARE, p. 910.) Harlem use.

Harlem toothpick n. (1930s–1940s) a switchblade knife carried in the pocket. (DB, OHHJ, p. 139.) Harlem use.

Harp n. (1800s–1940s) a harmonica. (FGC, DARE, p. 912.) SNU.

Harpie n. (1880s–1940s) an old woman with an ulterior romantic motive; comparable to the Jewish yenta. (DB, OHHJ, p. 139.) SNU.

Harping v. (1960s) (RDA, TB, p. 50.) See "Signifying."

Hash n. (1930s–1990s) short for hashish. (RSG, JT, pp. 122–123.) SU.

Hassle n. (1920s–1940s) to fight or argue; worry. (ZNH, MM, p. 218; CS, vol. 3, no. 2, p. 29.) SNU.

Hassling v. (1920s–1940s) panting. (ZNH, MM, p. 218.) Example: "Aaron come in here just hassling like a bear on his tail, and Nowell didn't help none, just kept right on eating supper." SNU.

Hat n. (1940s–1950s) any female; wife; sweetheart. (RSG, JT, p. 123.) Rare. JMFU.

Hatchet-thrower n. (1930s–1940s) any Spanish-speaking male living in Harlem. (DB, OHHJ, p. 140.) Harlem use.

Hat rack n. (1930s–1940s) the human head. (FGC, DARE, p. 919.) SNU.

Hat size n. (1990s) inflated self-image. (FR.) Example: "He's got a hat size problem"; or, "His hat size is pretty large." YCU.

Hat up v. (1960s) to make a departure; to leave. (DC, BJ, p. 68.) Example: "Mary, sorry, I gotta hat up and split." Rare. MWU. See "Get [one's] hat."

Haul ass v. (1940s–1950s) to run; go. (ZNH, AM, p. 95.) Example: "I saw Benny and them coming around the school building and I hauled ass the other way." SNU.

Haunty adj. (1700s–1940s) haunted. (FGC, DARE, p. 921.) Example: "If you children go down to that old haunty house again, I'm going to skin you 'live." SU.

Haunty; hanty adj. (1940s) haunted. (FR.) SNU.

Have a cub v. (1930s–1940s) to stack the deck in a game of cards. (ZNH, MM, JL, LBE, p. 154.) SU.

Have a thing about v. (1960s) to have an obsession with a person or idea, but not necessarily negative like "hang up." (FR.) SNU.

Have it covered adj. (1950s) to be completely in command. (RSG, JT, p. 123.) JMFU, SNU.

Have [one's] legs open v. (1930s–1950s) said of women who are or who are thought to be promiscuous. (FR.) Example: "Katrina always got her legs open, no wonder she got so many children." SNU.

Have [one's] mouth on v. (1930s–1940s) gossip; to speak with contempt or malice about someone. (AW, CP, p. 8.) Example: "You can't walk down the street in this here town less you got somebody who going to have his mouth on you." SU.

Have [one's] nose open v. (1940s–1960s) said of a man who is a fool for a woman. (FR.) SNU. See "Nose open."

Have off v. (1930s–1940s) to act in a mean-spirited way, especially to shout at someone. (ZNH, DTR, p. 234.) Example: "If I go in there I know she's just gonna have off at me." SNU.

Having yourself v. (1980s–1990s) masturbation. (WKB, JMC, PS, p. 49.) Example: "Sebert stay in his bunk like that so he can have himself while we out in the yard." PU, SCU.

Haw adj., n. (1700s–1930s) left; opposite of "gee" (right). (BJ, BLH, SD, p. 208; AEG, BB, p. 193.) See "Gee."

Hawk Coleman Hawkins, tenor saxophonist; born 1904.

Hawk n. (1930s–1990s) the crisp, cold blast of winter winds that sweep city streets, as in Chicago from Lake Michigan; also, some minor use of "hawk" to refer to strong LSD-25.) (HLF, RJPD, p. 170; RRL, DAZ, p. 97; DC, BJ, p. 68; JH, PBL, p. 84.) Chicago; NCU.

Hawk v. (1960s–1970s) to move quickly; walk at a brisk pace. (JH, PBL, p. 84.) Harlem; Brooklyn use.

Hawkins n. (1930s–1940s) variant of "Hawk"; cold winter winds. (DB, OHHJ, p. 140; MHB, JS, np; MM, RB, p. 333.) Chicago; NCU. See "Hawk."

Hawking v. (1970s) to observe in an unwavering fashion. (FR.) Example: "They were hawking the drunk as he headed across the street." YCU, NCU.

Hawk riding (1940s) refers to music made by Coleman Hawkins. (DB, OHHJ, p. 140.) JMFU.

Hay now n. (1940s–1950s) a greeting, like hello. (FR.) SNU.

Hay-eater n. (1880s–1930s) any white person. (FR.) SU.

He pron. (1900s–1930s) his. (FR.) Example: "He face was dirty." SU.

Head adj., n. (1920s–1930s; 1990s) in jazz, any improvised musical arrangement well-known by the players; in the thirties, drug user; from the forties to the nineties, fellatio; rarely among black speakers, bathroom. (RSG, JL, p. 141; TW, CH, p. 149; DW, TL, p. 183; CS, vol. 3, no. 2, p. 29.) SNU.

Headbone n. (1900–1990s) the human skull. (FR.) SNU.

Headcheese n. (1840s–1990s) various cheap grades of pork meat prepared and sold as lunch meat; smegma. (FGC, DARE, p. 937.) SNU.

Head-chick n. (1930s–1940s) a man's favorite woman; a woman skilled in oral lovemaking. (DB, OHHJ, p. 140.) PPU, SCU.

Head-handkerchief n. (1850s–1890s) a large handkerchief used to cover the hair, tied in the back; part of slave servant costume. (FGC, DARE, p. 939.) SNU. See "Handkerchief head."

Head hen n. (1930s–1940s) a landlady or female manager of a rooming house. (DB, OHHJ, p. 140.) Harlem use.

Head Knock n. (1930s–1940s) God, the Lord, or Jesus. (MM, RB, p. 333.) SNU.

Headlight(s) n. (1930s–1940s) a light-complexioned Afro-American girl—because she tended to stand out in a crowd of darker people; any woman's breasts; diamonds. (FGC, DARE, p. 939; DB, OHHJ, p. 140; EF, RDSL, p. 241.) SNU.

Head Nigger in Charge; H-NIC n. (1960s–1990s) a pejorative reference to any black person in any position of authority; used ironically to refer to a black boss. (Cecil Brown, "The Black Literary Critic as Melville's Confidence Man," *American Review*, vol. 14, no. 16, February–March, 1993.) See "Nigger in charge." NSCU.

Headquarters n. (1920s–1950s) a person with an usually large skull bone. (FR.) SNU.

Headrag n. See "Head handkerchief."

Head shop n. (1960s–1990s) very likely a term picked up from the white youth culture of the sixties, sometimes known as hippies; a store where drug paraphernalia can be bought. (TW, CH, p. 149.) DCU.

Head stick n. (1920s–1930s) a wooden board at the head of a grave. (HMH, HCWR, p. 1292.) SU.

Heap n. (1700s–1950s) a great quantity; large amount; in the midwest, an old automobile in poor repair, but this use is not common among black speakers. (ECLA, NN, p. 266; FGC, DARE, p. 942.) SU.

Hear v. (1920s–1960s) to experience jazz with "understanding." (RSG, JL, p. 142.) Example: "Cathleen ain't asleep, man, she hear the music when she look like that." JMFU.

Hearing n. (1800s–1930s) a spell or curse; a verbal attack. (ZNH, MM, p. 107.) Example: "Addis the goof doctor in this here town, and when she put a hearing on you it stays put." SU.

Heart n. (1960s–1990s) courage; bravery; strong will. (HLF, RJPD, p. 170.) Example: "You've got to have a lot of heart to succeed in this business." SNCU.

Heartleaf n. (1890s–1940s) a leaf shaped like a heart and used for medicinal purposes; an herbal remedy, thought to be good for the heart. (RW, AAGYRS, p. 84.) SU.

Heart-mad(ness) adj., n. (1920s–1930s) extreme anger. (FR.) Example: "She's crazy from heart-madness." North Carolina use.

Heat n. (1960s) police; law-enforcement officer; gun. (IS, PSML, p. 315; DC, BJ, p. 68; CS, vol. 3, no. 2, p. 29.) Example: "The dude's got some heat. Leave him alone." PPU, SCU.

Heaven n. (1850s–1890s) a free country; free land; Promised Land. (FR.) See "Promised Land."

Heavy; hebby adj. (1700s–1990s) anything eminent and profound; anything positive; good. (CCJ, NMGC, p. 118; AEG, BB, p. 306; CS, vol. 3, no. 2, p. 29; DC, BJ, p. 68.) SU, SNU, SCU, NCU.

Heavy D (1990s) a popular rap artist.

Heavy heat stretch n. (1940s) the months of summer. (DB, OHHJ, p. 140.) Example: "If we going to get through this heavy heat stretch together, we got to get along." SNU.

Heavy lard n. (1940s) a very impressive, verbally rendered story; tall tale; unbelievable story. (DB, OHHJ, p. 140.) Harlem use.

Heavy Lump n. (1940s) the section known as Sugar Hill in Harlem. "Lump," as in "lump of sugar." (DB, OHHJ, p. 140.) Harlem use.

Heavy shit n. (1960s–1990s) an important event or important information. (RDA, TB, p. 47.) SNU.

Heavy soul n. (1950s) heroin. Rare.

Heavyweight n. (1970s–1990s) a person of profound knowledge; person with social vision; a successful pimp or hustler. (EF, RDSL, p. 242.) DCU, PPU, PU, YCU.

Heavy wet n. (1930s–1940s) a rainstorm. (DB, OHHJ, p. 140.) Harlem use.

Heifer n. (1830s–1960s) disparagingly used to describe a woman or a girl; a pretty woman; a young woman who refuses to conform to prescribed proper behavior; a woman who defies a narrowly defined moral or sexual role; immoral woman; slut; hussy; an ugly female. (HLF, RJPD, p. 170; AW, CP, p. 40.) See "Hussy" and "Streetcleaner."

Hell adj. (1920s–1990s) excellent; good; an impressive person. (WF, DAS, 252.) Example: "The youngsters are hell today, man—they'll bring about changes we couldn't make happen in our time." SNU.

Hellacious adj. (1930s) remarkable or outstanding. (FCG, DARE, p. 959.) See "Hell."

Hem [in]; hemmed [in] v., adj. (1930s) to obtain; catch; surround; corner. (ZNH, DTR, p. 138.) SNU.

Hem-haw [hemming and hawing] v. (1930s–1940s) to be indecisive; to be unclear or unfocussed. (FGC, DARE, p. 967.) SU.

Hemp n. (1950s–1960s) hashish; also marijuana. (DB, HHJ, p. 14; DB, OHHJ, p. 140.) See "Bush," "Grass," and "Joint."

Hen n. (1920s–1940s) usually any woman over thirty; an older woman. (DB, OHHJ, p. 140.) SNU.

Hep adj. (1900s–1960s) incorrect spelling of "hip," which means awareness; to be well-informed. (RSG, JL, pp. 145–146.) See "Hip."

Hep-cat n. variant spelling of "hip cat." See "Hip."

Hep to the jive adj. See "Hip."

Herb n. (1960s–1990s) marijuana; also, in the nineties, a person who is unaware of street life. (DW, TL, p. 183; RDA, DDJ, p. 266; DC, BJ, p. 68.) SCU, PPU.

Herb v. (1990s) to rob. (FR.) Example: "They got Aubert in the alley just off Clemence Place and herbed him." SCU.

Herbs n. (1950s) marijuana. (RDA, DDJ, p. 266; DC, BJ, p. 68; EF, RDSL, p. 242.) See "Grass," "Joint," and "Weed."

Herd [of camels] n. (1930s–1940s) a pack of Camel cigarettes. (DB, OHHJ, p. 140.) Example: "Hey, Aaron, lay a nickel on me for a herd of camels." Harlem use.

Hereafter adv., n. (1850s–1930s) life after death; heaven. (FGC, DARE, pp. 977–978.) SU.

He-said-she-said n. (1960s–1970s) gossip; excessive chatter. (DR, BASL, p. 220; SH, GL, p. 212.) Example: "When them two get together all you hear is he-said-she-said." Philadelphia; NCU.

Heself; hisself pron. (1700s–1940s) himself. (LDT, AGD, p. 276; ECLA, CS, p. 37.) Example: "He be out here soon as he get heself together." SU. See "She-self."

He Who Diggeth the Digger Harlem name for Milton Mesirow (Mezz Mezzrow), clarinet player; born in Chicago, 1899. (FR; MM, RB.)

Hicky; hick adj., n. (1860s–1960s) rustic person, place, or thing. (FR.) Example: "They so countrified 'cause they from down in this little hicky town in Georgia somewhere." SNU.

Hickory n. (1850s–1940s) a cane; a walking stick. (CWC, CW, p. 106.) SU.

Hide n. (1930s–1950s) drums. See "Hide-beater."

Hide n. (1950s–1960s) a wallet. (DW, TL, p. 183; IS, PSML, p. 315.) Example: "To get my attention all you got to do is whip out that hide and un-ass some of that bread." PPU; SCU.

Hide-and-coop n. (1900s) variant of hide-and-seek; game played by southern black children. (FGC, DARE, p. 989.) SU.

Hideaways n. (1930s–1940s) one's pockets. (FR; DB, OHHJ, p. 140.) SNU.

Hide-and-woop n. (1930s–1940s) popular game among black children; variant of hide-and-seek. (ZNH, DTR.) See "Hide-and-coop" and "Hide-go-seek."

Hide-beater n. (1930s–1940s) drummer. (CC, OMMM, NCCHD, p. 256; DB, OHHJ, p. 140.) JMFU.

Hide behind v. (1950s) to avoid something or someone.

Hide-go-seek n. (1930s–1940s) popular game among black children, north and south; variant of hide-and-seek. (FGC, DARE, p. 989.) SU. See "Hide-and-coop."

Hides n. (1930s–1940s) drums. (DB, OHHJ, p. 140.) JMFU.

Higguhri-hee n. (1900s–1920s) Gullah word; an owl. (AEG, BB, p. 306; FGC, DARE, p. 991.) Coastal Georgia and South Carolina use.

High adj. (1700s–1930s) to possess conjuring power. (HMH, HCWR, p. 284.) SU.

High adj. (1900s–1950s) intoxicated; drunk; stimulated; emotionally or psychologically altered by narcotics. (RRL, DAZ, p. 109; MHB, JS, np; DC, BJ, p. 68.) DCU, SNU.

High as a Georgia pine adj. (1930s–1940s) intoxicated; drunk. (FGC, DARE, p. 993.) SU.

High as a kite adj. (1930s–1950s) drunk; intoxicated. (FGC, DARE, p. 993.) See "Sails high."

High balling v. (1920s–1930s) to signal with the hand. (ZNH, MM, p.) SU.

High behind n. (1940s–1950s) buttocks that jut up and out. (FR.) SNU.

High blood n. (1900s–1980s) variant of "high blood pressure." (Listen to Lightnin' Hopkins, "I Woke Up This Morning," *Double Blues*, Fantasy, 1989.) MWU, SU.

High brown [yellow] n. (1900s–1930s) African-American of black and white ancestry; picked up from white use. (FGC, DARE, p. 995.) SU.

High cotton v., n. (1930s–1940s) enjoying the good life; wealth; prosperity; the life-style of wealthy white folks. (FGC, DARE, p. 996.) SNU.

High five n. (1980s–1990s) palm slap of agreement with arms raised; one's open palm held above one's head, to be slapped against someone else's palm; gesture expresses approval, agreement, greeting. (FR.) Example: "Give me a high five." SNU. See "Give [one] five," "Give [one] some skin," and "Give the drummer some."

Highflyer; highflying n., adj. (1970s–1980s) a person who lives well or expensively; the good (expensive) life. The earlier (1900s) use referring to a hussy or "good time" woman was not common among black slang users. (FR.) SNU.

High hat; high hatted adj. (1920s–1940s) snobbish. (FGC, DARE, p. 998.) SNU. See "Hankty" and "Dicty."

High hat [it] v. (1920–1940) to act superior; to deliberately snub someone. (FGC, DARE, p. 998.) SNU. See "Hinkty" and "Dicty."

High Henry n. (1900s–1930s) variant of American hero John Henry ("steel driving man"); hero of the railroad camps; hero of a Negro work song; hero of songs sang in jook joints; the worker who tries to match his strength against a steam drill's speed and power. (ZNH, MM, p. 306; ZNH, JGV, p. 167.) SNU.

High on the hog adj., adv. (1900s–1950s) living well; eating well. (MA, PTO, BL, p. 96.) Example: "Since you folks been living high on the hog, we don't much of you any more." SNU.

High-powered adj. (1930s–1950s) timely; attractive; fashionable. (DB, OHHJ, p. 140.) Example: "The likes of you can't make no time with her—she a real high-powered lady, boy." Harlem; SNU.

High-prime (-priming) v. (1800s–1920s) showing off, especially with a swagger or strut. (FGC, DARE, p. 1004.) SU.

High season(ed) brown n. (1900s–1930s) a beautiful brown-skinned woman. (Mississippi John Hurt, "Lisa Jane, (God's Unchanging Hand," *Avalon Blues*, 1963.) Example: "Now, take a high season brown, you can trust her any day in the week, whereas a high yellow, now, that's a different story." SU.

High sign v. (1970s–1990s) to show off or best someone; to out-do someone; to strut and assert; brag. (EF, RDSL, p. 12, 80, 109, 242.) SCU, YCU, DCU, PU, PPU.

High sign n. (1970s–1990s) a gang's special colors, usually displayed on jackets or shirts; secret sign or gesture; since the eighties, a greeting accomplished by the slapping of raised palms; a signal of affiliation. (EF, RDSL, p. 242.) SCU, YCU, DCU, PU, PPU.

High tail [it] v. (1930s–1940s) to turn and leave quickly. (FR.) SU. See "Turn tail."

High tone adj. (1860s–1940s) high class; refers to behavior but ironically speaks also to the prospect of color. The expression is not of black origin but has been a favorite among black slang users. (Eddie "Cleanhead" Vinson, "High Class Baby," *Eddie "Cleanhead" Vinson and his Orchestra 1946–1947*, Trip Records, TLP 5590.) Example: "My baby so high tone, man, I can't even keep up with her. When she gets around her high tone friends I don't even know how to talk with her." SNU.

High yaller (yella) adj., n. (1700s–1950s) a relatively light complexion; light-skinned black person; light-skinned Afro-American, especially female; Creole; mulatto or quadroon. (CVV, NH, p. 285; DC, BJ, p. 68; Joel Williamson, *New People: Miscegenation and Mulattoes in the United States*. New York: The Free Press, 1980, pp. 56–57.) SNU.

Hike v. (1940s) to hide a valuable object; lay away a treasure. (DB, OHHJ, p. 140.) Harlem use.

Hincty adj., n. (1900s–1950s) snobbish; pretentious; pompous. (CC, OMMM, NCCHD, p. 256; DB, OHHJ, p. 140; GS, TT, p. 68; EF, RDSL, p. 47; MM, RB, p. 72; JH, PBL, p. 84.) Example: "Matilda too hincty, bring another girl next week when you make your rounds." SNU. See "Dicty," "Hinkty," "Siddity," and "Uppity."

Hind n. (1930s–1940s) variant of "behind"; buttocks; rear end. (FGC, DARE, p. 1014.) SNU.

Hinges n. (1930s–1940s) one's elbows. (DB, OHHJ, p. 140.) SNU.

Hinges creaking n. (1930s–1940s) old age; stiff joints; sore muscles. (DB, OHHJ, p. 140.) SNU.

Hinkty adj., n. See "Hincty."

Hip; hipping adj., v. (1700s–1990s) *hepi* ["to see"] *hipi* ["to open one's eyes"] (Wolof); correct term is "hip," not "hep"; sophisticated, independent, and wise; in fashion, alert, and courageous. Some of its popularity diminished in the sixties. (GS, TT, pp. 69–70; HV, AHAE, p. 142; RDA, TB, p. 52; DW, TL, p. 183; RSG, JL, pp. 145–146; CC, OMMM, NCCHD, p. 256; MHB, JS, np; DC, BJ, p. 68; CS, vol. 3, no. 2, p. 29.) JMFU; SCU; SNCU.

Hipcat n. (1700s–1960s) *hipicat* (Wolof); wise; intelligent; informed. (JEH, AHAE, p. 142.) SU.

Hip-hop (hiphop) n. (1960s–1990s) rap subculture; a cultural form; a type of rap with a heavily rhythmic musical style thought—according to Alex Pate—to have been identified as such by disc jockey Kool Herc in 1968 in the West Bronx. Nelson George said Kool Herc made the conscious leap not in 1968 but in 1975, when he started specializing in "break" sections of the records he played. It provided the fast-paced music that stimulated the break-dancing craze in the late seventies and through most of the eighties. "Hip-hop" is a lifestyle. "A broader term for rap culture" (Alex Pate, *USA Weekend*, May 7, 1993, p. 18; Nelson George, *Buppies, B-Boys, Baps & Bohos*, 1992, pp. 12–13). SNU. See "Rap."

Hippie (hippy) n. (1940s–1960s) from the word "hip"; a person who tries without success to be hip; overblasé; a would-be hipcat. In the 1960s the word fell largely into white use and took on a very different meaning, referring to the generation that followed the youngest of the Beat Generation of New York and San Francisco. (RSG, JT, pp. 129–130.) SNU.

Hippy dippy, sometimes piddy, cry for your bottle when you want your titty (1940s–1950s) an expression usually applied to one who is acting childish or stubborn. (CLC, TS, p. 220.) SNU.

Hip-slip n. (1960s) a woman's undergarment (slip) that starts at the waist and fits around the hips; half-slip. (FGC, DARE, p. 1019.) SNU.

Hipster n. (1930s–1940s) a hip person; knowledgeable; dropped by black speakers as early as the late forties; became popular among white speakers throughout the fifties and into the sixties. (CC, HDH, p. 16.) JMFU, SNCU.

Hisself pron. (1800s–1940s) variant of "himself." (CWC, WY, p. 145.) SU.

Hit v., n. (1960s–1990s) from the sixties through the eighties, to inhale smoke from marijuana or crack; a puff on a reefer; a puff on a cocaine pipe; a snort of cocaine; in the nineties, a puff on a cocaine pipe or a marijuana cigarette; a quantity of anything. (TW, CH, p. 149; TW, CK, p. 137; DC, BJ, p. 68.) DCU.

Hit [one] v. (1940s–1950s) to refill one's whiskey glass; to win; to say "hit me" while playing cards, for example, is to ask for a card from the deck. (FR.) SNU.

Hit a lick v. (1920s–1930s) to make an effort or to extend oneself at a physical task. Example: "He ain't about to hit a lick of work if he can help it." SU.

Hit it v. (1990s) to have sex. (FR.) Example: "What's happening with us, baby, it's been awhile since we hit it." YCU.

Hit on v. (1940s–1950s) propose; flirt; make a pass; to make a request, especially for lovemaking; aggressive flirting; sexual harassment. (EF, RDSL, p. 242; PM, UCLAS, p. 49.) SNU.

Hit of smack n. (1950s–1970s) heroin. (DG, ICH, p. 121.) Example: "If I could just get me a hit of smack I'd be straight till tomorrow." DCU.

Hit the road, Jack imper. (1950s–1960s) a command to someone to leave. (FR.) SNU.

Hit the street v. (1960s) to leave one's house suddenly; to go out for the night. (DC, BJ, p. 68.) Example: teenager to parent: "If you don't stop yacking at me I'm gonna hit the street." SNCU, YCU.

HN n. (1960s–1990s) house nigger. (FR.) SNU.

Ho; hoe n. (1890s–1980s) whore; a promiscuous female; prostitute. (HLF, RJPD, p. 170; CRM, BP, p. 302; PM, UCLAS, p. 49; EF, RDSL, p. 242; SH, GL, p. 212.) Example: "Belinda ain't nothing but a little ho." SNCU, PPU, DCU, PU, SCU, YCU.

Hobo cocktail n. (1940s) a glass of water, especially one requested in a restaurant or cafe. (MHB, JS, np.) Example: "Only thing I don't like about working in this diner, it's right by the railroad tracks and we get all kinds of drifters coming in asking for hobo cocktails." SU.

Ho boots n. (1970s–1980s) very tall, tightly fitting woman's boots with high heels. (EF, BVV, p. 53.) PPU, DCU, YCU, SCU, SNCU.

Hocks n. (1940s) feet. (DB, OHHJ, p. 140.) Rare. SNU.

Hocks n. (1930s–1940s) derogatory term for the feet. (FR.) Example: "Jasper, boy, get your hocks off the table before I break them off for you." SNU.

Hod Walter Howard O'Brien, piano player; born January 19, 1936.

Hoe cake n. (1700s–1890s) a cornmeal cake baked on a hoe held over a fire. "Hoe cake" is found in many African-American folk songs. (JSF, AON, p. 299.) SU.

Hoe darky n. See "Field nigger."

Hoe-down n. (1700s–1890s) the dance the slaves did when they put down their hoes for the day; a loud, joyous "negro" dance. (JSF, AON, p. 299.) SU.

Hoe nigger n. See "Field nigger."

Hog n. (1950s–1960s) a big car; a Cadillac automobile—"hog" for size and the amount of fuel it uses; also, some minor use of the word to refer to a motorcycle and to refer to general greediness. (CLC, TS, p. 255; CRM, BP, p. 302; IS, PSML, p. 315; DC, BJ, p.68; CS, vol. 3, no. 2, p. 29.) Example: "Since Gavin got himself a hog, the chicks been sticking to him like flies to flypaper." SNU.

Hog v. (1930s–1940s) to cast a spell, especially an evil one. (FR.) Example: "I'm going to put a hog on you if you don't leave my woman alone." SU.

Hog fashion adj. (1700s–1940s) refers to feet tied together as hogs are tied. (ECLA, NN, p. 266.) SU.

Hog hoof tea n. (1900s–1940s) commonly used remedy for coughs in Louisiana; a special favorite of hoodoo doctors. It consists of ground swine hoof mixed in hot water and whiskey. (FGC, DARE, pp. 1040–1041.) SU.

Hog-killing n., v. (1860s–1930s) Before the turn of the century the term referred solely to the slaughter of hogs at a certain time of the year. It later referred to both the slaughter and outdoors ceremonious cooking and eating of pork. (ZNH, DTR, p. 36.) SU.

Hog maw n. (1930s–1950s) a pork dish prepared from the stomach of the hog. (FGC, DARE, p. 1042.) See "Chitlins."

Hog pen n. (1920s–1940s) a messy or filthy place; a fenced enclosure where hogs and pigs are kept. The word "pen" may be derived from "penitentiary." (ZNH, DTR, p. 130.) SU.

Hogs n. (1970s–1990s) variant of "pigs"; the police. (EF, RDSL, p. 242.) DCU, SCU, PPU, PU.

Hoing v. (1890s–1990s) whoring. (TW, CK, p. 137.) PPU, DCU, SCU. See "Ho."

Ho layer n. (1980s–1990s) any man who constantly has sex with easily available women or prostitutes; a ladies' man; used frequently in rap songs. (FR.) SCU, PPU.

Hold; holding v., adj. (1940s–1990s) to be in possession of illegal drugs—especially to have such drugs in one's pocket or hidden in some way on one's body or in one's clothing, such as in a bra. (FR; RRL, DAZ, p. 110; CS, vol. 3, no. 2, p. 29.) Example: "Madge ain't holding today 'cause she heard the feds going to swoop down this way this afternoon." DCU.

Holding the bag v. See "Hold."

Hole n. (1960s) variant of "ho" for whore. (CRM, BP, p. 302.) Rare. PPU. See "Ho."

Hole n. (1980s–1990s) a woman's vagina. (EF, RDSL, p. 242.) SCU, PPU, YCU.

Hole card n. (1960s) withheld information about anything or anyone; use picked up from blackjack, a card game. (DW, TL, p. 183.) Example: "If she tries to wiggle out of this one, I bring out my hole card on her and destroy her." PPU, DCU.

Hole-in-the-wall n. (1930s–1960s) a small, uncomfortable apartment. (FR.) SNCU.

[Cornfield/Cotton field] Holler n. (1800s–1940s) a type of yodeling call done with a particular musical rhythm. This is a vocal means of communication used in the cotton and corn fields in the south. (AEG, BB, p. 307; LDT, AGD, p. 268.) SU, JMFU.

Holler n. (1900s–1950s) a spontaneous or improvised technique in jazz. (SL, RJON, p. 25.) JMFU.

Holler v. (1980s–1990s) to loud-talk someone; to ridicule with a verbal attack. (EF, RDSL, p. 242.) Example: "That nigger can holler you down even when he owes you some money." SCU.

Hollywood swoop(ing) n., v. (1980s–1990s) in fast automobile traffic, when one car—usually without signalling—crosses several lanes suddenly in front of other cars. (EF, RDSL, p. 242.) Watts and South-central Los Angeles use.

Holy dance n. (1800s–1930s) feverish dancing done in church or at the site of a religious gathering. (FGC, DARE, p. 1063.) SU.

Holy roller n. (1920s–1940s) pejorative term for a fire-and-brimstone preacher or church member; probably from "holey" (bumpy), as in an unpaved, gutted road. (FGC, DARE, p. 1057.) SU.

Home; homes n. (1930s–1960s) a term of address used by two black people either from the same southern state or simply from the south. (WKB, JMC, PS, p. 49.) NU. See "Homeboy" and "Homegirl."

Home cooking adj., n. (1930s–1940s) See "Soul food"; anything outstanding or positive. (CC, OMMM, NCCHD, p. 256; DB, OHHJ, p. 140.) Example: "Now, that's swinging, that's truly home cooking, when you turn like that." NCU.

Homeboy n. (1930s–1990s) term of informal, friendly address; male or female person from one's own town, usually down south; in the eighties—especially in Los Angeles and southern California—the expression came to mean any male from one's own neighborhood; any black male. (TW, CH, p. 149; WKB, JMC, PS, p. 49; JH, PBL, p. 84.) Example: "Hey! Homeboy!" SNCU.

Homegirl n. (1930s–1990s) term of informal, friendly address; any female person. (*Essence*, November 1992, p. 26.) See "Homeboy."

Homeland n. (1960s) one's own neighborhood. (DC, BJ, p. 68.) Example: "The brothers in the homeland got a beef going with the cats up in Forest Hills." Rare. MWU.

Home squeeze n. (1980s–1990s) one's wife or domestic mate. (EF, RDSL, p. 242.) Example: "I don't need nobody but my good home squeeze to make me feel good." SNCU.

Homey; homie n. (1930s–1940s; 1980s–1990s) a newly arrived southerner in a northern city; from the thirties to the fifties, male or female person from one's own town or city; from the eighties into the nineties, male or female person from one's own neighborhood; popular in southern California, especially Los Angeles, but frequent in other large cities. (DB, OHHJ, p. 140.) Example: "Hey, Homey, give me some skin!" See "Home," "Homeboy," and "Homegirl."

Honey [up] v. (1850s–1940s) flattery; sweet talk; kind words; praise; play; a beautiful thing or person. (FGC, DARE, p. 1072.) Example: "Lisa likes me to honey her up fore we do that thing." SU.

Honkey; honky; honkie n. (1650s–1990s) *honq* ("pink man") [Wolof]; a pink man or woman; derisive term; a white person— southern use, originally; in Los Angeles use, sometimes a light-complexioned Chicano or Chicana; an ice-cream bar. (DC, BJ, p. 68; FGC, DARE, p. 1078; JH, PBL, p. 85.) SNU.

Honking brown n. (1940s) a flashy tan suit of clothes. (DB, OHHJ, p. 140.) Harlem use.

Honkytonk (1900s–1920s) in jazz, a low style of life; the type of music played in the juke joints. (MM, RB, p. 371.) See "Gutbucket" and "Barrelhouse." JMFU, SNU.

Hooch n. (1920s–1930s) homemade liquor of doubtful quality; bootleg liquor; term not of black origin but common among black speakers during the twenties and thirties because of the availability of bootleg liquor. (FGC, DARE, p. 1079; WF, DAS, p. 266.) SNU.

Hoochie-choochie; Hoochy-choochy [man or woman] n. (1880s–1930s) one who preaches voodoo. "Hooch" was known generally as homemade whiskey of poor quality in the twenties, but black speakers had been referring to conjure "doctors" as hoochie-choochie men or women for as long as the term had been in use. (FGC, DARE, p. 1079.) SU.

Hoochie-choochie; Hoochy-choochy [dance] n. (1880s–1930s) a very erotic dance. (FGC, DARE, p. 1079.) SU. See "Hoochie-choochie (man or woman)".

Hoochie-pap n. (1920s) See "Boody." (CVV, NJ, p. 286.) Harlem; SNU.

Hood n. (1960s–1990s) neighborhood where one grows up; community or neighborhood, especially where a gang lives or congregates. (TW, CH, p. 149; DC, BJ, p. 68.) SCU.

Hoodoo n. (1880s–1930s) the spirit or essence of everything; an early African-American religion with origins in West African spiritual life; magic; a conjurer; charm; jinx; spell. (ZNH, MM, p. 229; HMH, HCWR, p. 776; JLD, LBE, p. 127.) Example: "Andrew going 'round here swearing up and down he can fix anybody—make a wife leave a husband, make a child turn on a mother—like he got the gift of hoodoo." SU.

Hoodoo bag n. (1920s–1930s) a bag containing graveyard dust and/or other magic potions used in conjuring. (HMH, HCWR, p. 227.) See "Bag."

Hoodoo doctor (HMH, HCWR, p. 776.) See "Hoodoo" and "Hoodoo bag."

Hoof; hoofing v. (1920s) to dance; dancing. (CVV, NH, p. 287.) Harlem use.

Hoogies n. (1940s–1960s) white people; same as "honkey"; (CM, CW, Gayle Jones, "White Rat," p. 375.) Kentucky use.

Hook(ed) adj., v. (1860s–1940s) originally from the sense of being hooked as on a cow's or bull's horns; by the late 1920s it came to mean addicted, especially to drugs or liquor or love. (Hear W. C. Handy, "Hooking Cow Blues," 1949.) DCU, SCU, PPU.

[Get] Hooked up v., adj. (1980s–1990s) to date or go out with someone. (FR.) YCU.

Hooker n. (1940s–1960s) a saxophone player who delivers poor-quality music. (RSG, JL, p. 150.) JMFU.

Hooker n. (1900s–1990s) a prostitute; from fishing talk; picked up by PPU life because a prostitute "hooks" a "trick" like a fisherman hooks a fish. (DW, TL, p. 183.) PPU, SNU.

Hooking v. (1980s–1990s) searching for a much-desired thing. (TW, CH, p. 149.) Example: "Lupe out hooking for crank." DCU, SCU, YCU.

Hooks n. (1950s) the human hands. (IS, PSML, p. 315; DB, OHHJ, p. 140.) SNU.

Hooky v. (1940s–1950s) truancy. School children's term.

Hooky party n. (1990s) a gathering of teens staying out of school and drinking "liquid crack" (malt liquor). (MM, NYT, p. 12.) Bronx, New York, use.

Hoop n. (1900s–1940s) a ring for the finger. (DB, OHHJ, p. 140.) Harlem; SNU.

Hoopdie swoop v. (1980s–1990s) to make a sudden romantic connection with a stranger; to succeed in "hitting on" someone. (EF, RDSL, p. 242.) Example: "Since Robert got that new ride he be making a hoopdie swoop at every stoplight." (EF, RDSL, p. 242.)

Hoop down v. (1980s) to play excellent basketball. (FR.) Basketball players' and fan use.

Hoop out v. (1980s) to play excellent basketball. (FR.) Basketball players' and fan use.

Hoopty; hoopdee n. (1990s) an old ugly car. (FR.) WCU, YCU.

Hoopty-mack n. (1990s) a girl or young woman singled out for macking. (FR.) See "Mack" and "Macking."

Hoosier; Hoogie n. (1940s–1950s) a word sometimes applied to white racists in the midwest; redneck; hillbilly; filthy, uncouth person; rustic person. (FGC, DARE, p. 1091.) SU, MWU.

Hooter n. (1990s) marijuana; a marijuana cigarette. (FR.) DCU.

Hootie Jay McShann, bandleader and piano player; born January 12, 1909; worked with Charlie Parker, et al.

[A] Hoove n. (1990s) a casual prostitute; an "unfresh" woman. (FR.) SCU, PPU, YCU.

Hop n. (1930s–1940s) in the twenties and thirties, any illegal drug; dope; in the forties, to dance. "Hop," as a term for a dance, has since become popular among white American teenagers. (DB, OHHJ, p. 140; AL, MJR, p. 47; MHB, JS, np.) SNU.

Hop a twig v. (1940s) to die. (DB, OHHJ, p. 140.) SNU.

Hoppergrass n. (1800s–1940s) grasshopper. (ECLA, NN, p. 266.) SU.

Hopping John n. (1700s–1940s) nineteenth-century term for cowpeas or black-eyed peas; usually cooked with rice, pork, and corn pone; or, a stew of bacon and peas native to the blacks of South

Carolina, who, of course, cooked also for the whites. (JSF, AON, p. 305; FGC, DARE, p. 1097.) SU.

Hops n. (1960s) any kind of beer. (DC, BJ, p. 69.) SNU.

Horn n. (1900s–1960s) a reed or brass wind instrument; short for "green horn." (RSG, JT, p. 132.) JMFU, SNU.

Hors d'oeuvre(s) n. (1970s–1990s) capsules of amphetamines or barbiturates. (EF, RDSL, p. 242.) DCU.

Horse n. (1950s–1960s) a knife; heroin. (DW, TL, p. 183; WF, DAS, p. 270.) DCU, PPU.

Horse n. (1930s–1950s) heroin. (CLC, TS, p. 255.) DCU.

Horse; hoss n. (1880s–1960s) a form of address, one male to another; common expression in the midwest during the forties; in the fifties and sixties it sometimes meant penis. (FR.) Examples: "How ya doing, horse?"; or, "I have to go [to the toilet] and let my horse out of my stable [pants; fly]." MWU, SU.

Horse blanket n. (1940s) an overcoat. (MHB, JS, np.) SU.

Horse heavy n. (1940s) a fat person. (MHB, JS, np.) SU.

Horse-mint tea n. (1890s–1940s) a tea made from mint and used as a medicine for "cleaning out" children in the spring. (RW, AA-GYRS, p. 84.) SU.

Hot adj. (1920s) in jazz, exciting in general; sexually exciting. (RF, WJ, p. 301; CC, OMMM, NCCHD, p. 256.) JMFU, SNCU. See "Hot mama."

Hotbed n. (1920s–1940s) in a flophouse, a public bed for the price of twenty-five cents per eight hours. (DB, OHHJ, p. 140; WF, DAS, p. 272.) SNU, SCU.

Hot cha! [got you?] interj. (1930s–1940s) an oath often heard during a crap game. (WM, DBD, p. 130.) SNU.

Hot comb n. (1900s–1950s) a heated straightening comb used to press kinky hair in an effort to make it straight. (GS, TT, p. 64.) SNU.

Hot dog! interj., n. (1900s–1960s) a cry of excitement; a quick-tempered, unpopular person. (WF, DAS, p. 272.) SNU.

Hot foot [it] v. (1900s–1940s) to hurry; run. (LA, SM, p. 39.) SU.

Hot for adj. (1940s–1950s) desiring someone sexually; eager for. (WF, DAS, p. 273.) SNU.

Hot jazz n. (1920s–1940s) a loud, unpolished style of music, usually with a very heavy beat, far removed from "popular" or "commercial" music. (RF, WJ, p. 301; MM, RB, p. 141.) JMFU.

Hot lips Oran Page, trumpet player and singer; born January 27, 1908, died November 5, 1954; worked with Chuck Berry, Artie Shaw, and others.

[Red] Hot mama n. (1920s–1940s) a frequent phrase used in the blues, it refers to a stout woman who is friendly and fun-loving, and one who can be found frequently in the barrelhouses and the juke joints. (WF, DAS, p. 424.) See "Flapper."

Hot oil n. (1980s) an important or self-important person. Example: "You think you hot oil, don't you?" Rare. (FGC, DARE, p. 1127.) See "Hot shit" and "Hot shot."

[To have the] Hots for [one] n. (1900s–1960s) sexual attraction. (FR.) Example: "Vita worse than some of these billy goat men around here—she got the hots for everything in pants." SNU.

Hot shit adj., n. (1960s–1970s) excellent; charming; used negatively, an important or self-important person. (FR.) Example: "That creep thinks he is hot shit." SNU.

Hot shot n. (1930s–1940s) bad homemade liquor; bootleg whiskey. (FGC, DARE, p. 1128.) SU.

Hot shot n. (1950s–1960s) a poisonous injection of heroin. (FR.) DCU.

Hot supper n. (1900s–1940s) a switchblade knife used for fighting. (FGC, DARE, p. 1128.) SU.

Hot supper n. (1930s–1950s) a backyard picnic or some other such gathering of friends and/or family; "hot" refers to the excitement, the fun, not the food, which is often cold cuts. (FGC, DARE, p. 1128.) South Carolina; SU.

Hound v. (1860s–1950s) to pester, annoy; Greyhound bus. (FR.) SNU.

House band (1900s–1950s) a jazz orchestra engaged on a permanent basis in one location. (RSG, JL, pp. 153–154.) JMFU.

House fee n. (1980s–1990s) the admission charge for entry to a crackhouse. (TW, CH, p. 149.) DCU.

House nigger [house negro] n. (1620s–1960s) a black person (such as Phillis Wheatley, 1753–1784) who worked in the slaveholder's house; the term was made popular in the fifties and sixties by Malcolm X. It refers to the fact that during slavery blacks working in the big house tended to be looked upon by fellow slaves working in the field as traitors because they often seemed more loyal to the slaveholders than to their own people. Also, a "house nigger" might be described as any black person guilty of cultural suicide or cultural contempt; an Uncle Tom. (SBF, IHAT, p. 36.) SNU. See "Field nigger."

House of countless drops n. (1930s–1940s) a barroom in which grilled food as well as liquor is sold. (DB, OHHJ, p. 140.) Harlem use.

House of knowledge n. (1940s) a school, especially a college. (MHB, JS, np.) Southern Negro college student use.

House of pain n. (1940s) a dentist's office. (MHB, JS, np.) Example: "Babette just back from the house of pain and her jaw is all swollen black and blue." SU.

House piece n. (1980s–1990s) a gift of crack cocaine, especially to one's host. (TW, CH, p. 149.) DCU.

House-rent party n. (1920s–1940s) (FGC, DARE, p. 1134.) See "Rent party."

House without chairs n. (1920s–1940s) an apartment or flat where dancing is permitted. Especially good for "rent parties." (DB, OHHJ, p. 140.) Example: "Me and Jerome hit the house without chairs and the babes all dig on our zoot suits and go crazy trying to be the first to dance with us." Harlem use.

How come? adv. (1700s–1940s) why. (ECLA, p. 266.) Example: "How come you do me like you do?" SU.

Howlin' Wolf blues singer Chester Burnett (1910–1976).

How low can you go? (1990s) taunt heard in rap songs: What's your staying capacity? Can you last in the act of lovemaking? (FR.) YCU.

How-so-ever; howsomever conj., adv. (1700s–1930s) however. (CC, CW, p. 140.) SNU.

How you be (1940s–1980s) how are you? Hello. (FR.) SNU.

Hubba n. (1980s–1990s) crack cocaine pellet. (FR.) DCU.

Hubba hubba exclam. (1930s–1940s) an expression of approval. (MHB, JS, np.) SU.

Huck n. (1880s–1930s) derogatory; a black person; probably picked up from title of Mark Twain's novel *Huckleberry Finn*, and used as a reference to Jim, the slave. (FGC, DARE, p. 1140.) Example (one rural black person to another): "Why you coming on so high and mighty? You just a huck like me." SU.

Huckabuck n. (1940s) dance; a song and dance term probably picked up from the huckabuck bath towel reference. (FR.) SNCU.

Hulla-balloo n. (1730s–1950s) *halwa balwalua* [Bantu]; the noise made by the arrival of many people; the noise of a crowd; the gaiety of a drinking party. (HV, AHAE, p. 142.) SU.

Hully n. (1980s–1990s) an overweight person. (EF, RDSL, p. 243.) SNU.

Hully-gully n. (1650s–1990s) *halakala* (Bantu): "compare"; a children's game. (HV, AHAE, p. 142.) SU.

Humbug n. (1950s–1990s) any false or fabricated condition or claim; anything perplexing or complicated or both; problems; difficulties. (CRM, BP, p. 302; EF, RDSL, p. 231.) SNU.

Humbugging v. (1960s–1980s) fighting or brawling. (REK, G, p. 97.) Example: "The dudes got to humbuggin', then I left out of there." SNU, YCU, SCU.

Humdinger n. (1960s–1970s) anything perplexing or baffling. (FR.) MWU. See "Humbug."

[A] Hummer n. (1930s–1940s) anything of outstanding quality or exceptional value. (CC, OMMM, NCCHD, p. 252.) Harlem use.

Hummer n., v. (1940s–1950s) a small error. Used as a verb, it's a variant of "humbug," meaning to get something free; to deadbeat. (DB, OHHJ, p. 140.) Example: "Mr. Taylor, that jive-ass dude, fired me for a hummer, man. I made a mistake and gave a customer too much change for a ten." Harlem use. See "Humdinger," "Humbug."

Hump n., v. (1950s–1990s) a difficulty; to perform sexual intercourse; the more physical aspects of sexual intercourse. (EF, RDSL, p. 243.) See "Getting over the hump."

Humpty Hump (1990s) rapper for Digital Underground.

Hung to; hang to adj. (1950s–1960s) to be obsessive about something or someone. (RDA, DDJ, p. 266.) Example: "Vance is really hung to the idea of marrying Alma." Philadelphia use.

Hung up adj. (1940s–1970s) to be obsessed with something or someone; to have a psychological problem. (EF, RDSL, p. 243.) SNU, DCU. See "Hang up," and "Hung out."

Hung out adj. (1980s–1990s) to be "hooked" on drugs or obsessed with something or someone. (EF, RDSL, p. 243.) SNU, DCU.

Hunky-fucking-dory [hunkie] adj. (1970s–1990s) excellent; good; fine; pleasing. "Hunky-dory" is not of black origin but is popular among black slang users, especially when improvised. (Terry McMillan, "The Love We've Lost," *Essence*, May 1993, p. 78; FGC, DARE, p. 1160.) SNU.

Hurryment n. (1800s–1930s) hasty movement; frenzied action. (FGC, DARE, pp. 1165–1166.) Example: "I heard that my sister was dying, so I drove all night and in my hurryment hit a tree on a dark road." SU.

Hurt (hurting) adj., v. (1700s–1990s) to be in great need; to experience great misfortune, especially due to a magic spell (hoodoo). (HMH, HCWR, p. 172; HLB, LSS, p. 179; AEG, BB, p. 307; CRM, BP, p. 302.) Examples: "I'm really hurting for some cash," or, "I really be hurting when pay day comes round and you tell me you can't meet payroll." SNU.

Hush-hush n. (1930s–1940s) a pistol with a silencer—especially a revolver; picked up from underworld use. (DB, OHHJ, p. 140; HEG, DAUL, pp. 104–105.) Harlem use.

Hush mouth n. (1940s) of Gullah origin; a glass or sip of whiskey. (ZNH, DTR, p. 176; LDT, AGO, p. 232.) Example: "Take this hush mouth and be happy." SU.

Hush [one's] mouth v. (1920s–1990s) a friendly imperative retort of playful disbelief; a request to stop and take back what has just been said; not a command or request at all to stop talking. (XC,

MEB, p. 156.) Example: in response to having just been told that her son's just been arrested for theft, a mother says, "Hush your mouth!" SNU.

Hush; hush [one's] mouth v. (1920s–1990s) a command to stop speaking. (CVV, NH, p. 13; ECLA, CS, p. 37.) Example: "Girl, hush your mouth!" SNU.

Husk v. (1940s) to undress. (DB, OHHJ, p. 140.) Example: "Are you gonna husk, or am I going to have to do it for you?" MWU, SU.

Huskings n. (1940s) clothing, especially in a pile after stripping. (DB, OHHJ, p. 140.) MWU, SU.

Hus-no-harra n. (1920s–1930s) a conjuring potion made from jasmine lotion. "Brings good luck to gamblers" (ZNH, MM, p. 337). SU.

Hussy; huzzy n. (1800s–1940s) a young woman with a tainted reputation. (FGC, DARE, p. 1170.) Example: "Wilhelmina is one sneaky gal—there ain't a wife down here who ain't worried about that hussy." SU.

Hustle v. (1650s–1860s) to move fast. Many white speakers still use this term in this early sense. (JSF, AON, pp. 310–311.) SU.

Hustle; hustling; [a] hustle v., n. (1650s–1990s) making money by pimping or selling drugs or running a "game"; to survive by any means possible; self-employment on a makeshift job; to gesture at someone in an intense manner. (TW, CH, p. 149; DW, TL, p. 183; RDA, DDJ, p. 266; DB, OHHJ, p. 140; DC, BJ, p. 69; EF, RDSL, p. 243; CS, vol. 3, no. 2, p. 30; JH, PBL, p. 85.) SCU, DCU, SNU.

Hustler n. (1650s–1860s) one who moves fast. (JSF, AON, pp. 310–311.) SU.

Hustler n. (1900–1990s) see "Hustle."

Hustlers don't call show downs (1960s–1970s) In other words, one on the receiving end does not instigate a confrontation that might terminate the hand-outs he or she is totally dependent on. (JH, PBL, p. 85.) PPU, DCU, SCU.

Hype; hyping n., v. (1960s–1990s) used in drug culture as early as the first decade of the twentieth century, "hype" (for hypodermic); became popular in black street culture in the fifties and remained so, used to refer to deception; an addict; phoney situation; scheme. (RDA, TB, pp. 42–43; FR; WF, DAS, p. 278; DW, TL, p. 183; CC,

OMMM, NCCHD, p. 256; IS, PSML, p. 315, DB, OHHJ, p. 140; CS, vol. 3, no. 2, p. 30.) See "Jeffing," and "Talking shit."

Ice n. (1950s–1990s) a diamond; an illegal drug synthesized from methamphetamine. From the sixties to the eighties, a cold personality; the cold shoulder. (HLF, RJPD, p. 170; TW, CH, p. 149; DW, TL, p. 183.) Examples: "Betty walked right by him and gave him the ice"; "She's got money to burn; she wears nothing but ice in her ears and around her neck"; and, "He stays high on ice all the time, that's why you can't talk to him." SCU, PPU, PU, YCU.

Iceberg Slim n. (1960s) Robert Beck, author of *Pimp: The Story of My Life* and other books; a pimp; any man or unpopular person who takes advantage of others. (DC, BJ, p. 69.) SCU, YCU, PPU.

Iced v. (1960s–1990s) to be refused by someone; rejected; imprisoned and in solitary confinement; to kill someone. (EF, RDSL, p. 243; DC, BJ, p. 69; JH, PBL, p. 85.) Example: "The Mandingos from over on Thirty-third iced a dude from the Maumaus last night." SCU.

Ice-palace n. (1940s) a jewelry store. (DB, OHHJ, p. 141.) Harlem use.

Ice T (1990s) rapper and MTV star; supplied music for the movie *Colors*.

Icky adj. (1930s–1940s) especially in jazz, sentimental; tasteless; a "conservative" musician. (DB, OHHJ, p. 141; SL, RJON, p. 150.) JMFU, NCU.

Icky n. (1930s–1940s) a "square" or stupid person. (CC, OMMM, NCCHD, p. 256.) NCU.

Idea-pot n. (1930s–1940s) the human skull; one's mind. (BD, OHHJ, p. 141.) Harlem use.

Idiot-box n. (1960s) television. (FR.) Example: "All you kids do is sit in front of that idiot box. Why don't you go outside and jump and run like normal children?" SNU.

If he hollers let him go (1920s–1940s) well-known line from a children's counting-out rhyme; this is an expression from the Negro folk rhyme: "Catch a nigger by the toe, if he hollers, let him go. . . ." (FR.) SNU.

If I'm lying, I'm dying (1930s–1990s) an oath expressing the assumed incontestable nature of what is being said. (FR.) Example: "I swear I saw your mama with her boyfriend. If I'm lying, I'm dying." SNU.

If I'm lying, I'm flying (1930s–1990s) an oath expressing the unshakable nature of one's position. (ZNH, AM, p. 87.) Example: "Lily gave this to me to give to you. If I'm lying, I'm flying." SNU.

If it ain't you, it's somebody else (1940s–1950s) in other words, trouble is always coming. SU.

If you feel froggish, take a leap (1970s–1980s) invitation to fist-fight. (EF, BVV, p. 48.) South-central Los Angeles; SCU.

Ig; igg v. (1960s) to ignore; to shun. (DC, BJ, p. 69; DB, OHHJ, p. 141.) NSU.

Ignite n. (1980s–1990s) whiskey. (EF, RDSL, p. 243.) South-central Los Angeles; SCU, YCU.

Ignorant oil; ig'nant oil n. (1960s) wine; especially fortified "rotgut" wine—the type sold only in ghetto liquor stores; liquor. (DC, BJ, p. 69; RDP, SRO, p. 6.) NSU.

I hear you (1960s) an expression meaning, "You are telling the truth." (FR.) Example: "I hear you, girl, ain't it the truth." NSU.

Illin v. (1980s–1990s) suffering from severe stress. (TW, CK, p. 137.) DCU.

I mean v. (1960s) I wish to say. NSU.

Imey-wimey n. (1920s–1930s) a voice that is meek sounding; cowardly voice. (CM, CW, Claude McKay, "Truant," p. 42.) SNCU.

Immo n., adj. (1940s–1960s) variant of and short for imitation. (FR.) SNU.

In a bad way adj. (1800s–1990s) having misfortune or sickness. (JAH, PBE, p. 175.) SNU.

In [there] n., adj. (1930s–1960s) to have an advantage. (DB, OHHJ, p. 141.) Examples: "I have an in with the boss"; and, "My mother's really in there when it comes to doing her own taxes." NSU.

[Put] In a cross n. (1960s) complication; difficulty. (DW, TL, p. 183.) Example: "They put me in a cross when they sent me to the wrong address." SCU. See "Put on a crosstown bus."

In-and-out-of n. (1930s–1940s) any doorway. (DB, OHHJ, p. 141.) Harlem; SNU.

[Put] In a sling n. (1960s) complication; difficulty. (DW, TL, p. 183.) See "[Put] In a cross" and "Put on a crosstown bus."

In a minute (1980s–1990s) in the future, perhaps a month from the time said, but not immediately. (TW, CK, p. 137; WKB, JMC, PS, p. 49.) Example: "Catch you in a minute." SCU.

In a nod adj. See "Nod."

In [one's] face adv., adj. (1980s–1990s) to invade one's aura; to provoke one by wolfing in his or her face. (PM, UCLAS, p. 18.) YCU, SCU.

In the groove adj. (1930s–1940s) (CC, OMMM, NCCHD, p. 256.) See "Groove."

In the street (1960s–1970s) open to public display. "Don't put my business in the street." (RDA, TB, p. 3.) SNU.

Into adv. (1960s–1970s) to be deeply involved in something, especially making music; to possess drugs; to possess a lot of money; to have the outward appearance of success—such as a new expensive car and expensive, well-made clothes. (RSG, JT, p. 139; RRL, DAZ, p. 117.) Examples: "Roach is really into the music"; and, "How you doing, Joseph? I'm not into anything." DCU, JMFU.

Indo n. See "Indonesia."

Indonesia n. (1990s) marijuana. (FR.) See "Weed."

Index n. (1930s–1940s) the human face. (DB, OHHJ, p. 141.) Harlem use.

Indoor aviator n. (1930s–1940s) elevator operator. (FR.) Example: "You can't even get a job at Sears as an indoor aviator and fly from bargain basement to apparel fifth floor all day long." NECU, MWU.

In front of adj. (1960s–1990s) a causal sequence. (FR.) Example: "Then she came back and in front of all that told me she was finished with me." SNCU.

Ink n. (1980s–1990s) cheap wine. (R.) SCU, PPU, YCU.

Inky-dinky adj., n. (1900s–1940s) a loosely used negative connotation; sometimes refers to a very dark Afro-American who happens also to be untidy. (ZNH, AM, p. 95; WF, DAS, p. 280.) SNU.

Innocent n. (1960s) a negative term for a white liberal anxious to help in the African-American struggle for justice during the sixties. (WF, DAS, p. 691.) NSU.

Insane adj. (1940s) positive; in a healthy state of mind. (FR.) SNU.

Insiders n. (1940s–1950s) one's pockets. (DB, OHHJ, p. 141.) Harlem use.

International nigger n. (1950s–1960s) black person dressed in a variety of expensive imported clothes. (DC, BJ, p. 69.) Rare. MWU.

Interplanetary mission n. (1990s) the act of making the rounds of the crack houses. (TW, CH, p. 149.) Example: "Jones run himself raggedy making his interplanetary mission round the clock." DCU.

In the mix adv., adj. (1990s) in process; picked up from recording use.

In there adj. (1930s–1940s) sophisticated; hip; informed. (DB, OHHJ, p. 141.)

Into something adj. (1950s–1960s) creative; special; involved; intelligent; lucky; unusual or exciting. (RSG, JT, p. 139.) SNCU, JMFU.

Iron lips n. See "Chops" and "Freak lips."

Ironing the yard (1920s–1940s) sweeping the yard with a straw broom. (RW, AAGYRS, p. 84.) SU.

Irregardless prep. See "Disregardless."

[Charlie] Irvine n. (1980s–1990s) any police officer. (EF, RDSL, p. 232.) Watts and South-central Los Angeles use.

I shot [one] lightly and [one] died politely (1930s–1940s) to best someone. (ZNH, AM, p. 95.) Harlem use.

Israelite n. (1940s) any Jewish person. (DB, OHHJ, p. 141.) Harlem use.

Issue n. (1930s–1940s) possibly short for "free issue"; any situation or thing or person; from nineteenth-century use or military use. (DB, OHHJ, p. 141.) Harlem; SNU.

[Free] Issue n. (1860s–1930s) a black person set free; African-American with a white mother and a black father during the Civil War; ex-slaves with Indian, Anglo, and African ancestry. (ECLA, CS, p. 56; BB, ASW, p. 34; *Federal Writer's Project Guide: North Carolina*, p. 336.) SNU. See "Free issue."

It's like that; it be's like that (1990s) that's the reality of the situation. (FR.) SNU.

It must be jelly 'cause jam don't shake like that (1920s–1940s) sex; an expression often heard in the blues. (ZNH, AM, p. 84.) JBWU, SNU.

Ivories n. (1900s–1940s) piano keys. (RSG, JT, p. 140.) Rare. JMFU.

Ivory tickler n. (1900s–1940s) a pianist—Eubie Blake's term. (RSG, JT, p. 140.)

J

J n. (1980s–1990s) a joint; marijuana cigarette. (Fr.) DCU.

Jaam n. (1700s–1860s) a gathering of slaves for the purpose of fun. (HV, AHAE, p. 142.) SU.

Jaambuur n. (1650s–1860s) Wolof word used by slaves to describe a free man. (HV, AHAE, p. 242.) SU.

Jack n. (1930s–1960s) male form of address to another male; any male; an all-purpose intensifier. Example: "You better believe it, Jack!" (DW, TL, p. 183; DB, OHHJ, p. 141; CC, OMMM, NCCHD, p. 256; DC, BJ, p. 69.) SNU.

Jack n. (1960s–1970s) money. (JH, PBL, p. 85.) NCU.

Jack around v. (1960s–1970s) to waste time. (FR.) Example: "That man don't do nothing but jack around all the time." SNU.

Jacked up adj. (1990s) in trouble; hurt; broke; depressed. (FR.) YCU, SCU.

Jacker n. (1990s) short for "car hijacker." (FR.) YCU, SCU.

[A] Jackie Robinson n. (1940s–1990s) any black person who is the first to penetrate a social or professional category. (FR.) SNU.

Jackie Robinson n. (1950s) the penis. (FR.) Rare. SNU.

Jack in the bean stack n. (1950s–1960s) term of address; variant of "Jack and the Bean Stalk"; an adventurous fellow. (DG, CP, p. 113.) SNU.

Jack-leg mechanic n. (1960s–1990s) an automobile mechanic who works on the street. (DR, BASL, p. 92.) Philadelphia use; NECU.

Jack-leg preacher n. (1930s–1950s) storefront preacher. (FR.) SNU.

Jack off v. (1930s–1940s) to masturbate; from "ejaculate." (PM, UCLAS, p. 52.) SNU.

Jackson n. See "Jack."

Jackson whites n. (1880s–1940s) persons of both black and white —possibly also Indian—ancestry native to Passaic, Bergen, and Morris counties in New Jersey and Orange and Rockland counties in New York; their ancestry can usually be traced back to the Revolutionary War period. (BB, AW, pp. 85–86.) New York and New Jersey use.

Jack up v. (1980s–1990s) to assault someone, especially suddenly. (EF, RDSL, p. 243.) SCU, DCU, PPU, PU. See "Jack[ed] up."

Jack(ed) up v. (1960s–1980s) in the sixties, to rob; from the late seventies into the eighties, to beat up or abuse in some way. (DC, BJ, p. 69; CS, vol. 3, no. 2, p. 31.) Example: "Victor and Wade pulled a jack up down at the grocery store." SCU.

Jag n. (1880s–1930s) intoxication from alcohol; drunk. (AB, DSJC, p. 465.) SNU.

[Marijuana] Jag n. (1930s–1940s) the state of mind induced by smoking marijuana; "a marijuana jag is a condition of the mind that rapidly and continually changes while each stage through which it passes contains only the present, the immediate moment, absolute and irrevocable" (Chester Himes, "Marijuana and a Pistol," *The Collected Stories of Chester Himes*, 1991, p. 372). DCU. See "Jag."

Jam v., n. (1860s–1990s) a party of musicians making music; to make exciting music; to have a good time socially; to "party." (DB, OHHJ, p. 141; CC, OMMM, NCCHD, p. 256; DC, BJ, p. 70; PM, UCLAS, p. 52; JH, PBL, p. 85.) SNCU, JMFU.

Jam n. (1980s–1990s) the vagina. (EF, RDSL, p. 243.) See "Jam pot."

Jam n. (1960s–1970s) cocaine. (CRM, BP, p. 303.) WCU, PPU.

Jam v. (1960s–1970s) to inhale cocaine. (CRM, BP, p. 303.) WCU, PPU.

Jama n. (1700s–1890s) a Wolof word meaning crowd; word used by early slaves to describe gatherings. (HV, AHAE, p. 142.) SU.

Jam back v. (1930s–1970s) to dance. "They can really jam back" (DC, BJ, p. 70). "Boy, you should see them sisters Adalia and Marcia, when they get out on the dance floor and the joint is jumping, they really jam back something terrible." SNCU, JMFU.

Jambalaya n. (1800s–1990s) cooked corn; from *tshimboebole* (Bantu). (HV, AHAE, p. 151.) See "Gumbo."

Jamboree n. (1840s–1990s) from the West African word *jama*, meaning a celebration. (HV, AHAE, p. 142.) SU.

[The] James Brown n. (1950s) a dance originated by singer James Brown.

Jam house n. (1950s) an apartment or house where drug users gather to buy cocaine and to get high on it. (CRM, BP, p. 12, 303.) WCU, DCU, PPU.

Jamming v. (1980s–1990s) to party; also, to fight. (TW, CK, p. 137; JH, PBL, p. 85.) DCU.

Jammy n. (1990s) a gun, especially a handgun or pistol. (FR.) WCU, DCU, SCU.

Jam pot n. (1980s–1990s) the vagina. (EF, RDSL, p. 240.) SNU.

Jams n. (1950s) phonograph records, especially 33 rpms. (FR.) JMFU, SNCU.

Jam session n. (1930s–1940s) an occasion where jazz musicians get together to play strictly for their own pleasure. (RSG, JT, p. 142.) JMFU, SNCU.

[Aunt] Jane n. (1960s) female Uncle Tom. See "Uncle Tom."

Janky n. (1990s) bad luck; negative; probably a variant of "jinxed." (FR.) YCU.

Jar-head n. (1930s–1940s) a black male. (ZNH, AM, p. 95.) SNU.

Jas n. (1820s) a slave on a plantation near New Orleans. Some researchers believe the word "jazz" may be derived from his name. (FR.) See "Jazz."

Jasper n. (1960s) lesbian. Earlier, and in general American use, "Jasper" meant a theological student or just any fellow, especially a meek one. (WF, DAS, p. 285; DW, TL, p. 183; IS, PSML, p. 315; RRL, DAZ, p. 117; EF, RDSL, p. 243.) SCU.

Jass n. See "Jazz."

Jasy adj. See "Jazzy."

Jawing v. (1800s–1940s) talking. (JAH, MLN, p. 175.) SU.

Jazz n. (1620s–1990s) very likely a modern word for *jaja* (Bantu), which means to dance, to play music; early variants are "jas," "jass," and "jasy"; a type of black music derived from blues, work songs, spirituals; possibly a Creole version of the Ki-Kongo word *dinza,* and the early New Orleans variant "jizz"; also, from Creole *patois* ("to speed things up"); another, less likely theory has it that "jazz" is a French word meaning sexy or sensuous; the word "jazz" attempts to define various kinds of musical forms created and developed primarily by black Americans—from the African beat, spirituals, and work songs, to the music of New Orleans marching bands, the Storyville district, the barrelhouse and cathouse innovations; also high-spirited; known for years as a word of uncertain origin, but thought to have possibly derived from the name Jasper, a slave in Louisiana whose dancing elicited shouts of encouragement in which he was addressed by his nickname Jas; music with instruments or voice or both. Another theory has it that "jazz" is derived from the African word *jaiza*—the sound of far-off drums; also means sexual intercourse. (RFT, FS, p. 104; HV, AHAE, p. 142; WF, DAS, pp. 286–288; AL, MJR, pp. 56–60, 62–63, 80–85, 193–194.) SNU.

Jazz Five (1970s–1980s) rap group, originally of the Bronx.

Jazznocracy Jimmie Lunceford, bandleader; born June 6, 1902, died July 13, 1947.

Jazzy adj. (1930s–1960s) brash; after the forties, old-fashioned; from the fifties to the sixties, in style, up-to-date. (SL, RJON, p. 4.) JMFU.

Jazzy Jeff and the Fresh Prince (1990s) a popular rap team.

Jaybird Ray a baseball player in the old Negro leagues.

Jeep n. (1940s) a drunk. (MHB, JS, np.) See "Jick head."

Jeep n. (1960s) the tiny strip of paper a heroin addict inserts between the hypodermic needle and the eyedropper. (CS, vol. 3, no. 2, p. 31.) DCU.

Jeff n., v. (1930s–1960s) loosely used term; a white person; to inform on someone; a dull person; a horrible square; a pest. (HLF, RJPD, p. 171; DB, OHHJ, p. 141; CC, OMMM, NCCHD, p. 257.) SCU, PPU, PU, DCU.

Jeff; jeffing v. (1960s–1990s) loosely used term; to act subservient to a white person; tomming; acting stupid to achieve an objective. The term derives from the widespread belief that whites in authority do not trust or respect or even believe in the possible existence of intelligent blacks. (CLC, TS, p. 255; RDA, TB, p. 53.) SCU.

Jeffing n. (1950s) loosely used term; an especially lowdown con game. (FR; IS, PSML, p. 315.) SCU, PPU, DCU. See "Hype."

Jelly n., v. (1630s–1940s) *jeli* [Mandingo] means minstrel; or virile man. (HV, AHAE, p. 143.) SU.

Jelly n. (1930s–1940s) sex; without charge; "on the house." (DB, OHHJ, p. 141; CC, OMMM, NCCHD; ZNH, AM, p. 95.) Harlem use.

Jelly n. (1890s–1900s) the vagina; sexual intercourse. (RSG, JT, p. 145.) SNU.

Jellybean n. (1930s–50s) a term of address.

Jelly-roll; jellyroll n. (1890s–1900s) one's lover; spouse; from the twenties to the forties, a term for the vagina. (EF, RDSL, p. 243.) SNU.

Jelly Roll Morton Ferdinand Joseph La Menthe, composer, pianist, bandleader, singer; born in Gulfport, Louisiana, September 20, 1885, died in Los Angeles, California, July 10, 1941; a great figure in jazz history.

Jelly sandwich n. (1970s–1990s) a pejorative term for sanitary napkin. (EF, RDSL, p. 243.) South-central Los Angeles; SCU, YCU, WCU.

Jerking pole n. (1740s–1860s) a tree limb for the sisters and brothers to cling to at a camp-fire "church" meeting during slavery; used to steady themselves during the frenzy of shouting and thrashing. (SK, PC, p. 76.) SU.

Jersey highball n. (1940s) cow's milk. (MHB, JS, np.) SU.

Jersey side of snatch play adj. (1940s) to be past thirty-eight years of age. (DB, OHHJ, p. 141.) Harlem use.

Jesse James Killer n. (1940s) any heavy, gluey hair pomade with a sharp scent. (DB, OHHJ, p. 141.) Harlem use.

Jessie n. (1940s) a red-headed vixen.

Jet v. (1980s–1990s) to move quickly; to leave. (FR.) (JM, WPC, p.) Example: "Let's jet before it rains." SCU. See "Ghost move."

[The] Jew n. (1940s–1950s) any boss on a job, not necessarily Jewish. (HLF, RJPD, p. 171.) Example: "I got to go downtown and see if the Jew will give me a job." Harlem use.

Jewcanoe n. (1930s–1940s) anti-Semitic word for a Cadillac; may stem from assumption that many dealerships are owned by Jews. (Fr.) NCU.

Jezebel n. (1800s–1860s) a pejorative term for a black woman, especially a young and attractive one, during and after slavery; usually considered a threat to the southern white family because white men were so attracted to such women. (Clarence E. Walker, *Deromanticizing Black History: Critical Essays and Reappraisals*, 1991, p. 11.) SU.

Jib n. (1970s–1990s) talk, especially excessive. (EF, RDSL, p. 243.) South-central Los Angeles; WCU.

Jib(s) n. (1960s) lips; buttocks. (IS, PSML, p. 315; DC, BJ, p. 70.) Example: "Just keep your jibs closed and you won't get in trouble." SCU, PPU.

Jibba n. (1800s–1890s) slave use; variant of gibblets—the leftovers from the white folks' table. (HV, AHAE, p. 143.) SU.

Jibs n. (1950s–1960s) teeth. (RDA, DDJ, p. 266.) Philadelphia use; NECU.

Jick n. (1920s–1940s) whiskey; liquor; especially bootleg alcohol. (MHB, JS, np; hear Lightnin' Hopkins's "Chicken Minnie," *Lightnin' Hopkins and Friends/Lost Texas Tapes, Vol. 5*.) SU.

Jick-head n. (1940s) a drunk; an alcoholic. (MHB, JS, np.) SU.

Jiffy n. (1700s–1950s) *tshipi* [Bantu]; short span of time; in a hurry; quickly; brief. (HV, AHAE, p. 143.) SNU.

Jig n. (1650s–1920s) a dance; possibly from African word *juge*, which means a fast-stepping dance done with great excitement. (JH, PBL, p. 85.) SU.

Jig n. (1650s–1920s) an African-American; a very black person; short for "jiggaboo." (CVV, NH, p. 286.) Harlem use. See "Jiggerboo."

Jig-chaser n. (1900s–1920s) a downtown Manhattan white person who actively sought the company of Negroes. (CVV, NH, p. 286.) Harlem use.

Jiggaboo; jigabo n. (1630s–1950s) *tshikabo* [Bantu] means a meek or servile person; a very dark-skinned African-American of pure African descent; a slave term, it was always pejorative. (HV, AHAE, p. 143; SBF, IHAT.) SU.

Jigging contest n. (1800s–1890s) nineteenth-century slave game in which the contestants tried to balance cups of water on their heads then tried to dance without dropping them or spilling water. (FR.) SU.

Jig-jagging v. (1900s–1920s) to dance without restraint. (CMC, HH; B65, p. 16) Harlem use. See "Foop."

Jig-tunes n. See "Corn song."

Jim n. (1940s–1950s) term of address to a male. (DW, TL, p. 183; DC, BJ, p. 70; JH, PBL, p. 85.) Example: "I'm not worried about it, Jim, 'cause I got the situation covered." See "Jack."

Jim Crow n. (1800s–1950s) enforced segregation; term comes from the song "Jim Crow," featured in a Negro minstrel show by Thomas Rice (1808–1860). (LA, SM, p. 14; SL, RJON, p. 18.) SNU.

Jim Crow n. (1860s–1890s) a picklike comb used by slaves and ex-slaves in the south. Also, in the 1850s, a "jim crow" was sometimes the name for a poor man. (FR.) SU.

Jim jam v. (1940s–1950s) to have a "ball"; a lively party; to make "hot" music. (SL, RJON, p. 148.) JMFU.

Jimmies n. (1990s) condoms. (TW, CH, p. 149.) SCU, DCU, YCU, PPU.

Jimmy Gall n. (1920s–1930s) a mythical place referred to by the "Negroes" of Eatonville, Florida. (ZNH, MM, p. 190.) Florida use. See "Bee-luther-hatchee."

Jimmy hat n. (1990s) condom. (TW, CH, p. 149.) DCU.

Jinky n. (1950s–1960s) variant of "jinx"—any negative or uncomfortable situation. (IS, TB, p. 312.) SNU.

Jism n. (1950s) juice; energy; semen. (IS, TB, p. 312.) SNU.

Jitter (JH, PBL, p. 85.) See "Jitterbug."

Jitterbug n. (1650s–1940s) *jito-bag* [Mandingo]; a dance done to swing music; the Lindy Hop; a dance-crazed person. (HV, AHAE, p. 138; DB, OHHJ, p. 141; MHB, JS, np; CC, OMMM, NCCHD, p. 257.) SNU.

Jitterbug n. (1970s–1990s) a person who "runs off at the mouth"; person who talks a lot. (EF, RDSL, p. 243.) South-central Los Angeles; WCU.

Jitterbug(s) n. (1960s–1970s) city street guys, but not necessarily gang members. (DR, BASL, p. 58.) Philadelphia use.

Jitterbugging n. (1960s) any kind of wild party dancing, not specifically the Jitterbug, as known in earlier times; extravagant behavior. (CS, vol. 3, no. 2, p. 31.) WCU, YCU.

Jitterdoll n. (1940s) a woman who loves dancing. (DB, OHHJ, p. 141; JH, PBL, p. 85.) See "Jitterbug."

Jitterjane n. (1940s) any woman who dances a lot and enjoys it. (FR.) See "Jitterbug."

Jive n. (1630s–1990s) *jev* and *jew* [Wolof] mean gossip, false talk, con game; loose talk; to sneer; from the forties to the fifties "jive" meant deceit, nonsense, to put someone on. Some researchers believe it may be a distortion of the English word "jibe." (HV, AHAE, p. 143; RDA, DDJ, p. 266; EF, RDSL, p. 243; DW, TL, p. 183; DB, OHHJ, p. 141; CC, OMMM, NCCHD, p. 257.) SNU.

Jive n. (1960s) marijuana. (CS, vol. 3, no. 2, p. 31; JH, PBL, p. 85.) YCU.

Jive-ass n. (1950s–1970s) an insincere person. (CRM, BP, 303.) SNU.

Jiver n. (1920s–1950s) a person who talks "jive." (MHB, JS, np.) See "Jive."

Jivetime adj. (1960s) not sincere; dishonest. (DC, BJ, p. 70.) Example: "I can't be bothered with a jivetime dude like him." SNU, SCU, YCU.

Jive turkey n. (1960s–1990s) a pejorative expression directed at someone who is considered insincere, undependable, or without ethics. (EF, RDSL, p. 244.) SNU, SCU, YCU.

Jizz n. (1700s–1930s) semen; probably from the Ki-Kongo word *dinza*, meaning "live force" or "life force"; energy or vitality. (RFT, FS, p. 104.) New Orleans; SU.

J.O. n. (1990s) one's job. (HC, WSJ, p. B1.) Example: They just cut everybody's salary by five percent on my j.o." YCU.

Jocking v. (1990s) to imitate or annoy someone. (FR.) Example: "I'm not surprised Marie quit, cause that dude Erroll, he was always jocking her and she was sick of it." SNCU.

Jodie n. (1940s) a Second World War serviceman's term meaning any civilian male not accepted by the military; a young male with a deferment. A "Jodie" is back home making love to the enlisted man's wife. (WF, DAS, p.692.) SNU.

Joe Blow n. (1900s–1920s) originally any horn-blowing musician but came to mean any male person, especially one who whose name is unknown. (FR; WF, DAS, p. 294.) JMFU.

Joe Moore n. (1920s–1930s) "a piece of gamblers' lucky hoodoo" (ZNH, MM, p. 190). SU.

Joe Sad n. (1900s–1930s) one without friends; unpopular. (WF, DAS, p. 295.) SNU.

Joey n. (1950s–1960s) any white man. (HLF, RJPD, p. 171.) NCU.

John n. (1630s–1860s) *jon* [Mandingo] means a person owned by another person; a slave. (HV, AHAE, p. 143.) SU. See "John Henry."

John n. (1920s–1960s) any man; when used by a prostitute, means same as "trick" but especially a white man. The word as a reference for a toilet has been rare among black speakers. (LH, LKFC, p. 120; DW, TL, p. 183; DB, OHHJ, p. 141; DC, BJ, p. 70.) SNU.

John Canoe n. (1800–1860s) an African festival observed by slaves both in North Carolina and other parts of the south and in the Caribbean; carnival time; dancing with hands behind the back. (HV, AHAE, p. 158.) SU.

John Constant n. (1800–1860s) cornbread; slave name for cornbread. (JLD, BN, p. 8.) SU.

[Big] John the Conqueror n. (1850s–1930s) the mythic man who beat the Devil's ass—he tore off the Devil's arm and whipped him with it. (SK, PC, pp. 153–154.) SU.

John [the] Conqueror n. (1850s–1930s) a root used in hoodoo doctoring. (ZNH, MM, p. 332, 334.)

John Henry n. (1890s–1940s) a hardworking black man; a black man with courage and endurance in the face of inhuman work; the legendary folk hero of railroad camp fame; a "Negro" work song. (ZNH, MM, p. 306.) SNU.

Johnny-be-good n. (1970s–1990s) a policeman. (EF, RDSL, p. 244.) South-central Los Angeles; WCU.

Johnson n. (1970s–1980s) human penis; probably stems from the image of Jack Johnson pounding his opponent. (HLF, RJPD, p. 171; TW, CH, p. 149.) Example: "He's always grabbing at his johnson like he thinks every girl he sees wants him." See "Jack Johnson."

Joint n. (1930s–1950s) through the thirties and into the fifties, where one lives or a tavern, poolroom, or dancehall. (MHB, JS, np; DC, BJ, p. 70.) SNU.

Joint n. (1930s–1970s) from the forties to the seventies, marijuana wrapped in cigarette paper. (CRM, BP, p. 303; CLC, TS, p. 255; TW, CH, p. 149; RRL, DAZ, p. 117; DC, BJ, p. 70.) SNU.

Joint n. (1940s–1980s) a man's penis. (RDA, DDJ, p. 266.) SNU.

Joint n. (1950s–1960s) prison; any correctional facility. (CRM, BP, p. 303; CS, vol. 3, no. 2, p. 31.) SCU, PPU, PU, DCU.

[The] Joint is jumping (1930s–1940s) the place—such as a ballroom where musicians are performing—is alive with joyous entertainment. (DB, OHHJ, p. 141; CC, OMMM, NCCHD, p. 257.) SNCU.

Jojo n. (1960s) nickname for penis. (DW, TL, p. 183.) Rare. SCU, YCU, PPU. See "Johnson."

Joke n. (1950s–1960s) a penis, especially a small one. (HLF, RJPD, p. 171.) Example (young woman speaking): "I guess you think that little joke of yours impresses me, huh?" New York City use.

Jollof rice n. (1700s–1990s) a style of rice cooking introduced in the south by Africans as early as the 1700s. (HV, AHAE, p. 151.) SU.

Jones n. (1950s–1980s) a fixation; a drug habit; compulsive attachment; also a job. (HLF, RJPD, p. 171; TW, CH, p. 149; EF, RDSL, p. 244; JH, PBL, p. 85.) SNU.

Jook v. (1700s–1950s) African word meaning to jab or poke—as in sexual intercourse; also used in the Caribbean. (AEG, BB, p. 308; MC, NTH, p. 210.) SU. See "Juke."

Jook n. (1860s–1940s) a shack where one can have a good time; tavern; whorehouse; "a fun house where they sing, dance, gamble, love, and compose 'blues' songs incidentally." There seems little doubt that this sense of "jook" is derived from the earlier sense of it: to jab or poke. The word "jukebox" is based on this African word. (ZNH, MM, p. 82; SK, PC, 183–191.) SU. See "Juke."

Jookass n. (1800s–1990s) a donkey; jackass. (AEG, BB, p. 308.) SU.

Jook it v. (1890s–1930s) to play the piano in a low-class night spot. (ZNH, AM, p. 95; MT, DAF, p. 162.) JMFU, SNU. See "Juke."

Jooking it v. (1890s–1900s) playing piano in a whorehouse. (ZNH, AM, p. 95; MT, DAF, p. 162.) JMFU, SNU. See "Juke."

Jordan John n. (1800–1890s) variant name for John the Baptist; used in spirituals. (FR.) SU.

Journey n. (1700s–1860s) the slave's term for life on earth. (FR.) SU.

Jower n. (1620s–1890s) talking; quarrelling; "a negro expression" (AB, DSJC, p. 480). SU. See "Jawing."

Joy box n. (1930s–1940s) radio. (MHB, JS, np.) SU.

Joy hemp n. See "Hemp" and "Weed." (DB, OHHJ, p. 141.)

Joy juice n. (1940s) liquor. (MHB, JS, np; DC, BJ, p. 70.) SNU.

Joy pop v. (1950s–1960s) the occasional use of drugs—but especially heroin—without developing a habit. (CLC, TS, p. 255.)

Joy roots n. (1920s–1940s) marijuana. (DB, OHHJ, p. 141.) Harlem use. See "Hemp" and "Weed."

Judas Caesar n. (1850s–1920s) slave and free black name for Julius Caesar. (AEG, BB, p. 308.) SU.

Juba n. (1620s–1900s) *nguba, kingooba* [Bantu]; peanut. (HV, AHAE, p. 144.) SU.

Juba n. (1620s–1800s) an African day name—that is, a family nickname—for a girl born on Monday; name used by early slaves for a female child. Such a child was thought to be impish. "Juba" is also one of seven day names for a Guinea male child. (HV, AHAE, p. 143; AB, DSJC, p. 480.) SU. See "Cudjo."

Juba n. (1790s–1900s) minstrel show dance done by a large or small group of slaves in which hands, knees, and thighs are clapped in a rhythmic pattern; a popular plantation dance. The Charleston may have been derived from the Juba. The dance very likely started before the 1790s since it was known by the earliest slaves and passed on. (HV, AHAE, p. 143, 157; SBF, HAT, p. 32.) SU.

Juba n. (1790s–1990s) slave name for leftovers from the white folks' table; also called "jiba" and "jibba"; nineteenth-century Virginia slave term for leftover food from the white folks' table. (HV, AHAE, pp. 143–144.) SU.

Jubilee n. (1790s–1990s) slave expression for free land; a symbol of Heaven. (FR.) See "Camp ground," "Canaan," and "Juba."

Jug n. (1900–1930s) bottle containing liquor. (DB, OHHJ, p. 141.) SNU.

Jug; jugging v. (1960s–1970s) to engage in verbal jousting. (DR, BASL, p. 176.) Philadelphia use.

Jug Eugene Ammons, tenor saxophone player; born April 14, 1925; worked with Sonny Stett, James Moody, et al.

Jug band n. (1900–1930s) usually a small, informal musical group in which a washboard, a homemade fiddle, and a bottle or a jug are used as music-making instruments. (RSG, JT, p. 149.) JMFU, SNU, YCU.

Juice n. (1930s–1990s) liquor, especially whiskey; after the eighties, human energy or personal charm or power. (CLC, TS, p. 255; TW, CH, p. 149; RRL, DAZ, p. 118; DB, OHHJ, p. 141; DC, BJ, p. 70; ZNH, AM, p. 95.) SNU. See "Juicer."

Juice n. (1960s) pay-off or protection money given to the police to look the other way. (CS, vol. 3, no. 2, p. 31.) DCU, PPU, SCU.

Juice back v. (1980s–1990s) to drink liquor; to get drunk. (FR.) YCU.

Juiced adj. (1930s–1950s) drunk. (FR.) SNU.

Juicehead; juice head n. (1930s–1960s) a person who is frequently drunk. (RRL, DAZ, p. 118.) SNU.

Juice joint n. (1930s) tavern, bar, cabaret. (HEG, DAUL, p. 112.) SNU.

Juice out of a brick bat n. (1860s–1900s) the impossible. (JAH, MLN, p. 175.) Example: "What'd you expect him to do—get juice out of a brick bat?" SNU.

Juicer n. (1980s–1990s) a woman who buys or may sell sex in exchange for crack cocaine. (TW, CH, p. 149.) DCU.

Ju ju n. (1650s–1940s) *njiu* [Bantu]; danger; a fetish against harm. (HV, AHAE, p. 144.) SU.

Juke v. (1800s–1940s) of African-Gullah origin; to be unruly; loud and boisterous; to have a good time dancing; to dance in a whorehouse; to get drunk; to dance to the music of a jukebox. (SBF, IHAT, p. 33.) SU.

Juke n. (1880s–1930s) person of Indian, African, and European ancestry in upstate New York. (BB, AW, p. 22.) Upstate New York use.

Juke; jook n. (1650s–1960s) *juka* [Bantu]; *dzug* [Wolof]; from Gullah; "juke-house"; related to West African words *dzug, dzog, dzugu*; a whorehouse; roadside-inn life-style; the type of music played in a juke joint; jukebox house. The music itself is characterized by an excessive use of string instruments. (HV, AHAE, p. 144; RSG, JL, p. 171; DW, TL, p. 184.) SU.

Juke box n. (1930s–1940s) public coin-operated record-playing machine; from "Negro" word "juke" or "jook." (WF, DAS, p. 298.) SNU.

Jumbo n. (1630s–1890s) one of the seven day names for an African male. (AB, DSJC, p. 480.) SU.

Jumbo(s) n. (1980s–1990s) very large vials of crack cocaine ready for street sale. (TW, CK, p. 137.) DCU.

Jump n. (1930s–1960s) any lively dance done to swing music; music with a bouncing rhythm; during the sixties, "jump" meant a fight between gang members. (DB, OHHJ, p. 141; DC, BJ, p. 70.) SCU.

Jump; jumped v., adv. (1990s) to fight; to attack someone; to be beaten in a physical fight. (*USA Weekend*, August 13–15, 1993, p. 10.) YCU.

Jump all over v. (1930s–1960s) to get angry with. (FR.) Example: "You don't have to jump all over my case!" SNU.

Jump bad v. (1940s–1960s) to become angry; to instigate a fight. (FR.) See "Jump salty."

Jumped in (1980s–1990s) the ritual of being initiated into a gang. (FR.) Example: "I swear I didn't expect Yates to make it through being jumped in, 'cause he such a cry-baby." SCU.

Jumpers n. (1960s) gym shoes. (DC, BJ, p. 70.) MWU.

Jump in v. (1940s–1960s) to become involved; when a musician enters an ongoing performance. (RSG, JT, p. 151.) JMFU.

Jumping Jody v. (1920s–1950s) exercising an infant's legs by jumping him or her up and down on the knee while chanting "Jump that Jody" or "Jump for Jody." (BJ, BLH, SD, p. 10.) SU.

Jump(ed) in port v. (1930s–1940s) to have just arrived in the city. (CC, OMMM, NCCHD, p. 257; DB, OHHJ, p. 141.) Example: "Thomas just jumped in port and he's hot to trot, wants to see some fine browns and do some jig-jagging." NCU.

Jump salty v. (1930s–1950s) to suddenly become angry. (ZNH, AM, p. 95.) Example: "She got a lot of nerve being the one to jump salty at me when she started the whole mess." SNU.

Jump steady imper., v. (1900–1950s) command to be honest and regular in a love relationship. (Hear Lucille Bogan's "Jump Steady Daddy," *Lucille Bogan/Walter Roland* (*1927–1935*), Yazoo, 1992.)

Jump steady n. (1920s–1990s) liquor—whiskey or wine. (EF, RDSL, p. 244; HEG, DAUL, p. 112.) SCU, DCU, YCU, PPU.

Jump street tn. (1980s–1990s) from the beginning. Example: "I tried to make it clear from jump street that I wasn't interested." (TMc, DA, p. 1.) SNCU. See "Get-go."

Jump(ing) the broom v. (1700s–1860s) to get married. Slaves had no legal means of marriage, so an engaged couple ritually jumped over a suspended broom as the symbolic gesture of announcing their commitment to each other. (SK, PC, p. 74.) SU.

Junebug n. (1850s–1950s) a variant of "Junior Boy," nickname for one who is named after his father. (FR.) SU.

Juneteenth n. (1940s–1990s) term refers to June 19, 1862, the date Abraham Lincoln signed the Emancipation Proclamation; Black Independence Day celebration. The Emancipation Proclamation became official January 1, 1863. Juneteenth has traditionally been taken more seriously in the South than in the North; it became a state holiday in Texas in 1972. (HV, AHAE, p. 158.) SNU.

Junior Walker and the All-Stars n. (1970s–1990s) the police patrolling South-central Los Angeles. (EF, RDSL, p. 244.) South-central Los Angeles use.

Junior Wells Amos Blackmore, blues singer.

Junk n. (1920s–1960s) from the underworld word "junker," for addict; from the twenties to the mid-forties, narcotics, especially heroin; in the fifties and later, miscellaneous items; things. (HEG, DAUL, p. 112; RSG, JL, p. 172; RRL, DAZ, pp. 118–119; CS, vol. 3, no. 2, p. 31.) DCU.

Junkanoo n. (1720s–1940s) a festival of African origin; John Canoe, also John Connu; a Caribbean Festival with a possible North Carolina counterpart. The Caribbean festival has at its center a legendary trickster figure named Junkanoo who may have a prototype in an actual man named John Canoe. Junkanoo is dressed in rags and he dances like a clown. The North Carolina festival takes place on Christmas day, and the participants entertain in the streets in exchange for presents. It's called "Coonering." See "Coonering." (FGC, DARE, pp. 256–262.) SU.

Junkie; junky n. (1930s–1960s) drug addict; a chronic user of morphine or heroin. (RSG, JL, p. 173; RRL, DAZ, p. 119; CS, vol. 3, no. 2, p. 32.) SCU, DCU.

Just like a bear adj. (1920s–1940s) to feel dejected or bored; hopeless. (ZNH, AM, p. 86.) SNU.

Just like the bear's brother [can't go no further] (1920s–1940s). See "Just like a bear."

Just like the bear's daughter [ain't got a quarter] See "Just like a bear."

Juvey; juvie n. (1970s–1990s) juvenile court; reform school. (EF, RDSL, p. 244; RP, C.) NECU.

K

Kack n. (1900s–1950s) a respected person; a person of integrity or character; used in much the same way as "fellow" or "dude." (WF, DAS, p. 300) SNU.

Kaiser baby (1920s–1930s) "to have a child by the Kaiser." "Kaiser" signifies wealth and power, so in this context the phrase refers to a woman who returns home married to a wealthy and usually white man or one who has a baby by a wealthy man. (ZNH, MM, p. 18.) SNU.

Kale n. (1940s) paper money. (MHB, JS, np; WF, DAS, p. 300.) SU.

Kansas Carl Donnell Fields, drummer; born December 5, 1915; worked with Benny Carter, Cab Calloway, and others.

Kapow! Kapow! n. (1960s) vocal sound made in imitation of a gun being shot; probably picked up from comic-strip use. The speaker points his finger at his would-be victim and says the words. (FR.) SNU, SCU.

Keeber n. (1980s) a white person. (TW, CH, p. 149.) DCU, NECU.

Keep cool v. (1940s–1980s) maintain the status quo; stay in one's place. (MHB, JS, np; EF, RDSL, p. 244.) SNU.

Keep [one's] feet in [one's] pants v. (1960s) follow the status quo; keep "cool"; don't complain. (DW, TL, p. 184.) NECU.

Keep on keeping on interj. (1960s) request to remain loyal; perseverance; keep trust.

Keep on top of the game interj. (1970s–1980s) offered as a word of encouragement; to succeed; to survive; to try to stay in charge of one's direction. (EF, RDSL, p. 244.) SNU.

Keep the faith, baby! interj. (1960s) a request for loyalty; perseverance; a slogan made popular by the congressman from Harlem, Adam Clayton Powell, during his self-exile and much-publicized expulsion from Congress. It was addressed to black people and means, remain optimistic, despite everything, regarding the goal of self-determination. (DC, BJ, p. 70.) SNCU.

Keg William Purnell, jazz drummer; born January 7, 1915. Worked with Benny Carter, et al.

Keg Frederic H. Johnson, trombone player; born November 19, 1908; worked with Louis Armstrong's band in the early thirties, later with Benny Carter.

Keister; kiester; keester; keyster n. (1930s–1960s) the buttocks. (DW, TL, p. 184; IS, PSML, p. 315; CS, vol. 3, no. 2, p. 32; WF, DAS, p. 301.) SNU, SCU, PPU.

Kelsey n. (1950s–1960s) a hairstyle worn by many black prostitutes in northeastern cities; a prostitute. (DW, TL, p. 184; WF, DAS, p. 301.) NECU.

Kelt; ketch v. (1700s–1890s) *kelekeja* [Bantu], means to catch or filter or strain, as through cheesecloth; also, an African-American of mixed ancestry. (HV, AHAE, p. 144.) SU.

Kelt, keltch n. (1900s–1960s) white person; black person passing for white. (WF, DAS, p. 301.) SNU.

Kemels n. (1940s) shoes. (DB, OHHJ, p. 142.) Harlem use.

[The] Kennedy swoop n. (1970s–1980s) hair straightened and brushed to one side in the manner of John and Robert Kennedy. (EF, RDSL, p. 244.) South-central Los Angeles use.

Key n. (1970s–1990s) unit of measurement, kilogram. (TW, CH, p. 150; TW, CK, p. 137; EF, RDSL, p. 244.) DCU.

Keyholing a round tripper adj. (1930s–1940s) to be witness to an extraordinary event, such as a homerun at a baseball game or love-making through a keyhole. (DB, OHHJ, p. 142.) Harlem use.

Ki-yi; ki; kwi; kway exclam. (1700s–1920s) of African-Gullah origin; an expletive sound often made by early slaves on plantations. (AEG, BB, p. 309; JSF, AON, p. 333.) SU.

Ki n. (1960s–1980s) about two pounds of marijuana. (SL, RJON, p. 146; CS, vol. 3, no. 2, p. 32.) DCU.

Kick n. (1940s) money in cash. (FR.) SNU.

Kick n. (1930s–1940s) pants pockets or shirt pockets. (DB, OHHJ, p. 142; CC, OMMM, NCCHD, p. 257.) Harlem use.

[A] Kick n. (1930s–1950s) a thrill; in the forties, one's passion or activity; satisfaction; a fad. (WF, DAS, pp. 302–303.) See "Kicks."

Kick; kicking n., v. (1930s–1950s) to overcome a drug habit. (CLC, TS, p. 255; DW, TL, p. 184.) DCU.

Kick ass v. (1950s–1990s) to perform a task quickly and well. (PM, UCLAS, p. 54.) SCU, DCU, PPU.

Kick back v. (1970s–1980s) to relax or sleep; enjoy oneself; rest. (EF, RDSL, p. 244; PM, UCLAS, p. 54.) SNU.

Kickeraboo n. (1700s–1950s) early slave word derived from *kekrebu* [Krio/Sierra Leone] and *kekre* [Ga], meaning to die. It is the source of the American expression "kick the bucket." (HV, AHAE, p. 144; AB, DSJC, p. 489.) SU, SNU.

Kick it [off] v. (1900–1990s) play music in an especially pleasing manner; get started. (RSG, JT, p. 155.) Example: "Kick it like this" (said before playing). JMFU.

Kick mud v. (1950s–1960s) to do hard and/or dirty work; to work as a prostitute soliciting on the street. (DW, TL, p. 184.) PPU, DCU.

Kicks n. (1930s–1950s) one's pleasure; excitement; thrills; entertainment. (DB, OHHJ, p. 142; CS, vol. 3, no. 2, p. 32.) SNU.

Kicks n. (1930s–1950s) a pair of shoes. (DB, OHHJ, p. 142; DC, BJ, p. 70; EF, RDSL, p. 244; DW, TL, p. 184; WF, DAS, p. 692.) Example: "Hey, man, where you get them bad alligator-skin kicks?" SNU.

Kick stick n. (1950s–1960s) a marijuana cigarette. (RRL, DAZ, p. 120.) DCU.

Kick [one] to the curb v. (1990s) to reject. (HC, WSJ, p. B1.) Example: "Man, she kicked me clean to the curb." YCU, SCU.

Kick up a dust v. (1840s–1900s) to cause an uproar or commotion. (FR.) SNU.

Kick up sand (1950s–1960s) to complain. (DR, BASL, p. 123.) See "Pitch a bitch."

Kid Edward Ory, bandleader and trombone player; born December 25, 1886; a pioneer of New Orleans jazz.

Kid Shots Louis Madison, cornet player; born February 19, 1899, died September 1948; worked with Louis Armstrong in 1915.

Kill [one] v. (1680s–1950s) variant of "thrill"; to affect strongly; to fascinate; to thrill. The same expression exists in several West African languages. (HV, AHAE, p. 144; DB, OHHJ, p. 142; CC, OMMM, NCCHD, p. 257; PM, UCLAS, p. 54.) Example: "Jimmy kills me with all those funny faces he makes!" SNU.

Killer-Diller adj., n. (1930s–1940s) inscrutable but exciting; a ladies' man (DB, OHHJ, p. 142; MHB, JS, np; CC, OMMM, NCCHD, p. 257.) SNU.

Killing floor n. (1970s–1980s) any location used for sexual activity of any type. (EF, RDSL, p. 244.) South-central Los Angeles use.

Killjoy n. (1940s) a policeman or any official person. (DB, OHHJ, p. 142.) Harlem use.

Killout n. (1930s–1940s) variant of "Killer-Diller"; a fascinating person or an extremely exciting situation or thing. (FR.) SNU.

King Pleasure Clarence Beeks, jazz singer; born March 24, 1922; worked with James Moody and others.

King singer and pianist Nat King Cole; born Nathaniel Coles, March 17, 1917.

[The] King's English n. (1920s–1960s) formal American English. (DC, BJ, p. 70.) Example: "Excuse me for not using the King's English, but I got to get to the gig to cop that bread for the juice and the pecks." SNU.

Kinky adj. (1850s–1950s) frizzy hair; in the nineties, unusual in a pleasing way. (FR.) SNU.

Kinky-head n. (1850s–1950s) a person with kinky hair. (WF, DAS, p. 306.) SNU.

Kinkout (1900s–1930s) a hair straightening formula sold in bottles or jars. (CVV, NH, p. 286.) Harlem; SNU.

Kiss-off v. (1940s) to die. (DB, OHHJ, p. 142.) Harlem use.

Kisser n. (1700s–1990s) mouth. See "Smacker."

Kiss(ing) Mary v. (1960s) smoking marijuana. (CS, vol. 3, no. 2, p. 32.) DCU.

Kiss where the sun don't shine exclam. (1940s–1950s) an expletive euphemism hurled in anger at one. (FR.) SNU.

Kitchen n. (1940s) nappy hair at the nape of the neck, especially on a woman or girl. (FR.) SU.

Kitchen n. (1870s–1880s) a short skip in a child's jumping-rope game in vogue during and after Reconstruction. (FR.) SU.

Kitchen mechanic n. (1930s–1940s) professional home cleaner; a woman working as a domestic; housecleaner. (ZNH, AM, p. 89, 95.) Harlem; SNU.

Kite n. (1920s–1940s) a note delivered in prison from one prisoner to another; a letter smuggled out of prison; air mail letter. (DB, OHHJ, p. 142; DW, TL, p. 184.) PU, SCU, SNU.

Kite with no string n. (1930s–1940s) a first-class or air mail letter. (DB, OHHJ, p. 142.) SNU.

Kitty, kitten n. (1930s) very young and inexperienced person, especially a girl. (FR.) SNU.

Kitty n. (1930s–1970s) a Cadillac car. (EF, RDSL, p. 244.) See "Hog."

Klook Kenneth Spearman Clarke (also known as Liaquat Ali Salaam), drummer; born in Pittsburg, Pennsylvania, January 9, 1914; worked with Ella Fitzgerald and other bands.

Kluxer; klucker n. (1870s–1990s) black term for a member of "The Invisible Empire of the South," better known as the Ku Klux Klan, a southern secret organization of terrorists—originally composed primarily of young white men—that formed in June 1866, following the Civil War. Their primary purposes were to maintain white supremacy and to terrorize blacks in an effort to keep them from enjoying rights of full citizenship. (JSF, AON, p. 336; SBF, IHAT, pp. 294–295.) SNU.

Knits n. (1960s–1970s) shirts; sweaters, especially those imported from Italy; Banlon pullovers. (DC, BJ, p. 70; HLF, RJPD, p. 171.) SNCU.

Knobs n. (1940s–1980s) one's knees. (DB, OHHJ, p. 142; EF, RDSL, p. 244.) SNU.

Knock v. (1930s–1940s) to give; to criticize negatively; to borrow or loan; to speak or walk. (DB, OHHJ, p. 142; CC, OMMM, NCCHD, p. 257; WF, DAS, p. 307.) Examples: "No wonder she left him; he is always knocking her"; and, "Can you knock a dime on me till payday?" SNU.

Knock a Joe v. (1900s–1940s) to mutilate oneself to escape the brutal slavery of penitentiary work; this was one way of prolonging one's life, since many black men dropped dead while working on the chain gangs of the Deep South. (AL, LWBB, p. 258.) SU, PU.

Knock a nod v. (1940s) to go to sleep. (DB, OHHJ, p. 142.) SNU.

Knock-down-drag-out fight n. (1930s–1940s) a serious fight or a beating. (Gwendolyn Brooks, *A Street in Bronzeville*, p. 37.) SNU.

Knocker n. (1990s) a foolish person; an annoying fool.

Knocking boots [with] v. (1980s) having sexual intercourse. (PM, UCLAS, p. 54.) YCU.

Knocking her dead one on the nose each and every double trey (1940s) to get a paycheck every sixth—second third—day. (DB, OHHJ, p. 142.) Harlem use.

Knocking off hen tracks on a rolltop piano v. (1940s) to type a personal letter on a typewriter. (DB, OHHJ, p. 142.) Harlem use.

Knock it out v. (1970s–1980s) to perform sexually; sexual intercourse. (EF, RDSL, p. 244.) SNU.

Knock off v. (1930s–1940s) to die; to stop. (DB, OHHJ, p. 142.) SNU.

Knockos n. (1980s–1990s) special police officers assigned to narcotics investigation. (RP, C.) DCU, PPU, PU, SCU.

Knock out v. (1940s) to finish work quickly; to clean house or one's room. (WF, DAS, p. 309.) SNU.

Knockout n. (1930s–1940s) expression of bewilderment or astonishment; amazement; some thing or person not easily understood but nevertheless considered very excellent and thrilling. (WF, DAS, p. 309.) Example: "Boy, you a knockout, the way you went out there and handled that crowd." SNU.

Knock the jive out v. (1940s) to play the piano. (MHB, JS, np.) SU, JMFU.

Knock up v. (1920s–1990s) to impregnate. (WF, DAS, p. 310.) SNU.

Knock [one's] wig v. (1940s) to comb one's hair. (MHB, JS, np.) Example: "That boy always in front of the mirror knocking his wig." SU.

Knock yourself out v. (1930s–1960s) an expression inviting one to enjoy oneself. (ZNH, AM, p. 95; CS, vol. 3, no. 2, p. 32.) Example: "Come on in, relax, get a drink, knock yourself out—the party is just starting." SNU.

Knot n. (1950s–1970s) one's head. (HLF, RJPD, p. 171; DW, TL, p. 184.) Example: "When will anything ever penetrate that knot of yours?" NECU; SNU.

Knotholes n. (1940s) doughnuts. (DB, OHHJ, p. 142.) Harlem use; MWU.

Know about it (1960s–1970s) expression of approval or agreement. (JH, PBL, p. 85.) NECU.

Knowledge box n. (1860s–1940s) the head. (DB, OHHJ, p. 142; MHB, JS, np; AB, DSJC, p. 498.) SNU.

Knuckle with [one] v. (1800s–1930s) to fight physically.

Knuckles n. (1960s–1980s) brass knuckles. (EF, RDSL, p. 244.)

Kong n. (1890s–1940s) *nkongo* [Bantu] is homemade whiskey. (HV, AHAE, p. 144; DB, OHHJ, p. 142.) SNU.

Konk n. (1930s–1950s) the human head; grease; greased hair. (FR.) SNU.

Konk-buster n. (1930s–1950s) a difficult problem. (FR.) SNU.

Kook; kooky (1700s–1950s) *kuku* [Bantu], means a fool or a stupid person. (WF, DAS, p. 310; HV, AHAE, p. 144.) Example: "I don't know how I manage to get hooked up with so many kooky blind dates." SNU.

Kool Herc (1980s) rapper. He coined the term "hip-hop," which has Jamaican origins. It's a form of rap people can dance to. (Bronx.)

Kool Moe Dee (1990s) rapper.

Kopasetic adj. (1940s) excellent. (DB, OHHJ, p. 142; CC, OMMM, NCCHD, p. 257.) SNCU.

Ku Kluxer n. (1870s–1880s) Reconstruction term for a Ku Klux Klan member. (FR.) Su. See "Kluckers."

Kwanza n. (1700s–1990s) first fruit [Swahili]; a word made popular in this century by the Black Muslims of Chicago. (SBF, IHAT, p. 46.) SNU.

L

La Baker Josephine Baker, dancer, singer, and actress.

Lac n. (1980s–1990s) short for "Cadillac." (FR.) YCU, SNCU.

Lady n. (1950s–1960s) a pimp's term for his prostitute; associated with but not exclusively derived from "lady of the evening." (CRM, BP, p. 303.) PPU.

Lady Bellson Louis Bellson, jazz drummer; born in Rock Falls, Illinois, on July 26, 1924; married Pearl Bailey.

Lady Day Lady Eleanora Gough McKay, better known as Billie Holiday, singer; born in Baltimore, Maryland, April 7, 1915, and died in New York City, July 17, 1959.

Lady Snow n. (1950s–1960s) white female; cocaine (RRL, DAZ, p. 122.) SNU.

Lady Soul Aretha Franklin, singer; born in Memphis, Tennessee, in 1942; raised in Detroit.

Lagniappe n. (1920s–1940s) a gift; a tip; a token of gratitude; extra thing. (LA, SM, p. 178.) SU.

Laid back adj. (1970s–1980s) literally, relaxed in a comfortable manner; music that is easygoing, lacking in intensity. (RSG, JT, p. 159.) JMFU, SNCU.

Laid crib n. (1960s) a nice house or apartment. (DC, BJ, p. 71.) MWU, SNU, YCU.

Laid [them] in the aisle v. (1950s–1960s) the effect a well-dressed person has on others; to "knock" people out with one's stylishness. (JH, PBL, p. 85.) NECU.

Laid to the bone adj. (1960s) drunk. (DC, BJ, p. 71.) YCU, MWU.

Laid to the natural bone adj. (1970s–1980s) to be completely naked; undressed. (EF, RDSL, p. 244.) SNU.

Laid up adj. (1960s) sick. (DC, BJ, p. 71.) YCU, MWU.

Lam v., n. (1800s–1940s) lam [Igbo]: to leave, to go; to be on the run; in the state of being an escapee from prison or prosecution. For the early slaves, it is likely that the African Igbo word "lam" became interchangeable with the English "lam"—especially because the idea of escaping bondage was for many a primary concern. (HV, AHAE, p. 144; HEG, DAUL, p. 121; JH, PBL, p. 85.) SNU, PU.

Lam v. (1800s–1940s) probably from Old English "lambasting," meaning to beat; to hit; to strike; to trash. Although not originally a black expression, "lam" has long been popular among black slang users. (MHB, JS, np; JSF, AON, p. 339.) Rare. SU.

Lam black n. (1930s–1940s) (ZNH, AM, p. 94.) See "Dark black." SNU.

Lamb n. (1940s) an innocent person who is easily deceived. (DB, OHHJ, p. 142.) Harlem; SNU.

Lame n., adj. (1950s–1990s) a weak, cowardly, ineffective male; an unsophisticated act or person; a square; to be unaware of street culture; a wrong deed. (AY, S, p. 16; RDA, TB, p. 91; CLC, TS, p. 255; DC, BJ, p. 71; HLF, RJPD, p. 171; PM, UCLAS, p. 55; EF, RDSL, p. 244; DW, TL, p. 184.) SCU, DCU, PU, YCU, SNU.

Lame scene n. (1960s–1970s) a boring party or a dull event. (CS, vol. 3, no. 2, p. 32.) YCU, SCU.

Lamp(ing) v. (1920s–1940s) the act of seeing; to look. (CC, OMMM, NCCHD, p. 257; DB, OHHJ, p. 142.) Example: "Don't you young men have nothing better to do than standing on the corner lamping the girls?" SNU.

Lamps n. (1920s–1940s) one's eyes. (DB, OHHJ, p. 142.) SNU.

Land of Darkness n. (1930s–1940s) Harlem; the African-American section in any town or city; used with humor and irony. (CC, OMMM, NCCHD, p. 257; DB, OHHJ, p. 142.) SNU.

Lane n. (1930s–1940s) a "square"; a rustic person; literally, one who lives on a country lane; an inexperienced prison inmate; any male; a nonprofessional. (MM, RB, p. 372; WF, DAS, p. 313; DB, OHHJ, p. 142; CC, OMMM, NCCHD, p. 257.) SNU.

Larceny n. (1940s–1960s) an unkind or evil feeling; an open condemnation of another person. (FR.) Example: "I swear I don't have no larceny in my heart fo that dude." SCU, PPU, PU, DCU.

Large adj. (1930s–1940s) successful; thrilling; well-to-do. (WF, DAS, p. 312.) JMFU, SCU.

[Living] Large v. (1990s) doing well; to conduct one's life in a grand and flashy manner; living expensively. (HC, WSJ, p. B8; RCC, SOC, p. 26.) SNCU.

Large charge n. (1930s–1950s) great excitement. (FR.) SNCU.

Last debt n. (1940s) death. (DB, OHHJ, p. 142.) Harlem; SNU.

[One's] Last heartbeat n. (1940s) one's sweetheart. (MHB, JS, np.) SNU.

[The] Last mile [walk] n. (1930s–1970s) the last few paces from one's prison cell to the electric chair or gas chamber; not originally a black term but common among black prisoners and ex-prisoners. (HEG, DAUL, p. 122; DW, TL, p. 184.) PU.

Last out n. (1940s) death. (DB, OHHJ, p. 142.) Harlem; SNU.

Latch n. (1960s–1970s) variant of "leech"; person who is a parasite; a beggar. (CS, vol. 3, no. 2, p. 32.) YCU; SCU.

Latch for the gate to your front yard n. (1930s–1940s) one's collar pin; zipper or buttons on a man's fly. (DB, OHHJ, p. 142.) Harlem use.

Latch on [to] v. (1930s–1940s) to understand or take part in an activity; to become aware; grab or snatch; term borrowed from obsolete Old English. (CC, HDH, p. 16; CC, OMMM, NCCHD, p. 257; LH, BNF, p. 488; DB, OHHJ, p. 142.) SNU.

Late black n. (1930s–1940s) a very dark, starless, moonless night. (DB, OHHJ, p. 142.) SNU.

Later interj. (1950s) a manner of saying good-bye; short for "see you later"; also, a put-down. (DC, BJ, p. 71; RSG, JT, pp. 160–161.) Example: "Later for that jive, man!" SNU.

[Catch you] Later on v. See "Later."

[The] Law n. (1900s–1920s) the police; officer of the law. (WF, DAS, p. 313.) Example: (wife to husband) "If you ever hit me again I'm gonna get the law on you." SCU, PPU, PU.

Lawfully lady n. (1870s–1920s) a black man's legal wife. (AEG, BB, p. 309.) Example: "What you got to say to me you can say to her, too—Dixie here my lawfully lady." SU.

Lay back v. (1930s–1950s) to follow the lead; to supply the follow-up rhythm in a jazz set. (RSG, JT, p. 161.) JMFU, SNU.

Lay back v. (1960s–1990s) to relax; rest. (EF, RDSL, p. 244.) SNU. See "Lay dead."

Lay bread on [one] v. (1930s–1950s) to lend or give money. (FR.) SNCU.

Lay dead v. (1930s–1950s) to become inactive; to "cool" it; slow down; rest; stop what one has been doing; to hide. (RSG, JT, p. 162.) SNCU; SCU, JMFU.

Lay [something] down v. (1930s–1970s) to explain; to speak; to outline a theory; to present. (DB, OHHJ, p. 142; DW, TL, p. 184.) SNU.

Lay down v. (1970s–1980s) to give in to another's position; to acquiesce; to act sheepish; lay down defeated like a dog. (EF, RDSL, p. 244.) Example: "You can't count on Trent 'cause he's likely to lay down the minute they come at him with a different proposition." SNU.

Lay down some cow v. (1940s) to walk—especially in the sense of wearing out shoe leather. (DB, OHHJ, p. 142.) Harlem; MWU.

Lay for v. (1950s–1970s) to wait, especially with a plan to ambush or to surprise someone. (DW, TL, p. 184.) Example: "I'll stay here and lay for him while you go around to the front to make sure he don't come that way." SCU, DCU, PU, PPU. See "Lay in the cut."

Lay in the cut v. (1960s–1970s) to hide, or remain out of sight, while waiting for something or someone. (DW, TL, p. 184.) SCU, DCU, PU, PPU.

Lay [some] iron [down] v. (1930s–1950s) to tap dance, especially professionally. (CC, HDH, p. 16; CC, OMMM, NCCHD, p. 257; MM, RB, p. 212.) JMFU.

Lay it on [one] v. (1940s–1960s) to fully explain; entreaty to tell the truth; to give someone something. (DC, BJ, p. 71.) Example: "I'm ready to hear why you left me baby, so lay it on me." SNCU, YCU, SCU.

Lay on v. See "Lay it on [one]."

Lay [something] on [one] v. (1930s–1950s) to relay a message; to give. (RSG, JT, p. 162.) SNCU.

Lay out v. (1920s–1930s) to stop—especially suddenly—participating in an activity; to avoid something or someone; to step aside; to become inactive. (RSG, JT, pp. 162–163.) JMFU, SNCU, SCU.

Layout n. (1930s–1940s) one's apartment or house. (DB, OHHJ, p. 142.) SNCU.

Layout across the drink n. (1940s) the continent of Europe. (DB, OHHJ, p. 142.) Harlem; NECU.

Lay pipe v. (1980s–1990s) to have sex, especially sexual intercourse; male term. (EF, RDSL, p. 144; PM, UCLAS, p. 18.) YCU, SCU.

Lay [one's] racket v. (1930s–1940s) to "jive" one; to tease; to con. (DB, OHHJ, p. 142; CC, OMMM, NCCHD, p. 257.) Example: "Mack runs that gas station, but when he gets you in the back room he lay his real racket on you with them dice." DCU, SCU, PU, PPU.

Lay some iron down v. See "Lay [some] iron [down]."

Lay some rubber v. (1970s–1990s) to burn one's tires as one speeds off, leaving black marks on the pavement. (EF, RDSL, p. 244.) South-central Los Angeles; YCU, SCU.

Lay some pipe v. See "Lay pipe."

Lay two ways v. (1960s–1970s) to shortchange or otherwise deceive someone in a money transaction. (DW, TL, p. 184.) DCU, PPU, SCU, PU.

Lay up v. (1930s–1950s) the same as "lay dead." (DC, BJ, p. 71; DW, TL, p. 184.) SNCU. See "Lay dead."

Lazy n., adj. (1900s–1950s) to make easygoing music; to be calm, relaxed. (RSG, JT, p. 163.) JMFU, SNU.

LD n. (1950s–1960s) the Cadillac Eldorado. (DC, BJ, p. 71.) MWU.

Lead sheet n. (1930s–1940s) one's topcoat or overcoat. (DB, OHHJ, p. 142; CC, OMMM, NCCHD, p. 257.) Harlem; NECU.

Lead sheet n. (1940s–1950s) a crude musical score hastily written for a jazz session. (RSG, JL, p. 186.) JMFU.

Leadbelly Huddie Ledbetter, singer, guitarist; born in Moorings-port, Louisiana, in 1888, died in New York City, December 6, 1949; world-famous as a folk singer.

Lean on v. (1970s–1980s) humiliate; ridicule; harass; torment; insult. (EF, RDSL, p. 245.) SNU.

Leap and [one] will receive imper. (1970s–1990s) a warning that the speaker is willing to fight; a challenge to fistfight. (EF, RDSL, p. 245.) YCU, SCU.

Least adj., n. (1950s) mediocre; dull person or situation. (RSG, JL, p. 186.) Example: "I'm feeling the least today." Rare. See "Blue."

'Lection Day n. (1750s–1860s) African holiday celebrated by slaves from the mid-eighteenth through the mid-nineteenth centuries. (JEH, A, p. 196.) See "pinkster."

Left town v. (1900–1950s) to have died; to "split." (RSG, JT, p. 164.) JMFU, SCU, SNU.

Left raise n. (1930s–1940s) one's left side, arm, shoulder; the left side of a person's body. (CC, OMMM, NCCHD, p. 257.) Example:

"Don't look now, but there's a very funny man on your left raise." Harlem use.

Leg n. (1960s–1980s) a girl or woman; female sexuality. (EF, BVV, p. 46; DC, BJ, p. 71; JH, PBL, p. 85.) SNU.

Leg sacks n. (1930s–1940s) socks. (DB, OHHJ, p. 142.) SNU.

Legit n., adj. (1920s–1970s) in jazz, a "straight" or conservative musician or music. (RSG, JT, pp. 164–165; RSG, JL, p. 187.) JMFU.

Lemon n. (1900s–1950s) light-skinned Afro-American; mulatto. (WF, DAS, p. 317; DB, OHHJ, p. 142.) SNU. See "High yellow."

Leon Leon Leon Spinks, prizefighter, boxer.

Less-than-nothing n. (1980s–1990s) male heterosexual term; male homosexual preceived to be weak or unable to defend himself. (WKB, JMC, PS, p. 49.) PU.

Let [one] down for [one's] chimer v. (1930s–1940s) to steal someone's watch. (DB, OHHJ, p. 143.) Harlem use.

Let [one] hold some change v. (1960s–1980s) a request to borrow money. (EF, RDSL, p. 245.) SNU.

Let [one's] game slip v. (1960s–1980s) to blunder; to "blow" one's front; to lose control one holds over a potential victim or victim. (EF, RDSL, p. 245.) PPU, PU, SCU.

Let go v. (1950s) to discharge from employment. (FR.) SNU.

Let it all hang out v. (1960s–1970s) to be uninhibited, free; to truthfully state what's on your mind. (JH, PBL, p. 85.) SCU, NECU, JMFU.

Let it lay v. (1940s) to forget something. (MHB, JS, np.) SCU, YCU.

Let it slide v. (1950s–1970s) to let something pass without responding to it. (FR.) SNU.

Let's [take it; go] home v. (1900s–1990s) in jazz, a call to stop playing—especially something outside the usual repertoire. (RSG, JL, p. 188.)

Let the deal go down v. (1940s–1960s) to play with a full deck; not to cheat; to play with all the cards. (FR.) SNCU.

Let the good times roll v. (1900s–1940s) a cry for enjoyment—music, talk, drinking, etc. (RSG, JT, p. 165.) JMFU.

Let up v. (1860s–1970s) to restrain from verbally abusing someone; cease; rest; pause; stop. (AB, DSJC, p. 13.) SNU.

Letter from home n. (1950s–1960s) euphemism for watermelon. (JH, PBL, p. 85.) NECU, MWU.

Lettuce n. (1960s) money; cash, especially paper money. (DC, BJ, p. 71.) SNU. See "Bread" and "Cabbage."

Let your backbone slip v. (1900s–1940s) get loose all over; a black addition to "Little Sally Walker," a children's game song. (BJ, BLH, SD, p. 107.) SU.

Liberate v. (1960s) to steal. (DC, BJ, p. 71.) See "Burn," "Cop," and "Rip off."

Liberty n. (1940s) a quarter. (MHB, JS, np.) SNU.

Library game n. (1960s–1970s) the code of silence observed in a library. (GS, TT, p. 58.) College students' use.

Lick n. (1930s–1940s) a plan; an idea; an outline of a situation. Probably no direct relation to early use of "lick" as saline deposits (licked by cows) or with the cant meaning of it: "to coax." (JSF, AON, p. 345.) SNU.

Lickety-split n. (1850s–1950s) straight ahead at full speed; quick movement; the sound of fast motion; working fast; running. (WFDAS, p. 318; JSF, AON, p. 345; AB, DSJC, p. 15.) SNU.

Lickety-splup n. (1850s–1900s) a hard-luck song, sung by Negro crapshooters in Georgia. It goes: "Lickety-splup / the more you put down, the less you pick up." (JSF, AON, p. 345; Newman I. White, *American Negro Folksongs*, 1928, p. 365.) See "Lickety-split."

[A good] Licking n. (1800s–1950s) a whipping, usually done with a switch or a belt. (CCJ, NMGC, p. 168.) Example: "Boy, come in this house before I give you a good licking." SU.

Licking the chops n. (1930s–1940s) the tuning up musicians do before a jam session. (CC, HDH, p. 16; DB, OHHJ, p. 142.) JMFU.

Licks n. (1930s–1990s) musical phrases; "riffs;" the "idea behind the musical composition, borrowed from the idea of striking something or somebody." (RSG, JT, pp. 165–166.) JMFU.

Licorice stick n. (1930s–1940s) a clarinet. (SL, RJON, p. 147; RSG, JT, p. 166.) JMFU.

Lieutenant n. (1990s) one who manages the activities of a team of young illegal-drug sellers. (RP, C, np.) DCU.

Lid n. (1930s–1970s) about twenty-two grams of marijuana sold in a pipe tobacco can. (RRL, p. 127; EF, RDSL, p. 245; CS, vol. 3, no. 2, p. 33.) DCU.

Lid n. (1920s–1960s) the sky; one's mind. (DW, TL, p. 184.) SNU.

Lid n. (1930s–1960s) a hat or cap. (BH, LSB, p. 20; DC, BJ, p. 71; HLF, RJPD, p. 171; MHB, JS, np; DB, OHHJ, p. 143.) MWU.

Lifts n. (1970s–1990s) automobile hydraulic lifts; a switch in the car allows the motorist to raise or slower the body of the car. These "lifts" are popular among so-called "inner city" young people. (EF, RDSL, p. 245.) South-central Los Angeles; NCU, YCU, SCU.

Light bread n. (1940s–1950s) white bread. (FR.) SNU.

Light drip-drizzle n. (1940s) a spring shower. (DB, OHHJ, p. 143.) SNU.

Lighten up v. (1960s–1980s) a plea for compassion or restraint; a request or command to go easy. (EF, RDSL, p. 245; CS, vol. 3, no. 2, p. 33.) SNU, SCU, YCU.

Lightfoot n. (1970s–1980s) one who is lacking in street smarts; one innocent of the rougher sections of the "ghetto." (EF, RDSL, p. 245.) SCU, YCU, PPU, DCU. See "Lame."

Lightly, slightly and politely adv. (1930s–1940s) to effect smoothly, as though without effort; perfection. (ZNH, AM, p. 95.) SNU.

Lightning bug n. (1800s–1950s) firefly. (FR.) SU.

Lightning bugs n. (1940s) cigarette tips burning in a dark room.

[White] Lightning n. (1880s–1940s) homemade corn liquor. (WF, DAS, p. 318.) SNU.

Lightning Sam Hopkins, blues singer and guitar player; born March 15, 1912, in Centerville, Texas; died January 31, 1982. His first guitar teacher was Blind Lemon Jefferson.

Light out v. (1680s–1940s) to start; to leave quickly; to go off to another place. (AEG, BB, p. 310; JSF, AON, p. 346.) Example: "They ain't likely to get here with they lynch rope fore late in the morning.

I reckon you won't never see me again, Sally, cause I'm gone light out fore early bright." SU.

Light pockets adj., n. (1940s–1970s) to be without money; to have very little money. (FR.) SNU.

Light splash (1940s) a bath. (DB, OHHJ, p. 143.) Harlem; SNU.

Light stuff n. (1940s–1950s) any nonphysically addictive but illegal drug, such as marijuana. (RRL, DAZ, p. 127.) DCU.

Light up v. (1930s–1960s) to light a marijuana cigarette or a tobacco cigarette; to strike someone. (CC, HDH, p. 16; DC, BJ, p. 71; RRL, DAZ, p. 128.) DCU, SNCU.

Lightweight n. (CS, vol. 3, no. 2, p. 33.) See "Lightfoot."

Like; lyke adv. (1650s–1940s) almost; nearly accomplished. (*The Oxford English Dictionary*, vol. 1, A–O, 1971, pp. 1624–1625.) Example: "She like to laugh herself crazy." SU.

Like interj. (1940s–1970s) "as" or "as if"; a filler word often used to link fragmented sentences. (DC, BJ, p. 71; WF, DAS, p. 319; RSG, JT, pp. 167–168; PM, UCLAS, p. 56.) Example: "Like, man, I was out in Wyoming, like two years and it was like, wow!" SNCU, JMFU, SCU.

Like a bat out of hell (1950s) to move fast.

Like a mojo (1980s–1990s) grand; excellent; big. (PM, UCLAS, p. 56.) Example: "I never been so lucky at the wheel before; I was hitting it like a mojo." YCU. See "Mojo" and "Mojo working."

Like cheese adv. (1940s) any strong odor. (DB, OHHJ, p. 143.) Example: "What's that I smell like cheese?" SNU.

Like crazy adj. (1960s) with enthusiasm.

[Tell it] Like it is v. See "Tell it like it is."

Like Jack the bear [just ain't nowhere] (1930s–1940s) See "Just like Jack the bear."

Like stink on shit adv., adj. (1950s–1960s) intrinsic; close; intimate. (DW, TL, p. 184.) Example: "Marvin, if you don't get out of my face with your mess, I'm gone be all over you like stink on shit, boy." SCU, YCU, PPU, PU, DCU.

Liked to [something] adv. (1700s–1990s) nearly; almost. (EF, RDSL, p. 245.) Example: "I'll never eat there again—I liked to died." SNU.

Like [something] was going out of style adv. (1960s–1980s) to perform a task exuberantly. (FR.) Example: "I want you to make love to me like love was going out of style." SNU.

[Miss] Lillian n. (1960s) white female. (FR.) SNU. See "Miss Ann."

Lilly n. (1970s–1990s) a capsule of seconal made by the Lilly drug manufacturing company; Lilly F-40. (EF, RDSL, p. 245.) DCU.

Lily n. See "Lily-white."

Lily-white n. (1800s–1960s) a derogatory reference to the U.S. political and social category "white"; Anglo-Saxon Protestants; American who strives to assert superiority on the basis of color. (JSF, AON, p. 346; WF, DAS, p. 319.) SNU.

Lily whites n. (1920s–1940s) bed sheets. (DB, OHHJ, p. 143, CC, OMMM, NCCHD, p. 257.) Harlem; MWU.

Limp-dick n. (1900s–1950s) a weak man. (FR.) SNU.

Lindy Hop n. (1930s–1940s) a popular dance first done at the Savoy; named after Charles A. Lindberg. (RSG, JT, p. 168.) SNCU.

Line n. (1940s–1960s) money or the purchase price of an item. (DC, BJ, p. 71; HEG, DAUL, p. 126; IS, PSML, p. 315; DB, OHHJ, p. 143; CC, OMMM, NCCHD, p. 257.) PPU, DCU, PU, SCU.

Line n. (1940s–1980s) a seductive line of talk aimed at winning someone over—usually a male flirting with a female. (EF, RDSL, p. 245.) SNU.

Line v., n. (1950s–1960s) in the fifties, short for "mainline"; needle-injected heroin; later, in the sixties and after, the same term meant a quantity of cocaine sniffed into the nose. (RRL, DAZ, p. 128.) DCU.

Lines n. (1980s–1990s) cocaine is measured out in what dealers call "lines"; gram measure. (TW, CK, p. 137.) DCU.

Line the flue v. (1930s–1940s) to eat. (DB, OHHJ, p. 143.) SNU.

[The] Link Between the Races n. Harlem name for Mezz Mezzrow. See "Mezz Mezzrow."

Lip n. (1850s–1970s) chatter; talk, especially harsh complaining; impudence; a defense lawyer; talking back in self-defense; prattle. (IS, PSML, p. 315; SL, RJON, p. 50; RSG, JT, p. 169; AB, DSJC, p. 19.) See "Chops."

Lip music n. (1980s–1990s) slang; rapping; hip-hop talk, jive talk; jitterbug talk; rhyming. (WKB, JMC, PS, p. 49.) PU; SCU, YCU.

Lip off v. (1950s–1960s) to talk back; backtalk. (SL, RJON, p. 50; DC, BJ, p. 71.) SCU, YCU, SNU.

Lip service n. (1950s) ingratiating talk; flattering, empty talk.

Lip-splitter n. (1930s–1950s) jazz musician who in blowing his horn is frantic; inflammatory; a deadly fighter. (SL, RJON, p. 150; DB, OHHJ, p. 143.) JMFU.

Lipton's n. (1940s–1970s) fake or poor marijuana; a reference to Lipton tea. (RSG, JT, p. 167.) DCU, JMFU.

Liquid crack n. (1990s) malt liquor, so called because of the "quick fix" it gives. (MMNYT, p. 1.) Bronx, New York, use.

Liquored up adj. (1920s–1950s) drunk. (FR.) SNU.

[One's] Liquor told [one] (1900s–1950s) an explanation for drunken, erratic behavior. (ZNH, AM, 96.) SNU.

Little Africa n. (1860s–1870s) a black New York City neighborhood south of Washington Square; early African-American name for any black section in any city. (ILA, CS, p. 238.) New York; NCU.

Little Boy Blue n. (1960s–1990s) a police officer. (EF, RDSL, p. 245.) South-central Los Angeles use.

Little Eva n. (1960s) a loud-mouth white girl.

Little Frield n. See "Friend."

Little Jazz David Roy Eldridge, trumpet player; born January 30, 1911; in the 1950s, worked with Coleman Hawkins, Ella Fitzgerald, and others.

Little Joe n. See "Little Joe in the Snow."

Little Joe in the Snow n. (1980s–1990s) cocaine. (WKB, JMC, PS, p. 49.) Example: "Bobby been sniffing Little Joe in the Snow so long he burned inside his nose out." PU, DCU. See "Blow."

Little John the Conqueror n. (1920s–1930s) a conjuring potion. (FR.) See "John the Conqueror." SU.

Little red wagon n. (1960s) a problem, any problem; an individual's private, personal business. (CS, vol. 3, no. 2, p. 33.) Examples: "If you choose to put yourself out like that, it's your own little red wagon"; and, "I couldn't care less whether or not she comes back to you—it's your own little red wagon." SNU.

Little mama n. (1800s–1950s) a black girl, usually attractive. (FR.) SNU.

Liver-lip n. (1930s–1950s) thick purple lips. (ZNH, AM, p. 95.) SNU.

Living large v. (1990s) enjoying the good life, wealth, prosperity. (FR.) SNCU.

Living low v. (1980s–1990s) living by a low standard; to be depressed. (FR.) SNCU.

Living room gig n. (1940s–1950s) in jazz, a television appearance. (WF, DAS, p. 321.) JMFU.

[Bad] Lizards n. (1950s–1970s) attractive shoes made of lizard skin. (HLF, RJPD, p. 171; EF, RDSL, p. 245.) SCU.

L.L. Cool J (1990s) a popular rap artist.

Load n. (1950s–1960s) twenty or thirty packets of heroin held together with a rubber band. (RRL, DAZ, p. 128.) DCU.

Load n. (1990s) a car. (FR.) YCU.

Loaded adj. (1950s–1960s) possessing a great amount of something; very "high" or "stoned." (RRL, DAZ, p. 128; EF, RDSL, p. 245.) DCU, SCU, PPU, PU, SNU.

Lobo n. (1940s) an ugly girl. (MHB, JS, np.) SU.

Lobstertails n. (1940s–1960s) usually refers to a case of crabs; sometimes a venereal disease; crotch crabs. (RDA, DDJ, p. 266.) Philadelphia; NECU, YCU, SCU, PPU.

Lock(ed) up vt. (1940s) to possess completely. (DB, OHHJ, p. 143; CC, OMMM, NCCHD, p. 257.) Example: "I got that situation locked up—they have to pay or else." SNCU.

Lockjaw Eddie Davis, jazz saxophone player.

Long adj. (1940s–1970s) describing a large quantity; a lot; plenty. (DW, TL, p. 185.) SNCU.

Long bread n. (1940s–1970s) a great deal of money. (EF, RDSL, p. 245.) SNCU. See "Bread."

Long con n. (1950s–1960s) a complex, drawn-out confidence scheme. (RRL, DAZ, p. 128.) DCU; PPU; SCU; PU.

Long Dong Silver n. (1990s) penis; term used by Anita Hill at the Clarence Thomas Senate hearing, 1991. (U.S. Senate Hearings, October 1991.) SNU.

Long green n. (1920s–1970s) a great deal of money. (EF, RDSL, p. 245.) SNU. See "Long bread."

Longhairs n. (1930s–1940s) musicians who play from written music; the kind of commercial music they play; a deep subject or an intellectual. (WF, DAS, p. 324; SL, RJO, p. 16.) JMFU.

Long house n. (1900s–1940s) a jook joint; whorehouse, especially one in a long building with a line of small rooms strung along a narrow hallway; most whorehouses in the south were of this type around the turn of the century and during the first two decades or so of the present century. (ZNH, MM, p. 307.) SU.

Long-shoe game n. (1950s–1970s) pimping; "long shoe" refers to the shiny, pointed-toe shoes pimps wear. (DW, TL, p. 185.) PPU, DCU, SCU.

Long underwear [gang] n. (1930s–1940s) among jazzmen, any music that is old-fashioned or conservative, such as supper club music; musicians who play from written scores. (RSG, JT, p. 171.) JMFU.

Looker n. (1980s) an attractive female. (FR.) Example: "The woman who sells flowers down at the corner, man, is really some looker." SNU.

Lookout n. (1980s–1990s) one who scouts the neighborhood on the watch for policemen. (TW, CH, p. 150.) DCU.

Loose adj. (1960s–1970s) feeling good or happy; in high spirits; having lots of money. (CS, vol. 3, no. 2, p. 33.) SNU.

Loose link n. (1980s–1990s) a person who informs on another to the police or prison authorities. (WKB, JMC, PS, p. 50.) PU.

Loosies n. (1980s–1990s) cigarettes bought unpackaged across the counter. (TW, CH, p. 150.) SCU.

Loot n. (1930s–1940s) money; cash. (RSG, JT, p. 171.) See "Bread."

Lord have mercy interj. (1700s–1990s) an interjection of acknowledgment or agreement. (GS, TT, p. 57; JSF, AON, p. 341.) SNU.

Lose [one's] cool v. (1960s–1990s) to become explosively angry or to act in an irrational manner. (EF, RDSL, p. 245.) SNCU.

Loud adj., adv. (1950s–1980s) "wolfing" at someone; making a scene; to embarrass one. (HLF, RJPD, p. 171.) Example: "She was all loud and everything, man. I had to get the hell out of there." SCU, DCU, YCU, SNCU. See "Loud talking."

Loud talking n. (1950s–1980s) talk done to annoy the listener. (RDA, TB, p. 17; DR, BASL, p. 171, 179.) See "Bad mouthing" and "Wolfing."

Louisville Lip Muhammad Ali, born Cassius Clay.

Love come down n. (1920s–1940s) orgasm; ejaculation; a Gullah expression that found its way into general use among southern African-Americans; can be heard in blues songs. (FR.) Example: "Baby, baby, you sure know how to make my love come down early in the morning." SU.

Love letter n. (1940s) a bullet or a rock thrown at someone. (DB, OHHJ, p. 143.) SNCU, PU, PPU, DCU, SCU.

Low black n. (1930s–1940s) (ZNH, AM, p. 94.) See "Dark black."

Low blood n., adj. (1900–1980s) term refers to anemia. (FR.) Example: "She got that low blood condition." MWU.

Low down n., adj. (1900–1940s) the blues; an economically depressed life-style; without money; having bad luck. (AB, DSJC, pp. 30–31.) See "Barrelhouse," "Blues," and "Gutbucket."

Lowland n. (1930s–1960s) the south side of the city where blacks usually live. (DC, BJ, p. 71.) MWU.

Low-rating v. (1950s–1960s) attacking verbally; telling someone off; denigrating someone. (RDA, TB, p. 53.) Example: "I don't even like to go home no more 'cause my mother always low-rating me—if it ain't my hair, it's my clothes." SNU.

Low-quarters n. (1930s–1940s) oxford shoes. (DB, OHHJ, p. 143.) SNCU.

Low-rider n. (1960s–1980s) one whose car has been hydraulically adjusted so that it rides low to the pavement. This is considered "cool." (CS, vol. 3, no. 2, p. 33.) Watts, South-central Los Angeles; YCU, SCU.

L-Seven adj., n. (1950s–1960s) out of fashion; strange; a square; a weird guy; an odd woman. (DC, BJ, p. 71.) MWU.

Luck up n., v. (1930s–1950s) sudden good luck; to be lucky after a period of bad luck. (LA, SM, p. 25.) Example: "Dean thinks he's going to luck up and get to take Lorena to the prom." SNU.

Luck out on v. (1960s–1970s) to win something, especially unexpectedly; to succeed when one had not expected success. (DW, TL, p. 185.) SNCU.

Lucky dog n. (1920s–1930s) a conjuring potion used by gamblers. See "Hus-no-harra."

[Drop a] Lug [on] v. (1960s) to chastise someone. (CRM, BP, p. 303.) PPU, SCU.

Lugs n. (1940s) one's ears. (DB, OHHJ, p. 143.) SNU.

Lumpy adj. (1940s–1950s) in jazz, playing that sounds uneven. (WF, DAS, p. 329.) JMFU.

Lunchbox n. (1970s) the stomach. (FR.) SNCU.

Lung-dusters n. (1940s) cigarettes. (DB, OHHJ, p. 143.) SNU.

Lurking v., n. (1960s) to go on a joy ride, in one's own car or a stolen car. (CS, vol. 3, no. 2, p. 33.) Watts, South-central Los Angeles; YCU, SCU.

Lush n. (1850–1940s) from *loschen* [German], meaning strong beer; a person who drinks a great deal. Not originally a black term but very common among black slang users; black slang users have rarely used "lush" to mean "dainty" or to refer to "luxury." (RRL, DAZ, p. 138; AB, DSJC, p. 34.) SNU.

Lush head n. (1900–1940s) (DB, OHHJ, p. 143.) See "Lush."

Lush hound n. (MHB, JS, np.) See "Lush."

Lushie n. (DB, OHHJ, p. 143.) See "Lush."

Lush stash n. (1900–1940s) a tavern; a drinking salon; a good-time house. (DB, OHHJ, p. 143.) SNU, SCU, PPU. See "Lush."

Lying v. (1950s) to play music without sincere emotion. (RSG, JT, p. 173.)

Lynch v. (1860s–1990s) to kill a person by any means. (LH, LKFC, p. 205.) SNU.

M n. (1930s–1950s) morphine. (WF, DAS, p. 330; RSG, JT, p. 174.) DCU.

M n. (1960s–1970s) marijuana. (CS, vol. 3, no. 2, p. 33.) Watts, Los Angeles; YCU.

Ma n. (1940s–1950s) a prefix often added to an older male homosexual's name by his intimate friends. (WF, DAS, p. 330.) Homosexual; SNCU.

Ma See "Ma Rainey."

Machine n. (1950s–1960s) an automobile; one's car. (DC, BJ, p. 71.) SNCU. See "Short" and "Wheels."

Mack n. See "Mackman."

Macking n. (1900s–1990s) pimping. (CLC, TS, p. 255; IS, PSML, p. 315.) See "Mackman."

Macking v. (1900s–1990s) male term; to use pimp talk while flirting; to try to pick up a young woman using the language of hustling. (DC, BJ, p. 72.) SCU, YCU. See "Mackman."

[Make] Mac(k) v. (PM, UCLAS, p. 57.) See "Macking."

Mackman n., v. (1900s–1990) "mackarel" and "mackawl"—both Old English cant for "bawd"; also, *maquereau, maquerelle* [French]; short for "mackerel man"; or possibly derived from "mackintosh raincoat"; when a pimp talks a young woman into hustling for him he is "macking" her; a violent pimp; to hurt or harm someone; injure. (CRM, BP, p. 35, 303; 302; Chuck D, *Essence*, September 1992, p. 118; CLC, TS, p. 208; DW, TL, p. 185; EF, RDSL, p. 245.) Example: "Lester thinks he's the toughest mackman on the scene; that chump thinks it's hip to be always knocking his bitches upside the head, but I bet you anything one of these days Mari, his bottom woman, is gonna blow him away." PPU.

Mack on [one] v. (1970s–1990s) to make an aggressive verbal attempt at seduction. (EF, RDSL, p. 245.) Example: "I don't want Rodney at my party, girl, 'cause he'll try to mack on all my girl friends —plus he'll get drunk and somebody will have to drive his fool-ass home." See "Hit on."

Mad adj. (1930s–1940s) fine, excellent, wonderful. (DB, OHHJ, p. 143.) Example: "That's a mad hat you're wearing, Susie." Harlem; SNCU.

Mad [about something] adj. (1940s–1950s) used loosely, this has a positive connotation: great, exciting. (WF, DAS, p. 330; RSG, JT, p. 174.) Example: "I'm mad about that woman," meaning, "I love that woman." SNU.

Mad dog n. (1970s–1990s) an incorrigible person; a "bad nigger"; a "mean motherfucker." (EF, RDSL, p. 246.) South-central Los Angeles; SCU.

Made adj. (1960s) finished; accomplished. (CS, vol. 3, no. 2, p. 33.) Example: "She's got it made any way you look at the situation."

Made v. (1900s–1950s) to have one's hair straightened; female term. (ZNH, AM, p. 95; WF, DAS, p. 330.) SNU.

Made; make v. (1950s–1970s) to be tricked or seduced; to take or be "taken" (cheated). (RRL, DAZ, p. 139.) Example: "She made two tricks before she had enough to buy her shit." DCU, SCU, YCU.

Magic Earvin Johnson, basketball player for the Los Angeles Lakers.

Magnolia Curtain n. (1940s) the Mason-Dixon Line; dividing the South from the North; a play on "Iron Curtain." (Johnny Otis, *Listen to the Lambs*, 1968, p. 145.) NCU.

Maharishee n. (1970s–1990s) marijuana. (EF, RDSL, p. 246.) South-central Los Angeles use; SCU, YCU.

Mah-shu-ka-tin n. (1900s–1940s) gossip. (FR.) New Orleans use.

Main bitch n. (1950s–1990s) a pimp's most trusted woman; a male's most reliable and regular sexual companion. (EF, RDSL, p. 246.) PPU, SCU, YCU.

Main drag n. (1930s–1940s) Seventh Avenue in Harlem. (DB, OHHJ, p. 143.) Harlem use.

Main Drag of Many Tears n. (1940s) 125th Street, Harlem; so called because of its many poverty-stricken and disappointed people who try to laugh away their tears. (DB, OHHJ, p. 143.) Harlem use.

Main girl n. (DW, TL, p. 185.) See "Bottom woman" and "Main queen."

Main ho n. See "Main whore."

Main-Line n. (1930s–1990s) the main railroad line into Philadelphia. (Stephen Longstreet, *The Pedlocks*, 1951, p. 16.) Philadelphia use.

Mainline; mainlining v. See "Mainliner."

Mainliner n. (1930s–1990s) one who injects heroin or another type of addictive drug directly into her or his veins. (WF, DAS, p. 331; RRL, DAZ, p. 139; CS, vol. 3, no. 2, p. 33.) DCU.

Main kick n. (1930s–1940s) the stage or theater; one's favorite activity; a drug habit; liquor. (CC, OMMM, NCCHD, p. 257; DB, OHHJ, p. 143.) JMFU, SCU, YCU, DCU.

Main man n. (1950s–1960s) a favorite male friend; one's hero. (RSG, JT, p. 174; DW, TL, p. 185.) SCU, DCU, JMFU.

Main on the hitch n. (1940s) a woman's favorite man, especially her husband. (CC, OMMM, NCCHD, p. 257; DB, OHHJ, p. 143.) Harlem; SNU.

Main queen n. (1940s) a man's wife or a favorite girlfriend; a pimp's most trusted woman. (CC, OMMM, NCCHD, p. 258; WF, DAS, p. 331; DB, OHHJ, p. 143.) Rare. SCU.

Main squeeze n. (1960s) lover; favorite girlfriend. (JH, PBL, p. 85; EF, RDSL, p. 246.) SCU, YCU, PPU, SNCU.

Mainstay n. (1980s) a dealer's most trusted friend or lover. DCU.

Main stem n. (1930s–1940s) the street in the ghetto where people tend to promenade. (DB, OHHJ, p. 143.) Harlem; SNCU. See "Corner."

Main stuff n. See "Main bitch" and "Main whore."

Maintain [one's] cool v. (1950s–1970s) keeping an even temper; to maintain self-control. (EF, RDSL, p. 246.) SNU, YCU, SCU.

Main thrill n. (1930s–1940s) Seventh Avenue in New York City; the main drag; one's choice of drugs. (DB, OHHJ, p. 143.) Harlem; SNCU.

Main whore n. (1940s–1960s) a pimp's most trusted woman. (RDA, DDJ, p. 266.) PPU.

Maison joire n. (1900s–1950s) a whorehouse; brothel. (SL, RJON, p. 55.) Storyville, New Orleans, use.

Major adj. (1980s–1990s) describes any extreme. (PM, UCLAS, p. 57.) Example: "If you get caught, man, you gone be doing some major time in a monkey cage." YCU, SCU.

Major nasty adj. (1980s–1990s) describes anything negative or anything negative that is done in a grand fashion. (JM, WPC, np.) Example: "Billy and Shorty had a major nasty time getting their drunk daddy home from the tavern." SCU, DCU, YCU.

Make v. (1890s–1990s) to achieve a desired goal. (RRL, DAZ, p. 141; CS, vol. 3, no. 2, p. 33.) DCU, SCU, YCU.

Make [it with] v. (1890s–1950s) to do; to have sexual intercourse. (AL, MJR, p. 125; RSG, JT, p. 175.) Example: "If you can make it with her, I'll eat your hat." SNU.

Make a payday v. (1940s) to get money other than by working for it. (FR.) SNU.

Make a play for v. (1960s) try to seduce. (FR.) SNU.

Make change v. (1940s–1950s) work or do something to obtain money. (FR.) SNU.

Make it v. (1950s–1960s) to go; to cope; to leave a place. (DC, BJ, p. 72; CS, vol. 3, no. 2, p. 34) SCU, YCU, SNCU.

Make it with see "Make [it with]."

Make like v. (1900s–1960s) to pretend; to imitate. (FR.) SNU.

Make like a banana v. (1960s) to leave. (CS, vol. 3, no. 2, p. 34.) Example: "Catch you jive dudes later, I'm going to make like a banana and split." Watts, Los Angeles, use.

Make like a cow pie v. (1960s) to leave. (FR.) Example: "Catch you suckers later, I'm going to make like a cow pie and hit the trail." YCU.

Make like a paper doll v. (1960s) to leave. (CS, vol. 3, no. 2, p. 34.) Example: "See you punks later, I'm gonna make like a paper doll and cut out." Watts, Los Angeles, use.

Make [one's] love come down v. (1950s–1960s) orgasm; to make love; to be aroused passionately. (MM, RB, p. 35; RSG, JT, p. 176.) SNCU.

Make-out artist n. (1930s–1950s) sexually active male. (WF, DAS, p. 332.) NCU.

Make(s) over v. (1900s–1990s) to flatter or praise someone. (CS, vol. 3, no. 2, p. 34.) Example: "It's a disgrace the way he makes over her when she won't even give him a second glance." SNU, YCU.

Make the fist v. (1960s–1970s) a salute to the struggle for justice made in the form of a clenched (Black Power) fist; a Black Panther Party salute. (EF, RDSL, p. 246.) SCU, YCU.

Make the scene v. (1930s–1950s) to go to the place, usually a street corner, where one's friends gather, or a poolroom, barbershop, or some other public place; also, one "makes the scene" especially if one is dressed distinctively. To "make the scene" is to be involved with the "happenings" or with what is "going down" in the area—on the streets—where the "hip" or acceptable people hang out. Two novels dealing with the subject: *The Scene* (Clarence L. Cooper Jr.) and *Corner Boy* (Herbert A. Simmons). (RSG, JT, p. 176.) SNCU, DCU, SCU, YCU.

Make [one's] self scarce v. (1750s–1940s) to leave under pressure; to be sent away. (JAH, PBE, p. 175.) SNU.

Make tracks v. (1840s–1950s) to leave; to run; to go away in a hurry. (FR.) SNU.

Make up n. (1950s) an injection of heroin into the arm; a heroin addict's equipment. (CLC, TS, p. 255.) DCU.

Make water v. (1930s–1950s) to urinate. (FR.) SNU. See "Pass water."

Making it v. (1950s–1960s) to barely subsist; to succeed; to leave a place. (FR.) SNCU.

Malaria n. (1980s) sweat. (FR.)

Mallet n. (1970s–1980s) the police; law enforcement officer. (EF, RDSL, p. 246.) South-central Los Angeles use.

Mallets n. (1960s–1970s) percussion instrument such as vibraphone or xylophone. (RSG, JT, p. 176.) JMFU.

Mama n. (1650s–1990s) male term for girlfriend or wife; any woman; any girl. (CVV, NH, p. 286.) SNU.

[Your] Mama n. (1940s–1990s) an expression of good-natured abuse—if that's possible—or an outright insult. Holloway found evidence of similar expressions in West African languages, especially in Wolof. (HV, AHAE, p. 145.) SNU. See "[The] Momma's game."

Mama's boy n. (1900s–1990s) derogatory term meaning a sissy; a weakling; not of black origin but popular among black slang users. (WF, DAS, p. 333.) SNU.

Mama's boss n. (1930s–1940s) a woman's husband. This may be more a male term than female. If a term such as "daddy's boss" existed, it probably would be used in jest or ironically. (MHB, JS, np.) Rare. SU.

Mammy n. (1700s–1930s) a pejorative and ironic term when used by black people; form of address for a mother or grandmother; used as a positive term by white children in addressing their black female caretakers during slavery and after. (JSF, AON, p. 356; AB, DSJC, p. 40; ZNH, AM, p. 95.) Example: "All the white folks over the divide think we go for is to be they mammies and they uncles." SU.

Mammy jammer; mammy jamming n., adj., v. (1940s–1950s) anything excellent; enjoyment or enjoyable; to do something exciting. (FR). Examples: "I just bought Bird's new album and man, it's a mammy jammer" and, "You better come with us, Bonita, me and Cordance gonna have a mammy jamming good time at the dance." YCU.

Mammy's boy n. See "Mama's boy."

Man n. (1900s–1990s) *ce* [Mandingo]; form of address carrying respect and authority; a word brought into popular use by black males to counteract the degrading effects of being addressed by whites as "boy"; black males address each other as one man to another. (HV, AHAE, p. 145; DW, TL, p. 185; DC, BJ, p. 72.) SNU.

[The] Man n. (1900s–1990s) policeman; any white authority figure; one's white boss. (HLF, RJPD, p. 171; WF, DAS, p. 694; RRL, DAZ, p. 142; DW, TL, p. 185; JH, PBL, p. 85.) DCU, SCU, SNU.

[The] Man About Town Harlem name for Mezz Mezzrow during the thirties and forties.

M and M n. (1970s–1990s) Seconal; barbiturates. (EF, RDSL, p. 245.) DCU.

Mango n. (1780s–1920s) the offspring of a sambo and a full-blooded African. (EBR, MUS, p. 13.) SU. See "Cascos."

Man in gray n. (1930s–1940s) the letter carrier from the post office. (CC, OMMM, NCCHD, p. 258; DB, OHHJ, p. 143.) Rare. Harlem; NCU.

Mannish adj. (1960s) a child's way of acting rebelliously grown-up; said of a male child acting like an adult. (DC, BJ, p. 72.) Example: "Stop trying to act so mannish." SNU.

Mantan-black adj. (1960s) physically very black; after Mantan Moreland, actor. (FR.) SNCU.

[The] Man That Hipped the World Harlem name for Mezz Mezzrow during the thirties and forties.

[The] Man That Made History Harlem name for Mezz Mezzrow during the thirties and forties.

Man who rides the screaming gasser n. (1930s–1940s) policeman in a patrol car. (DB, OHHJ, p. 143.) Harlem use.

Man with a paper asshole n. (1950s–1970s) a person—usually male—who says stupid things; a silly person who talks too much. (EF, RDSL, p. 246.) SNU.

Man with fuzzy balls n. (1960s–1980s) white man. (EF, RDSL, p. 246.)

Man with headache stick n. (1950s–1960s) policeman. (FR.) SCU, DCU, PU, PPU.

Man with the book of many years n. (1940s) judge in a courtroom. (DB, OHHJ, p. 143.) Harlem use.

[The] Man with the Righteous Bush Harlem name for Mezz Mezzrow during the thirties and forties.

Map n. (1930s–1940s) the face. (DB, OHHJ, p. 143.) Harlem; SNU.

Maps n. (1930s–1960s) in jazz, sheet music. (WF, DAS, p. 333.) JMFU.

[To] Map [someone] v. (1980s–1990s) to hit a person, especially in the face. (TW, CK, p. 137.) DCU.

Marabou n. (1780s–1900s) an African-American of mulatto and griffe descent. (JSF, AON, p. 358; EBR, MUR, p. 12.) SU.

Marble Town n. (1900s–1940s) a cemetery. (DB, OHHJ, p. 143.) SNU.

Mariweegee n. (1970s–1980s) marijuana. (EF, RDSL, p. 246.) South-central Los Angeles; DCU.

Mark n. (1950s–1960s) an innocent man who can be used; a trick; a sucker. (DW, TL, p. 185; IS, PSML, p. 315.) DCU, SCU.

Marking v. (1960s–1970s) variant of "mocking"; to torment or annoy by mocking. (RDA, TB, p. 8.) SCU, YCU.

Marking house n. (1840s–1850s) jail; a "sweat box" where "Negro" slaves and freed men were locked, usually for curfew violations. (SK, PC, pp. 70–71). Palmetto County, Florida, use.

Maroon; marooning n., v. (1780s–1860s) a runaway slave; escaping from slavery. (JSF, AON, p. 358.) SU.

Mary n. (1930s–1950s) derogatory term for a woman. (Gwendolyn Brooks, *A Street in Bronzeville*, p. 7.) Rare. Chicago use.

Mary n. (1940s) marijuana; morphine. (RRL, DAZ, p. 154.) Rare. DCU. See "Mary Jane."

Mary Ann; Maryanne n. (1940s–1950s) marijuana. (WF, DAS, p. 334; EF, RDSL, p. 246.) DCU.

Mary Jane; Maryjane n. (1940s–1950s) marijuana. (RSG, JL, p. 118; RRL, DAZ, p. 154; EF, RDSL, p. 246.) DCU.

Mary Warner n. (1940s–1950s) marijuana. (RRL, DAZ, p. 154.) DCU.

Maserati n. (1980s–1990s) an improvised crack cocaine pipe primarily composed from a spark-plug cover and a plastic bottle. (TW, CH, p. 150.) DCU.

MASH v. (1930s–1940s) to give something to someone. (DB, OHHJ, p. 143.) Harlem; JMFU, SCU.

Mash [one] a fin v. (1930s–1940s) a request for five dollars; to give one five dollars. (CC, OMMM, NCCHD, p. 258; DB, OHHJ, p. 143.) Example: "Mash me a fin till the weekend, will ya?" Harlem; JMFU, SCU.

Mashed Potatoes n. (1950s) a dance originated by James Brown. (FR.) See "The James Brown."

Mash(ing) the fat v. (1970s–1980s) to have face-to-face sexual intercourse. (EF, RDSL, p. 246.) SNU.

[The] Mason n. See "Mason line."

Mason line n. (1760s–1950s) the main street, especially one indicating the boundary between a black and a white community. An obvious takeoff on the Mason-Dixon line, which, surveyed by two Englishmen, Mason and Dixon, in 1763–1766, served to put to rest a dispute between three states: Pennsylvania, Maryland, and West Virginia. On the fortieth parallel of the northern latitude, the marker was thought of as a demarcation between the North and the South —between the slave states and nonslave states. (MHB, JS, np; JSF, AON, pp. 359–360; DB, OHHJ, p. 143.) SU.

Massa n. (1650s–1860s) *mande, masa,* ("chief") [Mandingo]; a slave term of address to the slaveholder-master; boss, master. (HV, AHAE, p. 145.) SU.

Massa planter n. (1960s–1970s) one's boss; especially a white person in charge; the expression is always used ironically or with satiric intentions. (JH, PBL, p. 85.) SNCU.

Master adj. (1980s–1990s) a superlative for the finest or the best; anything excellent or well done. (WKB, JMC, PS, p. 50.) PU, SCU.

Master blaster n. (1980s–1990s) a large amount of cocaine free base. (TW, CH, p. 150.) DCU.

Mat n. (1700s–1930s) *Hausa mata, muso* [Mandingo]; *musu* [Vail]; in the nineteenth century and later, "mat" was thought by casual observers and researchers to be derogatory because of the assumed association with "doormat"; despite any tone of obvious affection— a man's female mate; wife; common-law wife; female companion; variants are "chick," "pharaoh," and "bree;" all identified by H. L. Mencken in the thirties as African-American jazz names for "girl." In 1993 Holloway published what appears to be evidence of their African origins. (HV, AHAE, p. 145; WF, DAS, p. 335.) Rare. SNU. See "Mouse."

Mater Mazuma n. (1940s) a female college teacher. (MHB, JS, np.) Southern "Negro" college student use.

Mau Mau n. (1960s) any revolutionary-minded American young black person during the sixties who identified with the Mau Mau fighters of Kenya, who helped topple the white government. (WF, DAS, p. 694.) SCU, PU, YCU, SNCU.

Max n. (1950s–1990s) the maximum sentence for an offense. (CS, vol. 3, no. 2, p. 34.) PU, DCU, SCU.

Max n. (1950s–1990s) a maximum security prison. (CS, vol. 3, no. 2, p. 34.) PU, DCU, SCU.

Maxxed out adj. (1980s) adjusted up. (FR.) YCU.

MC n. (1980s–1990s) master of ceremonies; head rapper of a musical group; anybody in control of anything. (FR.) SNCU, YCU.

McDaddy n. (1950s–1960s) variant of "Big Daddy." (CM, CW, James A. McPherson, "The Story of a Scar," p. 360.) MWU.

MC Lyte (1990s) a popular rap artist.

Meamelouc n. (1780s–1920s) the offspring of a metif and a white parent. (EBR, MUS, p. 12.) SU.

[It's going to be] Me and you imper. (1940s–1950s) an invitation to fight. (RDA, DDJ, p. 266.) Example: "Put up your dukes, it's going to be me and you." SCU.

Mean adj. (1900s–1940s) the finest; good; down-to-earth; honest; strong; possessing soul; gutbucket spirit; funky. (RSG, JL, p. 202; WF, DAS, p. 335; DC, BJ, p. 72.) JMFU. See "Down" and "Game."

[The one who is] Mean enough to steal acorns from a blind hog n., adj. (1850s–1890s) crude, rustic, and poor white person; a slave expression for the indigent white population; a white person who could not afford even one slave; "poor white trash." (JSF, AON, p. 362.) SU. See "Mean-white."

Mean tune n. (1940s–1990s) good, fine, beautiful music. (RCC, SOC, p. 34.) SCU, YCU, SNCU.

Mean-white n. (1950s–1890s) a crude, rustic, and indigent white person, especially one who cannot afford to own even one slave. (AB, DSJC, p. 47.)

Meat n. (1900s–1990s) male term; one's penis; vagina. (EF, RDSL, p. 246.) SCU, YCU, SNCU.

Meathooks n. (1940s–1950s) the fingers. (FR.) See "Grabbers."

Meatwagon n. (1930s–1950s) an ambulance. (SL, RJON, p. 7.) SNCU.

Medium groove n. (1950s–1980s) in jazz, a pace or tempo that is faster than slow but not as fast as "hot." (KG, JV, p. 181.) JMFU.

Meet n. (1940s–1950s) a jazz gathering; gig; jam session; appointment to pick up drugs. (WF, DAS, p. 336; RRL, DAZ, p. 154.) JMFU, DCU.

Mellow adj. (1930s–1970s) gentle, sincere, satisfying; cool; one's best or close friend. (CC, OMMM, NCCHD; DB, OHHJ, p. 143; DC, BJ, p. 72.) JMFU, SCU, SNCU.

Mellow adj. (1950s–1970s) high or tipsy; feeling good, but not drunk or stoned. (CS, vol. 3, no. 2, p. 34; EF, RDSL, p. 246.) Example: "Here, have a sip or two of these, it'll get you nice and mellow." SNCU.

[One's] Mellow n. (1950s–1960s) one's best or closest friend; one's lover. (DW, TL, p. 185; EF, RDSL, p. 246; EF, RDSL, p. 246.) DCU, SCU.

Mellow-back adj. (1950s–1960s) fashionably dressed. (WF, DAS, p. 337.) SNCU. See "Mellow drag with the sag."

Mellow-black [woman] n. (1930s–1940s) attractive young black woman. (DB, OHHJ, p. 143.) SCU, JMFU, SNCU.

Mellow drag with the sag n. (1930s–1940s) a suit, popular in Harlem, with an extremely long jacket; a cutaway-type suit jacket; suit jacket similar to a frock. (DB, OHHJ, p. 143.) See "Cute suit with the loop droop."

Mellow roof n. (1930s–1940s) one's head. (DB, OHHJ, p. 143.) Harlem, MWU.

Mellow yellow n., adj. (1960s) dried banana skins; to be high from smoking dried banana skin fibers. (RRL, DAZ, p. 155; CS, vol. 3, no. 2, p. 34.) Watts; DCU.

Mellow yellow n. (1950s–1960s) male term; a light-skinned African-American woman or girl. (EF, RDSL, p. 246.) SNU.

Melons n. (1950s–1960s) a woman's breasts. (FR.) SNU.

Melted butter n. (1950s–1960s) male term; a light-skinned African-American woman or girl. (EF, RDSL, p. 246.) SNU.

Melted out adj. (1940s) to be without money and desperate. (CC, OMMM, NCCHD, p. 258; DB, OHHJ, p. 143.) SNU.

Melungeon n. (1870s–1960s) a person of black and white ancestry who is native to Tennessee. (FR.) Tennessee; SU.

Member n. (1890s–1970s) originally, any member of the black race; one black person to another; in the seventies, a black person. (DC, BJ, p. 72; EF, RDSL, p. 246.) SNU.

Memorial time n. (1920s–1930s) the distant past. (CM, CW, Zora Neale Hurston, "The Gilded Six-Bits.") SU.

Mercedes n. (1970s–1980s) an attractive and shapely young woman. (EF, RDSL, p. 246.) YCU.

Meserole n. variant of "mezzrole." (RRL, DAZ, p. 161.) See "Mezz's roll."

Mess adj. (1900s–1950s) ironic statement meaning good; a large quantity. (CC, OMMM, NCCHD, p. 258; DB, OHHJ, p. 143.) Example: "You're a mess with the way you handle that piano, boy," is to imply that the piano player is remarkable or puzzling but exciting. JMFU, SNU.

Mess around v. (1920s–1930s) popular improvisational jazz dancing; to act or perform in a less-than-serious manner. (RSG, JT, p. 179.) JMFU.

Message n., v. (1950s) the sensation felt from music well communicated; to understand something that is not clearly or not at all stated. (FR.) JMFU.

Messed up adj. (1980s–1990s) troubled; confused; victim of bad luck; wrong or illogical. (EF, RDSL, p. 246.) Example: "You want to kill him over it? That's messed up." SNU.

Mess up [one] v. (1950s–1990s) to attack physically; to verbally assault. (EF, RDSL, p. 246.) YCU, SCU, SNU.

Mess up [one's] action v. See "Mess up [one's] game."

Mess up [one's] game v. (1970s–1980s) to interfere with someone's attempt at romance. (EF, RDSL, p. 246.) YCU, SCU.

Mess up [one's] mind v. (1950s–1970s) to confuse someone through manipulation; to overwhelm someone with unexpected behavior. (EF, RDSL, p. 246.) SNU, YCU, SCU.

Mess up [one's] play v. See "Mess up [one's] game."

Mess up [one's] style v. See "Mess up [one's] game."

Mess with v. (1800s–1990s) to harass; interfere with; annoy; laugh at; to compromise someone; to intimidate or ridicule. (AS, SM, p. 202; DC, BJ, p. 72; EF, RDSL, p. 246.) SNU.

Mess with nature v. (1970s–1980s) to interfere with two people who are about to have sex. (EF, RDSL, p. 246.) South-central Los Angeles; SCU, YCU, SNCU.

Messy adj. See "Mess."

Messy attic n. (1950s) hair in need of a "do." (FR.) SNCU.

Mestizo n. (1880s–1940s) generic term for a person of mixed racial ancestry. (BB, AW, p.. 39–40.) SU. See also "Brass ankle," "Croatan," "Melungeon," and "Red bone."

Meter n. (1940s) a twenty-five-cent coin. (CC, OMMM, NCCHD, p. 258; DB, OHHJ, p. 143.) Example: "I ain't got a meter in the mouse." Harlem use.

Metif n. (1780s–1920s) the offspring of a Quadroon and a white parent. (EBR, MUS, p. 12.) SU.

Mexican green n. (1960s–1970s) a light-green, largely ineffective type of mariuana. (EF, RDSL, p. 247.) Watts and South-central Los Angeles; DCU.

Mezz Harlem name for Mezz Mezzrow, legally known as Milton Mesirow, clarinet and saxaphone player; born in Chicago, November 9, 1899. Author of the autobiography, *Really the Blues*, Mezzrow was born white, but, like Johnny Otis, chose to live all his life as a black man. Harlem use.

Mezz n. (1940s) anything good and true. (CC, OMMM, NCCHD, p. 258; DB, OHHJ, p. 143.) Harlem use.

Mezzrole n. See "Mezz's roll."

Mezz's roll n. (1940s) variant of "messy roll" with a play on the name "Mezzrow"; a generously rolled marijuana cigarette; a potent stick of marijuana, the "fat" kind rolled by well-known jazz personality Mezz Mezzrow, a white man who for many years lived, and sold marijuana, in Harlem; author of *Really the Blues*. (WF, DAS, p. 337; RR1, DAZ, p. 167.) Harlem use.

MF n. (PM, UCLAS, p. 59.) See "Motherfucker."

Mice n. (1900s–1930s) in jazz, violins. (RSG, JT, p. 180.) JMFU.

Mickey Mouse [music] n. (1930s–1960s) popular, commercialized music, put down by jazzmen; weak background music. (SJ, RJON, p. 338; RSG, JT, p. 180.) JMFU.

Mickey-mouse adj., n. (1930s–1960s) anything inferior; a thing made of shoddy material; a cheap, unethical scheme; anybody unprofessional. (SJ, RJON, p. 338; DC, BJ, p. 72.) JMFU, SNU, SCU.

Mickey-mouse n. (1960s–1970s) pejorative term for a white person. (JH, PBL, p. 85.) SNCU.

Middle leg n. (1950s) the penis. (WF, DAS, p. 338.) SNU.

Middle name n. (1940s–1950s) something that is intrinsic to one; that which one identifies; said when someone likes something intensely. (FR.) SNU.

Midnight n. (1950s–1960s) a very dark-skinned African-American. (DC, BJ, p. 72.) SNU. See "Midnight the cat."

Midnight the cat n. (1950s–1960s) a very dark-skinned African-American." EF, RDSL, p. 247.) South-central Los Angeles; SNU.

Midway n. (1900s–1940s) a hallway or corridor. (DB, OHHJ, p. 143.) Example: "Tell the mailman to leave the package in the midway. " Harlem use.

Miff Irving Mifred Mole, trombonist; born in Roosevelt, Long Island, March 11, 1898; best known for his Dixieland music.

Mighty Dome n. (1930s–1940s) House of Congress or any government building. (DB, OHHJ, p. 143.) SNCU.

Mighty Mezz n. See "Mezz."

Mikes n. (1940s) ears. (DB, OHHJ, p. 143.) Harlem; JMFU.

Milk a duck v. (1930s–1940s) to try the impossible. (ZNH, AM, p. 89.) SNU.

Mind n. (1800s–1990s) attention. (FR.) Example: "Don't pay him no mind." SNU.

Mind in the mud (1900s–1940s) to have vulgar thoughts. (MHB, JS, np.) SNU.

Mind-boggling adj. (1960s) amazing; incomprehensible. (FR.) SNU.

Mind-fuck n., v. (1970s–1990s) to deliberately confuse someone by exhibiting unexpected behavior or by saying "crazy" things. (EF, RDSL, p. 247.) Example: "Alphonso thinks he can get his way with any chick if he do his mind-fuck on her before hitting on her." See "Blow [one's] mind" and "Mess up [one's] mind."

Mink n. (1950s–1960s) a girlfriend; a beautiful young woman. (CRM, BP, p. 300; DC, BJ, p. 72; JH, PBL, p. 85; JM, WPC, p.) Example: "That mink couldn't be a day over twelve." Rare. WCU, PPU. See "Hammer."

Miscegenationist n. (1860s–1890s) variant of "nigger lover"; after the Civil War, white southerners used this term to refer to any white person who was even friendly toward the ex-slaves; "miscegenation" is a word coined by David Goodman Croly, editor of *New York World*, in an unsigned pamphlet outlining a hysterically stupid theory of race; a term used ironically—and rarely—by black people; "nigger lover" was always more common among black speakers. (SBF, IHAT, p. 39.) SU.

Misery n. (1780s–1900s) "a favorite negro synonym for pain" (JSF, AON, p. 368). Example: "Mary, I got a misery in my leg that's been hounding me for three days." SU.

Miss Amy n. (1960s–1980s) variant of "Miss Ann"; a young white female. (EF, RDSL, p. 247.) SNU.

Miss Ann n. (1890s–1960s) a white woman—carryover from southern terminology, but now used with a good-natured sneer or with outright maliciousness. (CVV, NH, p. 286; WF, DAS, p. 340; ZNH, AM, p. 95; CS, vol. 3, no. 2, p. 35.) SNU.

Miss Lillian n. (1980s) an older white female. (EF, RDSL, p. 247.) SNU.

Miss Thing n. (1940s–1990s) derogatory term for male homosexual. (FR.) SCU, PPU, PU, DCU.

Mission n. (1980s–1990s) any trip made in search of cocaine. Probably picked up from Trekkie (as in "Star Trek") talk. (TW, CH, p. 150.) DCU.

Mister B William Clarence Eckstein, singer; born in Pittsburgh, Pennsylvania, July 8, 1914; became a very famous nightclub soloist.

Mister Charlie n. (1900s–1960s) a white man—carryover from southern use, with no friendly over- or undertones. (ZNH, AM, p. 95; WF, DAS, p. 340; JH, PBL, p. 85; CS, vol. 3, no. 2, p. 35.) See "Charlie."

Mister Cracker n. (1970s–1990s) a derogatory term for any white male. (EF, RDSL, p. 247.) SCU, PU.

Mister Eddie n. (1900s–1930s) any white man. (CVV, NH, p. 286.) Harlem use.

Mister Hawkins n. (1930s–1960s) a cold winter's wind. (DB, OHHJ, p. 143; WF, DAS, p. 340.) See "Hawk."

Mister Sin n. (1970s–1980s) a vice squad police officer. (EF, RDSL, p. 247.) South-central, Los Angeles; SCU, PU.

Mister Speaker n. (1940s) A pistol, especially a revolver. (DB, OHHJ, p. 143.) Harlem; SCU.

Mister Tom; Thomas n. (1960s–1980s) derogatory term for a middle-class African-American or "Negro." (EF, RDSL, p. 247; WF, DAS, p. 695.) See "Tom" and "Uncle Tom."

Mitt man n. (1890s–1950s) a religious imposter, or unethical minister, who capitalizes on devoutly religious people; a crooked preacher who swindles his congregation out of its money; "mitt" may refer to the white gloves common in the Negro church before and just after the turn of the century. (IS, PSML, p. 315.) SNU.

Mitt pounding n. (1940s) applause. (CC, OMMM, NCCHD, p. 258; DB, OHHJ, p. 143.) JMFU.

Mitts n. (1940s–1970s) hands. (MHB, JS, np.) SNU.

Mix n. (1980s–1990s) an unfavorable situation; memory. (WKB, JMC, PS, p. 50.) Examples: "I should never have gone up there because the mix was all wrong"; and "Don't think I'm going to forget how to treated me, no way, it's going in the mix and you'll hear from me again." PU, SCU.

Mixed adj. (1860s–1990s) a term for racial integration; it and "miscegenation" (along with violently racist cartoons showing black men with baboon lips, kissing white women) became popular the minute Abraham Lincoln signed the Emancipation Proclamation document. (SBF, IHAT, p. 39.) SNU.

Mixed bag n. (1960s) a situation that is complex; both good and bad. (FR.) SNU.

Mizzy n. (1840s–1890s) "A Louisianian negro expression for the stomach-ache" (JSF, AON, p. 369). Example: "I got the mizzy something terrible." Louisiana; SU.

Mocha n. (1900s–1950s) a rich, dark, reddish brown complexion. (WF, DAS, p. 341.) Rare. NCU.

Mod adj. (1970s) fashionable. (EF, RDSL, p. 247.) SNCU.

Mod bag n. (1970s) one's fashionable style of dressing. (EF, RDSL, p. 247.) SNCU.

Mod squad n. (1970s) plainclothes young police officers who dress like "hippies" or "street people" while on assignments or sting operations; term made popular by the TV series "Mod Squad" starring Clarence Williams III. (EF, RDSL, p. 247.) SNU.

Mojo n. (1700s–1950s) charm; amulet; conjuring object; a good-luck charm used by gamblers and lovers. A variant is "Joe Moore. (RSG, JT, p. 181; WF, DAS, p. 695; PM, UCLAS, p. 56.) SU. See "Joe Moore."

Mojo working n. (1700s–1950s) good luck; success. (Toni Cade Bambara, *Gorilla, My Love*, p. 164.) SU.

Moke n. (1850s–1920s) probably from "mocha"; a black person or a white person in blackface in a minstrel show; picked up from white use. (WF, DAS, p. 341.; SBF, IHAT, p. 56.) SNU.

Moldy adj. (1940s–1960s) in jazz, music out of style. (RSG, JT, pp. 181–182.) JMFU.

Moldy Fig n. (1940s–1950s) a musician or fan who rejects the new jazz in favor of the older forms of the twenties and thirties. (RSG, JT, pp. 181–182.) JMFU.

Momma n. (1680s–1960s) form of address by black male to black female; a very attractive black female. (DC, BJ, p. 72.) See "Hammer" and "Mink."

[Your] Momma n. See "[Your] Mama."

[The] Momma's game n. (1950s–1970s) a verbal game for two in which participants insult each other's mother; "signifying"; playing the "dozens"; "capping." The object of the game is to build emotional strength. (EF, RDSL, p. 247.) SNU.

Moms n. (1900s–1990s) one's mother. (EF, RDSL, p. 247.) NECU.

Money n. (1980s–1990s) one's best, most trusted friend. (WKB, JMC, PS, p. 50.) Example: "Gil is pure money. I'd trust him with my life." PU, SCU, DCU.

Money ain't long enough [to do something] (1960s–1990s) in this context money is insufficient. (EF, RDSL, p. 247.) Example: "Your money ain't long enough to make me change my mind about going out with you." YCU.

Moneyfoot n. (1900s–1940s) disqualified foot; children's counting game in which the foot counted out becomes useless for walking or anything else; game picked up and changed from the way white children of English descent played it. (BJ, BLH, SD, pp. 159–160.) SU.

Moneymaker n. (1950s–1970s) a woman's vagina; buttocks; genitals; ass; female body; female mouth. (Hear Elmore James, "Shake Your Money Maker," *Dust My Broom*, Tomato, 1991, recorded in the early sixties; CRM, BP, p. 304.) PPU, SCU.

Money's mammy adj. (1930s–1940s) rich; very rich. (ZNH, AM, p. 92.) Example: "I don't have to ask you or nobody for money, I'm money's mammy." Harlem; SNU.

Monk v. (1900s–1990s) short for "monkey" or "monkey chaser" [West Indian]. (CVV, NH, p. 286.) Harlem use.

Monkey n. (1890s–1990s) a heroin- or cocaine-user's addiction or habit; from use regarding nineteenth-century Chinese immigrant opium addicts. (CLC, TS, p. 255; TW, CH, p. 150; RRL, DAZ, p. 170.) DCU. See "Crack attack."

Monkey n. (1920s–1960s) a band or orchestra leader; from the fifties to the sixties, drug addiction, the habit; a white person. (WF, DAS, p. 343.) NCU.

Monkey n. (1960s) pejorative term for any white person. (DC, BJ, p. 72.) MWU.

Monkey cage n. a jail or prison cell; picked up from prison use. (WF, DAS, p. 343.) PU.

Monkey catcher n. (1850s–1940s) of African origin (by way of Jamaica); a shrewd individual; one who knows how to live by his or her wits; one who avoids mistakes. (AB, DSJC, pp. 58–59.) See "Monkey chaser."

Monkey chaser n. (1850s–1940s) of African origin; person from the West Indies. (CVV, NH, p. 286; WF, DAS, p. 343; ZNH, AM, p. 95.) NCU.

Monkey on [one's] back n. See "Monkey."

Monking v. (1980s) passing time in solitude or isolation, as in prison or self-imposed isolation. (KCJ, JS, p. 123.) Harlem; PU, SCU.

Mooch n. (1920s–1950s) a slow dance similar to the "Drag" in the forties and fifties. (WF, DAS, p. 345.)

Mooch n. (1920s–1950s) to beg or borrow. (DB, OHHJ, p. 143.) SNU.

Moo juice n. (1930s–1940s) cow's milk. (CC, OMMM, NCCHD, p. 258; DB, OHHJ, p. 143.) SNU.

Moonack n. (1700s–1890s) of African origin; a hoodoo (mythical) animal respected by the slaves brought from Africa; to meet this beast face-to-face brings insanity or a horrible disease upon the human being unfortunate enough to happen upon it. (AB, DSJC, p. 60.) SU.

Moon rock n. (1990s) heroin and crack cocaine mixed. (TW, CH, p. 150.) DCU.

Moonwalk n. (1980s) dance imitating the motion of the astronauts walking on the moon; dance step created by Michael Jackson. (FR.) SNU.

Mootah (mooter; mootie; moota; moocah; muta; mu) n. (1930s) variant of "muta" for marijuana (RRL, DAZ, p. 171.) Rare. DCU.

Mop n. (1940s–1960s) the last beat at the end of a jazz number with a cadence of triplets; the end of anything. (DB, OHHJ, p. 143; SL, RJON, p. 147.)

Mop n. (1940s–1960s) one's natural hair; hair like a rag mop; in the fifties and early sixties, processed hair. (SL, RJON, p. 147; IS, PSML, p. 315; DC, BJ, p. 73.) SCU, SNU.

More better; mo' better adv. (1700s–1950s; 1990s) of Gullah origin; an improvement; better. The expression became popular and for the first time accessible to American popular culture when Spike Lee's movie *Mo' Better Blues* was released in the early 1990s. (AEG, BB, p. 313.) SU.

Morning wake-up n. (1980s–1990s) an addict's first snort or puff of the morning. (TW, CH, p. 150.) DCU.

Morph n. (1950s–1960s) short for "morphine." (CLC, TS, p. 255.) DCU.

Mose n. (1850s–1940s) derogatory term for a "Negro." (DB, OHHJ, p. 144; WF, DAS, p. 345.) SU.

Mosey v. (1820s–1960s) to walk slowly; meander. (WF, DAS, p. 345.) SU.

Moss n. (1940s–1960s) one's hair; kinky hair; African hair. (DB, OHHJ, p. 144; WF, DAS, p. 345.) SNU.

Mostest adj., superl. (1890s–1950s) the largest amount; the best of something; the finest of its kind. (WF, DAS, p. 345.) Example: "She got to be the hostess with the mostest." SNU.

Mother n. (1960s–1990s) Some variations: mutheree, motherfeyer, motherfouler, motherhugger, motherjiver, motherlover, mothersuperior, mammyjammer, mammysucker, mammyfucker, mammyhugger. (RSG, JT, p. 184.) SNU.

Mother n. (1960s–1990s) a difficult dilemma; a hard task. (FR.) SNU.

Mother n. (1960s–1990s); an effeminate male; homosexual.

Mother n. (1960s–1990s) drug pusher. (FR.) DCU.

Motherfucker n. (1790s–1990s) profane form of address; a white man; any man; anybody; of black origin; sometimes derogatory, sometimes used affectionately; other times used playfully. (SBF, IHAT, p. 159; RHdeC, NB, pp. 32–33; WF, DAS, pp. 695–696; CRM, BP, p. 304; DR, BASL, p. 217; DW, TL, p. 185.) SNU.

Motherfucker n. (1950s–1990s) a disappointing situation; bad luck; misfortune; betrayal. (DW, TL, p. 185; EF, RDSL, p. 247.) SCU, YCU, DCU, PPU, PU.

Mother Mezz Harlem name for Mezz Mezzrow during the thirties and forties.

Mother nature's own tobacco n. (1970s–1990s) marijuana. (EF, RDSL, p. 247.) YCU, DCU, SCU.

Mother of the Blues Gertrude Malissa Nix Pridgett, better known as Ma Rainy, blues singer; born in Columbus, Georgia, April 26, 1886, and died December 22, 1939, in Rome, Georgia.

Mother's Day n. (1940s–1960s) a woman's Aid to Dependent Children (ADC) or welfare check arrives on this day. (CS, vol. 3, no. 2, p. 35.) SNCU.

Mother-wit n. (1800s–1960s) common sense. (DC, BJ, p. 73.) SNU.

Motivate v. (1960s) to move; to put forth energy or drive. (CRM, BP, p. 304.) Example: "I'll be back on the scene this afternoon, but right now I got to motivate up the hill to see my mama." Rare. PPU, DCU.

Motor v. (1990s) to run or walk. (FR.) Example: "I got to motor. I'm late for work." SNU, YCU, SCU.

Motor City n. (1960s) Detroit. (FR.) Detroit; NECU.

Motorcycle n. (1950s) derogatory term for a woman; the implication is that one can "ride" either. (FR.) SNU.

Motorcycle bull n. (1930s–1940s) traffic law enforcement officer. (MHB, JS, np.) SNCU.

Motown n. (1960s) Detroit. (FR.) YCU, SNCU.

Mount n. (1970s–1980s) a woman who is casual about sex; promiscuous woman. (EF, RDSL, p. 247.) SCU, YCU.

Mount v. (1960s–1990s) to perform sexual intercourse. (EF, RDSL, p. 247.) SCU, YCU.

Mount v. (1960s–1980s) to brag or use any form of verbal aggression. (RDA, TB, p. 45; RDA, DDJ, p. 266.) Philadelphia; SCU, DCU, YCU, PU, PPU. See "Dozens" and "Signifying."

Mouse n. (1940s) one's pocket. (CC, OMMM, NCCHD, p. 258; DB, OHHJ, p. 144.) SNU.

Mouse n. (1800s–1890s) wife: *muso* (Mandingo); short for "mousetrap" (old cant for marriage). (AB, DSJC, p. 66; HV, AHAE, p. 145.) See "Mat."

Mouth n. (1940s–1950s) excessive talk. (FR.) Example: "The clerk's daughter sure brings a lot of mouth to the job." SNU.

Mouth harp n. (1920s–1940s) harmonica. (Ruby Pickens Tartt, *Toting the Lead Row*, 1981, p. 108.) SU.

Move v. (1950s–1970s) to become impressive, exciting musically. (RSG, JT, p. 185.) Example: "When they start making it move, that's when I like it." JMFU.

Move on [one] v. (1980s–1990s) to attack or shoot someone. (EF, RDSL, p. 247.) SCU, PU.

Moving out v. (1950s–1960s) in jazz, demonstrating innovative ability or originality in an energetic style. (RSG, JT, p. 185.) JMFU.

Mow the lawn v. (1930s–1940s) to comb the hair. (DB, OHHJ, p. 144.) Harlem; MWU.

Mr. B William Clarence Eckstein, singer; born July 8, 1914; as bandleader, worked with Charlie Parker, Sarah Vaughan, and others.

Mr. Cleanhead Eddie Vinson, singer, alto saxophone player; born December 18, 1917, in Houston, Texas; worked with Cootie Williams; had his own band in 1945.

Mr. Five-by-Five Jimmy Rushing, blues singer.

Much adv. (1930s–1960s) in black slang "much" often refers to quality rather than the usual quantity. (RSG, JT, p. 186.) JMFU, SNCU, YCU.

Mucty-muck n. (1950s–1990s) variant of "muck-a-muck" and "mucky-muck"; nonsense; silly talk; lies; aimless, aggressive talk. (RCC, SOC, p. 17; IS, PSML, p. 315.) SNCU, SCU.

Mud n. (1950s–1960s) opium. (CS, vol. 3, no. 2, p. 35.) DCU.

Mudear n. (1800s–1950s) term of address; variant of "mother dear." (FR.) SU.

Mud-kicker n. (1940s–1950s) a prostitute. (WF, DAS, p. 347.) PPU.

Muddle along (1900s–1940s) to walk slowly as from depression or exhaustion. (MHB, JS, np.) SNU.

Muddy waters n. (1980s) the loss of erection while engaged in sex. (EF, RDSL, p. 247.) Example: "He can't go five seconds without getting muddy waters." South-central Los Angeles; SCU; SNCU.

Mug n. (1940s) the human face. (DB, OHHJ, p. 144; HeG, DAUL, p. 142; CS, vol. 3, no. 2, p. 35.) SNU.

Mugged behind five v. (1930s–1940s) speaking with the hand shielding the lips. (DB, OHHJ, p. 144.) Harlem use; PU.

Mugging v. (1900s–1940s) kissing and hugging. (MHB, JS, np.) Rare. SNU.

Mugging v. (1930s–1940s) deliberately causing laughter by making funny faces or telling jokes. (CC, OMMM, NCCHD, p. 258.) SNCU.

Mugging heavy [or light; lightly] (1930s–1940s) in jazz, the term refers to the beat, its quality. (RSG, JT, p. 186.) JMFU.

Mugging up v. (1900s–1940s) sexual intercourse. (MHB, JS, np; WF, DAS, p. 348.) Rare. SNU.

Muggle n. (1940s–1950s) cigarette with marijuana stuffed into its tip. (HEG, DAUL, p. 142; SL, RJON, p. 144.) See "Roach."

Mug man n. (1900s–1940s) a petty gangster. (ZNH, AM, p. 95.) Harlem; SCU.

Mulatto n. (1700s–1990s) *mulato* (Spanish), from mule, meaning half-breed; one with a "touch of the tar brush"; a person with one white and one black parent; other related terms: Quarteron (or Quadroon); Mustafina; Griffe; Marabou; Sacatra. (JSF, AON, p. 376.) SU.

[Dope] Mule n. (1990s) a person—usually young and male—who delivers illegal narcotics for a dealer. (RP, C, np.) New York, New Jersey; DCU. See "Clocker."

Mule-skinner n. (1870s–1940s) a man who tends to and drives mules. (WF, DAS, p. 349.) SU.

Mulligrubs n. pl. (1940s) the blues. (WF, DAS, p. 349.) See "Blues."

Mullion n. (1960s) an ugly woman or man. (DC, BJ, p. 73.) MWU.

Mumbo jumbo n. (1660s–1950s) derived from *Mama Dyumbo* (Mandingo), protective spirit of the Khassonkee tribe of Senegal; also, ancestor spirit, with fetish pompom; a play; trick; later, nonsense. (See Mungo Park's *Travels in the Interior of Africa*.)

Mummy pussy n. (1970s–1980s) a woman who does not respond— or pretends to be a corpse—during intercourse. (TMc, WE) SNCU.

Murder [number] one n. (1940s–1950s) first-degree homicide. (IS, TB, p. 312.) DCU, SCU, PPU, PU.

Murder adj. (1930s–1940s) excellent; the best. (CC, OMMM, NCCHD, p. 258; DB, OHHJ, p. 144.) SNCU, DCU, SCU, PU.

Murphy n. (1940s–1960s) a confidence game played on an innocent man (especially white) who is expecting sex with a prostitute (usually black). The pimp or hustler steers the "trick" toward a vacant place, where he waits for a woman who does not appear. The pimp has, of course, already collected the "bread" (money) and "split" (gone). Or, the con game involves the victim receiving a sealed envelope which he—rarely she—believes contains valuable information or drugs in exchange for money he's already handed over. (IS, PSML, p. 316; DC, BJ, p. 73; WF, DAS, p. 696.) SCU, DCU.

[Miss or Mrs.] Murphy n. See "Murphy."

Murphy-man n. See "Murphy."

Muscle n. (1940s) a bluff; a bully; a false show of courage. (WF, DAS, p. 349.) SCU, PU.

Mush; mushing n., v. (1940s) a kiss. (DB, OHHJ, p. 144; WF, DAS, p. 349.) Example: "Those two love birds always mushing on the love seat." SNU. See "Mugging."

Mustafina n. (1760s–1900s) a "white" person with one-sixteenth African blood but legally classified a Negro. (JSF, AON, p. 381.) SU.

Mustard seed n. (1920s) a light-skinned African-American. (CVV, NH, p. 286.) See "High yellow" and "Lemon."

Mustifee n. (1780s–1920s) the offspring of an octoroon and a white parent. (EBR, MUS, p. 13.) SU.

Mustifino n. (1780s–1920s) the offspring of a mustifee and a white parent. (EBR, MUS, p. 13.) SU. See "Mustifee" and "Quadroon."

Must-I-holler n. (1980s–1990s) vagina. (FR.) SCU, YCU.

Musty n. (1880s–1990s) unclean body smell; a bad house odor; smelly clothes. (EF, RDSL, p. 247.) SNU.

Mutt Thomas Carey, trumpeter; born in New Orleans, Louisiana, 1892; died in Los Angeles, California, September 3, 1948; worked with Johnny Dodd, Kid Ory, and King Oliver in Dreamland.

My gun n. (1980s–1990s) one's most trusted friend. (WKB, JMC, PS, p. 50.) PU, DCU, SCU.

My man (1930s–1990s) an especially friendly term of address by one male to another. (EF, RDSL, p. 246.) See "Man."

My people n. (1950s–1970s) one's gang members. (DC, BJ, p. 73.) See "Boot."

My people! n. (1880s–1990s) an exclamation; sometimes said ironically or with satiric or cynical humor. (ZNH, AM, p. 95; DC, BJ, p. 73.) SNU.

Mysterious adj. (1950s–1990s) describes anything—especially music—that is "weird" or innovative or avant garde. (RSG, JT, p. 186.) JMFU, SCU, YCU, SNCU.

Nail n. (1960s) a male; if the female is the "hammer" then the male is the "nail." (DC, BJ, p. 73.) MWU. See "Cat," "Dude," and "Man."

Nail n. (1950s–1960s) heroin addicts use "nail" as a variant of "spike." (RRL, DAZ, p. 179.) DCU.

Nail-em-and-jail-em n. (1970s–1990s) the police. (EF, RDSL, p. 247.) Example: "Here comes Nail-em-and-jail-em. Just hang, be cool." Watts and South-central Los Angeles; SCU.

Nailers n. (1950s–1960s) police; those who "nail" people engaged in illegal acts. (HEG, DAUL, p. 144.) SCU, PU.

Nail head n. (EF, RDSL, p. 247.) See "B.B. Head."

Naked dance n. (1940s–1950s) "a real art" dance; lewd or obscene dance. (AL, MRJ, p. 47.) JMFU.

Naked jazz n. (1940s–1950s) gutbucket; lowdown. (FR.) JMFU.

Nam black n. (1960s–1970s) a very dark green type of marijuana grown in or associated with Vietnam. (EF, RDSL, p. 247.) DCU.

Nam shit n. (EF, RDSL, p. 247.) See "Nam black."

Nam weed n. (EF, RDSL, p. 247.) See "Nam black."

Napoleon n. (1930s–1940s) an insane man; an eccentric-acting man. (DB, OHHJ, p. 144.) Harlem use.

Nappy adj. (1800s–1950s) kinky; wooly; usually said of someone's hair. (SL, RJON, p. 150; EF, RDSL, p. 147.) SNU.

Nappy edges n. (1870s–1950s) brittle and broken hair along the hairline. (SL, RJON, p. 150; Ntosake Shange, *Nappy Edges*, 1978.) See "Go back."

Nappyblack adj. (1960s) very African looking. (FR.) SNU.

Naps n. (1870s–1950s) kinky hair. (ZNH, AM, p. 95; WF, DAS, p. 351.) SNU.

Narc; nark n. See "Narco."

Narco n. (1970s–1990s) special narcotics agents of the police department; federal (FBI) narcotics agents. (DW, TL, p. 186; CS, vol. 3, no. 2, p. 35; EF, RDSL, p. 247.) DCU.

Nasties n. (1900s–1980s) sexual desire. (FR.) SNU.

Nasty adj. (1930s–1990s) sexy; down-to-earth; in jazz, good; good-terrible; good-mean. (RSG, JT, p. 187; WF, DAS, p. 351; PM, UCLAS, p. 61.) Example: "That's some nasty sounds you putting out there, Buddy." JMFU, SNU.

[Do the] Nasty n. (1970s–1990s) sexual intercourse. (EF, RDSL, p. 247.) SCU, YCU, SNU.

[On the] Natch adj. (1950s–1960s) free from the use of any artificial stimulants or narcotics. (RRL, DAZ, p. 181.) DCU.

Natch adv. (1940s–1950s) variant of "natural" or "naturally." (MHB, JS, np; WF, DAS, p. 351; EF, RDSL, p. 247.) SNU.

Natch trips n. (1960s–1970s) "highs" induced by smoking the skins of or drinking the broth from banana, nutmeg, mace, cinnamon, peanut shells, peppers, or wild rice. (RRL, DAZ, p. 181.) DCU.

Natchie n. (1960s) variant of "natural"; an untrimmed, natural black hairstyle. (DC, BJ, p. 73.) MWU.

Nat King Cole Nathaniel Coles, singer, pianist; born in Montgomery, Alabama, March 17, 1917; became a very popular vocalist; his first big hit, "Straighten Up and Fly Right."

Natural adj. (1930s–1960s) an intensifier used with many other words such as "a natural-born freak"; in the sixties, a look, among American black people, inspired largely by positive racial identification with emerging "free" Africans who are bringing their countries onto the stage of the technological world. (RSG, JT, p. 187; EF, RDSL, p. 248.) Example: "I laughed till I cried—that boy is a natural-born comedian." SNU.

Natural [-born] (EF, RDSL, p. 248.) See "Natural."

Natural-born man (EF, RDSL, p. 248.) See "Natural."

Natural [hair] n. (1960s) hair worn cut and combed but without oils or grease; groomed or ungroomed bushy hair. The hair is usually sculpted in a tall and rounded fashion like a crown. (DC, BJ, p. 73; EF, RDSL, p. 249.) SNU.

Natural pick n. (1960s–1970s) a large comb, made of wood or plastic, for combing an Afro or a "natural." (EF, RDSL, p. 248.) See "Fork."

Nature's call n. (1900s–1990s) the need to urinate. (FR.) Example: "I feel nature's call." SNU.

Natural woman n. (1960s–1970s) a very positive term for a heterosexual female; a woman who commands respect; a well-adjusted woman. (EF, RDSL, p. 248.) SNCU.

Naughty by nature (1990s) a popular rap group ("O.P.P." and "Ghetto Bastard").

Nearer-my-God-to-Thee n. (1930s–1940s) "good" hair or straight, silky hair; used with irony and humor. (ZNH, AM, p. 95.) Example: "You got that righteous moss—or do you call it Nearer-my-God-to-Thee?—no wonder all the chicks all for you." SNU. See "Righteous moss."

[The] Needle n. (1930s–1990s) a drug addict's hypodermic needle. (HEG, DAUL, p. 144.) DCU.

Needle park n. (1960s) a narrow strip of green in a sea of concrete and metal traffic at Broadway and Amsterdam Avenue, West 71st Street, Sherman Square, New York City, where narcotics addicts congregate to get high. (RRL, DAZ, p. 182.) DCU.

Neck-breaking it v. (1950s–1990s) to move swiftly. (FR.) SNU.

Ned n. (1970s) any extremely dark-complected African-American male. (FGC, DARE, p. 296.) Chicago use.

Nefertiti Flattop n. (1990s) male hairstyle with a flat top. ("Guilt Trips," *The New Yorker*, April 5, 1993, p. 112.)

Negatory adj. (1900s–1950s) variant of "negative." (FR.) Example: "Kathleen is a nice lady and everything and God knows she's a good neighbor and she treats her children right, but I swear 'fore God I can't understand how she lets herself get into one negatory situation after another with these dead-beating men what keep coming along." SNU.

Negro n. (1630s–1990s) To call someone a "Negro" is another way of calling that person an "Uncle Tom." The word "Negro," in itself, does not qualify as a slang term except in this sense of renaming something. The acceptability (or the lack of acceptability) of terms black people use for self-identification has always been in a state of flux. A new generation traditionally rejects the terminology of the preceding one; after the mid-seventies, a "Negro" was a black person accused of cultural or racial disloyalty. (JSF, AON, p. 386; DC, BJ, p. 73; EF, RDSL, p. 248.) See "Uncle Tom."

[The] Negro fever n. (1750s–1860s) the drive to own slaves as a status symbol; in order to elevate oneself from the class of "poor white," this was one of the country's earliest emblems of the class struggle. Some ironic black use. (FB, STOS, p. 345.) SNU.

Negro overseer n. (1740s–1860s) a slave driver. (SBF, IHAT, p. 36.) SU.

Negro quarters n. (SBF, IHAT, p. 36.) See "Quarters."

Negro thief n. (1820s–1860s) anyone, white or black, who helped slaves escape to freedom. (SBF, IHAT, p. 36.) SU.

Neigho, pops (1900s–1930s) offhand response meaning no, did not; don't; to disagree. "Neigho" is a variant of "nay" or "no way," "nothing doing"; "pops" is any Joe or pal. (DB, OHHJ, p. 144; WF, DAS, p. 352; CC, OMMM, NCCHD, p. 258.) SU.

Nellie's belly adv. (1980s) playing it as it is. (GS, TT, p. 58.) Black golfers use.

New double six n. (1930s–1940s) a new year; said as one faces the new year; twelve forthcoming months. (DB, OHHJ, p. 144.) Harlem; SNU.

New Jack City n. (1990s) any black neighborhood like the one presented in the film *New Jack City*; South-central Los Angeles. YCU.

New Jerusalem n. (1860s) After the Civil War, slaves thought of their new condition as freed people as a "New Jerusalem." As such it was "a day of great rejoicing." (Elizabeth Botume, *First Days Amongst the Contrabands*, 1969, reprinted from the 1893 edition, p. 218.) SU.

New nigger n. (1630s–1860s) in the early days of slavery, a black person newly arrived in chains from Africa; later, a new slave recently purchased and brought to live on the plantation. (CCJ, NMGC, p. 169.) SU.

New school n. (1990s) musicians with a new vision of musical composition.

New thing n. (1960s) in jazz, an aggressive and original attitude and feeling, as demonstrated in the music of artists like Ornette Coleman, Eric Dolphy, Cecil Taylor, John Coltrane, Sun Ra, Pharoah Sanders. (RSG, JT, p. 188.) JMFU.

[Get] Next to [someone] v. (1950s–1960s) to attempt or to succeed in becoming intimate with someone. (AL, MJR, p. 16.) SNU.

NG adj. (1920s–1940s) short for "no good." (AL, MJR, p. 238.) SU.

Nice adj. (1950s–1980s) to feel very well in all or many respects; to be high. (FR.) Example: "I'm nice. I don't need anything." SNU.

Nickel n. (1940s–1960s) five-dollar bill. (DB, OHHJ, p. 144; RSG, JT, p. 188; DC, BJ, p. 73; CS, vol. 3, no. 2, p. 35.) See "Nickle Note."

[Make a] Nickel cry v. (1930s–1990s) budgeting to the penny; same as "penny pinching." (FR.) SNU.

Nickel-dime; nickel-dime [someone or it] n., v. (1960s–1980s) any "small-time" operation; to deal, operate, go, or work in small terms or with very little cash. (EF, RDSL, p. 248.) Example: (woman speaking) "That nigger came round here every day last week with his no-count, nickel-dime ass, trying to hit on me." SNU.

Nickel note n. (1940s–1960s) five-dollar bill. (DB, OHHJ, p. 144; RSG, JT, p. 188; CC, OMMM, NCCHD, p. 258; DC, BJ, p. 73; CS, vol. 3, no. 2, p. 35.) JMFU.

Nickelette n. (1930s–1940s) a jukebox into which a music listener places a nickel. (DB, OHHJ, p. 144; CC, OMMM, NCCHD, p. 258.) Harlem; SNCU.

Nickynacks n. (1760s–1860s) of Gullah origin; knicknacks or snacks. (AEG, BB, p. 315.) SU.

Nig n. (1840s–1940s) short for "nigger." (See Harriet E. Wilson, *Our Nig*, 1859; WF, DAS, p. 354.) SNU.

Nigger n. (1620s–1990s) pejorative term for African-American; appellation for an African-American. Some researchers believe the word "nigger" may be derived from "nick," as in nicking a coin; a "niggler" clips and files gold coins; "niggling" is "cutting awkwardly"; "nig" is also a variant form of nick; to "niggle," in early English, is to have sex. SBF believes the word originated in northern England in the Irish dialect (*Negar*)—an attempt to pronounce the Spanish word *negro*—around 1587; in any case, by the seventeenth century the word "negar" was widely accepted as a variant pronounciation of "negro." Others believe "nigger" possibly came from the French *negre*. Clarence E. Walker writes (in *Deromanticizing Black History: Critical Essays and Reappraisals*, 1991, p. xxi) that "the word 'nigger' was and is a crucial component in [the] . . . process of objectification." When used by a white person in addressing a black person, usually it is offensive and disparaging—and has been so since the end of the Civil War; used by black people among themselves, it is a racial term with undertones of warmth and goodwill—reflecting, aside from the irony, a tragi-comic sensibility that is aware, on some level, of the emotional history of the race. In the nineties members of the black youth culture say that "nigger" is no longer derogatory, that it's used to mean friend, brother, man, person, girl, woman. Even white people can be niggers, too, they say; "nigger" does not imply race; speaking of the U.S. government, Queen Latifah was quoted in *Newsweek*: "Those niggers don't know what the fuck they doing." (JSF, AON, p. 390; EP, DU, p. 469; FG, DVT, np; CRM, BP, p. 304; EF, RDSL, p. 248; SBF, IHAT, pp. 56–57.) SNU.

[Bad-assed] Nigger n. (EF, RDSL, p. 248.) See "Bad-assed nigger" and "Nigger."

[Dog] Nigger n. (EF, RDSL, p. 248.) See "Bad-assed nigger" and "Nigger."

[No-count] Nigger n. (EF, RDSL, p. 248.) See "Bad-assed nigger" and "Nigger."

Nigger babies n. (1860s) a term coined by Confederate General Hardee; refers to the projectiles shot from "swamp angels" (cannons) at Charleston under the direction of General Gilmore. Some black ironic use. (JSF, AON, pp. 390–391.)

Nigger boy n. (1820s–1950s) a common name for a young African-American. (SBF, IHAT, p. 57.) SNU.

Nigger breaker n. (1740s–1860s) a slave driver; an overseer on a plantation. (SBF, IHAT, p. 36.) White and black plantation use.

Niggerdemos n. (1800s–1990s) slave variant term for Nicodemus of the Bible. (FR.) SU.

Nigger driver n. (1900s–1950s) a white man hired to oversee and drive black prisoners in picking cotton or some other fieldwork; specifically, the overseer at Parchman Penitentiary, which, as late as

1957, was still being run like a brutal plantation. (AL, LWBB, p. 257.) SU, PU.

Nigger flicker n. (1950s–1970s) a long-blade knife or a razor carried in the pocket as a weapon of self-defense or attack. (EF, RDSL, p. 248.)

Nigger flipper n. (1850s–1930s) device for flinging or propelling small rocks and such; a slingshot; some black use but primarily white use. (FGC, DARE, p. 480.) SU, MWU.

Nigger front n. (1970s–1980s) fashionably dressed. (EF, RDSL, p. 248.) Watts and South-central Los Angeles; YCU, PPU. See "Front."

Nigger heaven n. (1870s–1940s) the balcony in a theater where black people had to sit if they were to see a film or a performance; Harlem. (SBF, IHAT, p. 57; See Carl Van Vechten, *Nigger Heaven*, 1926; WF, DAS, p. 354.) Harlem use; SNU.

Nigger-hounds n. (1780s–1860s) bloodhounds used to track runaway slaves. (JSF, AON, p. 386.) SU.

Niggerhouse n. (1700s–1860s) a plantation term; a slave's personal shack in the quarters. (AEG, BB, p. 315.) SU.

Niggerhouse yard n. (1700s–1860s) a plantation term; the yard around a slave's house in the quarters. (AEG, BB, p. 315. SU.

Nigger in Charge (NIC) n. (1960s) any African-American in a leadership position in business or industry; used ironically to refer to a black boss. See "Head Nigger in Charge." (FR.) SNU.

Niggerish adj. (1930s) stingy and selfish. (AW, CP, p. 115.) SNU.

Niggerism n. (1800s–1960s) refers to the philosophies, customs, and culture of African-Americans. (JSF, AON, p. 391; RHdeC, NB, p. 35.) Rare. SNU.

Nigger jail n. (1800s–1860s) a holding house for slaves; slave pen. Creating great symbolism, many of these brick houses were turned into black tenements after the Civil War. (FB, STOS, p. 171.) Example: "Before the war they kept us in these nigger jails as slaves, and now after the war we stuck in the same same slave pens." South Carolina and Georgia use.

Nigger killer(s) n. (1850s–1860s) usually a young white man or boy on horseback looking for runaway or stray slaves; after the Civil War "nigger killers" rode by night in all the slave states, terrorizing blacks when and where they could find them. (FR.) SU.

Nigger-lover n. (1780s–1990s) a white person who associates with or who relates to black people on a human level; a white term, originally offensive and disparaging. (FR.) SNU.

Nigger luck n. (1870s–1920s) a term used ironically referring to good luck; putting the best face on a bad, if not tragic, situation. (JSF, AON, p. 391.) SU.

Nigger monger n. (1730s–1860s) a slave trader. (SBF, IHAT, p. 36.) SU.

Nigger night n. (1930s) Saturday night. (FR.) SNU.

Nigger-pot n. (1900s–1930s) homemade whiskey; bootleg liquor; moonshine liquor; picked up from whites and used ironically. (WF, DAS, p. 697.) SU.

Nigger rich n. (1930s–1960s) having a pocket roll of singles covered with a twenty-dollar bill; maintaining outward signs of wealth without any real money. (CRM, BP, p. 304.) SNU.

Nigger rig n. (1980s–1990s) a homemade ramp used for skating; any makeshift skateboard ramp. (JM, WPC, p. 31.) Oakland, California, and SCU.

Nigger's bankroll n. (1970s–1990s) a roll of singles with a large bill, such as a twenty- or a fifty-dollar bill, on top. (EF, RDSL, p. 248.) See "California bankroll" and "Chicago bankroll."

Nigger show n. (1870s–1900s) a minstrel show with performing white men in blackface. (SBF, IHAT, p. 57.) SNU.

Nigger spit n. (1880s–1890s) "the lumps of demerara in sugar"; picked up from white use. (AB, DSJC, p. 82.) Some plantation and later use.

Nigger steak n. (1930s) beef liver.

Nigger-toe n. (1880s–1950s) a dark brown walnut; Brazil nut; picked up from white use, used ironically. (CM, CW, Gayl Jones, "White Rat," p. 378; WF, DAS, p. 354; SBF, IHAT, p. 57.) SU.

Nigger trader n. (SBF, IHAT, p. 36.) See "Nigger Monger."

[The] Nigger War n. (1860s–1880s) the American Civil War; picked up from white use. (FGC, DARE, p. 4.) SNU.

Nigger worshipper n. (1840s–1870s) any white person who believed in the humanity of black people; any white person who spoke out against slavery; members of the Republican party. Picked up from whites and used ironically. (JSF, AON, p. 391.) SU.

Niggery adj. (1700s–1890s) pertaining to black people; acting like a "nigger." (JSF, AON, p. 391.) SU.

Niggra n. (1700s–1940s) a variant of "nigger"; used only ironically and in cynical imitation of southern white use. (WF, DAS, p. 354.) SU.

Night riders n. (1860s–1990s) terrorist groups organized after the Civil War; Klu Klux Klan and related groups, composed of young white men out for some "rough fun," rode in the night on horseback on black killing missions. These young men were descended, professionally speaking, from the earlier patterollers who tracked down runaway slaves. (SBF, IHAT, p. 294.) See "Nigger killer[s]."

Nightstick n. (1920s–1940s) penis. (FR.) SNU.

Nina n. (1990s) a gun. (FR.) WCU.

Nine n. (1990s) a gun, especially a handgun. SGU.

Nip n. (1970s–1990s) Japanese male or female. (EF, RDSL, p. 248.) Watts and South-central Los Angeles use.

Nip joint n. (1950s–1960s) a place where bootleg liquor is sold. (RDP, SRO, p. 8, 13.) Harlem; NECU.

Nipsey Russell a popular black comedian.

Nitty-gritty n. (1960s–1970s) unvarnished facts; underbelly of a situation; core; the basics. (RSG, JT, p. 188; WF, DAS, p. 697.) JMFU, SCU, YCU, SNU.

Nix out v. (1900s–1940s) to throw away. (DB, OHHJ, p. 144; CC, OMMM, NCCHD, p. 258.) Harlem; SNU.

No account [person] adj., n. (1800s–1950s) of little worth; without a sense of responsibility; a person on whom it is not possible to depend; shiftless person; a manipulative or "criminal-minded" person. (JSF, AON, p. 392; WF, DAS, p. 356; EF, RDSL, p. 248.) SU.

Noble n. (1960s–1970s) inmate term for a popular fellow inmate who is respected for his strength of character, courage, and leadership qualities. (DW, TL, p. 186.) PU.

No-brand cigarette n. (1970s–1990s) a marijuana cigarette, better known as a "joint." (EF, RDSL, p. 248.) DCU.

No class adj. (1960s–1990s) one who is uncouth; lacking social grace or simple dignity; deficient in social skills. (CS, vol. 3, no. 2, p. 35.) SNCU, YCU, DCU, PU, PPU.

[The] Nod n. (1930s–1990s) sleep or nap; the lethargic, sluggish, drowsy posture of one on heroin; stuporlike state experienced by a junkie succumbing to drugs, usually in a standing position; falling from drowsiness caused by narcotics. (CLC, TS, p. 255; RSG, JT, p. 189; WF, DAS, p. 356; DB, OHHJ, p. 144; DC, BJ, p. 73; RRL, DAZ, pp. 185–186; CS, vol. 3, no. 2, p. 35.) JMFU, DCU. See "Nodding out."

[On the] Nod adj. (RRL, DAZ, p. 186.) See "[The] Nod."

Nodding out v. (1960s) to be in a drug stupor. (DB, OHHJ, p. 144; RSG, JT, p. 189; CC, OMMM, NBCCHD, p. 258; JH, PBL, p. 85; DC, BJ, p. 73; RRL, DAZ, pp. 185–186; CS, vol. 3, no. 2, p. 35.) JMFU, DCU. See "High."

Nod out v. (EF, RDSL, p. 248.) See "[The] Nod."

Noggin n. (1850s–1940s) in Old English this word meant "small quantity of drink," but later, among black speakers, it meant the human head. (HEG, DAUL, p. 145; WF, DAS, p. 357.) SU.

Nohow adv. (1700s–1950s) anyhow. (JSF, AON, p. 392.) Example: "It don't make no difference nohow."

Noise [off] n., v. (1930s–1990s) loud, silly talk; to engage in such talk. (WF, DAS, p. 357; HEG, DAUL, p. 146.) Examples: "The fucker likes to noise off all the time—that's why I don't want him at the party"; and "Fuck that noise, man—get out of my face." YCU, SCU, DCU, SNCU. See "Wolfing."

Noisola n. (1930s–1940s) a record player; jukebox. (DB, OHHJ, p. 144.) Harlem; NCU.

No jive n. (CS, vol. 3, no. 2, p. 35.) See "Jive."

No Jonas trip played on me adj. (1950s–1960s) Nobody can take me for a chump. (CLC, TS, p. 255.) DCU, SCU, PU.

No-name brand [cigarette] (EF, RDSL, p. 248.) DCU. See "No-brand cigarette."

Nontoucher n. (1980s–1990s) a crack user who resists physical contact while or directly after smoking crack cocaine. Many smokers crave human contact at such times. (TW, CH, p. 150.) DCU.

Noodle v., n. (1930s–1960s) in jazz, to play in a testy manner; also, the human head. (RSG, JT, p. 189.) JMFU.

Nookie n. (1920s–1950s) derogatory term for the vagina; sexual intercourse; the female as "body." (WF, DAS, p. 357.) SNU.

Nose flute v. (1950s) to make a loud snorting sound through the mouth and nose in a deliberately rude manner. (CM, CW, Toni Cade Bambara, "The Lesson," p. 351.) NCU.

Nose habit n. (1960s–1970s) having the habit of sniffing narcotics through the nose. (CS, vol. 3, no. 2, p. 36.) DCU.

[To have a] Nose job n. (1960s–1970s) to be in love with or obsessive or preoccupied about someone. (CS, vol. 3, no. 2, p. 36.) Watts and South-central Los Angeles; YCU, SCU.

Nose [wide] open adj. (1950s–1960s) to be under another's spell, especially to be in love. (HLF, RJPD, p. 171; DC, BJ, p. 73.) Example: "That boy's nose is so wide open you could drive a ten-ton truck up in it." SNU, YCU, SCU.

No shit exclam. (1890s–1990s) an exclamation; a declaration of truth; absolute truth. (WF, DAS, p. 358.) SNU.

No stuff (1940s–1960s) an expression that implies sincerity. (FR.) SNU.

No sweat (1970s–1990s) easy to manage; no problem. (FR.) SNU.

Not adv. (1990s) variant of no; usually a response to a question. (FR.) SNU.

Nothing happening (1940s–1950s) often a response to "What's happening?" The implication is that things are status quo or more than simply slow. (RSG, JT, p. 189.) JMFU, DCU, SCU, YCU, SNCU.

Nothing shaking (1940s–1950s) the usual response to "What's happening?" (RSG, JT, p. 189.) JMFU, DCU, SCU, YCU, SNCU.

Nothing to nobody (1840s–1950s) request or resolution to keep quiet. (FR.) Example, "Don't say nothing to nobody." SU.

Nothing to the bear but his curly hair (1930s–1940s) an expression explaining someone's cowardice; lack of courage. (ZNH, AM, p. 95.) SNU.

Not wrapped too tight adj. (1970s) to be slightly odd in behavior. (FR.) Example: "That dude over there playing with his food ain't wrapped too tight." SNCU.

Nowhere adj. (1930s–1950s) applied to a really dull or square person who is also undesirable; also, a place or thing of the same quality. (MM, RB, p. 373; DC, BJ, p. 7; WF, DAS, p. 697.) SNU. See "Like Jack the bear."

Now you cooking with gas v., adj. (1930s–1940s) an expression of approval; agreement. (ZNH, AM, p. 95.) NCU.

Nubbin pron., adv., adj. (1800s–1890s) variant of "nothing" or "nuffin"; Indian corn. (JSF, AON, p. 394.) SU.

Number n. (1930s–1990s) in jazz, a tune or composition. (FR.) JMFU.

Number one n. (1950s–1990s) first-degree murder. (EF, RDSL, p. 248.) PU, SCU, DCU.

Number-one n. (1960s–1990s) a person's best-loved spouse or sweetheart. (EF, RDSL, p. 248.) SNCU.

Numbers n. (1920s–1950s) policy numbers or lottery numbers based on daily official numbers from legal sources such as the racetrack, the clearinghouse, or the stock market; illegal gambling game of chance in which the winning numbers are taken from the bank exchange and balances each day, using the seventh and eight digits of the exchanges, and the seventh of the balances. The source is the daily newspapers. (CVV, p. 286; HEG, DAUL, p. 146.) SNCU.

Nusering v. (1890s–1980s) variant of "nursing." (FR.) SNU.

Nut n. (1900s–1990s) a crazy-acting person; an eccentric; irrational. (SL, RJON, p. 10; HLF, RJPD, p. 171.) SNU.

Nut roll n. (1940s–1950s) one who acts foolish; a stupid-acting person; eccentric; "crazy nigger." (IS, PSML, p. 316; WKB, JMC, PS, p. 50.) PPU, DCU, SCU, PU.

Nuts n. (1700s–1950s) testicles. (FR.) SNU.

[Get one's] Nuts off v. (1930s–1990s) to have an orgasm or to ejaculate. (FR.) SNU.

Nutted out v. (1960s) usually a positive term; exhibited eccentric behavior. (RSG, JT, p. 190.) Example: "The audience nutted out when he put down his sax and picked up Billy's trumpet and started blowing all this funky shit." JMFU, SNCU.

Nutty adj., interj. (1950s) superior. (RSG, JT, p. 190.) See "Nutted out."

Nutty as a fruitcake adj. (1950s–1990s) insane; crazy-acting. (FR.) SNU.

O

O n. (1930s–1960s) short for "opium." (WF, DAS, p. 361; RSG, JT, p. 191; RRL, DAZ, p. 188.) DCU.

Oaktown n. (1970s–1990s) variant of "Oakland" (California); name of a black community in Oakland. (JM, WPC) Oakland, Bay Area use.

Obeah n. (1700s–1920s) an African witchcraft system practiced in the Caribbean and to some extent during the early years of slavery in slave states. (JSF, AON, p. 396; JEH, AAC, p. 231.) SU.

Octoroon n. (1950s–1950s) a white-looking African-American; a person with one-eighth African ancestry and the rest of any of the various European lines. (SBF, IHAT, p. 56.) SNU.

Ofaginzy n. (1800s–1950s) white person; a longer form of "ofay," "ofaginzy" may be of African origin. (HV, AHAE, p. 145; SL, RJON, p. 361; WF, DAS, p. 361.) SNU.

Ofay n. (1800s–1950s) white man; possibly of African origin, stemming from *bama fe* or *Gola fua* or *Ndob fowe*; commonly believed to be derived from "foe" in Pig Latin. (HV, AHAE, p. 145; ZNH, AM, p. 95; LA, SM, p. 147; CVV, NH, p. 286; JH, PBL, p. 85; DB, OHHJ, p. 144; DC, BJ, p. 74.) SNU.

Ofay watcher n. (1960s) an oppressed person who carefully observes whites and their actions. (See Eldridge Cleaver, *Soul on Ice*.) (FR.) SCU.

Off v. (1950s–1960s) to beat up; to kill; to get rid of something; crazy. (CLC, TS, p. 255; DC, BJ, p. 74; DW, TL, p. 18; EF, RDSL, p. 248; HLF, RJPD, p. 171.) Example: "I'll off the dude if he comes around my number-one again." See "Blaze on [one]."

Off beat n., adj. (1900s–1960s) in jazz, a cymbal note hit by the drummer on the off beat; odd; fantastic. (WF, DAS, p. 362; RSG, JT, p. 191.) JMFU.

Offed vt. (1970s) murdered. (FR.) SCU.

Off-brand adj. (1970s–1990s) a person whose behavior is considered unusual or different from one's own. (EF, RDSL, p. 248.) South-central Los Angeles; SCY, YCU.

Off-brand cigarette n. (EF, RDSL, p. 248.) See "No-brand cigarette."

Office piano n. (1940s) a typewriter. (DB, OHHJ, p. 144.) Harlem; JMFU.

Off note n. (1900s–1960s) a note that is off pitch. (RSG, JT, p. 191.) JMFU. See "Off-beat."

Off the cob adj. (1930s–1940s) out of style or backwards. (DB, OHHJ, p. 144.) Harlem; SNU.

Off the wall adj. (1950s–1960s) a weak excuse; insincere; outlandishly incorrect; misinformed; foolish; irrelevant. (CRM, BP, p. 304; DC, BJ, p. 74; EF, RDSL, p. 248.) Example: "He's totally off the wall, man. Pay him no mind." SNCU, YCU, PPU, SCU.

Off-time jive n. (1930s–1940s) a weak excuse. (DB, OHHJ, p. 144.) Harlem; JMFU, SNCU.

O.G. n. (1900s–1950s) Old Girl; mother. (DC, BJ, p. 73.) Example: "My O.G. just started getting her social security checks in the mail." SU, MWU.

Oil n., v. (1940s–1960s) whiskey; hard liquor; graft; money to pay off the police; to beat; whip. (IS, PSML, p. 316; DB, OHHJ, p. 144; DC, BJ, p. 74; EF, RDSL, p. 248.) SCU, DCU.

Oil bags n. (1960s) a person's rear end; buttocks. (CS, vol. 3, no. 2, p. 36.) Rare. Watts, Los Angeles; YCU.

Oil burner adj. (1950s–1960s) a heavy drug habit. (CLC, TS, p. 255.) DCU.

Oiled behind n. (DB, OHHJ, p. 144.) See "Oiled Head."

Oiled head n. (1930s–1940s) a whipped head—one beaten by a police nightstick. (DB, OHHJ, p. 144.) Harlem; SNCU.

Oiler n. (1930s–1940s) one who is prone to fistfights. (DB, OHHJ, p. 144.) Harlem; SNCU.

Oink n. (1960s) a cop; policeman; law-enforcement officer. (FR.) SCU.

Okay; O.K. n. (1620s–1990s) yes; all right; probably from West African sources: *o-ke* (Djabo); *waw-kayk, waw ke* (Wolof); *o-kay* (Dogno); *o-key* (Mandingo) *eeyi-kay* (Fula West). Also these possibly converged with American "okay," as used by Martin Van Buren in his abbreviation of "Old Kinderhook." "OK" ("orally korrect") was, according to Vere, an abbreviation Gen. Andrew Jackson used to initial paperwork as a symbol of his approval; an early American abbreviation of the (incorrect) spelling of orally correct ("orally korrect"). But it seems much more likely that the original African form influenced all such later variations. "Oh ki" was being used by blacks in the South by the 1770s and in Jamaica at least twenty years before evidence of "okay" in the speech of New England. (HV, AHAE, p. 146; WF, DAS, p. 362; JH, PBL, p. 85; JSF, AON, p. 398.) SNU.

Okey-doke n. (1930s–1950s) a con game; stupid talk; this is a variant of white use of "hokey-dokey" for anything positive; all right—but black use refers to anything negative, "jive." (IS, PSML, p. 316; WF, DAS, pp. 362–363; MHB, JS, np.) SNU.

Okey-dokey n. See "Okey-doke."

Okra n. (1770s–1990s) *kingombo* [Bantu]; once a slang word, okra has its origins in the word *nkru* [Tshi]. (HV, AHAE, p. 146; JSF, AON, p. 398.) SNU.

Old [woman or man] n. (1780s–1900s) a spouse; wife; husband; archaic. (WF, DAS, p. 363.) See "Old lady."

Old Chocolate George Godfrey, prizefighter popular in the 1880s; fought Professor Hadley, another Negro fighter, in 1882. John L. Sullivan refereed the fight.

Old country n. (1960s–1990s) the Deep South; Africa. (DC, BJ, p. 74.) See "Down home."

Old cuffee n. (1650s–1900s) a black person; an African; an African-American; Negro; colored person. (ZNH, AM, p. 95.) SNU.

Old-fogeyism n. (1900s–1940s) a derogatory term for a blues singer's style; a blues style with strong African and Delta roots; a blues style not much dependent on the European diatonic scale. (AL, LWBB, p. 454.) SU.

Old Glory n. (1880s–1940s) anything out of fashion; stale. (MHB, np.) SU.

Old Hannah n. (1700s–1900s) the sun; sunlight. (HV, AHAE, p. 146.) SU.

Oldie(s) n. (1900s–1990s) an old song or tune; an old record; anything old. (WF, DAS, p. 363.)

Old lady n. (1900s–1950s) a man's female mate; from the twenties to the fifties, male term for wife; common-law wife; a pimp's prostitute. (LA, SM, p. 122; RSG, p. 192; DR, BASL, p. 251; CRM, BP, p. 304; DC, BJ, p. 74; EF, RDSL, p. 248; RDA, TB, p. 69.) SNU. See "Old" and "Old man."

Old Maker n. (1900s–1940s) the Christian God. (AW, CP, p.) SU.

Old man n. (1900s–1950s) a woman's male mate; a husband. (RSG, p. 192; EF, RDSL, p. 248.) SNU.

Old man Mose n. (1940s) death or time. (DB, OHHJ, p. 144.) SNU.

Old massa [marster] n. (1680s–1860s) Negro slave term of address to a white slaveholder; variant pronunciation of old master. (FR.) SU.

Old Ned n. (1830s–1860s) slave name for bacon. (JLD, BN, p. 8.) SU.

Old saw n. (1870s–1940s) one's wife. (DB, OHHJ, p. 144.) SNU.

Olorum n. (1620s–1860s) a Yoruba god worshipped by black people from various Yoruba ethnic groups during slavery. (SK, PC, pp. 175–179.) SU.

On adj. (1940s–1950s) informed, sophisticated; "in"; having an advantage; having an addictive drug habit. (RSG, JT, p. 192.) Example: "Look at him go! He's really on tonight!" JMFU.

On a mission v. (1990s) to have a goal or project in mind. (FR.) YCU.

On a tight leash adj. (1950s–1960s) restricted; restrained; being faithful in marriage or in a love relationship. (EF, RDSL, p. 248.) SNCU.

On [one's] case v., adv. (1950s) giving unsolicited advice. (FR.) Example: "She was on his case day and night." SNU.

One bill n. (1980s–1990s) a hundred dollars. (FR.) YCU, SCU.

One-nighter n. See "One-night stand."

One-night stand n. (1920s–1960s) for jazz musicians, a one-night —or brief—engagement in a club; a booking for one appearance in a nightclub or theater; a term picked up from show business slang. (John A. Williams, *Night Song*, 1961, p. 100.) JMFU.

Onest; onst n., adj., conj. (1700s–1940s) variant of "once." (JSF, AON, p. 402.) Example: "Onest you finish the dishes, take out the garbage." SU, MWU.

On flake v. (1970s–1980s) to pass out from using narcotics. (EF, RDSL, p. 248.) DCU.

On [one's] J adj. (1990s) to be alert. (FR.) YCU.

On [one's] job adj. (1950s–1980s) to be alert and in charge. (EF, RDSL, p. 248.) SNU.

On ice n. (1950s–1960s) in prison; in solitary confinement. (FR.) PU, SCU.

On it adj. (1950s–1960s) to be "hooked" or addicted to a narcotic. (DC, BJ, p. 74.) DCU. See "On."

Onion act n. (1930s–1940s) any thing or situation considered extremely wrong; an unacceptable, offensive act. (DB, OHHJ, p. 144.) SNU.

On the avenue n. (1990s) in the streets; where the common people live. (FR.) Example: "Check it out down on the avenue." YCU, SCU.

On the beam adj. (1940s) smart, alert. (DB, OHHJ, p. 144.) Harlem; SNCU.

On the beam on short-cut plays adj. (1940s) smart, alert. (DB, OHHJ, p. 144.) See "On the beam."

On the DL adj. (1990s) "down low"; feeling depressed or tired. (FR.) Example: "I'm on the DL today. Catch you tomorrow." SCU, YCU.

On the down beat adj. (1940s) losing popularity; to be depressed; to be without money. Apparently this use of "down beat" has nothing to do with its meaning in jazz. (MHB, np.) Rare. SU.

On the make adj. (1950s–1970s) sexually aggressive. (FR.) SCU, YCU.

On the mike v. (1980s–1990s) to rap to a large audience from a stage. (FR.) Rap and hip-hop performers use.

On the needle adj. (1940s–1960s) to inject heroin or some other narcotic into one's veins on a regular basis. (RRL, DAZ, p. 188.) DCU.

On the nut adj. (1960s–1970s) to be penniless; without cash; broke. (DW, TL, p. 186.) SCU.

On the Q.T. n. (1950s–1970s) a secret or something whispered; undercover action. (FR.) YCU, SCU.

On the rag adj. (1930s–1970s) a woman's term for her menstrual time, "rag" referring to a sanitary napkin. (EF, RDSL, p. 248.) SNU.

On the roam v., n. (1950s–1960s) to wander in a deliberate or apparently directionless manner; prostitute walking the streets. (DW, TL, p. 186.) SCU, PPU.

On the set adj. (1960s–1970s) to be in a particular location, especially a street corner. (FR.) See "Scene."

On the [something] side adj. (1950s–1970s) aspect; part; degree. (CRM, BP, p. 304; EF, RDSL, p. 248.) Example: "He's not much to look at, but on the taking-an-interest-in-the-kid's side he's a real good man." SNU.

On the square adj., n. (1930s–1950s) innocence; sincerity; to declare one's innocence; to be confronted to declare one's honesty; truthfulness. (RDA, TB, p. 49.) SNU.

On the under adj. (1990s) on the sly; secretly done. (FR.) YCU, SCU.

[To be] On to [one or something] (1960s–1990s) to have knowledge of. (FR.) SNU.

Oo-bla-dee n. (1700s–1950s) well-known jazz expression, may have African origins: *abada* (Mandingo); *abadaa, abadaa-aabaadi* (Hausa); used in modern times as a playful improvisational jazz sound. (HV, AHAE, p. 146; RSG, JL, pp. 219–220.) See "Oo-bop-she-bam." JMFU.

Oo-bop-she-bam n. (1940s–1960s) playful, improvisational jazz sounds; an existential jazz phrase; perhaps a mystic effort to comment on the inscrutable in the black man's social, moral, and spiritual condition in the United States, or simply another way of talking to that "sense" of mystery often referred to as God. (Hear Dizzy Gillespie, "Oo-Bop-She-Bam;" RSG, JL, pp. 219–220.) JMFU. See "Oo-bla-dee."

Oofay n. (WF, DAS, p. 367.) See "Ofay."

Oofus n. (1930s–1960s) a dumb, awkward person. (WF, DAS, p. 367.) Harlem; NSCU.

Oo-pappa-da (1940s–1950s) playful, improvisational verbal jazz sounds. (BH, LSB, p. 207.) JMFU.

Oowee! interj. (1940s–1950s) an expression of shock or delight or excitement. (RSG, JT, pp. 193–194). Example: "Oowee! Look at all these people!" SNU.

Oozing v. (1930s–1940s) to "cruise" the streets, especially in search of members of the opposite sex. (ZNH, AM, p. 94.) SNU.

OP's [something] n. (1930s–1960s) other people's [anything]. (WF, DAS, p. 368.) Example: "I've been smoking op's so long I forget what my own brand taste like." SNU.

OPB n. (1930s–1950s) other people's brand; reference to a hypothetical brand of cigarettes. (FR.) SCU, YCU.

Open adj. (1970s) short for open-minded. (FR.) SNU.

[Nose] Open adj. (CRM, BP, p. 304.) See "[To have one's] Nose open."

OPP n. (1990s) Other people's property (somebody's wife or husband). (FR.) SNU.

Oprah (Oprahed, O-pray) v. (1990s) to engage in persistent intimate questioning. (FR.) Example: "Girl, Collette Oprahed the whole story out of Danita about what she and Dennis did while Amber was in the hospital having her twins." SNU.

Orchestration n. (1940s) an overcoat. (DB, OHHJ, p. 144; CC, OMMM, NCCHD, p. 258.) Harlem; JMFU.

Oreo n. (1960s–1970s) derogatory; black person who is culturally Anglo-American; "white on the inside, black on the outside." (EF, RDSL, p. 248; SBF, IHAT, p. 49.) SNU.

Oscar n. (1950s–1960s) a man's nickname for his penis. (HLF, RJPD, p. 171.) Rare. New York City use.

Ossified adj. (1950s–1970s) to be blind drunk or very high from narcotics. (EF, RDSL, p. 248.) DCU, SNCU.

[All] Original(s) n. (1920s–1970s) any person of African descent; a party or gathering to which only black people are invited. (CRM, BP, p. 304.) SNU, SCU, PPU, YCU.

Other man n. (1930s–1940s) the white man, especially one who is a merchant in a black neighborhood. (RSG, JT, p. 195.) SNU.

[The] Other shore n. See "[The] Other side."

[The] Other side n. (1850s–1940s) Heaven; used in spirituals and blues. (Hear Charlie Patton, "I'm Goin' Home," *King of the Delta Blues*, 1991.) SNU.

[Far] Out adj. (1940s–1950s) a show of great imagination and skill; also, extremely unusual. (WF, DAS, p. 369; RSG, JT, p. 195.) Example: "His music is way out!" JMFU.

Out box n. (1990s) the start or beginning of something.

Outfit n. (1950s–1960s) the various artifacts used by an addict. (CLC, TS, p. 255; IS, PSML, p. 316; RRL, DAZ, p. 191.) DCU. See "Works."

Outlaw n. (1950s–1970s) a pimp's derogatory term for a prostitute working on her own. (CRM, BP, p. 305.) PPU.

[Go] Out of [one's] head adj. (1950s–1990s) to be overcome with emotion or excitement; overcome with grief; overcome with sorrow or sadness. (FR.) SNU.

Out of it adj. (1950s–1970s) unfashionable; unpopular idea; excluded. (RSG, p. 196.) Example: "Right after I broke up with my wife I was out of it for a long while, so much so that my friends stopped wanting me around." SNCU.

Out of it adj. (1950s–1960s) (EF, RDSL, p. 248.) See "Ossified."

Out of pocket adj. (1940s–1970s) a poolroom term: to miss the pocket; also used by pimps and in street culture in general to refer to anything that has gone wrong, to bad news, to erratic behavior. (CRM, BP, pp. 304–305). Poolroom; SCU, PPU.

Out of sight adj. (1950s–1960s) wonderful; extremely exciting idea or person or thing. (RSG, JT, p. 196; DC, BJ, p. 74; CS, vol. 3, no. 2, p. 36.) JMFU, SNCU.

Out of [one's] skull adj. (1950s–1970s) variant of "out of [one's] head;" to be distraught; to be crazed; deranged; mentally and emotionally dislocated; disoriented; drunk; high from drugs. (RSG, JT, p. 196.) JMFU, SNU.

Out of this world adj. (1920s–1940s) often used as exaggeration to mean beyond "mortal experience"; to be in touch with the extrasensorial. (RF, WJ, p. 303; DB, OHHJ, p. 144; CC, OMMM, NCCHD, p. 258.) See "Out of sight."

Out of town adj. (1960s) that which is unacceptable; off. (CS, vol. 3, no. 3, p. 9.) Example: "This dress is just out of town—no way am I going to wear it to the dance tonight." YCU, SCU.

Outside adj. (1870s–1950s) to be born out of wedlock. (AL, MJR, 33.) SU.

Out to lunch adj. (1960s–1970s) to be off; to miss the point; to be confused; neurotic; vague. (WF, DAS, p. 370; JH, PBL, p. 85; CS, vol. 3, no. 2, p. 36.) SNCU.

[Get] Over v. (1950s–1960s) to succeed; to get "over" is to accomplish an objective. (RSG, JT, p. 197.) See "Get over."

Over town n. (1930s–1950s) on the other side of town. (FR.) SCU, YCU, MWU.

Oxford n. (1940s) a Negro whose complexion is very dark; expression borrowed from Oxford shoe polish. (DB, OHHJ, p. 144.) SNU.

Oxidize v. (1800s–1900s) of Gullah origin; in the black humor of folklore and myth, to undergo a physical or spiritual transformation from human into that of an ox. (AEG, BB, p. 317.) SU.

P

Packer n. (1980s–1990s) one who performs anal intercourse. (FR.) See "Packing."

Packer n. (1980s–1990s) a long slender stick—sometimes a chopstick—used for packing in the cocaine pipe screen. (TW, CH, p. 150.) DCU.

Packing v. (1960s–1990s) carrying a gun. (DC, BJ, p. 74.) Example: "I woulda taken him out but the dude was packin', man." SCU, DCU, PU.

Packing v. (1980s–1990s) heterosexual term for performing anal intercourse. (FR.) See "Pack peanut butter." SCU.

Pack peanut butter v. (1970s–1990s) to perform anal intercourse; not a homosexual term. (EF, RDSL, p. 249.) YCU, SCU.

Pacifier bulb n. (1940s–1950s) an infant's rubber pacifier that is connected to an eyedropper in preparation for an injection of heroin. (IS, PSML, p. 317.) DCU.

Pad n. (1800s–1990s) one's home; room; apartment; bed; residence. Frances Grose lists "pad" as a "bed" as early as 1811, and Cab Calloway lists it as such as late as 1944. (DG, ICH, p. 139; WF, DAS, p. 371; LA, SM, p. 8; FG, DVT, np; CC, HDH, p. 16; MM, RB, p. 373; DB, OHHJ, p. 144; MHB, JS, np; CC, OMMM, NCCHD, p. 258; DC, BJ, p. 74; DW, TL, p. 186.) SNCU.

Paddles n. (1930s–1940s) the hands. (DB, OHHJ, p. 144.) Harlem; SNU.

Paddy n. (1940s–1990s) a white person; usually mildly pejorative but not necessarily always derogatory. (IS, TB, p. 312; WF, DAS, p.

698; EF, RDSL, p. 249; JH, PBL, p. 85; EF, BVV, p. 49; DC, BJ, p. 74.) SCU, SNU.

Padhouse n. (1930s–1940s) one's home. (SL, RJON, p. 372.) SU.

Pad of cold cream n. (1940s) an ice cream shop or parlor. (MHB, JS, np.) SU.

Pad of dry scarfs n. (1940s) a grocery store. (MHB, JS, np.) SU. See "Scarf."

Pad of galloping snapshots n. (1940s) motion picture theater. (MHB, JS, np.)

Pad of stiffs n. (1940s) a funeral parlor. (MNB, JD, np.) SNU.

Pad of stitches n. (1940s) a hospital. (MHB, JS, np.) SU.

Pad of togs-in-the-rough n. (1940s) a tailor's shop. (MHB, JS, np.) SU.

Pad of wet scarfs n. (1940s) a restaurant. (MHB, JS, np.) SU.

Pad room n. (1930s–1950s) a room in an apartment or house where drug addicts gather to get high. (WF, DAS, p. 372.) DCU.

Pail n. (1940s) the stomach. (WF, DAS, p. 372; DB, OHHJ, p. 144.) SNU.

Pain in the ass n. (1980s–1990s) something or someone difficult. (WF, DAS, p. 372.) SNU.

Pale adj. (1900s–1940s) a white person. (WF, DAS, p. 373.) SNU.

Pale faces n. (1860s–1870s) a southern group of young white men committed to violence against black people after the Civil War. (SBF, IHAT, p. 294.) SU.

Paleface n. (1880s–1960s) white person. (FR.) SNU.

Palmer House; Palmer House-ing it v., n. (1930s–1940s) flat feet; flat-footed; to walk in a flat-footed manner; fallen arches; from the excessive walking done by black waiters at the Palmer House Hotel restaurant in Chicago. (ZNH, AM, p. 95.) Chicago; NCU.

Palooka (paluka; palooker) n. (1700s–1950s) *paluka* (Bantu); violent, involuntary muscular spasms; to shake violently with convulsions; a dumb person; a less-than-first-rate boxer; average prizefighter. (HV, AHAE, p. 146; EP, DU, p. 494; WF, DAS, p. 373.) SNU.

Pammy Christy beans n. (1800s–1890s) slave term for magic or conjuring beans. (FR.) SU.

Pamper adj. (1800s–1950s) *pamba* (Bantu); to feel unsettled, uneasy, scared, anxious, or upset. (HV, AHAE, p. 146.) SU.

Pan n. (1940s) one's face. (MHB, JS, np.) Rare. SU.

Panama red n. (1970s–1990s) marijuana believed to be native to Panama; any locally grown marajuana. (EF, RDSL, p. 249; RRL, DAZ, pp. 193–194.) DCU.

Panatella; panatela n. (1930s–1960s) the finest grade of marijuana; a marijuana cigarette the size of a cigar; marijuana from Central and South America. (BH, LSB, p. 53; RSG, JT, p. 198; RRL, DAZ, p. 194.) DCU.

Pancake n. (1890s–1940s) an Uncle Tom or servile person; meek Negro. (WF, DAS, p. 374; ZNH, AM, p. 95.) SNU.

[To] Pancake [a car] v. (1980s–1990s) to drop the back end of a car, then the rear end; to drop the body of a car. (EF, RDSL, p. 249.) Watts and South-central Los Angeles use.

Panic n. (1950s–1960s) a period when drugs are scarce. (CLC, TS, p. 255.) DCU.

Panicky adj. (1940s) experiencing unusually intense pleasure or excitement; a variant of the standard meaning of overwhelming fear or hysterical response to something. (DB, OHHJ, p. 144.) Harlem; NCU.

Panther piss n. (1930s–1990s) cheap liquor; bootleg liquor; homemade liquor. (RCC, SOC, p. 19; WF, DAS, p. 375; EF, RDSL, p. 249.) SCU.

[Pair of] Pants n. (1930s–1940s) any male person. (MHB, JS, np.) SNU.

Papa n. (1920s–1990s) affectionate name a woman uses to address her sweetheart, husband, or pimp. (CVV, NH, p. 286; DW, TL, p. 1861.) SNU.

Papa Oscar Celestin, cornetist, bandleader; born in Napoleonville, Louisiana, January 1, 1884; died in New Orleans, Louisiana, December 15, 1954; played with Henry Allen, Sr.'s Excelsior Brass Band.

Papa-tree-top-tall n. (1930s–1940s) an extremely tall male. (ZNH, AM, p. 84.) SU.

Paper n. (1900s–1980s) sheet music; money. (RSG, JT, p. 198.) JMFU.

Paper-hang n. (1950s–1970s) forgery as a means of income; cashing bad checks. (DW, TL, p. 186.) Example: "I don't know how much time David got for the paper-hang he had going." SCU, PU.

Paper man n. (1900s–1940s) pejorative term for a musician, especially a drummer, who plays according to written music. (RSG, JT, pp. 198–199.) JMFU.

Papers n. (1940s–1990s) marriage documents. (EF, RDSL, p. 241.) SNU.

Papers n. (1900s–1990s) cigarette papers used to roll marijuana in. (EF, RDSL, p. 249.) DCU.

Paradiffle n. (1900s–1930s) an onomatopoeic term for a very basic drum roll. (RSG, JT, p. 199.) JMFU.

Parakeet n. (1960s) a Puerto Rican. (DC, BJ, p. 74.) See "PR."

Paralyzed adj. (1970s–1990s) drunk. (FR.) YCU.

Park ape n. (1930s–1940s) pejorative term for any black person thought to be extremely ugly and blue-black. (ZNH, AM, p. 95.) Harlem; NCU.

Partner; pot'ner n. (1930s–1990s) male expression; any stranger, especially a black male stranger. (Hear Lightnin' Hopkins, "Big Black Cadillac Blues," *Drinking in the Blues*, Collectable Records, 1989; HEG, DAUL, p. 291; EF, RDSL, p. 249.) See "Bro."

Party [girl] n. (1920s–1950s) any person, especially a woman, who likes to have a good time dancing or kissing and touching. (WF, DAS, p. 376.) Rare. SNU.

Party v. (1960s–1990s) to have a good time at a social event. (FR.) Example: "Let's party." YCU. See "Ball."

Party n. (1930s–1970s) a "party" happens when two or more prostitutes turn a trick on one man. (SH, GL, p. 212.) PPU.

Partying v. (1960s–1990s) having a good time at a social gathering, especially where drugs are shared. (RRL, DAZ, p. 196.) YCU, DCU, SCU.

Party piano n. (1920s–1940s) a fast-moving style, like Lil Hardin's; early boogie-woogie; a blues pattern as theme; a style of piano playing developed in association with the rent parties of the twenties and thirties. (RSG, JT, p. 199.) JMFU.

Pasmala n. (1890s–1900s) variant of *pas mele* (French); "mixed step"; "La Pas Ma La" (song); a popular jazz dance. (RSG, JT, p. 199.) New Orleans; JMFU.

Pass v. (1800s–1930s) to pass for white because of a fair or light complexion. (AL, MJR, p. 3; WF, DASp, p. 377; CVV, NH, p. 286; see Nella Larsen, *Passing*, 1929.) SNU. See "Passing."

[The] Pass n. (1950s–1970s) the transfer of heroin, cocaine, marijuana, or some other narcotics in a drug deal. (RRL, DAZ, p. 197.) Example: "She meets Jimmy down at State and Yekwana Avenue to make the pass." DCU.

Passel n. (1890s–1920s) several; an uncounted number of things. (ECLA, NN, p. 268.) SU.

Passing v. (1800s–1930s) short for "passing for white"—something done by a considerable number of light-skinned, free, African-Americans during and after slavery. (See Nella Larsen, *Passing*, 1929; CVV, NH, p. 286; KG, JV, p. 181.) SNU.

Passing v. (1970s–1990s) short for passing the cocaine pipe around or sharing a marijuana cigarette. (TW, CH, p. 150.) DCU.

Passion kiss n. (1960s) open-mouthed kiss. (FR.) SNU.

Passport n. (1960s) verbal consent from gang leaders to enter their territory. (DC, BJ, p. 74.) Example: "What you doing over here, man, you got a passport?" NCU, SCU.

Pass water v. (1900s–1990s) to urinate; picked up from white use. (FR.) See "Make water."

Past cool adj. (1980s–1990s) very "hip." (Jess Mowry, *Six Out of Seven*, 1993, p. 17.) SCU.

Past gorgeous adj. (1990s) female expression; extremely attractive. (TMc, WTE, p. 231.) SNCU.

Pat Juba n. (1680s–1900s) a type of dance during which the dancer pats out the rhythm of the dance against his body. (FR.) See "Juba."

Patteroller; patter-roller; patteroler n. (1700s–1860s) patroller; a "thrill-seeking [young white male] hoodlum" paid to track down runaway slaves; predecessor to the klansmen; a tracker; slave's term for slave-catcher; a slave guard; "Old Bill the Rolling Pin" is a children's song about a patteroller. (SK, PC, p. 68; BJ, BJH, SD, pp. 208–209.) SU.

Patting v. (1900s–1940s) body slapping during dancing or playing —as in the games "Hambone" and "Juba." (BJ, BLH, SD, p. 22.) See "Hand jive."

Patting leather v. (1930s–1990s) walking the streets looking for work. (EF, RDSL, p. 249.) SNCU.

Pawnhost n. (1870s–1890s) variant "negro term" for Liverwurst, liver sausage made by the Pennsylvania Dutch. (JSF, AON, p. 411.) NCU.

Paws n. (1940s) the hands. (DB, OHHJ, p. 144.) Harlem; NCU.

[Make a] Payday n. (1920s–1940s) southern gambler's term; often a stranger from out of town, the gambler would arrive on, say, a Friday, when the men of a particular company or a particular town got their pay (often in cash) and gathered to gamble in a well-established gambling house, usually someone's home. (AL, MJR, p. 106; WF, DAS, p. 378.) Gamblers; SU.

Payback v. (1930s–1950s) to take revenge on someone. (FR.) SCU, YCU.

Pay dues v. (1940s–1990s) to have hard luck; to suffer as a result of race prejudice; to come up the hard way. (EF, RDSL, p. 249; DC, BJ, p. 74.) SNU.

Pay no mind v. (1930s–1990s) to ignore or deliberately snub or avoid. (EF, RDSL, p. 249.) YCU, SNU.

Payoff n. (1940s–1990s) a person who is free with his or her money; in the nineties; the end result. (FR.) Example: "Now we come to the payoff." SCU, SNU.

Pay school n. (1900s–1990s) a private school that charges tuition. (RP, C.) SCU, SNU.

Pay [one's] water bill v. (1970s) to urinate. (FR.) SNU, SCU.

PC n. (1990s) piece of crack. (TW, CH, p. 150.) DCU.

PC n. (1980s–1990s) short for "part commission" in a drug deal. (TW, CK, p. 137; TW, CH, p. 150.) DCU.

Peaches n. (1960s–1990s) Dexedrine. (CS, vol. 3, no. 2, p. 37.) DCU.

Peanut n. (1960s) white person. (FR.) SNU.

Peanuts n. (1960s) small amount of pay. (FR.) Example: "I'm working for peanuts." SNU.

Pearlie Mae Pearl Bailey, dancer and singer; born March 29, 1918; appeared in *St. Louis Woman* (1946) and other films.

Pedigree n. (1960s–1970s) one's vita; vital information about one's background, family history, work record, education, and so on. (DW, TL, p. 186.) Example: "Did they ask you your whole damned pedigree too?" SCU.

Peck n. (1830s–1950s) short for peckerwood; a white person. (WF, DAS, p. 380; EF, RDSL, p. 249.) SU, SNU.

[The] Peck n. (1950s–1960s) in jazz, movement happening at irregular intervals in time; choppy music. (RSG, JT, pp. 199–200.) JMFU.

Peck v. (1940s–1950s) to eat. (WF, DAS, p. 380; DC, BJ, pp. 74–75.) SNU. See "Pecking" and "Pecks."

Peck John Morrison, bass player; born September 11, 1919; worked with Tiny Bradshaw, Horace Silver, Lou Donaldson, et al.

Pecker n. (1930s–1950s) a white man. (EF, RDSL, p. 249.) SU. See "Peckerwood."

Peckerwood n. (1830s–1950s) originally, a very poor white Anglo-Saxon Protestant. The word came into use as a result of the vivid presence in the south of the red woodpecking birds that black people saw as a symbol of whites; on the other hand, they saw the common blackbird as a symbol of themselves. The word was turned around, in a halfhearted effort, to preserve the privacy of its meaning and origin. Later, it took on a more general meaning—any white person; and especially during the 1950s it was used widely even in many northern black communities; also, a hostile term for any white man; poor white trash. (IS, TB, p. 312; WF, DAS, p. 380; ZNH, AM, p. 96; EF, RDSL, p. 249; JH, PBL, p. 85; EF, BVV, p. 49; DC, BJ, p. 75.) SNU.

Peck horn n. (1900s–1920s) mellophone or saxophone. (FR.) JMFU.

Pecking n. (1950s) in jazz, a fast, abbreviated style like Charlie Parker's or, before him, Art Tatum's. (FR.) JMFU.

Pecking n. (1930s–1940s) a jitterbug dance step originated at the famous Cotton Club, according to Cab Calloway and Dan Burley, in 1937; done to a sporadic movement in music; "pecking" dance-step motion. (RSG, JT, p. 200; DB, OHHJ, p. 144; CC, OMMM, NCCHD, p. 258.) JMFU.

Peckings n. (1940s–1950s) food. (WF, DAS, p. 380; DB, OHHJ, p. 144.) See "Peck."

Pecks n. (1940s–1950s) food. (CLC, TS, p. 255; WF, DAS, p. 698.) SCU, YCU, SNCU.

Peculiar Institution n. (1850s–1890s) political slang for slavery; believed first used in *The South Carolina Gazette* in 1852 in the following manner: the "peculiar domestic institutions of the South"; one wonders if "particular" was not really intended; picked up from white use during the last years of, and after, slavery. (JSF, AON, p. 413.) SNU.

[To] Pee between two heels v. (1950s–1960s) refers to the posture of a female urinating; an expression of contempt for a woman. (DG, W, p. 105.) Example: "She the best ho ever peed between two heels." PPCU, SCU.

Peekers n. (1940s) the eyes. (DB, OHHJ, p. 144; DC, BJ, p. 75.) SNU.

Peeking through [one's] liquor; peeking through [one's] likker v. (1930s–1940s) drunk but trying to act normal. (ZNH, AM, p. 96.) Harlem; SNU.

Peeling a fine green banana v. (1940s) making love to a very pretty light-skinned girl. (DB, OHHJ, p. 145.) Harlem; YCU, SCU.

Peel off v. (1940s–1960s) to carefully remove one or two of the large bills covering a roll of singles, so as not to reveal that the roll does not consist solely of large bills. (IS, PSML, p. 317.) PPU, DCU, SCU.

Peep(ed) vi. (1940s–1990s) in jazz, to read sheet music; in the nineties, to look at closely; to see, especially with great understanding. (RSG, JT, p. 200; DC, BJ, p. 75; DW, TL, p. 186.) Example: "Peep this, y'all." YCU, SNCU.

Peepers n. (1960s) eyes. (FR.) SNU.

Peeps dig the range v. (1930s–1940s) to scan the immediate scene; look around at what is happening. (DB, OHHJ, p. 144.) Harlem; SCU, YCU.

Pee wee n. (1900s–1950s) small; a very narrowly rolled marijuana cigarette; (1960s) a short person. (FR.) DCU.

Peg; pegged v. (1930s–1940s) to categorize. (FR.) Example: "I pegged him as a loser." Harlem; SNU.

Peg Leg Clayton Bates; one-legged tap dancer.

Peg(s) n. (1930s–1960s) trousers tapered down to the cuffs. (DB, OHHJ, p. 145.) Harlem; SNU.

Pellet n. (1970s–1990s) green grass; the green area where golf is played. (GS, TT, p. 58.) Black golf lingo.

Pen n. (1900s–1960s) penitentiary. (FR.) PU, SCU.

Penny n. (1940s–1960s) a dollar. (WF, DAS, p. 698; DC, BJ, p. 75.) Rare. JMFU.

Penocha n. (1960s–1990s) a woman's vagina; picked up from Spanish-speaking people by blacks who live among or near Latino neighborhoods. (EF, RDSL, p. 249.) Watts and South-central Los Angeles use.

Peola n., v. (1700s–1950s) *peula* [Bantu]; to peel off skin, such as the skin of fruit; human skin; a fair or light-complexioned Afro-American girl or young woman. (HV, AHAE, p. 146; WF, DAS, p. 382; DB, OHHJ, p. 145; ZNH, AM, p. 96; CC, OMMM, NCCHD, p. 259.) Rare.

People n. (1950s–1960s) narcotics agents; police. (RRL, DAZ, p. 197.) DCU.

People n. (1940s–1960s) one person. (FR.) Example: "See that boy there, he's good people—he won't let you down." SNU.

People n. (1950s–1960s) one's friends or the members of one's gang. (HLF, RJPD, p. 171.) SCU.

Pep-em-ups n. (1960s–1990s) any of the variety of amphetamines in capsule form. (EF, RDSL, p. 249.) DCU.

Pepper Park Adams, alto saxophone player; born November 8, 1930.

Pepper and salt n. (1960s–1970s) a mix of black and white people. (FR.) SNU.

Pepper-kissing v. (1970s–1990s) to try to present bad news in a less than negative light; to send mixed signals; to sugarcoat the facts. (EF, RDSL, p. 249.) South-central Los Angeles; YCU, SCU.

Percolating v. (ZNH, AM, p. 94.) See "Cruise."

Percolator n. (1930s–1940s) a pay party launched so the host can pay rent; rent party; a "shake." (SL, RJON, p. 126; WF, DAS, p. 384.) See "Rent party" and "Shake."

Perfume it v. (1940s) to cover up a misdeed; to put the best face on a bad situation. (MHB, JS, np.) SNU.

Perico n. (1980s–1990s) cocaine. (TW, CK, p. 137; TW, CH, p. 150.) New York City; DCU.

Peter n. (1930s–1950s) a little boy's penis. (WF, DAS, p. 384.) SNU.

Peter Jay n. (1980s–1990s) any policeman patrolling South-central Los Angeles. (EF, RDSL, p. 249.) South-central Los Angeles use.

[To] Pet up [one] v. (1960s–1990s) any attempt to comfort or console an upset child or adult. (EF, RDSL, p. 249.)

Pez n. (1940s–1950s) mustache, goatee, beard, or the hair on one's head. (WF, DAS, p. 385.) JMFU.

Pfat (1990s) superb; really wise and classy; "cool"; "hip." (FR.) YCU.

Pharaoh n. (1800s–1920s) *fero* [Kanuri]; a young woman; girl; used in early blues songs. (HV, AHAE, p. 146.) SU.

Philadelphia bank roll n. (WF, DAS, pp. 698–699.) See "California bank roll."

Philly Joe Joseph Rudolph Jones, drummer; born July 15, 1923. He worked with Dexter Gordon and later with Ben Webster.

[The] Philosopher n. (1930s–1940s) Harlem name for Mezz Mezzrow. (FR.) See "Mezz Mezzrow."

Phiz n. (1940s) the face. (DB, OHHJ, p. 145.) Harlem use.

Phone ho [whore] n. (1990s) a woman who talks on the phone in detail about sexual activity for a fee. (FR.) PPU.

Phone booth baby n. (1960s–1970s) any child whose father's identity is uncertain; term used in a cynical, playful, or pejorative way. (DR, BASL, p. 149.) Example: "Mabel, I know, had two by John, one by Bob, the twins by Sonny, and that last one was just a phone booth baby." Philadelphia; NCU.

Phony; foney adj., n. (1760s–1960s) *foni, fani* [Mandingo] false; pretense; deceptive value; counterfeit; insincere; insincere person. (HV, AHAE, p. 146) SNU.

Phony jazz n. (1950s) a lie; a trick; deliberate misinformation. (CW, TM, p. 107.) JMFU.

PI n. (1900s–1930s) a pimp. (RSD, JT, pp. 200–201.) SCU, JMFU, PPU.

Piano n. (1930s–1940s) spare ribs. (WF, DAS, p. 387; ZNH, AM, p. 88.) SU.

Pianoing v. (1980s–1990s) down on hands and knees searching with one's fingers for cocaine accidentally dropped on the floor. (TW, CH, p. 150.) DCU.

Piano kid n. (1900s–1930s) an early jazz term: any teenage pianist working the rundown joints; teenage piano players were common in the brothels and cabarets of this period. (RSG, JT, p. 201.) JMFU.

Piano on a platter n. (1930s–1940s) barbecued (Bar BQ) ribs on a plate. (ZNH, AM, p. 88.) Harlem use.

Pic; piccolo n. (1930s–1940s) jukebox; Victrola. (RSG, JT, p. 201; DB, OHHJ, p. 145.) JMFU.

Pick n. (1960s–1990s) a large West African–style wooden or plastic comb used for fluffing out hair. (DC, BJ, p. 75.) SNU.

Pickaninny; pickney n. (1650s–1950s) an African word for "child"; common word for any small black child in the old slave states; however, used in the West Indies to refer to any small child of any color or race; sometimes used humorously by adults to refer to themselves.

(JSF, AON, p. 418; Michelle Cliff, *No Telephone to Heaven*, 1987, p. 210; FGC, JT, p. 82, 270.) SNU.

Picker n. (1900s–1940s) in jazz, any player of a guitar or bass; one who plays a stringed instrument in a band. (RSG, JT, p. 201.) JMFU.

Pickers n. (1930s–1940s) the fingers. (DB, OHHJ, p. 145.) Harlem; SNU.

Picking the box v. (1890s) playing guitar. (FR.) JMFU.

Picking v. (1990s) frantically searching for particles of rock cocaine on the ground.

Pick(ing) cherries v. (1900s–1930s) playing bass or guitar. (RSG, JT, p. 201; CVV, NH, p. 242.)

Picking [one's] cherry v. (1930s–1950s) to seduce a virgin. (HEG, DAUL, pp. 42–43; DW, TL, p. 60.) SNU. See "Cherry."

Pick up v. (1930s–1950s) to do, understand, act, take action, gather, perceive, start. (DB, OHHJ, p. 145.) SNU.

Pick up v. (1930s–1940s) to put together lunch or dinner from leftovers. (DB, OHHJ, p. 145.) Harlem; SNU.

Pick up [on] v. (1930s–1950s) to listen; to observe; to take; to obtain.

Pick-up band n. (1930s–1990s) a quickly brought together assortment of musicians for the purpose of a recording or a concert. (FR.) JMFU.

Pickney (1920s–1950s) variant of "pickaninny"; transported to the States from the West Indies by immigrating West Indians. (MC, NTH, p. 210.) Harlem; NCU. See "Pickaninny."

Pick style n. (1920s–1950s) a form of guitar playing done with a plectrum or a "pick." (RSG, JT, p. 201.) JMFU.

Picnic v. (1980s–1990s) to have fun; a pleasant experience. (FR.) YCU.

Pickup n. (1920s–1990s) in jazz, the first few notes introducing a chorus. (RSG, JT, p. 201.) JMFU.

Piece n. (1900s–1980s) a pistol; handgun. (EF, RDSL, p. 249; DC, BJ, p. 75; CRM, BP, p. 305; DW, TL, p. 186.) SCU, DCU, YCU, PU.

Piece n. (1930s–1950s) short for "piece of ass"; female sexuality. (WF, DAS, p. 388; RDA, DDJ, p. 266.) SCU, SNU.

Piece n. (1950s–1960s) an ounce of heroin; a hundred narcotics capsules; any measure of street drugs. (CLC, TS, p. 255; IS, PSML, p. 316.) DCU.

Piece n. (1900s–1950s) musical instrument. (RSG, JT, p. 202.) JMFU.

Piece of shit n. (1930s–1960s) anything without value. (FR.) SNU.

Piece of ass n. See "Piece."

Piece of stuff n. (1950s–1960s) an ounce of cocaine; narcotics in any form. (IS, PSML, p. 316; CRM, BP, p. 305; CS, vol. 3, no. 2, p. 37.) DCU.

Pieces n. (1970s–1990s) one's clothes: pants, jackets, dresses, slips, shirts, socks, underwear. (EF, RDSL, p. 249.) South-central Los Angeles; YCU.

Pies n. (1940s) the eyes. (DB, OHHJ, p. 145.) Harlem use.

Pig n. (1840s–1990s) probably originally from "stool pigeon"; police informer; common among black youth during the 1960s as a term for a racist policeman; any policeman. (WF, DAS, p. 389; EF, RDSL, p. 249; DC, BJ, p. 75; EP, DU, p. 511.) YCU, SCU.

Pig n. (1950s–1960s) variant of "hog" for Cadillac. (HLF, RJPD, p. 171.) See "Hog."

Pig n. (1900s–1990s) pejorative term for any fat woman; anyone who overeats. (EF, RDSL, p. 249.) SNU.

Pig brother n. (1960s–1990s) derogatory term for a black male who has turned police informer. (EF, RDSL, p. 249.) South-central Los Angeles; SCU, PU, DCU.

Pigeon n. (1900s–1940s) affectionate male term for a girl or young woman. (DB, OHHJ, p. 145; CC, OMMM, NCCHD, p. 259.) Harlem; YCU, SCU.

Pigeon n. (1880s–1940s) a person who informs on another. (WF, DAS, p. 389.) SCU, PU, PPU, DCU.

Pigeon dropping v. (1940s) playing a confidence game. (DB, OHHJ, p. 145.) Harlem; SCU, DCU, PPU, PU.

Pig heaven n. (1960s–1990s) any police station but especially one in a black neighborhood. (EF, RDSL, p. 249.) South-central Los Angeles; YCU, SCU, DCU.

Pig-meat n. (1880s–1940s) an older, loose woman; a dumb girl; female whore; young girl. (WF, DAS, p. 389; ZNH, Am, p. 96.) SU.

Pigmeat Dewey Alamo Markham, comedian.

Pig-mouth n. (1900s–1990s) any obese woman or one who overeats. (EF, RDSL, p. 249.) SNU.

Pigger n. (EF, RDSL, p. 249.) See "Pig-mouth."

Piggin n. (1850s–1920s) of Gullah origin; a relatively small pail or bucket made from cedar and used for toting or carrying water. (AEG, BB, p. 318.) Coastal Georgia and South Carolina; SU.

Pilch n. (1930s–1940s) one's residence; apartment or house; may be related to "pilfer" (pilch), nineteenth-century American cant. (ZNH, AM, p. 96; EP, DU, p. 513; JSF, AON, p. 420.) Harlem use.

Pile n. (1970s–1990s) male term for the act of sexual intercourse or anal sex. (EF, RDSL, p. 249.) SCU.

Pile of bricks n. (1940s) any building in a city. (DB, OHHJ, p. 145.) Rare. Harlem use.

Pill n. (1960s–1970s) basketball. (DC, BJ, p. 75.) Example: "She can really shoot the pill." Basketball players' and fan use.

Pillars n. (1930s) human legs. (DB, OHHJ, p. 145.) Rare. Harlem; SNU.

Pillow pigeons n. (1940s) bedbugs. (MHB, JS, np.) SNU.

Pimp n. (1890s–1990s) may have pre-nineteenth-century English origin—meaning "small" or "petty" or "mean"; a man who controls the lives of one or more prostitutes; a man who receives money from prostitutes in exchange for controlling (managing?) their lives; a person who takes advantage of others; man who directs prostitutes; a "cool" or "smart" man; a con artist. (EP, DU, p. 513; SH, GL, p. 212; RDA, DDJ, p. 266; JSF, AON, p. 420; DC, BJ, p. 75; CRM, BP, p. 305; CS, vol. 3, no. 2, p. 37.) SNU. See "Player."

Pimp v. (1890s–1990s) to live off money a woman earns selling sex; to get something for nothing; freeloading. (EF, RDSL, p. 249; CRM, BP, p. 305.) PPU, SCU. See "Pimping."

Pimp adj. (1950s–1990s) male term for a flashy or expensive appearance. (EF, RDSL, p. 249.) SCU, PPU, YCU.

Pimp's arrest n. (1950s–1960s) for a prostitute to be arrested resulting from her own ex-pimp informing the police that she's turning tricks; if the woman is out on bail, the pimp retrieves the bail money and she goes to jail. (CRM, BP, p. 305.) PPU.

Pimp-crazy adj. (1950s–1970s) a woman ("ho") who goes from one abusive pimp to another. (CRM, BP, p. 34, 305.) Example: "That bitch, she must like to get her ass beat 'cause she goes for meanest gorillas out here." PPU.

Pimp dust n. (1970s–1990s) cocaine. (EF, RDSL, p. 249.) DCU.

Pimped down adj. (1960s) male term; to be sharply or smartly dressed in expensive clothes, especially an expensive suit, shoes, hat, and tie. (CRM, BP, p. 305.) PPU.

Pimp front n. (1950s–1990s) expensive and fancy clothes, especially suits and hats and mink coats. (EF, RDSL, p. 249.) SCU.

Pimping v. (1890s–1990s) to accept money from someone who cannot afford to give it. (EF, RDSL, p. 249.) SNU, PPU, SCU.

Pimp rest n. (1970s–1990s) the armrest in a luxury car on which pimps—and those who imitate them—lean while driving or while parked watching the scene. (EF, RDSL, p. 249.) SCU.

Pimp ride n. (1960s–1990s) any high-priced car such as a Cadillac, Lincoln, Mercedes-Benz, or Porsche. (EF, RDSL, p. 249.) SCU, PPU.

Pimp roll n. (1980s–1990s) a slow, confident strut. (FR.) SCU, YCU, PPU.

Pimp shades n. (1960s–1990s) sunglasses. (EF, RDSL, p. 249; CRM, BP, p. 305.) SCU, PPU.

[The] Pimp's sign n. (1930s–1940s) any gesture of invitation to a woman; a pimp in this sense is a male prostitute. (ZNH, AM, p. 85.) Harlem use.

Pimp socks n. (1950s–1960s) long, expensive dress socks in various colors. (CRM, BP, p. 305.) SCU, PPU.

Pimp steak n. (1930s–1950s) a frankfurter; hotdog. (DB, OHHJ, p. 145.) PPU, SCU, YCU.

Pimp sticks n. (1930s–1960s) a wire weapon consisting of two coat hangers opened out and braided; and used by some pimps for beating the women who work for them. (DG, W, p. 199; CRM, BP, p. 305.) PPU.

Pimp stride n. (1950s–1990s) a proud, arrogant, pompous rhythmic and strutting style of walking done with bobbing and swaggering motions. (EF, RDSL, p. 249.) SCU.

Pimp talk n. (1950s–1960s) a monologue by a pimp in an effort to convince a young woman to work for him. (DC, BJ, p. 75; CRM, BP, p. 305.) SCU. See "Hype."

Pimp tints (EF, RDSL, p. 249.) See "Pimp shades."

Pimp walk n. (1920s–1960s) a very flashy style of strutting; the distinctive strut African-American men do that denotes a sense of pride and individuality—if not arrogance. (DC, BJ, p. 75.) SCU, YCU.

Pin; pinning; pinned v. (1700s–1960s) *pind* (Temne); *pin* (Sierre Leone); *pin* (British English); to watch closely. (IS, PSML, p. 316; MHB, JS, np; EF, RDSL, p. 249; DW, TL, p. 186.) SNU, YCU, SCU.

Pinch n. (1880s–1990s) any minute portion; a tiny amount of snuff; a small amount of marijuana. (EF, RDSL, p. 249; CS, vol. 3, no. 2, p. 37.) SNU, DCU.

Pinchers n. (1920s–1950s) shoes. (DB, OHHJ, p. 145.) SNU.

Pinders n. (1800s–1890s) "a Florida negro term for peanuts." (JSF, AON, p. 421.) Florida use. See "Gobers."

Pine drape n. (1900s–1940s) a coffin. (DB, OHHJ, p. 145.) SNU.

Pinetop Clarence Smith, 1904–1929; well-known blues and vaudeville singer, pianist, and songwriter.

Piney wood people n. (1840s–1900s) the poor whites who did not own property in rural Georgia during slavery. (ALA, AL, p. 51.) See "Cracker" and "White trash."

Pink n. (1870s–1940s) a white girl or young woman; white person; Anglo-Saxon; (CVV, NH, p. 157, 286; RSG, JT, pp. 202; DB, OHHJ, p. 145; DW, TL, p. 186.) SNU.

Pink boy n. (1960s–1990s) any white male of any age. (EF, RDSL, p. 249.) SCU.

Pink chaser(s) n. (1890s–1940s) any black person who aggressively or deliberately cultivates friendships with or seeks the company of white people. (CVV, NH, p. 286.) NCU.

Pinkie; pinky n. (1870s–1950s) light-skinned young woman; black person; term popularized by the movie *Pinky*, starring Jeanne Crain. (WF, DAS, p. 392.) SU.

Pink lady; pink ladies (1950s–1990s) Darvon (propoxyphene) capsules; barbiturates. (EF, RDSL, p. 249; CS, vol. 3, no. 2, p. 37.) DCU.

Pink pimp suit n. (1960s) playful expression for a baby's crib; baby as "freeloader." (FR.) Rare. New York.

Pinkster Day n. (1750s–1860s) festival day; African holiday celebrated on plantations by slaves "from the mid-eighteenth through the mid-nineteenth centuries." (JEH, A, p. 196.)

Pinkster frolic (James Fenimore Cooper, *Satanstoe*, 1845, pp. 122–123.) See "Pinkster Day."

Pinktoes n. (1890s–1920s) a black man's term of affection for a light-skinned African-American young woman. (WF, DAS, p. 392; ZNH, AM, p. 96.) SU.

Pinktoes n. (1930s–1950s) a black man's term of affection for a white woman. (CH, P, p. 7; GS, TT, p. 68; DB, OHHJ, p. 145.) NCU.

Pins n. (1940s) the legs. (DB, OHHJ, p. 145.) Rare. Harlem; YCU.

Pinto n. (1700s–1930s) *bentho* (Temne); a bier; a coffin. (HV, AHAE, p. 146; WF, DAS, p. 392.) Georgia and South Carolina use.

Pipe n. See "[Agony] Pipe" and "[Gobble] Pipe."

Pipe n. (1980s–1990s) penis. (EF, RDSL, p. 249.) SCU.

[Agony] Pipe n. (1930s–1940s) clarinet. (RSG, JT, p. 203.) JMFU.

[Gobble] Pipe n. (1930s–1940s) a saxophone. (RSG, JT, p. 203.) JMFU.

Pipe v. See "[Hit the] Pipe."

[Hit the] Pipe (1930s–1950s) to smoke cocaine, opium, or marijuana in a pipe. (WF, DAS, p. 393.) DCU.

Pipehead n. (1980s–1990s) one who's addicted to smoking cocaine in a pipe. (FR.) DCU.

Pipero n. (1980s–1990s) one who smokes free base; one who smokes crack cocaine. (TW, CH, p. 150.) New York; DCU.

Pipes n. (1930s) lungs, especially of a singer. (FR.) JMFU.

Pipe up v. (1980s–1990s) to fill a pipe with cocaine; to smoke a pipe containing cocaine. (FR.) DCU.

Piss-poor adj (1940s–1980s) extremely poor in any respect. (FR.) SNU.

Pissed-off adj. (1940s–1990s) annoyed or angered. (FR.) SNU.

Pistols n. (1940s) zoot suit trousers. (DB, OHHJ, p. 145.) Harlem; NCU, YCU, SCU.

Pitch a bitch v. (1930s–1990s) to complain; to fight; to cause noise. (DR, BASL, p. 123.) SNCU.

Pitch a ball v. (1940s) to give an exciting party; to have fun at a party. (MHB, JS, np.) SNU.

Pitcher n. (1980s–1990s) a drug dealer; a middleman in street drug dealing. (TW, CH, p. 150.) DCU.

Pitch out v. (1970s–1990s) to shake the ball. (GS, TT, p. 59.) Black golfers lingo.

Pixie n. (1960s–1990s) standard meaning refers to a short hairstyle; female: hair curled with a hot iron; male: processed hair. (DC, BJ, p. 75.) SNCU.

Plain lie n. (1920s–1950s) an undisputed lie. (FR.) SNU.

Plain people n. (1820s–1890s) "a negro term for white folks—a tit-for-tat in connection with the term colored people" (JSF, AON, p. 424). SU.

Plant; planted n., v. (1960s–1970s) a "plant" is when a policeman runs a hand containing drugs into one's empty pocket and pulls the hand out, exposing the drugs; to be framed by narcotics officers. (CS, vol. 3, no. 2, p. 37.) DCU, SCU, PU.

Plantation n. (1630s–1930s) large farm; in the southern states, any large private farm owned by a white planter and worked by black slave labor; picked up from white use. (JSF, AON, p. 425.) SNU.

Plantation darky n. (1770s–1860s) derogatory term for a black slave. (SBF, IHAT, p. 36.) See "Plantation."

Plantation nigger [Plantation Negro] n. (1770s–1860s) (SBF, IHAT, p. 36.) See "Plantation."

Planter n. (1630s–1930s) white owner of a plantation. (JSF, AON, p. 425.) See "Plantation."

Plant show n. (1890s–1900s) a blackface comedy show; a minstrel show; picked up from circus use. (WF, DAS, p. 395.) SNU.

Plant you now, dig you later v. See "Dig."

Plastered adj. (1960s) drunk. (FR.) SNU.

Plates n. (1940s) the feet. (DB, OHHJ, p. 145.) Rare. Harlem use.

Plat-eye v. (1760s–1940s) *platatayi* (Bantu); doglike scratching at the back or front door. (HV, AHAE, p. 146.) South Carolina, Georgia, SU.

Plat-eye; platt-eye n. (1760s–1940s) a female ghost, believed to be as physically strong as a powerful animal. (HV, AHAE, p. 146; AEG, BB, p. 319.) Example (spoken by an adult to a small child still awake past bedtime: "Old Plat-eye come round after midnight and get you for sho if you ain't sleep." South Carolina, Georgia; SU.

Platt-eye (plat-eye) prowl n. (1760s–1940s) of Gullah origin; the time between nine o'clock and midnight. (FGC, DARE, p. 867.) SU.

Platter n. (1940s) a record album of music. (MHB, JS, np.) SNU, YCU.

Platter(s) n. (1940s) the feet. (DB, OHHJ, p. 145.) Rare. Harlem use.

Play n. (1930s–1960s) in jazz, the particular plan a group of musicians have for a performance. (MM, RB, p. 63; RSG, p. 203.) JMFU.

Play n., v. (1800s–1990s) situation; any condition; idea; program; a proposal; a scheme; plan; in the sixties, a greeting that employs a palm slap, in the nineties; to behave in a certain way. (DB, OHHJ, p. 145; EF, RDSL, p. 250; TW, CH, p. 150; DC, BJ, p. 75.) Examples: "I don't play that shit any more"; and, "Give me the play so I'll know what to expect when I get there." SCU, YCU, NCU.

Play n. (1960s–1990s) money; valuable objects; investments. (DW, TL, p. 186.) PPU, SCU.

Play a part v. (1930s–1960s) to talk, walk, and generally pretend to be a type of person one is not; picked up from theater use. (RSG, JT, p. 203.) NCU, JMFU.

Play [one's] ass off v. See "Blow [one's] ass off" and "Blow away."

Play brother n. (1880s–1990s) a friend who is like a relative; a female's or male's closest or close friend. (EF, RDSL, p. 250.) SNU.

Play chicken v. (1980s–1990s) to interrupt a romantic or flirtatious conversation between a male and a female. (EF, RDSL, p. 250.) South-central Los Angeles use.

Play-children n. (1880s–1930s) children; children with the leisure to play as opposed to children doomed to work all the time. (Virginia Pound Brown and Laurella Ownes, *Toting the Lead Row: Ruby Pickens Tart, Alabama Folklorist*, 1981, p. 94.)

Play cousin n. (EF, RDSL, p. 250.) See "Play brother."

Play dead; lay dead v. (1940s–1950s) to wait patiently for something or someone. (MHB, JS, np.) SNU. See "Lay dead."

Play [one] down v. (1930s–1950s) in jazz, in a battle of instruments, when one musician "defeats" or out "blows" another in a contest of energetic playing. (RSG, JT, p. 203.) JMFU.

Played out adj. (1930s–1990s) used up; passé; exhausted; old-fashioned. (HC, WSJ, p. B8.) Example: "Our options had been played out." SNU.

Player n. (1950s–1990s) a pimp or a person—usually male—in "the [hustling] life"; also any male who can manipulate rich women into giving him money or supporting him and his expensive habits; a man who manages to convince people—usually women—to invest in crooked schemes. (CRM, BP, p. 33, 297, 306; SH, GL, p. 212; TW, CK, p. 137; EF, RDSL, p. 250; DW, TL, p. 186.) PPU, DCU, SCU.

Player n. (1950s–1990s) a lady's man; a sexually active male; male with more than one woman. (EF, RDSL, p. 250; CS, vol. 3, no. 2, p. 37.) SCU, PPU.

Play in [one's] family; play in the family (1920s–1930s) to play the dozens. (ZNH, DTR, p. 194; WF, DAS, p. 396.) Example: "Listen, jack, I don't play in your family, so don't you play in mine or you gone be sorry." SU. See "Dirty Dozens."

Playing v. (1900s–1960s) pretending; kidding; joking. (DC, BJ, p. 75.) Examples: "Sally, don't let Mack get you down, he's just playing." SNU.

Playing the dozens with [one's] uncle's cousin v. (1940s) having the wrong approach to everything. (DB, OHHJ, p. 145; DC, BJ, p. 75.) SNU, SCU, YCU. See "Dirty Dozens."

Playing with [one's] stuff out the window v. (1900s–1940s) to proceed with caution; to commit infidelity with extreme caution; to play cards without risk. (FR.) SNU.

Play it cool v. (1940s–1960s) to be unemotional, cautious, composed. (RSG, JT, pp. 204–205; DC, BJ, p. 76.) SCU, JMFU.

Play mother n. (EF, RDSL, p. 250.) See "Play brother."

Playoffs n. (1930s–1940s) patrons. (DB, OHHJ, p. 144.) Harlem; NCU.

Play on the line v. (1900s–1940s) in jazz, to work in any of the various jazz "joints" along Basin Street in New Orleans. (RSG, JT, p. 204.) JMFU.

Play past v. (1960s) ignoring or avoiding any difficulty or stumbling block. (CRM, BP, p. 306.) Example: "The bitch hardheaded and stubborn, but I can play past her bullshit long as she get her ass out there and get them biscuits." PPU.

Play possum v. (1850s–1940s) to make believe; to deceive or trick someone. (AEG, BB, p. 319.) SU.

Play sister n. (Ef, RDSL, p. 250.) See "Play brother."

Play that shit v. (1950s–1990s) to take a course of action. (TMc, DA, p. 1) Example: "Don't leave your things in here, man, I don't play that shit." SNU.

Play the dozens n. (WF, DAS, p. 397; ZNH, AM, p. 96; EF, RDSL, p. 250.) See "Dirty Dozens."

Play the fool v. (1880s–1990s) pretending to be stupid or crazy. (EF, RDSL, p. 250.) Example: "Willie-Boy act like he ain't got good sense; he play the fool every time white folks come 'round." See "Putting on" and "Putting on white folks."

Play the skin v. (1900s–1990s) beating drums with the palms of one's hands. (DC, BJ, p. 76.) JMFU, SNU.

Play the Tom v. (EF, RDSL, p. 250.) See "Play the fool."

Plenty adj. (1800s–1940s) large amount; in jazz, after the turn of the century, good or excellent. (RSG, JT, p. 204.) Example: "That sho is a plenty good-looking woman over there by the levy." SU, SNU, JMFU.

Plow; plowing v. (1900s–1940s) metaphor for the male role in sexual intercourse. (Hear Mississippi Fred McDowell, introductory comments, *I Do Not Play No Rock 'Roll*, Capitol Industries.) SU.

Pluck; plug n. (1960s–1990s) wine, especially cheap wine. (EF, RDSL, p. 250; EF, BVV, p. 50; DC, BJ, p. 76.) SCU, SNCU.

Pluck n. (1960s–1980s) a good-looking, sexy woman. (EF, RDSL, p. 250.) SCU, NSU.

Pluck v. (1970s–1990s) to perform sexual intercourse. (EF, RDSL, p. 250.) YCU, SCU.

Plucked adj. (1970s–1990s) a sense of peace or comfort or well-being following sexual intercourse. (EF, RDSL, p. 250.) Example: "I get that plucked feeling all I want to do is kick back and listen to some jams and smoke bush." SCU.

Plug v. (1970s) shoot someone. (FR.) SCU, PU.

Plug the mug v. (1940s) to stop talking. (MHB, JS, np.) SNU.

Plum adv. (1800s–1950s) completely. (FR.) Example: "He was plum broke by the time he got to Atlanta." (JAH, PBE, p. 171.) SU.

Plumber n. (1970s–1990s) a male with a reputation for female sexual conquests. (EF, RDSL, p. 250.) YCU, SCU.

Plunger n. (1940s) a bathtub. (DB, OHHJ, p. 145.) Harlem; NCU.

PO n. (1950s–1990s) a parole officer. (DW, TL, p. 186.) Example: "My PO is real cool, man, she wants to see me make it out here." SCU, PU.

Pocket roast n. (1970s–1990s) baked chuck roast; stale bread, oysters, onions, celery, parsley, and various spices cut together and stuffed into pockets of a ground chuck roast. (Dooky Chase Restaurant term, New Orleans.) New Orleans use.

Pod n. (1890s–1930s) marijuana; "pot" may be a variant of "pod." (WF, DAS, p. 399.) See "Grass" and "Pot."

Poke n. (1750s–1900s) *-poko* (Bantu); a sack or bag; anything with a pocket or deep cavity; container; purse; a wallet. (HV, AHAE, p. 146; DB, OHHJ, p. 145.) SU.

Poke n. (1940s–1950s) a puff of a marijuana cigarette or pipe. (RSG, JT, p. 205.) DCU, JUMFU.

Poke n. (1940s–1950s) roll of money—probably derived from wallet as a container for carrying money. (IS, PSML, p. 316; DB, OHHJ, p. 145; DW, TL, p. 186.) SCU, PU, DCU, PPU.

Poke (poking) v. (1980s–1990s) to perform sexual intercourse. (EF, RDSL, p. 250.) SCU.

Point n. (1950s–1990s) a hypodermic syringe used by a heroin addict. (EF, RDSL, p. 250; CS, vol. 3, no. 2, p. 38.) DCU.

Point blank adj. (1900s–1990s) without doubt; without question; no further comments are necessary. (Heavy D, *Newsweek*.) Example: "She a tough bitch, period, point blank."

Poison people n. (1950s–1960s) heroin addicts. (RRL, DAZ, p. 205; Claude Brown, *Manchild in the Promised Land*, 1965) DCU.

Pole n. (1970s–1990s) penis. (EF, RDSL, p. 250; HM, GL, p. 32.) SCU.

Pole hole n. (1970s–1990s) vagina. (EF, RDSL, p. 250.) SCU.

Polluted adj. (1970s) drunk. (FR.) YCU, SCU.

Pollydo n. (1850s–1920s) of Gullah origin; male term; variant of "Polydore"; also variant of Apollo; affectionate name for a male friend. (AEG, BB, p. 319.) SU.

Polo Paul D. Barnes, soprano saxophone player; born November 22, 1901; worked with Chick Webb, Jelly Roll Morton, et al.

Pone n. (1920s–1940s) a roll of fat on the neck. (CM, CW, ZNH, "The Gilded Six-Bits," p. 71.) SU.

Pony Norwood Poindexter, alto saxophone player; born February 3, 1926; worked with Billy Eckstine's band, Lionel Hampton, and others.

Poontang; poon tang; puntang n. (1700s–1940s) variant of *puntuny* (Lima) and/or *mu ntanga* (Bantu); sexual intercourse; the vagina; a black woman's sexuality; converged with *putain* (French) for prostitute. (EF, BVV, p. 50; HV, AHAE, p. 147; EF, RDSL, p. 250.) SU, SNU.

Poop n. (1800s–1940s) *pup* (Wolof); a small child's bowel movement; closely related in sound to a Dutch term meaning the same thing. (HV, AHAE, p. 147.) SU, SNU.

Poop out v. (1930s–1940s) to fail; to lose one's mind. (DB, OHHJ, p. 145.) Harlem; SNU.

Poor boys n. (1960s) unemployment checks. (FR.) SCU.

Poor Buckruh n. (1760s–1920s) a poor white man or poor white family, especially one that cannot afford to own slaves. (AEG, BB, p. 319.) SU. See "Poor white trash."

Poor Buckruh Nigger n. (1760s–1860s) a slave who is owned by a poor white man or a poor white family with a plantation. (AEG, BB, p. 319.) SU.

Poor Jo n. See "Poor Joe."

Poor Job n. See "Poor Joe."

Poor Joe n. (1730s–1930s) *pojo* (Liberia/Sierra Leone), Val dialect; a blue heron. (HV, AHAE, p. 147.) SU.

Poor Joe [Po' Joe] Joe Williams, blues singer.

Poor whites (JSF, AON, pp. 431–432.) See "Poor white trash."

Poor white trash [po white trash] n. (1650s–1990s) indigent white people; destitute white population of the southern slave states; a white person who works as an indentured servant; white person or family who cannot afford to own slaves; poor white southern farmers; outcasts, vagrants, criminals "spirited away" from England, Scotland, and Ireland, legally and illegaly, to work as bondsmen, often as punishment; homeless poor white person. (JSF, AON, pp. 431–432.) SNU.

Poot n.,v. (1900s–1960s) a fart; to break wind; to release intestinal gas from the rectum. (FR.) SU.

Poot-butt [poop-butt] n. (1970s–1990s) a lazy person; unmotivated person; a "square"; a fool. (EF, BVV, p. 50; EF, RDSL, p. 250; JMC, PS, p. 50; CRM, BP, p. 306.) SCU, YCU, SNCU.

Pop n. (1930s–1950s) any handgun, but especially a revolver. (WF, DAS, p. 402.) SCU, DCU, SNCU.

Pop n. (1930s–1960s) in jazz, short for "popular" (music) as opposed to "progressive," "standard," or "classical" (jazz); swing music such as that played by Benny Goodman. (RSG, JT, p. 205.) JMFU.

Pop vt. (1950s–1970s) male sexual penetration of the female. (DW, TL, p. 186.) Example: "I can pop that chick, man, in five minutes—what you wanna bet?" SCU.

Pop(ped) v. (1950s–1960s) arrest; to be apprehended and taken into custody by the police. (DC, BJ, p. 76; CS, vol. 3, no. 2, p. 38.) SCU, YCU, DCU, PPU, SNCU.

Pop(ping) v. (1940s) to spend an excessive amount of money on someone in a social situation. (FR.) Example: "Look at Willy, he's really popping tonight." SNU.

Pop a roll v. (1970s–1990s) to throw four or five pills into one's mouth at one time and swallow with water or beer. (EF, RDSL, p. 250.) DCU.

Popcorn n. (1950s–1990s) not to be taken seriously; "lightweight" as opposed to "heavyweight"; mentally deficient. (CRM, BP, p. 306.) SCU, PPU. See "Popcorn pimp."

Popcorn pimp n. (1950s–1990s) any pimp who stoops to solicit for his "ho"; a small-time pimp. (CRM, BP, pp. 33, 306; EF, RDSL, p. 250.) SCU, PPU. See "Player."

Poppa-stoppa n. (1930s–1940s) term of address for any older man who is effective at what he does; term of address for any male. (RE, IM, p. 420; RSG, JT, p. 205; DB, OHHJ, p. 145.) SNCU, JMFU, SCU.

Poppa Mezz n. (1930s–1940s) Harlem name for Mezz Mezzrow. (FR.) See "Mezz Mezzrow."

Popper n. (1940s) a gun. (DB, OHHJ, p. 145.) PU, SCU.

Poppers n. (1940s) the fingers. (MHB, JS, np.) YCU, SNU.

Popping v., adj. (1930s–1960s) in jazz, to make outstanding music; a great performance (such as Jimmy Smith's twelve-bar blues classic "The Sermon," recorded at Manhattan Towers on February 25, 1958, under the direction of Rudy Van Gelder for Blue Note). (RSG, JT, pp. 205–206.) JMFU.

[Finger] Popping v. (1940s–1970s) having a good time at a party, a nightclub, or dance hall, or anywhere where music and entertainment are present. (CS, vol. 3, no. 2, p. 38.) SNU, YCU.

Popping v. (1980s–1990s) snapping the body while dancing. (FR.) YCU.

Pops n. (1920s–1950s) a complimentary term of address for an older man; term of address by one male to another. (WF, DAS, p. 402; CC, HDH, p. 16; RSG, JT, p. 206; DB, OHHJ, p. 145; EF, RDSL, p. 250; CC, OMMM, NCCHD, p. 259; DC, BJ, p. 76.) SNU, JMFU.

Pops Louis Armstrong, singer and trumpet player. See "Satch."

Pork chop [music] n. (1900s–1920s) a slow, barrelhouse style of jazz; earthy blues or jazz. (RSG, JT, p. 206.) JMFU.

Poro-Sande n. (1700s–1860s) of African origin; divine order; "Poro-Sande was law. Poro-Sande was order. And Poro-Sande came from God" (JEH, A, p. 78). SU.

Porsche n. (1980s–1990s) a shapely woman. (EF, RDSL, p. 250.) South-central Los Angeles; YCU.

Portrait n. (1900s) one's face. (DB, OHHJ, p. 145.) Harlem; NCU.

Portuguese n. (1930s–1940s) nickname for persons of Black, Indian, and Anglo ancestry native to Tennessee. (FR.) Tennessee use.

Posse n. (1990s) in third person, oneself. (HC, WSJ, p. B1.) Example: "The posse can't handle this, so he's splitting—catch you on the rebound."

Posse n. (1980s–1990s) a gang; group of young drug runners; musical group; group of close friends. (TW, CK, p. 137; PM, UCLAS, p. 68.) YCU, SCU, DCU.

[Let's] Posse up v. (1990s) a request or command that the group —or gathering of friends—should get ready to depart its present location, such as a cafe. (FR.) YCU.

Possum-la n. (1900s–1940s) a jumping dance step; "Possum Up-a That 'Simmon Tree." (BJ, BLH, SD, p. 127, 221.) SU.

Pot n. (1930s–1990s) marijuana; especially in the form of a cigarette; term may derive from the practice of city dwellers growing marijuana (cannabis sativa) in city flower pots on the window ledge; or, possibly from earlier cant use of "pot" as a woman. (CLC, TS, p. 255;

SL, RJON, p. 146; WF, DAS, p. 403; RSG, JT, pp. 206–207; FN, JS, p. 292; DC, BJ, p. 76; DW, TL, p. 186; CS, vol. 3, no. 2, p. 38.) DCU, SNU.

Potato man n. (1900s–1960s) a nonplaying, instrument-carrying "musician" assigned to a ten- or twelve-man marching band. (RSG, JT, p. 207.) Example: "His horn is plugged with potatoes." JMFU.

Pothead n. (1950s–1960s) a person who habitually smokes marijuana. (WF, DAS, p. 700; CS, vol. 3, no. 2, p. 38.) DCU.

Pot-licking v. (1960s) ingratiate; "ass-kissing"; to win favor by being solicitous. (CS, vol. 3, no. 2, p. 38.) SCU, SNU.

Pot liquor n. (1860s–1940s) of black southern origin; juice from greens. (WF, DAS, p. 404.) SU.

Pot liquor n. (1950s) marijuana juice; derived from the black southern expression of juice from greens; brew from marijuana seeds and stalks. (RRL, DAZ, p. 206.) DCU.

Pot party n. (1960s) a gathering of friends and acquaintances in an apartment or house for the purpose of smoking pot and listening to music. (CS, vol. 3, no. 2, p. 38.) DCU, SCU.

Pots [are] on v. (1950s–1960s) in jazz, to really be "cooking"; means the music is very beautiful and very effective. (RSG, JT, p. 207.) JMFU.

Potted v. (1960s) to be intoxicated on marijuana smoke. (CS, vol. 3, no. 2, p. 38.) DCU, SCU.

Pounder n. (1940s) a policeman or detective—so called because of excessive walking, especially on sidewalks. (DB, OHHJ, p. 145; CC, OMMM, NCCHD, p. 259.) Harlem; SNCU.

Pounds n. (1960s) dollars; money; five dollars. (JH, PBL, p. 85; DC, BJ, p. 76; DW, TL, p. 186.) SCU, DCU, NECU.

Pour-man n. (1940s) a bartender. (DB, OHHJ, p. 145.) Harlem; JMFU, SNCU.

Power n. (1890s–1930s) money. (FR.) Rare. SNU.

Power Dance; Black Power Dance n. (1960s) the mood of reacting physically to oppression; looting. (FR.) SCU.

Powerhouse n. (1970s) person who has charisma; extremely competent person. (FR.) SNU.

Power to the people interj. (1960s) greeting indicating political solidarity. (FR.) SCU.

PR n. (1960s) a Puerto Rican male or female. (DC, BJ, p. 74.) NCU.

Prat; pratting n. (1930s–1950s) a term usually applied to women; coyness; erotic or sexual teasing; playing hard-to-get during love-making in order to prolong foreplay. (IS, PSML, p. 317.) SCU, PPU, DCU, SNCU.

Prayer-bones n. (1880s–1940s) the knees. (JSF, AON, p. 436; DB, OHHJ, p. 145.) SNU.

Prayer-dukes n. (1920s–1940s) one's knees. (DB, OHHJ, p. 145.)

Prayer-handles n. (1920s–1940s) the knees. (DB, OHHJ, p. 145.) SNU.

Preg adj. (1940s–1990s) short for pregnant. (EF, RDSL, p. 250.) SNU.

Prescription red(s) n. (1970s–1990s) Seconal (secobarbital) in red capsules. (EF, RDSL, p. 250.) DCU.

Prescriptions n. (1970s–1990s) any type of amphetamine, tranquilizer, or barbiturate in capsule form sold on the street by "clockers" (drug dealers). (EF, RDSL, p. 250.) DCU.

Press the flesh v. (1960s) to shake hands. (FR.) Rare. NCU.

Pressed adj. (1960s–1990s) well-dressed, especially in expensive clothes; "clean." (EF, RDSL, p. 250; DC, BJ, p. 76; DW, TL, p. 186.) SCU.

Press roll n. (1900s–1950s) in jazz, a drum roll that builds in intensity and volume; drum-roll momentum. (WF, DAS, p. 407; RSG, JT, pp. 207–208) JMFU.

Pretty adj. (1900s–1940s) loosely used, in jazz, for poor-quality music; "white" music; fake blues or jazz. (RSG, JT, p. 208.) JMFU.

Prez n. (1950s–1960s) a leader or power figure; from the nickname Billie Holiday gave Lester Young. (DC, BJ, p. 76.) Example: "The prez won't dig it."

Prez [Pres; President] Lester Willis Young, jazz tenor saxophone player; called the "president" of the tenor saxophone; born in Woodville, Mississippi, August 27, 1909, and died in New York City on March 15, 1959, worked with Count Basie, Billie Holiday, Fletcher Henderson, and many others.

[The] Price [of one's] hat isn't the measure [of one's] brain 1800s–1940s) that is, one's intelligence cannot be measured in terms of a person's material value or worth. (FR.) SNU.

Prince n. (1970s–1980s) charismatic male. (FR.) YCU.

[One's] Privates n. (1900s–1950s) penis or vagina. (HLF, RJPD, p. 171.) Example: "Sadie, that boy too old to be walking round with his privates hanging like that—I don't care if he is only three, put some pants on that boy." SNU.

Prison-yard queen n. (1980s–1990s) male homosexual in prison. (KCJ, JS, p. 141.) PU.

Prob n. (1990s) short for "problem." (FR.) Example: "Yes, I changed the record. You got a problem with that?" YCU.

Process n. (1930s–1960s) straightened hairstyle for men. (EF, RDSL, p. 250; HLF, RJPD, p. 171; DC, BJ, p. 76; CS, vol. 3, no. 2, p. 38.) SNU.

Processed mind n. (1960s) the type of black mind which seems to see things solely from a white perspective. (DC, BJ, p. 76.) SNCU.

[The] Product n. (1980s–1990s) illegal narcotics; already processed street drugs. (KCJ, JS, p. 152.) New York City; DCU.

Professional woman n. (1950s–1990s) a pimp's term for a prostitute he respects. (CRM, BP, p. 306.) PPU.

Professor [prof] n. (1900s–1930s) an ironic term for a pianist who works in a juke joint, cabaret, or longhouse. (RSG, JT, pp. 208–209.) JMFU.

Profile; profiling v. (1960s–1990s) exhibitionistic behavior; strutting; an arrogant walk; proud walk. (FR.) YCU, SCU, YCU, SNCU.

Profile for the fans v. (1960s–1990s) to show off; stroll in a flashy manner. (CS, vol. 3, no. 3, p. 9.) Example: "When you see her stepping like that she's profiling for the fans." Watts; SCU, YCU.

Program n. (1960s) one's way of life; the way one conducts one's affairs; one's personal business or style. (DC, BJ, p. 76.) Example: "That's her program."

Progressive jazz n. (RSG, JT, p. 209.) See "Bebop" and "Bop."

Projects n. (1930s–1990s) any large urban housing development unit that has become a black ghetto. (FR.) SNU.

[The] Promised Land n. (1800s–1950s) Negro slaves' concrete expression for the concept of freedom—usually referred to the northern states of the union, sometimes to Heaven. (FR.) SU.

Pronging v. (1940s) having a good time, especially at a lively party. (MHB, JS, np.) SNU.

Prop n. (1950s–1960s) a proposition, especially by police, to inform for a lighter sentence. (CLC, TS, p. 255; DW TL, p. 186; CS, vol. 3, no. 2, p. 38.) PU, DCU, SCU.

Prop(s) n. (1990s) in the show business side of rap, a forum or platform, such as a radio or television program, which can offer exposure to the artist. (MC Lyle, *Essence*, September 1992, p. 85.) Rap "show business" use.

[Fine] Props n. (1940s–1970s) a young woman's or girl's legs; legs. (MHB, JS, np; DB, OHHJ, p. 145;) Harlem; SNU.

Props n. (1980s) weapons or people who can protect you. (FR.) YCU, SCU.

Props n. (1990s) to give credit where credit is due. (FR.) YCU, SCU.

Props n. (1990s) the proper respect or recognition for an accomplishment or achievement. (FR.) Example: "When Jake comes here he always shows me props in front of the kids." SNCU.

Pross n. (1950s–1970s) short for prostitute. (SH, GL, p. 212; DW, TL, p. 186.) SCU, PPU.

Protection n. (1950s–1990s) usually a condom. (FR.) SNU.

Prune(s) n. (1920s–1950s) a black person's head; "nigger-head"; picked up from white use. (HEG, DAUL, p. 304.) SNU.

Psychedelic to the bone adj. (1970s–1990s) to be very high on any kind of drugs, such as amphetamines or barbiturates, not simply mescaline, DMT, cannabis, LSD, or psilocybin. (EF, RDSL, p. 250.) DCU.

Psych v. (1960s–1990s) to gain mental control over someone or to manipulate someone's mind. (DC, BJ, p. 76.) Example: "When Ralph puts his mind to it he can psyche any of them people coming in the shop borrowing money they and he know they'll never pay back." SNCU.

Psych out v. (1970s–1980s) to understand another's point of view. (DC, BJ, p. 76.) See "Psych."

PTS (1970s–1980s) "secret" term for an unwashed and unpleasant-smelling woman or girl; abbreviation for "pussy, titties, armpits." (EF, RDSL, p. 249.) South-central Los Angeles; YCU, SCU.

Puddinghead Ed Battle, jazz musician.

Pudenany n. See "Poontang."

Puffed air n. (1940s) no food; a play on puffed wheat. (DB, OHHJ, p. 145.) Example: "My refrigerator is empty, so I'm eating puffed air till payday." Harlem; SNU.

Pull n. (1960s–1990s) influence; personal charm; possessing the ability to win favor; power, force. (EF, RDSL, p. 250.) SNU. See "Catch."

Pull v. (1950s–1990s) to take; to win; to attract. (CRM, BP, p. 306; DW, TL, p. 186.) Example: "Robert the kind of pimp who can pull a ho from any punk even if she's being treated right." PPU.

Pull a quick park v. (1980s–1990s) to succeed quickly in "picking up" a stranger as a sexual partner. (EF, RDSL, p. 250.) South-central Los Angeles; YCU.

Pull [one's] coat v. (1930s–1960s) to alert someone to something; to inform; to expose. (DG, DC, p. 25; RDP, SRO, p. 103; IS, TB, p. 312; RSG, JT, p. 209; EF, RDSL, p. 250; JH, PBL, p. 85; CS, vol. 3, no. 2, p. 39.) SCU, PPU, YCU, JMFU.

Pull [one's] cover v. (1950s–1970s) to expose; to reveal one's secret activities. (CS, vol. 3, no. 2, p. 39.) SCU, YCU.

Pull dude n. (1980s–1990s) one who informs on fellow inmates to the prison authorities. (JMC, PS, p. 50.) PU.

Pulleys n. (1940s) suspenders. (DB, OHHJ, p. 145.) Harlem; SNU.

Pull off v. (1950s–1960s) to do something; accomplish. (DG, DC, p. 35; DW, TL, p. 186.) SNU.

Pull shoe strings v. (1930s–1940s) variant of "pull strings" as does the ventriloquist behind the dummy; to make a secret deal; to make an underhanded arrangement; a crooked deed. (MHB, JS, np.) SNU.

Pull to a set v. (1980s–1990s) to go to a party or where the "action" is. (EF, RDSL, p. 250.) Example: "When I pull to the set with Lisa, dig how Bill and John react." YCU.

Pull wool [to the white folks] v. (1800s–1920s) of Gullah origin; in the absence of a hat, to touch or "pull" a few strands of hair at the front of the head; a subservient and self-effacing gesture; a salutation of humility and respect—same as tipping one's hat to someone out of respect. (AEG, BB, p. 321.) SU.

Pump n. (1970s–1990s) a machine gun or any type of shoulder or handgun requiring pumping action. (EF, RDSL, p. 250.) SCU, PU, DCU.

Pump the stump v. (1940s) to shake hands. (MHB, JS, np.) SU.

Pumpkin n. (1940s) the moon or the sun. (DB, OHHJ, p. 145.) SNU.

Pumpkin-seed n. (1800s–1920s) a mulatto; light-skinned person. (CVV, NH, p. 286.) Harlem; SNU. See "Pumpkin-skin."

Pumpkin-skin n. (1800s–1920s) a mulatto; light-skinned person. (AEG, BB, p. 321.) See "Pumpkin-seed."

Punch Ernest Miller, trumpet player and singer; born December 24, 1897; worked with Big Bill Broonzy, the blues singer, and others.

Punch n. (1920s–1940s) a spontaneous or planned free party where dancing, eating, and drinking are done; a lively gathering of friends. (LA, SM, p. 411; WF, DAS, p. 411.) SNCU.

Punk n. (1940s–1990s) derogatory term for male homosexual; a homosexual's companion. (EF, RDSL, p. 250; RDA, DDJ, p. 266; DC, BJ, p. 76.) SNU, SCU, PPU.

Punk n. (1950s–1990s) male pejorative term for any other male without similar interest; a weak man; any male who gives in to anal intercourse in prison; same as "sissy"; "Punk . . . was a warrior word slung at those who lacked 'manly' courage," says Elaine Brown. "It addressed not sexuality but power" (Alice Walker, "They Ran on

Empty"; Elaine Brown, "Attack Racism, Not Black Men," *The New York Times*, May 5, 1993, p. A17; EF, RDSL, p. 250; CRM, BP, p. 306; CS, vol. 3, no. 2, p. 39.) SCU, DCU, YCU, PPU, PU, SNU.

Punk n. (1950s–1990s) pejorative term for any male. (DG, DL, p. 124.) PPU, DCU, SCU, YCU.

Punk(ing) v. (1970s–1990s) to perform anal intercourse. (EF, RDSL, p. 250.) SCU.

Punk pills n. (1960s–1970s) any type of tranquilizers. (CS, vol. 3, no. 2, p. 39.) Watts; DCU, SCU, YCU.

Punk's run n. (1980s–1990s) a unit in a prison where an inmate is kept in protective custody. (JMC, PS, p. 50.) PU.

Pup pup n. See "Poop."

Puppy n. (1970s–1990s) a half-pint size bottle of fortified "rotgut" wine sold exclusively in ghetto liquor stores. (EF, RDSL, p. 250.) SCU.

Puppy n. (1960s–1980s) any young man who's head-over-heels in love, especially one who's affection is not being returned. (EF, RDSL, p. 250.) SNU.

Puppy n. (1900s–1990s) a pet name for one's wife or husband or sexual partner and companion. (EF, RDSL, p. 250.) SNU.

Puppy n. (1950s–1960s) a teenage male who's sexually active, especially with an older woman or older women. (EF, RDSL, p. 250.) SNU.

Puppy n. (1880s–1990s) female pet name for her husband's or lover's penis. (EF, RDSL, p. 250.) SNU.

Pure silk n. (1960s) neutral heterosexual term for a male homosexual. (DC, BJ, p. 77.) Rare. MWU.

Push v. (1930s) to sell or distribute something—usually drugs. (FR.) DCU.

Push v. (1970s) to drive, especially a car. (DW, TL, p. 186.) New York; SCU, PPU.

Push; pushing n., v. (1920s–1930s) in jazz, energetic music; music with a strong rhythm section. (MM, RB, p. 373; RSG, JT, pp. 209–210.) JMFU.

Pusher n. (1930s–1990s) one who delivers and sells narcotics. (CLC, p. 255; RSG, JT, p. 210.) DCU.

Pusher n. (1980s–1990s) a slender stick or chopstick used to stuff cocaine residue farther down into the pipe stem. (TW, CH, p. 150.) DCU. See "Packer."

Puss n. (1940s) the face. (DB, OHHJ, p. 145.) SNU.

Puss'ed adj. (1940s–1950s) to be henpecked or submerged by one's wife. (FR.) See "Pussy-whipped."

Pussy n. (1940s–1950s) a weak man; a coward; a "sissy." (RDP, SRO, p. 103; DW, TL, p. 187.) SCU, PPU, DCU, NCU.

Pussy n. (1800s–1990s) the vagina. (EF, RDSL, p. 250.) SNU. See "Pussycat."

Pussy n. (1930s–1950s) any beautiful woman; considered derogatory by women because it reduces them to a sexual object. (EF, RDSL, p. 250.) SNU.

Pussycat n. (1800s–1990s) the vagina. (EF, RDSL, p. 250.) SNU.

Pussy-clot n. (1980s–1990s) a male coward; an informer. (JM, WPC, p. 41.) SCU, YCU.

Pussy tickler n. (1940s–1950s) mustache. (FR.) SNU.

Pussy-whipped adj. (1900s–1990s) to be henpecked or submerged by one's wife; patriarchal vulgar expression referring to a man perceived to be dominated by a woman. (EF, RDSL, p. 250.) SNU.

Puta n. (1950s–1990s) whore; prostitute; picked up by blacks from Spanish-speaking neighbors in New York and Los Angeles. (Peri Thomas, *Down These Mean Streets*, p. 316: EF, RDSL, p. 251.) PPU, SCU.

Put a damper on [one's] high v. (1950s) to take the edge off a drug "high" by eating or drinking. (FR.) DCU.

Put a hurt on [one] v. (1960s–1970s) to carry out revenge on someone; to cause physical or mental pain; abuse. (KCJ, JS, p. 151.) SCU, PU, DCU, YCU.

Put a spell on [one] v. (1800s–1940s) to work magic on a person. (FR.) SU.

Put(ting) down v. (1940s–1950s) to perform, do, say, act. (DB, OHHJ, p. 145; RSG, JT, pp. 210–211.) Example: "You can't tell what they putting down unless you go out there and see them for yourself." JMFU, SCU, YCU, SNCU.

Put down; put-down v., n. (1940s–1970s) an insult; reject someone. (SL, RJON, p. 147; WF, DAS, pp. 413–414) Example: "He had nothing but put-downs for me." SCU, JMFU, YCU.

Put [something] down v. (1970s–1990s) a command to desist; order to stop or to surrender something. (EF, RDSL, p. 251.) Example: "He came in here with his ass on his shoulder and I just told him to put that shit down right this minute." SNU.

Put [one's] foot in [one's] ass v. (1950s–1990s) usually uttered as a threat of physical violence. (DW, TL, p. 187.) SCU, PPU, PU.

Put [one's] foot up v. (1920s–1930s) to make an arrogant and forceful presence; tell one off. (ZNH, DTR, p. 194.) SNU.

[To be] Put in check v. (1980s–90s) to be restrained from making a mistake.

Put [one] in the alley v. (1900s–1920s) in jazz, to play earthy blues or jazz; to play or sing with vigor; to play real soul music, down-home style. (RSG, JT, p. 212.) JBWU, SU.

Put [one] in the wind v. (EF, RDSL, p. 250.) See "Get in the wind" and "Split."

Put it in lay-away v. (1960s–1970s) to hold back; refrain from telling someone something; to save something for another time. (DC, BJ, p. 77.) NCU.

Put [one] on v. (1680s–1990s) originated among slaves; popular among jazz musicians during the forties; to fake or tease or mislead; in the seventies, eighties, and nineties, to ridicule a person who is not aware he or she is a victim of malicious fun; obviously related to earlier use of "putting on white folks" and faking or teasing. (RSG, JT, p. 211; WF, DAS, p. 700.) See "Putting on white folks."

Put on a crosstown bus v. (1960s) to deliberately confuse someone. (RRL, DAZ, p. 211.) New York; YCU.

[To be] Put on the block v. (1680s–1860s) to be sold on an auction block as a slave. (FR.) SU.

Put [one] on the block v. (1930s–1990s) pimp term; send a woman out to sell sex for money. (EF, BVV, p. 50; EF, RDSL, p. 251.) PPU.

Put [one] on the corner v. (EF, RDSL, p. 251.) See "Put [one] on the block."

Put on [one's] traveling shoes v. (1780s–1950s) symbolic of going to heaven; to get ready to leave home or some other place; heard in and picked up from the spirituals. (FR.) SU.

Put out v. (1950s–1970s) to be promiscuous; in the seventies, to give sexual favors on demand. (FR.) YCU, SCU.

Put [one's] stuff down v. (1970s–1990s) to ridicule or insult one. (EF, RDSL, p. 251.) See "Base."

Put the freeze on v. (1970s) command to stop. (EF, RDSL, p. 251.) Rare. See "Put [something] down."

Put the issue on [one] v. (1940s) to give an inducted young man an army uniform, a gun, and the required military training before sending him to the frontline. (FR.) Military use.

Putting down v. See "Put down."

Putting on v. (1680s–1990s) pretending. (Hear Lightnin' Hopkins, "That's My Story," *Prison Blues*, Collectables, 1989.) See "Put [one] on."

Putting on white folks v. (1680s–1990s) smiling and grinning at and yes-ing white folks; giving white strangers a "line"; telling white folks what they want to hear. (RDA, TB, p. 33.) SNU.

Put wise v. (1960s–1970s) to explain something; inform; spell out in detail. (DW, TL, p. 187.) SCU, SNCU.

Puzzlegut n. (1900s–1940s) a large stomach, especially on a man. (CM, CW, Zora Neale Hurston, "The Gilded Six-Bits," p. 71.) SU.

Q n. (1940s–1950s) short for "barbecued ribs." (FR.) Example: "Let's go down to Mae's Rib Shack and get's some Q's." SNU.

[On the] QT adj. (1940s–1960s) short for "quiet." (FR.) See "On the QT" and "Quiet as it's kept."

Quadroon n. (1780s–1920s) the offspring of a mulatto and a white parent. (EBR, MUS, p. 12.) SU.

Quail n. (1930s–1950s) an attractive young woman. (LA, SM, pp. 414–415.) SU.

Quarter bag n. (1980s–1990s) a plastic sandwich bag of marijuana sold for twenty-five dollars. (EF, RDSL, p. 251; RRL, DAZ, p. 212.) DCU.

Quarteron n. (1780s–1920s) the offspring of a mulatto and a white parent. (EBR, MUS, p. 12.) SU.

Quarters n. (1750s–1860s) the section of the plantation where the slaves lived; the area the slaves called "home." (JSF, AON, p. 445.) SU.

Quashee n. (1620s–1850s) one of the seven day names for a West African male. (AB, DSJC, p. 480.) SU.

Queen n. (1900s–1960s) a beautiful young woman; man's wife; companion; sweetheart; girlfriend; lover. (CC, OMMM, NCCHD, p. 259; EF, RDSL, p. 251; CC, HDH, np; Chester Himes, *Black on Black*, p. 196.) SNU.

Queen n. (1960s–1990s) a lesbian. (DC, BJ, p. 77.) Rare. MWU.

Queen n. (1960s–1990s) male homosexual; black (and white) male homosexual use. (HM, GL, p. 34.) Gay life.

Queen Latifah (1990s) a popular female rap artist.

Queen of de Nile [denial] n. (1990s) a woman who refuses to face reality; self-deceiver.

Queen of Soul Aretha Franklin, rhythm-and-blues singer.

Quickie n. (1940s–1990s) quick sexual encounter. (WF, DAS, pp. 415–416.) SNU.

Quick one n. (1950s) a quick drink of liquor. (WF, DAS, p. 416.)

Quiet as it's kept adj. (1940s–1950s) an expression used prior to revealing what is assumed to be a secret. (FR.) SNU.

Quiet village n. (1980s–1990s) Venice, California. (EF, RDSL, p. 251.) Watts and South-central Los Angeles use.

Quill n. (1950s–1970s) a folded matchbook cover in which a narcotic is held and smoked or sniffed. (RRL, DAZ, p. 212.) Rare. DCU.

Quill n. (1950s–1960s) the genuine article; the authentic thing. (IS, TB, p. 312.) DCU, SCU, PU.

Quit it v. (1940s–1950s) to die. (WF, DAS, p. 701.) SNU.

Quit the scene v. (1950s) to leave a place such as a street corner or a bar; also, said of someone who has just died; to die. (RSG, JT, p. 213.) JMFU, SNCU, SCU.

R

Rabbit John C. Hodges, born 1906, an alto saxophonist; also Richard Brown, born around 1880 in New Orleans, a country blues singer.

[A] Rabbit n. (1970s–1990s) a white person. (EF, RDSL, p. 251.) South-central Los Angeles, YCU, SCU.

Rabbit foot n. (1890s–1930s) attention; good luck. (MT, DAF, p. 244.) SNU.

[The] Rabbit prizefighter Floyd Patterson.

Race music n. (1900s–1950s) African-American music, especially the blues and jazz; ethnic black music produced by and sold almost exclusively to black people during the twenties and thirties—black music was separate from white music from its beginning through the fifties, a situation that started changing in the sixties; the type of music generally known as rhythm-and-blues. (RSG, JT, p. 215; WF, DAS, p. 416.) JMFU.

[A] Rack n. (1970s–1990s) a card with birth control pills for one month: three or five capsules contained in plastic bubbles. (EF, RDSL, p. 251.) SNCU.

Racket-jacket n. (1930s–1940s) a zoot suit. (WF, DAS, p. 416; DB, OHHJ, p. 145.) SCU.

Rack pick n. (1970s–1990s) an afro-comb; a comb with widely spaced teeth; a pick. (EF, RDSL, p. 251.) YCU. See "Fork."

Racktify (wreck-tify) v. (1850s–1920s) of Gullah origin, meaning to break something. (AEG, BB, p. 322.) SU.

Rado n. (1970s–1990s) short for Cadillac El Dorado, a popular car in "the ghetto." (EF, RDSL, p. 251.) SNCU.

Rag n. (1890s–1920s) in jazz, a simple piano syncopation. (RSG, pp. 216–217; WF, DAS, p. 417.) JMFU. See "Ragtime (music)."

[The] Rag n. (1800s–1990s) during slavery times and in the rural South up to the forties, a rag; since the forties, a sanitary napkin. (EF, RDSL, p. 251.) Example: "Your wife must be on the rag, Joe, you been mean as a snake all morning." SNU.

Rag n. (1940s–1950s) a magazine or newspaper. (DB, OHHJ, p. 145.) SNU.

Rag v. (1950s) to complain. (RSG, JT, p. 216; WF, DAS, p. 417.) Example: "He ragged all the time about any and everything." JMFU.

Ragged down heavy adj. (1950s–1990s) dressed in expensive and attractive clothes. (EF, RDSL, p. 251.) SNCU, YCU.

[To] Rag out v. (1950s–1970s) to put on one's finest clothes. (FR.) YCU.

Raggedy adj. (1960s) poor-looking; destitute in appearance; drunk; unkempt. (DC, BJ, p. 77; EF, RDSL, p. 251.) Example: "He drives a raggedy car." Also, incomplete; ineffectual. Example: "I know my shit is raggedy. I haven't paid my bill this month."

Raggedy Ann n. (1970s–1990s) any unattractive or unpleasant woman. (EF, RDSL, p. 251.) SNU.

Raggedy-ass, raggedy-assed adj. (1950s–1960s) state of shabbiness; lacking neatness; dirty or unkempt. (FR.) SNU.

Raghead n. (1900s–1960s) a black male who wears a scarf or kerchief tied around his head to protect an expensive hairdo. (FR.) SNU.

Ragmen n. (1900s–1920s) jazzmen who play ragtime music. (RSG, JT, p. 216.) JMFU. See "Ragtime (music)."

Ragmop adj. (1940s–1950s) messy, unkempt. (FR.) JMFU, SCU.

Rags n. (1960s) one's clothes, especially good-looking garments. (DC, BJ, p. 77; HLF, RJPD, p. 171; EF, RDSL, p. 251; CS, vol. 3, no. 2, p. 39.) Example: "Those are some bad rags." See "Vines."

Ragtime [music] n. (1890s–1920s) a simple sixteen-bar piano style, usually with a quick gay tempo and fast breaks, combined with complex figures; "hot" music that probably originated in Missouri; a distinct form of music that preceded jazz (or, as it came to be known in the 1970s, "the sound of the black experience" or "the black experience in sound"), usually a very "hot" style. (RSG, JT, p. 216; WF, DAS, p. 417; SL, RJON, p. 7.) JMFU, SNU.

Ragtime shuffle n. (1900s–1920s) a drum break in the ragtime manner. (RSG, JT, p. 217.) JMFU. See "Ragtime [music]."

Rah-rah n. (1940s) clothes—especially drapes—fashionable among college students in Negro colleges. (DB, OHHJ, p. 145; MHB, JS, np.) Negro college student use.

Raifield v. (1950s–1960s) to steal openly and contemptuously without regard for personal safety; to go about stealing in a reckless manner. (CLC, TS, p. 255.) SCU, PU.

Railroad Bill (1890s) Morris Stater, a black hero who robbed trains, stealing from the rich and giving to the poor; like Robin Hood, he became the subject of legends and ballads. (MT, DAF, pp. 245–246; Ruby Pickens Tartt, *Toting the Lead Row*, 1981, pp. 148–149.) SNU.

Railroad whiskey n. (1970s–1990s) Santa Fe wine; any cheap "rotgut"; fortified wine sold exclusively in "the ghetto." (EF, RDSL, p. 251.) South-central Los Angeles, SCU.

Rain v., n. (1880s–1950s) to complain, especially about hard times, being without money or food or shelter; used as a symbol of hard times. (WF, DAS, p. 701.) Example: "Rain keep on falling in my life every time I turn around." SNU.

Rain coat n. (1950s–1960s) a condom or prophylactic. (JH, PBL, p. 85.) SNCU, SCU, YCU.

Rainbow(s) n. (1970s–1990s) barbiturate or secobarbital in colorful red and blue capsules; Tuinal. (EF, RDSL, p. 251; CS, vol. 3, no. 2, p. 39.) DCU.

Rainbow Queen n. (1980s–1990s) from the Reverend Jesse Jackson's phrase "rainbow coalition," any gay person who is involved in a black-white interracial relationship. (HM, GL, p. 35.) Homosexual use.

[A] Raise n. (1940s–1950s) a pocket. (IS, TB, p. 312.) SCU, PPU.

Raise n. (1950s–1960s) parents. (DC, BJ, p. 77.) Example: "My raise won't go for it." YCU.

Raise v. (1850s–1960s) to go; leave; start moving; procure; obtain; make; to get out of, be bailed out of, or be released from jail. (DC, BJ, p. 77; JH, PBL, p. 85; JSF, AON, pp. 449–450.) MWU, SCU, YCU.

Raise Cain v. (1840s–1940s) to make trouble and noise; to brawl; fight; cause a ruckus. A distant echo of the bibilical Cain. (WF, DAS, p. 418.) SNU. See "Raise sand."

[The] Raise n. (1950s–1970s) the police; from the 1850s to about the 1920s, the word "raise" was used in the streets to mean a burglary, or to steal. (EP, DU, p. 553; JSF, AON, pp. 449–450.) SCU, PU.

Raise hell v. (1840s–1950s) cause a ruckus; make trouble. (FR.) SNU.

Raise sand v. (1840s–1940s) to make an outcry; to brawl; to fight; to complain loudly; to stop. (MM, RB, p. 374; RSG, JT, p. 217.) SNU.

Rale adj. (1850s–1890s) very, really, truly. (CCJ, NMGC, p. 169.) SU.

Ramify v. (1850s–1920s) of Gullah origin, meaning to smash something all to pieces; "to act like a ram." (AEG, BB, p. 322.) SU.

Rank adj. (1920s–1990s) faulty; filthy; bad; unpleasant; stupid flaw. (RDA, TB, p. 56; RSG, JT, p. 217; CC, OMMM, NCCHD, p. 259; HLF, RJPD, p. 171; PM, UCLAS, p. 70; EF, RDSL, p. 251; CS, vol. 3, no. 2, p. 40.) YCU, SCU.

[To] Rank [one] v. (EF, BVV, p. 50.) See "Rank."

Ranking [on] (1920s–1990s) to insult; to denigrate. Also "capping," "sounding," "mounting," "playing the dozens." (RDA, TB, p. 56; WF, DAS, pp. 418–419; DB, OHHJ, p. 145; EF, RDSL, p. 251; CS, vol. 3, no. 2, p. 40.) YCU, SCU. See "Dirty dozens" and "Base."

[A] Ranky dank n. (1960s–1970s) an uninformed, "square" person; one who is not mindful of what is fashionable in terms of behavior, dress, and vocabulary. (CS, vol. 3, no. 2, p. 40.) YCU.

Ranky tank n. (1950s) dance motion that imitates riding a bicycle. (FR.) YCU.

Rap v., n. (1730s–1990s) In Sierra Leone usage, rap means to con, fool, flirt, tease, or taunt; as a noun "rap" was used as early as 1753 to refer to the theft of a purse. Another early meaning (1732) was a false oath or to perjure oneself. "Rap" has been in use as cant, in one form or another, since the seventeenth century. It's meant to talk or converse since the 1870s, and by 1916 the noun "rapper" was used generally to refer to a police informer or a talking witness to a crime; "to rap," therefore, has carried the implication of talking long before it was taken up by black speakers in its present-day form, in the late forties or early fifties, and transformed, to be used in none of the other previous ways: to refer to an arrest, a criminal charge, a conviction, a prison term, going to jail, and so on. There's a remote possibility that the word was derived from prisoners tapping or rapping on walls as a means of communication. Since the late forties, "rap" has meant to hold a conversation; a long, impressive, lyrical social or political monologue; rapid, clever talk; rhyming monologue; conversation as a highly self-conscious art form. At least among black speakers, European and African uses may have converged. (HV, AHAE, p. 147; EP, DU, pp. 555–556; WF, DAS, p. 419; CRM, BP, p. 306; DC, BJ, p. 77; CS, vol. 3, no. 2, p. 40; RRL, DAZ, p. 212; HLF, RJPD, p. 171; JH, PBL, p. 86; EF, RDSL, p. 251; DW, TL, p. 187.) SCU, YCU, SNCU, PU, PPU.

Rap Jack n. (1900s–1940s) a game played by black adults and children in the South. Players whip each other's legs with switches; apparently the first one to give in to pain or to cry is the loser. (BJ, BLH, SD, p. 186.) SU.

Rapper n. (1940s–1990s) a talker; a singer who performs rhyming political or socially conscious songs; in the latter part of the nineteenth century, a contemptuous term for a spiritualist. (JSF, AON, p. 452.) See "Rap."

Rapping v. (1940s–1980s) talking; singing a type of poetry fused with a strong beat. (RRL, DAZ, p. 212.) See "Rap."

Raptavist n. (1990s) a rap singer who is also politically active. Also "Sister Soldier." Rap artists and fan use.

Raspy [rasty] adj. (1970s–1990s) unpleasant or unappealing; unattractive; dirty. (EF, RDSL, p. 251.) SCU, YCU.

Rat n. (1930s) a wig. (Hear Lightnin Hopkins's "Short Haired Woman," *The Complete Aladdin Recordings* 1, EMI Records, 1991.) SU.

[A] Rat n. (1900s–1990s) an informer or informant. (CS, vol. 3, no. 2, p. 40.) See "[To] Rat on [one]."

Ratamacue n. (1920s–1930s) an onomatopoeic construction representing a drum phrase. (RSG, JT, p. 218.) Rare. JMFU.

Rat hole n. (1940s) one's pocket. (DB, OHHJ, p. 145.) Harlem, SNU.

[To] Rat on [one] (1900s–1990s) to inform the police of a crime; to turn someone in to the police for a crime; to plead guilty to a crime and to inform on one's accomplices; picked up from underworld use. (EP, DU, pp. 556–557; CS, vol. 3, no. 2, p. 40.) SCU, PU.

Rattle [one's] chain (1990s) to annoy. (FR.) Example (said to one who is agitated): "Who rattled your chain?" YCU, SCU, SNU.

Raunchy (ronchie) adj., n. (1940s–1990s) very bad, cheap in quality. (WF, DAS, pp. 420–421; PM, UCLAS, p. 70.) SCU, YCU.

Raw adj. (1940s–1950s) short for "in the raw," or naked. (WF, DAS, p. 421.) YCU.

Raw adj. (1980s–1990s) natural, unpretentious; pleasantly accommodating; excellent; beautiful. (Big Daddy Kane, "R.A.W.," by Antonio Hardy p/k/a Big Daddy Kane (© 1988 Def Jam Music; PM, UCLAS, p. 71.) Example: "I like him because he's so raw." YCU, SCU.

Raw deal n. (1950s–1960s) a very unpleasant situation; a swindle. (WF, DAS, p. 421.) YCU, SCU.

Raw Head n. (1920s–1950s) a conjure doctor (Hurston).

Raw soul(s) n. (1840s–1860s) during slavery, a person not yet admitted to a black society; a secret society requiring initiation. (JEH, AAC, p. 79.) SU.

Razzmatazz n. (1930s–1940s) out of style; old-fashioned; anything outdated; popular but corny; poor-quality jazz. (WF, DAS, p. 421; SL, RJON, p. 421.) SNCU, YCU, JMFU.

Read v. (1960s) to understand another's motives. (WF, DAS, p. 422.) Example: "I can read you like a book." SNU.

Ready adj. (1930s–1990s) to be alert, able and willing to deal with the situation at hand; prepared for anything; receptive; "hip"; knowledgeable; attractively dressed. (RSG, JT, p. 218; WF, DAS, p. 423; CC, OMMM, NCCHD, p. 259; DB, OHHJ, p. 145; EF, RDSL, p. 251.) JMFU.

Reaganania n. (1980s) the United States of America, so called because of its then-current president, Ronald Reagan. (FR.) SCU, YCU.

[For] Real adj. (1940s–1960s) sincere, genuine; honest. (AL, MJR, p. 30; WF, DAS, p. 422; PM, UCLAS, p. 71.) SNU.

[A] Real woman n. (1970s–1990s) any heterosexual woman. (EF, RDSL, p. 251.) SNU.

Rearview n. (1980s) variant of rear end. (KCJ, JS, p. 140.) SCU, YCU.

Rebop (re-bop) n. (1940s–1950s) in jazz, staccato two-note phrase or four-beat music; early term for complex jazz. (Hear Lionel Hampton's "Hey-Baba-Rebop," 1946; RSG, JT, pp. 218–219; WF, DAS, p. 423.) JMFU.

Reckless eyeballing v. (1900s–1970s) obvious ogling of the opposite sex; looking with desire at "forbidden" persons; flirting. (FR.) See "Eyefuck."

Reckon v. (1800s–1950s) to guess; to imagine; conjecture. Picked up from southern white use. (FR.) SU.

[To] Reconstitute v. (1980s–1990s) to chemically alter cocaine so that it appears to be pure, to make it crystalline in appearance. (TW, CK, p. 137.) DCU.

Red Henry Allen, Jr., born 1908, trumpeter and singer.

Red, black and green n. (1960s–1990s) symbol of international black unity; the colors of Africa; used to invoke black unity. Example: "Get with the red, black and green."

Red bone (redbone) n. (1850s–1960s) a pale-skinned African American, from the French *os rouge*, spoken of a black person with American Indian blood. (DC, BJ, p. 77; BB, AW, pp. 26–27.) SNU. See "High yellow."

Red devil(s) n. (1970s–1990s) secobarbital or barbiturate compound in red capsules. (EF, RDSL, p. 251.) DCU.

Red dog on the white horse n. (EF, RDSL, p. 251.) See "Red Mary."

Red Fast Luck n. (1920s–1930s) hoodoo luck formula; a conjuring solution made with cinnamon, oil of vanilla, and wintergreen. (ZNH, MM, p. 336.) SU.

Red gravy n. (1940s) blood. (MHB, JS, n.p.) SU.

Red hot adj. (1900s–1930s) sexy; erotic. (WF, DAS, p. 424.) SNU, JMFU.

Red knight on the white horse n. (EF, RDSL, p. 251.) See "Red Mary."

Red Mary n. (1900s–1990s) a woman's menstrual flow; menses; period. (EF, RDSL, p. 251.) SNU.

Redneck n. (1870s–1950s) pejorative term for a countrified white person of the Deep South, usually a racist; from the thirties to the fifties, a poor white person in rural areas of the Deep South, especially one who is bigoted and crude. (WF, DAS, p. 424; ZNH, AM, p. 96; EF, RDSL, p. 251.) See "Country Cracker," "Cracker."

Red Shirts of South Carolina (1860s–1870s) a group of young white thugs committed to random violence against black people, especially active directly following the Civil War. (SBF, IHAT, p. 294.) SU.

Reefer n. (1920s–1960s) marijuana wrapped in cigarette paper; may be a variant of Mexican *grefa*. (CLC, TS, p. 255; CC, HDH, p. 16; RSG, JT, p. 219; SL, RJON, p. 144; WF, DAS, p. 424; RRL, DAZ, p. 213; ZNH, AM, p. 96; IS, PSML, p. 316; DB, OHHJ, p. 145; EF, RDSL, p. 251.) DCU.

[The] Reefer King (1930s–1940s) Harlem name for Mezz Mezzrow.

Reefer man n. (1920s–1950s) one who sells marijuana; a pusher. (RSG, JT, p. 219.) DCU.

Reefer weed (WF, DAS, p. 424.) See "Reefer."

Reet adv., adj. (1930s–1940s) variant of "right" in "all right"; good; yes; excellent. (RSG, JT, p. 219; LA, SM, p. 152; WF, DAS, np.; WF, DAS, p. 424.) SCU, JMFU, SNCU.

Reet pleat n. (1930s–1940s) a zoot suit pleat with a knife blade-sharp point; "zoot suit with the reet [right] pleat." SCU, YCU, JMFU, SNCU.

[The] Refrigerator William Perry, a Chicago football star.

[To] Register v. (1960s–1990s) heroin users' term for dropping blood in an eyedropper while injecting a vein. (CS, vol. 3, no. 2, p. 40.) DCU.

Regular n., adj. (1960s) any popular and respected pimp or hustler; to have a reputation for fair-dealing among one's fellow pimps and prostitutes. (CLC, TS, p. 255.) Example: "I'd trust Buster with the stash cause he's regular and you know he ain't gone prop for the nailers." DCU, PPU, SCU, PU.

Regular Hell n. (1900s–1940s) the place before one reaches West Hell, sometimes called Ginny Gall. (SK, PC, pp. 153–154.) SU.

Reliefer n. (1930s–1940s) a person receiving public assistance; on welfare; on relief. (CM, CW, Dorothy West, "Jack in the Pot," p. 123.) SNU.

Remembery v. (1680s–1920s) to remember. (FR.) Example: "The old folks remembery the time back before slavery ended." SU. See "Disremember."

Rent party [stomp; strut] n. (1920s–1940s) a party given in one's home to make money to pay the rent. Entertainment includes live or recorded "race music," and the guests pay for admission and for food and drinks. (RSG, JT, p. 220; WF, DAS, p. 425.) NCU.

Rep n. (1950–1990s) one's reputation. (DC, BJ, p. 77; MHB, JS, np.) SNU.

Repent pad n. (1940s) a bachelor's apartment, where a girl may be led to engage in an act she may later regret. (DB, OHHJ, p. 145.) Harlem, NCU.

Res n. (1980s–1990s) the "dew" or oil left in the pipe after smoking freebase. (TW, CH, p. 151.) DCU.

Rescue station n. (1970s–1990s) any liquor store. (EF, RDSL, p. 251.) South-central Los Angeles, SCU.

Rest v. (1940s–1960s) in jazz, when a musician stops playing to allow others to work out a section where his or her instrument isn't needed, or to allow someone to do a solo. (RSG, JT, p. 220.) JMFU.

Re-up v. (1980s–1990s) to replenish or restock one's supply of cocaine. (FR.) DCU.

Rhode n. (1940s) a young male's best male friend; one's "running mate." (MHB, JS, np.) Southern Negro college student use.

Rhythm n. (1990s) sexual advances. (FR.) Example: "I'm not sure, but I think Carl is giving me rhythm." YCU.

Rhythm-and-Blues [R and B] n. (1930s–1990s) music with a definite boogie base; before the seventies, a relaxed style of singing and playing so ethnically oriented that it had little appeal to other groups, unless transformed so that it had a less "nitty-gritty" character. (RSG, JT, p. 220.) JMFU, SNU. See "Race music."

Rhythm section n. (1920s–1960s) in a jazz band, the instrumental accompaniment that maintains the beat; the bass; drums. (RSG, JT, p. 221.) JMFU.

Rib n. (1960s) a girl or woman; from the biblical story of Adam making his mate Eve from one of his own ribs. (CS, vol. 3, no. 2, p. 40.) Watts, Los Angeles, use; YCU, SCU.

Rib joint n. (1900s–1990s) a restaurant or cafe where spareribs are offered. (FR.) SNU.

Ribs n. (1900s–1990s) short for "spareribs," but usually also refers to a full, hot supper, including ribs. (WF, DAS, p. 426.) SNU.

Riceman n. (1930s–1990s) mildly pejorative term for a Chinese male; usually used in reference to the workers in the many Chinese restaurants in black communities in northern cities. (DB, OHHJ, p. 145.) NCU.

Ricer n. (1930s–1990s) mildly pejorative term for any person of Asian descent; Chinese, Japanese. (EF, RDSL, p. 251.) South-central Los Angeles, NCU.

Ride n. adj. (1920s–1950s) in jazz, a solo chorus improvised brilliantly and artfully, such as those Charlie Parker was well known for; to keep "perfect" time. (CC, HDH, p. 16; RSG, JT, pp. 221–222; CC, OMMM, NCCHD, p. 259; DB, OHHJ, p. 145.) JMFU.

[To] Ride in the [one or something] seat (riding in the [one or something] seat) v., n. (1970s–1990s) derogatory expression for the seat in a car where a girl or woman is expected to sit; to be seated in the middle portion of the front or back seat of a car; for a girl or young woman to be seated in the front or back seat of a car, especially in the middle between two males; sexist and pejorative term meaning in the middle: to ride "pussy," "bitch," or "punk." (EF, BVV, p. 50; EF, RDSL, p. 251.) Examples: "I don't care what you dudes say, I'm not riding in the bitches' seat" or (one of three males about to get into a car) "Somebody got to ride pussy." South-central Los Angeles, SCU, YCU. See "[To] Ride bitch."

[Get on your pony and] Ride n. (1930s–1950s) a dance in the motion of one riding a horse; doing the Pony, a popular dance in the fifties. (WF, DAS, pp. 426–427.) YCU.

Ride n. (1950s–1960s) a car. (DC, BJ, p. 77; EF, RDSL, p. 251; CS, vol. 3, no. 2, p. 40.) Example: "That's a bad ride." SNCU, YCU, SCU.

[To] Ride bitch v., n. (1970s–1990s) to ride, either in the front or back seat, in the middle between two others. (PM, UCLAS, p. 71.) Example: "Cliff rather walk 'fore he'd ride bitch." YCU, SCU.

[To] Ride Punk v., n. (EF, RDSL, p. 251.) See "[To] Ride bitch."

[To] Ride Pussy v., n. (EF, RDSL, p. 251.) See "[To] Ride bitch."

Ride [one] down to the ground v. (1950s–1990s) to ridicule someone in a particularly aggressive manner; to "wolf" someone; disparage; to "down" a person. (EF, RDSL, p. 251.) SNU.

Ride man n. (1920s–1940s) the player who "rides out" the chorus of a composition; player of the last chorus in a jazz performance. (RSG, JT, p. 222.) JMFU.

Rideout (ride out) v. (1920s–1940s) (WF, DAS, p. 427; SL, RJON, p. 149.) See "[Let's] Go home."

[To] Ride shotgun v. (1950s–1970s) to ride in the passenger's seat of a car, from the nineteenth-century western stagecoach expression; to serve as armed "lookout." (EF, BVV, p. 50; PM, UCLAS, p. 71.) SCU, YCU.

Ride the rag v. (EF, RDSL, p. 252.) See "Red Mary."

Ride the white horse v. (EF, RDSL, p. 252.) See "Red Mary."

Ridiculous n. adj. (1930s–1960s) in jazz, a technique or style of playing that is surprisingly delightful. (RSG, JT, p. 222.) JMFU.

Riff n., adj. (1900s–1990s) in jazz, a repeated musical phrase; a "hot lick"; a "short ostinato melodic figure"; one's style; close harmony playing; improvisation. (AL, MJR, p. 58; WF, DAS, p. 427; *Harvard Dictionary of Music*, p. 378; p. 90; RSG, JT, p. 223; CC, OMMM, NCCHD, p. 259; DB, OHHJ, p. 145; EF, RDSL, p. 252.) JMFU.

Riff n., adj. (1940s–1960s) one's style, borrowed from jazz talk. (Chandler Broassard, *Who Walk in Darkness*, p. 90; RSG, JT, p. 223.) SCU, YCU.

Riff v. (1990s) to inform on; to offend in some way. (De La Soul, "Millie Pulled a Pistol on Santa," (© 1991 by T-Girl Music Publ., Inc./ MCA Bridgeport Music, Inc.) Example: "If you riff on me I'll make you sorry you were ever born." YCU, SCU.

Riffs and rills n. (1940s) ideas; strategy; a mapped-out plan; a proposal. (DB, OHHJ, p. 145.) NCU, JMFU.

Rig city n. See "Rigor mortis."

Right adj. (1920s–1950s) in jazz, perfection; playing with great skill and soul or heart. (RF, WJ, p. 304; RSG, JT, p. 223.) JMFU. See "Reet."

[Make or Get] Right n., v. (1950s–1990s) intoxication induced from narcotics. (EF, RDSL, p. 246.) DCU.

Right ahead v. see "Straight ahead."

Right hand n. (1940s–1960s) in jazz, the playing done and the music made with the right hand. (RSG, JT, p. 224.) JMFU.

Righteous adj. (1940s–1990s) all-purpose intensifier meaning genuine; good; correct; fine; beautiful; terrific; outstanding; satisfactory. (RSG, JT, p. 224; WF, DAS, pp. 427–428; CRM, BP, p. 307; CC, OMMM, NCCHD, p. 259; DB, OHHJ, p. 145; EF, RDSL, p. 252.) SNU.

Righteous bush n. (1940s) marijuana. (RRL, DAZ, p. 213.) DCU.

Righteous cool n. (1940s) a nice sunny, breezy day. (DB, OHHJ, p. 146.) NCU.

Righteous egg n. (1960s) a pleasant, trusted person; a "good guy." (CS, vol. 3, no. 2, p. 40.) Watts, Los Angeles; YCU.

Righteously adj., adv. (EF, RDSL, p. 252.) See "Righteous."

Righteous moss [or grass] (1930s–1950s) white folks' hair; straight, silky hair. (WF, DAS, p. 428; ZNH, AM, p. 96.) SNU.

Righteous nod n. (1940s) a good night's sleep. (MHB, JS, np.) SU; SNU.

Righteous rags n. (1930s–1950s) attractive and expensive clothes; a zoot suit; flashy clothes. (ZNH, AM, p. 96.) SNCU.

Righteous riff n. (1940s) a lively and fascinating conversation; a great line of thought. (DB, OHHJ, p. 146.) NCU.

Righteous yellow n. (1920s–1940s) an attractive, light-skinned young woman; "pretty mulatto girl." (DB, OHHJ, p. 146.) SNCU.

Right on! interj., adj. (1950–1970s) cry of approval, affirmation; agreement; endorsement; truth; remote possibility, short for "right on the nose" or "right on target." (CRM, BP, p. 307; DC, BJ, p. 77; JH, PBL, p. 86; CS, vol. 3, no. 2, p. 40.) SCU, YCU, PPU, PU.

Rigor mortis n. (1940s–1950s) a bad urban situation, especially in terms of finding employment; any bad situation; unemployment in the music business. (John A. Williams, *Night Song*, 1961, p. 47; RSG, JT, pp. 224–225.) NCU.

Rigville n. See "Rigor mortis."

Rimshot; rim-shot n. (1930s–1940s) in jazz, the sound produced when the drummer hits both the rim and the skin at the same time. (RSG, JT, p. 225.) JMFU.

Rinctum n. (1890s–1950s) variant of "rectum." (WF, DAS, p. 428.) SU.

Rind n. (1940s) one's skin. (DB, OHHJ, p. 146.) Harlem, SNC.

[The] Ring n. (1980s–1990s) anal intercourse. (EF, RDSL, p. 228.) SCU, SNU.

Ring through [one's] nose n. (1980s) to be in love; to be obsessed with someone. (EF, RDSL, p. 241.) SNU.

Rinky-dink adj., n. (1920s–1950s) poor quality; cheapness; broken-down things; cheap or worn-out objects. (WF, DAS, p. 429; SL, RJON, p. 147.) SNU.

Rinky-dink [joint] n. (1920s–1950s) a low-down juke-joint; "gut-bucket" tavern; honky-tonk tavern. (WF, DAS, p. 429.) SNU.

Riot season n. (1960s–1990s) summer, especially July and August. (FR.) YCU, SCU.

Rip n. (1920s–1940s) in jazz, fragmented sound; the sound made when a quick, short glissando is juxtaposed with a quickly inter-rupted sforzando. (RSG, JT, p. 225.) JMFU.

Rip and run v. (1900s–1970s) to move about in an unstable and unsettled manner; to be in a frenzy; restless; to move from one sweet-heart to another. (CS, vol. 3, no. 2, p. 40.) SNU.

Rip off v. (1950s–1970s) cheat, rob, steal; to physically attack; beat. (CRM, BP, p. 307; DC, BJ, p. 77; JH, PBL, p. 86; EF, BVV, p. 50; EF, RDSL, p. 252; CS, vol. 3, no. 2, p. 40.) SCU, YCU, PU, PPU, DCU.

[To] Rip off [a piece of ass] v. (1950s–1970s) male pejorative for sexual intercourse. (EF, BVV, p. 50.) SNU, SCU; YCU.

Rip on v. (EF, RDSL, p. 252.) See "Rip off."

Ripped adj. (1950s) unhappy; in grief; drunk; high; in jazz, fragmentation. (RSG, JT, p. 225; EF, RDSL, p. 252.) NCU, JMFU.

Ripper n. (1940s) one who has a reputation for cutting others with a knife. (DB, OHHJ, p. 146.) Harlem, SNU, SCU.

Rithers n. (1920s–1930s) same as "druthers"; both are corruptions of "rather," meaning "choice." (Hurston.)

Riv [Rivie] n. (1970s–1990s) short for Buick Riviera automobile. (EF, BVV, p. 50; EF, RDSL, p. 252.) South-central Los Angeles, YCU, SCU.

Roach n. (1930s–1950s) a policeman. (SL, RJON, p. 144; WF, DAS, p. 429.) PU, SCU.

Roach n. (1930s–1960s) the butt end of a reefer; usually smoked "cocktailed" in the cleaned-out end of a cigarette, held with tweezers or a roach clip, or impaled on the end of a toothpick. (CC, HDH, p. 16; RSG, JT, p. 225; RRL, DAZ, p. 214; DB, OHHJ, p. 146; EF, RDSL, p. 252.) DCU. See "Cocktail" and "Reefer."

Roach clip n. (CS, vol. 3, no. 2, p. 41.) See "Roach."

Roach holder n. (RRL, DAZ, p. 214.) See "Roach."

Robocop n. (1990s) brutal name taken from the movie of the same name. (Nelson George, *Buppies, B-Boys, Baps & Boho's*, 1992, p. 31.) YCU.

Rochester Actor Eddie Anderson, nicknamed after Rochester, New York.

Rock n. (1940s) a dollar. (MHB, JS, np; DB, OHHJ, p. 146.) SU.

Rock n. (1960s–1990s) pure cocaine; crystalline cocaine. (JM, WPC, p. 42; Alice Walker, "They Ran on Empty," *The New York Times*, May 5, 1993, p. A17; Mareva Brown, "Dynamic Duo," *Sacramento Bee*, June 5, 1993; TW, CK, p. 137.) DCU.

Rock n. (1900s–1990s) rhythm; a type of swing music; rock and roll music; music to stomp, jump, jitterbug, and swing to. (WF, DAS, p. 430; CC, OMMM, NCCHD, p. 259; DB, OHHJ, p. 146.) JMFU, YCU, SNU.

Rock [one] v. (CC, HDH, p. 16.) See "Rock."

[To] Rock vi., vt., (1900s–1990s) to dance with great vigor; to sway, jump, stomp, jitterbug, bop, shimmy, hop to boogie or rock and roll music. (RSG, JT, p. 225; SL, RJON, p. 149; WF, DAS, p. 430; DB, OHHJ, p. 146.) JMFU, YCU, SNU.

Rock; rocking v. (1900s–1990s) to have sexual intercourse. (RSG, JT, p. 225.) SNU.

Rock and roll; rock 'n' roll n. (1940s–1990s) a two-beat type of popular music with roots in "race music"; a style of "rough" or "crude" music with a simple melodic line; the type of music associated with Chuck Berry, whose hits included "Hail! Hail Rock 'n' Roll" and "Go Johnny Go." John Lennon once remarked: "If you tried to give Rock 'n' Roll another name, you might call it 'Chuck Berry.'" (WF, DAS, p. 431.) SNU. See "Rock" and "[To] Rock."

Rock candy n. (1940s) diamonds. (DB, OHHJ, p. 146.) Harlem, NCU.

Rockets n. (1990s) bullets. (FR.) SCU, YCU.

Rocking a beat v. (1990s) playing music. (FR.) SCU, YCU.

Rocking chair n. (1930s–1940s) metaphor for sexual intercourse used frequently in blues music. (JLD, LBE, p. 38.) Example: "Baby, if you wanna rock, just put me in your rocking chair, cause I'm a good rocking daddy." SU, SNU.

Rock out v. (1970s–1990s) to pass out from drug intoxication. (EF, RDSL, p. 252.) DCU. See "Flake out."

Rockpile n. (1940s) any tall building. (DB, OHHJ, p. 146.) Harlem, NCU.

Rocks n. (1960s) testicles. (FR.) SCU.

Rod n. (1930s–1940s) freight train—a variant reference to the rails on which the train rides. (LH, LKFC, p. 60; WF, DAS, p. 431.) Also a "Negro" hobo. SNU.

Rod n. (1920s–1960s) a handgun, picked up from underworld use. (WF, DAS, p. 431; DC, BJ, p. 78.) SCU.

Rod n. (1950s–1990s) penis. (EF, RDSL, p. 252; DW, TL, 187.) SCU.

[Hit the] Rods v. (1930s–1940s) to ride a freight train, picked up from hobo use. (WF, DAS, pp. 431–432.) See "Rod."

Rodda n. (1960s) a Cadillac. (DC, BJ, p. 78.) MWU.

Rogue n. (1960s–1990s) any male who spends an abnormal amount of time in pursuit of sexual intercourse. (EF, RDSL, p. 252.) South-central Los Angeles, SNCU. See "Cock hound."

Roll n. (1900s–1940s) a ripping quality in piano music; a piano roll. (SL, RJON, p. 129; WF, DAS, p. 432.) JMFU.

Roll n. (1950s) a wad of paper money. (WF, DAS, p. 432.) SCU.

[A] Roll n. (1970s–1990s) a month's supply of birth-control pills. (EF, RDSL, p. 252.) See "[A] Rack."

[To] Roll [a marijuana cigarette] v. (EF, RDSL, p. 252.) See "Reefer."

Roll v. (1900s–1990s) to have sex. (FR.) SCU.

Roll n. (1960s–1980s) street robbery. (FR.) SCU.

Roll; rolling v., n. (1990s) to laugh; laughter. YCU.

Roll v. (1990s) to ride; to walk; walking. (TW, CK, p. 137.) YCU.

Roll v. (1940s) riding in a car; driving a car; to go for a ride in a car. (MHB, JS, np.) Example: "Come on, sugar, hop in, let's roll." SU, SNU.

Roller(s) n. (1900s–1990s) from "patteroller" (patroller), the police, police detectives, law inforcement officers, cops. (CLC, TS, p. 255; IS, PSML, p. 316; EF, RDSL, p. 252; DW, TL, p. 187.) SCU, DCU, PU. See "Patteroller."

Rolling base [or piano] n., v. (1900s–1950s) in jazz piano, the effect of train wheels ("rolling") created by the left hand. (RSG, JT, p. 227.) JMFU.

Roll them; roll 'em imp. (1950s–1990s) command to open the sliding doors of prison cells. (DW, TL, p. 187.) Example (prisoner to guard): "Come on, man, you're two minutes late—roll 'em." PU.

[Pull a] Rommel v. (1940s) to do an about-face, like the Nazi general. (DB, OHHJ, p. 146.) Example: "You see Albert? When his mama saw him with the stolen stuff he pulled a Rommel and high-tailed it out the back door." Harlem, NCU.

Romp vi. (1900s–1940s) to dance to music; to stomp and prance; stamp one's feet. (RSG, JT, p. 227; DW, TL, p. 187.) SNU.

Romp vi. (1900s–1940s) to make "gutbucket" music. (MM, RB, p. 73; RSG, JT, p. 227.) JMFU.

Rookie; rooky n. (1920s–1990s) a newcomer in town; someone who is inexperienced on the scene; excluded person. (LA, SM, p. 37; WF, DAS, p. 433; EF, RDSL, p. 252; CS, vol. 3, no. 2, p. 41.) SU.

Rookus n. (1890s–1920s) variant of "ruckus"; fracas; commotion; a disturbance; noise of any argument or fight. Joseph Holloway believes there may be a connection between "ruckus" and the Bantu word "lukashi," which refers to cheering and applause. (ECLA, NN, p. 268; HV, AHAE, p. 147.) SNU.

[Listening] Room n. (1950s–1960s) a small bar or lounge without a dance floor, where jazz bands play to devoted fans. (RSG, JT, p. 227.) JMFU

Roost n. (1940s–1950s) where one lives; home. (MM, RB, p. 374; RSG, JT, p. 227; DB, OHHJ, p. 146.) SNU.

Rooster n. (1950s–1970s) a man. (EF, RDSL, p. 252.) SNU. See "Alligator."

Rooster Ben Ben Webster, a jazz saxophone player.

Root n. (1960s–1980s) in jazz, the bottom or last note of a chord. (KG, JV, p. 181.) JMFU.

Rooty-poot adj. (1960s–1980s) inferior; not serious. (EF, RDSL, p. 252.) SCU, YCU.

Rooty-poot n. (1960s–1980s) a person who is not informed; a "square;" a dumb person. (EF, DVV, p. 50; EF, RDSL, p. 252.) SCU, YCU.

Rooty-toot; rooty-toot-toot n. (1700s–1960s) "rutu-tuti" [Wolof]: the sound of fast drum-beating; music no longer fashionable; loud noise. (HV, AHAE, p. 147.) SU, SNU.

Rope n. (1940s) a marijuana cigarette. (DB, OHHJ, p. 146.) DCU.

Roscoe n. (1930s–1970s) a pistol; a handgun. (WF, DAS, p. 433; MHB, JS, np; EF, RDSL, p. 252.) SU.

Rosewood n. (1920s–1950s) a billystick, otherwise known as a policeman's nightstick. (FR.) Example: "James won't go in Jump's anymore since that time the roller hit him with his rosewood." SNCU.

Rot-gut n. (1860s–1950s) bad or cheap whiskey; poor-quality wine; fortified wine sold exclusively in black communities. (FR.) SNU.

Rough adj. (1960s–1970s) attractive; stylish. (FR.) SNU.

Rough-dried hair n. (1930s–1940s) very kinky hair. (ZNH, AM, p. 84.) Harlem, SU, SNU.

Round about n. (1950s–1960s) anywhere; everywhere; in this area. (DG, KLH, p. 128.) Example: "I never seen him round about before." SCU, SNU.

Round ball n. (1970s–1990s) basketball. (EF, RDSL, p. 252.) Basketball players and fan use.

Rounder n. (1880s–1920s) a person who "makes the rounds" of the juke joints and whorehouses, picked up from white use for a man who likes the "company of the demi-monde." (Barbecue Bob, "It's Just Too Bad," *Chocolate to The Bone*, Yazoo, 1992; WF, DAS, p. 434; JSF, AON, p. 464.) SU.

Round head n. (1970s–1990s) a blunt-ended capsule containing a barbiturate compound. (EF, RDSL, p. 252.) DCU. See "Blunt."

Round-eye n. (1950s–1990s) the anus as a sexual aperture. (DW, TL, p. 187.) SCU, SNU.

Roupy v. (1860s–1890s) to be hoarse, as heard in a "negro minstrel song." (AB, DSJC, p. 182.) SU, SNU.

Roust v. (1850s–1990s) to be harassed, especially by the police. (IS, PSML, p. 316; PM, UCLAS, p. 72.) YCU, SCU.

Rowdy adj. (1950s–1990s) troublesome; noisy; violent. (EF, RDSL, p. 252.) SNU.

Royal n. (1900s–1920s) mildly pejorative and ironic term for any West Indian black born in or associated with any former British colony in the Carribbean. (FR.) Harlem use.

Rub v. (1680s–1990s) to rob or steal; burglary; "sting"; remote possibility: variant of "rob." (EP, DU, p. 580; DW, TL, p. 187.) PU, SCU.

Rub down v. (1820s–1990s) term often used in connection with robbery, meaning to frisk or search someone; pat a person's pockets and clothing in search of something. (EP, DU, p. 580; DW, TL, p. 187.) SCU, PU.

Rubber n. (1940s–1950s) a car, derived from automobile tires. (RSG, JT, p. 227; MHB, JS, np; DB, OHHJ, p. 146.) SNU.

Rubber n. (1940s–1990s) a condom; device used for contraceptive purposes. (CS, vol. 3, no. 2, p. 41.) SNU.

Rubies n. (1940s) one's lips, especially large or full lips. (MHB, JS, np.) SU.

Rub-joint n. (1930s–1940s) a jook-joint where dancing is allowed; a seedy dance hall where young women dance with men for a price or for the price of a drink; they bellyrub and the women often "wear nothing under their dresses." (SL, RJON, p. 57; WF, DAS, p. 437.) SCU, JMFU.

[Pull a] Rudolph Hess v. (1940s) to fade away; to vanish, disappear. (DB, OHHJ, p. 146.) SNCU.

Ruff n. (1940s) a quarter. (CC, OMMM, NCCHD, p. 259; DB, OHHJ, p. 146.) Harlem, JMFU.

Rug n. (1950s–1960s) a wig worn by women. (FR.) SNU.

Rug-cut v., n. (WF, DAS, 436.) See "Rugcutter" and "Rugcutting."

Rugcutter (rug cutter) n. (1920s–1950s) one who dances a lot and well, especially at parties; a good dancer. (RSG, JT, pp. 227–228; WF, DAS, p. 436; CC, OMMM, NCCHD, p. 259; ZNH, AM, p. 96; MHB, JS, np; DB, OHHJ, p. 146.) Example: "We go down to Lenny's place every Saturday night and do a little rocking 'cause that's were all the best rugcutters go." SNU.

Rugcutting v. (1920s–1950s) dancing, especially with great energy and technical skill. (RSG, JT, pp. 227–228; MHB, JS, np; DB, OHHJ, p. 146.) SNU. See "Rugcutter."

Rugy adj. (1970s–1990s) unattractive or unpleasant; shabby; mean-spirited. (EF, RDSL, p. 252.) South-central Los Angeles, YCU.

Ruint n. (1960s–1990s) to be extremely intoxicated from narcotics; ugly; hurt, as in an accident or fight. (EF, RDSL, p. 252; CS, vol. 3, no. 2, p. 41.) YCU, DCU, SCU.

Rum n. (1950s–1960s) a square; a dupe. (CLC, TS, p. 255.) See "Chump."

Rumble n. (1930s–1990s) fight between gang members, picked up from underworld use. (HEG, DAU, p. 182; DC, BJ, p. 78; EF, RDSL, p. 252.) SCU.

Rumble in the jungle (1970s) Muhammad Ali's famous expression, used as a promotion slogan for the 1974 heavyweight title fight in Zaire.

Rumpkin (rumpskin) n. (1970s–1990s) a stupid person; dumb individual; a fool; silly person. (EF, RDSL, p. 252.) See "Poot butt."

[To] Run v. (1880s–1990s) to associate with. (EF, RDSL, p. 252.) SNU.

Run a double train v. (1940s–1990s) vaginal and anal intercourse with one woman between two men. (EF, RDSL, p. 252.) SNU.

Run a game on [one or something] v. (1940s–1990s) to deceive; mislead; trick; "con;" manipulate. (EF, RDSL, p. 252.) SCU. See "Hustle."

Run away v. (1900s–1960s) in jazz, to be ahead of the other players in terms of rhythm or harmonics. (RSG, JT, p. 228.) JMFU.

Run down v. (1930s–1970s) in jazz, to rehearse a composition or a performance. (RSG, JT, p. 228.) JMFU.

Run down some lines v. (1950s–1990s) usually a male expression, meaning to talk in an impressive, seductive, overwhelming, or winning way while flirting with a member of the opposite sex. (EF, RDSL, p. 252.) SCU.

Run off of [something]; running off of [something] v. (1970s–1990s) to be sustained by something such as cocaine or alcohol. (EF, RDSL, p. 252.) Example: "You been talking all night, you must be running off of all that coke you pigged out on." DCU, SCU, YCU.

[To] Run off at the jibs v. (1970s–1980s) to talk excessively. (EF, BVV, p. 51.) YCU, SCU.

Run it down v. (1930s–1990s) disclose; provide or relate information; to tell the whole truth of whatever is in question. (RSG, JT, p. 228; JH, PBL, p. 86; EF, RDSL, p. 252; DW, TL, p. 187.) SNCU, SCU, YCU.

Run [one's] mouth v. (1960s–1980s) to talk excessively; to complain.

[To] Run [or roll] sets on [one] v. (1970s–1980s) to punch someone hard and quickly with double-fisted blows. (EF, BVV, p. 51.) South-central Los Angeles, SCU, YCU.

Run the Streets v. (1930s–1990s) to spend a lot of time away from home. (EF, RDSL, p. 252.) SNU.

Runner n. (1980s–1990s) one who delivers drugs, especially cocaine. (TW, CH, p. 151.) DCU.

Running a game v. (1960s) attempting to manipulate; "hustling" someone or "sweet-talking." (RDA, TB, p. 42; DC, BJ, p. 78.) Example: "Micky a smooth dude, he be running a game on somebody and they don't even know it, think he trying to help." SCU. See "Hype."

Run a gorilla game v. (1960s–1970s) to aggressively con someone; to strong-arm someone; rob. (FR.) SCU, PPU, PU.

Running buddy n. (1930s–1990s) one's best friend or companion; a person one socializes with frequently. (FR.) YCU, SCU.

Running changes n., v. (1920s–1940s) in jazz, fast movement from one key change to another; also to undergo a number of emotional and psychological changes in a very short span. (RSG, JT, p. 229.)

Running [something] down v. (1950s–1990s) giving one important news. (RDA, TB, p. 42; DC, BJ, p. 78.) SCU, YCU.

Running feet n. (1900s–1930s) in voodoo, an evil spell cast on one's enemy. (ZNH, MM, p. 334.) SU.

[One's] Running partner n. (1930s–1990s) a person with whom one spends most of his or her time; a close friend. (EF, RDSL, p. 252.) SNU.

Running range n. (1920s–1950s) gonorrheal discharge. (ZNH, MM, p. 340.)

Running wild v. (1920s–1940s) in jazz, to make music with great energy and excitement, without restraint. (RSG, JT, p. 229.) JMFU.

Run with [one] v. (1950s–1990s) to be friends with and to socialize with. (Richard Price, *Clockers*, np.) DCU, SCU.

[A] Rush n. (1950s–1990s) the first exhilarating effects of a narcotics high. (EF, RDSL, p. 252; DW, TL, p. 187.) DCU.

Rushing v., n. (1890s–1950s) raising animals or crops; an attempt to raise crops or animals quickly; to speed up the process of growth. (Richard Westmacott, *African-American Gardens and Yards in the Rural South*, 1992, p. 96.) SU.

[A] Russian n. (1930s–1940s) a "Negro" who has "rushed" from the South to the North. (ZNH, AM, p. 91, 96; WF, DAS, p. 439.) Harlem use.

Rusty dusty n. (1930s–1950s) one's buttocks. (Hear Jimmy Rushing, "Harvard Blues," 1942; RSG, JT, p. 229; WF, DAS, p. 439.) SNU.

Ruth Buzzy n., adv. (1960s–1970s) after the TV character on "Laugh-In," any woman whose appearance is plain and unchanging; old-maidish looking. (EF, RDSL, p. 252.) Example: "Sally looks too Ruth Buzzy to be running with us, girl." SNU.

S

Sabe v. (1800s–1890s) from Spanish, to know. (CCJ, NMGC, p. 169.) SU.

Sacatra n. (1850s–1890s) person of European and African descent; a mulatto. (JSF, AON, p. 468.) SU, SNU. See "Mulatto."

Sack n. (1960s–1980s) a bed; sometimes, though rarely, an overcoat or jacket. (DC, BJ, p. 78.) SCU.

[A] Sack n. (1980s–1990s) an ineffective athlete. (EF, RDSL, p. 252.) Rare. YCU.

Sack lunch n. (1980s) cunnilingus. (EF, RDSL, p. 241.) SCU.

Sack mouth n. (1980s–1990s) an incessant talker; a gossip. (EF, RDSL, p. 252.) YCU.

Sack-shaker n. (1880s–1930s) a cotton picker. (Lightnin' Hopkins, "Cotton," *Nothing But the Blues*, Collectable Records, 1989.) SU.

Saddity adj. see "Dicty" and "Uppity."

Safety n. (1940s–1950s) one's bed. (FR.) SU.

Safety n. (1950s) a condom. (FR.) Example (mother to son): "I hope you use some kind of safety with that slut you fooling around with." SNU.

Sails n. (1940s) the ears. (FR.) SNU.

[To have one's] Sails high (1940s–1950s) to be drunk. (WM, DBD, p. 169.) See "High as a kite."

St. Louis flats n. (1900s–1930s) flat, moccasin-like shoes with a gambler's design on the toe, worn by early jazz musicians and others in St. Louis and New Orleans; later called "low cut" or "Italian style" shoes. (AL, MJR, p. 16; WF, DAS, pp. 440–441.) SU.

Salbe n. (1960s–1970s) nickname for King Solomon sweet wine, a fortified wine sold exclusively in black communities; "rot-gut" wine. (DR, BASL, p. 74.) Philadelphia, SCU.

Salt n. (1990s) interference; trouble; annoyance. (FR.) YCU.

Salt-and-pepper n. (1960s–1990s) an interracial couple or interracial friends. (FR.) SNU.

Salt-and-pepper n. (1980s–1990s) a police team consisting of one black and one white officer; policeman; a police squad car. (EF, RDSL, p. 252.) South-central Los Angeles, YCU, SCU.

Salt and pepper queens n. (1970s–1990s) an Anglo and African-American gay couple. (HM, GL, p. 37.) Gay culture use.

[To] Salt [one's] game v. (1990s) intruding on someone who is attempting to seduce a third person. (FR.) YCU.

Salt-N-Pepa (1980s–1990s) three rap artists—Sandy, Dee Dee Roper, and Cheryl James—originally of Queens, New York.

Salt-water Negro n. (1620s–1860s) a black person "fresh" from Africa; not yet broken in. (SBF, IHAT, p. 55.) SU.

Salty adj. (1920s–1970s) irritated; ill-tempered; angry. (Hear Washboard Sam, "My Feet Jumped Salty," *Rockin' My Blues Away*, BMG/ Bluebird, 1992; RSG, JT, p. 230; MM, RB, p. 371, 374.; MHB, JS, n.p.) See "Jump salty."

Sam n. (1940s–1950s) from "Ol' Black Sam," a Negro who conforms to the patterns of racial oppression. (FR.) SNU.

Sam and Dave n. (1980s) any two policemen. (EF, RDSL, p. 252.) South-central Los Angeles, YCU.

Sambo [zambo] n. (1650s–1990s) samba [Bantu]: to give comfort; common African name: Samb, Samba [Wolof], Sambu [Mandingo], Sambo [Hausa]; black male child; black man; originally the child of a full-blooded African and a mulatto; the offspring of a full-blooded African and a member of one of the Native American tribes; "yellow complexion;" "Little Black Sambo," a popular story about a "sambo," is probably derived from an African folktale; in the early part of the present century "sambo" became a white pejorative term for any person of African descent; used ironically by blacks since the 1930s. (JSF, AON, p. 470; EF, RDSL, p. 252; HV, AHAE, p. 147.) SNU.

Same-old same-old n. (1930s–1960s) the usual; a routine thing or situation. (FR.) SNU.

Same lick at the same pop (1860s–1900s) two different things happening at the same time. (JAH, PBE, p. 175.) SU.

[The] Sand n. (1900s–1940s) dance step originated by black vaudville dancers; also a popular Harlem dance. (RSG, JT, p. 230.) YCU, SNCU. See "Suzie Q."

[Making a] Sandwich n. (1970s–1990s) two males having sex with one woman in the middle. (EF, RDSL, p. 246.) SNU.

Sandy Ree (1870s–1920s) a "pretty" dance step and a song of the same name; children's game-song. (BJ, BLH, SD, pp. 133–136.) SU.

Sang v. (1630s–1950s) to sing. (FR.) SU.

Sang-mele n. (1780–1920s) the offspring of a quarteron and a white parent. (EBR, MUS, p. 12.) SU.

Santa Claus n. (1970s–1980s) a person who wears gaudy colors and flashy clothes. (EF, RDSL, p. 253.) South-central Los Angeles, YCU.

Sapphire n. (1940s–1960s) derogatory term for a disagreeable woman; in the sixties, an unpopular black female. (GS, TT, p. 68; DC, BJ, p. 78.) SNU.

Sashay (sashaying; sachay; sachaying) v. (1890s–1940s) to cavort; stroll leisurely. (ECLA, NN, p. 268; RDA, DDJ, p. 267; WF, DAS, p. 443.) SU

Sass adj., n. (1800s–1990s) to be too driven by one's own sense of importance or power; asserting one's own will without consideration for others; mean-spirited. Among English-speaking Africans on the West Coast of Africa during the 1860s, anyone—including the chief —found guilty of "sass" was forced by "the people" to drink a "remedy" called "sass water," a very bitter liquor; sometimes the people threw the sassy person into the surf and rolled him or her around in the water; extreme cases were said to be cut at with knives till they died. In the South during and after slavery, "sass" was a common word among black people. (AB, DSJC, p. 195.) SU, SNU.

Sassfrass [sassafras] n. (1940s) marijuana; marijuana cigarette. (RRL, DAZ, pp. 215–216.) Rare. DCU.

Sassy adj. (1930s–1950s) usually used to describe a little girl who is disobedient; vibrating and radiating with youthful energy. (RSG, JT, p. 230; EF, RDSL, p. 253.) SNU.

Sassy Sarah Vaughn, a singer.

Satch n. (1900s–1940s) a mouth abnormally large for one's face. (WF, DAS, p. 443.) SNU. See "Satchel mouth."

Satch [Satchmo] The famous and important jazz figure Daniel Louis Armstrong (1900–1972), trumpeter, singer, band leader. See "Pops."

Satch n. (1940s–1950s) a jacket, perhaps the type worn by Louis Armstrong or Satchel Page. (RDA, DDJ, p. 267.) Philadelphia, SCU.

Satchel-mouth n. (1900s–1940s) person with a big mouth; "Satchmo," for Louis Armstrong, was the corruption of this term. (WF, DAS, p. 443.) SU.

Satchel Paige a famous baseball player in the Negro leagues.

Satin n. (1970s–1990s) short for Italian Swiss Colony Silver Satin wine. (EF, RDSL, p. 253.) South-central Los Angeles, SCU, YCU.

Saturday-night fish-fry n. (1930s–1940s) a very popular weekend social event in small southern towns that did not survive very long in the urban environment. (FR.) SU.

Save it interj. (1970s–1990s) shut up. (FR.) YCU.

Saw n. (1900s–1950s) any unpleasant or mean person. (WF, DAS, p. 444.) SNU.

Sawed-off adj., n. (1970s) short; a short person. (FR.) SNU.

Sax n. (1900s–1990s) short for saxophone—baritone, tenor, soprano, or alto. (WF, DAS, p. 444; RSG, JT, p. 231.) JMFU, SNU.

Saying something v. (1950s–1960s) speaking with profundity; refers to anything impressive or profound. (RSG, JT, p. 231.) YCU, SNCU, JMFU.

Saying nothing v. (RSG, JT, p. 231.) See "Saying something."

Say what? interrog. (1970s–1990s) an expression of mock disbelief. (FR.) See "Do what?"

Say which? interrog. (1800s–1990s) short for "What did you say?" (WF, DAS, p. 445.) SU, SNU. See "Say what?"

Scab n. (1960s–1990s) pejorative male term for any girl or young woman he considers ugly or undesirable or both. (EF, RDSL, p. 253; HLF, RJPD, p. 171.) YCU, SCU.

Scag (skag) n. (1960s) heroin. (RRL, p. 216.) DCU.

Scan on vt. (1960s–1970s) to examine something closely; to look closely at something one wishes to steal. (DW, TL, p. 187.) SCU.

Scare n. (1940s–1970s) in jazz, a pleasant surprise or a feeling of terror; to be so caught up in the music that one is shaken to a mortal level of fear or delight. (RSG, JT, p. 232.) JMFU.

Scare party n. (1940s–1950s) Halloween party. (FR.) SNU.

Scare up v. (1970s) find; gather. (FR.) SNU.

Scarf [scoff] v. (1920s–1990s) to eat; to eat heartily; to gorge oneself; food. Picked up from hobo use. (EF, BVV, p. 51; MHB, JS, np; RSG, JT, p. 232; EF, RDSL, p. 253; DC, BJ, p. 78; EP, DU, p. 599.) SNU.

Scarification n. (1900s–1940s) fear. (Jane Cortez, *Scarifications*, 1973.) Example: "Don't be coming 'round here, boy, with no funny scarification, making these children wild, causing them to run and break my antique furniture." SNU.

Scars n. (1930s–1990s) black embossed marks on the arms or legs resulting from injecting heroin into the veins. (RRL, DAZ, p. 216; CB, MPL.) DCU.

Scat; scatting v. (1900s–1990s) in jazz and blues singing, to keep the rhythm going verbally, as a novelty, by using pure sounds without regard to their meaning. Scat singing has been generally attributed to Louis Armstrong, who, when he forgot the words to a song, would make up syllables. But scat singing was done by blues and jazz singers long before Louis Armstrong came on the scene. Such singers were often trying to imitate verbally the sounds of musical instruments. Also a kind of spontaneous "sound" poetry that may sound like "doubletalk" to unfamiliar ears. In the seventies, to move quickly. (AL, MJR, p. 120; SL, RJON, p. 147; WF, DAS, p. 446; KG, JV, p. 181.) JMFU, SU, SNU.

Scat n. (1970s–1990s) the vagina; female sex. (EF, RDSL, p. 253.) YCU, SCU.

[The] Scene n. (1940s–1950s) the main area of popular group activity, such as a street corner, a bar, a poolroom. (RSG, JT, p. 233; EF, RDSL, p. 253; DC, BJ, p. 78.) SCU, JMFU.

Scene n. (1960s–1990s) any happening, event, or circumstance. (EF, RDSL, p. 253.) SCU, YCU.

[The] Scene is clean (1940s–1950s) among jazz musicians, this expression meant that one had just found a job or would be working soon. (RSG, JT, p. 233.) Rare. JMFU.

[To] Scene on [one] v. (1970s–1990s) to try to gain an advantage over a rival by out-talking him or her; to belittle someone; to "front off." (EF, RDSL, p. 253.) YCU, SCU.

Scheme on vt. (1950s–1970s) to plan or plot to rob or violate or abuse someone in some way; to "take advantage" of a person. (DW, TL, p. 187.) SCU.

School [one] v. (1940s–1990s) to teach; to inform. (EF, RDSL, p. 253.) Example: "Hey, man, let me school you to what's happening." SCU.

Schoolbook chump n. (1970s–1990s) a student who spends a lot of time studying or reading; a young intellectual; a "pootbutt" or "square." (EF, RDSL, p. 253.) YCU, SCU.

Schoolboy scotch n. (1970s–1990s) cheap wine or "rot-gut"; a fortified wine sold exclusively in black neighborhoods. (EF, RDSL, p. 253.) YCU, SCU.

School of hard knocks n. (1890s–1990s) learning by making mistakes and bad experiences. (FR.) Example: "I came from the school of hard knocks." SCU.

Schooly n. (1980s–1990s) any student who is interested in studying and staying in school; a "chump" or "square." (FR.) YCU, SCU.

Schooly D (1990s) Jesse Barnes Weaver, Jr., a rapper.

Scobe n. (1940s) a black person. (WF, DAS, p. 702.) Rare. SNU.

Scoff v. see "Scarf" and "Grease."

Scoffing fishheads and scrambling the gills (1940s–1950s) having a very difficult time. (FR.) SU, SNU.

Scoobydoo interj. (1940s–1950s) in jazz, an onomatopoetic expression often heard in scat singing; a verbal approximation of a musical phrase. (RSG, JT, p. 234.) JMFU. See "Oo-bla-dee," "Oo-bop-she-bam," and "Oo-pappa-da."

Scoops George Dorman Carry (b. 1925), an alto saxophone player.

Scooping pitch n. (1930s–1950s) in jazz, a change of key or pitch. (SL, RJON, p. 149; WF, DAS, p. 449.) JMFU.

[A] Scoot n. (1960s–1990s) short for motor scooter, a motorcycle. (CS, vol. 3, no. 2, p. 41.) SCU.

Scope (scoping) v. (1980s–1990s) to look; to gaze. (EF, RDSL, p. 253; EF, BVV, p. 51.) Example: "Ralph, don't scope me like that, I don't like it—it feels like rape." YCU, SCU.

Score v. (1930s–1990s) to obtain something of value—a date with a member of the opposite sex, narcotics, marijuana, a musical engagement; to gain another's compliance; in the late fifties and early sixties, to buy drugs. (CLC, TS, p. 255; DG, CR, p. 47; RSG, JT, p. 234; CS, vol. 3, no. 2, p. 41; RRL, DAZ, p. 218.) DCU, SCU, YCU, JMFU.

Scotty n. (1970s–1990s) cocaine or crack cocaine; after Mr. Scott in "Star Trek," the TV series. (TW, CK, p. 137; TW, CH, p. 151.) New York, DCU.

Scram n. (1940s–1950s) a black man, picked up from white use but origin unknown. (WF, DAS, p. 450.) Rare.

Scrambling n. (1960s–1990s) street hustling by any means necessary. (TW, CK, p. 137; DR, BASL, p. 217.) DCU, SCU.

Scramboose v., interj. (1940s–1960s) to leave; variant of "scram." (FR.) SU, SNU.

Scrape v. (1970s–1990s) to lower the body of one's car so low that it occasionally hits the pavement and causes sparks; this is considered cool or hip. (EF, RDSL, p. 253.) SCU, YCU.

Scraping Dixie v. (1940s) walking the streets in any large southern city, especially in search of a job. (MHB, JS, np.) SU.

Scrap iron n. (1940s) bad liquor; homemade whiskey. (MHB, JS, np; ZNH, AM, p. 96.) SU.

Scratch n. (1940s–1960s) money, short for "chicken scratch." (IS, TB, p. 312; CS, vol. 3, no. 2, p. 41; DC, BJ, p. 78.) See "Chicken scratch."

Scratch n., v. (1980s) in rap music, a technique that involves playing a record in short bursts, which gives the music a rhythmic, scratchy sound. (FR.) YCU.

Scratch-crib n. (1940s) a cheap hotel or rooming house, so called because the expected bedbug bites cause one to scratch one's flesh. (FR.) SNU.

Scratching n. (1950s–1960s) penmanship; handwriting; writing. (DC, BJ, p. 78.) YCU.

Scream n., v. (1930s–1960s) in jazz, a high-pitched trumpet sound; in the sixties, to complain about oppression and exploitation: "scream, don't cry" [Don Lee]. (RSG, JT, pp. 234–235.) JMFU, SCU.

Scream down some heavy lines v. (1970s–1990s) to talk or "rap" in a fast, rhyming, clever and forceful manner, but especially in an attempt to out-talk someone else. (EF, RDSL, p. 253.) SCU, YCU.

Screamer n. (1930s–1960s) a jazzman who produces a screamlike effect through his trumpet; high trumpet notes. (RSG, JT, p. 235.) JMFU.

Screamer n. (1960s–1990s) a siren, especially on a police car. (FR.) YCU, SCU.

[A] Screaming fairy n. (1940s–1950s) a very flamboyant and loud-talking homosexual. (HM, GL, p. 38.) Chicago, Harlem, homosexual use.

Screaming gasser n. (1940s) police squad car or patrol wagon moving through traffic with its siren going full-blast. (FR.) Harlem, NCU.

Scream on [one]; screaming on [one] v. (1960s–1970s) to give away a secret or to betray the confidence of someone; to tell; to inform; to attack; to betray. (RDA, TB, p. 56; EF, RDSL, p. 253.) Example: "He screamed on me when I thought I could trust him." SCU, YCU.

Screech n. (1920s–1940s) homemade liquor; rot-gut whiskey; cheap, inferior liquor; fortified wine. (WF, DAS, p. 702.) SU.

Screen n. (1960s–1990s) any type of television set. (DC, BJ, p. 78.) Example: "The neighbors buy a new screen about every other year." YCU, SNU.

Scribe n. (1870s–1940s) a letter. (WF, DAS, p. 453.) Example: "Baby, you been gone so long, look like you could send me some kind of scribe to let me know how you doing." SNU.

Scrip (script) n. (1960s–1970s) short for "prescription," a prescription for narcotics. (CS, vol. 3, no. 2, p. 41; RRL, DAZ, p. 219; DW, TL, p. 188.) Example: "I got some nice shit now and it's strictly scrip." DCU.

Scrooch (scooch) adj. (1920s–1940s) drunk; heard in early blues songs. (WF, DAS, p. 453.) SU. See "Screech."

[The] Sconch (scraunch; scrontch; scrunch; scronching) n., v. (1900s–1940s) a dance step popular in Harlem during the twenties; belly-rubbing while dancing; a slow, dragged-out dance. In the thirties, the same dance steps carried over into such dances as the Drag and the Mooch. (ZNH, AM, p. 95; CVV, NH, p. 286; RSG, JT, p. 234.) SNU.

[A] Scrub n. (1980s–1990s) a fool; stupid person; dumb individual. (JMC, PS, p. 50.) PU.

Scrunch; scrunching v. (1900s–1930s) to stoop or crouch; drop down low by bending at the knees. (FR.) Example: "I scrunched down and talked to the little boy face to face." SNU.

Scuffle n., v. (1890s–1950s) difficulty; great hardship; a struggle; to just get by on little or no money. (SL, RJON, p. 147; WF, DAS, p. 454; MM, RB, p. 374.) SU, SNU.

Scuffle (skuffle) n. (1920s–1930s) a generic term for any kind of fast, energetic, frenzied dancing. (RSG, JT, p. 235.) JMFU.

Scuffler n. (1890s–1950s) a person who does hard but honest work to make a living. (DB, OHHJ, p. 146.) SNU.

Scurvy adj. (1970s–1980s) shabbiness; ugliness; unpleasantness of any sort. (EF, RDSL, p. 253.) YCU, SCU.

Scuttle n. (1900s–1920s) a "Negro" taxi passenger, picked up from derogatory white taxi drivers' use. (WF, DAS, p. 454.) Rare. Chicago use.

Seal n. (1920s–1930s) a "Negro" woman; any "Negro"; picked up from derogatory white use. (WF, DAS, p. 455.) Rare. SNU.

Seal-a-Meals n. (1980s) small plastic bags used for packaging set amounts of cocaine for sale. (FR.) DCU.

Search me interj. (1930s–1950s) a statement expressing innocence or ignorance. (FR.) SNU.

Second base n. (1930s–1950s) a woman's breasts. (FR) SNU.

Second burial n. (1650s–1860s) an Igbo or African custom practiced by slaves. The first burial is the "burying" and the second is the "funeral preaching," held sometimes as much as three months later. (JEH, AAC, p. 112.) SU.

Second line n. (1900s–1930s) the line of children who playfully trailed the marching jazz bands of parades or funerals in New Orleans. (RSG, JT, p. 236.) JMFU.

Second mind n. (1820s–1940s) the unconscious mind. (FR.) Example: "If I hada listened to my second mind, I wouldn't be in this mess today." SU.

Seddity n., adj. (1960s–1980s) bourgeois black person; snobbish and pretentious. (EF, RDSL, p. 253.) SNU.

Seed n. (1960s) a baseball; one's child; children. (DC, BJ, p. 78.) Rare. MWU.

Seeking [time] n. (1840s–1860s) the specific time between a person's "expressed desire" to live as a Christian and the full acceptance in the church by the elders; a time when "raw souls" begin their "striving." (JEH, AAC, pp. 79–80.) SU.

See (seeing) v. (1930s–1940s) in jazz, to read music. (FR.) Example: "Half these cats who be seeing the music can't get no soul into it, ya know what I mean." JMFU.

Sell a woof (sell a wolf) (1970s–1980s) to brag or boast or show off; to loud-talk; tell a lie. (EF, RDSL, p. 253.) SCU, YCU.

Sell a woof ticket (EF, RDSL, p. 253.) See "Sell a woof."

[To] Sell [one] down the river (1830s–1880s) to betray; misuse; a threat made or an actual punishment. To punish a slave, a Georgia or South Carolina slave-holder might sell him or her to a Mississippi sugar-cane plantation. After the 1880s, the expression fell into wide use to mean betraying or abusing someone. (SBF, IHAT, p. 36.) Example: "If you don't stop that hoodoo stuff, Norton, I'm gwine sell you down the river and I promise you you won't like it one bit."

Sell out v. (1930s–1940s) to run in fear. (ZNH, p. 96.) SNU.

Sell out to the Yankees (1880s–1890s) to move to a northern industrial area. (FR.) SU.

Semolia n. (1890s–1930s) a fool; stupid person. (WF, DAS, p. 457.) SU.

Send(s) v. (1900s–1950s) to arouse emotionally; to be deeply moved by music. (SL, RJON, p. 104; WF, DAS, p. 457; LA, SM, p. 126; CC, HDH, p. 16; RSG, JT, p. 237; DB, OHHJ, p. 146.) Example: "Bird really sends me." SNU, JMFU. See "Gas."

[Solid] Sender n. (1920s–1940s) one who arouses emotionally; one who inspires excitement. (LA, SM, p. 457; WF, DAS, p. 457; RSG, JT, p. 237; ZNH, AM, p. 96.) SNU, JMFU.

Send on a humbug (send on a hombug) (1950s–1990s) to deliberately mislead someone by misdirecting them. (EF, RDSL, p. 253; EF, BVV, p. 51.) YCU, SCU. See "Humbug" and "Humbugging."

Send on a merry-go-round (EF, RDSL, p. 253.) See "Send on a humbug."

Send on a trip (EF, RDSL, p. 253.) See "Send on a humbug."

Send to Long Beach (1960s–1970s) when the narcotics agents are coming, to flush illegal drugs down the toilet. (CS, vol. 3, no. 2, p. 41.) Watts, DCU.

Serious adj. (1980s–1990s) large; intense; important. (FR) Example: "He has a serious record collection." YCU, SCU.

[Jam] Session n. (1940s–1970s) in jazz, usually an informal after-hours gathering of musicians who play for themselves and maybe a few friends; a jazz performance in a club; a social; a dance. (WF, DAS, p. 458; RSG, JT, p. 237.) JMFU.

Set n. (1930s–1990s) a party; a dance; in jazz, the length of time—twenty or thirty minutes—a combo or band spends playing before taking a break or quitting. (WF, DAS, p. 703; RSG, JT, p. 237; CS, vol. 3, no. 2, p. 41.) SNU, YCU, JMFU, SCU.

Set n. (1960s–1990s) a clique of friends who tend to party and generally hang out together; a place where friends meet. (EF, RDSL, p. 253; DW, TL, p. 188.) YCU.

Set-ending n. (1930s–1990s) the musical composition a group of musicians use as a closing number; it is kept short and is usually identified with and known as their theme. (RSG, JT, p. 238.) JMFU.

Set horses v. (1980s–1990s) to get along. (FR.) YCU.

Set of drapes n. (WF, DAS, p. 458; SL, RJON, p. 150.) See "Zoot suit."

Set of seven brights n. (1930s–1940s) a week; seven days. (DB, OHHJ, p. 146; CC, OMMM, NCCHD, p. 259.) Harlem, NCU.

Set of threads n. (1930s–1950s) fine clothing. (SL, RJON, p. 105; WF, DAS, p. 458.) YCU, NCU.

Set [one] on [one's] ass (1970s–1990s) to be knocked out from drug intoxication. (EF, RDSL, p. 253.) Example: "That chronic is some bad stuff, man, it'll set you on your ass." DCU.

Set mouth [on] v. (1970s–1990s) to tell someone off; to give one a tongue-lashing. (EF, RDSL, p. 253.) Example: "If you get in her way, man, she'll set her mouth on you and you'll wish you were dead." South-central Los Angeles use.

[Roll] Sets on v. (1970s–1990s) to deliver double-fisted blows in quick succession. (EF, RDSL, p. 253.) YCU, SCU.

[Run] Sets on v. (EF, RDSL, p. 253.) See "[Roll] Sets on."

[Throw] Sets on v. (EF, RDSL, p. 253.) See "[Roll] Sets on."

Setting up n. (1880s–1920s) a wake for the dead. (ECLA, p. 264.) South Carolina and other southern areas use.

Set-up v. (1950s–1960s) to arrange with the police for a pusher or dealer to be "busted" by marking the money to be used in the transaction; to trick someone; to be framed by the police; picked up from police use. (CLC, TS, p. 256; CS, vol. 3, no. 2, p. 41; RRL, DAZ, p. 222.) SCU, PU.

Set up v. (1900s–1990s) in jazz, to get things—chairs, etc.—arranged for a performance. (RSG, JT, p. 238.) JMFU.

Setup n. (1940s–1950s) whiskey, ice, and chaser served in a barroom. (FR.) SNU.

Seventeen-forty-seven B n. (1960s) New York State code for possession of barbiturates, which is a misdemeanor. (RRL, DAZ, p. 222.) New York, DCU.

Sexed in n. (1990s) the gang rape of a female; variant of "done in." YCU, SCU.

Shack v., n. (1890s–1930s) male term for living alone; a bachelor living alone. (WF, DAS, p. 460.) SU.

Shack n. (1880s–1960s) one's home; a house; an apartment. (JSF, AON, pp. 478–479; DC, BJ, p. 78; DW, TL, p. 188.) SNU.

Shack up with [one] v. (1900s–1960s) to live temporarily with a lover; man and woman living together without benefit or restraint of marriage; expression picked up from itinerant workers during the Depression. Also to have sexual intercourse with someone. (FR.) SNU.

Shad Lester Rallingston Collins, a trumpeter (b. 1910 in Elizabeth, N.J.) who played with Benny Carter and Cab Calloway.

Shade n. (1850s–1900s) a Negro, picked up from derogatory white use. (WF, DAS, p. 461.) Rare. SU.

[To] Shade v. (1980s–1990s) to hide; to conceal something. (TW, CH, p. 151.) New York, SCU, DCU.

Shades n. (1940s–1950s) dark glasses, from bop musicians' use. (WF, DAS, p. 703; RSG, JT, p. 234; HLF, RJPD, p. 171.) JMFU, SCU, YCU.

Shad mouth n. (1930s–1940s) picked up from derogatory white use, a person with a big upper lip; a Negro. (WF, DAS, p. 460.) Rare. SU, SNU.

Shadow n. (1880s–1930s) a Negro, picked up from derogatory white use and used ironically. (WF, DAS, p. 460.) SU, SNU.

Shadow Rossiere Wilson, a drummer (b. 1919) who worked with Earl Hines, Louis Jordan, Count Basie, Ella Fitzgerald, and others.

Shady adj. (1960s) stupid or dense. (CS, vol. 3, no. 2, p. 41.) Rare. Watts, Los Angeles, use.

Shaft v. (1970s) to cheat; trick; deceive; abuse. (FR.) SCU, YCU.

Shafts n. (1930s–1940s) one's legs. (DB, OHHJ, p. 146.) Harlem, SCU.

Shag [and stomp] n. (1900s–1920s) a fast jump dance; nervous, earthy hop dance; crude, down-home dance done to a type of blues of the same name; jitterbugging. Shag anticipated the jitterbug. (RSG, JT, pp. 238–239.) JMFU.

Shag; shagging v. (1960s–1970s) to perform sexual intercourse. (DW, TL, p. 188.) New York, SCU.

Shag; shagging v. (1980s–1990s) to walk slowly or in a lazy or tired manner; variant of "drag." (JM, WPC.) Example: "He come shagging his ass home three in the morning." WCU, SCU.

Shake n. (1920s) a rent party. (SL, RJON, p. 126; WF, DAS, p. 461.) See "Rent party" and "Rug-cutter."

Shake n., v. (1900s–1930s) an Oriental dance style done in sensuous jazz terms; to dance erotically; shaking added to Oriental dance motions. (RSG, JT, p. 239; BH, LSB, p. 51; MHB, JS, n.p.) SNU.

Shake v. (1940s–1950s) to extort. (IS, PSML, p. 316.) PPU, SCU.

Shake n. (1980s–1990s) diluted cocaine. (TW, CK, p. 138.) DCU.

Shake and bake v. (1990s) to dribble a basketball from left to right, this is the "shake," then going past your opponent to score a basket, this is the "bake"; a trick played on the other team for a score in a basketball game. (FR.) Basketball players' and fans' use.

Shake [oneself] apart v. (1900s–1940s) to lose self-control either while dancing, laughing, or crying. (BH, LSB, p. 179; RSG, JT, p. 240.) SCU.

Shake baby n. (1920s–1930s) a dress very tight across the hips, but with a full short skirt. (ZNH, MM, p. 125.) SU.

Shake [one] down v. (1980s–1990s) to engage in heterosexual or homosexual activity; to rape. (WKB, JMC, PS, p. 50.) PU.

Shake-em-up n. (1970s–1990s) cocktail mixture of lemon juice and white port. (EF, RDSL, p. 253.) South-central Los Angeles, YCU, SCU.

Shake it! interj. (1900s–1950s) a cry or command to dance fast and with great feeling. (RSG, JT, p. 240.) JMFU.

Shake it! interj. (1900s–1990s) a cry of encouragement to a dancer, usually a dancing woman; also from children's counting-out or playing song, a black version of "Little Sally Walker": shake it to the east/shake it to west/shake it to the very one you love the best. (BJ, BLH, SD, pp. 107–111.) SNU.

Shaker n. (1980s–1990s) a tiny glass bottle used by cocaine addicts to cook the drug. (TW, CH, p. 151.) DCU.

Shake that thing! interj. (RSG, JT, p. 240.) See "Shake it."

[A] Shake-up [shakeup] n. (1930s–1940s) a potent alcoholic drink made with a variety of liquors, such as scotch whiskey, wine, gin, and bourbon. (WF, DAS, p. 462; SL, RJON, p. 148.) SU.

Shaking n. (1950s) that which is taking place at the present; event; happening or occurrence. (FR.) Examples: "What's shaking, man?" and "Ain't nothing shaking but the leaves on the trees." SCU, SNU.

Shaky adj., adv. (1960s–1980s) exhibiting irrational or erratic behavior. (DC, BJ, p. 79.) Example: "Marty is too shaky to have all that responsibility Mr. Weaver gave him." SNU.

Sham on [one] v. (1970s–1990s) to outsmart; mislead; deceive; trick. (EF, RDSL, p. 253.) YCU, SCU.

Shank n. (1970s–1990s) a switchblade knife carried as a weapon. (EF, RDSL, p. 253.) SCU.

Sharecropping n. (1860s–1930s) "share of the crop" system. Black people newly freed from slavery were victims of this system. (Richard Wright, *Twelve Million Black Voices*, Viking, 1941, pp. 32–43.) SU.

Sharks n. (1970s–1990s) a sharkskin suit. (EF, RDSL, p. 253.) South-central Los Angeles, YCU.

Sharp adj. (1920s–1950s) stylishly and attractively dressed. (MM, RB, p. 374; RF, WJ, p. 305; WF, DAS, p. 463; LA, SM, p. 164.) SNU.

Sharp as a mosquiter's peter (1970s–1990s) to be beautifully or handsomely dressed in expensive clothes. (EF, RDSL, p. 253.) YCU.

Shattered n. (1990s) variant of "short"; term used in rap songs. (FR.) WCU.

Shaw (EF, BVV, p. 51.) See "Short."

Shawl (EF, BVV, p. 51.) See "Short."

Shebang n. (1880s–1890s) place; public place; home; residence; may be the source of "sh-bam," in the jazz expression "Oop-Bop-Sh'bam." (JSF, AON, pp. 481–482; Dizzy Gillespie, "Oop Bop Sh'bam," 1946.) SU.

Shecoonery n. (1860s–1890s) corruption of "chicanery." (JSF, AON, p. 482.) SU.

Shed v. (1900s) to rid oneself of. (FR.) Example: "I tell you boys, got shed of my wife and I'm a happy man this morning." SU.

Shed n. (1940s–1950s) a bus or train station waiting room. (IS, TB, p. 312.) SCU, PU, NCU.

Sheen (chine) n., v. (1950s–1960s) a car; to drive an automobile. (CS, vol. 3, no. 2, p. 41; DC, BJ, p. 79.) See "Chine."

[The] Sheet n. (1940s–1950s) an official police record. (IS, PSML, p. 316.) SCU, DCU, PPU.

She-he n. (1940s–1950s) a lesbian. (FR.) See "Bulldagger." SCU.

Sheisty adj. (1990s) underhanded; immoral; unethical; criminal. (FR.) College students, YCU.

Sheisty-trickster n. (1990s) a person who gets away with a crime or a misdeed; an immoral or unethical person. (FR.) College students, YCU.

Sherlock Holmes n. (1960s–1990s) a police detective (despite the fact that Sherlock Holmes was a private investigator and did not work for Scotland Yard). (EF, RDSL, p. 253.) SCU.

Sherm n. (1980s–1990s) nickname for the narcotic PCP, named after the cigarette brand Sherman, which is sometimes soaked in PCP before being smoked. (WKB, JMC, PS, p. 50.) PU.

She-self n. see "Herself."

She-she [talk] n. (1850s–1920s) male term; pejorative for "woman's talk." (AEG, BB, p. 326.) SU, SNU.

Shield n. (1940s–1950s) detective or police badge. (FR.) SCU, PU.

Shimmy n. (1950s–1920s) variant of "chemise." (AEG, BB, p. 326.) SU.

Shimmy [shimmie-she-wobble; shim-shim-shimmy] n. (1920s–1940s) a dance, from the word "chemise." Women dancing at the Cotton Club in Harlem would shake their shoulders, and the part of their chemise that covered the breasts shook to the rhythm of their dancing bodies; thus the dance became known as the Shimmy. There is no agreement on when or where the Shimmy was introduced. (RSG, JT, p. 241.) JMFU.

Shine n., adj. (1800s–1930s) a black person; blue-black skin. (CVV, NH, p. 286; WF, DAS, p. 467; LH, LKFC, p. 60; CVV, NH, p. 286.) Examples: "He's so black he shines!" and "I don't call you shine 'cause you mine!" SU, SNU.

Shine n. (1920s–1940s) short for moonshine. (WF, DAS, p. 467.) SU.

[Monkey] Shine n. (1900s–1950s) foolishness. (FR.) SU, SNU.

Shine box n. (1940s–1950s) a "Negro"-owned tavern or dancehall; a bar or club where black people congregate. Picked up from derogatory white use and used ironically. (WF, DAS, p. 467.) SU, SNU.

Shine [one] on v. (1950s–1990s) to avoid; to ignore; to deceive. (EF, BVV, p. 51; EF, RDSL, p. 253; CRM, BP, p. 307.) YCU, SCU, PPU.

Shiney [shinny] n. (1890s–1930s) a "Negro." Picked up from derogatory white use and used ironically. (WF, DAS, p. 467.) SU, SNU.

Shit n., adj., interj. (1630s–1990s) a word loosely used as an abbreviation for or variant of "bullshit." Stuff, nonsense; jive; personal affairs; drugs; whiskey; conversation. Used to describe almost any subject from the nineteenth century to the 1990s; an all-purpose intensifier. Also refers to offensive or worthless talk or action. An expression of surprise or anger. Not originally a black expression but popular among black slang users. (WF, DAS, pp. 467–468, 703; RSG, JT, p. 241; John A. Williams, *Night Song*, 1961, p. 89; EF, RDSL, p. 253.) SNU.

Shit n. (1940s–1950s) narcotics; marijuana; poor quality heroin. (RSG, JL, p. 118; EF, RDSL, p. 253; RRL, DAZ, p. 222.) DCU.

[Chicken] Shit adj. (1940s–1950s) insignificant; cowardly. (FR.) SU, SNU. See "Chickenbone special," "Chicken feed," "Chicken scratch."

[One's] Shit n. (1970s–1990s) one's gun, especially a handgun. (EF, RDSL, p. 253.) SCU, PU.

Shit comes in piles (1990s) metaphoric way of saying that when trouble comes, it comes in large portions; "shit happens." (JM, WPC, p. 55.) SCU.

Shiv (sheive; chiv; chive; shive; chev) n. (1660s–1990s) a knife used as a weapon; a switchblade. In prison after the 1950s, a homemade knife. (IS, PSML, p. 316; EP, DU, p. 616; OHHJ, p. 146; WF, DAS, p. 468; DC, BJ, p. 79.) SCU, PU, PPU, DCU.

Shoddy-doo n. (1960s–1970s) the hand-slapping performance ("Give [one] five") common in a meeting of two friends. (DW, TL, p. 188.) New York, SCU.

Shoeshine-black n. (1960s) the ideology of black consciousness; black nationalist phrase. (FR.) SCU.

Sho nuff [sure enough] (1700s–1950s) variant of "sure enough"; an expression of affirmation; without doubt. (JAH, PBE, p. 172.) Example: "I sho nuff did try to get that man to change his ways but he weren't studying me so I had to leave him." SU.

Shoo v. (1800s–1940s) a command to be quiet or to whisper. (FR.) SU.

Shoo-shooing v. (1800s–1940s) to whisper. (FR.) SU.

Shoot (1960s–1990s) used to give someone the go-ahead to speak. (EF, RDSL, p. 253.) SNU.

Shoot a brick v. (1970s–1990s) In basketball, to make a shot off the mark. (EF, RDSL, p. 254.) Basketball players' and fans' use.

Shoot a good shot (1970s–1990s), in verbal combat, to out-"shoot" or defeat the other talker in "rapping" or "capping." (EF, RDSL, p. 254.) SCU, YCU.

Shoot [one's] best mack (1970s–1990s) to flirt in the most seductive manner one can manage. (EF, RDSL, p. 254.) YCU. See "Mack on [one]."

Shoot [a] blank(s) (1970s–1990s) to say something or to tell someone something that is of no interest to them. (EF, RDSL, p. 254.) SNU.

Shoot [a] dud(s) (EF, RDSL, p. 255.) See "Shoot [a] blank(s)."

Shoot [one] down (WF, DAS, p. 703.) See "Shot down."

Shoot jokes on [one] (1970s–1990s) to belittle someone in a jocular manner. (EF, RDSL, p. 254.) YCU, SCU.

Shoot on v. (1960s–1970s) to belittle; insult; verbally attack. (CS, Vol. 3, No. 2, p. 42.) SCU. See "Shoot jokes on [one]."

Shoot skin (1950s–1960s) to miss the vein in attempting to inject heroin. (CS, vol. 3, no. 2, p. 42.) DCU.

Shoot the dozens (1950s–1970s) (EF, RDSL, p. 254.) See "Dirty Dozens."

Shoot the gift (1980s–1990s) to talk in rhyme or rhythm; to converse; to rap. (FR.) YCU.

Shoot up v. (1940s–1990s) to inject narcotics—especially heroin—into one's veins. (CS, vol. 3, no. 2, p. 42.) DCU.

Shoo, turkey n. (1960s–1990s) post-Civil War children's jumping motion in dance and song of the same name. (BJ, BLH, SD, p. 53, 220.) SU.

Shoot [one's] wad (1950s–1970s) for males, to have an orgasm; to spend all one's money. (FR.) SCU, YCU.

Shooting n. (1960s–1970s) violent or brutal talk; fighting talk. (CS, vol. 3, no. 2, p. 42.) SCU.

Shooting gallery n. (1950s–1990s) usually a house, apartment, or abandoned building where drug addicts go to shoot up. (RRL, DAZ, p. 222; WF, DAS, p. 470.) DCU.

Shooting gravy (1950s–1990s) when an addict re-injects his own cooked blood. (RRL, DAZ, p. 222.) DCU.

Shooting it off (1990s) for males, to have an orgasm. (FR.) YCU.

Shooting the agate n. (1900s–1920s) a kind of "hip" strut done in parades or often anywhere on the street in New Orleans and Memphis; parade "hip" stepping. (RSG, JT, p. 242.) JMFU.

Shooting the marbles from all sides of the ring (1930s–1940s) to be in a very dangerous position. (DB, OHHJ, p. 146.) SCU.

Short n. (1930s–1980s) an automobile; a car. (EF, BVV, p. 51; RSG, JT, p. 242; EF, RDSL, p. 254; IS, PSML, p. 316; DC, BJ, p. 79.) See "Rubber" and "Sheen."

Short [line] adj. (1940s–1950s) gambler's term meaning to be without money or to have very little money; expression picked up from gamblers. (RSG, JT, p. 242.) Gamblers' use, SNU.

Short dog n. (1960s–1990s) bottle of cheap wine; small bottle of "rot-gut" fortified wine. (EF, BVV, p. 51; EF, RDSL, p. 254; CS, Vol. 3, No. 2, p. 42.) South-central Los Angeles use, SCU.

Short money game n. (1960s) the money a pimp makes off a prostitute who is with him for only a brief time. (CRM, BP, p. 298.) PPU.

Short nail n. (1960s–1970s) a black woman with short, kinky hair. (EF, RDSL, p. 254.) South-central Los Angeles use, SCU.

Short stop n. (1950s–1960s) a temporary arrangement, thing, or length of time. (CRM, BP, p. 307.) PPU.

Short stop v. (1970s) to suddenly prevent someone or something from proceeding. (FR.) SCU, YCU.

Shortstop n. (1960s–1970s) anyone considered to be stupid, a fool, a coward, a "sucker," or a likely victim. (DW, TL, p. 188.) New York, NECU, SCU.

Short-stop money n. (1950s–1970s) temporary money a man gets from "pimping" a woman on welfare. (CRM, BP, p. 247.) PPU, SCU.

Short trill n. (1940s) a short walk. (DB, OHHJ, p. 146.) SCU.

Shortie Harold Baker (b. 1914), a trumpet player who worked with Duke Ellington's band.

Shot adj. (1950s–1990s) finished; defeated; ugly. (CS, vol. 3, no. 2, p. 42.) SCU.

[A] Shot n. (1960s–1970s) a professional pickpocket. (DW, TL, p. 188.) SCU, PU, NECU.

Shot down v. (1960s–1980s) to suffer a verbal attack; to be insulted or rejected. (WF, DAS, p. 703; DC, BJ, p. 79.) Example: "Shorty got shot down by Mabel so he's not making the scene." See "Cap on," and "Dirty Dozen."

Shotgun seat n. see "[To] Ride shotgun."

Shot through the grease (1950s–1960s) to be duped; betrayed; abused. (RDA, TB, p. 49; JH, PBL, p. 86.) SCU, YCU.

Shout n., adj. v. (1800s–1950s) the kind of hymn-singing that went on at revival meetings; a slow blues or spiritual done as a chant; gospel-singing in church on Saturday or Sunday nights; in jazz, when music is both played and sang; having a "ball"; a "prom." (RF, WJ, p. 305; WF, DAS, p. 473; RSG, JT, pp. 242–243.) SU, SNU.

Shout n. (1870s–1930s) from Arabic word "*Saut*": to dance; a dance step—not a sound. (BJ, BLH, SD, pp. 45–46, 144; JH, PBL, p. 86.) SU.

Shouter n. (1890s–1920s) a gospel singer, or a blues singer with a gospel orientation such as Charlie Patton and, more recently, Mississippi Fred McDowell. (RSG, JT, p. 243.) SU.

Shouter n. (1890s–1920s) a "Negro" church. Picked up from white use. (FGC, DARE, p. 678.) See "Clapper."

Shouting n. (1750s–1990s) sounds resulting from being "possessed," especially in a church. (GS, TT, p. 56.) SNU. See "Getting the spirit."

Show 'em what you got (1990s) show how talented you are. (FR.) YCU.

Showcase nigger n. (1960s–1970s) "Negro" hired by a white-owned firm to sit out front as a living example of the "fair" hiring practices of the company. (FR.) SNCU.

Show [one's] color (1950s–1970s) to behave foolishly in public; act like a clown; behave like a spoiled or difficult child. (EF, RDSL, p. 254.) SNU.

Show out; showing out v. (1890s–1930s) to flaunt oneself or one's possessions; to put on airs; "showing off." (RSG, JT, p. 243.) SU, SNU.

Shuck; shucking n., v. (1870s–1990s) variant of "shit"; any deed without value or one considered unethical or immoral; false flattery; to be insincere; to "jive" someone; to tease; to lie. (RSG, JT, p. 243; CS, vol. 3, no. 2, p. 42; CRM, BP, p. 307; DW, TL, p. 188; RDA, DDJ, p. 267.) SU, SNU. See "Jive."

Shuck dropping v. (1940s) taking advantage of an unsuspecting person. (DB, OHHJ, p. 146.) SCU.

Shucking and jiving (1870s–1960s) originally, southern "Negro" expression for clowning, lying, pretense. (DC, BJ, p. 79.) SU, SNU. See "Shuck."

Shuffle n. (1900s–1960s) a style of dancing and dance music done in four/four time, with eight tones to a measure creating the effect of a slow but heavy, serious, boggie-woogie rhythm, a "back beat"; later, in the sixties, a subservient black person, one who shuffles along. (RSG, JT, p. 244.) JMFU.

Shug n. (1850s–1990s) variant of and short for "sugar"; often a nickname for a girl in the south. (AW, CP.) SU, SNU.

Shut-eye n. (1900s–1940s) sleep. (SL, RJON, p. 79; WF, DAS, p. 475.) SNU.

Shutter clicker n. (1940s) the projector operator in a movie theater. (MHB, JS, np.) SNU.

Shutters n. (1940s) one's eyelids or eyes. (DB, OHHJ, p. 146.) SNU.

Sick and tired of [one or something] (1930s–1970s) to have had enough. Example: "I'm sick and tired of the way we live." (WF, DAS, p. 476.) SNU.

Sick adj. (1940s–1970s) the feeling and discomfort of being without drugs when the craving is present. (FR.) DCU.

Sick as a dog (1840s–1930s) very ill. (FR.) SNU.

Side(s) n. (1930s–1980s) disk played on a phonograph machine; phonograph records also called LPs, 33s, 45s, 78s. They replaced the Victrola just as compact discs have replaced LPs. (EF, RDSL, p. 254;

RSG, 244; CS, vol. 3, no. 2, p. 42; DC, BJ, p. 79.) Example: "Let's go up to my place and listen to some Charlie Parker sides." JMFU.

Side n. (1960s–1970s) male term for woman, from the idea of one's woman being at one's side through thick and thin. (JH, PBL, p. 86.) Rare. New York, SCU.

Side n. (1960s) sometimes short for South Side [of Chicago, et al.]; area of any town where black community is located. (FR.) SNCU, SNU.

Sideman n. (1930s) in jazz, any musician in a group other than the soloist; one's supporting friend in a situation. (RSG, JT, p. 244.) JMFU, SCU.

Sides n. (1920s–1940s) padding used by some women to make their hips appear larger. (LA, SM, p. 476.) SU.

Siding v. (1980s–1990s) leaning to the side in a "cool" manner while driving. (FR.) South-central Los Angeles use, YCU.

Sig v. (1920s–1990s) short for signify. (FR.) SNU. See "Signification."

Sigging v. (1940s) variant of "signifying." (MHB, JS, np.) See "Signifying."

Signification v., n. (1900s–1990s) to berate someone; negative talk, using irony. (GS, TT, p. 82; DB, OHHJ, p. 146.) See "Dirty Dozens."

Signify v. (1900s–1990s) to censure in twelve or fewer statements; to goad; to harrass; to show off. (EF, RDSL, p. 254; CC, OMMM, NCCHD, p. 259; CRM, BP, p. 307; RDA, DDJ, p. 267.) See "Dirty Dozens."

Signifying v. (1900s–1990s) "performance" talk; to berate someone; to censure in twelve or fewer statements; speaking ironically. (RDA, TB, p. 46; EF, RDSL, p. 254; CRM, BP, p. 307; RDA, DDJ, p. 267.) See "Dirty Dozens."

[A] Silk n. (1930s–1950s) a white girl or woman. The reference is to her hair. (CLC, TS, p. 256.) SNU. See "Silk broad."

Silk and satin n. (1970s–1990s) amphetamines and barbiturates mixed together. (EF, RDSL, p. 254.) DCU.

Silk and satin n. (1970s–1990s) a good-looking white or light-skinned woman. (EF, RDSL, p. 254.) SCU, YCU.

Silk broad n. (1930s–1950s) a white girl or woman. (CLC, TS, p. 256; WF, DAS, p. 477.) SNU.

Silked adj. (1980s–1990s) dressed up. (EF, BVV, p. 51.) SCU.

Silks n. (1950s) any clothing made of silk such as shirts, socks, handkerchiefs. (DC, BJ, p. 79.) Example: "Bobby be in his bad silks Saturday night when he hit the scene." SCU.

Silked to the bone (1980s–1990s) to be dressed extremely well and expensively. (EF, BVV, p. 51.) SCU.

Simon Legree n. (1870s–1900s) a mean foreman or boss. Based on the character in *Uncle Tom's Cabin*. (WF, DAS, p. 477.) SU, SNU.

Simple pimp n. (1950s–1970s) an unsuccessful pimp. "Simple" is used as in "simple-minded" to mean a pimp who is unable to escape the lowest order of "pimp-prostitute culture." (CRM, BP, pp. 33, 307.) PPU.

Since time adj. (1930s) a very long time; since the beginning of time. (AW, CP, p. 186.) Example: "The Africans been making them things way back since time." SU.

Sing v. (1920s) in jazz, to make one's instrument sound lyrical. (RSG, JT, pp. 244–245.) JMFU.

Sip at the fuzzy cup (1970s–1990s) to perform cunnilingus. (EF, RDSL, p. 254.) SCU, YCU.

Sissy n. (1940s–1990s) derogatory term for male homosexual, from "sister." (EF, RDSL, p. 254; WF, DAS, 478; RDA, DDJ, p. 267.) See "Snake." SNU.

Sissy soft sucker n. (1980s–1990s) a weak man. (FR.) YCU, SCU.

Sister n. (1940s–1990s) male term for a black woman; soul sister. (EF, RDSL, p. 254; WF, DAS, p. 704; DC, BJ, p. 79.) SNU. See "Brother," "Brother in blackness," and "Brotherman."

Sister n. (1800s–1990s) female member of a black church. (FR.) SNU.

Sister n. (1950s–1990s) among black male homosexuals, a lesbian. (FR.) Homosexual use.

Sister-in-law n. (1940–1990) the relationship of other women in a pimp's stable to the main or bottom woman. (DW, TL, pp. 191–192.) PPU.

Sit in v. (1920s–1950s) to join any group of people already engaged in some activity such as gambling, playing cards, or checkers. (LA, SM, p. 123.) SU, SNU.

Sit-in; sitting in v. (1920s–1990s) in jazz, when a nonprofessional or outside musician is invited to join a working group on the stand. (RSG, JT, p. 246; KG, JV, p. 181.) JMFU.

Sit-in(s) n. (1950s–1960s) during the civil rights movement "sit-in" referred to protests at lunch counters in the South, staged in a dramatic attempt to break down the entrenched walls of segregation in public places where black people had been systematically rejected. (WF, DAS, p. 715.) SNU.

Sit on a beast (1970s–1980s) to drive or sit in the front seat of a car that has been "lifted" rather than "lowered"; this is thought to be "cool." (EF, RDSL, p. 254.) South-central Los Angeles use, YCU.

Sit on a dago (1970s–1980s) to drive or sit in the front seat of a car that has been so "lowered" in the front that it nearly touches the pavement; this is thought to be "cool." (EF, RDSL, p. 254.) South-central Los Angeles use, YCU.

Sitting chair n. (1920s–1930s) any chair; one's most comfortable chair. (FR.) SU.

Sitting on tight (1990s) any acceptable calm and self-assured behavior; acting "cool." (FR.) YCU.

Situation n. (1900s–1990s) problem; condition. (RP, C, p. 148.) Example: "I got to make an appointment to see the doctor about my situation." SNU.

Six n. (1940s) short for "six feet under"; a grave. (DB, OHHJ, p. 147.) Harlem use, SNU.

Six-foot subway n. (1940s) a grave. (MHB, JS, np.) SU.

Six months in front and nine months behind (1930s–1940s) unattractive appearance due to obesity. (ZNH, AM, p. 88.) SU, SNU.

Six-pack n. (1990s) a tight, flat stomach; tight stomach muscles. (FR.) YCU.

[The] Sixteens v. (1900s–1920s) in boggie woogie jazz, to roll sixteen piano bass notes. (RSG, JT, p. 246.) JMFU.

Six-trey n. (1930s–1990s) Sixty-third Street in Chicago; sixty-three. "Trey" is commonly substituted for "three." (DC, BJ, p. 79.) Chicago use, SCU.

[To] Sizzle adj., n., v. (1930s–1960s) to be dangerously subject to arrest, usually for the possession of illegal drugs; "sizzle" is from Old English meaning "hot." In American tramp use from the early part of this century: a cook; cooking; also, to electrocute. (IS, PSML, p. 316; RRL, DAZ, p. 223; JSF, AON, p. 489; EP, DU, p. 629.) DCU, SCU.

Skag n. (1930s–1990s) an ugly girl or young woman. (EF, RDSL, p. 254.) SCU, YCU.

Skag n. (1940s–1990s) heroin. (EF, RDSL, p. 254.) DCU.

Skag n. (1940s) bad liquor. (MHB, JS, np.) SU.

Skank n. (1970s–1990s) variant of "stank," or "skunk"; a girl or woman with a very foul body odor; a "slut"; a cheap-looking girl or woman. (EF, RDSL, p. 254; PM, UCLAS, p. 76.) South-central Los Angeles use, YCU.

Skanky adj. (PM, UCLAS, p. 76.) See "Skank."

Skate v. (1940s) to escape paying a debt. (DB, OHHJ, p. 147.) Harlem, NCU.

Skee n. (1920s–1930s) short for whiskey. (FR.) SU.

Skeeter Clifton Best (b. 1914), a guitarist who worked with Kenny Clarke and Oscar Pettiford.

Skeezer n. (1980s–1990s) a woman who sells sex in exchange for crack cocaine; promiscuous female; a girl or woman. (TW, CH, p. 151.) See "Juicer."

Skeezer n. (1980s–1990s) a female groupie; female fan of a hip-hop or rap artist. (*Essence*, Sept., 1992, p. 120.) Rap and hip-hop culture use.

Skid-bid n. (1980s–1990s) prison term or time in juvenile detention. (FR.) YCU.

Skied adj. (1980s–1990s) very "high" on cocaine; drunk out of one's mind. (TW, CK, p. 138.) DCU, SCU.

Skiffle [music or band] n. (1900s–1940s) a shuffle type of music or the band that makes it; a band of rhythm instruments; amateur musicians. Term is said to have been coined in 1930 by Dan Burley, journalist and pianist, and his group, "Dan Burley and His Skiffle Boys," but Eubie Blake says the term existed as early as the first decade of the present century. (LF, EJ, p. 148; RSG, JT, p. 246.) JMFU.

Skiffle n. (1930s–1940s) a rent party where the music is supplied by non-professional musicians. (WF, DAS, p. 481.) NCU, JMFU.

Skiffling and shuffling v. (1940s) frantic activity. (DB, OHHJ, p. 147.) Harlem use, NCU.

Skillet n. (1930s–1950s) a black person. (WF, DAS, p. 481.) SU, SNU.

Skillet blonde n. (1920s–1930s) a black woman in a blond wig. (FR.) SNCU.

Skimmer n. (1960s) a hat; cap; helmet; tam. (DC, BJ, p. 79.) MWU. See "Brim," "Sky piece," and "lid."

[Give one some] Skin (1700s–1980s) of African origin: *botme-der* [Temme]: to "put skin"; *i golo don m bolo* [Mandingo]: "place your hand in my hand." The human hand. Among black Americans, to slap hands with someone as a friendly gesture or as a symbol of agreement; an expression of cultural solidarity; considered manly. (RSG, JT, p. 246.) Example: "I like the way you handled that deal man, give me some skin." SCU, YCU.

Skin n. (1990s) a girl. (FR.) YCU.

Skin n. (1920s–1930s) a drum or set of drums. (RSG, JT, p. 247; CS, vol. 3, no. 2, p. 42.) JMFU.

Skin-beater n. (1930s–1940s) a drummer. (WF, DAS, p. 482; MHB, JS, np.) JMFU.

Skin-popping n. (1920s–1990s) to inject heroin or some other drug into a muscle to achieve a mild effect. Practiced by neophytes as opposed to mainliners. (RRL, DAZ, p. 224.) DCU.

Skin-shot n. (CS, vol. 3, no. 2, p. 42.) See "Shoot skin."

Skin the cat (1970s) to perform sexual intercourse. (EF, RDSL, p. 254.) South-central Los Angeles, YCU, SCU.

Skinner v., n. (1870s–1940s) based on "skin," meaning "to cheat"; a shyster; also based on "skin the lamb," meaning to fix a horse race; a game of cards; a man who cuckolds another. (Hear Lightnin' Hopkins, "Jailhouse Blues," *Blues in my Bottle*, Prestige, 1961; AB, DSJC, p. 237.) SU.

Skins n. (1930s–1970s) in jazz, drums. (DB, OHHJ, p. 147; WF, DAS, p. 482; CC, OMMM, NCCHD, p. 259.) JMFU.

Skippy n. (1930s–1940s) a homosexual or effeminate male. (WF, DAS, p. 482.) Rare. SNU.

Skis n. (1940s–1960s) extremely big shoes, especially comical shoes. (DC, BJ, p. 79.) SNU, YCU, MWU.

Skits n. (1960s) shoes; clothes. (CS, vol. 3, no. 2, p. 42.) Rare. Watts, Los Angeles, use.

Skoofer [skrufer; skoofus; skrufus] n. (1970s–1990s) marijuana cigarette. (EF, BVV, p. 51; EF, RDSL, p. 254.) YCU, SCU.

[A] Skull n. (1940s) one who gives a first-rate performance; smart individual; an "ace slicker." (DB, OHHJ, p. 147.) Harlem use, JMFU, NCU.

Skull-drag n. (1950s–1960s) any performance or task that taxes the mind heavily. (FR.) YCU.

Skunked adj. (1990s) deceived; tricked; misled. (FR.) YCU.

Sky n. (1930s–1940s) refers to the blue uniform of a law-enforcement officer. A policeman; prison guard. (WF, DAS, p. 483.) NCU.

Sky-piece n. (1930s–1940s) a hat; cap; helmet. (RSG, JT, p. 247; DB, OHHJ, p. 147; MHB, JS, np; DC, BJ, p. 79.) SNU, JMFU.

Sky-pocket n. (1940s) pocket inside one's outer garments, such as a vest pocket. (DB, OHHJ, p. 147.) Harlem, NCU.

Slab n. (1940s) bread. (DB, OHHJ, p. 147.) Harlem, JMFU, NCU.

Slab n. (1980s–1990s) weakened or impure crack cocaine. (TW, CH, p. 151.) DCU.

[Give one some] Slack (1960s–1990s) a plea for money, compassion, kindness, understanding, opportunity, consideration, or "cover." (EF, RDSL, p. 254; CS, vol. 3, no. 2, p. 43; DC, BJ, p. 79.) SNU.

Slag n. (1970s–1990s) a disreputable or unattractive girl or woman; a "slut." (PM, UCLAS, p. 77.) YCU. See "Skank."

Slam; slammer n. (1930s–1950s) a jail; prison; door; portal; entrance. (WF, DAS, p. 704; MM, RB, p. 371; RSG, p. 247; DB, OHHJ, p. 147.) PU, SCU.

[A] Slam n., v. (1960s–1990s) an insult. In the eighties and nineties, to fight, especially with the fist. (FR.) YCU. See "Slamming."

Slam Leroy Stewart (b. 1914), a bass player who worked with Charlie Parker and Art Tatum.

Slamming; slamminest adj. (1980s–1990s) fashionable; first rate; beautiful; wonderful; the best; delicious. The term is loosely used as a surperlative. Rap duo Black Sheep used the word in a song titled "Flavor of the Month." (*Essence*, Nov., 1992, p. 26.) Examples: "That's a slamming dress," or, "He has the slamminest car in the hood." YCU.

Slamming v. (1980s–1990s) fighting with fists or knives. (TW, CH, p. 151.) SCU.

Slanguage n. (1930s–1990s) African-American slang. (HC, WSJ, p. B1.) YCU.

Slant(s) n. (1950s–1990s) pejorative term for an Asian man or woman. (EF, RDSL, p. 254.) South-central Los Angeles use.

Slanters n. (1940s) one's eyes. (DB, OHHJ, p. 147.) Harlem use, NCU.

Slap [the doghouse] (1920s–1950s) in jazz, to slap or pluck the strings of a instrument such as a base violin. (RSG, JT, p. 248.) JMFU.

Slap [one] five (1940s–1990s) when two friends meet one might request, with this expression, that they slap the palms of their hands together as a variant of a handshake. The practice has evolved into many fancy versions of the simple business of slapping hands, for example, one might hold both palms open at about thigh level and receive two slaps, or one might hold the open palm behind his back and wait for the slap. 'Til the sixties, the practice was almost exclusively black, but has since become national if not international. (EF, RDSL, p. 254; DC, BJ, p. 79.) See "[To] Give [one] five." SNU.

Slap-happy n. (1940s) a devoted swing music fan. (DB, OHHJ, p. 147.) Example: "Hey, Sla-happy, when you gone get up off that old swing kick and dig some of these new bop sounds?"

Slap-tongue [tongue-slap] v. (1920s–1940s) in jazz blowing, to hit or strike the tongue against the mouthpiece. (RSG, JT, p. 248.) JMFU.

Slapped with an ugly stick (1960s–1970s) used to describe one who is ugly. (PM, UCLAS, p. 18.) YCU, SCU.

Slat n. (1940s–1950s) sometimes refers to the length of a prison term or quantities of other things, such as money. (IS, PSML, p. 316.) PU, SCU, DCU.

Slaughter house n. (1970s–1990s) any place, such as a bedroom, where sexual intercourse is performed. (EF, RDSL, p. 254.) South-central Los Angeles use, YCU. See "Killing floor."

Slave n. (1620s–1990s) derived from "*Sclavus*" or "*Slav*" a thirteenth-century word for the slaves [Slavic people] of Germans in the Middle Ages. An African captured or bought and sold into American slavery; a person bound to the "peculiar institution." (JSF, AON, pp. 492–493; SBF, IHAT, p. 36.)

Slave n., v. (1930s–1960s) a job; to work. In jazz, any job not involving music. In the sixties, an oppressed person; a drug addict. (Chester Himes, *Black on Black*, 1973, p. 201; RSG, JT, p. 248; DB, OHHJ, p. 147; CS, vol. 3, no. 2, p. 43.) SU, SNU. See "Gig," and "Hame."

Slave breeder n. (1700s–1860s) the owner of a slave breeding plantation. Picked up from white use and used ironically. (SBF, IHAT, p. 36.) SU.

Slave car n. (1750s–1860s) a railroad boxcar for moving large numbers of slaves from one location to another; a cattle car used for slaves. (SBF, IHAT, p. 36.) SU.

Slave catcher (SBF, IHAT, p. 36.) See "Patteroller."

Slave name n. (1960s–1990s) one's family or given name or both. (JM, WPC, p. 48.) YCU, SCU.

Slave pen n. (1650s–1860) a holding place for slaves about to be sold. (Joel Williamson, *New People: Miscegenation and Mulattoes in the United States*, 1980, p. 69.)

Slavery n. (1620s–1990s) a fourteenth-century word; the "peculiar institution." (JSF, AON, pp. 492–493; SBF, IHAT, p. 36) See "Slave."

Slave tip n. (1940s) information regarding a job opportunity. (DB, OHHJ, p. 147.) NCU.

Slay [one] v. (1900s–1950s) a request to be told stunning news. (MHB, JS, np.) SNU.

[The] Sleep n. (1940s) a college professor's lecture, especially one given in a large hall. (MHB, JS, np.) Southern black college student use.

Sleepers n. (1960s–1990s) barbiturates. (CS, vol. 3, no. 2, p. 43.) DCU.

Sleeping in chapters n. (1960s) the frequent bouts of sleep following heroin withdrawal. (CS, vol. 3, no. 2, p. 43.) Rare. DCU.

Sleeping white (1960s–1970s) to be sexually involved with a white person. (FR.) SNU.

Slicer n. (1960s–1980s) a knife, especially one carried in the pocket and used in street fights. (EF, RDSL, p. 254.) SCU.

Slicing [one's] chops (1940s) talking. (DB, OHHJ, p. 147.) Harlem use, JMFU, NCU.

Slick n., adj. (1850s–1990s) originally, in England, a provincial variant of "sleek" [glossy]; as an Americanism it became unquestionably distinct from "sleek." Among black speakers, an underhanded person; the "art" of being clever; deception; deceptive charm; in the nineteen-fifties, good, pleasing. Though not of black origin, "sleek" has been exceptionally popular among black slang users since before the turn of the century. (EF, RDSL, p. 254; DC, BJ, p. 80; JsF, AON, pp. 493–494; WF, DAS, pp. 486–487; RDA, DDJ, p. 267.) Example: "That's cool; that's pretty slick." SNU.

Slick as greased-lightning see "Slick."

Slicker n. (EF, RDSL, p. 254.) See "Slick."

Slick-em-plenty n. (1970s) a deceptive, fast-talking, con artist. (EF, RDSL, p. 254.) See "Slick."

Slick Rick (1980s) Ricky Walters, a rapper.

Slickster n. (EF, RDSL, p. 254.) See "Slick."

Slide n. (1920s) in jazz, a glissando way of playing the piano. (RSG, JT, p. 248.) JMFU.

[To] Slide; sliding v. (1930s–1940s) to dance, especially on a polished wooden floor; "slipping and sliding." (Hear Lightnin' Hopkins, "I'm Taking a Devil of a Chance," *Double Blues*, Fantasy, 1989; MHB, JS, np.) SU.

Slide v. (1950s–1960s) to depart. (DC, BJ, p. 80.) Example: "I'm going to finish this last case then slide on toward home—I got a big weekend coming up." SNCU.

Slide [one's] jib (1930s–1940s) to talk; to talk freely and at random. (DB, OHHJ, p. 147; CC, OMMM, NCCHD, p. 259.) Harlem use, JMFU, NCU.

Slide Locksley Wellington Hampton (b. 1932), trombonist and composer who worked with Lionel Hampton.

Slides n. (1930s–1940s) shoes. (DB, OHHJ, p. 147.) See "Skies."

Slim n. (1940s–1960s) a regular cigarette, as opposed to a marijuana cigarette; "square" cigarette. (WF, DAS, p. 704.) Example: "Say, man, lay a slim on me, I left mine in the dressing room." DCU.

Sling sassy v. (1860s–1900s) to suddenly show contempt or impertinence. (JAH, PBE, p. 175.) SU.

Slingshot n. (1960s–1980s) a Cadillac El Dorado. (EF, RDSL, p. 254.) South-central Los Angeles use.

Sling-shot n. (1970s–1990s) a sanitary napkin, so-called because of its shape. (EF, RDSL, p. 254.) YCU.

Sliphorn n. (1900s–1940s) a trombone. (RSG, JT, p. 249.) JMFU.

Slipstick n. (1930s–1950s) trombone. (FR.) JMFU.

Slipping v. (1970s–1990s) nodding from a heroin high. (FR.) DCU.

Slit n. (1800s–1990s) vagina. (EF, RDSL, p. 254.) SNU.

Slit(s) n. (1960s–1990s) EF, RDSL, p. 254.) See "Slant[s]."

Slob; slobbing v. (1950s–1960s) to kiss; kissing. (DC, BJ, p. 80.) SNU.

[A] Slop n. (1940s) a saxophone, so called because of the saliva that collects in it. (MHB, JS, np.) JMFU, SNU.

Slops and slugs n. (1940s) coffee and doughnuts. (DB, OHHJ, p. 147.) Harlem use, NCU.

Slow drag (LH, BNF, p. 483; RSG, pp. 249, 76–77.) See "Drag."

Slow-em-up(s) n. (1970s–1990s) any one of a variety of barbiturates or tranquilizers; sometimes used by addicts to calm the effects of amphetamines. (EF, RDSL, p. 254.) DCU. See "Downers."

[The] Slows n. (1980s–1990s) to move slowly while high on narcotics. (EF, RDSL, p. 241.) DCU.

Slow the row (1940s) a request to take it easy; slow down; be "cool." (MHB, JS, np.) SU.

Slow track n. (1960s) the hustling scene in a quiet, small city or town. (CRM, BP, p. 309.) PPU, DCU, SCU.

Slum n. (1940s–1960s) fake jewelry; cheap costume jewelry sold as the real thing. (IS, TB, p. 312.) SCU, PU, NCU.

Slum hustler n. (1940s–1950s) one who peddles cheap costume jewelry as the real thing in black ghettos. (IS, PSML, p. 316.) SCU, NCU.

Slumming v. (1900s–1940s) to visit a slum area out of curiosity; the use has remained literal among black speakers. (FR.) SNU.

Slurp n. (1940s–1950s) in jazz, glissando piano style; an onomatopoeia: the sound is like a "slurp." (SL, RJON, p. 150; WF, DAS, p. 490.) JMFU.

Slush pump n. (1930s–1950s) a trombone, so called because of the spittle that tends to collect in the slide. Infrequent usage among black jazz musicians. (WF, DAS, p. 490; RSG, JT, p. 249.) Rare. JMFU.

Sly adj. (1920s) hip; excellent. (FR.) SNU, SCU.

Smack n. (1880s–1950s) a slap, especially on the cheek. (WF, DAS, pp. 490–491.) SU, SNU.

Smack n. (1900s–1940s) a kiss. (WF, DAS, pp. 490–491; CS, vol. 3, no. 2, p. 43.) SU, SNU.

Smack n. (1950s–1960s) sexual intercourse; sex. (HLF, RJPD, p. 171.) Rare. New York use, YCU, SCU.

Smack James Fletcher Henderson (b. 1898), bandleader, composer, pianist.

Smack [smock] v., n. (1940s–1990s) a variant of the Yiddish *schmeck*, to sniff; heroin. (IS, PSML, p. 316; EF, RDSL, p. 255; CS, vol. 3, no. 2, p. 43; RRL, DAZ, pp. 216, 224; CLC, TS, p. 256.) DCU.

Smack n. (1960s–1990s) flirtatious talk; "nonsense" talk. (CS, vol. 3, no. 2, p. 43.) SCU.

Smack down v. (1880s–1950s) to strike hard, especially on the face. (WF, DAS, p. 491.) SU, SNU.

Smacker n. See "Kisser."

Smacko n. (1940s) a street person; unemployed person; "hoodlum." (WF, DAS, pp. 490–491.) Rare. Harlem use.

Small bread (WF, DAS, p. 491; RSG, JT, p. 249.) See "Chicken feed."

Small pipe n. (1940s–1950s) alto saxophone. (WF, DAS, p. 491.) Rare. JMFU.

Smart-ass see "Smart mouth."

Smart mouth n. (1930s–1990s) belligerent, loud talk; disagreeable talk; a caustic person. (EF, RDSL, p. 255.) SNU.

Smart stuff n. (1940s–1950s) tricky, underhanded activity. (FR) SCU.

Smarty-pants n. (1940s–1950s) a boy who has begun to feel mature sexual desire. (FR.) SU.

Smash(ed) adj. (1940s–1950s) very drunk; intoxicated. (WF, DAS, p. 492; CS, vol. 3, no. 2, p. 43.) SNU. See "Smash."

Smash n. (1960s–1990s) wine. (EF, RDSL, p. 255; DC, BJ, p. 80.) Example: "Sam can't get along without his smash first thing in the morning." SCU, YCU.

Smash and grab (1990s) to hurt or kill someone, then rob them. (FR.) See "Bump."

Smear n. (1920s–1950s) in jazz, a slightly flat tonal quality. (RSG, JT, p. 249.) JMFU.

Smell [one] (1990s) to understand. (HC, WSJ, p. B1.) Example: "I'm gon' tell you straight, man. Do you smell me?" New York, YCU, SCU.

Smit smoke n. (1940s) a very intelligent black person. (DB, OHHJ, p. 147.) Harlem use, NCU.

Smoke n. (1890s–1920s) a "Negro." (CVV, NH, p. 286; WF, DAS, p. 492.) SNU.

Smoke n. (1930s–1940s) marijuana or opium. (EF, RDSL, p. 255; WF, DAS, p. 492; SL, RJON, p. 104; DC, BJ, p. 80.) Example: "This wine ain't hitting the spot, I need me some smoke to get right." SCU, DCU.

Smoke v. (1990s) shot; to be murdered in a drive-by shooting. (FR.) YCU. See "Drive-by."

Smoked [windows] adj. (1970s–1990s) dark-tinted car windows; considered "cool," very "gangster." (EF, RDSL, p. 255.) SCU, YCU.

Smoke the nigger out of the woodpile (1850s–1890s) describes slave catchers or patrollers searching for runaway slaves, who would flush the slaves out of places where anti-slavery whites had hidden them on their journey north or to Canada. Picked up from white use. (FR.) SU.

Smoke out (1970s–1990s) to arrogantly impress others; to best someone; defeat another. (EF, RDSL, p. 255.) YCU.

Smoke [one or something] out (1900s–1950s) derived from "smoke the nigger out of the woodpile"; to locate a person or to gather information. (WF, DAS, p. 492.) SNU.

Smoke [them] out (1950s–1960s) in jazz, to play really fantastic, exciting, energetic music. (RSG, JT, p. 249.) See "Cook."

Smoke pad n. (1940s–1950s) an apartment, bed, or cot where several people gather to smoke marijuana or opium. (SL, RJON, p. 145; WF, DAS, p. 492.) DCU.

Smoke screen n. (1940s) underarm deodorant. (DB, OHHJ, p. 147.) Harlem, NCU.

Smokestack n. (1980s) dark-skinned black person. (EF, RDSL, p. 255.) YCU, SCU.

Smoking v. (1950s–1960s) in jazz, exhibiting great technical skill; generally, performing with energy and outstanding ability. (RSG, JT, p. 250.) JMFU.

Smoking; smoking over v. (1930s–1940s) looking closely at someone. (ZNH, AM, p. 96.) SNU.

Smoking adj. (1980s–1990s) dressed beautifully or elegantly, especially in expensive clothes. (TW, CK, p. 138.) SCU.

Smoky [the fire bear] adj., n. (1930s–1980s) blackness; the sense or spirit of black people gathered in one place. Picked up from extremely derogatory white use. (WF, DAS, p. 492; EF, RDSL, p. 255.) Rare. SNU.

Smooth adj. (1920s–1950s) very adept; clever. (WF, DAS, p. 493.) SNU.

Smudge n. (1940s) variant of "smoky"; picked up from extremely derogatory white use. (WF, DAS, p. 493.) Rare. SNU.

Snack n. (1950s–1960s) penis. (HLF, RJPD, p. 171.) Rare. New York, SCU.

[A] Snag n. (1950s–1960s) pejorative term for an unattractive female; a rude and physically ugly woman. (DC, BJ, p. 80; JH, PBL, p. 86.) MWU, SCU. See "Bat."

Snag; snagging n., v. (1970s–1980s) sexual intercourse; to perform sexual intercourse. (EF, RDSL, p. 255.) South-central Los Angeles use, YCU, SCU.

Snags Clifford Jones (1900–1947), drummer who worked with King Oliver and later with Bunk Johnson.

Snake n. (1950s–1970s) a sneaky person; one who's deceptive. (WF, DAS, p. 704.) SNU.

Snake n. (1970s) derogatory expression for male or female homosexual. (FR.) Rare. Harlem use. See "Sissy."

[Blowing] snakes (1940s–1960s) to blow or play "snake charmer music"; to play music badly. (RSG, JT, p. 250.) JMFU.

[Make] Snakes (1920s–1940s) in jazz, playing a saxophone fast, the way "Bird" did; playing any reed instrument with great skill; using one's tongue in a snake-like manner on the mouthpiece. (RSG, JT, p. 251.) JMFU.

Snake doctor n. (1920s–1940s) dragonfly. (FR.) SU.

Snake eyes n. (1930s–1940s) black gambler's term for the black dots on white dice when only two such dots are showing. (WF, DAS, p. 494.) Black gamblers' use, SU, PU.

Snake Hips n. (1900s–1930s) dance in which the hip movements are snake-like; a Baltimore- and New York-oriented jazz dance; referred to in "Snake Hips," by the Blue Rhythm Boys. (RSG, JT, p. 250.) JMFU. See "Pasamala," Camel Walk," "Fox Trot," "Turkey Trot," and "Bunny Hug."

Snap n. (1980s–1990s) a wisecrack; quick retort; fast repartee. (AL, LWBB, p. 137.) NCU, SCU.

Snap v. (1960s) to move fast. (FR.) New York's Lower East Side use.

Snap v. (1960s–1980s) to tease someone; to laugh with or at someone. (WF, DAS, p. 704.) YCU.

Snap a snapper v. (1940s) to light a match. (DB, OHHJ, p. 147.) Harlem, use, NCU.

Snapper n. (1940s) a match. (DB, OHHJ, p. 147.) Harlem, NCU.

Snatch n. (1930s–1950s) the vagina; female sexuality. (IS, PSML, p. 316; WF, DAS, p. 495.) SNU.

Snatcher n. (1900s–1940s) a policeman; police detective; private detective. May be left over from and short for "slave-snatcher." (DB, OHHJ, p. 147; CC, OMMM, NCCHD, p. 259.) Harlem, use, NCU.

Snatch up (1980s–1990s) an arrest by the police. (TW, CK, p. 138.) DCU, SCU.

Sneaky Pete n. (1940s–1950s) cheap fortified wine; cheap liquor. (WF, DAS, p. 495; AL, MJR, p. 230.) SCU, SNU.

Sneezer n. (1940s) a handkerchief. (DB, OHHJ, p. 147.) Harlem, NCU.

Sniff; sniffing v. (1900s–1990s) inhaling cocaine or powdered heroin. (CS, vol. 3, no. 2, p. 43; RRL, DAZ, p. 224.) See "Snort."

Sniff a powder (1940s) to run away or leave. (DB, OHHJ, p. 147.) Harlem, SCU, PU, DCU.

Sniffer n. (1940s) one's nose. (DB, OHHJ, p. 147.) See "Snuffer."

Snip a dolly (1940s) to go away; leave; depart. (DB, OHHJ, p. 147.) Harlem, use, NCU.

Snipe n. (1940s) a cigarette or cigar stub. (DB, OHHJ, p. 147.) Harlem, SCU. See "Slim."

Snipe on [one] (1970s–1980s) to insult; verbally abuse. (EF, RDSL, p. 255.) YCU.

Snipe one (1970s–1990s) murder; to kill someone. (EF, RDSL, p. 255.) SCU.

Snitch v. (1930s–1960s) to tell; inform against someone; to relay secret information; to plead guilty in a courtroom. (DG, BGL, p. 123; CS, vol. 3, no. 2, p. 43; CLC, TS, p. 256.) SNU, SCU.

Snitch-pad n. (1930s–1940s) a notebook. (DB, OHHJ, p. 147.) Harlem use, NCU, SCU.

Snitch-sheet n. (1930s–1940s) a newspaper. (DB, OHHJ, p. 147.) Harlem use, NCU, SCU.

Snitcher n. (1930s–1940s) a newspaper reporter; columnist; an informer; a writer. (DB, OHHJ, p. 147.) Harlem, NCU, SCU.

Snookie Eugene Edward Young (b. 1919), trumpet player who worked with Count Basie, Miles Davis, Ray Eldridge, and others.

Snookum Isaac Russell (b. 1913), bandleader, gave Fats Navarro, J.J. Johnson, Ray Brown, and many others their start.

Snort v. (1940s–1990s) to inhale cocaine or any drug in powder form. (IS, PSML, p. 316; WF, DAS, p. 704; EF, RDSL, p. 255; RRL, DAZ, p. 225.) DCU. See "Sniff."

Snot-rag n. (1900s–1940s) handkerchief. (FR) SU.

Snow n. (1900s–1990s) cocaine. (CVV, p. 286; SL, RJON, p. 144; WF, DAS, p. 497; EF, RDSL, p. 255.) DCU.

Snow n. (1950s–1960s) white female. (FR.) See "Silk broad."

Snowball n. (1850s–1900s) a "Negro" male with white hair; based on *a tort et a travers*. Picked up from derogatory white use. (JSF, AON, p. 501; WF, DAS, p. 497.) SU.

Snow Queen n. (1970s–1990s) a black gay male who prefers white sexual partners; a black gay male in love with a white male. (Melvin

Dixon, *Vanishing Rooms*, 1991, p. 90; HM, GL, p. 40.) Homosexual use.

Snub Laurence Leo Mosley (b. 1909), trombone player who worked with Louis Armstrong and trained for the USO during WWII.

Snuff [one] out v. (1950s–1990s) to kill a person. (EF, RDSL, p. 255; CLC, TS, p. 256; DW, TL, p. 189.) SCU. See "Snipe one."

Snuffer n. (1940s) one's nose. (DB, OHHJ, p. 147.) See "Sniffer."

Sock n., v. (1960s) originally, a drummer's double cymbals. Also, to hit; move fast; to jab; to inform; to move decisively. Not of black origin but popular among blacks in the sixties. (WF, DAS, pp. 499–500.) SNU, JMFU.

Sock chorus n. (1920s–1940s) the last chorus of a jazz or blues composition. (RSG, JT, p. 250.) JMFU. See "Sock."

Sock cymbal n. (1920s–1940s) in jazz, the cymbal is an instrument used in a decisive way during the "sock chorus." (RSG, JT, p. 251.) JMFU. See "Sock."

Sock frock n. (1940s) one's best suit. (DB, OHHJ, p. 147.) Harlem, NCU.

Sock it [to one or something] (1960s) a popular saying implying readiness; it carries an erotic or sexual connotation. (FR.) SNU.

Sock it to me (1960s–1970s) phrase made popular by Aretha Franklin in "Respect." (FR.) See "Sock it [to one or something]."

Sock rhythm n. (1920s–1940s) in jazz, a heavy rhythm produced by the excessive use of bursts of sounds produced primarily by drums, piano and tuba; a jabbing effect. (RSG, JT, p. 251.) JMFU.

Soda n. (1900s–1940s) nitrate used with fertilizer in farming and gardening in the rural South. (Richard Westmacott, *African-American Gardens and Yards in The Rural South*, 1992, p. 78, 96.) SU.

[Hard head and a] Soft behind (1880s–1940s) phrase meaning that stubbornness can have negative consequences. (WF, DAS, p. 501.) Example: "If that boy don't listen to me, he'll find out that a hard head makes a soft behind." SU, SNU.

[A] Soft-leg n. (1950s–1970s) a woman, especially an attractive woman. (JH, PBL, p. 86.) SCU.

Soft sucker n. (1990s) a weak man. (FR.) See "Sissy soft sucker." SCU.

Soft-top n. (1940s) a padded stool, especially in a bar. (DB, OHHJ, p. 147.) Harlem, NCU.

So help me (1800s–1990s) an oath; short for "So help me God"; the truth; common among black speakers both south and north. (DB, OHHJ, p. 147.) SNU.

Sojourner Truth Isabella Baumfree [born free], nineteenth-century anti-slavery crusader, lecturer, feminist.

Solid adj. (1920s–1960s) describes a fine state of affairs; great; exciting; anything marvelous or truly wonderful; loyal; outstanding; trustworthy. (ZNH, AM, p. 96; DB, OHHJ, p. 147; WF, DAS, p. 502; LA, SM, p. 126; RSG, JT, p. 251; CC, HDH, p. 16.) SNU.

Solid sender n. (1930s–1960s) a very "together" and satisfying person. (WF, DAS, p. 502; RSG, JT, p. 252.) JMFU. See "Solid."

Solitaire n. (1940s) suicide. (DB, OHHJ, p. 147.) Harlem use, NCU.

Some n. (1900s–1940s) vagina; female sex. Heard in early blues songs. (FR.) Example: "Come on, Lucy, give me some, just a little bit." SU.

Some lip n. (1930s–1950s) back-talk, usually in self-defense. (FR.) See "Lip."

Some pig (1940s–1950s) talk, conversation. (FR.) SU.

Some skin See "[Give one some] skin."

Something else (1950s–1960s) very special; any extraordinary person, place, thing or idea; above average. (WF, DAS, p. 502; RSG, JT, p. 252.) SNU.

Sometimey (sometimesy) adj., v. (1840s–1990s) changeable; moody; possessing a very inconsistent personality; to frequently change moods. (DC, BJ, p. 80.) Example: "She's sometimey—happy one minute, then miserable the next." SU, SNU.

Sonny Theodor W. Rollins (b. 1929), famous tenor saxophonist; also, Charles Liston, prizefighter.

Sonny Boy Williamson blues singer and harmonica player, born Aleck Miller 1908 or 1909 in Glendora, Mississippi. Worked with Willie Dixon, Otis Span, Muddy Waters and many others.

Soon n. (1700s–1940s) early, as in "early in the morning"; used frequently in spirituals and work songs. (JSF, AON, p. 505.) SU.

Sooner n. adj. (1930s–1940s) cheap or shabby clothing; a raggedy person; dirty. (ZNH, AM, p. 96; WF, DAS, p. 503.) SNU.

[A] Soon-man n. (1800s–1890s) a smart, alert, wide-awake man; early riser. (CCJ, NMGC, p. 169.) See "Soon."

[A] Soon-woman see "[A] Soon-man."

Sophisticated lady n. (1970s–1990s) cocaine. (EF, RDSL, p. 255.) DCU.

Sophisticated scum n. (1950s–1960s) any educated city person; monied citizen of New York City. (CW, TM, p. 27.) Rare. New York use.

Sorry adj. (1700s–1940s) lazy; lacking in ambition or motivation. (FR.) SU.

Sot n. (1630s–1930s) variant of "set." (JSF, AON, p. 506.) SU.

Soul n., adj. (1930s–1990s) essentially the essence of blackness; the sensitivity and emotional essence that derives from the blues; the heritage that is black; a natural process; black authenticity; feeling for one's roots, as demonstrated in black music and literature; a synonym for African-American culture; cultural truth or validity; deep racial feelings; deep cultural feelings; a sense of racial history or of the suffering of the thousands of black people killed or tortured or worked to death since the 1620s. (WF, DAS, p. 705; RSG, JT, pp. 252–253; EF, RDSL, p. 255; CS, vol. 3, no. 2, p. 44.) SNU.

Soul brother n. (1930s–1960s) form of address for one black man to another; an expression of cultural solidarity. Also, often used by white males on the hip scene in addressing black males, in fact, white speakers had, by the mid-sixties, taken over the phrase entirely. Rare among black speakers after the mid-sixties. (EF, RDSL, p. 254; WF, DAS, p. 705; RSG, JT, p. 254.) SNU. See "Soul" and "Blood brother."

Soul Brother Number One singer James Brown, born May 3, 1933, in Augusta, Georgia, R&B recording artist.

Soul City n. (1960s) Harlem. (WF, DAS, p. 705.) New York use.

Soul [hand-]clap n. (1920s–1950s) traditional black church expression; a handclap on the beat quickly followed by another off beat. (GS, TT, p. 57.) SNU.

Soul dancing v. (1950s–1990s) dancing in a manner or style characteristic to African-American popular dance culture. (DC, BJ, p. 80.) SNU, YCU.

Soul food n. (1780s–1990s) southern-style cooking done by black Americans, includes chitterlings, tripe, hominy grits with bacon and biscuits, ham hocks and black-eyed peas, turnip greens, cornbread, collard greens, mustard greens, neckbones, neckbones and greens, sweet potatoes, sweet potato pie, barbecue ribs, fried chicken, and potato salad. (WF, DAS, p. 705; EF, RDSL, p. 255; RSG, JT, p. 254; DC, BJ, p. 80.) See "Blackplate," "Chitlins," "Cow pea soup," "Crackling biscuit," "Ham-bone soup."

Souling v. (1950s–1990s) doing anything well, but especially playing exciting jazz. (CS, vol. 3, no. 2, p. 44.) SCU, JMFU.

Soul kiss n. (1950s–1960s) a deep kiss involving tongues. (WF, DAS, p. 504.) SNU.

Soul language n. (1940s–1990s) African-American slang. (CS, vol. no. 2, p. 44.) See "Slanguage."

Soul minority n. (1960s–1970s) African-Americans. (CS, vol. 3, no. 2, p. 44.) Rare. SNU.

Soul music n. (1930s–1990s) uniquely black music composed and performed by black musicians; gospel; blues; early and modern jazz. (WF, DAS, p. 705; EF, RDSL, p. 255; DC, BJ, p. 80.) JMFU.

Soul on (1960s–1970s) phrase encouraging one to continue to be authentic or successful. (FR.) SNCU.

Soul power n. (1960s–1970s) variant of "Black Power"; the social and political strength of black Americans as voters or in civil disobedience. (CS, vol. 3, no. 2, p. 44.) SNU. See "Black Power."

Soul session n. (1960s–1970s) any sort of informal gathering of black people. (CS, vol. 3, no. 2, p. 44.) SNCU.

Soul [hand] shake n. (1960s–1990s) an elaborate and intricate "handshake" carried out by "juxtaposing" one's right thumb to that of the other person's, then by grabbing his or her fingers and locking them in one's palm while he or she does the same in one's palm, followed by pushing forcefully away with the thumbs; a thumb-locking handclasp representing solidarity. (GS, TT, p. 57; EF, RDSL, p. 255; DC, BJ, p. 80.) SNU, SCU, YCU. See "Slap [one] five," and "[To] give one five." Also see "Black power handshake."

Soul sister n. (1930s–1990s) respectful or affectionate term of address for a black girl or woman to whom one is not related. The term is expressive of cultural solidarity. (WF, DAS, p. 705; EF, RDSL, p. 255; CS, vol. 3, no. 2, p. 44; DC, BJ, p. 80.) SNU, SCU, YCU. See "Soul brother."

Soul sound(s) n. (1950s–1970s) (CS, vol. 3, no. 2, p. 44.) See "Sound(s)."

Soul talk n. (1950s–1970s) informal conversation among two or more African-Americans. (CS, vol. 3, no. 2, p. 45.) SNCU.

Soulville n. (1950s) any black neighborhood; Africa. (WF, DAS, p. 705.) JMFU, SNCU. See "Soul City."

Sound n. (1940s–1950s) point of view; in jazz, one's doctrine as expressed musically in rhythm, concept, harmonics. (RSG, JT, p. 254.) Examples: "How you sound?" and "I really dig Monk's sound." SNU, JMFU.

Sound [one] v. (1940s–1950s) inform; to tell someone something; to insult; to play the dozens with one. (MHB, JS, np; RDA, DDJ, p. 267.) SNU.

[To] Sound off v. (1940s) to start a conversation with one or more than one person. (DB, OHHJ, p. 147.) Harlem, use, NCU, SCU.

Sound on; sounding on [one] v. (1950s–1960s) flirting. (FR.) SNU, YCU, SCU.

Sounds n. (1950s–1960s) music, especially bebop jazz; records. (EF, RDSL, p. 255; DC, BJ, p. 80.) See "Sound."

Sound the bugle (1940s) a request to start the music. (MHB, JS, np.) SNU.

[One's] Southern can n. (1930s–1950s) the buttocks. (FR.) SNU.

[A] Sow n. (1930s–1940s) a nickel; any coin. (DB, OHHJ, p. 147.) SNU.

[To] Space v. (1960s) to depart; go; leave. (DC, BJ, p. 80.) SCU, YCU.

Space-base n. (1980s–1990s) a cigar hull stuffed with crack cocaine and angel dust. (TW, CH, p. 151.) DCU.

Spaced v. adj. (1950s–1990s) to be high on narcotics; from the eighties on, to be mentally off. (RRL, DAZ, pp. 225–226.) DCU, YCU, SCU, SNCU.

Spaces n. pl. (1950s–1970s) in jazz and blues, the pauses between notes or words or phrases. Derived from the phrase to "space out" one's playing. (RSG, JT, p. 255.) JMFU.

Spade n., adj. (1930s–1960s) Derived from playing-card spades, a black person. Picked up from white "hip" or "beat" use, and used primarily by blacks in the "Bohemian life" of Greenwich Village and other such places in the late fifties and early sixties. (RSG, JT, p. 255; WF, DAS, p. 505; SL, RJON, p. 147; EF, RDSL, p. 255; DB, OHHJ, p. 147; IS, PSML, p. 316.) Rare. New York use, NCU.

Spagingy-spagade [spaginzy] (1900s–1920s) Pig Latin for "Negro." (CVV, p. 286; SL, RJON, p. 147; WF, DAS, pp. 505–506.) Rare. SU, SNU.

Spare n. (1940s) a friend. (MHB, JS, np.) Rare. SU.

Spark jiver n. (1950s) electric organ. JMFU.

Spark n. (1940s) a match, cigarette, or a diamond. (DB, OHHJ, p. 147.) Harlem, NCU, SCU.

Sparky James de Brest (b. 1937), bass player who worked with Lee Morgan, Art Blakey, Jay Johnson, and others.

Spasm band n. (1900s–1920s) a group of musicians who get together with homemade instruments—washtubs, washingboards, bones, etc.—and form a marching band. So called because of the disjointed sounds made by the makeshift instruments. (RSG, JT, pp. 255–256) JMFU. New Orleans use, JMFU.

Speak softly and carry a big stick (1900s) West African expression made popular in America by Teddy Roosevelt. (FR.)

Speaker n. (1930s–1940s) a gun. (Wf, DAS, p. 506.) Example: "Baltimore came busting in the joint with his two speakers drawn like Wild Bill himself." SCU, PU.

Spearchucker n. (1960s) a young adult, especially a college student. "Chucker" may be a variant of "chunker." (CS, Vol. 3, No. 3, p. 10.) College students' use, YCU.

Speck n. (1970s) black person. (EF, RDSL, p. 255) NSU.

Specs Charles Weight (b. 1927), drummer who worked with Dizzy Gillespie, Carmen McRae, and others.

Speed n. (1960s–1990s) amphetamines; C9H13N; methedrine. (EF, RDSL, p. 255; CS, vol. 3, no. 2, p. 45.) DCU.

Speedball n. (1940s–1990s) a mixture of cocaine or an amphetamine [for example Desoxyn] and heroin injected into the veins. (IS, PSML, p. 316; RRL, DAZ, p. 226; CLC, TS, p. 256.) DCU.

Spewing out v. (1990s) to engage in an angry diatribe or tirade; to participate in a bitter argument. (FR.) SCU, YCU.

Spic n. (1930s–1990s) east-coast derogatory term for a Puerto Rican; in the midwest and on the west coast, refers to a Mexican-American. (DB, OHHJ, p. 147; IS, PSML, p. 316.) Harlem use, Los Angeles use, NCU.

Spic and span n. (1950s–1990s) a pejorative term for an African-American and Puerto Rican couple. (WF, DAS, p. 508.) Harlem use, Brooklyn use.

[A] Splash n. (1940s) water; a bath; lake; ocean; river; stream; pond. (DB, OHHJ, p. 147.) Harlem use, NCU, SCU.

Splib n. (1940s–1970s) a black woman or man; an African-American; a "Negro"; a colored person. (CRM, BP, p. 308.) SNU.

Spliff n. (1960s–1990s) a marijuana cigarette. (Michelle Cliff, *No Telephone to Heaven*, 1987, p. 211.) Example: "Wait till I get a whiff of this good spliff, then I'll be ready." YCU, SCU. See "Joint," "Weed," and "Bush."

Spiel v., n. (1940s–1990s) to talk; to confess; speak at length; make a declaration. A term used by older hustlers. Sales talk; a fancy speech. Picked up from circus barker talk. (IS, PSML, p. 316; DB, OHHJ, p. 147; WF, DAS, p. 508.) SCU, DCU, PU, PPU. See "Rap."

Spike n. (1940s–1990s) a hypodermic needle used to inject drugs into the veins. (WF, DAS, p. 705; EF, RDSL, p. 255; CS, vol. 3, no. 2, p. 45; DC, BJ, p. 81; RRL, DAZ, p. 226.) DCU.

Spike Lee filmmaker Shelton Jackson Lee (b. 1957).

Spill n. (1940s–1950s) a person of Puerto Rican and African-American descent; a Puerto Rican or an African-American. (WF, DAS, p. 705.) Rare. New York use.

Spilling v. (1900s–1930s) older term with the same meaning as "rapping"—talking. (FR.) YCU, SCU. See "Rap."

Spin a hen (1940s) to dance with an older woman. (DB, OHHJ, p. 147.) Harlem use, NCU, SCU.

Spindle-shanked adj. (1930s–1940s) possessing a heavy rear end and thin legs. (CM, CW, Ann Petry, "Has Anybody Seen Miss Dora Dean," p.) SNU.

Spinning at the track on a fool's dime (1940s) to go dancing with a girl (who works as a maid) on her night off. (DB, OHHJ, p. 147.) Harlem use, NCU, SCU.

Spit-valve n. (1900s–1950s) among jazz musicians, the sliding part of a slide instrument—such as a trombone or a baritone saxophone—where saliva gathers. (RSG, JT, p. 256.) JMFU.

Splap n. (1940s–1950s) an onomatopoeia. A variant pronunciation of "slap." (FR.) SCU; JMFU.

Splash n. (1940s–1960s) an onomatopoetic device. Water; a bath; the ocean; lake. (DC, BJ, p. 81.) SCU, YCU.

Splay n. (1940s) marijuana. (WF, DAS, p. 705.) Rare. DCU.

Splib n. (1940s–1960s) reference to any black person; from the existential jazz word "splibby," suggesting "soul." (WF, DAS, p. 705; CS, vol. 3, no. 2, p. 45; DC, BJ, p. 81.) SNCU, YCU, SCU.

Splibby n. (1930s–1960s) a good feeling; "soul"; a feeling of wholeness; jazzy feeling. (FR.) JMFU, YCU, SCU.

Split v. (1780s–1990s) to leave; to leave quickly. (AB, DSJC, p. 274; Chester Himes, *The Real Cool Killers*, 1959, p. 15; SBF, IHAT, p. 314; RSG, JT, p. 256; EF, RDSL, p. 255.) SU, SNU.

Split the scene (RSG, JT, p. 256.) See "Split."

Sponge hair n. (1930s–1950s) hair that is difficult to manage; hair that resists a comb; hair with texture like a sponge. (FR.) SU.

Spook n. (1800s–1960s) originally used by black slaves as a reference to ghosts, and later as a reference to white people as "ghostlike." A black person; a "Negro"; picked up from derogatory white use and used ironically. (RHdeC, NB, pp. 37–38; CS, vol. 3, no. 3, p. 10; WF, DAS, p. 510; EF, RDSL, p. 255; IS, TB, p. 312.) SNU.

Spoon n. (1950s–1990s) about one-sixteenth of an ounce of heroin. (RRL, DAZ, p. 227; CS, vol. 3, no. 2, p. 45.) DCU.

Spoon Jimmy Witherspoon, blues and jazz singer.

Sporting house n. (1940s) whorehouse; brothel. (FR.) SU. See "Barrelhouse," and "Juke joint."

Spot n. (1900s–1990s) among jazz musicians, usually a nightclub, but can signify any popular place such as Harlem, the Village, or Hollywood. (RSG, JT, p. 257.) SNCU, JMFU.

Spot n. (1980s–1990s) an after-hours club. (TW, CK, p. 138.) SCU, DCU.

Spotlight n. (1940s–1960s) a light-complected African-American woman; an American of mixed white and black ancestry. (DC, BJ, p. 81.) SNU.

Spots n., pl. (1920s–1930s) music symbols on sheet music. (RSG, JT, p. 257.) JMFU.

Spotter n. (1980s–1990s) in drug culture, one who serves as a lookout for the police. (TW, CH, p. 151.) DCU.

Spotters n. (1940s) one's eyes. (DB, OHHJ, p. 147.) Harlem use, NCU, SCU.

Spouting n. (1930s–1940s) excessive talking. (DB, OHHJ, p. 147; CC, OMMM, NCCHD, p. 260.) NCU.

Spread [one's] jenk (1920s–1930s) to have a good time; to sing or enjoy music; to have sex. (ZNH, MM, p. 91.) Example: "I went to Big Mabel's last night and spread my jenk like nobody's business." SU.

Spud Webb (1990s) basketball player for the Sacramento Kings.

Spudding (spuddin) v. (1920s–1930s) to play cards for a small amount of money. (ZNH, MM, p.) SU.

Spring v. (1920s–1950s) to bail someone out of jail; to obtain the release of a person from prison. (LA, SM, p. 126.) SU, SNU, PU.

Sprung adj., adv. (1990s) in love. (FR.) YCU.

Spy v. (1930s–1940s) to see; look. (ZNH, AM, p. 85.) SNU.

Spyglass n. (1900s–1950s) magnifying glass; picked up from Sherlock Holmes mysteries. (FR.) SNU.

Square n., adj. (1900s–1990s) an old word dating back before 1811, meaning, at that time, "not roguish"; an orthodox person; one who supports popular mainstream values; a conventional person; unenlightened; innocent; not "hip" to the jazz or "cool" scene; sincere person; honesty. (FG, DVT, np; MM, RB, p. 375; SL, RJON, p. 147; WF, DAS, p. 513; RSG, JT, p. 257; CC, HDH, p. 14; EF, RDSL, p. 255.) SCU, YCU, SNU, JMFU.

Square(s) n. (1950s) an ordinary cigarette sold legally and commercially rather than a marijuana cigarette; a "square" smoke. (WF, DAS, p. 705; DC, BJ, p. 81.) DCU, SCU, YCU. See "Slim(s)."

Square brain (EF, RDSL, p. 255.) See "Square."

Square broad n. (1940s–1970s) any woman not hustling "tricks" for a pimp; a woman not in the "life" of prostitution. (CRM, BP, p. 308.) PPU.

Squaring out v. (1960s–1980s) ridiculing a person in his or her presence. (FR.) SCU, YCU.

Square in a social circle (1930s–1940s) a person who is out of place in a particular group; misfit. (MHB, JS, np.) SNU.

Square john n. (1950s–1970s) any male who is not actively engaged in "street" or "pimp-prostitution" culture; a "trick." (DW, TL, p. 189.) PPU, SCU.

Square setting n. (1950s–1960s) a house party of orthodox persons and mainstream music. (CLC, TS, p. 256.) SCU, DCU.

Squaresville n. (1950s–1970s) anything not worth one's attention; a place dominated by squares; conventional people. (FR.) YCU.

Square to the wood (EF, RDSL, p. 255.) See "Square."

Square up v. (1940s–1960s) to leave the scene and start a new life along more conventional lines; in the sixties, to double-cross. (IS, PSML, p. 316; SH, GL, p. 212.) Example: "I'm going to square up, get married, settle down to me a little white house with a picket fence." SCU, PU, DCU.

Square up v. (1960s) to betray. (DC, BJ, p. 81.) Rare. MWU.

Squaring out v. (1960s) verbally harrassing someone; "signifying"; "capping"; trying to engage someone in the "dozens." (DC, BJ, p. 81.) Rare. MWU.

Squasho n. (1950s) a "Negro." Picked up from derogatory white use. (WF, DAS, p. 513.) Extremely rare. NCU.

Squat v., n. (1940s) to sit down; a chair. (DB, OHHJ, p. 147; DC, BJ, p. 81.) Example: "Come in, brother, and take a squat." NCU.

Squat-pad n. (1940s) a lounge or lobby. (DB, OHHJ, p. 147.) NCU.

Squatter n. (1940s) a stool or chair. (DB, OHHJ, p. 147.) NCU.

Squeak box n. (1940s–1950s) violin. (FR.) SNU.

Squeeze n. (1940s–1990s) a difficult situation. (FR.) SNU.

[A] Squeeze n. (1940s) a belt. (DB, OHHJ, p. 147.) Harlem, use, NCU, SCU.

Squeeze [one] v. (1940s) inform; to tell one something; pass on information. (MHB, JS, np.) SU.

[One's] Squeeze n. (1970s–1990s) a person's mate or lover. (EF, RDSL, p. 255; JH, PBL, p. 86; WKB, JMC, PS, p. 50.) SNU.

[One's main] Squeeze See "[One's] Squeeze."

Squeeze-box n. (1900s–1950s) accordion. (FR.) See "Groan box." JMFU, SNU.

Stable n. (1940s–1970s) a big-time pimp's prostitutes. (IS, PSML, p. 316; WF, DAS, p. 515; DC, BJ, p. 81.) PPU.

Stacked n. (1930s–1950s) refers to a well-shaped woman's body; shapely hips and rear-end. (MHB, JS, np; CS, vol. 3, no. 2, p. 45.) SNU.

Stag n. (1940s–1950s) a detective. (WF, DAS, p. 515.) NCU.

Stagger Lee (1890s–1990s) a character in "Negro" folklore who accuses someone called Billy of cheating at dice, goes home, and returns with his gun. At gunpoint, Billy begs for his life to no avail. Not only is Billy shot, but the bullet passes through his body and breaks the bartender's glass. (FR.) SNU.

Stagolee (1890s–1990s) a character in an African-American folktale. Stagolee shoots Billy Lyon during a card game, claiming Billy has cheated him out of his Stetson. (Cecil Brown, *Coming Up Down Home*, 1993, p. 57.) SU, SNU.

Stairway to heaven (1960s) a woman's thighs. (FR.)

Stalks n. (1960s) one's legs. (DC, BJ, p. 81.) MWU. See "Stems."

Stall n. (1940s–1950s) one who works with a pickpocket. The "stall" attracts the victim's attention while the "cannon" does his work. (IS, PSML, p. 316.) SCU, PU

Stallion n. (1900s–1990s) a tall, thin, attractive young woman; a good-looking black girl or woman; beautiful girl or woman. (EF, RDSL, p. 255; DC, BJ, p. 81; CRM, BP, p. 308; DW, TL, p. 189; JH, PBL, p. 86.) See "Cock."

Stanch [out] v. (1930s–1940s) to begin; starting; to "step out." (ZNH, AM, p. 96.) SNU.

Stand-in n. (1950s–1960s) black and white people standing in line in front of a racially segregated public place, such as a restaurant, both waiting to enter and to dramatize the racial policies of the establishment. (WF, DAS, p. 715.) SU, SNU.

Stand tall v. (1960s–1970s) go forth with pride; to be ready for any occasion. (FR.)

Stand-up (stand up) adj., v. (1940s–1950s) showing remarkable strength or a capacity for survival under poor odds. (IS, PSML, p. 317.) Examples: "Black people in the United States are stand-up people!" and "She's something else, man, to be able to stand up under that shit he be putting down." SNU.

Stank n. (1970s–1990s) pejorative term for vagina; female sexuality. (EF, RDSL, p. 255.) SCU.

Stanky adj. (1970s–1990s) odoriferous; smelling bad. (EF, RDSL, p. 255.) SNU.

Star adj. (1950s–1980s) the best quality; a pimp's term for his most dependable and successful prostitute; male term of endearment. (EF, RDSL, p. 255; CLC, TS, p. 256.) SNCU, SCU, PPU.

Starting shit (1950s–1990s) to instigate an argument or trouble. (DR, BASL, p. 176.) Example: "Every time Mike come over here he come starting some shit, man." SCU.

Stash v., n. (1920s–1990s) conceal; to hide something, especially drugs or bootleg liquor; illegal narcotics; stolen goods such as jewelry or other booty. (MM, RB, p. 375; IS, PSML, p. 317; WF, DAS, p. 517; SL, RJON, p. 158; RSG, JT, p. 258; EF, RDSL, p. 255.) SCU, PU, DCU.

Stash v. (1940s) to stay; to remain. (DB, OHHJ, p. 148.) Example: "Make sure the kids stash themselves here till we get back." Harlem use, NCU, SCU.

Stash catcher n. (1980s–1990s) person who stands outside to catch drugs thrown from a window during raid. (TW, CH, p. 151.) DCU.

Stash pad [apartment] n. (1980s–1990s) the place where a drug dealer ("lieutenant") keeps narcotics prior to street sales; a storage place for drugs. (FR.) DCU.

Static n. (1950s–1970s) unwanted talk; back-talk; verbal abuse. (HLF, RJPD, p. 171.) SCU, SNU.

Stavin Chain n. (1900s–1920s) name of a man who became the mythical black southwestern sexual hero of the ballad, "Wining Boy Blues," by Jelly Roll Morton; Jelly Roll Morton's peer in "prowess"; a lady's man; a rambling man. (WF, DAS, pp. 517–518; AL, MJR, p. 45.) Southwestern use, JMFU.

Stay down low (1970s–1990s) to appear in an ordinary or normal manner; refrain from wearing flashy clothes; to be inconspicious. (EF, RDSL, p. 255; CS, vol. 3, no. 2, p. 46.) SCU, YCU.

[One should have] Stay(ed) in bed (1900s–1950s) expression suggesting that the day has gone very badly and that getting up that morning was, after all, not worth the effort; the idea is given full expression by the various blues singers since the twenties who've sang the "Buddy Brown Blues." (FR.) SU, SNU.

Stay on [one's] case (1970s–1990s) to verbally harass or intimidate for a prolonged period. (EF, RDSL, p. 255.) SCU, YCU.

St. Brew (1940s–1950s) nickname for St. Louis, Missouri. MWU.

[One's] Steady n. (1950s–1970s) one's regular partner in a romantic relationship. (CS, vol. 3, no. 2, p. 46.) YCU.

Steady on the case v. (1950s–1960s) to take unrelenting approach to a task; persistence. (DC, BJ, p. 81.) SCU, YCU.

Steal away (1800s–1940s) escape; originally slave's expression for escape from bondage or death and deliverance. (FR.) SU.

Stealers n. (1940s) the fingers; especially the fingers of a professional thief. (DB, OHHJ, p. 148.) SCU.

Steam n. (1950s–1960s) beer; wine. (DC, BJ, p. 81.) SCU.

Steel adj. (1940s–1950s) whiteness as a reference to an American of Anglo-Saxon descent. (WF, DAS, p. 518.) Rare. SNU.

Steel n. (1990s) a gun. (FR.) SCU, YCU.

Steerer n. (1950s–1990s) one who guides those seeking drugs or prostitutes to the dealer's place of business, or whorehouse, or the proper location on the street. (TW, CK, p. 138; TW, CH, p. 152; DC, BJ, p. 81.) DCU.

Stem n. (1980s–1990s) a crack cocaine pipe. (TW, CH, p. 152.) See "Demo."

Stems n. (1940s–1950s) the legs; especially the shapely legs of a young woman. (WF, DAS, p. 518; DB, OHHJ, p. 148; MHB, JS, np.) SNCU.

Stencil n. (1970s–1980s) an especially long and thin marijuana cigarette. (EF, BVV, p. 52; EF, RDSL, p. 255.) DCU.

Step v. (1950s–1990s) to dance; to run; to leave. (EF, RDSL, p. 255; DC, BJ, p. 81.) YCU, SCU.

Step fast (1960s–1990s) to work hard for success; walk briskly. (EF, RDSL, p. 256.) SNCU.

Stepin Fetchit Lincoln Theodore Monroe Andrew Perry, actor, born May 30, 1902, in Key West, Florida. Famous for playing sleepy-eyed, lazy-acting, stupid, stereotypical Hollywood "nigger" roles from the late twenties to the fifties. Early in his career, Perry took his screen name from a racehorse that came in for him.

Stepinfetchit n. (1930s–1950s) an Uncle Tom; a slave; a Sambo; name derived from the Negro Hollywood character actor and the subservient roles he played. (FR.) See "Stepin Fetchit."

Step it down (1890s–1940s) a hand-clapping, side-stepping movement and dance step done by children while singing "Draw Me a Bucket of Water" or "Way Down Younder in the Brickyard;" "step down" the "claps." (BJ, BLH, SD, pp. 20–21, 90.) SU.

[A] Step-off n. (1940s) a street curb. (DB, OHHJ, p. 148.) NCU.

Step off; stepping off v. (1930s–1950s) to leave a place; a command meaning, "Go away." (TW, CH, p. 152.) SCU.

Step on; stepping on v. (1990s) to dilute cocaine with a harmless or inert substance to increase the quantity. (FR.) DCU.

Step out v. (1800s–1970s) to leave home for a party or a dance; to die. (JSF, AON, p. 516; WF, DAS, p. 519.) SNU.

Step out on [one]; stepping out on [one] (1900s–1970s) to commit adultery. (WF, DAS, p. 519.) SNU.

Step out on the green (1970s) an invitation to fist-fight or to fight with weapons. (EF, RDSL, p. 256.) SCU.

[A] Stepper n. (1970s–1990s) a prostitute. (EF, RDSL, p. 255.) PPU, SCU. See "Stepping."

Stepping v. (1970s–1990s) practicing prostitution. (EF, RDSL, p. 255.) PPU, SCU.

Step [to one]; stepping to (1990s) to challenge someone in a hostile manner; to make sexual advances. (FR.) Rapculture use, YCU.

Step up; stepping up (1980s–1990s) to get promoted from dealing in the street to buying drugs wholesale. (FR.) DCU.

Stewer n. (1900s–1940s) pejorative term for an old woman who gossips and spreads rumors. (DB, OHHJ, p. 148.) SNU.

Stewie n. (1940s) a drunk; one who gets "stewed." (DB, OHHJ, p. 148.) SCU, SNU.

Stick n. (1940s–1990s) variant of the Yiddish *"shtik,"* or *"shtick,"* [chunk of horse fat] which refers to "behavior," among other things; one's preference; style; way of doing things; manner; technique. (Gene Bluestein, *Anglish/Yinglish: Yiddish in American Life and Literature,* 1989, p. 93; John A. Williams, *Sons of Darkness, Sons of Light,* 1969, p. 263; CC, HDH, p. 16; RSG, JT, p. 259; EF, RDSL, p. 256; DW, TL, p. 190.) New York use, NCU.

Stick n. (1920s–1970s) short for "stick of tea," marijuana; a reefer. (WF, DAS, p. 519; EF, RDSL, p. 256; DB, OHHJ, p. 148; RRL, DAZ, p. 228.) DCU.

[Dope] Stick (WF, DAS, p. 519.) See "Stick."

[Dream] Stick (WF, DAS, p. 519.) See "Stick."

[Joy] Stick (WF, DAS, p. 519.) See "Stick."

[Pimp] Stick (WF, DAS, p. 519.) See "Stick."

Stick n. (1920s–1950s) a clarinet. (RSG, JT, p. 259.) JMFU.

Stick n. (1940s) a drunk person. (DB, OHHJ, p. 148.) Harlem, SCU.

[Are you] Sticking? (1920s–1940s) phrase meaning, "Are you supplying the marijuana?" (Hear "Are You Sticking?" by Duke Ellington and his Orchestra, 1941; RSG, JT, pp. 259–260.) JMFU.

[To] Stick it in the ground (1960s–1990s) to tee up the ball. (GS, TT, p. 59.) Black golf players' use.

[The] Stick man n. (1950s–1970s) a policeman, especially one carrying a nightstick, sometimes called a belly. Billy-club, billy-stick. "Billy" or "stick" in use since the eighteen-fifties. (CS, vol. 3, no. 2, p. 46.) SCU.

Stick of gage (WF, DAS, p. 520.) See "Stick."

Stick of tea (WF, DAS, p. 520.) See "Stick."

Stick-up artist n. (1980s–1990s) a person who robs at gunpoint. (FR.) SCU.

Stick-up man n. (1920s–1940s) one who commits armed robbery, from underground use. (EP, DU, p. 687; WF, DAS, p. 520.)

Sticks n. (1900s–1990s) drumsticks; tambourine sticks. (RSG, JT, p. 260; WF, DAS, p. 520; AL, MJR, p. p. 10.) JMFU.

Sticking adj. (1920s–1930s) variant of stinking, as in "stinking rich." (LA, SM, p. 212; WF, DAS, pp. 519–529.) Example: "I know you stinking, man, so why don't you lay some bread on me for this next round." SU.

Stiff n. (1950s–1960s) a square; chump; a dupe; "useless" person in a gathering. (CLC, TS, p. 256; WF, DAS, p. 521.) SCU, DCU, YCU.

Stiffing and jiving (1930s–1950s) in jazz, a big show with very little expertise behind it. In general, deception; pretense; an impressive showing but with very little actual substance. (RSG, JT, p. 260.) JMFU.

Stiffing the stroll (1930s–1940s) loitering on the corner; "hanging out" on the scene. (DB, OHHJ, p. 148.) SCU, NCU.

Stilts n. (1940s) one's legs, especially long legs. (DB, OHHJ, p. 148.) SCU, NCU.

Sting v., n. (1920s–1950s) to rob; also refers to booty gained from a robbery. (IS, PSML, p. 317; WF, DAS, p. 521; CLC, TS, p. 256.) SCU, PU.

Stingy-brim n. (1940s–1950s) narrow-brimmed hat; a porkpie hat. (EF, RDSL, p. 256; RDA, DDJ, p. 267.) SCU, SNCU.

Stink-finger n. (1940s–1970s) the middle finger. So-called because of its use in sexual play. (EF, RDSL, p. 256.) SNU.

Stink pot n. (1950s–1970s) vagina. (EF, RDSL, p. 256.) SNU.

Stinky-pie rich (1900s–1920s) very wealthy. (FR.) SNU.

Stir n. (1940s) jail; prison. (DB, OHHJ, p. 148.) PU, SCU.

Stir v. (1960s–1970s) to strip a car; to steal. (DR, BASL, p. 111.) Philadelphia use, SCU.

St. Joseph's mixture n. (1920s–1930s) a conjuring potion made of buds, berries, beans and anise. (ZNH, MM, p. 337.) SU.

Stogie n. (1960s–1980s) an extremely thick, cigar-like marijuana cigarette. (EF, RDSL, p. 256.) DCU.

Stole on (1990s) to throw an unexpected punch. (FR.) YCU.

Stomach habit n. (1950s–1970s) heroin addiction. (CS, vol. 3, no. 2, p. 46.) DCU.

Stomp n., adj. (1900s–1950s) the word "stomp," for "stamp," has been common in American speech since before the mid-nineteenth century; but black speakers have had a very specific use for it: a heavy-footed, action-packed dance; a jazz instrumental competition; in jazz, a fast-moving, rhythm- and riff-packed, lively composition. (Hear Frank Stokes, "Stomp That Thing," 1928, *Creator of the Memphis Blues*, Yazoo, 1990; Blind Blake, "Seaboard Stomp," *Ragtime*

Guitar's Foremost Fingerpicker, Yazoo, 1990; Jelly Roll Morton, "King Porter Stomp"; AL, MJR, p. 112; WF, DAS, p. 522; ZNH, AM, p. 96; JSF, AON, p. 518.) JMFU.

[A] Stomp down [woman] adj. (1960s–1970s) a pimp's term for his hardest-working prostitute. (DW, TL, p. 190.) New York use, PPU.

Stomp on [one] (1940s–1990s) to beat someone, to kick, stamp under the feet. (EF, RDSL, p. 256; RDA, DDJ, p. 267.) SCU.

Stomp off n. (1900s–1940s) a rhythmic foot-stamping signal used by the lead musician to set the beat for the start of a performance; the "kick off." (RSG, JT, p. 261.) JMFU.

Stompers (stumpers) n. (1900s–1940s) one's shoes or feet. (WF, DAS, p. 706; DB, OHHJ, p. 148; DC, BJ, p. 81; JH, PBL, p. 86.) JMFU, NCU, SCU.

Stomps n. (1900s–1940s) one's shoes. (DB, OHHJ, p. 148.) SCU, JMFU, NCU.

Stoms (EF, BVV, p. 52.) See "Stumblers."

Stone adv., adj. (1940s–1990s) very; completely; perfect; unquestionable; ultimately; finally; desirable; attractive. All-purpose intensifier. A greater degree of anything; precise. Also, an intensifying prefix. (EF, RDSL, p. 256; WF, DAS, p. 522; RRL, DAZ, p. 228; RDA, DDJ, p. 267.) Examples: "She's a stone fox," "Man, I was so stone high I couldn't see straight," and, "The dude is a stone junkie." SCU, YCU, SNCU.

Stone addict (RRL, DAZ, p. 228) See "Stone."

Stone broke see "Stone."

Stone cold (WF, DAS, p. 523; DW, TL, p. 190.) see "Stone."

Stone dead (WF, DAS, p. 523.) see "Stone."

Stoned adj. (1940s–1990s) nearly immobile from the effects of a drug or drugs; drunk on liquor; ecstatic. (RSG, JT, p. 261; CS, vol. 3, no. 2, p. 46; RRL, DAZ, p. 228.) DCU, JMFU, YCU, SCU. See "High."

Stone fox n. (1940s–1960s) a beautiful black girl or woman. (WF, DAS, p. 706; CS, vol. 3, no. 2, p. 46.) YCU, SCU, SNCU.

Stone soul see "Soul."

Stooling v. (1940s) informing on someone—especially one black person informing on another to a white authority figure. (DB, OHHJ, p. 148.) SCU.

Store-bought hair n. (1900s–1930s) a wig or wigs. (FR.) SNU.

Stormbuzzard n. (1930s–1940s) a homeless person; man or woman without work; poor person who begs. (ZNH, AM, p. 96.) SNU.

Story n. (1800s–1990s) not exactly a lie but not the truth either; an elaborate form of verbal self-defense; a person's problems or situation, but especially an explanation; philosophy; sense of reality; condition; excuse. (RSG, JT, p. 262.) Examples: "He come in here with that same old story every time he miss work," and, "He thinks no one can see through his story," and, "He's got a story for every fuckup he causes." SU, SNU.

[What's your] Story morning glory see "What's your story morning glory?"

Storyville n. (1890s–1900s) a thirty-eight-block district of New Orleans nicknamed after Sidney Story, a New Orleans alderman who led the fight to restrict the "red-light district"; the [brothel] district in New Orleans commonly credited as the birthplace of formal jazz. It was an area where whorehouses were openly and legally maintained (1896–1917) and where black musicians could actually find employment; legal prostitution was formally and officially discontinued when the U.S. Navy closed the whorehouses in 1917. (MM, RB, p. 375; AL, JRM, 38; RSG, JT, pp. 262–263; WF, DAS, p. 523.) SU, SNU.

Stove-lid n. (1900s–1930s) a "Negro." Picked up from derogatory white use and used ironically. (WF, DAS, p. 523.) Rare. SU, NSU.

Straight adj., n. (1920s–1990s) honest; legitimate; faithful; conventional; acceptable; euphoria; a good feeling; above suspicion. (MM, RB, p. 163; WF, DAS, p. 524; RSG, JT, p. 263; EF, RDSL, p. 256; DW, TL, p. 190.) NCU, PPU, SCU, YCU, PU.

Straight adj. (1940s–1960s) to feel especially well after taking drugs; without exaggeration. (WF, DAS, p. 706; RRL, DAZ, p. 231.) Example: "Thanks for the stuff, it really got me straight." DCU.

Straight ahead (1950s–1970s) in jazz, describes playing in an unwavering manner; making lively, expert, soulful music; continuing to play no matter what. (RSG, JT, p. 264.) JMFU.

Straighten v. (1930s–1960s) to straighten someone is to tell him or her the truth or to pay back money borrowed. (MM, RB, p. 375; RSG, JT, p. 264.) SCU.

Straighten up and fly right (1850s–1950s) to behave properly. Expression from a Negro folktale about a buzzard that takes other animals and eventually a monkey for a ride as part of a scheme to drop them to their deaths and eat them; but the monkey outwits the buzzard. Probably first recorded by Joel Chandler Harris in *Daddy Jake the Runaway*, and *Short Stories Told After Dark*, 1889. Also, title of a popular song by Nat King Cole. (AMD, ANF, pp. 116–117.) SNU.

Straight up on a Columbo tip (1990s) secret, true knowledge of the facts. (FR.) Example: "If you put your money on seven and thirteen you can't go wrong—straight up on the Columbo tip." YCU.

Straight up six o'clock girl (1940s) a very thin girl or young woman; skinny female. (MHB, JS, np.) SU.

Strap n., adj. (1990s) a handgun; to be armed, especially with a handgun. The word is derived from the holster-strap used for securing the weapon to the upper body. (FR.) Example: "We be strapped when we go out in the street." NCU.

Straps n. (1930s–1960s) suspenders. (DB, OHHJ, p. 148.) SNU.

[A] Straw n. (1960s–1970s) a hat, though not necessarily a straw hat. (DW, TL, p. 190.) New York, SCU.

Streamer issue n. (1930s–1940s) necktie. (DB, OHHJ, p. 148.) SNU.

[The] Street n. (1940s–1990s) among prisoners, the world beyond prison walls; the world beyond the U. S. Public Health Service Hospital, Lexington, Kentucky. (RRL, DAZ, pp. 231–232.) PU, DCU.

[The] Street n. (1940s–1990s) metaphor for the unsafe world beyond the home. Before the forties, many black city dwellers (recently from the South) referred to "the street" as a "road," a habit left over from the rural South, but after the forties the word "street" itself became common and was immediately identified with violence, underworld or criminal activity, immorality and unethical practices.

(EF, RDSL, p. 256; DB, OHHJ, p. 148; WF, DAS, p. 706.) NCU, SNCU.

[The] Street n. (1930s–1940s) among jazz musicians, the strip where jazz night clubs were located along Fifty-second Street, between Fifth and Sixth Avenues. (Hear Thelonious Monk, "52nd Street Theme;" RSG, JT, p. 265.) JMFU.

[On the] Street v. (1940s–1990s) drug addicts' jargon, to be actively "using" and "buying" every day; the addict's world. (RRL, DAZ, p. 231.) DCU.

Street Arabs n. (1940s–1950s) the more orthodox, robe-wearing Moslems in Harlem. (FR.) Harlem use, SCU.

Street buy (1980s–1990s) a drug purchase, on the street from a "clocker"—a person who delivers drugs to customers. (RP, C, np.) DCU.

Street cleaner n. (1930s–1950s) a whore; a woman who makes herself available to many men. (AW, CP, p. 40, 49.)

Streevus mone on the reevus cone (1940s) an existential jitterbug expression. (FR.) JMFU.

Stretch n. (1950s–1990s) a prison sentence. (FR.) PU, SCU.

Stretch out (1950s–1960s) in jazz, to play without restraint or without being mindful of a time limit; to play "straight ahead" music. (RSG, JT, p. 265; WF, DAS, p. 706.) JMFU.

Stretch out (1950s–1960s) to operate without restraint; to explore; to be uninhibited. (WF, DAS, p. 706.) JMFU.

Stretcher n. (1930s–1940s) a belt, suspenders, or a necktie. (DB, OHHJ, p. 148.) SNU.

Stride [piano] n. (1920s–1950s) an early jazz piano style evolved from ragtime; a "ten-key stretch"–piano style associated with James P. Johnson; piano style in which single notes are alternated with the bass during the first and third beats. (WF, DAS, p. 525; RSG, JT, p. 265.) JMFU.

Striders n. (1940s) trousers. (DB, OHHJ, p. 148.) NCU.

Strides n. (1940s–1950s) trousers. (DB, OHHJ, p. 148; IS, PSML, p. 317.) NCU.

Strides n. (1940s–1950s) shoes. (DB, OHHJ, p. 148.) See "Kicks."

Striding v. (1920s–1950s) in jazz, playing a ten-key stretch in bass on a piano. (DB, OHHJ, p. 148.) JMFU. See "Stride."

Striding v. (1960s–1970s) doing anything extremely well. (EF, RDSL, p. 256.) Example: "When I get to college, dude, I'm going to be striding." YCU, SCU.

Strike and fade! (1960s) commit the deed, then vanish; slogan used as instruction for those working in the "organized" area of a riot. (FR.)

String band n. (1890s–1940s) "the classic jazz [bands] . . . small string bands—fiddle, guitar, mandolin, string-bass." (AL, MJR, p. 525; SL, RJON, p. 48; WF, DAS, p. 525.) JMFU.

String bean n. (1970s) a long thin penis. (EF, RDSL, p. 256.) Rare. South-central Los Angeles use.

String out see "Strung out."

Striving [time] n. (1840s–1860s) the time between announcing one's desire to be a Christian and acceptance by the church elders; a time for "raw souls" to "strive." (JEH, AAC, pp. 79–80.) See "Seeking [time]."

Stroking v. (1960s–1980s) performing sexual intercourse. (EF, RDSL, p. 256.) SNU.

Stroll n. (1930s–1940s) a road or street; walkway. (WF, DAS, p. 525; DB, OHHJ, p. 148.) SU, SNU.

Stroll n. (1940s) a light "gig"; a task not requiring much effort; any easy commitment; to do something well. (ZNH, Am, p. 96; WF, DAS, p. 525.) SU, SNU, JMFU.

[The] Stroll n. (1950s–1960s) the "main drag" where prostitutes display themselves. (SH, GL, p. 212.) PPU.

Stroll v. (1930s–1970s) in jazz, to rest while someone is doing a solo; to pause so two other instruments can work out a theme. (RSG, JT, p. 266.) JMFU.

[To come on] Strong (RSG, JT, p. 266.) See "Come on strong."

Struggle n. (1900s–1960s) in jazz, a bad performance. (RSG, JT, p. 266.) JMFU.

[The] Struggle n. (1960s) short for the civil rights struggle. (FR.) SNU.

Struggle buggy n. (1920s–1940s) a very old, rundown car; a early model Ford. (CVV, NH, p. 286; WF, DAS, p. 526; MHB, JS, np.) SNCU.

Strung out adj. (1950s–1990s) to be addicted, especially to a "heavy" narcotic such as heroin. (WF, DAS, p. 706; RSG, JT, p. 267; DC, BJ, p. 81; RRL, DAZ, p. 232.) DCU, SNU.

Strung out [behind, over or on] adj. (1950s–1990s) in love; infatuated. (RSG, JT, p. 267; CS, vol. 3, no. 2, p. 46.) Example: "Cal is really strung out behind that Lake Meadows chick." YCU, SNU.

Strut n. (1900s–1930s) a fancy-step slow dance. (WF, DAS, p. 526; RSG, JT, pp. 266–267; CVV, NH, p. 242.) JMFU, SNU.

Strut your stuff (1900s–1930s) a cry encouraging someone to show off. (CVV, NH, p. 242; WF, DAS, p. 526.) Example: "That's it, Mary! Strut your stuff, girl." See "Strut."

Strutter n. (1900s–1930s) one who does the "Strut"; used in the 1922 all-black Broadway revue, *Darktown Strutters' Ball*. (FR.) See "Strut." JMFU, SNU.

Stud n. (1900s–1970s) any male; a hip male (without the usual sexual connotation). Used ironically. (RSG, JT, p. 267; DB, OHHJ, p. 148; DC, BJ, p. 82; DW, TL, p. 190; RDA, DDJ, p. 268.) Example: "How ya doing, Stud?" SCU, YCU.

Stud n. (1940s–1950s) pejorative term for a lesbian. (DC, BJ, p. 82.) Rare. MWU, SCU.

Stud-horse (stud-hoss) n. (1850s–1940s) term of greeting used by one male to another. Probably picked up from rural white use. (DB, OHHJ, p. 148.) SRU.

Stud with many fingers n. (1940s) refers to J. Edgar Hoover and his Federal Bureau of Investigation agents. (DB, OHHJ, p. 148.) SCU, SCU.

Study on v. (1930s–1950s) to give attention to; to think about. (FR.) Example: "You say you want me to drive to New York with you; well, I say, I'll study on it and let you know in a day or so."

Studying v. (1900–1930s) thinking. Carries a mental image of a serious facial expression. (FR.) Examples: "I told him I was studying on it"; "Don't bother me, I'm studying."

Stuff n. (1800s–1990s) almost anything: sex; drugs; loose talk; money, etc. (RF, WJ, p. 305; WF, DAS, p. 526; RSG, JT, p. 267; EF, RDSL, p. 256.) SNU, SCU. See "Shit."

[To] Stuff v. (1960s–1990s) when a basketball player leaps high enough to seem to literally drop the ball in the net; to "dunk" a basketball. (EF, RDSL, p. 256.) Basketball players' and fans' use.

[Good] Stuff see "Stuff."

[Green] Stuff (WF, DAS, p. 526.) See "Stuff."

[On or off the] Stuff (1940s–1960s) on or off heroin. (FR.) DCU.

[White] Stuff (WF, DAS, p. 526.) See "Stuff."

[To put some] Stuff on [one] (1940s–1950s) to deceive; trick; betray. (IS, PSML, p. 317.) SCU, PPU, PU.

[One's] Stuff out the window (1900s–1930s) to take no chances; to be ready to run in case of trouble; to be prepared. (ZNH, MM, p. 71.) Examples: "I always play with my stuff out the window cause these niggers think nothing of cutting you with they razor"; and, "Baby, I don't mind going up there to your bedroom with you but you got to understand I got to love you with my stuff out the window 'cause no telling when your husband might show up." SU.

Stuff Hezekiah Leroy Gordon Smith, born 1909 in Portsmouth, Ohio, singer and songwriter who worked with Dizzy Gillespie, among others.

Stuff cuff n. (1940s) zoot suit's padded cuff. (WF, DAS, p. 526.) JMFU, NCU, YCU. See "Zoot suit," "Drapes," and "Reet pleat."

Stum; stumming v. (1970s–1980s) to get intoxicated on narcotics. (EF, RDSL, p. 256.) DCU.

Stumble v. (1940s) to encounter serious misfortune. (DB, OHHJ, p. 148.) SCU.

Stumble and fall (1940s) to get into a great deal of trouble, especially with the police; to be arrested; to be murdered. (DB, OHHJ, p. 148.) SCU.

[A] Stumble bumble n. (1970s–1980s) any powerful narcotic. (EF, RDSL, p. 256.) DCU.

Stumblers n. (1960s) barbiturates. (CS, vol. 3, no. 2, p. 46; EF, BVV, p. 52.) DCU.

Stumps n. (1940s) one's legs, especially short legs. (DB, OHHJ, p. 148.) See "Stilts."

Stums (EF, BVV, p. 52.) See "Stumblers."

Style (EF, RDSL, p. 256.) See "Front."

Styles n. (1960s–1990s) expensive and attractive clothes. (EF, RDSL, p. 256.) Example: "Every time I see that dude, he be in some nice styles and he be stepping, too." SCU.

Styling v. (1950s–1990s) to show off; strutting; self-parody; exaggerated display of one's self and clothes, manner, or presence. (EF, RDSL, p. 109; CS, vol. 3, no. 2, p. 46; CRM, BP, p. 308.) SCU, YCU.

Stymie Matthew Beard, Jr.; "Our Gang" child actor.

Such-a-such-a-thing (1930s–1950s) a generic term for any possible comment or statement. (FR.) Example: "If I say to him such-a-such-a-thing he always turns right around and got some lip for me." SNU.

Suckass adj., n. (1940s–1990s) servile; a flunky. (FR.) SCU.

Sucker n. (1850s–1990s) originally a professional gambler's term; a duped or foolish person; one easily misled; greenhorn. Picked up from gamblers, thieves and hobos. (AB, DSJC, p. 306; EP, DU, p. 701; EF, RDSL, p. 256; JSF, AON, p. 521.) Professional gamblers' use, SCU, YCU, PU, PPU. See "Chump."

Suckler n. (1700s–1860s) a slave woman with "an abundant supply of milk whose duty it was to nurse the babies of mothers who worked." (SK, PC, p. 75.) SU.

Sucker snow n. (1950s–1990s) diluted, weak cocaine. (FR.) DCU.

Sucker weed n. (1950s–1990s) diluted, weak marijuana. (EF, RDSL, p. 256.) DCU.

Sucking suds (1940s) drinking beer. (MHB, JS, np.) YCU, SNU.

Suction (HLF, RJPD, p. 171.) See "Static."

Suede n. (1940s–1950s) a dark-complected "Negro." (WF, DAS, p. 528.) Rare. SNCU.

[A] Suffer n. (1940s) a long story, especially one told in a drawn-out and dull manner. (MHB, JS, np.) SNU.

Suffering with the shorts (1940s) to be without money; to be short on cash. (DB, OHHJ, p. 148.) Harlem, SCU, NCU.

Sugar n. (1900s–1990s) a kiss; "neck-sugar"; "mouth-sugar"; etc. (FR.) SNU.

Sugar n. (1900s–1990s) a term of affection or endearment for either sex. (EF, RDSL, p. 256.) SNU.

Sugar n. (1900s–1930s) money. (FR.) SNU.

Sugar daddy n. (1900s–1950s) a woman's affectionate name for her husband or lover, especially one who supports her. (EF, RDSL, p. 256; WF, DAS, p. 528.) SU, SNU.

Sugar Hill Gang (1980s) Big Bank Hank, Wondermike, and Master Gee, a rap group.

Sugar Hill n. (1930s–1950s) a whorehouse district in a black community in the South. (ZNH, AM, p. 96; WF, DAS, p. 528.) PPU, SCU, SU.

Sugar Hill n. (1900s–1930s) in Harlem, a very popular middle-class neighborhood, signifying "the sweet and expensive life that money afforded." (ILA, CS, p. 240; WF, DAS, p. 528; ZNH, AM, p. 96.) New York use, NCU. See "Bacon."

Sugar papa see "Sugar daddy."

Sugar Ray Robinson Walker Smith, welterweight and middle-weight prizefighter.

Sugar shack n. (1960s) space for putting someone up, usually temporarily; extra-sleeping space such as a hideaway bed. (CS, vol. 3, no. 2, p. 47.) Rare. Watts, Los Angeles, use.

Sugar weed n. (1960s–1970s) diluted, weak marijuana. (EF, RDSL, p. 256.) See "Sucker weed."

Suitcase n. (1930s–1940s) drums. (FR.) JMFU.

Suited down adj. (1960s–1990s) to be dressed beautifully, especially in expensive clothes. (EF, RDSL, p. 256.) SCU, YCU.

Suits [one] down to the ground (1980s–1990s) an expression meaning, "It is pleasing"; attractive. (FR.) YCU.

Sumption n. (1800s–1940s) firmness; strength. (SK, PC, p. 147.) Florida use, SU.

Sunday-go-to-meeting clothes n. (1800s–1940s) a black slave's best clothes; one's best-looking, finest garments. (SK, PC, p. 73; WF, DAS, p. 528.) SU, SNU.

[The] Sun's going to shine in my back door some day (1700s–1920s) an expression of hope often voiced by slaves and passed on to later generations. If the sun could make it through the back door, the rest of the house, so to speak, would automatically be in good shape. Slaves were always required to enter the "big" house through the back door. (FR.) SU. See "Back door."

Super glue n. (1990s) any type of stiff holding gel used on the hair. (FR.) YCU.

Superhonkie n. (1960s) an especially authoritarian white person. (FR.)

Super-spade n. (1940s–1960s) a black person who is extremely racially self-conscious. The term—with a different meaning—may be of white origin and picked up and transformed by black slang users. (FR.) Rare. JMFU.

Susie-Q; Suzie-Q; Suzy-Q n. (1930s–1940s) a frenetic jazz dance. According to Cab Calloway, the "Susie-Q" originated at the Cotton Club in 1936. (MM, RB, p. 230; RSG, JT, p. 268; DB, OHHJ, p. 148; CC, OMMM, NCCHD, p. 260.) YCU, JMFU. See "Sand."

Swabble v. (1940s) to gulp food; probably a variation of "gobble." (DB, OHHJ, p. 148.) Harlem use, NCU.

Swag n. (1960s–1970s) money; stolen goods. (DW, TL, p. 190.) New York use, SCU, PU.

Swag n. (1970s–1990s) liquor; bad liquor. (EF, RDSL, p. 256.) South-central Los Angeles use, YCU, SCU.

Swamp boss n. (1920s–1930s) in the Deep South, a white man who drives black sawmill workers. (ZNH, MM, p.) SU.

Swat(s) n. (1920s–1950s) Jelly Roll Morton tells a story about a drummer who hit his drums so hard and made so much noise that

Jelly Roll gave him a couple of fly-swatters as a joke. The drummer, unexpectedly, used them, and to good effect. That's how the "swats" effect got started. (AL, MJR, p. 59; WF, DAS, p. 530.) JMFU.

Sweat v. (1980s–1990s) to embarrass; upset; hassle; annoy. (FR.) Example: "I don't like it when a teacher sweat me just 'cause I come to class late." YCU.

Sweet adj. (1900s–1990s) calm and self-assured behavior, in other words, "cool." (FR.) YCU.

[A] Sweet n. adj. (1950s–1970s) gay or effeminate male. (EF, RDSL, p. 256; SH, GL, p. 212.) Rare. South-central Los Angeles use, SCU.

Sweet daddy (EF, RDSL, p. 256.) See "Sugar daddy."

Sweet [music] adj., n. (1920s–1940s) jazz played by white musicians. This does not apply to white-musicians-turned-black such as Mezz Mezzrow and Johnny Otis, or to white musicians like Art Pepper. (RSG, JT, p. 268.) JMFU.

Sweet-back [man] n. (1900s–1950s) lady's man. A sweet-back man is one who attracts a lot of women; a man with a back women like to stroke, touch, or hold. (AL, MJR, p. 15; WF, DAS, p. 531.) SU, SNU.

Sweetheart v. (1900s–1920s) to be romantically involved, courting, or dating. (LA, SM, p. 57; WF, DAS, p. 531.) Example: "Now, that Lilly, she's the kind of gal you can't sweetheart no time of the day or night. She won't give none of these chumps the time of day." SU.

Sweet lucy n. (1960s) marijuana. (RRL, DAZ, p. 232.) Rare. DCU.

[A] Sweet mack (1950s–1960s) a gentle, considerate, compassionate pimp; a non-violent pimp. (SH, GL, p. 212.) PPU.

Sweet mama n. (1900s–1940s) a black man's black female lover; a woman who is generous and kind. (WF, DAS, p. 531.) SU, SNU.

Sweet Mama Stringbean Ethel Waters's stage name before she became a film star.

Sweet papa (WF, DAS, p. 531.) See "Sugar daddy."

Sweet Pea Billy Strayhorn (b. 1915), composer, piano player who worked with Duke Ellington.

Sweet potato pie n. (1900s–1990s) soul food dessert made with yams or sweet potatoes. (FR.) SNU.

Sweet-potato-pie n. (1900s–1990s) term of endearment for either sex. (EF, RDSL, p. 257.) SNU.

Sweets trumpeter Harry Edison, born in Columbus, Ohio, October 19, 1915, who worked with Count Basie, Benny Carter, and Josephine Baker.

Sweet talk n. (1700s–1990s) flattery. Probably derived from the Krio [Sierra Leone] expression, *"suit mot,"* which means flattery or sweet mouth. (RDA, TB, p. 28; WF, DAS, p. 532; EF, RDSL, p. 257.) SU, SNU.

Sweet tooth n. (1750s–1990s) a craving for sweets. (FR.) SU, SNU.

Swift adj. (1960s–1990s) intelligent. (EF, RDSL, p. 257.) Example: "The boy is swift, he's gone grow up to go to college, you mark my words." SNU.

Swim-in n. (1950s–1960s) black and white people protesting segregated swimming pools in the North and the South staged swim-ins in an effort to change the policies of racial exclusion. (WF, DAS, p. 715.) SU, SNU.

Swine eater n. (1950s–1990s) pejorative term for a white person; white policeman; anyone who eats pork. (EF, RDSL, p. 257.) Muslim use.

Swing [music] n. (1930s–1940s) the music white jazz musicians adopted from the longhouse and gutbucket blues and jazz created earlier by black musicians; white teenager's dance music; "square" music. (RSG, JT, pp. 268–269; WF, DAS, p. 533.) JMFU, SNU. See "Sweet."

Swing v. (1930s–1960s) to enjoy oneself at a party; to dance and drink and laugh and generally have fun. (DC, BJ, p. 82.) SNCU.

Swinging gate (1930s–1940s) metaphor for the moments when the members of a swing band are playing well together. (SL, RJON, p. 135; WF, DAS, p. 533.) Rare. JMFU. See "Swing like a rusty gate."

Swing like a rusty gate (1930s–1940s) black jazz musicians' snobbish expression for a good and characteristic performance of swing music by a typical swing band. (WF, DAS, p. 533.) JMFU.

[A] Swing out n. (1950s–1960s) a violent street fight between rival gangs in any large urban city. (DC, BJ, p. 82.) SCU, YCU, SNCU.

Swing n. (1930s–1950s) in jazz, a style of white music that developed from hot jazz. Also, a type of black music developed by Duke Ellington. (RSG, pp. 268–270.) JMFU.

Swinger n. (1950s–1960s) originally a very thrilling musician; anyone who goes all-out to have a good time; a professional pleasure-seeker, especially one who enjoys listening to jazz in clubs. (RSG, JT, pp. 270–271.) JMFU.

Swingformation n. (1930s–1940s) variant of information; information about swing music. (Cab Calloway.) Rare. JMFU.

Swinging the dice (1990s) simile implying the element of chance. (FR.) Example: "Every black man's life is like swinging the dice."

Swinging n. (1950s–1960s) an expression of approval. (RSG, JT, p. 271.) SNCU, JMFU.

Swipe n. (1950s–1970s) penis. (HLF, RJPD, p. 171; DW, TL, p. 190.) Rare. New York use, SCU.

Swish v. (1960s–1990s) to flaunt homosexual characteristics or what are thought to be such; to flaunt the body. (FR.) Homosexual use.

Switch n. (1800s–1950s) a tree branch or several branches wrapped together for the purpose of whipping someone, usually a child. (FR.) SU.

Switch n. (1940s–1950s) short for switchblade knife. (DB, OHHJ, p. 148.) SCU.

Switch a mean fanny in the kitchen (1930s–1940s) to be an excellent cook. (ZNH, TEWWG, p. 19.) SU.

Switch hips n. (1880s–1940s) a dance motion done mainly by children of the Sea Islands. While playing the game and singing "Johnny Cuckoo" with knees together, the children jerk their hips at the child selected to be Johnny Cuckoo while he or she selects from among them soldiers to defend his or her kingdom. The game is descended from the English children's game, "Three Dukes A-Riding," but transformed from a courtship-marriage ritual to a military one. (BJ, BLH, SD, pp. 71–73.) Sea Islands use, SU.

Swith v. (1940s–1950s) to smell; may be a variant of "sniff." (RDA, DDJ, p. 268.) Philadelphia use, SCU, YCU.

Swobble v. (1930s–1940s) to eat too fast; eating in a hurry without chewing one's food. (WF, DAS, p. 534.) Rare. SU.

Swoop v. (1950s–1990s) to go, leave; to move fast; to run; approach quickly. (EF, RDSL, p. 257; CS, vol. 3, no. 2, p. 47.) See "Split."

Swopping slob (swooping slop) n., v.(1940s) a quick goodbye kiss; fast kissing. (MHB, JS, np.) SU. See "Slob."

Sylvester n. (1950s) variant of "Charlie," a white man. (FR.) See "Mister Charlie," and "Charlie."

T

Tab v., n. (1930s–1940s) to hit someone; a physical blow. (MHB, JS, np.) Rare. SU.

Tab (WF, DAS, p. 534; SL, RJON, p. 105.) See "Tab action."

Tab action (1930s) to borrow something, especially money; to request or to have credit at a bar or another type of business establishment. (DB, OHHJ, p. 148; SL, RJON, p. 105; WF, DAS, p. 534.) Example: "John, you know ya long bread, how about giving me some tab action till payday?" Harlem, SNU.

Tabbed adj. (1970s–1990s) to be dressed beautifully or handsomely in expensive clothes. (EF, RDSL, p. 257.) South-central Los Angeles use, YCU.

Tabby (HV, AHAE, pp. 147–148.) See "Tabby house."

Tabby house n. (1630s–1870s) mudhouse [*tabaz*]; *ntaba* [Bantu]: the place where the mud comes from. On the plantations, slaves built their own homes in the West African manner using sand, lime, oyster shells and the local saltwater. (HV, AHAE, pp. 147–148; JH, PBL, p. 86.) SU.

Tab issue n. (1940s) the business of borrowing. (DB, OHHJ, p. 148.) SNU. See "Tab action."

Tabs n. (1940s) one's ears. (DB, OHHJ, p. 148.) SNU.

Tack n. (1940s–1960s) a nickel. (WF, DAS, p. 534.) SU, SNU.

Tack n. (1950s–1960s) in the fifties and early sixties, a dumb person; a "square"; in the late sixties, a clever person. (HLF, RJPD, p. 171.) Example: "Look out, ya'll, here comes Mister Tack, you know what you can expect." New York, use, NCU.

Tacked down adj. (1960s) nicely dressed; neatly dressed. "The dude was tacked down. (DC, BJ, p. 82.) SCU.

Tackhead [tackyhead] n. (1960s–1980s) pejorative male term for a woman who is not beautiful; an ugly woman. (EF, RDSL, p. 257.) SCU, YCU.

Tackie(s) (tacky) n. (1800s–1900s) horse [*taki*/ West African]; the small horses running wild in coastal Georgia and Carolina marshes.

Tacky adj. (1960s–1970s) damaged; cheap; ill-composed; bad manners. (FR.) SCU, YCU.

Taco [bender] n. (1960s–1990s) a pejorative term for a Chicano or Latino male or female. (EF, RDSL, p. 257.) South-central Los Angeles use.

Tag n. (1920s–1960s) in jazz, a footnote-like music phrase at the end of a chorus. From the thirties to the forties, a nickname or label. (LF, EJ, p. 272; RSG, JT, p. 272.) JMFU.

Tagged the play with the slammer issue (1940s) the act of putting a troublesome person in jail. (DB, OHHJ, p. 148.) Harlem use.

Tagging v. (1960s–1990s) to create public graffiti; spray-painting or writing one's individual name or the name of one's gang on fences, walls of buildings, subway trains, and sidewalks. (See photographs in [Kurlansky; Naar; Mailer] *The Faith of Graffiti*, 1974; TW, CH, p. 152.) SCU.

Tail n. (1750s–1990s) male pejorative term for buttocks, vagina, female sexuality; a sexually attractive female. (WF, DAS, p. 535; EF, RDSL, p. 257.) SNU.

Tail-gate n. adj. (1900s–1960s) in the early blues or jazz, music played with accents on the second and fourth beats; a hard-driving, simple rhythm-driven manner of playing blues or jazz; music in the New Orleans street-parade style. (WF, DAS, p. 535; RSG, JT, p. 272.) JMFU, SU, SNU. See "Jazz."

'Taint n. (1700s–1940s) "It is not." (FR.) Example: "Your mother's a man." response: "'Taint so!" SU.

Take n. (1920s–1990s) in jazz, one in a series of recordings made of a series of trial performances of a song or instrumental number in a recording studio; the best take is the one released; picked up from film industry use. (RSG, JT, p. 273.) JMFU.

[Double-] Take v. (1930s–1940s) to rob; to swindle. (WF, DAS, p. 536; AL, MJR, p. 50.) SCU, SU.

Take a powder v. (1940s) to leave. Picked up from Hollywood movies. (DB, OHHJ, p. 148.) NCU.

Take care of business (TCB) (1950s–1970s) expression picked up from jazz use; to meet one's commitments with efficiency; to perform effectively, skillfully. (EF, RDSL, p. 257; RSG, JT, p. 274.) SNU, JMFU.

Take charge (1900s–1960s) in jazz, to out-perform someone else in a "battle"; to leap out front, musically speaking, of the rest of the band and to dominate the performance, the way Charlie Parker often did. (RSG, JT, p. 278.) JMFU.

Take down (1850s–1880s) (AEG, BB, p. 295; CCJ, NMGC, p. 92.) See "Cut down."

Take for a long ride (1990s) to enlighten. (FR.) YCU.

Take five (1930s–1990s) in jazz, to take a five-minute break from performing; intermission. (RSG, JT, p. 274.) JMFU.

Take home the iron (1960s–1970s) to win the prize. (GS, TT, p. 59.) Black golf players' use.

Taking care of business (TCB) (1960s–1970s) maintaining one's social standing in the community; to have a mission; to be committed to a task. (RDA, TB, p. 40; HLF, RJPD, p. 172.) SNCU.

Take it easy greasy (1930s–1940s) an expression of farewell. (FR.) SNU. See "Take it slow."

Take it from the top (1930s–1990s) in jazz, start at the beginning. (RSG, JT, pp. 274, 284.) JMFU.

Take it home [out] (1920s–1940s) an agreement among jazzmen to do the final chorus of a number. (RSG, JL, p. 126; RSG, JT, p. 274.) JMFU.

Take it light (1960s) go slowly, don't overdo it; a friendly comment used when parting company with a friend or an acquaintance. (DC, BJ, p. 82.) SNU, SCU.

Take it slow [easy] (1930s–1940s) said in farewell to someone; "be careful." (CC, OMMM, NCCHD, p. 260; DB, OHHJ, p. 148; RSG, JT, p. 274.) SNU.

Take it to the limit (1950s–1960s) in jazz, to reach the highest achievement; to push for the finest performance. (FR.) JMFU.

Take [one's] mind (1940s–1950s) control over one's mind, especially for negative purposes. (WF, DAS, p. 707.) SCU.

Take no shorts (1980s–1990s) refusing to be duped or placed at a disadvantage. (FR.) SCU.

Take-off (take off; takeoff) n. (1930s–1950s) in bebop jazz, to "fly," so to speak; sometimes called "getoffs" or "takeoffs"; to experiment, especially during a solo; to start playing a solo; to do something different. (CC, OMMM, NCCHD, p. 260; DB, OHHJ, p. 148; RSG, JT, p. 274.) JMFU, SNU.

Take [one] off (1940s–1990s) to steal from one; to rob; to kill or shoot someone. (CLC, TS, p. 256; DW, TL, p. 190; TW, CH, p. 152; WF, DAS, p. 707; RRL, DAZ, p. 234.) Example: "Don't mess with Billy, he'll take you off in the blink of an eye." SCU, DCU, PU. See "Sting."

Take on some backs (1970s–1990s) to perform anal intercourse. (EF, RDSL, p. 257.) SCU.

[That] Takes the cake (1890s–1990s) expression of surprise; the most; the final word on something; expression of astonishment or bewilderment; originated during the contest dance, "The Cakewalk." One of the many African-American expressions that has become a standard Americanism. (HV, AHAE, p. 157.) See "Cakewalk."

Take the weight (1950s–1970s) to accept, without tears or grief, one's punishment; to go to prison for a crime. (DW, TL, p. 190.) SCU, PU.

Take [one] to the bridge (EF, RDSL, p. 257.) See "Take [one] to the hoop."

Take [one] to the cleaners (1930s–1960s) to strip one of everything; to cheat one out of all or most of their wealth or possession. (WF, DAS, p. 536.) SNCU, YCU, SCU.

Take [one] to the hoop (1970s–1990s) "driving" hard to make a basket. (EF, RDSL, p. 257.) Basketball players' and fans' use.

Talcum Queen n. (1980s–1990s) a black gay male who prefers white sexual partners. (HM, GL, p. 12.) Homosexual use.

Talk v. (1920s–1960s) to touch someone deeply in ways other than verbal. When a jazzman is really communicating through his music people often cry out "Talk to me!" or they might say, "He's really saying something." (RSG, JT, p. 275.) JMFU.

Talk [one's] business (1960s–1990s) to speak with authority and intelligence; flirtatious and seductive talk. (EF, RDSL, p. 257.) YCU, SCU.

Talk out of the side of [one's] neck (1970s–1990s) to talk aimlessly, especially in a boastful manner; just talking for the sake of talking. (EF, RDSL, p. 257.) SCU, YCU.

Talk shit (1920s–1990s) to romance a member of the opposite sex (usually female); rapping; smooth talk; a verbal con. (RDA, TB, p. 38; CRM, BP, p. 309; EF, RDSL, p. 257.) SCU.

Talk that shit [stuff; trash] (EF, RDSL, p. 257.) See "Talk shit."

Talk that [one's] talk (1960s–1990s) commendation for having great and "hip" verbal skill; for being in style verbally; encouragement to be one's self. (EF, RDSL, p. 257.) SCU, YCU.

Talk [one's] talk and walk [one's] walk (EF, RDSL, p. 257.) See "Talk that ([one's] talk)."

Talk trash (1920s–1990s) to use insincere-sounding romantic talk; smooth talk; a verbal con; to rap. (CRM, BP, p. 309.) YCU, SCU.

Talking bullshit [shit] (1940s–1970s) talk that is deliberately and obviously designed to con someone; "sounding," "rapping," or "hitting on" someone. (RDA, TB, p. 39, 41, 43, 49, 51.) SCU, YCU.

Talking trash v. (1940s–1960s) to "jive-talk;" lie; pretend; use performance talk. (FR.) SCU.

Tall money n. (1940s–1960s) a great deal of wealth. (FR.) See "Long bread."

Tall habit n. (1950s–1970s) a very serious addiction, especially to heroin. (DW, TL, p. 190.) DCU.

Tambourine n. (1700s–1990s) an African musical instrument. (HV, AHAE, p. 155.) SNU.

Tampon braces n. (1930s–1940s) pejorative term for a girl's or young woman's legs. (MHB, JS, np.) Southern Negro college student use.

Tap v. (1960s–1970s) to inject a hypodermic needle (containing heroin or cocaine) into one's flesh. (DW, TL, p. 190.) DCU.

Tape; taped v. (1950s–1960s) to control with understanding or a show of sympathy. (RSG, JT, p. 275.) Example: "Mooch comes in here with his jive thinking he's got everybody taped, but he himself is the sucker and don't even know it." JMFU, SCU.

Tapped out (1950s–1970s) depleted; without money; desperate. (FR.) SCU.

Taste n., v. (1940s–1960s) whisky, wine, scotch, gin, any kind of liquor; drinking liquor; to sample or take drugs. Also, any small amount of anything; a small quantity. (CRM, BP, p. 309; HLF, RJPD, p. 172; DC, BJ, p. 82; RSG, JT, pp. 275–276.) Example: "Would you mind turning down your music a taste?" SNU, SCU, DCU. See "Oil."

Taters n. (1800s–1940s) variant of "potatoes," a basic soul food staple. (FR.) SU, SNU.

Tattler n. (1940s) an alarm clock. (DB, OHHJ, p. 148.) NCU.

Tax n. (1980s–1990s) crackhouse entrance fee. (TW, CH, p. 152.) Example: "You stand here at the door, Bobby, and don't let nobody in 'less they got tax." DCU.

T-Bone Aaron Walker, born 1913 in Linden, Texas; singer and blues guitar player who worked with Ida Cox, Blind Lemon Jefferson, Ma Rainey, and others.

TCB (1960s–1970s) take care of business. (HLF, RJPD, p. 172; DC, BJ, p. 82.) SNCU. See "Taking Care of Business."

Tea n. (1920s–1950s) marijuana. (RSG, JL, p. 118, pp. 316–317; DW, TL, p. 190; DB, OHHJ, p. 148; DC, BJ, p. 82.) DCU. See "Grass," and "Pot."

Tea head n. (1940s–1950s) a marijuana addict. (RRL, DAZ, p. 234.) DCU.

Tea pad n. (1920s–1950s) a place where one can purchase and smoke marijuana; Harlem rooftop "pup tents" used for getting high in the thirties and forties. (RRL, DAZ, p. 235; RSG, JT, p. 276.) DCU.

Tea party n. (1920s–1950s) a gathering of friends or acquaintances for the purpose of smoking marijuana and socializing. (WF, DAS, p. 538.) DCU.

Teach n. (1900s–1990s) any person who sounds intelligent and projects a sense of authority. (DC, BJ, p. 82.) SNU.

Tear [it] up (1920s–1940s) in jazz, to give a great performance. (RSG, JT, p. 278.) JMFU.

Tear up (1950s–1990s) generally, to have a wonderful time having sex or attending a party, etc. (EF, RDSL, p. 257.) SCU.

Tear out (1900s–1950s) to move fast. Also, in jazz, to give a great performance. (RSG, JT, p. 277.) SU, SNU, JMFU.

Tears n. (1940s) pearls. (DB, OHHJ, p. 148.) SU, SNU.

Teed adj. (1940s) drunk. (MHB, JS, np.) SU.

Teenybop; teenybopper n. (1960s) a devoted teenage rock-and-roll fan. (WF, DAS, p. 707; CS, vol. 3, no. 2, p. 47; EF, RDSL, p. 257.) Example: "You can't even walk by the Trans-Lux for all the teenyboppers lined up to see the latest rock 'n roll star." SCU.

Tell a story (RSG, JT, p. 277) See "Talk" and "Story."

Tell a green man (1900s–1940s) a request for information; let one know what's going on; "green" refers to one who is innocent of experience. (WF, DAS, p. 539; SL, RJON, p. 147.) Example: "I just got in town, partner; can you tell a green man where he might get some food and a room for the night?"

Tell it like it is (1950s–1990s) an statement of support made to one who is, in the listener's judgment, speaking with wisdom or saying something of great importance; an exclamation of affirmation. (RSG, JT, p. 168; DC, BJ, p. 82.) See "Tell the truth."

Tell the truth (1950s–1990s) an exclamation of affirmation to a statement someone has made, similar to, "Preach the word!" (GS, TT, p. 57.) See "Tell it like it is."

Tell the truth [snagger-tooth] (1930s–1950s) a playful expression encouraging one not to lie. (FR.) SU.

Ten n. (1940s) one's toes. (DB, OHHJ, p. 148.) SNU.

Ten bones n. (1940s) the fingers of both hands. (DB, OHHJ, p. 148.) SNU.

Ten-cent bag n. (1950s–1990s) a ten-dollar plastic bag of marijuana. (EF, RDSL, p. 257.) DCU.

Terrible adj. (1950s–1970s) to be really wonderful, great. Also, in jazz, to give a beautiful or great performance. (EF, RDSL, p. 257; RSG, JT, p. 278.) DCU, JMFU.

Testify v. (1840s–1990s) to confess one's sins, bad deeds, life story (originally in church but now in music, in literature, and through other forms of art; to ritually comment upon any cultural experience understood by all black people; a secular or religious confession. (FR.) Example: "I want to testify this evening to the goodness of my Lord and to the fact he directed me away from a life of sin." SU, SNU.

Testimony n. (1920s–30s) a Protestant confessional. (ZNH, MM.) See "Testifying."

Texas piano n. (1930s–1950s) boogie-woogie; the original name of the "Boogie Woogie," a fast piano style associated with Texas blues and jazz musicians. (RSG, JT, p. 278.) JMFU.

Texas shuffle n. (1930s–1950s) in jazz, a "stride" rhythm; a 1938 Count Basie recording; good Basie stride. (FR.) JMFU.

That thing [thang] (1900s–1940s) sex; vagina; penis. Phrase often heard in the blues. (ZNH, AM, p. 94.) SU, SNU.

That's [one's] weight (1950s–1970s) one's responsibility or obligation. (JH, PBL, p. 86.) NECU, SCU.

The article. (1920s–1990s) in jazz and show business culture, used as a prefix to some names, such as "The Bird," for Charlie Parker; "The Hawk," for Coleman Hawkins; "The Monk," for Thelonius Monk. (WF, DAS, p. 540.) Show business use, JMFU.

The bear n. (1930s) poverty. (ZNH, AM, p. 96.) Example: "Honey, the bear is at my door so bad I ain't got food to feed my children." SNU.

The Big Apple (ZNH, AM, p. 96.) See "Apple," and "Big Apple."

The carpet n. (1960s) a type of street hustler's confidence game. (CS, Vol. 3, No. 2, p. 47.) Watts, Los Angeles, use, SCU.

The end adj. (1950s–1970s) the best; the finest; the greatest; wonderful. (DC, BJ, p. 82.) Example: "If I hit the jackpot, boy oh boy, that would be the end." SNU. See "Out of sight."

The Fat Boys (1980s) Prince Markie Dee, Kool Rock-Ski, and the Human Beat Box, aka Buffy, a rap group.

The folk(s) n. (1900s–1950s) one's family. (FR.) SU, SNU.

The half of it (1800s–1950s) an expression referring to difficulties originating during slavery. (FR.) Example: "In slavery times things were so bad you ain't heard the half of it." SU, SNU.

The hots (1940s) love; sexual desire; admiration. (RF, WJ, p. 301.) SNU.

The Life (1940s–1990s) the hustler's, pimp's, or con man's life on the street. (SH, GL, p. 213.) SCU, PPU, PU.

The Man n. (1930s–1960s) an American male of European descent in a position of authority, such as a boss on a factory job or in an office, or a policeman; the Establishment; the supplier of drugs. (ZNH, AM, p. 96; DC, BJ, p. 82; CS, vol. 3, no. 2, p. 47.) DCU.

The Real Roxanne (1980s) a popular female rap artist.

There you go! (1930s–1950s) an expression of agreement; giving assent; approval. (RSG, JT, p. 279.) JMFU.

The Virus (1990s) HIV, the virus that causes Acquired Immunodeficiency Syndrome (AIDS). (FR.) SNU.

Thick 'n thins n. (1950s–1960s) stylish nylon socks, usually black or brown; dress socks worn by "hip cats." (DC, BJ, p. 82.) SCU. See "Silks."

Thin adj. (1930s–1960s) in jazz, a musician who plays without full body to his or her tone; a tone without depth. (RSG, JT, p. 279.) JMFU.

Thin one n. (1930s–1940s) a dime. (MHB, JS, np; DB, OHHJ, p. 148.) SNU.

Thing [thang] n. (1950s–1990s) almost anything; one's main interest; life style; talent; skill; hobby; occupation; party; politics; philosophy; vagina; penis. (EF, RDSL, p. 257; RSG, JT, p. 279.) "Photography is his thing." SNU. See "That thing [thang]."

[One's own] Thing (1950s–1970s) a personal way of doing something; an individual's life style, ideas or career; in jazz, a very personal approach to the instrument. (DC, BJ, p. 83; RSG, JT, p. 279; RSG, JT, p. 279.) SNCU, SCU.

Things n. (1950s–1960s) capsules of illegal drugs; heroin; cocaine. (CLC, TS, p. 256.) DCU.

Thinkbox n. (1930s–1940s) one's head, brain, mind. (DB, OHHJ, p. 148.) SNU.

Thinkpad (DB, OHHJ, p. 148.) See "Thinkbox."

[One] Thinks [one's] pretty (1900s–1960s) pejorative phrase describing a person who flaunts him- or herself in a flamboyant and overconfident way. (DC, BJ, p. 82.) Example: "Tommy thinks he so pretty he can't even see nobody else—prancing around here with that slicked-down hair and his nose in the air." YCU, SNU.

[One] Thinks [one's] cute See "[One] Thinks [one's] pretty."

Third Base (1990s) MC Search and Grandmaster Pete Nice, a rap group.

Third base n. (1940s–1950s) the vagina. Equated with baseball's "home" or "all the way." (FR.) YCU.

Third stream (thirdstream; third-stream) n. (1960s) a type of music (by people like Charlie Mingus and John Lewis) that reflects to a very noticeable degree both the European and black technical experience. (RSG, JT, pp. 279–280.) JMFU.

Thirst n. (1980s–1990s) a strong desire for crack cocaine. (TW, CH, p. 152.) DCU.

Thirty-three-o-five n. (1950s–1960s) the New York State code for the misdemeanor of possession of drugs for the purpose of personal use. (RRL, DAZ, p. 235.) Example: "Teddy got two months under thirty-three-o-five and all he had on him was less than an ounce." New York, use, DCU.

This is an A and B conversation, C yourself out (1990s) a rebuff hurled at someone who has deliberately or innocently wandered into the hearing range of a private conversation between two or more persons. (FR.) YCU.

This man's country (1930s–1950s) the United States; "this man" refers to white people. (FR.) JMFU.

This time around (1990s) the next occurrence of an event. (FR.) Example: "This time around the revolution will not fail." SCU.

Thomas D. Rice (SBF, IHAT, p. 39.) See "Jim Crow."

Thoroughbred n. (1950s–1980s) a person held in high esteem; a champ; one who's dependable; a sophisticated hustler; an expert. (CLC, TS, p. 256; DW, TL, p. 190.) SCU, DCU, PU.

Thoroughfare n. (1930s) of West Indian origin; a woman sexually active with a large number of men. (FR.) Brooklyn use, Harlem use, New York use, SCU.

[A pair of] Thousand-eyes n. (1970s–1980s) shoes perforated at the toe—often Florsheim shoes with such perforations. (EF, BVV, p. 52; EF, RDSL, p. 257.) South-central Los Angeles use.

Thousand-on-a-plate n. (1930s–1940s) beans or peas. (ZNH, AM, p. 96.) SNU.

Threads n. (1930s–1950s) one's garments, especially a suit; expensive, good-looking clothes. (CC, OMMM, NCCHD, p. 260; IS, PSML, p. 317; CRM, BP, p. 309; DW, TL, p. 190; DB, OHHJ, p. 148.) SCU. See "Rags."

[A] Three n. (1950s–1970s) a three-dollar glassine or plastic bag of heroin. (DW, TL, p. 190.) DCU.

[Mister] Three Balls n. (1940s–1950s) pejorative term for a white (usually Jewish) shop owner—especially a pawn-shop owner—in a black community. (EF, RDSL, p. 257.) NCU.

Three-bullet Joey n. (1960s–1980s) any police officer driving a squad car through a black neighborhood. (EF, RDSL, p. 257.) South-Central Los Angeles use.

Three Jacks and a King (1920s–1930s) a conjuring potion made from carnation-based perfume. (ZNH, MM, p. 337.) SU.

Three-fifths compromise (1850s–1860s) expression picked up from white use; refers to the Constitutional order that a slaveholder could count each of his slaves as three-fifths of a human being in order to satisfy congressional appointments. (FR.) SU.

Three pointer n. (1940s) a street corner in a city. (DB, OHHJ, p. 148.) Harlem, use, NCU.

Three-pointer of the ace trill in the twirling top (1940s) any busy corner of Seventh Avenue in Harlem; a corner on a main street. (DB, OHHJ, p. 148.) Rare. Harlem use.

Three-quarter kelt adj., n. (1700s–1890s) one quarter African and three-quarters European descent; a person of such ancestry. (WF, DAS, p. 543.) SU. See "Kelt."

Three-times seven (1880s–1950s) of legal or adult age; to be twenty-one years old. (Sleepy John Estes, "Black Mattie Blues," *I Ain't Gonna Be Worried No More 1929–1941*, Yazoo, 1991.) Example: "You three-times-seven, girl, you can make up your own mind about that sometimey man." SU, SNU.

Thriller-diller (WF, DAS, p. p. 543, 716.) See "Kill [one]" and "Killer-diller."

Thriller in Manila n. (1970s) Muhammad Ali's famous expression and fight promotion slogan for the prizefight against Joe Frazier in Manila. (FR.) SNU.

Through adj. (1990s) literally bad; unpleasant; ugly. (FR.) Example: "Mary came in the lunchroom this morning, girl, with her nappy hair standing all over her head—she looked through." YCU.

Throw v. (1950s–1970s) to overcome something, such as a drug habit or the habit of smoking. (DW, TL, p. 190.) Example: "I'm going to throw this habit and get my life straight and maybe she'll come back." DCU, SCU.

Throw a brick (1950s–1960s) to commit a violent act, such as to overdose and die as a result, or kill somebody. (CB, MPL.) SCU.

Throw a buttonhole on [one] (1960s–1990s) to perform anal intercourse. (EF, RDSL, p. 257.) SCU.

Throw down v. (1980s–1990s) to "party" with great vigor; to begin working at a big, complicated project. (FR.) YCU.

Throw down v. (1980s–1990s) to fight violently with fists or knives. (TW, CK, p. 138.) SCU, DCU.

Throw [ass; some ass] n., v. (1950s–1990s) a woman walking in a sexy manner; performing sexual intercourse. (EF, RDSL, p. 257.) SCU.

[What's the word?] Thunderbird! (1950s–1960s) a rhyming slang expression of greeting based on the fortified sweet red wine, Thunderbird, sold in "ghetto" liquor stores; a common greeting used by winos as well as non-wine-drinking neighborhood people. (WF, DAS, p. 544.) NCU.

Thunder chicken [thunder chick] n. (1970s–1980s) pejorative male term for a girl or young woman thought to be unattractive or unappealing. (EF, RDSL, p. 257.) SCU.

Thunderdom n. (1990s) the sound and feeling of being beaten by a prison guard. (FR.) West-coast prison use.

Thunk v. (1960s) playful variant on "thought." (FR.) Example: "Who would have thunk it?" YCU.

[A] Thump n. (1960s–1990s) a fight, especially a fist- or knife-fight on the street. (EF, BVV, p. 52; DC, BJ, p. 83; EF, RDSL, p. 257.) SCU.

[To] Thump v. (1960s–1990s) to fight; fighting. (EF, BVV, p. 52; DC, BJ, p. 83; CS, vol. 3, no. 2, p. 48.) Example: "I swear 'fore God, if he pull some shit like that again me and him gonna thump all over this place." SCU. See "[A] Thump."

[A] Tick (1930s–1940s) a minute. (DB, OHHJ, p. 148; CC, OMMM, NCCHD, p. 260.) SNU. See "Few ticks."

Ticker n. (1940s–1950s) the human heart. (MHB, JS, np; DB, OHHJ, p. 148.) SNU.

[Ivory] Ticklers (RSG, JT, p. 281.) See "Ivories," and "Ivory tickler."

Tick-tock n. (1940s) the heart-beat. (DB, OHHJ, p. 148.) SNU.

Ticky [ricky-tick; ricky-ticky; tick-tock] adj. (1930s–1960s) in jazz, an onomatopoeia for monotony of rhythm or tone; but also in general use, old-fashioned; corny; stick; mechanical; stale; particular. (SL, RJON, p. 149; WF, DAS, p. 545; RSG, JT, pp. 280–281.) SNU.

Tiger [by the tail] n. (1900s–1940s) what one has been "dealt" in life; one's condition; fate; bad luck; in longhouse and barrelhouse talk, to hold a "tiger by the tail" referred to the ability to endure. (AL, MJR, p. 62; WF, DAS, p. 545.) SU, SNU.

Tiger-breath (1980s–1990s) a playful, teasing form of greeting. (Jess Mowry, *Six Out of Seven*, 1993, p. 44.) YCU.

Tiger-brother; tiger-bro (1980s–1990s) form of greeting. (Jess Mowry, *Six Out of Seven*, 1993, p. 42.) YCU.

Tiger sweat n. (1930s) badly made homemade or bootleg gin or whiskey with a bitter, raw taste. (SL, RJON, p. 4, 148; WF, DAS, p. 545.) SU, JMFU.

Tight adj. (1920s–1960s) originally, the term carried a sexual connotation that can be heard in early blues ("tight like that"); but later came to be used in general: close as in close friends; close to someone; "tight with the cops"; sharing a friendship or companionship. (RDA, DDJ, p. 268; CRM, BP, p. 309; HLF, RJPD, p. 172; DC, BJ, p. 83; BH, LSB, p. 32; RSG, JT, p. 281.) Example: "Brayat and Ted, they been tight for years; you can't tell one something and expect the other not to know." SCU, YCU. See "Ace."

Tight adj. (1900s–1920s) tautness or hardness. (RF, WJ, p. 306.) Harlem use.

Tight adj. (1970s–1980s) to be well-dressed, especially in expensive clothes. (EF, RDSL, p. 258.) Rare. South-Central Los Angeles use, YCU.

Tight-ass n. (1980s–1990s) hurled at one as an insult or used playfully as a put-down. (Jess Mowry, *Six Out of Seven*, 1993, p. 44.) YCU.

Tight cheeks adj. (1950s–1990s) anger so visible it can be seen in the face; cheeks puffed out with anger. (DC, BJ, p. 83.) Example: "Rose, she gets these tight cheeks when she don't get her way, just watch when you tell her you've changed your mind." SNU. See "Wind in [one's] jaws."

Tighten v. (1990s) short for "tighten up"; to correct one, especially verbally. (FR.) Example: "Benny's been making a fool of himself, man, running after Trish like that, somebody needs to tighten him —and fast." YCU.

Tighten up [one's] game (1950s–1990s) to get one's life organized or to improve one's life style; gain self control; avoid stupid mistakes. (EF, RDSL, p. 258.) SCU, PPU.

Tighten [one's] wig (1940s) the tight feeling in the head resulting from smoking marijuana. (MM, RB; RRL, DAZ, p. 236.) Example: "Bradford is a good dude, he'll bring you in his pad and tighten your wig anytime he's got some weed on hand." DCU.

Tight eyes n. (1960s–1970s) derogatory term for any Asian person. (EF, RDSL, p. 258.) South-central Los Angeles use.

Tight head n. (1930s–1940s) a head of nappy or kinky hair. (ZNH, AM, p. 96.) SNU.

Tight jaws n. (1950s–1970s) excessive anger. (DC, BJ, p. 83.) Example: "I told him to take it back to the store, and the dude come getting tight jaws like I was in the wrong and not him." SCU, YCU. See "Tight cheeks."

Tight-assed adj. (1950s–1960s) stingy. (FR.) SCU.

Till death do us part (1780s–1990s) of African origin; expression used by American slaves in their wedding ceremonies which consisted of jumping or stepping over a broom together. (FR.) SU, SNU.

Tilltapper n. (1950s–1960s) one who takes money from a cash register, especially while working as a cashier. (CS, vol. 3, no. 2, p. 48.) SCU.

Timber n. (1930s–1940s) a toothpick. (CC, OMMM, NCCHD, p. 260; DB, OHHJ, p. 148.) SCU, YCU.

Tin n. (1960s–1970s) an ounce of marijuana. (CS, vol. 3, no. 2, p. 48.) DCU.

Tin-ear [ten ear] adj., n. (1920s–1960s) tone deafness; a person who can't hear music on its own terms; one who dislikes jazz or "swing" music. (SL, RJON, p. 150; WF, DAS, p. 547.) JMFU.

Tinkler n. (1930s–1940s) a bell, such as a doorbell. (DB, OHHJ, p. 148.) SNU.

Tints n. (1950s–1960s) any sunglasses, but especially fancy ones worn by "hip cats" or "cool chicks." (DC, BJ, p. 83; EF, RDSL, p. 258.) SCU, YCU.

Tip v. (1950s–1970s) to gain knowledge of or discern something; discovery; to see. (DW, TL, p. 191.) Example: "Now that I've tipped what you're putting down, baby, I'm getting hat." SCU.

Tip (1950s–1960s) (HLF, RJPD, p. 172.) See "Tip in the wind."

[One's] Tip n. (1950s–1960s) a girl; a young woman. (HLF, RJPD, p. 172; WF, DAS, p. 708.) Example: "I'll be late for the gig 'cause I got to go see my tip at nine tonight." Rare. New York use, NCU.

Tip [out on; to; over to] (1890s–1990s) to have sex with someone other than one's spouse; sexual infidelity; to "cheat." (EF, BVV, p. 52; WF, DAS, p. 708; EF, RDSL, p. 258.) SNU. See "Creep."

Tip in the wind (1970s–1980s) to leave. (FR.) SCU, YCU.

Tipple (tiple) n. (1880s–1930s) a stringed ukulele; the tipple sound. (RSG, JT, pp. 281–282.) JMFU.

Tired adj. (1930s–1960s) stupid; boring; lame. (FR.) Example: "That's a very tired story he comes in here with every night about having missed the bus. If he can't make it to work on time tomorrow night I'm firing him." SNU.

Titties n. (1800s–1940s) a woman's breasts. (FR.) SNU.

Titty n. (1800s–1940s) nipple. (FR.) SNU. See "Tough titty."

THC n. (1960s–1990s) abbreviation for tetrahydrocannabinol, the essential chemical element in marijuana. (EF, RDSL, p. 257.) DCU.

TJ n. (1960s–1990s) abbreviation for Tijuana, Mexico. (EF, RDSL, p. 257.) South-central Los Angeles use.

TLC n. (1960s–1970s) tender loving care. (CS, vol. 3, no. 2, p. 48.) SNU.

Toad frog bread n. (1900s–1940s) a mushroom, especially one still in the ground. (FR.) See "Frog bread."

Toast adj. (1950s–1970s) very good; excellent; the best; fine or finest; acceptable. (DW, TL, p. 191; DC, BJ, p. 83.) SCU.

Toast n. (1950s–1970s) a rhyming "folk" song or poem in the vernacular celebrating some aspect of "street culture" or "the life," made up, memorized and recited by and among pimps and street hustlers. (DW, TL, p. 191; EF, RDSL, p. 258.) SCU, PU.

Toasted adj. (1970s–1980s) to be extremely intoxicated on drugs or alcohol. (EF, RDSL, p. 258.) SCU, SNCU.

Toby n. (1700s–1890s) *tobe* [Kongo]; an early black good-luck charm; a *tobe* was composed of wine and grave dust. (RFT, FS, p. 105.) See "Goofer [dust]."

Toddle n. (1920s–1930s) slow jazz tempo and dance. (RSG, JT, p. 282.) JMFU.

Toe-jam n. (1900s–1950s) dead skin and dirt stuck between the toes. (FR.) SNU.

Toe-party n. (1920s–1930s) a game played at a social gathering where all the women line up behind a sheet with only their toes showing. The men choose the women to spend the evening with on the basis of their toes. (ZNH, MM, p. 31.) SU.

Toffy [taffy; taffee] n. (1630s–1990s) a black person; blackness as a skin color. (JSF, AON, p. 526.) SU, SNU.

Tog v. (1920s–1950s) to dress fashionably and expensively. (RSG, JT, p. 282; CC, HDH, p. 16; MM, RB, p. 29.) SCU, JMFU.

Together (1950s–1970s) to have one's mind free of confusion; to be positive, functional; to emerge as a whole person; to be well dressed. (HLF, RJPD, p. 172; DC, BJ, p. 83; CS, vol. 3, no. 2, p. 48; RSG, JT, p. 282; CW, TW, p. 90.) See "Hip," "Down," and "Togs."

Togged down (1930s–1940s) to be dressed fashionably. (ZNH, AM, p. 94.) SCU, YCU.

Togged to the bricks (1930s–1940s) dressed extremely well and in fashion. (CC, OMMM, NCCHD, p. 260; DB, OHHJ, p. 149) SCU, YCU.

Toggle [woman; girl; broad] (1800s–1900s) *dzogal* [West African]: to rise as on a see-saw. (JH, PBL, p. 86.) SU.

Togs n. (1920s–1940s) clothes, especially good-looking clothes. (MM, RB, p. 41; RSG, JT, p. 283.) SCU, YCU. See "Tog."

Toke; toking n., v. (1950s–1970s) a drag on a marijuana cigarette; a puff of marijuana smoke; smoking. (WF, DAS, p. 548; EF, RDSL, p. 258; RSG, JT, p. 283.) DCU.

Tom (EF, BVV, p. 52; RSG, JT, p. 283; MHB, JS, np; WF, DAS, p. 708; SL, RJON, p. 147; BH, LSB, p. 116.) See "Uncle Tom."

Tom-a-Lee n. (1940s–1960s) an subservient black person who might as well serve as a flunky to General Robert E. Lee. (EF, RDSL, p. 258.) See "Uncle Tom."

Tom-and-try v. (1960s–1970s) to deprive one's self of a sense of identity or culture to obtain something such as employment or wealth. (DC, BJ, p. 83.) Example: "No way can I Tom-and-try just to make it to the top of this stupid company." SNCU.

Tomcat n. (1900s–1970s) a well-dressed dude who is out searching for a willing female sexual partner. (EF, RDSL, p. 258.) SNU.

Tomette n. (1960s) derogatory term for female Uncle Tom, usually a young woman. (FR.) SCU, YCU.

Tommy see "Uncle Tom."

Tom out n. (1950s–1970s) a black person informing on another to a white authority such as, but not necessarily, the police. To commit cultural disloyalty. (EF, RDSL, p. 258.) SCU, YCU, SNU.

Tom slick (EF, RDSL, p. 258.) See "Tom out."

Tonk n. (1900s–1920s) short for "honkytonk." (LA, SM, p. 60; WF, DAS, 549.) See "Honkytonk."

Tonto n. (1950s–1960s) an Uncle Tom. The Lone Ranger's sidekick's name is used in this context because he is considered a traitor to his particular Native American culture. (DC, BJ, p. 84.) SCU, YCU. See "Uncle Tom."

Tony adj. (1950s) stylish and snobbish. (FR.) Rare. NCU.

Toogoodoo n. (1850s–1920s) the name coastal Carolina black people used to refer to any creek or river. Probably has roots in one or more African languages. (AEG, BB, p. 334.) SU.

Took and run v. (1800s–1940s) ran; to have run. (FR.) SU.

Too-la-loo (1700s–1990s) *tulualua* [Bantu]: literally, "we are coming"; so-long, goodbye. (HV, AHAE, p. 148.) SU, SNU.

Too much (1930s–1960s) an expression of high praise; something inscrutable; the phrase can have a negative meaning but used to a far lesser degree: short for "too much to take." (CC, OMMM, NCCHD, p. 260; DB, OHHJ, p. 149; WF, DAS, p. 550; DC, BJ, p. 84; RSG, JT, p. 283.) Example: "Mother, when you start on Vernon you are just too much." SNU. See "Gas" and "Way out."

Too much like right (1900s–1950s) said to imply that a person willfully does the wrong thing. (FR.) Example: "She won't do that. It would be too much like right." SU, SNU.

Tool n., v. (1900s–1970s) penis; to drive an automobile. (FR.) Example: "Duke tool that sheen of his real slow up and down the street so all the pretty girls can see him." SNCU.

Tooth booth n. (1940s) a dentist's office. (MHB, JS, np.) SU.

Tooting cocaine (1980s–1990s) sniffing cocaine. (FR.) DCU.

Tooting stomps n. (1940s) fancy, low-quarter shoes, popular among "hip cats." (DB, OHHJ, p. 149.) Harlem use, NCU, SCU.

Tootmobile n. (1960s) an automobile. (DC, BJ, p. 84.) Rare. MWU, YCU.

Toothpick n. (1970s) a very thin marijuana cigarette; a slender switchblade pocketknife. (EF, RDSL, p. 258.) DCU.

Top n., v. (1950s–1990s) a maximum prison sentence; to be put to death by the state. (CS, vol. 3, no. 2, p. 48.) SCU, PU.

[From the] Top down (1930s–1990s) in jazz, to start playing at the beginning and continue till the end. (RSG, JT, p. 284.) JMFU.

Top-flat n. (1940s) one's head. (DB, OHHJ, p. 149.) SNU.

Top line n. (1960s–1990s) in jazz, the melody line on sheet music. (KG, JV, p. 181.) JMFU.

[On] Top of the beat (1920s–1970s) to perform just a bit ahead of the beat; singing or playing in correlation with the beat. (RSG, JT, p. 284.) JMFU.

Topper n. (1930s–1940s) a hat, especially one suitable for wearing with a suit and overcoat. (DB, OHHJ, p. 149.) NCU.

Top Sergeant n. (1940s) a lesbian. (DB, OHHJ< p. 149.) Harlem use, SCU.

Topside of the rockpile n. (1940s) the top floor of an apartment building. (DB, OHHJ, p. 149.) NCU.

Torch n. (1960s–1990s) a very big cigarette lighter; in the eighties, a butane lighter used by crack cocaine smokers to light the pipe. (TW, CH, p. 152; DC, BJ, p. 84.) SCU, DCU.

Torch cooking v. (1980s–1990s) making use of butane or propane gas for cooking cocaine base. (TW, CK, p. 138.) DCU, SCU.

Tore down adj. (1940s–1990s) distressed; ugly in appearance; generally bad. (FR.) See "Tore up."

Tore up adj. (1950s–1990s) from the fifties till the end of the seventies, "tore up," among jazz musicians and their fans, meant: upset, or distressed. After the seventies, in general use: drunk; unhappy; ugly in appearance; raggedy; to appear physically abused; generally bad. (RRL, DAZ, p. 237; DC, BJ, p. 84; CS, vol. 3, no. 2, p. 49; RSG, JT, p. 285.) SCU, YCU.

Toss gapper v. (1950s–1970s) to give someone something, especially drugs. (DG, D, p. 21.) DCU, SCU, PU.

Tostada (tostado) n. (1960s–1970s) a pejorative term for a Mexican-American. (EF, RDSL, p. 258.) SCU.

To the bone (1940s–1990s) completely; all the way; thoroughly. (EF, RDSL, p. 258.) SNU.

[Dressed] To the nines (1900s–1950s) to be well dressed, especially in expensive clothes. (RSG, JT, p. 285.) SCU, JMFU.

[To] Tote v. (1650s–1940s) *tota* [Konga/Kikonga/Gullah]: to pick up, to take; *tuta* [Kimbundu]: to carry; a load; *tot* [Sierra Leone]; *tut* [Cameroon]: to carry; also common in Bantu languages. Barrere, among many other more recent scholars, supports the African origin theory; Bartlett, according to Barrere, also believes it to be of African origin, although in his *The Dictionary of Americanisms* (1848) he says it is of unknown origin but probably derived "absurdly . . . from the Latin *tollit;*" rural southern word for "carry"; perhaps converged with the Latin *"tollit,"* the Anglo-Saxon *"teonhan," "teon,"* meaning to "carry" or "lead"; and the Dutch *"tot."* (AB, DSJC, p. 355; JH, PBL, p. 86; HV, AHAE, p. 148; JSF, AON, p. 68.) SU, SNU.

To the max adj. (1960s–1970s) short for "to the maximum degree or extent." (DC, BJ, p. 84.) YCU.

Toucher n. (1980s–1990s) a person who becomes physically intimate as a result of the high from crack cocaine. (TW, CH, p. 152.) DCU.

Tough adj. (1950s–1970s) great; wonderful; difficult; terrible; formidable; good; well. (DW, TL, p. 191; WF, DAS, p. 552; DC, BJ, p. 84; EF, RDSL, p. 258.) SCU, SNCU. See "Terrible," "Bad," and "Hard."

Tough fit n. (1950s–1960s) good-looking suit or dress, or other garment that fits one well. (DC, BJ, p. 84.) YCU.

Tough shit (1950s–1990s) a dismissive expression meaning "too bad—that's your problem"; bad luck; difficulty. (WF, DAS, p. 553.) SCU, YCU.

Tough titty n. (1950s–1960s) hard luck. (FR.) Example: "Working on this stupid job is a tough titty but the milk is good!" SNCU.

Tout n. (1980s–1990s) the middle man who purchases drugs for buyers. (TW, CK, p. 138; TW, CH, p. 152.) DCU, SCU.

Tower of Pisa v. (1940s) leaning, or to lean. (DB, OHHJ, p. 149.) Example: "Old Bill so drunk when he come out The Flagellants Tavern he be doing a Tower of Pisa all the way home." Rare. Harlem use.

Toy band n. (1930s–1940s) a group of musicians who produce popular, synthetic sounds. (RSG, JT, p. 285.) See "Mickey Mouse [music]."

Toys n. (1960s) a drug addict's paraphernalia. (DC, BJ, p. 84.) DCU.

Toy soldier(s) n. (1940s) a war-time phrase meaning an R.O.T.C. cadet, many of whom were training in Negro colleges during the Second World War. (MHB, JS, np.) Southern Negro college student use.

Track n. (1930s–1940s) a ballroom or dance hall; a musical piece on a phonographic record. (DB, OHHJ, p. 149.) Harlem, use, JMFU.

[The] Track n. (1930s–1990s) "racetrack" analogy; Harlem was the "track" for "hip" people in "the life" during the thirties and forties; the city pace as it applies to the hustling scene; the street or section of the city where a prostitute solicits; "hard track": east coast style; "soft track": west coast style; the Savoy Ballroom in the thirties; a ballroom. (CRM, BP, p. 309; DG, W, p. 160; WF, DAS, p. 553; MM, RB, p. 375; RSG, JT, p. 285; DB, OHHJ, p. 149.) PPU, SCU, YCU.

Tracks n. (1940s–1990s) marks and scars on the arm or other areas of the body from hypodermic injections of heroin; "police proof" of an addict's habit. (CRM, BP, p. 310; DW, TL, p. 191; RRL, DAZ, p. 238.) DCU.

Trade n. (1900s–1990s) sexual customers for a prostitute or homosexual. (FR.) PPU, SCU.

[Pull a] Train [on one] (1940s–1950s) when two or several males have sex with or rape one female. (IS, TB, p. 312; HLF, RJPD, p. 172; EF, RDSL, p. 258.) Example: "Christie got so drunk, girl, she don't even know how many of them clowns pulled a train on her last night." SCU.

Train v. (1960s–1970s) to have a number of foursomes pitted against each other in a golf contest. (GS, TT, p. 59.) Black golf players' use.

Tram n. (1920s–1940s) variant of and short for "trombone." (RSG, JT, p. 286.) JMFU. See "Bone."

Trane John William Coltrane (1926–1966), tenor saxophonist; a highly original musician and one of the greatest jazz figures of all time.

[The] Trap n. (1940s–1950s) the military draft board. (JH, PBL, p. 86; DB, OHHJ, p. 149.) SCU.

Traps n. (1930s–1950s) trap-drums. (FR.) JMFU.

Traps Arthur Benjamin Trappier (b. 1910), Drummer who worked with Tine Bradshaw, Fats Waller, Sy Oliner, Willie the Lion Smith, and others.

Trash (JSF, AON, p. 540.) See "Poor white trash."

Trashy see "Trashy-looking."

Trashy-looking adj. (1960s–1990s) derelict in appearance; shabby, unkempt look; neglected appearance; privation; dispossessed. (EF, RDSL, p. 258.) SCU, SNU.

Treaders n. (1940s) shoes. (DB, OHHJ, p. 149.) SNU.

[A] Tree n. (1960s) a Watts policeman who accepts bribes. (CS, vol. 3, no. 2, p. 49.) Rare. SCU.

Tree-suit n. (1940s) coffin. (DB, OHHJ, p. 149.) Example: "I don't know how long I'm gon' live but, man, I can tell you, I'm gon' have my fun before they put the tree-suit on me." SNU.

[A] Trey n. (1940s–1960s) a three-dollar plastic bag of heroin. (RRL, DAZ, p. 238.) DCU.

Trey of sous n. (1940s) three nickles. (DB, OHHJ, p. 149.) SNU.

Trey of sous and a double ruff n. (1940s) forty cents. (DB, OHHJ, p. 149.) Harlem use, SNU.

Trick; tricking n., v. (1900s–1990s) may be related to the unexpected and mysterious in hoodoo; converged with Modern English "trick" meaning "a bout of love-making"; but, in any case, we've known it in the current sense since the turn of the present century: a prostitute's customer or the transaction itself. Turning a trick refers to having any of various forms of sex for money; also, the victim of a crime; a "John." (LA, SM, p. 8; RDA, DDJ, p. 268; CLC, TS, p. 256; CRM, BP, p. 310; DW, TL, p. 191; WF, DAS, p. 554; MM, RB, p. 30; CVV, NH, p. 252; RSG, JT, pp. 286–287.) PPU, SCU.

Trick baby n. (1930s–1970s) a child conceived by a prostitute (accidentally) during intercourse with a customer; child born to a prostitute. (DG, W, p. 9.) PPU.

Trick bag n. (1940s–1970s) victimization; paying for sex. From the pimp's point of view, real men don't pay for sex, only chumps do, and they deserve to be the victims they are. To be on the receiving end of deception. (CRM, BP, p. 310; EF, RDSL, p. 258.) PPU, SCU. See "Trick."

Trickeration v. (1930s–1940s) to show off; flaunting one's self or objects of pride. (CC, OMMM, NCCHD, p. 260; DB, OHHJ, p. 149.) Rare. Harlem use, JMFU.

Trick house n. (1940s–1970s) a whorehouse; brothel; place of prostitution. (DW, TL, p. 191.) PPU, SCU.

Trick money n. (1940s–1990s) a prostitute's earnings passed on to her pimp. (CS, vol. 3, no. 2, p. 49.) PPU.

Tricks walking n. (1900s–1930s) available customers for street prostitutes. (Hear Lucille Bogan, "Tricks Ain't Walking No More," *Lucille Bogan/Walter Roland 1927–1935*, 1930, Yazoo, 1992.) PPU, SU.

Trig [one's] wig (1940s) to think fast; to prod one's brains. (DB, OHHJ, p. 149.) Harlem use, NCU.

Trilby v. (1930s) departure; leaving a place. (WF, DAS, p. 554.) Rare. SNU. See "Trill."

Trill [trilly] v. (1930s–1940s) a fancy way of walking; departure; leaving a place; possibly from Trilbys; the feet—based on the pretty feet of a fictional character in the novel *Trilby* (1894) by Dumaurier. (WF, DAS, p. 554; CC, OMMM, NCCHD, p. 260; DB, OHHJ, p. 149.) Examples: "Max be real cool when he trill down the boulevard all togged to the bricks," and, "When the clock strikes twelve midnight you trilly yourself on home, you hear me?" Rare. SNU.

Trilly-walk (1940s) (DB, OHHJ, p. 149) See "Trill."

Trim n., v. (1930s–1950s) vagina; sexual intercourse; a woman's sexuality; to have sex with a woman; pejorative for a girl or woman. (HLF, RJPD, p. 172; CS, vol. 3, no. 2, p. 49; EF, RDSL, p. 258; RSG, JT, p. 287.) SNU.

Trip; tripping v. (1960s–1990s) to be passionately involved in an activity such as sex or listening to music; to be on drugs; in the eighties, to be deranged by drugs; high on drugs; saying inappropriate things. (RCC, SOC, p. 70; TW, CK, p. 138; CS, vol. 3, no. 2, p. 49.) DCU, SCU.

Trip n. (1960s–1990s) line of thought; manner of behaving; one's life style. (CS, vol. 3, no. 2, p. 49.) SCU, YCU.

Trip down v. (1960s–1970s) to go or leave; to leave a place; to leave quickly. (CS Vol. 3, No. 2, p. 49; EF, RDSL, p. 258.) Example: "I'm hungry, let's trip down to the barbecue cafe." SCU, YCU.

Trip in v. (1960s–1970s) to arrive. (CS, vol. 3, no. 2, p. 50.) SCU, YCU.

Trip off of (1960s–1990s) to entertain oneself by watching something or somebody interesting. (EF, RDSL, p. 258.) Example: "Chico is too much, I really trip off of him every time he does his Eddie Murphy imitation." SCU, YCU.

Trip out v. (1960s–1990s) to get lost in one's own thoughts or imagination, without the use of drugs. (CS, vol. 3, no. 2, p. 50; EF, RDSL, p. 258.) See "Turn on."

Trip [one] out (1960s–1990s) to get extremely high ("stoned") either on drugs or an idea or situation; to upset or confuse someone. (CS, vol. 3, no. 2, p. 49.) Example: "I went home early and caught my husband with another woman. It really tripped me out." DCU.

Trip out [one] (EF, RDSL, p. 258.) See "Trip [one] out."

Tripping heavy (CS, vol. 3, no. 2, p. 50.) See "Trip."

Triple-clutcher motherfucker n. (1940s–1950s) a skilled black truck driver during the Second World War and the Korean so-called "conflict." (WF, DAS, p. 708.) Example: "Ben's the best triple-clutcher

motherfucker we got in this here man's battalion—he can throw
more clutches than Joe Louis can throw right hooks." Military use.

Triple-hip adj. (1940s–1950s) extremely wise; very "cool"; respected
on the "set" as a "thoroughbred." (FR.) SCU, YCU.

Triple-master blaster n. (1980s–1990s) for one to smoke crack-
cocaine or freebase while being fellated and sodomized. (TW, CH, p.
152.) DCU.

Trods n. (1940s) one's feet. (DB, OHHJ, p. 149.) SNU.

Trogans n. (1950s) variant of "Trojans," a brand of prophylactics.
(JH, PBL, p. 86.) New York use, SCU.

Trollop n. (1960s) an ugly woman; an unpleasant woman; no sexual
connotation or reference to prostitution. (DC, BJ, p. 84.) Rare. MWU,
SCU. See "Bear."

Trom n. (1990s) marijuana; derived from "traumatize." (FR.) DCU.

Trotters n. (1940s) pig's feet; also, a person's legs or feet, diarrhea.
(DB, OHHJ, p. 149.) SNU.

Trout n. (1950s–1960s) pejorative male term for a girl or young
woman. (EF, RDSL, p. 258.) SCU, YCU.

Truck v. (1890s–1940s) go; walk or run; to leave; moving. (DB,
OHHJ, p. 149; AJ, MJR, p. 10; WF, DAS, p. 555; RSG, JT, p. 287.)
Example: "You gonna have to truck, Tally, if you mean to get to work
before they lock the gate." SNU. See "Tricking," and "Jet."

Truck Charles Valdez Parham (b. 1913), bass player who worked
with Roy Eldridge, Art Tatum, Earl Hines, and others.

Truck driver n. (1950s–1960s) an extremely masculine homosexual.
(FR.) Homosexual use.

Trucking v., n. (1890s–1930s) strutting; strolling; walking in a fancy
manner; any kind of fancy walking or hip-slinging during a dance.
(BJ, BLH, SD, p. 137; DB, OHHJ, p. 149.) SU, SNU.

Trucking n., v. (1930s–1940s) a formal dance introduced in Harlem's famous nightclub, the Cotton Club, according to Cab Calloway,
who worked there with his band at the time, in 1933. (CC, OMMM,
NCCHD, p. 260; ZNH, AM, p. 96; DB, OHHJ, p. 149.) Harlem use,
SCU, SNCU.

True lie n. (1920s–1930s) a general assessment based more on immediate or long-range historical consensus rather than factual evidence. (Richard Wright, *Lawd Today*, 1963.) Example: "You say I'm lying about what you did last night, but I say even if you didn't cuss out the bartender, I'm telling a true lie about you cause you've done it so many times." SNU.

Trummy James Osborne Young (b. 1912), trombonist and singer.

Trump the hump (1930s–1940s) climb the hill. (DB, OHHJ, p. 149.) Example: "I have to trump the hump every morning half past six to get over Miss Lucy's house to let her dog out." SNU.

Truth n. (1940s–1950s) good, authentic jazz, played with great feeling. (RSG, JT, pp. 287–288.) JMFU.

[Every] Tub see "Every tub [on its own black bottom.]"

Tubby Alfred Hall (1895–1946), drummer who worked with Louis Armstrong and others.

[The] Tube n. (1930s–1950s) the New York City subway. (DB, OHHJ, p. 149.) Harlem, New York, use.

[The] Tube n. (1960s–1990s) a television set. (DC, BJ, p. 84; CS, vol. 3, no. 2, p. 50.) SNCU.

Tubesteak; tube n. (1970s–1980s) the penis. (EF, RDSL, p. 258.) SCU, YCU. See "Meat."

Tubs n. (1930s–1990s) originally, a homemade set of drums; drums. (RSG, JT, p. 288.) JMFU.

'Tude n. (1970s–1990s) short for attitude. (FR.) YCU.

Tuna [fish] n. (EF, RDSL, p. 258.) See "Trout."

Tune in our mikes (1940s) among jazz musicians, to listen. (DB, OHHJ, p. 149.) Harlem use, JMFU.

Tune n. (1940s–1960s) among jazz musicians, very loosely used, an idea, a story, or a woman. (RSG, JT, p. 288.) JMFU.

Tuned in adj. (1950s–1970s) in rapport with whatever is going on; the opposite is "tuned out." (RSG, JT, p. 288.) JMFU.

Tuned out adj. (1950s–1970s) out of touch or uninvolved or uninterested; inattentive; not in rapport. (RSG, JT, p. 288.) JMFU.

Turf n. (1930s–1970s) a city sidewalk; a city block or area of blocks claimed as private territory by a gang; the street one lives on; a city area defended by a gang; the Bronx; Harlem; East Harlem; Brooklyn; Bedford-Stuyvesant; New York City; South-central Los Angeles; Watts, Los Angeles, etc. (DB, OHHJ, p. 149; HLF, RJPD, p. 172; WF, DAS, p. 556; DC, BJ, p. 84.) New York use.

Turk n. (1950s–1960s) a variant of "turf"; neighborhood; the "hood"; one's "territory." (FR.) YCU, SCU.

Turkey n. (1960s) a fool; an uncool man. (FR.) SCU, JMFU, YCU.

Turkey on a string n. (1970s–1980s) a person who is head-over-heels in love or infatuated with another. (EF, RDSL, p. 258.) SCU, YCU.

Turkey Trot n. (1900s–1920s) a jazz dance in which the dancer imitates the movements of a turkey just as, in the "Camel Walk," camel motions are imitated. many African-American popular dances were based on animal motions. (RSG, JT, p. 289.) SU, SNU.

[To] Turn v. (1990s) short for "turn state's evidence." (FR.) SCU, PU.

Turn [one's] damper down (1900s–1930s) relax; calm down; don't get so excited. (RF, WJ, p. 307.) SNU.

Turned around (1960s–1970s) to be dislocated; baffled; disoriented or confused. (RSG, JT, p. 289.) SCU, YCU, JMFU.

Turned off (RSG, JT, p. 289.) See "Tuned out."

Turn on v., adj. (1900s–1970s) in the first two decades of the twentieth century, "turn on" meant simply to feel intense or extremely good, as, in Rudolph Fisher's terms, while "strutting one's stuff"; after the Depression: to get high; to give or sell drugs to someone; to give advice; to introduce someone to something; in the seventies, all previous meanings became current: something exciting, stimulating; a high degree of response to drugs, music, to almost anything. (RF, WJ, p. 306; CLC, TS, p. 256; RRL, DAZ, p. 239; EF, RDSL, p. 258; RSG, JT, p. 289.) Examples: "The show was really a turn on," and, "I like to turn on with Sue because her karma is like my own, restful in the room," and, "Nice thing about Bob is every time you drop by he turns you on." DCU, SCU.

[To] Turn [one] out (1940s–1970s) to initiate a beginner to the scene—drugs, conning, or whatever else is currently fashionable; to introduce someone to something, such as sex or drugs; pimp phrase: to convince a woman to sell her body for money. (DG, DC, p. 98; EF, BVV, p. 52; IS, TB, p. 312; EF, RDSL, p. 258.) PPU, SCU, YCU.

Turn out a set [turn the set out; turn the shit out] (1970s–1990s) to start fighting at a party or to pass out from alcohol or drugs; generally, to make a spectacle of oneself and cause disruption or confusion. (EF, BVV, p. 52; EF, RDSL, p. 259.) YCU, SCU.

Turn tail v. (1900s–1940s) to leave, especially suddenly; the image evoked is of a rabbit suddenly fleeing a prey. (CM, CW, "Jack in the Pot," p. 124) See "Split," and "High tail."

Turn the rhythm around (1920s–1990s) in jazz, a request to correct the false direction of the music being played. Sometimes communicated by the leader or some other member of the group in a non-verbal manner. (RSG, JT, p. 290.) JMFU.

Turn tricks v. (1900s–1990s) selling sex for money; practicing prostitution. (DG, ER, p. 101; DC, BJ, p. 84.) PPU. See "Trick."

Turnip greens n. (1970s–1980s) marijuana. (EF, RDSL, p. 259.) DCU.

Turtles n. (1940s) body turns, especially those made while dancing or fighting or even running. (DB, OHHJ, p. 149.) NCU.

Tush n. (1930s–1950s) wealthy, light-skinned society "Negro"; mulatto. (WF, DAS, p. 557.) SNU.

Tush adj. (1930s–1950s) high class; high society manners; sophistication. (WF, DAS, p. 557.) SNU.

Tusheroon; tusheroony n. (1900s–1950s) money. (WF, DAS, p. 557.) SNU.

Tuskee n. (1970s–1980s) a cigar-sized marijuana cigarette. (EF, RDSL, p. 259.) SCU.

Twat n. (1940s–1950s) the vagina. (FR.) SCU. See "Pussy."

Tweaking adj. (1990s) high on drugs; saying inappropriate things. (FR.) YCU, SCU, DCU.

Twelve o'clock high (1970s) a cry of alarm meaning the police are coming. (FR.) DCU.

Twenty-cents n. (1930s–1970s) twenty dollars. (CRM, BP, p. 310.) SCU, SNU.

[A] Twenty-four-seven [24–7] n. (1980s–1990s) refers to a convenience store that stays open around the clock, such as Seven-Eleven. (TW, CK, p. 138; TW, CH, p. 152.) New York use, SCU, DCU.

[The] Twich; twitches; twitchers n. (1980s–1990s) nerve disorder resulting from excessive use of crack cocaine. (TW, CH, p. 152.) DCU.

Twig n. (1930s–1940s) a tree. (DB, OHHJ, p. 149.) SNU.

Twigs n. (1930s–1940s) one's legs. (DB, OHHJ, p. 149.) SNU.

Twilight world n. (1950s–1960s) the world of all-night parties. (FR.) JMFU, SCU.

Twinkle n. (1940s) a doorbell, the sound it makes. (DB, OHHJ, p. 149.) NCU.

Twinklers n. (1930s–1950s) one's eyes. (DB, OHHJ, p. 149.) SNU.

Twisted adj. (1950s–1970s) to be intoxicated; high on drugs; to feel ill for lack of drugs; suffering withdrawal. (Hear Wardell Gray, "Twisted," *Central Avenue*, Prestige, 1976; CLC, TS, p. 256; WF, DAS, p. 709; RRL, DAZ, p. 239; DC, BJ, p. 84; RSG, JT, p. 290.) DCU, JMFU.

Twister n. (1930s–1940s) door key. (DB, OHHJ, p. 149.) NCU.

Twister to the slammer n. (1930s–1940s) the key to the door. (CC, OMMM, NCCHD, p. 260.) Example: "In case you get home before I do, here's the twister to the slammer." SCU, YCU.

Two-beat n. (1950s–1960s) a hard, driving Dixieland style of jazz in which the accent is placed on two bars in every four; "two-beat" music. (RSG, JT, p. 290.) JMFU.

Two bits n. (1940s–1960s) twenty-five dollars in cash. (CS, vol. 3, no. 2, p. 50.) SCU, DCU.

Two camels n. (1940s) ten minutes. (DB, OHHJ, p. 149.) SNU.

Two cents n. (1940s) two dollars. (CC, OMMM, NCCHD, p. 260; DB, OHHJ, p. 149.) SCU, YCU.

Two-faced adj. (1850s–1950s) guilty of deliberate deception; or misrepresentation; saying one thing and meaning another. (FR.) SNU.

[To be] Two-inched v. (1990s) female expression of discontentment with sexual intercourse with a man who has a short, small penis. (FR.) Example: "Listen, honey, ain't nobody got time to be two-inched by a two-minute-er, so just keep your sweet talk to yourself." YCU, SCU.

Two-story lorry n. (1940s) a double-decker bus. (DB, OHHJ, p. 149.) New York use.

Two wrongs don't make a right (1860s–1990s) a "Negro saying" suggesting that revenge never works. (FR.) SU.

U

Ugly n. (1700s–1990s) evil; "ugly" to mean evil is common both in the United States and in the West Indies. (FGC, JT, p. 187.) SNU.

Ugly as home-made sin adj. (1900s–1950s) an abusive remark. (FR.) SNU.

Ugly ways n. (1700s–1990s) ill-tempered behavior; bad manners. (FGC, JT, p. 187.) SNU.

Uh-uh n. (1620s–1990s) no; of African origin. (JH, PBL, p. 86.) SNU. See "Un-huh" and "uuh-huh."

Un-huh n. (1620s–1990s) yes; of African origin. (HV, AHAE, p. 148; JH, PBL, p. 86.) SNU. See "uuh-huh."

Ultracool adj. (1960s–1970s) possessing a high level of hipness and togetherness. (FR.) JMFU, SCU, YCU.

Umbrella n. (1960s–1970s) police protection (from arrest) bought with cash. (CS, vol. 3, no. 2, p. 50.) Watts use.

Un-ass v. (1940s–1960s) to give up something. (RHdeC, NB, p. 38.) Example: "Hey, Betty, un-ass my scarf! You can't wear it!" SCU, SNCU.

Unbleached American n. (1860s) a black person; picked up from contemptuous white use and used humorously. (JSF, AON, p. 159; AB, DSJC, p. 375.) SNU.

Uncle n. (1750s–1860s) an elderly Negro male; southern black and white use. (JSF, AON, p. 69.) SU.

Uncle n. (1940s) a pawnshop manager. (DB, OHHJ, p. 149.) Example: "If we going to make this month's rent I got to take my watch and my sax down to Uncle's again." Harlem; Chicago; NECU.

Uncle Ben-black n. (1960s) a deep sense of black racial consciousness. (FR.) Rare. YCU.

Uncle nab(s) n. (1970s–1990s) the police. (EF, RDSL, p. 259.) South-central Los Angeles; YCU, SCU.

Uncle Sam's action n. (1940s) induction into military service. (DB, OHHJ, p. 149.) Harlem; SNCU.

Uncle Sam's pets n. (1940s) enlisted or drafted foot soldiers during World War II. (MHB, JS np.) SNU.

Uncle Sham n. (1960s–1970s) a derogatory version of Uncle Sam; product of the movement for social justice and possibly also the antiwar movement. (FR.) YCU, SCU.

Uncle Thomas n. (1960s) variant of Uncle Tom. (FR.) SNU. See "Uncle Tom."

Uncle Tom n. (1860s–1990s) derogatory term for African-American; a servile "Negro" (originally a character in the novel *Uncle Tom's Cabin*, by Harriet Beecher Stowe); the creation of bop (in the 1940s) on the part of young black musicians to the "Uncle Tom" music that preceded it; a black person who is culturally disloyal; a black person who does not practice racial or cultural loyalty; a pejorative term for any African-American perceived by any other African-Americans to be "middle-class," to own property, and to have money in the bank. (DC, BJ, p. 84; EF, RDSL, p. 259; CS, vol. 3, no. 2, p. 50.) See "Handkerchief head."

Uncool adj. (1950s) not smart; not intelligent; too hasty; too overreacting; the opposite of Cool. (DC, BJ, pp. 84–85; RSG, JT, p. 291.)

Uncut adj. (1960s–1990s) narcotics in a pure or fairly pure state; strong, undiluted heroin or cocaine. (EF, RDSL, p. 259.) DCU.

Under cover n. (1950s–1990s) sex. (Hear Katie Webster, "Hold on to What You Got," *The Swamp Boogie Queen*, Alligator Records, 1988.) SNU. See "Under rations."

Underground Railroad n. (1830s–1860s) for runaway slaves, the escape route from the slave states to the North and to Canada. Such runaways were often led by Sojourner Truth (1777–1883), who herself escaped slavery in 1827. Politically active in the Abolitionist and the Suffrage movements, she is best remembered for her speech "Ain't I a Woman?" (JSF, AON, p. 546; Lisa Tuttle, *Feminism*, 1986, p. 328.) SNU.

Under rations n. (1930s–1940s) sex. (ZNH, AM, p. 95.) SNU.

[An] Understanding n. (1960s–1980s) the intimate arrangement between a wife and husband or between two people living together on intimate terms. (EF, RDSL, p. 259.) SNCU.

Undertaker n. (1970s–1980s) one who is able to bury the ball quickly. (GS, TT, p. 59.) Example: "You can get frustrated with playing with Bill because he's such an undertaker." Black golfers lingo.

Underworlded v. (1850s–1900s) in voodoo, to be cursed with an evil spell. (FR.) Example: "Sara Alice been so bad to her mama that that lady Miss Clarice underworlded her and can't nobody break the spell but her herself." North Carolina use.

Unhip adj. (1930s–1960s) unwise; foolish; frenetic; innocent; the opposite of hip. (RSG, JT, p. 291; DC, BJ, p. 85; DB, OHHJ, p. 149; CC, OMMM, NCCHD, p. 260.) JMFU, SNCU.

Unhipped adj. See "Unhip."

Union wage n. (1960s–1980s) the police. (EF, RDSL, p. 259.) South-central Los Angeles.

Unnecessary adj. (1900s–1940s) a dejected feeling; depression; to be blue. (FR.) Example: "I feel so unnecessary since my baby left." SU.

Unravel v. (1960s–1970s) to tell someone something, especially something complicated or complex. (DW, TL, p. 191.) Rare. SCU.

Unsheik v. (1920s) to divorce. Sheik is the brand name of a condom. (CVV, NH, p. 286.) Harlem use.

Untogether adj. (1960s) not functioning well; not socially adept; unpleasant. (DC, BJ, p. 85; Toni Cade Bambara, *Gorilla, My Love*, p. 70.) SNCU, YUC.

Up adj. (1950s–1960s) high; intoxicated. (RR1, DAZ, p. 240.)

Up against the wall, motherfucker exclam. (1960s) be aware of racism; be conscious of one's social condition; a popular phrase—mocking the police use of same—used ironically by socially and politically conscious, and angry, youths of the sixties. (FR.) SCU.

Up and say v. (1880s–1950s) to begin an utterance. (FR.) Example: "Just out of nowhere, he up and say he was gone leave me, and, girl, he was gone the next day." SNU.

Up for it adj. (1880s–1950s) to be motivated to do something. (FR.) "I'm just not up for it today, Joe." SNU.

Upper(s) n. (1960s–1990s) usually amphetamine in capsule form. (EF, RDSL, p. 259; CS, vol. 3, no. 2, p. 50.) DCU.

Uppity adj. (1900s–1990s) snobbish and pretentious. (EF, RDSL, p. 259.) See "Dicty," "Hincty," and "Seddity."

Upright(s) n. (1870s–1940s) one's legs. (JSF, AON, p. 546; DB, OHHJ, p. 149.) Rare. Harlem; NECU.

Ups n. (1960s) stimulant drugs. (RRL, DAZ, p. 240.) DCU.

Up side [one's] head (1950s–1960s) to land a fist-blow in the face; to fistfight someone; often used as a threat. (DC, BJ, p. 85.) Example: "Stay outta my way, man, or I'm gone go up side your head." SCU, PU, YCU.

Up South n. (1950s–1960s) the North; Maryland and Washington, D.C.; the phrase implying that racial bigotry in the North is no less vicious than in the South. (FR.) NECU.

Upstairs n. (1930s–1940s) the Christian concept of Heaven in the sky. (DB, OHHJ, p. 149.) Harlem; SNU.

Up-tempo adj. (1930s) fast-tempo music. (RSG, JT, p. 292.) JMFU.

Uptight adj. (1950s–1970s) in the fifties in jazz circles, to have good sex; a good feeling, especially in the music; also, to be short on cash; later, black ghetto use had it to mean "a good feeling"; also, to a minor degree, it meant having financial or personal troubles; later, in the late sixties, early seventies, it was adapted by white teenagers to mean mental or emotional disorder. (Hear Gene Ammons, *Up Tight*, Prestige PRLP 7208; WF, DAS, p. 709; IS, PSML, p. 317; CRM, BP, p. 310; DW, TL, p. 191; CS, vol. 3, no. 2, p. 50.) SNCU, JMFU.

Up to the notch adj. (1850s–1920s) to be in the best shape or form. (CCJ, NMGC, p. 170.) Georgia and the Carolinas use.

Uptown adj. (1930s–1950s) stylishness; wealth. (Hear Erskine Hawkins Orchestra, *Uptown Shuffle*, Bluebird 10506; RSG, p. 292.) JMFU.

Use v. (1950s–1990s) to practice the use of addictive drugs. (EF, RDSL, p. 259.) DCU.

User n. (1950s–1990s) a drug addict. (DC, BJ, p. 85; EF, RDSL, p. 259.) DCU, SCU.

Uuh-huh n. (1650s–1990s) no; of African origin. (HV, AHAE, p. 148.) SNU. See "Uh-huh."

Vacation n. (1930s–1960s) time spent in jail or prison. (DC, BJ, p. 85; WF, DAS, p. 563.) PU, SCU.

Vacuum cleaner n. (1940s) one's lungs. (DB, OHHJ, p. 149.) Harlem; Chicago; NCU.

V and X [store] n. (1930s–1940s) a ten-cents store; a store where cheap items are sold. (ZNH, AM, p. 96.) Harlem use.

VBD n. (1960s) abbreviation for "very bad date"; a disappointing romantic evening out with a member of the opposite sex. (CS, vol. 3, no. 2, p. 50.) Watts; YCU.

Vampire's tea bag n. (1980s–1990s) a sanitary napkin. (FR.) YCU.

Vanilla Queen n. (1980s–1990s) a black gay male who prefers white sexual partners. (HMGL, p. 12.) Black and white homosexual use.

V-8 n. (1940s) a female loner; woman who avoids contact with others, especially with men; unfriendly female. (DB, OHHJ, p. 149; CC, OMMM, NCCHD, p. 260.) Harlem use; NECU.

Vein n. (1950s–1960s) in jazz, a double bass. (WF, DAS, p. 564.) JMFU.

Vibes n. (1930s–1990s) short for "vibraphone," "vibraharp," and "vibrabells." (WF, DAS, p. 565.) JMFU.

Vibes n. (1960s–1970s) feelings; emotions. (EF.) Example: "I like coming here because this place gives me good vibes." SNCU, YCU.

Vic; vict n., v. (1930s–1990s) a victim of a crime; victimize; victimizing; also, convict, but rare in black slang. (TW, CK, p. 138; TW, CH, p. 152; WF, DAS, p. 565; IS, PSML, p. 317; CS, vol. 3, no. 2, p. 51.) Examples: "You go down there by yourself you'll be victed sure as shit"; and, "They say there's at least five hundred vics every minute in the Big Apple." DCU.

Vice(d) v. (1960s–1980s) to do harm; cheat; steal; rob someone; to inflict physical pain. (DW, TL, p. 191.) PU, SCU, PPU, DCU.

Viddle-de-vop n. (1940s) a low whistle. (MHB, JS, np.) Rare. SU.

-Ville (1940s) popular suffix often attached to any word as an intensifier. Example: "I'll dig you cats later, I'm splitsville—gotta go to the pad and cap some Zs."

[The] Vine n. (1970s–1990s) wine. (EF, RDSL, p. 259.) South-central Los Angeles; SNCU.

Vine(s) n. (1930s–1950s) a suit of clothing; clothes. (DB, OHHJ, p. 149; RDA, DDJ, p. 268; HLF, RJPD, p. 172; DC, BJ, p. 85; DW, TL, p. 191; CRM, BP, p. 310.) SCU, YCU, NECU.

Vinyl n. (1990s) a record album; compact discs. (MC Lyte, *Essence*, September 1992, p. 118.) YCU.

Vipe v. (1930s–1940s) to smoke marijuana. (RRL, DAZ, p. 241.) DCU.

Viper n. (1930s–1940s) drug dealer; a drug addict; anyone who survives either on narcotics or from its sale; marijuana smoker. (SL, RJON, p. 144; DW, TL, p. 191.) DCU.

Vitamins n. (1980s–1990s) amphetamines or barbiturates in capsules. (EF, RDSL, p. 259.) DCU.

Voguing v. (1980s–1990s) expressive black gay dancing, which started in Harlem; classy; out of *Vogue*. (FR.) Harlem; Homosexual use.

Volly Voltaire de Faut, saxophone player; born March 14, 1904; worked with New Orleans Rhythm Kings.

Voodoo [voudo; voudou; voodeux; voodouism] n. (1770s–1990s) *vodu* (Ewe); *vodum* [Ashanti]; probably related to *obosum*;

Dahomey fetish; witchcraft; deity trusted to guard those of strong faith; hoodoo; religion practiced in by early-American slaves and till this day in Haiti; in voodoo practice, sorcerers exercise supernatural power—they can create and destroy. Representing an ancient African religion, the word "voodoo," in the West, was first recorded in about the 1820s, fifty years before "hoodoo" (1875). (JSF, AON, p. 549; SBF, IHAT, p. 377; HV, AHAE, p. 148.) SNU. See "Hood" and "Zombie."

Wacky adj. (1920s) in jazz, eccentric, as in a rhythm or beat. (WF, DAS, p. 566.) Rare. JMFU.

Waders n. (1940s) boots. (DB, OHHJ, p. 150.) SNU.

Wagging n. (1800s–1890s) walking slowly. (FR.) YCU.

Wah-wah(s); wa-wa; wow-wow n., adj. (1920s–1940s) the expression may have some distant relation to the word "*WuWu*," meaning "evil," used by Africans sold into slavery; or to the more recent "wow"; but since the twenties, in jazz, it refers to the often muted sounds or brass effects made when musicians cause brass instruments to imitate the sounds of animals or humans; such effects were created with rubber or glass mute modifiers for, say, a trumpet or some other similar instrument; bell- and horn-distorted sounds. (AL, MJR, p. 59; WF, DAS, p. 566; RSG, JT, p. 297.) JMFU.

Wail n., adj. (1950s–1970s) in jazz, a truly beautiful performance, especially in the delivery of a solo; something that gives pleasure or that makes a person laugh. (SL, RJON, p. 146; WF, DAS, pp. 566–567; BH, SB, p. 17; EF, RDSL, p. 259; RSG, JT, p. 297.) JMFU. See "Smoke," "Burn," and "Blow fire."

[To] Wail on [one] (1960s–1970s) to fight someone; to attack a person. (CS, vol. 3, no. 2, p. 51.) SCU.

[A] Wailer n. (1950s) in jazz, a musician who gives a truly beautiful performance. (RSG, JT, p. 297.) JMFU.

Wake-up(s) n. (1970s–1990s) benzedrine capsules. (EF, RDSL, p. 259.) SCU, DCU.

Walk; walking n. (1950s–1970s) in jazz, four-beats-to-the-bar-rhythm. (WF, DAS, p. 567.) JMFU. See "Walking bass," "Cakewalk," and "Camel Walk."

Walk; walking v. (1960s–1990s) to move in a driving motion toward the hoop. (DC, BJ, p. 85.) Example: "Man, Michael Jordan can really do some heavy walking." Basketball players' and fans' use.

[A] Walk-back n. (1930s–1940s) a rear apartment. (DB, OHHJ, p. 150.) NCU.

Walk cool v. (1960s) to show an unhurried approach in all of one's affairs; affect an air of disinterest. (CS, vol. 3, no. 2, p. 51.) SCU, YCU.

[A] Walk-down n. (1940s) a basement apartment. (DB, OHHJ, p. 150.) NCU.

Walk heavy (1900s–1960s) to go forth in the world projecting one-self as important; to stride in a self-assured manner. (WF, DAS, p. 710.) SU, SNU.

Walking bass; walk the bass n. (1900s–1940s) in jazz, playing in an unbroken pattern at least two notes to the bar; whole bass tones and broken octaves; a progression with an up-and-down movement of semitones; or, in Langston Hughes' words, a sound "like marching feet." (RSG, JT, p. 299.) JMFU.

Walking papers (1800s–1990s) possibly "walking papers" had its origins in the idea of a legal document setting a slave free; notice of having been fired from a job. (Richard Wright, *Lawd Today*, 1963, p. 112; AB, DSJC, p. 386.) SU, SNU.

Walking the dog (1900s–1920s) a popular jazz dance done in a style mocking the sometimes arrogant and pretentious manner of a high society lady walking her little dog. (RSG, JT, p. 299.) Harlem use, JMFU, YCU.

Walk softly and carry a big stick (1700s–1940s) an African proverb common among early slaves in the slave states meaning proceed with caution; expression made famous by President Teddy Roosevelt. (FR.) SNU.

Walk that walk (1960s–1990s) commendation for having great style or appearance. (FR.) SCU, YCU. See "Talk that talk."

Waller n. (1950s) an expert pianist, but also any musician who is a true artist (from Thomas "Fats" Waller [1904–1943], pianist, singer, songwriter).

Wall-to-wall niggers n. (1970s–1990s) a packed dancehall in a black community; any crowded, standing-room-only, social gathering of black people; from "wall-to-wall carpet." (EF, RDSL, p. 259.) SNCU.

Wana n. (1970s–1980s) variant of, and short for, marijuana. (EF, RDSL, p. 259.) DCU.

Wannabe n. (1970s–1990s) any young white person who affects the manners and speech associated with black street-culture; an outsider who wants to be an insider. (EF, RDSL, p. 259.) See "Yo-Boy," and "Wigger."

War lord n. (1950s–1990s) in street culture, a gang member who lays out the strategy for gang fights. (DC, BJ, p. 85.) SCU.

War Water n. (1920s–1930s) a conjuring solution made with filtered oil of tar and used to create domestic chaos. (ZNH, MM, p. 336.) Florida use, SU.

War zone n. (1980s–1990s) among drug dealers, another dealer's territory. (FR.) DCU.

Washboard n. (1900s–1930s) an ordinary scrub-board used to improve a musical instrument. (RSG, JT, p. 299.) JMFU, SU.

Washboard band n. (1900s–1930s) a group of jazzmen utilizing washboards (by rubbing thimbles over the surfaces) as musical instruments. (RSG, JT, p. 299.) JMFU, SU.

Washed adj., n. (1990s) a black person who seems to have absorbed Anglo-American cultural values and attitudes; one accused of such a cross-over. (FR.) See "Oreo."

Washer n. (1940s) a tavern; a fast-food grill. (DB, OHHJ, p. 150.) Harlem use, NCU.

Washer-dryer n. (1970s–1990s) a rubber or plastic douchebag and a bath or face towel. (EF, RDSL, p. 259.) South-central Los Angeles use, SCU, YCU.

Washing n. (1980s–1990s) to change the taste and color of cocaine through a chemical process. (TW, CK, p. 138.) DCU.

Washing powder n. (1970s–1990s) any name-brand douching solution.

Wash-out; washout; washed out v., n. (1920s–1940s) to lose, especially in a contest such as gambling with dice or cards; defeat; loss; failure. (LA, SM, p. 123; WF, DAS, pp. 568–569.) SU, SNU.

Washtub base n. (1850s–1860s) a homemade stringed instrument made of a washtub and a broom; gutbucket instrument. (HV, AHAE, p. 154.) SU.

Waste; wasted v. (1950s–1990s) to murder or injure someone; destroy; wipe out; beat up. (EF, RDSL, p. 259; WF, DAS, p. 567; RSG, JT, p. 299; HLF, RJPD, p. 172; IS, TB, p. 312.) Example: "Perry got wasted 'cause he didn't know how to keep his mouth shut, so let that be a lesson to you, youngblood." SCU.

Wasted adj. (1950s–1960s) intoxicated; high on drugs; in bad physical condition resulting from any kind of external cause. (WF, DAS, p. 567; EF, RDSL, p. 259; RSG, JT, p. 300; DC, BJ, p. 85.) DCU.

Watch; watching v. (1900s–1940s) to look; looking. (Richard Westmacott, *African-American Gardens and Yards in the Rural South*, 1992, p. 94.) SU.

[To make] Water n., v. (1800s–1990s) urine, to urinate. (FR.) Example: "You run along now to the bathroom and make water before you go to bed." SNU.

Water Notre Dame n. (1920s–1930s) a conjuring solution made with the oil of white roses and used to bring about domestic tranquility. (ZNH, MM, p. 336.) SU.

Watermelon time n. (1800s–1990s) term for the time in the summer when watermelons are ripe. (FR.) SU.

Waters n. (1940s) rubber boots; galoshes. (DB, OHHJ, p. 150.) SNU.

Waterworks (water-works) n. (1940s) eyes wet with tears; tears. (DB, OHHJ, p. 150.) Example: I ain't studying Mary—every time she can't get her way she turns on the waterworks." SNU.

Watts rat patrol n. (1970s–1990s) any police patrolling Watts and South-central Los Angeles. (EF, RDSL, p. 259.) SCU, YCU.

Wax; waxing n. (1940s–1950s) a severe beating from the police. "Wax" has a relatively long history as slang; in the latter part of the nineteenth century, among thugs and robbers, it meant to "take note" of something such as a place one plans to rob). (CLC, TS, p. 256; EP, DU, p. 762.) SCU, PU.

Wax; waxing; waxed v., n. (1980s–1990s) to have sex; sexual intercourse. (FR.) YCU, SCU.

Wax; waxing v., n. (1950s–1960s) chewing gum; to chew chewing gum. (DC, BJ, p. 86.) Example: "Girl, if I have to tell you one more time to take that wax outta your mouth I'm going to go in there myself and yank it out." SCU, YCU.

Way in adj. (1950s–1960s) anything in vogue; anything popular among young people. (DC, BJ, p. 86.) YCU.

Way out adj. (1940s–1960s) in jazz, in the forties and fifties, "progressive" innovative music; anything pushed to the extreme, usually positive or beautiful; in the sixties, not very stylish; not understandable; outlandish. (WF, DAS, p. 570; RSG, JT, p. 300; DC, BJ, p. 86; CS, vol. 3, no. 2, p. 51.) SNCU, JMFU.

Way past bad (JM, WPC.) See "Way past cool."

Way past cool (1980s–1990s) to be super-cool; to be "hip" beyond measure. (JM, WPC.) SCU, YCU.

Weak adj. (1950s–1960s) unsuitable; inferior in quality; in bad taste. (DC, BJ, p. 86; HLF, RJPD, p. 172.) SCU, YCU.

Weaking down n., v. (1900s–1940s) failure; defeat; illness; to lose one's dignity; to show a lack of character; to become demoralized. (Hear Bukka White, "Sleepy Man Blues," and, "When Can I Change My Clothes," *The Complete Sessions 1930–1940*, Interstate Music, Ltd., 1990.) SU.

Weak mind; weak-minded (1950s–1990s) receptive to manipulation. (EF, RDSL, p. 259.) Example: "You see the way Sara let Brad mess her around, girl; she must be really weak-minded to take that kinda treatment." SCU.

[To] Wear a smile; wearing a smile (1900s–1940s) to be naked; nakedness; nude. (DB, OHHJ, p. 150.) Example: "I was looking for the bathroom and opened the wrong door and there was Annie wearing a smile, and I was so embarrassed I almost peed on myself." SNU.

Wear [the other band] out (1920s–1940s) phrase referring to two musical groups on the same stage and in good-natured competition; one may out "blow" the other in an attempt to win the greatest support from the audience. (RSG, JT, p. 300.) JMFU.

Wear the ring; wearing the ring (1960s–1990s) to avoid flirting or sexual involvement with persons other than one's spouse. (EF, RDSL, p. 259.) Example: "You won't get anywhere with Phil tonight, honey, he's wearing the ring." SNU.

Weave n. (1950s–1960s) one's garments, especially suits, jackets, wool dresses, topcoats. (DC, BJ, p. 86.) Example: "Hey, Miss Mary, that's a bad mink coat you're wearing there, honey." SCU, YCU, SNCU.

Weed n. (1920s–1970s) marijuana; a metonymy in the sense that marijuana is a weed; in the sixties, house or garden plants. (WF, DAS, p. 570; RSG, JT, p. 301; CC, HDH, p. 16; EF, RDSL, p. 259; DB, OHHJ, p. 150.) Example: "Charlie must have a green thumb, 'cause look at how he keeps his weeds growing—look at the red in them roses!" SCU, YCU, DCU.

Weed v. (1940s) to lend somebody something, especially money. (DB, OHHJ, p. 150.) Example: "Hey, man, can you weed me a dime till Friday when I get my check?" Rare. Harlem use, NCU.

[To] Weed a holler note until [one's] mother comes in (1940s) to lend one a hundred dollars till one's luck changes at the race track or, less literally, till one's luck changes period. (DB, OHHJ, p. 150.) Harlem use, SCU.

Weedhead n. (1950s–1960s) a person who is addicted to smoking marijuana. (CS, vol. 3, no. 2, p. 51.) SCU.

Weeding out v. (1950s–1970s) smoking marijuana excessively. (RRL, DAZ, p. 243.) DCU.

Weed tea n. (1920s–1930s) marijuana. (WF, DAS, p. 570.) DCU.

Weedy [flowers] n. (1900s–1950s) flowers that die in winter and come back in the spring, in rural southern yards. (Richard Westmacott, *African-American Gardens and Yards in the Rural South*, 1992, p. 107.) SU.

Weepers n. (1920s–1940s) one's funeral clothes, often the same as one's "Sunday-go-to-meeting" best. (DB, OHHJ, p. 150.) See "Sunday-go-to-meeting clothes."

Weeping Mary n. (1800s–1890s) slave expression for any of the biblical personalities named Mary: Mary of Bethany, Mary Magdalene, and Mary, mother of Christ. (FR.) SU.

Weight n. (1970s–1990s) one's influence. (FR.) See "Heavy."

Weight n. (1980s–1990s) a gun. (EF, RDSL, p. 232; KCJ, JS, p. 139.) SCU, PU.

[Carrying] Weight (KCJ, JS, p. 139.) See "Weight."

Weird n. (1940s–1960s) in jazz, innovation often thought to be "too much"; a surprise, sometimes a delightful surprise; anything unusual or different from the expected; a white hippie; a flaunting homosexual. (RSG, JT, p. 301; CS, vol. 3, no. 2, p. 51.) SCU, YCU.

Weirdbag n. (1950s–1960s) among jazz musicians, the inner resources an innovative performer depends on to make his or her often indefensible music. (RSG, JT, p. 301.) JMFU.

Weirdie; weirdy; weird-o n. (1950s) an unusual person. (RSG, JT, p. 301.) SNU.

We go way back (1940s–1950s) announcement of a long sustained friendship; in other words, "we are old friends." (WM, DBD, p. 2.) SNU.

Welfare mother n. (1960s–1990s) a judgment made about any woman who is tastelessly dressed in cheap, ill-matching clothes. (EF, RDSL, p. 259.) SCU.

Well, all right! (GS, TT, p. 57.) See "Tell the truth."

Wench n. (1840s–1930s) originated among white speakers: a black woman or girl. Black people have used the term ironically. (JSF, AON, p. 554.) SU, SNU.

Went down on [go down on] v. (1960s–1990s) to fight with, especially to defeat; fight with; to defeat. (DC, BJ, p. 86.) Example: "Ronnie really went down on Harvey last night in the parking lot next to Jugg's." SCU, MWU. See "Thump."

Wesorts n. (1880s–1940s) in Maryland, a "clan" of people of mixed black and white ancestry; derived from Sallie Thompson's "we sort of people," opposed, that is, to recently freed slaves. (BB, AW, pp. 35–36.)

West Coast jazz n. (1950s–1960s) cool jazz; among jazz fans, it is generally thought to be a "white" form, but some critics argue that black West Coast jazz musicians first developed the "cool" West Coast sound later picked up by people like Gerry Mulligan. (RSG, JT, p. 302.) JMFU.

Western style jazz n. (1920s–1930s) Chicago style; essentially a midwestern style, as opposed to a New Orleans style; "traditional" jazz. (RSG, JT, p. 302.) JMFU.

West Hell n. (1900s–1940s) far, far away; way past Hell. (ZNH, AM, p. 96; SK, PC, pp. 153–154.) SU. See "Ginny Gall."

Wethead n. (1970s–1990s) a lazy, unmotivated person. (EF, RDSL, p. 259.) See "Poot-butt."

Whack attack (1980s–1990s) a violently irrational reaction to an hallucinogenic drug. (WKB, JMC, PS, p. 51.) DCU, PU.

Whale (whail) v. (1940s–1960s) to throw dice or to be very active in some other gambling activity; to do anything very effectively; to run extremely fast; related to "wail." (JH, PBL, p. 86.) SCU. See "Whail."

Wham bam (1880s–1990s) quick, impersonal sexual intercourse. (WF, DAS, p. 573.) SNU. See "Wham bam (thank you ma'am)."

Wham bam [thank you ma'am] (1880s–1990s) quick, impersonal sexual intercourse followed by a perfunctory word of gratitude; used more as a description of such an event than by the participants. (WF, DAS, p. 573.) SNU.

What it is! (1980s–1990s) a friendly greeting. (EF, BVV, p. 53.) Harlem, SCU.

What the real deal is (1970s–1990s) what is really happening; the truth of the matter. (FR.) SCU, YCU, SNU.

What time it is (1990s) what's really occurring; the truth of a situation. (FR.) Example: "I'm going to show him what time it is." YCU.

What's cooking? (1930s–1960s) a greeting in the form of an inquiry, meaning, "what's going on in your life?" (WF, DAS, p. 574.) JMFU, SCU, YCU.

What's going down? (1960s–1970s) a greeting in the form of an inquiry, sometimes about a confusing situation; same as "What's happening?" (DC, BJ, p. 86.) SCU, YCU.

What's happening? (1960s–1990s) an inquiry and greeting similar to "hello"; what's going on? (EF, RDSL, p. 260; DC, BJ, p. 86.) SCU, YCU.

What-so-never (1700s–1940s) whatsoever. (FR.) SU.

What's on the rail for the lizard? (1930s–1940s) a playfully cynical request for suggestions for activity—usually recreational—excitingly depraved or joyously wicked. (ZNH, AM, p. 96.) Rare. Harlem use, SNU.

What's up? interj. (1960s–1990s) a greeting and request for information about the other person's situation or condition; used in friendly or potentially unfriendly circumstances. (WF, DAS, p. 574.) SCU.

What's your song, King Kong? (1940s) a playfully caustic inquiry about one's condition; same as "How do you feel?" (MHB, JS, np.) SNU.

What's your story [morning glory?] (1930s–1950s) playfully sarcastic inquiry; explain yourself; please justify what you are doing or saying. (DB, OHHJ, p. 150; CC, OMMM, NCCHD, p. 261.) SNU.

Wheelchair n. (1940s) an automobile; a car; any motor vehicle. (DB, OHHJ, p. 150.) Rare. Harlem use, NCU.

[To] Wheel v. (1930s–1990s) to drive any sort of vehicle, but especially a car. (EF, RDSL, p. 260.) SCU, SNCU.

Wheels n. (1930s–1980s) any kind of motor vehicle, but especially a car. (RSG, JT, p. 302; DC, BJ, p. 86; CS, vol. 3, no. 2, p. 51; HLF, RJPD, p. 172.) SNCU, SCU.

Where (1850s–1920s) in various parts of the Deep South, sometimes used as a variant of "who." (FR.) Example: "My brother, where's in the undertaking business, ..." SU.

Where [one] is at (1960s–1970s) one's essential nature or central philosophy. (RSG, JT, p. 302.) SCU, YCU.

Where [one's] head's at (1960s–1970s) someone's perspective. (FR.) YCU.

Where [one] is coming from (1970s–1990s) one's perspective; what one means; point of view. (EF, RDSL, p. 260; DC, BJ, p. 86.) Example: "I'm not down on you, Billy, just trying to figure out where you're coming from, boy." SCU, SNU.

Where it's at (1970s) the truth; what's important. (RSG, JT, p. 302.) SCU, YCU.

Where the action is (1950s–1960s) the place where "hip" people are doing exciting things; a dance; a social gathering; a card game; a cocaine house; the "scene." (RDA, TB, p. 89.) SCU, SNCU, YCU.

Whichaway See "Every which way."

Whichway (1700s–1940s) in any or all directions. (FR.) Example: "You shoulda seen them going every whichway when she came back in with that thing from the backyard."

Whiles (1700s–1940s) variant of "while." (FR.) SU.

Whing-ding n. (1890s–1940s) a loud crowd and boisterous party. (FR.) SU.

Whip [whup] v. (1700s–1990s) the standard punishment for a disobedient slave; to physically beat, especially as punishment for a misdeed. (DC, BJ, p. 86.) SNU.

Whip [one's] head to the red (1930s–1940s) threat of injury; a threat of retaliation; promise to return like for like; a bluff. (ZNH, AM, p. 96.) Harlem use, SCU.

Whip it on [one] v. (1940s–1970s) to speak in an honest and open manner; to tell the whole story. (DC, BJ, p. 86.) Example: "Now, Betty, she'll whip it on you, if you got a minute to spare." SNU.

Whip it on [one] (1950s–1990s) a non-gender-specific hortatory expression used during sexual intercourse. (FR.) SNU.

Whip out (1950s–1960s) to show; do; expose; give. (FR.) Example: "Every time Clark comes over here he has to whip out his baseball cards and start trying to trade." SCU, YCU.

Whipped adj. (1940s) hung-over. (MHB, JS, np.) SU.

Whipped cream n. (1970s–1990s) semen. (EF, RDSL, p. 260.) SCU, YCU.

Whipped up; whipped-up adj. (1930s–1950s) physically beaten; exhausted; tired. (CC, OMMM, NCCHD, p. 261; WF, DAS, p. 575; RSG, JT, p. 303; DB, OHHJ, p. 150.) SNU, SCU.

Whipping boss (1840s–1860s) an overseer on a slave plantation. (SK, PC, p. 67.) Palmetto County use.

Whipping the game on [one]; whupping the game on [one] (1940s–1990s) trying to "con" someone, especially in a drug deal or any kind of illegal street transaction. (DC, BJ, p. 86.) See "Murphy," and "Rip off."

Whip shack n. (1970s–1990s) any place where teenagers can go to have sex, such as an abandoned building, a closed-down movie theater, somebody's house when parents are away, etc. (EF, RDSL, p. 260.) YCU, SCU.

[The] Whips n. (1960s–1990s) the "white establishment" or "the police"; from "slave whip." (EF, RDSL, p. 260.) SCU, YCU.

Whip that thing (1900s–1940s) used by an audience to exhort or encourage musicians to continue to play. (RSG, JT, p. 303.) JMFU.

Whip that thing on [one] (1940s–1960s) hortatory expression used during sexual intercourse. (RSG, JT, p. 303.) SNU.

Whip the game (1960s–1990s) to overcome difficulties; to accomplish something important in life. (EF, RDSL, p. 260.) SCU, YCU.

Whip upside the head (1950s–1990s) administer a brutal beating, especially by the police. (EF, RDSL, p. 260.) SCU, YCU.

White adj. (1960s) pejorative term for anybody who is immoral, unethical, or sinful; bad. (WF, DAS, p. 711.) YCU, SCU.

White bricks n. (1980s–1990s) cocaine. (FR.) SNU.

White eyes n. (1970s–1990s) any white person. (EF, RDSL, p. 260.) SCU.

White folks n. (1860s–1990s) a white person. (FR.) Example: "Don't tease Jones like that, Hawk, he's good white folks." SNU.

White girl n. (1940s–1950s) cocaine. (FR.) DCU. See "White lady."

White hope n. (1900s–1920s) any white boxer who seemed to be a good bet for defeating Jack Johnson, the black champion prizefighter. (WF, DAS, p. 576.) Prizefighters' and fans' use.

[The] White house n. (1950s–1970s) white society. (FR.) SCU.

White lady n. (1950s–1960s) heroin. (RRL, DAZ, p. 243.) DCU.

White lightning n. (1930s–1950s) a colorless, homemade corn liquor; clear bootleg whisky. (WF, DAS, p. 576; EF, RDSL, p. 260.) See "Chain-lightning," and "Panther piss."

White lilies n. (1940s) bedsheets. (MHB, JS, np.) Rare. SU.

[The] White man's handsome woman n. (1750s–1860s) a white man's black slave or ex-slave mistress. (AB, DSJC, p. 399.) SU.

[The] White Mayor of Harlem Harlem name for Mezz Mezzrow during the 1930s–1940s.

White meat n. (1930s–1960s) pejorative term for a white woman as sexual object with focus on her genitalia; a white sexual partner. (WF, DAS, p. 576.) SCU.

White mouth n. (1920s–1930s) ash-gray skin around the mouth from hunger. (ZNH.) Example: "My children all got the white mouth. They ain't et in over a week." SU.

White mule n. (1920s–1930s) grain alcohol used in the rural south as a substitute for liquor; bootleg or homemade whiskey. (WF, DAS, p. 577.) See "White lightning."

White Negro n. (1750s–1950s) a mulatto; in the nineteenth century and before, a person legally black who in appearance seems white; in the twentieth century, especially after the fifties, a black person with white affectations; a white person with black affectations. (Norman Mailer, *The White Negro*.) NCU.

White nigger see "White Negro."

White-on-white; white-on-white-in-white adj., n. (1940s–1950s) a white Cadillac with white interior finish and upholstery; a person, usually a black male, who tries to obtain "white" status symbols such as a white girlfriend and a white Cadillac. (CS, vol. 3, no. 2, p. 51; DW, TL, p. 191.) Example: "That nigger, Joe Farmer, boy, he's something else! Sleeping white with a white bitch and driving a white-on-white Cadillac." SCU, YCU.

Whites n. (1970s–1990s) the amphetamine sulfate known as benzedrine in white tablet form. (EF, RDSL, p. 260; CS, vol. 3, no. 2, p. 51; RRL, DAZ, p. 243.) DCU.

White shit n. (1950s–1960s) cocaine. (DG, CR, p. 47.) DCU.

White slave n. (1700s–1860s) a white person sold into slavery; a person believed to be at least in part of African descent and held in slavery in the American South during the years of the self-defeating institution; a person such as Peter McCutcheon, the model for Fanny Howe's novel *The White Slave*. (Fanny Howe, *The White Slave*, Avon, 1980, p. 311.) SU.

White stone(s) n. (1940s–1950s) a fake diamond, especially one used in a street "hype" or con game. (IS, TB, p. 312.) SCU, PU.

White trash n. (1780s–1990s) a poor, immoral, uneducated white person, originally of the Deep South; lower-class white person with questionable morals and ethics; white prostitute, bum, whore, etc. (AB, DSJC, p. 400; WF, DAS, p. 577.) See "Cracker," and "Peckerwood."

Whitey n. (1960s–1970s) the white man; any American of European descent; a caucasian. Most often mildly pejorative. (WF, DAS, p. 711; DC, BJ, p. 86; CS, vol. 3, no. 2, p. 51; Julius Lester, *Look Out, Whitey! Black Power's Gon' Get Your Mama*, Dial, 1968.) YCU, SCU.

Whole lot of shit n. (1960s–1970s) confusion; disturbance; disorder; problems. (DR, BASL, p. 122.) SCU.

Whole wheat [bread] n. (1970s–1990s) a light-brown-skinned African-American. (EF, RDSL, p. 260.) SCU, YCU.

Whoopee mama n. (1920s) headstrong young woman. (SBF, IHAT, p. 309.) See "Flapper."

Whoopi Goldberg Caryn Johnson, actress, comedian.

Whore [ho] n. (1940s–1990s) a prostitute. (RDA, DDJ, p. 268.) PPU, SCU.

Whore boots n. (1970s–1990s) very tall, tightly fitting, high-heel leather boots. (EF, BVV, p. 53.) SCU.

Whore-chaser n. (1950s–1960s) any man who prides himself on sexual conquest and is addicted to sex with prostitutes or other women. (CS, vol. 3, no. 2, p. 51.

Whorehouse-girl [-chick; -woman; -broad] n. (1940s–1990s) a prostitute who is part of a stable located in one house or apartment;

a prostitute who does not work on the street. (CRM, BP, p. 247.) PPU.

Whore scars n. (1940s–1960s) needle-marks on the skin. (FR.) See "Tracks."

Whore strip n. (1980s–1990s) city block where prostitutes parade. (FR.) New Jersey use, New York use, SCU, NCU.

Who would've thunk it? (1960s–1970s) a variant of "Who would have thought it"; expression of bewilderment. (FR.) SCU, SNCU.

Wicked adj. (1970s) superb; wonderful; intense. (EF, RDSL, p. 260.) SCU, YCU.

Wienie n. (1900s–1950s) a small boy's penis. (FR.) SU.

Wife n. (1940s–1990s) a pimp's main or most trusted prostitute. (SH, GL, p. 213.) PPU.

Wife n. (1900s–1950s) a man's term for his commonlaw wife. (FR.) SNU.

Wife-in-law n. (1940s–1990s) in the family network of a pimp's stable of women, the name "wife-in-law" identifies the relationship of each woman to the main ("bottom") woman, also called a "wife." (DW, TL, pp. 191–192; SH, GL, p. 213.) PPU.

Wig n. (1930s–1960s) a man or woman's natural hair that has been processed or straightened; one's mentality, brain, skull, thoughts. (DC, BJ, p. 87; WF, DAS, p. 579; CW, TW, un-numbered first page.) SNU.

Wig n. (1930s–1950s) in the jazz world, a highly respected musician, respected because he or she "wigs" people out—reaching them on a mental level and causing reflection, rather than exciting them to dance. (BH, LSB, p. 221; WF, DAS, p. 579; RSG, JT, p. 303; DB, OHHJ, p. 150.) JMFU.

Wig [one] out; wigged [one] out (1950s–1960s) in jazz, to excite or thrill; respond with great enthusiasm; used also in the same way in street culture—to delight, etc. (WF, DAS, p. 711; DW, TL, p. 192) Example: "Man, Bags [Milt Jackson] really wigs me out when he starts tapping that vibraphone like he's making tender love to it." JMFU, SCU.

Wigged out adj. (1950s–1960s) to be extremely high on narcotics. (WF, DAS, p. 711; RRL, DAZ, p. 244.) See "Twisted."

Wigger n. (1990s) derived from a combination of "white" and "nigger"; refers to a young white person who affects the manners and speech associated with stock black street culture. (*American Heritage Dictionary of the English Language*, 1992.) See "Yo-boy," and "Wannabe."

Wigging v. (1940s–1950s) in jazz, playing unusually innovative music; talking strangely or doing something considered "weird." (FR.) SCU, YCU.

Wigglers n. (1940s) fingers. (DB, OHHJ, p. 150.) SNU.

Wiggy adj. (1930s–1950s) pleasing, especially when referring to a condition; "far out"; or "hip." (RSG, JT, p. 305.) SCU, JMFU.

Wig-head n. (1930s–1950s) derogatory term for an intellectual; the mind. (DB, OHHJ, p. 150.) SCU, YCU, SNU.

Wild adj. (1940s–1990s) anything intensely pleasurable; of great satisfaction; out of the ordinary; "strange"; in the nineties, extreme. (RSG, JT, p. 305; JH, PBL, p. 86.) SCU, JMFU.

[The] Wild thing n. (1990s) sex. (FR.) SCU, YCU.

Willie The Lion pianist and composer William Henry Joseph Berthol Bonaparte Berlholoff Smith, born 1897 in Goshen, N.Y.

Windbags n. (1830s–1940s) one's lungs. (DB, OHHJ, p. 150.) SNU.

Wind in his jaws adj. (1950s–1960s) to be very angry. (DC, BJ, p. 87.) Example: "Do you know Ron got wind in his jaws about that little incident, and we were just kidding him."

Winding boy [or man] (1920s–1930s) a young man who is well known and popular among women as a sexual partner; to "grind" expertly. (AL, MJR, p. 44; WF, DAS, p. 581.) SU. See "Grind [on]; (grinding)."

Wind pumps n. (1930s–1940s) one's lungs. (DB, OHHJ, p. 150.) SNU.

Wine n. (1950s–1960s) money in cash; paper money. (JH, PBL, p. 86.) Rare. New York use, SCU.

Wine-spoodee-o-dee (1930s–1960s) an expression of the joy of drinking wine; drinking wine; wine. (Hear Lightnin' Hopkins, "Wine-Spodee-o-Dee," *Blues in My Bottle*, Prestige, 1990.) SU, JMFU, SNU.

Wing it v. (1950s–1960s) in jazz, to improvise; in street culture, to pretend to understand; to leave; depart. (WF, DAS, p. 711.) SCU, YCU.

[To throw a] Wingding (1950s–1960s) pretend severe withdrawl pain in order to get a doctor to inject one with heroin. (RRL, DAZ, p. 244.) Example: "I got this doctor down at St. Vincent's I can throw a wingding on every time I can't get some smack on the street." DCU.

Wino n. (1930s–1990s) one who drinks wine, or any alcoholic beverage, to excess, especially a person who lives on the street and exists mainly for the next drink; a person addicted to drinking; picked up from "hobo" use. (WF, DAS, p. 582.) SNU.

Wipe(d) out adj., v. (1940s–1960s) drunk or exhausted; to astonish beyond expectation. (RHdeC, NB, p. 38.) SCU.

Wipe(d) out v. (1960s–1970s) to "defeat" in a "blowing" or playing competition. (RSG, JT, p. 305.) See "Wear [the other band] out."

Wire n. (1940s) the grapevine or community gossip or rumor mill. (DW, TL, p. 192; IS, PSML, p. 317.) SU, SNU.

[To be] Wired adj. (1980s–1990s) to be very high or drugs or alcohol; uncontrollable excitement. (EF, BVV, p. 53.) SCU. See "Wired-up."

Wired-up adj. (1970s–1990s) extremely high or excited; thrilled. (EF, RDSL, p. 260.) DCU, SCU.

Wise v. (1950s–1990s) understanding; intelligence; agreement; approval. (DC, BJ, p. 87.) SCU, YCU.

Wise up v. (1970s–1990s) to become aware. (FR.) SCU, YCU.

Wishbone n. (1880s–1940s) a forked chickenbone held and broken by two persons making a silent wish; the one who breaks off the larger portion will have his wish fulfilled. (FR.) SU.

Witch n. (1780s–1990s) derogatory term for a disagreeable woman. (FR.) SU, SNU.

[To be] With it (1650s–1990s) to be *a la* [Mandingo]; to have rapport with whatever is happening; in the 1990s, to be in agreement; in harmony with what is happening or going on; in jazz, since the

1940s, to be in rhythm, in harmony with music and life. (HV, AHAE, p. 138; RSG, JT, p. 305; DC, BJ, p. 87.) Example: "I wasn't with it the last time you saw me but I got my horn out of hock, so look out—I'm ready!" SU, SNU, JMFU.

[Fucked] With no vaseline (1990s) to be misused or abused in an extremely harsh way; not used in reference to sex. (FR.) YCU, SCU.

Wolf n. (1930s–1950s) an extremely aggressive male who is constantly attempting to seduce women; male on the make. (DB, OHHJ, p. 150.) SNU. See "Wolverine."

Wolf ticket; woolfing ticket (1950s–1960s) an invitation to fight with fists or weapons or both. (HLF, RJPD, p. 172.) SCU, YCU. See "Woofing."

Wollie n. (1980s–1990s) crack cocaine or base cocaine wrapped in a cigar leaf. (TW, CK, p. 138.) DCU.

Wolverine n. (1930s–1950s) a female flirt. (DB, OHHJ, p. 150.) Rare. SNU. See "Wolf."

Womanish n. (1900s–1940s) said of a female child acting like an adult. (FR.) SU, SNU.

Won't quit [or stop] (1960s–1970s) outstanding; great; truly beautiful; wonderful. (RSG, JT, p. 306.) Example: "James and Trey came in here together, not paying attention, and they both fell out when they saw Karen in a dress that wouldn't quit." YCU, SCU.

Woodpile; wood-pile n. (1930s–1940s) in "real" jazz talk, either a vibraphone, vibrasharp or xylophone with wooden keys or a marimba. The term went out of fashion once metal keys in the mid-forties replaced the wooden ones on these instruments. (SL, RJON, p. 150; WF, DAS, p. 586; RSG, JT, p. 306.) JMFU.

Wood-shed; woodshedding v., n. (1930s–1970s) in jazz, when a musician practices his instrument in private. In rural America the woodshed was often thought of as a perfect place for a moment of solitude away from the rest of the family; a place where one could think without interruption. (SL, RJON, p. 586; WF, DAS, p. 586; RSG, JT, p. 306.) JMFU.

Woofing; wolfing v. (1920s–1990s) aimless talking; flirting; forceful talk; meaningless talk; to bluff; bullying; threatening to fight; in the eighties and nineties, bluffing or intimidating someone. (ZNH,

MM, pp. 30, 305; AM, p. 96; RDA, TB, p. 19; KCJ, JS, p. 136; EF, RDSL, p. 260; DC, BJ, p. 87; HLF, RJPD, p. 172.) Examples: "He's just woofing, man—go on back in there. He don't own the place," and "I don't know what kind of luck you've had with other women but you won't get anywhere with me by woofing, because I don't like to be hustled." SCU, YCU, SNCU. See "Wolf ticket," "wolf," and "Hype."

Woolah n. (TW, CH, p. 152.) See "Wollie."

Word interj. (1950s–1990s) affirmation spoken in agreement; the truth; street culture gospel. (TW, CK, p. 138.) Example: "Word! I was there, I saw it with my own eyes." SCU, PPU, YCU, DCU.

Word up! interj. (1980s–1990s) call for attention; used as an expression of one's word of honor. (WKB, JMC, PS, p. 51.) Example: "Word up, the cops are down there right now busting Rickie." SCU.

[To] Work v. (1940s–1990s) to submit to sexual acts in exchange for money. (SH, GL, p. 213.) PPU.

Work v. (1960s–1970s) to administer a beating; to beat up someone. (DR, BASL, p. 164.) Philadelphia use, SCU.

Work [out] v. (1940s–1950s) sexual activity; in the fifties, in jazz, to play with great energy. (RSG, JT, pp. 306–307; WF, DAS, p. 711.) JMFU, SU, SNU, SCU. See "Trim."

Working girl [working woman; working broad; working chick] n. (1940s–1990s) a prostitute. (CRM, BP, p. 310; WF, DAS, p. 711; CS, vol. 3, no. 2, pp. 51–52; SH, GL, p. 213.) PPU.

[What are you] Working out of (1990s) in other words, what is your point of view, explain yourself. (FR.) YCU.

Works n. (1950s–1990s) drug paraphernalia. (CLC, TS, p. 256; WF, DAS, p. 711; CS, vol. 3, no. 2, p. 52.) DCU. See "Outfit."

[To] Worm v. (1950s–1970s) to study. (FR.) Student use.

Worrying the line (1960s–1970s) in jazz, stretching out or twisting notes or syllables; playing "with pitch"; an essential aspect of the jazz or blues solo. (JEH, AAC, p. 194.) JMFU.

WPLJ n. (1970s–1990s) white port and lemon juice. (EF, RDSL, p. 259.) South-central Los Angeles use, SCU.

Wren n. (1930s–1940s) a young woman or girl; an especially attractive female. (DB, OHHJ, p. 150; CC, OMMM, NCCHD, p. 261.) SCU, YCU.

Wringing the dishrag (1930s–1950s) holding hands; a children's term used in reference to holding hands during the game "Nana, Thread Needle"; derived from a British game but changed by black children in the South and the Caribbean. (BJ, BLH, SD, p. 81.) SU.

Wringling and twisting (1930s–1940s) resisting or putting up with racial oppression; severe racial or cultural discrimination in housing and public places; the practice of racial segregation in the United States. (DB, OHHJ, p. 150.) Harlem use, SCU, YCU.

Writer n. (1920s–1930s) one who writes songs or music. (RSG, 308.) JMFU.

Wrong adj. (1950s) defective quality. (FR.) SU, MWU.

[The] Wrong riff n. (1930s–1940s) originally a jazz term but came into general black use in the forties; anything out of order; a mistake. (CC, OMMM, NCCHD, p. 261; RSG, JT, pp. 222–223, 308; DB, OHHJ, p. 150.) JMFU. See "Riff."

WuWu n. (1800–1920s) an evil spell. (FR.) North Carolina use.

Wyacoo n. (1700s–1990s) variant of *Yacub*, powerful chief [Mandingo]; *Yaqub* [Arabic] for Jacob. (HV, AHAE, p. 148.) SNU.

X n. (1620s–1990s) a name; a signature; the mark of a person who cannot write; in-the-absence-of-a-name; unknown identity; Malcolm X; the names of Black Muslims representing unknown African identities. (WF, DAS, p. 589.) SNU.

X n. (1990s) "black re–nominalization . . . ground zero of a virtual nation . . ." (Houston A. Baker, Jr., *Black Studies, Rap and the Academy*, 1993, p. 35.) SNU.

X'ed out adj. (1970s) something formerly important that is no longer significant. (FR.) NECU.

X-ing v. (Houston A. Baker, Jr., *Black Studies, Rap and the Academy*, 1993, p. 36.) See "X."

XKE n. (1980s–1990s) short for the Jaguar XKE automobile. (EF, RDSL, p. 260.) SNCU.

X-ray v. (1960s) to look at something or someone closely. (DC, BJ, p. 87.) Example: "You go down there and x-ray the happenings and report back to me. Okay?" Rare. MWU.

Xerox v. (1990s) copy; imitate. (FR.) YCU.

Yackety-yack n. (1630s–1990s) chatter; aimless talking; very likely from *yakula-yakula* (Bantu); "yack" meant a stupid person but in the early part of this century and later was used to refer to a stupid conversation. (HV, AHAE, p. 148; RCC, SOC, p. 17.) YCU, SCU, SNU.

Yacoo (yakoo) n. (1960s–1990s) very derogatory; a white American racist; a bigot who happens to be white. (EF, RDSL, p. 260; CS, vol. 3, no. 2, p. 52.) SCU, YCU, SNCU.

Yah n. (1630s–1990s) *ya* (Crebo); *yo* (Temne); yes; yes, indeed; a conclusive particle used at the end of a direct order or emphatic statement; common in West African languages, in the Caribbean and in the southern former slave states. (HV, AHAE, p. 148.) SU; SNU.

Yaffner n. (1880s–1930s) sneaky, untrustworthy person. (FR.) SU.

Yam n. (1850s–1920s) a West Indian black person. (AB, DSJC, p. 410.) Plantation slave; SU.

Yam v. (1640s–1940s) among the earliest slaves, to eat; from *nyam* (Serer); *nyama* (Fula); *djambi* (Vai); *name* (Sengal); *njam* (Gullah). Although "yam" seems to have first appeared in written form in America in 1676, it had been in use for some time before. According to Dan Burley it was still current in Harlem in the 1940s. (AH, AHAE, p. 148; AB, DSJC, p. 410; SBF, IHAT, p. 33; DB, OHHJ, p. 150.) Plantation slave; SU.

Yam n. (1640s–1990s) food; sweet potato, *nyambi* (Bantu). (HV, AHAE, p. 148; AB, DSJC, p. 410.) Plantation slave; SU, SNU.

Yap n. (1890s–1960s) white person; Kentucky word for "honkey." (CM, CW, Gayle Jones, "White Rat," p. 376.) Kentucky use.

[A] Yard n. (1950s–1960s) a hundred dollars in cash. (CS, vol. 3, no. 2, p. 52.) Watts and South-central Los Angeles; DCU, SCU, YCU.

[Playing in somebody else's] Yard v. (1950s–1960s) adulterous sexual relations; illicit sex. (CLC, TS, p. 256.) Example: "He playing in his best friend's yard and it just might get him killed if he ain't careful." SNU.

Yard Negro n. (1860s–1960s) Uncle Tom. (FR.) SU, SNU.

Yardbird Charlie Parker or Charles Christopher Parker, Jr., alto saxophonist; born in Kansas City, Kansas, August 29, 1920, and died in New York City, March 12, 1955; see "Bird."

Yard dog n. (1930s–1940s) a dumb person; one easily misled. (DB, OHHJ, p. 150; CC, OMMM, NCCHD, p. 261.) Harlem; SNU.

Yea big adj. (1960s) expression indicating a small amount, usually demonstrated by bringing the index finger and the thumb so close together that they nearly touch. (DC, BJ, p. 87.) SNU.

Yeah n. (1620s–1990s) yes; an exclamation expressing approval. (DB, OHHJ, p. 150; CC, OMMM, NCCHD, p. 261.) SNU.

Yeah, boy interj. (1990s) an affirmation, spoken in agreement.

Yeasting v., adj. (1940s–1960s) to exaggerate; yeast is what makes bread rise. (IS, PSML, p. 317.) SCU, PPU, PU, DCU.

Yellow [person] adj. (1930s–1950s) light skin; describes a mulatto. (EF, RDSL, p. 260.) SNU. See "Bright."

Yellow-ass [person] adj. (1930s–1950s) light skin; describes a mulatto. (EF, RDSL, p. 260.) SNU. See "Bright."

Yellow eye n. (1920s–1940s) an egg—from the appearance of the yellow yoke in the center of a white oval space. (DB, OHHJ, p. 150.) Example: "No yellow eyes for me this morning, just a bowl of corn flakes." Harlem; SNU.

Yellow girl [boy] n. (1860s–1950s) a light-skinned male or female. (FR.) SNU. See "Bright" and "Yellow."

Yellow jacket(s) n. (1950s–1990s) Nembutal; a yellow capsule containing pentobarbital sodium; a depressant drug. (IS, PSML, p. 317; EF, RDSL, p. 260; CS, vol. 3, no. 2, p. 52; RRL, DAZ, p. 246.) DCU.

Yellows n. (CS, vol. 3, no. 2, p. 52.) See "Yellow jacket(s)."

Yen n. (1880s–1960s) the gut-grinding hunger a heroin addict feels when he or she needs a "fix"; a strong need for drugs; craving. (CS, vol. 3, no. 52; RRL, DAZ, p. 246.) DCU.

Yen hok n. (1880s–1960s) a needle used in the preparation of a pipe of opium for smoking. (CS, vol. 3, no. 2, p. 52.) DCU.

Yenning v. See "Yen."

Yen she n. (1950s–1960s) whiskey and opium ashes mixed. (CS, vol. 3, no. 2, p. 52.) DCU.

Yo n. (1980s–1990s) term of address; yes or hello; often used in response to a verbal address; a greeting. (TW, CH, p. 152.) YCU, SCU, SNU.

Yo Boy n. (1990s) term used to refer to a young white person who affects the manners and speech associated with black street culture, often in the belief that this mannerism represents the single true black identity as if there were only one. (FR.) YCU, SCU.

Yoke n. (1940s) the type of large collar on a formal dress shirt worn by a "hipcat" or a "jutterbug." (DB, OHHJ, p. 150.) Harlem; SCU, YCU.

Yo mama! [yo mammy!] exclam. (1880s–1950s) an insult used in the "dozens." (SNH, AM, p. 94.) SNU.

Yola n. (1900s–1940s) a light-complexioned young woman; mulatto. (MHB, JS, np.) SU.

You ain't saying nothing (1960s) a statement meant to tell someone that their opinion is of little or no importance. (DC, BJ, p. 87.) SNU.

You all [y'all; you-uns] n. (1660s–1990s) each of you; all of you; one and all; form, wedded with Spanish and French forms, very likely has African origins: *yow, yeen, yena* (Wolof); common form of address to a group in various parts of Africa from which slaves were sold or Africans captured and forced into slavery. (HV, AHAE, p. 149.) SU, SNU.

You better know it n. (1960s) an affirmation that what is being said is true. (DC, BJ, p. 87.) SNU, SCU, YCU.

You can say that again n. (1930s–1990s) an expression of affirmation; agreement or approval. (MHB, JS, np.) SNU.

You got it n. (1960s) indicates that nothing new has occurred. (DC, BJ, p. 87.) Example: question, "What's happening?"; answer, "You got it." SNU, SCU, YCU.

You know interj. (1900s–1990s) a questionlike interjection after a phrase or sentence. (FR.) SNU.

Younder adj. (1630s–1950s) in the distance. (FR.) SU.

Young bantam n. (1880s–1940s) a very young girl. (DB, OHHJ, p. 150.) SNU.

Young blood (youngblood) n. (1900s–1990s) usually a male-to-male term; an older black person's term for a younger black person. (EF, RDSL, p. 260.) SNU. See "Blood" and "Blood brother."

Young in the head adj. (1860s–1980s) a physically mature person whose behavior is still childish because of personality or retardation. (EF, RDSL, p. 260.) SNU.

[Go on with] Your bad self (1950s–1970s) a compliment; addressed to one who has accomplished a remarkable act or piece of work. "Bad," of course, means good. (FR.) See "Bad."

Your thing n. (1950s–1960s) one's own business; one's concerns; one's personality; one's manner of being. (CS, vol. 3, no. 2, p. 52.) SCU, YCU, SNCU.

Your own thing n. See "Thing."

You Sue n. (1840s–1860s) voodoo saint; early Africans in America found a similar figure in St. Anthony. (JEH, AAC, p. 54.) New Orleans; SU.

Young suit n. (1930s–1940s) an ill-fitting suit, especially one too small. (ZNH, AM, p. 96.) Example: "Hey, Terry, that young suit you wearing—your little brother's suit?" SNU.

You the man (1900s–1990s) a phrase or response meaning "you're in charge," "whatever you say goes," et cetera. This expression has changed in the ninety years or so that it has been popular in black informal speech. Originally a woman's line addressed to a man, usually her husband or lover, about half the time used ironically. In the thirties, black men used it ironically in addressing white men—and in some cases black men—who happened to be their bosses. In the eighties young black men began using it as an ironic compliment. (FR.) SNU.

Yo yo n. (1930s–1960s) a dumb person; victim of routine; someone who is manipulated. (FR.) SNU.

Zanzy adj. (1940s–1950s) from "Zanzibar"; the real thing; authentic thing; good-looking—especially applied to an attractive young woman; flashy; excellent. (DW, TL, p. 192; RSG, JT, p. 311.) JMFU, SNCU. See "Foxy" and "Zoot."

Zap v. (1950s–1990s) to move quickly; to strike; probably picked up from military use. (WF, DAS, p. 712.) SCU.

Zar n. (1900s–1940s) a faraway, damnable place. (SK, PC, pp. 153–154.) See "Ginny Gall" and "West Hell."

Zazzle n. (1930s–1960s) sexual desire; sexy; sexually attractive; exaggerated sensuousness; "original Negro use." (WF, DAS, p. 594.) YCU, SCU, SNCU. See "Zazzy."

Zazzy adj. (1930s–1960s) erotic attractiveness; sensuousness. (WF, DAS, p. 594.) YCU, SCU, SNCU.

Ziggaboo (Ziggerboo) n. (1700s–1940s) a very dark-skinned person; a Negro; an African-American; black person. (HV, AHAE, p. 149 ZNH, AM, p. 96.) SU.

Ziggerboo (Ziggaboo) n. (1930s–1940s) a crazy person. (MHB, JS, np.) Rare. SU.

Z'ing v. (1960s) sleeping. (DC, BJ, p. 87.) SNU.

Zip Coon n. (1980s) variant of "Uncle Tom." (Stanley Crouch, *Notes of a Hanging Judge*, 1990. p. 203.) Rare. SNU.

Zombie n. (1630s–1940s) in the Voodoo (Kongo/Bantu) religion, a deity; *Nzambi* (Tshiluba); *zombi* (Haitian French); *jombi* (Sierra Leone); *jumbi* (Cameroon); *zombie* (Jamaica/Guyana); God; deity;

spirit; ghost; supernatural presence, especially one that can raise the dead; dark-skinned black person; snake deity. Sensationalized in the press after the Civil War, the idea of zombies and other other aspects of voodoo caused a great deal of confusion and misunderstanding about the practice. (HV, AHAE, p. 149; SBF, IHAT, pp. 377–378.) SNU.

Zombie n. (1940s–1950s) a weird or strange-looking man or woman; from original "zombie"; some limited black use. (WF, DAS, p. 594.) YCU.

Zone out v. (1990s) to nod or doze, usually from a drug high; or to sit or lie around half awake. Examples: "The guy zones out too often to be driving a car"; and, "I was zoning out on some TV all afternoon." DCU.

Zonked adj. (1950s–1970s) intoxicated; drunk; stoned; a hallucinogenic high; may have been picked up from comic strip onomatopoeic use. (RR1, DAZ, p. 247; RSG, JT, p. 311; CS, vol. 3, no. 2, p. 52; WF, DAS, p. 712.) JMFU, SCU, YCU, DCU. See "Juiced" and "Stoned."

Zoom v. (1930s–1940s) to obtain something without paying for it; to sneak (without paying) into a public place (like a theater) where admission is charged. (DB, OHHJ, p. 150.) NCU, YCU, SCU.

Zoom; zooming v. (1970s) to deceive; betray; kid. (Hear Aretha Franklin, "Who's Zoomin' Who?") SCU, YCU. See "Zoom [one] out."

Zoom [one] out v. (1970s–1980s) to overwhelm someone by wolfing at or by praising them; gaining control of someone's mind. (EF, RDSL, p. 260.) SNCU.

Zoot interj. (1930s–1940s) usually a shouted expression of support; agreement; notice or recognition; encouragement or satisfaction. (SL, RJON, p. 150.)

Zoot adj. (1930s–1940s) to exaggerate; to overdress, especially in a flashy manner. (CC, OMM, NCCHD, p. 261.) JMFU; YCU; SCU.

Zooted up adj. (1980s–1990s) to be intoxicated from smoking or inhaling cocaine. (TW, CK, p. 138.) DCU. See "Skied."

Zoot suit (zoot soot) n. (1930s–1940s) a fashionable and flashy or extreme style in clothing with lots of drape shape to the jacket and pants. Zoot suits have huge padded shoulders, zippered narrow cuffs, very fancy lapels, and they expand at the knees; "reet," sharp pleats;

Harlem and other northern city ghetto fashion. Term originally of jazz origin. (ZNH, AM, p. 96; RSG, JT, p. 312.) SNCU. See "Zooty."

Zoot suit action n. (1930s–1940s) the competitive game of one zoot suit wearer trying to outdress the next zoot-decked person. (DB, OHHJ, p. 150.) NCU, YCU, SCU.

Zoot suiter n. (1930s–1940s) a flashy, silly, or arrogant young man, especially one who wears flashy, colorful clothes. (WF, DAS, p. 595.) NCU, YCU, SCU.

Zooty adj. (1920s–1930s) stylish; from New Orleans patois meaning "cute" (Zutty Singleton); to be well-dressed; dressed in an attractive manner; probably the origins of the term "zoot suit." (MM, RB, p. 311, 376; RSG, JT, p. 311.) New Orleans use.

Zutty Arthur James Singleton, drummer; born May 14, 1898, in Bunkie, Louisiana; worked with Louis Armstrong's Hot Five, with Jelly Roll Morton, Sidney Bechet, Lionel Hampton, et al.

BIBLIOGRAPHY

Abrahams, Roger D. *Deep Down in the Jungle: Negro Narrative Folklore from the Streets of Philadelphia*. Roger Abrahams. Hatboro, Penn.: Folklore Associates, 1964, 1970.

———. *Postively Black*. Englewood Cliffs, N.J.: Prentice-Hall, 1970.

———. *Talking Black*. Rowley, Mass.: Neubury House Publishers, Inc., 1976.

Albertson, Chris. *Bessie*. New York: Stein and Day, 1972.

Alexander, Adele Logan. *Ambiguous Lines: Free Women of Color in Rural Georgia 1759–1879*, Fayetteville: the University of Arkansas Press, 1991.

Allen, Samuel W. [Paul Vesey, pseud.] *Elfenbein Zahne (Ivory Tusks)*. Heidelberg, Germany: Wolfgang Rothe, 1956.

———. *Ivory Tusks and Other Poems*. New York: Poets Press, 1968.

———. *Paul Vesey's Ledger*. London: Paul Breman, 1975.

Allen, William Francis, Charles Pickard Ware, and Lucy McKim Garrison. *Slave Songs of the United States, 1867*. New York: Oak Publications, 1965.

Amini, Johari M. [a.k.a. Jewel C. Latimore]. *Images in Black*. Chicago: Third World Press, 1969.

———. *Let's Go Somewhere*. Chicago: Third World Press, 1970.

Andrews, Malachi, and Paul T. Owens. *Black Language*. Los Angeles: Seymour-Smith Publishers, 1973.

Andrews, William L. *Six Women's Slave Narratives*. New York: Oxford University Press (The Schomburg Library of Nineteenth-Century Black Women Writers), 1988.

Ansa, Tina McElray. *Ugly Ways*, New York: Harcourt Brace and Jovanovich, 1993.

Armstrong, Louis. *Satchmo: My Life in New Orleans*. Englewood Cliffs, N.J.: Prentice-Hall, 1954.

BIBLIOGRAPHY

Armstrong, Orlando Kay. *Old Massa's People: The Old Slaves Tell Their Story*, Indianapolis, Ind.: Bobbs-Merrill Co., 1931.

Asch, Moses, and Alan Lomaz. *The Leadbelly Songbooks*. New York: Oak Publications, 1962.

Austin, Doris Jean. *After the Garden*. New York: New American Library, 1987.

Baker, Houston A., Jr., *A Many-Colored Coat of Dreams: The Poetry of Countee Cullen*. Detroit: Broadside Press, 1974.

Bambara, Toni Cade. *The Black Woman: An Anthology*. New York: New American Library, 1970.

———. *Tales and Stories for Black Folks*. New York: Doubleday, 1971.

———. *Gorilla, My Love*. New York: Bantam, 1972; New York: Vintage, 1981.

Banks, C. Tillery. *Hello to Me with Love: Poems of Self-Discovery*. William Morrow, 1980.

Baraka, Amiri, and Amina Baraka. *Confirmation: An Anthology of African American Women*. Newark: Quill, 1983.

Baraka, Imamu [a.k.a. LeRoi Jones]. *Spirit Reach*. Jihad, 1972.

———. *In the Tradition (For Black Authur Blythe)*. Jihad, 1980.

———. *Reggae or Not: Poems*. Contact II Publications, 1981.

Barerer, Albert, and Charles G. Leland, eds. *A Dictionary of Slang, Jargon and Cant*. London: Ballantyne, 1890.

Barksdale, Richard, and Keneth Kinnamon. *Black Writers of America: A Comprehensive Anthology*. New York: Macmillan, 1972.

Barrax, Gerald. *Another Kind of Rain: Poems*. Pittsburgh: University of Pittsburgh Press, 1970.

———. *An Audience of One*. Athens: University of Georgia Press, 1980.

Barthelemy, Anthony G. *Collected Black Women's Narratives*. New York: Oxford University Press (The Schomburg Library of Nineteenth-Century Black Women Writers), 1988.

Bartlett, John. *The Dictionary of Americanism*, New York: Crescent, 1989. (Originally published in 1849.)

Bayliss, John F., ed. *Black Slave Narratives*. New York: Collier, 1970. Reprinted by permission of Macmillan Publishing Co.

Beam, Joseph. *In the Life: A Black Gay Anthology*. Boston: Alyson, 1986.

Bechet, Sidney. *Treat It Gently*. New York: Hill and Wang, 1960.

Beck, Robert [Iceberg Slim, pseud.] *Pimp: The Story of My Life*. Los Angeles: Holloway House, 1969.

———. *Mama Black Widow*. Los Angeles: Holloway House, 1969.

———. *Trick Baby*. Los Angeles: Holloway House, 1969.

Bell, Bernard W. *Modern and Contemporary Afro-American Poetry*. Allyn and Bacon, 1972.

Bentley, Robert H., and Samuel D. Crawford. *Black Language Reader*. Glenview, Ill.: Scott, Foresman and Co., 1973.

Blassingame, John W. *The Slave Community*. New York: Oxford University Press, 1972.

Bluestin, Gene. *The Voice of the Folk*. Amherst: University of Massachusetts Press, 1972.

Bontemps, Arna. *American Negro Poetry*. New York: Hill and Wang, 1963.

———. *Personals*. Paul Breman, 1963.

———. *Great Slave Narratives*. Boston: Beacon Press, 1969.

———. *Hold Fast to Dreams: Poems Old and New*. Follet, 1969.

Botkin, B. A., ed. *Lay My Burden Down*. Chicago: University of Chicago Press, 1945, 1965.

———. *A Treasury of Southern Folklore*. New York: Crown, 1949.

———. *A Treasury of Mississippi River Folklore*. New York: Crown, 1955.

Boulware, Marcus H., ed. *Jive and Slang*. Hampton, Va.: M. Boulare, 1947.

Brasch, Lla, and Walter Brasch. *A Complete Annotated Bibliography of American Black English*. Baton Rogue: Louisiana State University Press, 1974.

Brasch, Walter M. *Black English and the Mass Media*. Amherst: University of Massachusetts Press, 1981.

Brawley, Benjamine, ed. *Early Negro American Writers*. New York: Dover, 1970 (Originally published in 1935).

Brewer, J. Mason. *The World on the Brazos: Negro Preacher Tales from the Brazos Bottoms of Texas*. Austin: University of Texas Press, 1953.

———. *American Negro Folklore*. Chicago: Quadrangle Books, 1968.

———. *American Negro Folklore*. Chicago: Quadrangle Books, 1972.

Brooks, Gwendolyn. *Blacks*. David, 1987.

———. *Jump Bad, A New Chicago Anthology*. Detroit: Broadside Press, 1971.

———. *A Broadside Treasury, 1965–1970*. Detroit: Broadside Press, 1971.

———. *The World of Gwendolyn Brooks*. New York: Harper and Row, 1971.

———. *Blacks/Gwendolyn Brooks*. David, 1987.

———. *Gottschalk and the Grande Tarantelle/Gwendolyn Brooks*. David, 1988.

———. *Winnie*. David, 1988.

Broonzy, William, and Yannick Bruynoghe. *Big Bill Blues*. London: Cassell, 1955.

Brown, Cecil. *The Life and Loves of Mr. Jiveass Nigger*. New York: Farrar, Straus & Giroux, 1969.

———. *Coming Up Down Home*. Hopewell, NJ: The Ecco Press, 1993.

Brown, Claude. *Manchild in the Promised Land*. New York: Macmillan, 1965.

Brown, Sterling A. *Southern Road*. New York: Harcourt, 1932.

———. *The Last Ride of Wild Bill, and Eleven Narrative Poems*. Broadside Press, 1975.

Brown, Sterling A., Arthur P. Davis, and Ulysses Lee, eds. *The Negro Caravan*. New York: Dryden Press, 1941; New York: Arno, 1969.

Brown, William Wells. *Clotelle: Or, The President's Daughter: A Narrative of Slave Life in The United States*. New York: Carol Publishing Group, 1969. (Originally published in 1853.)

———. *My Southern Home: Or, The South and Its People*. Boston: A. G. Brown and Co., 1880.

———. *Clotelle: Or, The Colored Heroine, a Tale of the Southern States*, 1867. Miami: Mnemosyne Publishing Co., 1969.

Buerkle, Jack Vincent, and Danny Barker. *Bourbon Street Black*. New York: Oxford University Press, 1973.

Burley, Dan. *Dan Burley's Original Handbook of Harlem Jive*. Introduction by Earl Conrad. Published by Dan Burley. Copyright 1944 by Dan Burley.

———. *Diggeth Thou?* Chicago: Burley, Cross, 1959.

Cain, George. *Blueschild Baby*. New York: McGraw-Hill, 1971.

Calloway, Cab. *Hi De Ho*. New York: Mills, n.d.

———. *The New Cab Calloway's Hepsters Dictionary: Language of Jive*. New York: C. Calloway, 1944.

Cartiér, Xarm, *Muse-Echo Blues*. New York: Harmony Books, 1991.

Cassidy, Frederic G. *Dictionary of American Regional English*. Vols. I and II. Cambridge: Harvard University Press, 1985, 1991.

Chapman, Abraham. *Black Voices: An Anthology of Afro-American Literature*. New York: New American Library, 1968.

———. *Steal Away: Stories of the Runaway Slaves*. New York: Preager, 1971.

———. *New Black Voices: An Anthology of Contemporary Afro-American Literature*. New York: New American Library, 1972.

Chapman, Robert L. *Thesaurus of American Slang*. New York: Harper and Row, 1989.

Charters, Samuel B. *The Country Blues*. New York: Rinehart and Co., 1959.

———. *The Poetry of the Blues*. New York: Oak Publications, 1963.

———. *The Poetry of the Blues*. New York: Avon Books, 1970.

———. *The Bluesmen: The Story and the Music of the Men Who Made the Blues*. New York: Oak Publications, 1967.

———. *The Country Blues*. New York: Rinehart and Co., 1959.

Chestnutt, Charles Waddell. *The Conjure Woman*. Boston: Houghton Mifflin, Co., 1899.

———. *The Marrow of Tradition*. Boston: Houghton Mifflin, Co., 1901.

———. *The House Behind the Cedars*. Ridgewood, N.J.: Gregg Press, 1901.

———. *The Colonel's Dream*. New York: Doubleday, Page, 1905.

Claerbaut, David. *Black Jargon in White America*. Grand Rapids, Mich: William B. Ferdmans Publishing Co., 1972.

Clarke, John H. *American Negro Short Stories*. New York: Hill and Wang, 1966.

Clayton, Ronnie W. *Mother Wit: The Ex-Slave Narrative of the Louisiana Writers' Project*. Lawrence: University of Kansas, 1990.

Cliff, Michelle. *Bodies of Water*. New York: Dutton, 1990.

———. *Free Enterprise*. New York: Dutton, 1993.

Clifton, Lucille. *Good Times*. New York: Random House, 1969.

———. *Good News About the Earth*. New York: Random House, 1972.

———. *An Ordinary Woman*. New York: Random House, 1974.

———. *Two-Headed Woman*. Amherst: University of Massachusetts Press, 1980.

———. *Next: New Poems*. New York: BOA Editions, 1987.

———. *Good Woman: Poems and a Memoir, 1969–1980*. New York: BOA Editions, 1987.

Coleman, Wanda. *Mad Dog Black Lady*. Santa Rosa, CA: Black Sparrow Press, 1979.

Colter, Cyrus. *Night Studies*. Chicago: The Swallow Press, Inc., 1979.

———. *Heavy Daughter Blues*. Santa Rosa, CA: Black Sparrow Press, 1987.

Cone, James H. *The Spirituals and the Blues*. New York: Seabury Press, 1972.

Cook, Bruce. *Listen to the Blues*. New York: Charles Scribner's Sons, 1973.

Cooper, Helen. "Once Again, Ads Woo Teens with Slang," *The Wall Street Journal* (March 29, 1993), pp. B1, B8.

Cooper, J. California. *A Piece of Mine: Short Stories*. Navarro, CA: Wild Trees Press, 1984.

———. *Homemade Love*. New York: St. Martin's Press, 1987.

———. *Some Soul to Keep*. New York: St. Martin's Press, 1987.

———. *Family*. New York: Doubleday, 1991.

Corbin, Steven. *Fragments That Remain*. Boston: Alyson Publications, Inc., 1993.

———. *No Easy Place to Be*. New York: Simon and Schuster, 1989.

Cortez, Jayne. *Piss-stained Stairs and the Monkey Man's Wares*. Phrase Text, 1969.

———. *Scarifications*. New York: Bola Press, 1973, 1978.

———. *Mouth on Paper*. New York: Bola Press, 1977.

———. *Firespitter*. New York: Bola Press, 1982.

———. *Coagulations*. New York: Thunder's Mouth Press, 1984.

Costello, Mark and Wallace, and David Foster. *Signifying Rappers: Rap and Race in the Urban Present*. New York: Echo Press, 1990.

Courlander, Harold. *A Treasury of Afro-American Folklore: The Oral Literature, Traditions, Recollections, Legends, Tales, Songs, Religious Beliefs, Customs, Sayings and Humor of Peoples of African Descent in the Americas*. New York: Crown, 1976.

———. *Negro Folk Music*, New York: Columbia University Press, 1966. (First printed 1963.)

Cromwell, Otelia Lorenzo Turner, and Eva B. Dykes. *Readings from Negro Authors*. New York: Harcourt, 1931.

Cullen, Countee. *Color*. New York: Harper, 1925.

———. *The Ballad of the Brown Girl*. New York: Harper, 1927.

———. *Copper Sun*. New York: Harper, 1927.

———. *Caroling Dusk: An Anthology of Verse by Negro Poets*. New York: Harper, 1927.

———. *The Black Christ and Other Poems*. New York: Harper, 1929.

———. *One Way to Heaven*. New York: Harper, 1932.

———. *The Medea and Some Poems*. New York: Harper, 1935.

———. *The Lost Zoo*. New York: Harper, 1940.

———. *On These I Stand*. New York: Harper, 1947.

Cuney, Waring. *Puzzles*. Utrecht, Netherlands: Deroos, 1960.

———. *Storefront Church*. London: Paul Breman, 1973.

Dance, Daryl Cumber. *Shuckin' and Jiving': Folklore from Contemporary Black Americans*. Indianapolis: Indiana University Press, 1978.

Danner, Margaret. *Impressions of African Art Forms*. Detroit: Broadside Press, 1960.

———. *To Flower*. Hemphill Press, 1963.

———. *Iron Lace*. Kriya Press, 1968.

———. *Down of a Thistle.* Country Beautiful, 1976.

Davis, Arthur P., and Saunders Redding. *Cavalcade: Negro American Writing from 1760 to the Present.* Boston: Houghton Mifflin Co., 1971.

Davis, Arthur P., and Michael W. Peplow. *The New Negro Renaissance: An Anthology.* New York: Holt, Rinehart and Winston, 1975.

Davis, Miles, with Quincy Troupe. *Miles: The Autobiography.* New York: Simon and Schuster, 1989.

Davis, Thulani. *1959.* New York: Grove Weidenfeld, 1992.

———. *All the Renegade Ghosts Rise.* Middletown, Conn.: Anemone Press, 1978.

———. *Playing the Changes.* Middletown, Conn.: Wesleyan University Press, 1985.

deCoy, Robert H. *The Nigger Bible.* Los Angeles: Holloway House, 1967.

Derricote, Toi. *The Empress of the Death House.* Detroit: Lotus Press, 1978.

Dillard, J. L. *Black English: Its History and Usage in the United States.* New York: Random House, 1972.

———. *Black Names.* The Hague: Mouton, 1976.

———. *American Talk: Where Our Words Came From.* New York: Random House, 1976.

———. *Perspectives on Black English.* The Hague: Mouton and Co., 1975.

Dixon, Melvin. *Vanishing Rooms.* New York: Dutton, 1991.

Dixon, Robert, and John Godrich. *Recording the Blues.* New York: Stein and Day, 1970; *Recording the Blues* (CBS 52797).

Dodson, Owen. *Powerful Long Ladder.* Farrar, Straus and Giroux, 1946.

Dorson, Richard M. *American Negro Folktales.* Greenwich, Conn.: Fawcett Premier Book, 1967. (Reprint of the 1956, 1958 Indiana University Press edition.)

Dorson, Richard. *American Negro Folktales.* New York: Fawcett, 1967.

Douglass, Frederick, *Life and Times.* New York: Collier, 1962. (Originally published in 1881.)

———. *My Bondage and My Freedom.* New York: Arno Press and New York Times, 1969. (Originally published in 1855.)

———. *Narrative of the Life of Frederick Douglass, an American Slave.* New York: Signet, 1968. (Originally published in 1845.)

Dove, Rita. *Museum.* Pittsburgh: Carnegie-Mellon University Press, 1983.

———. *Thomas and Beulah.* Pittsburgh: Carnegie-Mellon University Press, 1986.

———. *Grace Notes.* New York: W. W. Norton, 1989.

———. *Through the Ivory Gate.* New York: Pantheon, 1992.

Dumas, Henry. *Play Ebony: Play Ivory*. Edited by Eugene B. Redmond. New York: Random House, 1975; originally published as *Poetry for my People*. Carbondale: Southern Illinois University Press, 1970.

———. *Ark of Bones, and Other Stories*. Southern Illinois University Press, 1974.

———. *Jonah and the Green Stone*. New York: Random House, 1976.

Dunbar, Paul Laurence. *Oak and Ivy*. Dayton, Ohio, 1893.

———. *Folks from Dixie*. New York: Dodd, Mead, and Co., 1898.

———. *The Sport of the Gods*. New York, 1902.

———. *Lyrics of the Lowly Life*. New York: Dodd, Mead, and Co., 1912.

———. *In Old Plantation Days*. New York: Dodd, Mead, and Co., 1903.

———. *The Heart of Happy Hollow*. New York: Dodd, Mead, and Co., 1904.

———. *The Sport of the Gods*. New York: Dodd, Mead, and Co., 1902, 1981; New York: Collier, 1970.

———. *The Complete Poems of Paul Laurence Dunbar*. New York: Dodd, Mead, and Co., 1913, 1980.

Dundes, Alan, ed. *Mother Wit from the Laughing Barrel*. Englewood Cliffs, N. J.: Prentice-Hall, 1973.

Duplechan, Larry. *Blackbird*. New York: St. Martin's Press, 1986.

Elder, Lonnie. *Ceremonies in Dark Old Men*. New York: Farrar, Straus and Giroux, 1965.

Ellison, Ralph. *Invisible Man*. New York: Random House, 1952.

Emanuel, James A., and Theodore Gross. *Dark Symphony: Negro Literature in America*. Free Press, 1968.

Emanuel, James A. *The Treehouse and Other Poems*. Detroit: Broadside Press, 1968.

Evans, David. *Tommy Johnson*. London: Studio Vista, 1967.

Evans, Mari. *Where Is All the Music?* London: Paul Breman, 1968.

———. *I am a Black Woman*. New York: William Morrow, 1970.

Exum, Pat Crutchfield. *Keeping the Faith: Writings by Contemporary Black American Women*. New York: Fawcett, 1974.

Faggett, Harry Lee, and Nick Aaron Ford. *Best Short Stories by Afro-American Writers (1925–1950)*. Meador, 1950; Krause Reprint, 1977.

Fahey, John. *Charley Patton*. London: Studio Vista, 1970.

Fair, Ronald. *Excerpts*. London: Paul Breman, 1975.

———. *Hog Butcher*. New York: Harcourt, 1966.

———. *We Can't Breathe*. New York: Harper and Row, 1972.

Farmer, John S., and W. E. Henley, eds. *A Dictionary of Slang and Colloquial English*. New York: Dutton, 1905, rev. 1921.

Fauset, Jessie R. *Comedy American Style*. New York: Frederick A. Stokes, 1933.

Ferris, William. *Blues from the Delta*. London: Studio Vista, 1970; *Blues from the Delta* (Matchbox SDN 226).

Fisher, Miles Mark. *Negro Slave Songs in the United States*. New York: Russel and Russel, 1968.

Fisher, Rudolph. *The Walls of Jericho*. New York: Alfred A. Knopf, 1928.

———. *The Conjure Man Dies*. New York: Covici, Friede, 1932.

Flowers, A. R. *De Mojo Blues*. New York: Dutton, 1985.

Flowers, Arthur. *Another Good Loving Blues*. New York: Viking, 1993.

Folb, Edith A. *A Comparative Study of Urban Black Argot*. Los Angeles: University of California at Los Angeles Occasional Papers in Linguistics, No. I, March 1972.

Ford, Nick Aaron. *Black Insights: Significant Literature by Black Americans, 1760 to the Present*. Ginn, 1971.

Forrest, Leon. *Divine Days*. Chicago: Another Chicago Press, 1992.

———. *The Bloodworth Orphans*. New York: Random House, 1977; rev. ed., Another Chicago Press, 1987.

———. *There Is a Tree More Ancient Than Eden*. New York: Random House, 1973; rev. ed., Another Chicago Press, 1988.

———. *Two Wings to Veil My Face*. New York: Random House, 1984.

Foster, Herbert Lawrence. "Dialect-Lexicon and Listening Comprehension." Dissertation, Columbia University, 1969.

———. *Ribbin', Jivin', and Playin' the Dozens: The Unrecognized Dilemma of Inner City Schools*. Cambridge, Mass.: Balinger Publishing Co., 1974.

Gaines, Ernest, J. *Bloodline*. New York: Dial Press, 1968.

———. *Catherine Carmier*. New York: Atheneum, 1964; Chatham, NJ: Chatham Booksellers, 1972; North Point Press, 1981.

———. *Of Love and Dust*. New York: Dial Press, 1967; New York: W. W. Norton, 1979.

———. *Bloodline*. New York: Dial Press, 1968; New York: W. W. Norton, 1976.

———. *The Autobiography of Miss Jane Pittman*. New York: Dial Press, 1971; New York: Doubleday, 1987.

———. *A Long Day in November*. New York: Dial Press, 1971.

———. *In My Father's House*. New York: Alfred A. Knopf, 1978; W. W. Norton, 1983.

———. *A Gathering of Old Men.* New York: Alfred A. Knopf, 1983.

Garland, Phyl. *The Sound of Soul.* New York: Pocket Books, 1971.

Garoin, Richard M., and Edmond G. Addeo. *The Midnight Special.* New York: Bernard Geis Associates, 1971.

Garon, Paul. *The Devil's Son-in-Law: The Story of Peetie Wheatstraw and His Songs.* London: Studio Vista, 1971.

Garren, Paul. *Blues and the Poetic Spirit.* London: Eddison Press, 1975.

Gert zur Heide, Karl. *Deep South Piano: The Story of Little Brother Montgomery.* London: Studio Vista, 1970.

Gibson, Donald B. *Black and White: Stories of American Life.* New York: Washington Square Press, 1971.

Giovanni, Nikki. *Black Judgement.* Detroit: Broadside Press, 1968.

———. *Black Feeling, Black Talk.* Detroit: Broadside Press, 1970.

Godfrey, Irwin, ed. *American Tramp and Underworld Slang.* New York: Sears, 1930.

Gold, Robert J. *Jazz Talk.* Indianapolis, Ind.: Bobbs-Merrill Co., 1975.

Gold, Robert S. *A Jazz Lexicon.* New York: Alfred A. Knopf, 1964.

Goldin, Hyman E., Frank O'Leary, and Morris Lipsius, eds. *Dictionary of American Underworld Lingo.* New York: Twayne, 1950.

Gonzales, Ambrose. *The Black Border.* Columbia, S.C.: The State Co., 1922.

Graham, Maryemma. *The Complete Poems of Frances E. W. Harper.* New York: Oxford University Press (The Schomburg Library of Nineteenth-Century Black Women Writers), 1988.

Greenlee, Sam. *The Spook Who Sat by the Door.* New York: R. W. Baron, 1969.

———. *Blues for an African Princess.* Chicago: Third World Press, 1970.

Griggs, Sutton E. *Imperium in Imperio.* New York: Orion, 1899; New York: Arno, 1969.

Guy, Rosa. *Bird at My Window.* New York: Lippincott, 1966.

———. *Ruby.* New York: Random House, 1976.

———. *Edith Jackson.* New York: Viking, 1978.

———. *The Disappearance.* New York: Delacorte, 1979.

———. *My Love, My Love; or, The Peasant Girl.* New York: Henry Holt, 1985.

Hague, Ron, and Sean Kelly. *Nick Names.* New York: Collier Books, 1987.

Haley, Alex. *Roots.* New York: Doubleday, 1976.

Hall, Robert A. *Pidgin and Creole Languages.* Ithaca, N.Y.: Cornell University Press, 1966.

Handy, W. C., *Father of the Blues*. New York: Collier Books, 1970. (First published in 1941.)

———. *Blues: An Anthology*. New York: Collier Books, 1972.

Hannerz, Ulf. *Soulside: Inquiries into Ghetto Culture and Community*. New York: Columbia University Press, 1969.

Harper, Frances E. W. *Iola Leroy; or, Shadows Uplifted*. Philadelphia, 1893; New York: Oxford University Press (The Schomburg Library of Nineteenth-Century Black Women Writers), 1988.

Harper, Michael S. *Images of Kin: New and Selected Poems*. Urbana: University of Illinois Press, 1977.

———. *The Collected Poems of Sterling Brown*. New York: Harper and Row, 1980.

Harper, Michael S., and Robert B. Stepto. *Chant of Saints: A Gathering of Afro-American Literature, Art, and Scholarship*. Urbana: University of Illinois Press, 1979.

Harris, Middleton. *The Black Book*. New York: Random House, 1974.

Hayden, Robert E. *A Ballad of Remembrance*. London: Paul Breman, 1962.

———. *Kaleidoscope: Poems by American Negro Poets*. New York: Harcourt, Brace and World, 1967.

———. *Angle of Ascent: New and Selected Poems*. New York: Liveright, 1975.

———. *Afro-American Literature: An Introduction*. New York: Harcourt Brace Jovanovich, 1971.

Heilbut, Tony. *The Gospel Sound: Good News and Bad Times*. New York: Simon and Schuster, 1971.

Hernton, Calvin. *Scarecrow*. New York: McGraw-Hill, 1970.

Heron, Gil Scott. *The Nigger Factory*. New York: Dial Press, 1972.

Herskovits, Melville J. *Life in a Haitian Valley*. New York: Octagon Books, 1937.

———. *Myth of the Negro Past*. Boston: Beacon Press, 1941.

———. *The Myth of the Negro Past*. Boston: Beacon Press, 1958. (Second Edition.)

Hill, Herbert. *Soon, One Morning: New Writings by American Negroes, 1940–1962*. New York: Alfred A. Knopf, 1963.

Himes, Chester. *Cast the First Stone*. New York: Coward-McCann, 1952, 1953.

———. *A Rage in Harlem*. New York: Avon, 1965.

———. *Run Man, Run*. New York: Putnam, 1966.

———. *Blind Man with a Pistol*. New York: William Morrow, 1969.

———. *Hot Day, Hot Night*. New York: Dell, 1969.

———. *Black on Black: Baby Sister and Selected Writings.* New York: Doubleday, 1973.

———. *A Case of Rape.* Targ Editions, 1980; Washington, D.C., Howard University Press, 1984.

———. *Lonely Crusade.* New York: Alfred A. Knopf, 1947; New York: Thunder's Mouth Press, 1986.

———. *If He Hollers, Let Him Go.* Doubleday, 1945; New York: Thunder's Mouth Press, 1986.

———. *The Real Cool Killers.* New York: Avon, 1959; New York: Berkeley Medallion Editions, 1966; New York: Vintage, 1988.

———. *Cotton Comes to Harlem.* New York: Putnam, 1965; New York: Vintage, 1988.

———. *Pinktoes.* New York: Dell and G. P. Putnam's Sons, 1966. (Reprint of the 1965 G. P. Putnam's Sons/Stein and Day edition.)

Holloway, Joseph E. *Africanisms in American Culture.* Bloomington: Indiana University Press, 1990.

Holiday, Billie. *Lady Sings the Blues.* New York: Doubleday, 1956.

Hopkins, Lee Burnett. *On Our Way: Poems of Pride and Love.* New York: Alfred A. Knopf, 1974.

Horne, Elliot. *Hiptionary.* New York: Simon and Schuster, 1963.

Houchins, Sue E. *Spiritual Narratives: Maria W. Stewart, Jarena Lee, Julia A. J. Foote, Virginia W. Broughton.* New York: Oxford University Press (The Schomburg Library of Nineteenth-Century Black Women Writers), 1988.

Hughes, Langston. *The Weary Blues.* New York: Alfred A. Knopf, 1926.

———. *Fine Clothes for the Jew.* New York: Alfred A. Knopf, 1927.

———. *Not Without Laughter.* New York: Alfred A. Knopf, 1930.

———. *The Dream Keeper.* New York: Alfred A. Knopf, 1932.

———. *The Ways of White Folks.* New York: Alfred A. Knopf, 1934.

———. *The Big Sea.* New York: Hill and Wang, 1940.

———. *Shakespeare in Harlem.* New York: Alfred A. Knopf, 1942.

———. *Fields of Wonder.* New York: Alfred A. Knopf, 1947.

———. *One-Way Ticket.* New York: Alfred A. Knopf, 1949.

———. *Montage of a Dream Deferred.* New York: Henry Holt, 1951.

———. *Laughing to Keep from Crying.* New York: Henry Holt, 1952.

———. *Simple Takes a Wife.* New York: Simon and Schuster, 1953.

———. *I Wonder as I Wander.* New York: Hill and Wang, 1956.

———. *Simple Stakes a Claim.* New York: Rinehart, 1957.

——. *Tambourines to Glory*. New York: John Day, 1959.

——. *Selected Poems*. New York: Alfred A. Knopf, 1959.

——. *Ask Your Mama: Twelve Moods for Jazz*. New York: Alfred A. Knopf, 1961.

——. *The Best of Simple*. New York: Hill and Wang, 1961.

——. *Something in Common, and Other Stories*. New York: Hill and Wang, 1963.

——. *New Negro Poets, U.S.A.* Bloomington: Indiana University Press, 1964.

——. *Simple's Uncle Sam*. Hill and Wang, 1965.

——. *The Book of Negro Humor*. Dodd, Mead, and Co., 1966.

——. *The Best Short Stories by Negro Writers: An Anthology from 1899 to the Present*. Boston: Little, Brown, 1967.

——. *The Panther and the Lash*. Knopf, 1967.

Hughes, Langston, and Arna Bontemps, eds. *The Weary Blues*. New York: Alfred A. Knopf, 1947.

——. *The Book of Negro Folklore*. New York: Dodd, Mead, and Co., 1958.

——. *Selected Poems*. New York: Alfred A. Knopf, 1959.

——. *The Best of Simple*. New York: Hill and Wang, 1961.

——. *Selected Poems*. New York: Alfred A. Knopf, 1970.

——. "Simply Heavenly." In *Five Plays*, edited by Webster Smalley. Bloomington: Indiana University Press, 1968.

——. *The Poetry of the Negro, 1746–1970*, 1970.

Hunter, Kristin. *God Bless the Child*. New York: Scribner's, 1964; Washington, D.C.: Howard University Press, 1987.

——. *The Landlord*. New York: Scribner's, 1966.

Hurston, Zora Neale. *Jonah's Gourd Vine*. Philadelphia: Lippincott, 1934, 1971.

——. *Tell My Horse*. Philadelphia: Lippincott, 1938.

——. *Mules and Men*. Philadelphia: J. B. Lippincott, 1935.

——. *Dust Tracks on a Road: An Autobiography*. Philadelphia: J. B. Lippincott, 1942.

——. *Their Eyes Were Watching God*. Lippincott, 1937; Urbana: University of Illinois Press, 1978.

——. *The Sanctified Church*. Turtle Island Foundation, 1983.

——. *Moses, Man of the Mountain*. Lippincott, 1939; Urbana: University of Illinois Press, 1984.

———. *Dust Tracks on a Road*. Lippincott, 1942, 1971; Urbana: University of Illinois Press, 1984.

———. *Spunk: The Selected Stories of Zora Neale Hurston*. Turtle Island Foundation, 1985.

Hyatt, Harry Middleton. *Hoodoo-Conjuration-Witchcraft-Rootworks*. 4 vols. Washington, D.C.: American University Bookstore, 1970.

Irving, Lewis Allen. *The City in Slang: New York Life and Popular Speech*. New York: Oxford University Press, 1993.

Jablow, Alta. *The Intimate Folklore of Africa*. New York: Horizon Press, 1961.

Jackson, Bruce. *Wake Up Dead Man (Afro-American Work Songs)*. Cambridge: Harvard University Press, 1972; *Wake Up Dead Man* (Rounder 2018).

———. *Get Your Ass in the Water and Swim Like Me*. Cambridge: Harvard University Press, 1974.

Jeffers, Lance. *When I Know the Power of My Black Hand*. Detroit: Broadside Press, 1974.

Joans, Ted. *Jazz Poems*. Rhino Review, 1959.

———. *Black Pow-Wow*. New York: Hill and Wang, 1969.

———. *Afrodisia: New Poems*. New York: Hill and Wang, 1970.

Johnson, Charles. *Faith and the Good Thing*. New York: Viking, 1974; New York: Atheneum, 1987.

———. *Oxherding Tale*. Bloomington: Indiana University Press, 1982.

———. *The Sorceror's Apprentice*. New York: Atheneum, 1986.

———. *Middle Passage*. New York: Atheneum, 1990.

Johnson, Clifton, H., ed. *God Struck Me Dead*. Boston: Pilgrim Press, 1969.

Johnson, Georgia Douglas. *Autumn Love Cycle*. H. Viral, 1928; Books for Libraries Press, 1971.

Johnson, James Weldon. *Gold's Trombones: Seven Negro Sermons in Verse*. New York: Viking, 1927.

———. *The Book of American Negro Poetry*. New York: Harcourt, Brace & World, 1931.

———. *God's Trombones: Seven Negro Sermons in Verse*. New York: Viking, 1927, 1969.

Jones, Bessie, and Bess Lomax Hawes. *Step It Down: Game, Plays, Songs and Stories from the Afro-American Heritage*. Athens: University of Georgia Press, 1972.

Jones, Edward. *Lost in the City*. New York: William Morrow and Co., Inc., 1992.

Jones, Gayl. *Corregidora: A Novel*. New York: Random House, 1975; Boston: Beacon Press, 1986.

———. *Eva's Man*. New York: Random House, 1976; Boston: Beacon Press, 1987.

———. *White Rat*. New York: Random House, 1977.

Jones, LeRoi [a.k.a. Imamu Baraka]. *The System of Dante's Hell*. New York: Grove, 1965.

———. *Tales*. New York: Grove, 1967.

———. *Black Magic Poetry: 1961–1967*. New York: Bobbs-Merrill, 1969.

Jones, LeRoi, and Larry Neal. *Black Fire: An Anthology of Afro-American Writing*. New York: William Morrow, 1968.

Jones, Robert B., and Marjorie Toomer Latimer. *The Collected Poems of Jean Toomer*. Durham: University of North Carolina Press, 1988.

Jordan, June. *Some Changes*. New York: Dutton, 1971.

———. *New Days: Poems of Exile and Return*. New York: Emerson Hall, 1974.

———. *Things That I Do in the Dark: Selected Poems*. New York: Random House, 1977.

———. *Passion: New Poems, 1977–1980*. Boston: Beacon Press, 1980.

———. *Living Room*. New York: Thunder's Mouth Press, 1985.

Kelley, William Melvin. *Different Drummer*. New York: Doubleday, 1962.

———. *Dancers on the Shore*. New York: Doubleday, 1964; Washington, D.C.: Howard University Press, 1984.

Kenan, Randall. *Let the Dead Bury Their Dead*. New York: Harcourt Brace and Jovanovich, 1992.

Kennedy, Robert Emmet. *Black Cameos*. New York: Albert and Charles Boni, 1924.

Killens, John O. *Youngblood*. New York: Dial Press, 1956.

———. *And Then We Heard the Thunder*. New York: Alfred A. Knopf, 1963; Washington, D.C.: Howard University Press, 1983.

———. *'Sippi*. New York: Simon and Schuster, 1967; New York: Thunder's Mouth Press, 1988.

King, Woodie. *Black Short Story Anthology*. New York: Columbia University Press, 1972.

———. *The Forerunners: Black Poets in America*. Washington, D.C.: Howard University Press, 1976.

Knight, Etheridge. *Poems from Prison*. Detroit: Broadside Press, 1968.

———. *Belly Song and Other Poems*. Detroit: Broadside Press, 1973.

———. *The Essential Etheridge Knight.* University of Pittsburgh Press, 1986.

Kochman, Thomas. "Rapping in the Black Ghetto." *Trans-action* 6 (February 1969):26–34.

———, ed., *Rappin' and Stylin' Out: Communication in Urban Black America.* Urbana: University of Illinois Press, 1972.

Krehbiel, H. E. *Afro-American Folksongs.* New York: G. Schirmer, 1914.

Labov, William. *Language in the Inner City.* Philadelphia: University of Pennsylvania Press, 1972.

Lane, Pinkie Gordon. *I Never Scream: New and Selected Poems.* Detroit: Lotus Press, 1985.

Larkin, Rochelle. *Soul Music.* New York: Lancer Books, 1970.

Lee, Don L. [a.k.a. Haki R. Madhubuti]. *Think Black.* Detroit: Broadside Press, 1967.

———. *Black Pride.* Detroit: Broadside Press, 1968.

———. *Don't Cry, Scream.* Detroit: Broadside Press, 1969.

———. *We Walk the Way of the New World.* Detroit: Broadside Press, 1970.

Lee, George W. *Beale Street: Where the Blues Began.* New York: Robert O. Ballou, 1934.

Lehman, Theo. *Negro Spirituals.* Berlin: Eckart-Verlag, 1965.

Liebow, Elliott. *Talley's Corner: A Study of Negro Street Corner Men.* Boston: Little, Brown and Co., 1966.

Lindo, Bernice. *Black Ghetto Dialect.* Los Angeles: Instant Phonics, 1972.

Locke, Alain L., ed. *The New Negro.* New York: Arno Press, 1968. (Originally published in 1925.)

Locke, Alain, L. *The New Negro: An Interpretation.* Boni, 1925; New York: Atheneum, 1968.

Lomax, Alan. *The Folk Songs of North America.* Garden City, N.Y.: Doubleday, 1960.

———. *The Land Where the Blues Began.* New York: Pantheon Books, 1993.

———. *Mister Jelly Roll.* New York: Duell, Sloan and Pearce, 1950.

———. *The Rainbow Sign: A Southern Documentary.* New York: Duell, Sloan, and Pearce, 1959.

Lomax, John A., and Alan Lomax. *American Ballads and Folklore.* New York: Macmillan. Copyright 1934 by Macmillan. Reprinted by permission of Alan Lomax.

———. *Negro Folksongs as Sung by Lead Belly.* New York: Macmillan. Copyright 1936 by John Lomax and Alan Lomax.

Lomax, John and Alan. *The Leadbelly Legend*. New York: Folkways Publishers, 1965.

Long, Richard A., and Eugenia W. Collier. *Afro-American Writing: An Anthology of Prose and Poetry*. 2 vols. New York: New York University Press, 1972.

Lovell, John Jr. *Black Song: The Forge and the Flame*. New York: Macmillan, 1972.

Mackey, Nathaniel. *Bedouin Handbook*. Lexington: Callaloo Fiction Series, 1986.

Major, Clarence. *The New Black Poetry*. New York: International Publications, 1969.

———. *Swallow the Lake*. Middletown, Conn.: Wesleyan University Press, 1970.

———. *Dictionary of Afro-American Slang*. New York: International Publishers, 1970.

———. *The Cotton Club: New Poems*. Detroit: Broadside Press, 1972.

———. *The Syncopated Cakewalk*. New York: Barlenmir, 1974.

———. *Calling the Wind: Twentieth-Century African-American Short Stories*. Edited and with an introduction. New York: An Edward Burlingame Book/Harper Perennial, 1993.

Margolies, Edward. *A Native Sons Reader: Selections by Outstanding Black American Authors of the Twentieth-Century*. Philadelphia: Lippincott, 1970.

Marshall, Paule. *Brown Girl, Brownstones*. New York: Random House, 1959; The Feminist Press, 1981.

———. *Soul Clap Hands and Sing*. New York: Atheneum, 1961; Washington, D.C.: Howard University Press, 1988.

———. *Reena and Other Stories*. The Feminist Press, 1983.

Mayfield, Julian. *The Hit*. New York: Vanguard, 1957.

———. *The Long Night*. New York: Vanguard, 1958.

———. *The Grand Parade*. New York: Vanguard, 1961.

Mberi, Antar S. K., and Cosmo Pieterse. *Speak Easy, Speak Free*. New York: International Publishers, 1977.

McCluskey, John, Jr. *The City of Refuge: The Collected Stories of Rudolph Fisher*. Columbia: University of Missouri Press, 1987.

McKay, Claude. *Harlem Shadows*. New York: Harcourt, 1922.

———. *Home to Harlem*. New York: Harper and Brother, 1928, 1956.

———. *Gingertown*. New York: Harper, 1932.

McMillan, Terry. *Disappearing Acts*. New York: Viking Penguin, 1989.

Mencken, H. L. *The American Language: An Inquiry Into the Development of English in the United States.* Alfred A. Knopf, Inc., 1919.

Mezzrow, Milton, with Bernard Wolfe. *Really the Blues.* New York: Random House, 1946.

Miller, E. Ethelbert. *Women Surviving Massacres and Men: Nine Women Poets, An Anthology.* Anemone Press, 1977.

———. *Migrant Worker.* The Washington Writers' Publishing House, 1978.

Mitchell, Henry. *Black Belief.* New York: Harper and Row, 1975.

Mitchell, Henry M. *Black Preaching.* Philadelphia: J. B. Lippincott Co., 1970.

Moon, Bucklin. *Primer for White Folks.* New York: Doubleday, 1945.

Moore, Carman. *Somebody's Angel Child.* New York: T. Y. Crowell, 1969.

Morrison, Toni. *The Bluest Eyes.* New York: Holt, Rinehart and Winston, 1970.

———. *Sula.* New York: Alfred A. Knopf, 1974.

———. *Beloved.* New York: Alfred A. Knopf, 1987.

Mosley, Walter. *Devil in a Blue Dress.* New York: Pocket Books, 1991. (Originally published by W. W. Norton and Co., Inc., 1990).

———. *White Butterfly.* New York: W. W. Norton and Co., 1992.

Murphy, Beatrice M. *Today's Negro Voices: An Anthology by Young Negro Poets.* Messner, 1970.

Murray, Albert. *Stomping the Blues.* New York: McGraw-Hill, 1976.

———. *Train Whistle Guitar.* New York: McGraw-Hill, 1974.

Naylor, Gloria. *Bailey's Cafe.* New York: Harcourt Brace and Jovanovich, 1992.

———. *Linden Hills.* New York: Ticknor and Fields, 1985.

———. *Mama Day.* New York: Ticknor and Fields, 1988.

———. *The Women of Brewster Place.* New York: Penguin, 1983.

Neal, Larry. *Black Boogaloo.* San Francisco: Journal of Black Poetry Press, 1969.

———. *Hoodoo Hollerin' Bebop Ghosts.* Washington, D.C.: Howard University Press, 1974.

Nicholas, A. X. *The Poetry of Soul.* New York: Bantam Books, 1971.

Oakley, Giles. *The Devil's Music: A History of the Blues.* London: British Broadcasting Corporation, 1976.

Odom, Howard W., and Guy B. Johnson. *The Negro and His Songs.* New York: New American Library, 1969. (First printed 1925.)

Oliver, Paul. *Bessie Smith.* New York: A. S. Barnes, 1971.

————. *The Blues Fell This Morning*. London: Cassell 1960.

————. *Conversation with the Blues*. New York: Horizon Press, 1961.

————. *Conversation with the Blues*. New York: Horizon Press, 1965; *Conversation with the Blues* (Decca LK 4664).

————. *The Meaning of the Blues*. New York: Collier Books, 1966.

————. *Screening the Blues*. London: Cassell, 1968.

————. *Savannah Syncopators*. New York: Stein and Day, 1970; *Savannah Syncopators* (CBS 52799).

————. *The Story of the Blues*. New York: Chilton Book Co., 1969.

Osofsky, Gilbert. *Puttin' on Ole Massa: The Slave Narratives of Henry Bibb, William W. Brown, and Solomon Northrop*. New York: Harper and Row, 1969.

Oster, Harry. *Living Country Blues*. Detroit: Folklore Associates, 1969.

Parrish, Lydia. *Slave Songs of the Georgia Sea Islands*. Hatboro, Pa.: Folklore Associates, 1965.

Partridge, Eric. *A Dictionary of Slang and Unconventional English*. New York: Macmillan, 1937.

————. *A Dictionary of the Underworld*. New York: Bonanza Books, 1949, (1961).

————. *Smaller Slang Dictionary*. New York: Philosophical Library, 1961.

Patterson, Lindsay. *A Rock Against the Wind: Black Love Poems, An Anthology*. Dodd, Mead, 1973.

Perry, Margaret. *The Short Fiction of Rudolph Fisher*. Westport, CT: Greenwood Press, 1987.

Petry, Ann. *The Street*. Boston: Houghton Mifflin Co., 1946; Pyramid Books, 1961; Boston: Beacon Press, 1985.

Pharr, Robert Deane. *The Book of Numbers*. Garden City, N.Y.: Doubleday, 1969.

Pipes, William H. *Say Amen, Brother! Old-Time Negro Preaching*. Westport, Conn.: Negro Universities Press, 1970.

Plumpp, Sterling D. *Portable Soul*. Chicago: Third World Press, 1969.

————. *Half Black, Half Blacker*. Chicago: Third World Press, 1970.

————. *The Black Poets*. New York: Bantam, 1971.

————. *The Mojo Hands Call, I Must Go*. New York: Thunder's Mouth Press, 1982.

————. *Somehow We Survive: An Anthology of South African Writing*. New York: Thunder's Mouth Press, 1982.

Price, Richard. *Clockers*. Boston: Houghton Mifflin Co., 1992.

BIBLIOGRAPHY

Puckett, Niles Newell. *Folk Beliefs of the Southern Negro*. Durham: University of North Carolina Press, 1926.

Ramsey, Frederick J. *Been Here and Gone*. New Brunswick, N.J.: Rutgers University Press, 1960; *Been Here and Gone* (Folkways FA 2659).

Randall, Dudley. *Cities Burning*. Detroit: Broadside Press, 1968.

———. *Black Poetry: A Supplement to Anthologies Which Exclude Black Poets*. Detroit: Broadside Press, 1969.

———. *Love You*. London: Paul Breman, 1970.

———. *The Black Poets*. New York: Bantam, 1971.

Randall, Dudley, and Margaret Burroughs. *For Malcolm: Poems on the Life and the Death of Malcolm X*. Detroit: Broadside Press, 1967.

Rawick, George P. *From Sundown to Sunup*. Westport, CT: Greenwood Publishing Co., 1972.

———. *Rope of Wind and Other Stories/Henry Dumas*. New York: Random House, 1979.

———. *Goodbye, Sweetwater: New and Selected Stories/Henry Dumas*. New York: Thunder's Mouth Press, 1988.

———. *New and Collected Poems*. New York: Atheneum, 1988.

Reed, Ishmael. *Yellow Black Radio Broke-Down*. Garden City, N.Y.: Doubleday, 1969.

———. *19 Necromancers from Now*. New York: Doubleday, 1970.

———. *Conjure: Selected Poems, 1963–1970*. Amherst: University of Massachusetts Press, 1973.

———. *The Last Days of Louisana Red*. New York: Random House, 1974.

———. *Chattanooga: Poems*. New York: Random House, 1974.

———. *Yardbird Lives*. Grove Press, 1978.

———. *Shrovetide in Old New Orleans*. New York: Doubleday, 1978; New York: Avon Books, 1979.

———. *Writin' is Fightin': 37 Years of Boxing on Paper*. New York: Atheneum, 1988.

Render, Sylvia Lyons. *The Short Fiction of Charles W. Chestnutt*. Washington, D.C.: Howard University Press, 1974.

Reuther, Edward Byron. *The Mulatto in the United States*. New York: Negro Universities Press/Greenwood Publishing Corp., 1969 [reprint of the 1918 Richard G. Badger edition].

Rodgers, Carolyn M. *The Heart As Ever Green*. Anchor Press, 1970.

———. *How I Got Ovah: New and Selected Poems*. Anchor Press, 1975.

Rosenberg, Burce A. *The Art of the American Folk Preacher*. New York: Oxford University Press, 1970.

Rosengarte, Theodore. *All God's Dangers: The Life of Nate Shaw*. New York: Alfred A. Knopf, 1974.

Ross, Fran. *Oreo*. New York: Greyfalcon House, 1974.

Sackheim, Eric, comp. *The Blues Line: A Collection of Blues Lyrics*. New York: Grossman Publishers, 1969.

Sackheim, Eric, comp. *The Blues Line: A Collection of Blues Lyrics*. New York: Schirmer Books, 1975.

Sanchez, Sonia. *Homecoming*. Broadside Press, 1970.

———. *We Be Word Sorcerors: 25 Stories by Black Americans*. New York: Bantam, 1973.

———. *Homegirls and Handgrenades*. New York: Thunder's Mouth Press, 1984.

Scarborough, Dorothy. *On the Trail of Negro Folk Songs*. Hatboro, Pa.: Folklore Associates, 1963. (First printed 1925.)

Schneider, Gilbert. *Cameroons Creole Dictionary: First Draft*. Southern Cameroons, 1960.

———. *West African Pidgin English: An Historical Over-View*. Athens, Ohio: Center for International Studies, 1967.

Schuyler, George. *Black No More*. Macaulay, 1931.

Scott-Heron, Gil. *Small Talk at 125th Street and Lenox*. Cleveland: World, 1970.

———. *The Vulture*. Cleveland: World, 1970.

Shaik, Fatima. *The Mayor of New Orleans*. Berkeley, Calif.: Creative Arts Books Co., 1989.

Shange, Ntozake. *Nappy Edges*. New York: St. Martin's Press, 1978.

———. *Three Pieces*. New York: St. Martin's Press, 1981; Penguin, 1982.

———. *Sassafrass: A Novella*. San Lorenzo, CA: Shameless Hussy Press, 1977.

———. *Sassafrass, Cypress & Indigo*. New York: St. Martin's Press, 1982.

———. *A Daughter's Geography*. New York: St. Martin's Press, 1983.

———. *From Okra to Greens: A Different Love Story*. Minneapolis: Coffee House Press, 1984.

———. *See No Evil: Prefaces, Essays, & Accounts, 1976–1983*. Momo's Press, 1984.

Sherman, Charlotte Watson. *One Dark Body*. New York: Harper Collins, 1993.

Sherman, Joan R. *Invisible Poets: Afro-Americans of the Nineteenth Century.* Urbana: University of Illinois Press, 1974.

———. *Collected Black Women's Poetry.* 4 vols. New York: Oxford University Press (The Schomburg Library of Nineteenth-Century Black Women Writers), 1988.

Shuman, R. Baird. *Nine Black Poets.* Moore, 1968.

———. *A Galaxy of Black Writing.* Moore, 1970.

Shields, John C. *The Collected Works of Phillis Wheatley.* New York: Oxford University Press (The Schomburg Library of Nineteenth-Century Black Women Writers, 1988.

Shockley, Ann Allen. *The Black and White of It.* Tallahassee, FL: Naiad, 1980, 1987.

Simmons, Herbert A. *Man Walking on Eggshells.* Boston: Houghton Mifflin Co, 1962.

Smith, Arthur L. *Rhetoric of Black Revolution.* Boston: Allyn and Bacon, 1969.

Smith, Barbara. *Home Girls: A Black Feminist Anthology.* Kitchen Table: Women of Color Press, 1983.

Smith, Reed. *Gullah.* Columbia: University of South Carolina Press, 1962.

Smith, William Gardner. *South Street.* New York: Farrar, Straus & Giroux, 1954.

Smitherman, Geneva. "A Comparison of the Oral and Written Styles of a Group of Inner-City Black Students." Ph.D. Dissertation, University of Michigan, 1969.

———. *Black Language and Culture: Sounds of Soul.* New York: Harper and Row, 1975.

———. *Talkin' and Testifying: the Language of Black America.* Boston: Houghton Mifflin Co., 1977.

Southern, Eileen, *The Music of Black Americans: A History.* New York: W. W. Norton, 1971.

———. *Readings in Black American Music.* New York: W. W. Norton, 1971.

Stadler, Quandra P. *Out of Our Lives: A Collection of Contemporary Black Fiction.* Washington, D.C.: Howard University Press, 1975.

Stanley, Lawrence A., ed. *Rap: the Lyrics.* New York, London: Penguin, 1992.

Stewart-Baxter, Derrick. *Ma Rainey and the Classic Blues Singers.* New York: Stein and Day, 1970.

Stuart Berg Flexner. *I Hear America Talking: An illustrated Treasury of American Words and Phrases.* New York: Van Nostrand Reinhold, Co., 1976.

Talley, Thomas. *Negro Rolk Rhymes*. Port Washington: Kennikat Press, 1968. (Originally published in 1922.)

Thomas, Lorenzo D. *Africanisms in the Gullah Dialect*. Chicago: University of Chicago Press, 1949.

Thorne, Tony. *The Dictionary of Contemporary Slang*. New York: Pantheon, 1990.

Thurman, Wallace. *The Blacker the Berry*. Macaulay, 1929.

———. *Infants of the Spring*. Macaulay, 1932.

Titon, Jeff. *Early Downhome Blues: A Musical and Cultural Analysis*. Urbana: University of Illinois Press, 1977.

Tolson, Melvin B. *Rendezvous with America*. New York: Dodd, Mead, 1944.

———. *Libretto for the Republic of Liberia*. Boston: Twayne, 1953.

———. *Harlem Gallery; Book I: The Curator*. Boston: Twayne, 1965.

———. *A Gallery of Harlem Portraits*. New York: University of Missouri Press, 1979.

Toomer, Jean. *Cane*. New York: Boni and Liveright, 1923.

Troupe, Quincy. *Embryo Poems*. New York: Barlenmir, 1972.

———. *Snake-Back Solos: Selected Poems, 1969–1977*. New York: I. Reed Books, 1978.

———. *Skulls Along the River*. Reed and Cannon, 1984.

Troupe, Quincy, and Rainer Schulte. *Giant Talk: An Anthology of Third World Writers*. New York: Random House, 1975.

Turner, Darwin T. *Black American Literature: Poetry*. New York: Chas. E. Merrill, 1969.

———. *Black Drama in America: An Anthology*. New York: Fawcett, 1971.

———. *The Wayward and the Seeking: A Collection of Writings by Jean Toomer*. Washington, D.C.: Howard University Press, 1980.

Turner, Lorenzo Dow. *Africanisms in the Gullah Dialect*. Chicago: University of Chicago Press, 1949.

Twain, Mark. *Huckleberry Finn*. Boston: Houghton Mifflin Co., 1958.

Van Den Bark, Melvin, and Lester V. Berrey. *The American Thesaurus of Slang: A Complete Reference Book of Colloquial Speech*. New York: Crowell, 1942; with new appendix, 1947; rev., 1953.

Walker, Alice. *The Third Life of Grange Copeland*. New York: Harcourt Brace Jovanovich, 1970.

———. *In Love and Trouble: Stories of Black Women*. New York: Harcourt Brace Jovanovich, 1973.

———. *Meridian*. New York: Harcourt Brace Jovanovich, 1976.

———. *I Love Myself When I am Laughing . . . And Then Again When I am Looking Mean and Impressive: A Zora Neale Hurston Reader.* New York: The Feminist Press, 1979.

———. *The Color Purple.* New York: Harcourt Brace Jovanovich, 1982.

Walker, Margaret. *For My People.* New Haven, Conn.: Yale University Press, 1942; New York: Ayer, 1969.

———. *This is My Century: New and Collected Poems/Margaret Walker.* Athens: University of Georgia Press, 1989.

Washington, Mary Helen. *Black-Eyed Susans: Classic Stories By and About Black Women.* New York: Anchor Press, 1975.

———. *Midnight Birds: Stories of Contemporary Black Women Writers.* New York: Anchor Press, 1980.

———. *Invented Lives: Narratives of Black Women's Lives, 1860–1960.* New York: Anchor Press, 1987.

Wasson, Ben. *The Devil Beats His Wife.* New York: Harcourt and Brace, 1929.

Watkins, Sylvester C. *Anthology of American Negro Literature.* New York: Random House, 1944.

Wentworth, Harold, and Stuart Berg Flexner, ed. *Dictionary of American Slang.* New York: Crowell, 1960, 1967.

Weseen, Maurice, ed. *A Dictionary of American Slang.* New York: Crowell, 1934.

White, Newman L. *American Negro Folk Songs.* Hatboro, Penn.: Folklore Associates, 1965.

Wideman, John Edgar. *A Glance Away.* New York: Harcourt Brace and World, 1967; Chatham, NJ: Chatham Booksellers, 1975; New York: Henry Holt, 1985.

———. *Dumballah.* New York: Schocken, 1981; New York: Random House, 1988.

———. *Hiding Place.* New York: Avon Books, 1981; Schocken, 1984; New York: Random House, 1988.

———. *Sent for You Yesterday.* New York: Bard, 1983.

———. *Reuben.* New York: Henry Holt, 1987.

———. *Philadelphia Fire.* New York: Henry Holt, 1990.

Wilkinson, Andrews. *Plantation Stories of Old Louisiana.* Boston: The Page Co., 1914.

Williams, John A. *The Angry Ones.* New York: Ace Books, 1960.

———. *Night Song.* New York: Farrar, Straus and Giroux, 1961.

———. *Sissie.* New York: Farrar, Straus and Giroux, 1963.

———. *The Man Who Cried I Am.* Little, Brown, and Co., 1967.

———. *This Is My Country, Too*. New York: New American Library, 1965; New York: Signet, 1966.

Williams, John A., and Charles F. Harris. *Amistad I: Writings on Black History and Culture*. New York: Vintage, 1970.

Williams, Sherley Anne. *The Peacock Poems*. Middletown, Conn.: Wesleyan University Press, 1978.

———. *Some One Sweet Angel Chile*. New York: William Morrow, 1982.

———. *Dessa Rose*. New York: William Morrow, 1986.

Williams, Terry. *The Cocaine Kids: The Inside Story of a Teenage Drug Ring*. Reading, Mass.: Addison-Wesley, 1989.

———. *Crackhouse*. New York: Addison-Wesley, 1992.

Williamson, Joel. *New People: Miscegenation and Mulattoes in the United States*. New York: The Free Press, 1980.

Wilson, Harriet E. *Our Nig*. Rand and Avery, 1859; New York: Vintage, 1983.

Work, John W. *American Negro Songs and Spirituals*. New York: Bonanza Books, 1940.

Wright, Charles. *The Wig. A Mirror Image*. New York: Farrar, Straus and Giroux, 1966.

———. *Absolutely Nothing to Get Alarmed About*. New York: Farrar, Straus and Giroux, 1973.

Wright, Richard. *Uncle Tom's Children: Four Novellas*. New York: Harper and Brothers, 1938.

———. *Uncle Tom's Children*. New York: Harper, 1938, 1969.

———. *Native Son*. New York: Harper and Brothers, 1940.

———. *Native Son*. New York: Harper, 1940.

———. *The Long Dream*. Garden City, N.Y.: Doubleday, 1958.

———. *Lawd Today*. New York: Walker and Company, 1963.

———. *Uncle Tom's Children*. New York: Harper and Row, 1965.

———. *Black Boy*. New York: Harper and Row, 1966.

———. *Eight Men: Stories by Richard Wright*. World, 1961; New York: Thunder's Mouth Press, 1987.

X, Malcolm. *Malcolm X Speaks*. New York: Grove Press, 1965.

X, Malcolm, with Alex Haley. *The Autobiography of Malcolm X*. New York: Grove, 1965.

Yetman, Norman R. *Voices from Slavery*. New York: Holt, Rinehart and Winston, 1970.

Young, Al. *Snakes*. New York: Holt, Rinehart and Winston, 1970.

BIBLIOGRAPHY

———. *Who Is Angelina?* New York: Holt, Rinehart and Winston, 1975.

———. *Ask Me Now.* New York: McGraw-Hill, 1980.

———. *The Blues Don't Change: New and Selected Poems.* Baton Rouge: Louisiana State University Press, 1982.

———. *Seduction by Light.* New York: Delta Fiction, 1988.

Young, Martha. *Plantation Bird Legends.* New York: Appleton and Co., 1916.

FOR THE BEST IN PAPERBACKS, LOOK FOR THE 🐧

In every corner of the world, on every subject under the sun, Penguin represents quality and variety—the very best in publishing today.

For complete information about books available from Penguin—including Pelicans, Puffins, Peregrines, and Penguin Classics—and how to order them, write to us at the appropriate address below. Please note that for copyright reasons the selection of books varies from country to country.

In the United Kingdom: For a complete list of books available from Penguin in the U.K., please write to *Dept E.P., Penguin Books Ltd, Harmondsworth, Middlesex, UB7 0DA*.

In the United States: For a complete list of books available from Penguin in the U.S., please write to *Consumer Sales, Penguin USA, P.O. Box 999— Dept. 17109, Bergenfield, New Jersey 07621-0120*. VISA and MasterCard holders call 1-800-253-6476 to order all Penguin titles.

In Canada: For a complete list of books available from Penguin in Canada, please write to *Penguin Books Canada Ltd, 10 Alcorn Avenue, Suite 300, Toronto, Ontario, Canada M4V 3B2*.

In Australia: For a complete list of books available from Penguin in Australia, please write to the *Marketing Department, Penguin Books Ltd, P.O. Box 257, Ringwood, Victoria 3134*.

In New Zealand: For a complete list of books available from Penguin in New Zealand, please write to the *Marketing Department, Penguin Books (NZ) Ltd, Private Bag, Takapuna, Auckland 9*.

In India: For a complete list of books available from Penguin, please write to *Penguin Overseas Ltd, 706 Eros Apartments, 56 Nehru Place, New Delhi, 110019*.

In Holland: For a complete list of books available from Penguin in Holland, please write to *Penguin Books Nederland B.V., Postbus 195, NL-1380AD Weesp, Netherlands*.

In Germany: For a complete list of books available from Penguin, please write to *Penguin Books Ltd, Friedrichstrasse 10-12, D-6000 Frankfurt Main 1, Federal Republic of Germany*.

In Spain: For a complete list of books available from Penguin in Spain, please write to *Longman, Penguin España, Calle San Nicolas 15, E-28013 Madrid, Spain*.

In Japan: For a complete list of books available from Penguin in Japan, please write to *Longman Penguin Japan Co Ltd, Yamaguchi Building, 2-12-9 Kanda Jimbocho, Chiyoda-Ku, Tokyo 101, Japan*.

FOR THE BEST IN REFERENCE, LOOK FOR THE Ⓟ